Alfred Beaven Beaven

Bristol Lists

Municipal and Miscellaneous

Alfred Beaven Beaven

Bristol Lists
Municipal and Miscellaneous

ISBN/EAN: 9783337405472

Printed in Europe, USA, Canada, Australia, Japan

Cover: Foto ©Suzi / pixelio.de

More available books at **www.hansebooks.com**

BRISTOL LISTS:

MUNICIPAL

AND

MISCELLANEOUS.

COMPILED BY

The Rev. ALFRED B. BEAVEN, M.A.

(Formerly Scholar of Pembroke College, Oxford.)

BRISTOL:
T. D. TAYLOR, SONS, AND HAWKINS, "TIMES AND MIRROR"
OFFICE, SMALL STREET.

TO

Francis Frederick Fox, Esq., J.P.,

Alderman and sometime High Sheriff of Bristol,
and Chairman of the Museum and Libraries Committees of the Bristol Corporation,

who, both by his private researches and in his
official character, has done so much to create and
foster a more general interest in the history of
our native city;

AND TO

Thomas David Taylor, Esq.,

Senior Proprietor of the "Bristol Times and Mirror,"

the "Grand Old Man" of Bristol Journalism,

inheritor and transmitter of the local traditions of an older day,

I beg leave to Dedicate this record of many
generations of prominent Bristol Citizens

as a memorial of kindred tastes,
and in recognition of invaluable assistance which
they have generously rendered me in its
compilation.

A. B. B.

August, 1899.

PREFACE.

The following pages are an expansion of some notes which originally appeared in the "Bristol Times and Mirror" nineteen years ago, and were revised, with considerable additions, in the same paper in 1897 and 1898. In their present much-enlarged form they constitute a nearly exhaustive collection of lists of those who have held official or quasi-official positions in Bristol, (with the exception of one important section), for a long period of years, going back, in the case of the Mayors, Sheriffs, Aldermen and Common Councillors, the Society of Merchant Venturers, and some of the more important offices under the Corporation, to the end of the 16th or the beginning of the 17th century.

The one important section which is omitted is that of the clergy, who are, as a class, not represented in these lists, except by the Mayors' Chaplains, though the names of several individual clerics are recorded in connection with the School Board, the Grammar School, the City Library, &c. I may hereafter supplement the present publication with an ecclesiastical series, for which I have accumulated considerable material.

The notes which form the basis of this collection were begun in my early boyhood, forty years since, and have been continued from time to time to the present day. The fact that I have not been resident in Bristol during the last thirty-one years, except at long intervals and for a few days at a time, has tended to increase the difficulty of securing the degree of accuracy and completeness at which I have aimed.

The somewhat sporadic arrangement of the book requires some apology. It is due to the original form of publication in a series of articles appearing periodically in a newspaper; the earlier sheets, dealing with the period since the Municipal Corporations Act of 1835, having been printed off before the whole work was completed, while its scope was being gradually widened by the inclusion, (in many instances in response to suggestions and requests), of matter which, although collected, I had not originally had it in contemplation to publish.

I hope that the Alphabetical Indexes, which comprise a summary of the offices held at various times by each one of nearly 3,800 individuals, will be found useful for reference. They have been compiled with great care, in the belief that they would add very materially to whatever value the rest of the work might possess.

It is impossible, in a collection dealing with so many names, dates, and facts, to ensure more than an approximation to perfect accuracy. In matters of date, especially, contemporary newspapers, (not to mention later authorities from which less minute accuracy is to be expected), often present considerable discrepancies, which, in the absence of any official record or family memoranda, render certainty impossible. The somewhat copious list of errata will, I fear, be evidence of some want of experience in proof-reading on my part, as well as of too many *lapsus plumæ* in transcribing for the Press. I trust, however, that the errors which still remain uncorrected are neither numerous nor important.

It has frequently been difficult to discriminate fully between contemporaries bearing the same name, but, wherever possible, I have had recourse to comparison of signatures to enable me to verify my identifications in cases of doubt.

It remains for me to record my acknowledgments of the material assistance I have received, (both unsolicited and in answer to inquiries), from public and private sources in preparing these lists for publication.

The original papers, as printed in 1880, had been revised throughout, and some of the lists contained in them had been altogether contributed, by the Town Clerk (Mr. D. Travers Burges), who continued to furnish me with additions and notes from time to time until his invaluable help was interrupted by his serious illness. The aid which he had so liberally afforded me has since been abundantly supplied, with equal readiness, by Mr. C. S. Sampson, of the Town Clerk's office. To both these gentlemen I am under lasting obligation.

I must also specially acknowledge my indebtedness to the City Treasurer (Mr. J. Tremayne Lane) and to the Clerk to the Bristol Board of Guardians (Mr. J. J. Simpson), who have not merely displayed their habitual courtesy in placing the records under their charge unreservedly at my command, but have been unsparing both of time and labour in facilitating my researches by making references and transcribing minutes for me, and supplying me with careful tracings of signatures.

Amongst other officials who have given me valuable information and, whenever required, access to documents and records, I must offer my thanks to Mr. H. J. Spear (Secretary to the Chamber of Commerce), Mr. F. W. Newton (Secretary to the Charity Trustees), Mr. W. A. Adams (Clerk to the School Board), Mr. Henley Lancaster (Clerk to the Barton Regis Board of Guardians), Mr. Norris Mathews (City Librarian), Mr. Acland Taylor (Librarian of the Museum and Reference Library), Mr. Girdlestone (General Manager of the Docks), Dr. Davies (Medical Officer of Health), Mr. R. C. Tombs (Postmaster), and the Secretary to the Board of Customs in London.

In connection with my papers on the Colston Societies, I received much help from Colonel Woodward, Mr. L. C. Danger, and Aldermen Fox, Thatcher, and Cope-Proctor, while those on the Gloucestershire Society and the Antient

Society of St. Stephen's Ringers owe their completeness to Mr. F. A. Jenkins and Mr. Fuller Eberle respectively.

To Alderman Fox and Mr. T. D. Taylor I have endeavoured, on another page, to express my sense of their kindness in giving me access to their valuable collections of Bristol books and newspapers respectively, as well as in supplying information from their vast stores of personal knowledge of men and things in relation to the last half century of local history.

To my friend, Mr. Fuller Eberle, my acknowledgments are due in an especial degree. His assistance has not been confined to matters connected with the Society whose records are in his custody, but he has, with characteristic promptitude and energy, applied himself to the task of searching for information for me on almost every point on which, from time to time, I have made him acquainted with any *lacuna* in my collection.

Mr. E. A. Harley's help, (most kindly volunteered, when I was personally unknown to him), has only been bounded by the limits which I have set myself in having recourse to it; and Mr. H. Napier Abbot and Mr. John Latimer, the careful and accurate historian of the city of his adoption, have been equally assiduous in providing me with material.

I must also acknowledge the courteous assistance of Mr. H. Meade King, Mr. Charles Nash, Mr. W. R. Barker, Mr. F. P. Lansdown, Mr. Arthur Lee, Mr. George White, and of my old schoolfellow, Mr. Edmund Gill, as well of many others who have answered particular inquiries by me in the "Times and Mirror," either directly or through the medium of that paper.

Finally, though I name him last, by no means the least entitled to my thanks is Mr. G. H. Pope, Treasurer of the Society of Merchant Venturers, who has made researches, involving some expenditure of time and labour, in the minutes of that Society on several occasions, in order to settle points on which I required official information. I trust he will not consider that his courtesy and kindness are inadequately appreciated by me, if I add that my gratitude to him is alloyed with a feeling of keen disappointment at being precluded by a rigid, not to say pedantic, adherence to a somewhat illiberal rule from having personal access to the records of the Society of which he is the representative, and being thereby deprived of the means of adding very materially to the comprehensiveness and accuracy of my work. I have been assured by one who has the best possible means of knowing, that there is nothing in the minutes of the Society which any one need mind being proclaimed to all the world, and, even if there were, I should have wished to use, or even to read, nothing contained in them beyond mere particulars of names and dates. I must confess to being somewhat surprised that such a rule should be enforced in the case of one who may, perhaps, claim to be entitled to be credited with worthier objects than mere idle curiosity, in seeking to inspect these records. Perhaps I may be permitted to hope that at some not very distant date, although too late for the purposes of the present publication, a renewed application on my part may be more favourably entertained.

I trust that the information put together in these pages may not be altogether without interest to Bristolians, and may be found useful for reference, both now and hereafter, if not to a wide public, at least to the members of that good old family of Dryasdust, which concerns itself with the records of persons and institutions of byegone times, and which, I hope, will always number some representatives among the natives and citizens of Bristol.

A. B. B.

August, 1899.

CONTENTS.

Bristol Municipal Elections since the Act of 1835:—

Bristol Ward	1
Clifton Ward	6
Redcliff Ward	12
St. Augustine Ward	16
St. Philip Ward	19
St. Philip Ward (South)	21
St. Philip Ward (North)	22
Bedminster Ward	23
Bedminster Ward (West)	26
Bedminster Ward (East)	27
St. Michael Ward	28
St. James Ward	31
St. Paul Ward	34
The District Ward	36
Westbury Ward	39
Horfield Ward	40
St. George Ward	40
Stapleton Ward	40
Somerset Ward	40
Easton Ward	40

See also pp. 413, 414, 417, 418, 423.

Aldermen 41, 414, 418, 423

Mayors 49, 415, 418, 424

Distribution of Seats in the Council	52
Political Composition of the Bristol Corporation, 1835-1898	53
Miscellaneous Notes on the Composition of the Bristol Corporation, 1835-1898	57
The Old Corporation at the date of the passing of the Municipal Corporations Act, 1835	90

Since 1835.

Lord High Stewards	92, 425
High Sheriffs	92, 415, 419, 425
Town Clerks	94, 415
City Treasurers	94
Clerks of the Peace	94, 425
Coroners	95
Registrars of the Tolzey Court	94, 425
Chief Constables	95
Haven Masters	95
Medical Superintendents of the Lunatic Asylum	95
Medical Officers of Health	95, 425
Surveyors	96
Inspectors of Nuisances	96, 425
Clerks to the Sanitary Authority	96
Inspectors of Weights and Measures	96
Sword Bearers	96, 426
City Librarians	96, 426

Auditors	97
Assessors	98, 426
Commissioners in Bankruptcy	98
Recorders since 1835	99
Judges of the County Court	99
Justices of the Peace	100, 415, 419, 426
Clerks to the Justices	103
Trustees of the Bristol Municipal Charities	104, 426
Bristol School Board	107, 415, 427

Bristol Incorporation of the Poor 115
Society of Merchant Venturers 122, 415, 419, 427
Chamber of Commerce 134, 416
The Colston Societies 138-152, 416, 419, 427
    Presidents of the Dolphin Society 138
    Presidents of the Anchor Society 142
    Presidents of the Grateful Society 144
    Presidents of the Colston Society 148
    Treasurers of the Colston Society 151
    Secretaries of the Colston Society 152
Antient Society of St. Stephen's Ringers...152, 267, 417
The Gloucestershire Society 160, 417
Members of Parliament for Bristol, 1529-1885......165, 428
Members of Parliament for Bristol West 174
Members of Parliament for Bristol South 175
Members of Parliament for Bristol North 175
Members of Parliament for Bristol East 175
Notes on Elections and Members for Bristol ... 176
    (See also pp. 54, 55.)
The Old Corporation of Bristol from 1599 to the passing of the Municipal Corporation Act of 1835:—
    Aldermen 184
    The Ancient Wards 190, 428
    Common Council 195
    Notes on the Knight Family 204, 430
    Mayors and Sheriffs, 1598-1835 222
Lord High Stewards, 1541-1835 231
Recorders, 1541-1835 .... 231, 430
Town Clerks, 1531-1835 234
Chamberlains, 1603-1835 235
Vice or Deputy Chamberlains, 1686-1835 .... 236, 430
Coroners, 1647-1835 .... 236, 431

Stewards of the Sheriffs' or Tolzey Court ... 237, 431
Court of Requests 238
Registrars of the Court of Conscience 238
Clerks and Registrars of the County Court ... 239
Sword Bearers, 1609-1835 239
Head Masters of the Grammar School 240, 431
Second Masters of the Grammar School 241
City Librarians before 1835 242
Chaplains of St. Mark's Church 242
Mayor's Chaplains 242, 431
Under Sheriffs 245
City Solicitors 245
Clerks of Arraigns 245
Mayor's Clerks 245
Quay Wardens 246
Water Bailiffs 246, 431
Haven Masters before 1835 247
Corn Measurers 247
Receivers of Town Dues 247
Secretaries to the Docks Estate 248
Superintendents of Works at Bristol Docks ... 248
Resident Engineers to the Bristol Docks ... 248, 417
Land Stewards 248
District Surveyors 248
City Surveyors 249
City Estates Surveyor 249
Lords-Lieutenant of Bristol 250
Postmasters 251, 432
Collectors of Customs 251
Registrars of the District Court of Bankruptcy 252
Official Assignees of the District Court of Bankruptcy 252

Official Receiver in Bankruptcy	252
Superintendent Registrars of Births, Deaths, and Marriages	252
Superintendent Registrars	252
Board of Guardians: Clifton Union	253, 432
Provincial Grand Masters of the Society of Freemasons	254
Principals and Vice-Principals of Bristol College, Park Row	254, 432
Principals of the Bishop's College	254, 432
Headmasters of Clifton College	254
Chairmen of Bristol Water Works Company	255
Bristol Royal Infirmary	255-263, 432
Treasurers	255
Presidents and Treasurers	255
Secretaries	255
Chaplains	256
Physicians	256
Obstetric Physicians	258
Surgeons	258
Ophthalmic Surgeon	260
Assistant Physicians	261
Assistant Surgeons	261
Apothecaries	261
House Surgeons and Apothecaries	262
Apothecaries	262
House Surgeons	262
Medical Superintendents	262
Assistant House Surgeons	263
House Physicians	263

Bristol General Hospital:—

    Presidents 263

    Secretaries 264

    Chaplains 264

    Physicians 264

    Physician Accoucheurs 265

    Surgeons 265

    Ophthalmic Surgeon 265

    Assistant Physicians 265

    Assistant Surgeons 266

    House Surgeons 267

Deputy Town Clerk 415

Bristol Board of Guardians 415

Chairmen of Docks Committee 420

Collectors of Mayor's Dues................................ 420

Trustees of Dr. White's Charity 420

Dock Masters 422

Presidents of Bristol Stock Exchange 422

Alphabetical Indexes:—

    I.—Mayors, Aldermen, and Town Councillors since the Municipal Corporation Act (1835-1899) 64, 269

    II.—Candidates for Seats in the Town Council who have not obtained Seats (1835-1899) 84, 274

    III.—Members of the Corporation (1599-1835) 275

    IV.—Persons not Elected to, or Candidates for, Seats in the Corporation (1599-1899).......................... 316

Errata and Addenda.. 433

The "Bristol Journals," of the Eighteenth Century 449

BRISTOL MUNICIPAL ELECTIONS SINCE THE ACT OF 1835.

NOTE.—The *first* election in all the wards took place on Dec. 26th, 1835. All subsequent elections were on Nov. 1st (or 2nd, if the 1st fell on a Sunday), unless when other dates are specified.

BRISTOL WARD.

1835.
James Wood (L) 388
Wm. Edward Acraman (C) 379
*Thomas Stock (L)..........377
Frederick Ricketts (L)...366
Peter Maze (C)................366
Charles Bowles Fripp(L)344
Henry Bush (C) 335
James Lean (C) 322
John Savage (C) 315
Richard Bligh (L) 314
Thomas Carlisle (L) 307
William Terrell (L) 302
Geo. Woodroffe Franklyn (C)...291
Samuel Waring (L)..........289
Samuel Morgan (L) 272
William Watson (C) 268
William Plummer (C) ...246
Aurelius John Drewe (C)238

*Mr. Stock was elected an alderman at the first meeting of the Council, but the vacancy thereby created in the representation of this ward was not filled till Nov. 1, 1837.

1836.
Harman Visger (L)..........364
Henry Bush (C) 363
Thomas Carlisle (L) 358
James Lean (C) 346
John Savage (C) 346
Samuel Waring (L)..........335

1837.
Charles Bowles Fripp(L)410
Stephen Prust (L) 403
Robert Fiske (L)............397
Peter Maze (C)................393
Peter Freeland Aiken (C) 384
Charles Grevile (C) 366

1837 (*vice* Stock elected an alderman).
*John Ballard Harwood (L) 363
Edmund Butcher (C) ...360
Peter Maze (C) 28
Charles Bowles Fripp (L) 10
P. Freeland Aiken (C) ... 9
Stephen Prust (L) 8
Charles Grevile (C)......... 3
Robert Fiske (L)............. 1

*Messrs. Harwood and Butcher were the only candidates for this vacancy, but as the election for three councillors to serve till 1840 was in progress at the same time, several votes were polled by mistake for the candidates who were standing for the other seats. The votes thus thrown away upon Mr. Maze would have sufficed to place him at the head of the poll at the contest in which he was actually a candidate.

BRISTOL WARD.—Continued.

1838.
Wm. Edward Acraman (C) 419
Peter Maze (C).........412
John Kerle Haberfield (C) 407
James Cunningham (L) 395
James Wood, J.P. (L) ...387
Thos. Richard Guppy (L) 371

1839.
Henry Bush (C) 389
James Lean (C).........387
Thomas Kington Bayly (C) 386
Harman Visger (L)......... 3
Michael Hinton Castle (L) 2
Robert Bruce (L)......... 0
[Messrs. Visger, Castle and Bruce retired before the poll].

1840.
Peter Freeland Aiken (C) 569
Valentine Helliear (C)...560
W. Weaver Davies (C) ...530
Charles Bowles Fripp (L) 501
M. Hinton Castle (L)......475
Harman Visger (L).........441

1841.
Wm. Edward Acraman (C)
Peter Maze (C)
John Kerle Haberfield (C)

1842, August 12 (vice Acraman, resigned).
Thos. Stock Butterworth (C) 366
James Wood, J.P. (L) .. 321

1842. Sept. 14 (vice Butterworth, deceased).
Thomas Green (C)

1842.
James Lean, J.P. (C)
Thos. Kington Bayly (C)
John George Shaw (C)

1843.
Thomas Carlisle (L)
Stephen Prust (L)
Robert Castle (L)

1844.
John Kerle Haberfield (C) 468
Thomas Green (C) 444
John William Miles (C) 439
George Jones (L) 362
Fredk. Charles Husenbeth (L)...356

1845.
John George Shaw (C)
Charles Joseph Vining (C)
Abraham Alexander (C)

1846.
Thomas Carlisle (L)
Stephen Prust (L)
Geo. Eddie Sanders, J.P. (L)

1847.
John Kerle Haberfield (C) 451
John William Miles (C) 431
Thomas Green (C) 427
Samuel Pim Jackson (L) 358
George Jones (L).........355

1848.
John George Shaw (C)
Abraham Alexander (C)
Arthur Hare Palmer (L)

1849.
Robert Bruce (L)........488
Geo. Eddie Sanders, J.P. (L) 372
Thos. Richard Sanders (L) 361
James Bush (C).........201
James Protheroe (L)......183
[This was not a political contest. Messrs. Bush and Protheroe stood in the "Free Port" interest. Mr. Bruce receiving votes from both parties.]

1850.
*John Kerle Haberfield, J.P. (C)
Thomas Green (C)
John William Miles (C)
 * Knighted Mar. 26, 1851.

1851. April 10 (vice G. E. Sanders, deceased).
John Cox (L)

1851.
John George Shaw (C)
Abraham Alexander (C)
Arthur Hare Palmer (L)

1852.
Thomas Canning (C)......461
Thos. Richard Sanders (L) 454
Richard Fuidge (C) 449
John Cox (L).........434
James Bush (C) 434
Francis Short (L) 423

BRISTOL WARD.—*Continued.*

1853.
Sir J. K. Haberfield, J.P. (C) 538
Robert Lang (L) 505
John William Miles (C) 466
Richd. Manning Hayman (L)...457
Thomas Green (C) 448
Robert Goss (L) 380

1854.
John George Shaw, J.P. (C) 638
John Bates (C).............. 468
Abraham Alexander (C) 459
Arthur Hare Palmer (L) 434
Thos.Wright Rankin (L) 398
[Mr. Shaw, being Mayor, received considerable support from the Liberals.]

1855.
Thomas Canning (C)
Richard Fuidge (C)
Arthur Hare Palmer (L)

1856.
Sir J. K. Haberfield, J.P.(C)
John William Miles (C)
Robert Lang (L)

1857.
John George Shaw, J.P.(C)
Abraham Alexander (C)
John Bates (C)

1858, Jan. 5 (*vice* Haberfield' deceased).
James Hassell (C)

1858.
Thomas Canning (C)......499
James Bush (C) 493
Richard Fuidge(C).........459
William Terrell (L) 437
Mark Whitwill (C).........401
Francis Tuckett (L) 374
[This was not a political contest. Messrs. Bush, Terrell, and Whitwill stood on the Dock interest. Mr. Whitwill was at this time a Conservative, and his name appeared on Mr. Slade's committee at the Parliamentary election of April, 1859. He subsequently became a Liberal leader.]

1859.
John William Miles (C)
Robert Lang (L)
James Hassell (C)

1860.
John Bates (C).............. 736
John George Shaw, J.P. (C) 556
Abraham Alexander (C) 451
Mark Whitwill (C) 366
Thos Wright Rankin (L) 243
[Mr. Bates, being mayor, was unopposed. Messrs. Whitwill and Rankin represented the Dock party.]

1861.
Thomas Canning (C)
James Bush (C)
Joseph Abraham (C)

1862, Jan. 10 (*vice* Hassell, deceased).
Wm. Hy. Harford, jun. (C)

1862.
John William Miles (C)
Wm. Hy. Harford, jun. (C)
William Henry Wills (L)

1863.
Abraham Alexander (C)
John Bates (C)
William Terrell, J.P. (L)

1864.
Thomas Canning, J.P. (C)
James Bush (C)
Joseph Abraham (C)

1865.
John William Miles (C)
Wm. H. Harford, jun. (C)
William Henry Wills (L)

1866, March 29 (*vice* Bush, deceased).
George Wills (L)............ 64
William Hathway (C) ... 0
Nominated without consent.

1866.
James Creswell Wall (C)609
Robert Bush (C) 608
John Bates, J.P. (C) 572
William Terrell, J.P. (L)528
Henry Overton Wills, jun. (L) 494
Joseph Dodge Weston (L) 493

1867, Feb. 13 (*vice* Abraham, deceased).
William Killigrew Wait (C)

1867.
Thomas Canning, J.P. (C)
George Wills (L)
William Killigrew Wait (C)

BRISTOL WARD.—Continued.

1868.
Wm. Hy. Harford, jun., J.P. (C)
William Henry Wills, J.P. (L)
William Henry Miles (C)
1869, Aug. 30 (vice Bates, deceased).
John Bartlett (C)
1869.
Robert Bush (C)
John Bartlett (C)
William Terrell, J.P. (L)
1870.
Thomas Canning, J.P. (C)
George Wills (L)
William Killigrew Wait (C)
1871.
Wm. Henry Harford, jun. J.P. (C)
William Henry Wills, J.P. (L)
William Henry Miles (C)
1872.
Robert Bush, J.P. (C)
John Bartlett (C)
William Terrell, J.P. (L)
1873.
Thomas Canning, J.P. (C)
George Wills, J.P. (L)
William Killigrew Wait, J.P. (C)
1874.
Wm. Hy. Harford, jun., J.P. (C)
William Henry Wills, J.P. (L)
William Henry Miles (C)
1875.
Robert Bush, J.P. (C)
John Bartlett (C)
William Terrell, J.P. (L)
1876.
George Wills, J.P. (L)
William Killigrew Wait. J.P. (C)
John William Stone Dix (C)
1877, August 24 (vice Bush, deceased).
Henry Napier Abbot (C)
1877.
William Henry Harford, J.P. (C)
*William Henry Wills, J.P. (L)
William Henry Miles (C)

1878.
John Bartlett (C)
Hy. Napier Abbot (C)
*James Derham (L)
1879.
William K. Wait, J.P. (C) 570
John Wm. Stone Dix (C)499
*George Wills, J P. (L) 394
Moss Levy (L) 247
* Transferred to St. Philip's (North), October 22, 1880, in accordance with a resolution passed on Sept. 28, the number of councillors for Bristol Ward being reduced to six by the Act of that year.
1880.
Wm. Hy. Harford, J.P. (C)
Wm. Henry Miles (C)
1881.
Hy. Napier Abbot (C)....576
John Bartlett (C) 575
Moss Levy (L) 445
William Stevens (C) 255
William Jennings (L)....243
[The two last were supported by the Ratepayers' Association.]
1882.
Wm. Killigrew Wait (C).655
John Wm. Stone Dix (C).617
Edwd. Gustavus Clarke (L) 525
1883.
Charles Wills (L) 695
William Hy. Miles (C) ...613
William Hy. Harford J.P. (C) 568
1884.
John Bartlett (C)
Henry Napier Abbot (C)
1885.
Joseph Thos. Board (C) 787
John William S. Dix (C).763
Thomas Baker (L) 577
1886.
Charles Wills (L) 644
William Ansell Todd(C)630
Robert Hy. Symes (C) ...577
1887.
John Bartlett (C)
Henry Napier Abbot (C)

BRISTOL WARD.—*Continued.*

1888.
John Wm. Stone Dix (C)
Joseph Thomas Board (C)

1889.
Charles Wills, J.P. (L)
William Ansell Todd (C)
1890, July 14 (*vice* Bartlett, elected an alderman).
George White (C)

1890.
Henry Napier Abbot (C)
George White (C)
1891, Feb. 25 (*vice* Dix, elected an alderman).
Robert Fenton Miles (C)

1891.
Joseph Thomas Board (C)
Robert Fenton Miles (C)

1892.
Charles Wills, J.P. (L)
William Ansell Todd (C)

1893.
Hamilton Wilfrid Killigrew Wait (C) 898
Henry Napier Abbot (C) 890
William Jennings (L)... 411

1894.
Joseph Thomas Board (C)
Charles Henry Cave (C)

1895.
William Ansell Todd, J.P. (C)...... 702
Richard Court Stephens (C) 683
Charles Wills, J.P. (L) 412

1896.
H.W.Killigrew Wait (C) 677
Henry Napier Abbot(C) 666
Solomon Leonard (L)... 224

1897.
Joseph Thomas Board (C)
Charles Henry Cave (C)

The BRISTOL WARD was represented by

5 Conservatives and 4 Liberals in Dec., 1835
5 Conservatives and 3 Liberals from Dec. 1835 to 1836
3 Conservatives and 5 Liberals from 1836 to 1837
2 Conservatives and 7 Liberals from 1837 to 1838
4 Conservatives and 5 Liberals from 1838 to 1839
6 Conservatives and 3 Liberals from 1839 to 1840
9 Conservatives from 1840 to 1843
6 Conservatives and 3 Liberals from 1843 to 1848
5 Conservatives and 4 Liberals from 1848 to 1852
7 Conservatives and 2 Liberals from 1852 to 1853
6 Conservatives and 3 Liberals from 1853 to 1854
7 Conservatives and 2 Liberals from 1854 to 1858
8 Conservatives and 1 Liberal   from 1858 to 1863
7 Conservatives and 2 Liberals from 1863 to March, 1866
6 Conservatives and 3 Liberals from March to Nov., 1866
7 Conservatives and 2 Liberals from 1866 to 1869
6 Conservatives and 3 Liberals from 1869 to Oct., 1880
6 Conservatives from Oct., 1880, to 1883
5 Conservatives and 1 Liberal from 1883 to 1895
6 Conservatives from 1895

58 individuals have represented Bristol Ward, of whom 37 were Conservatives and 21 Liberals

21 Councillors, viz., those after whose names " J.P." is appended above, and also Messrs. Stock, Savage, Cox, R. Castle, Fuidge, and Wall, were, or afterwards became, Justices of the Peace for the city.

1 (Sir J. K. Haberfield) was an Alderman up to the time of his election as Councillor

3 (Messrs. Stock, Bartlett, and Dix) were elected Aldermen whilst serving as Councillors

3 (Dr. Green and Messrs. Wall and W. K. Wait) were elected Aldermen after ceasing to be Councillors, the first-named (Dr. Green) at the first meeting of the Council after his defeat in this ward.

BRISTOL WARD.—*Continued.*

6 (Sir J. K. Haberfield and Messrs. Shaw, Bates, Abraham, W. K. Wait, and Canning) served the office of Mayor. Mr. Savage had been Mayor before the Act of 1835

5 (Messrs. Bayly, Harford, W. H. Miles, Todd, and Sir W. H. Wills) served the office of High Sheriff, which was also filled by Messrs. Savage and Lean before the Act of 1835.

8 Councillors (Sir J. K. Haberfield and Messrs. Butterworth, G. E. Sanders, Hassell, J. Bush, Abraham, Bates, and R. Bush) died in office: only one (Mr. Acraman) vacated his seat by resignation

The longest periods of office were those of Mr. J. W. Miles and Mr. Canning, each of whom served for 24 years: the shortest that of Mr. Butterworth, who died within a month of his election.

The highest poll in this ward was 898 for Mr. H. W. K. Wait in 1893.

CLIFTON WARD.

NOTE.—In most instances where a small number of votes is recorded for a candidate in this ward he was nominated without his consent, generally by the late Mr. Royall, who proposed candidates at almost (if not literally) every election for 40 years.

1835.
Charles Payne (C)......... 274
Gabriel Goldney (C) ... 268
James Norroway Franklyn (C) 258
Joseph Cookson (C)...... 238
Abraham Hillhouse (C) 223
William Singer Jacques (L) 204
James Ford (C) 204
Robert Edward Case (C) 204
Michael Hinton Castle (L) 198
John Warne (L)............. 196
Joseph Lax (C) 184
John Vining (C)............. 184
James Johnson (L)...... 177
Lachlan McBayne (L)... 165

1836.
Michael Hinton Castle (L.) 232
John Warne (L.)............. 226
Robert Edward Case (C) 209
James Ford (C) 204
James Johnson (L.) 200
William Oliver Bigg (C) 185

1837, Oct. 23 *vice* Warne, deceased).
*Cann Wilkins (C) 252
James Johnson (L.) 152
*Took the name De Winton, July, 1839.

1837.
Joseph Cookson, J.P. (C) 285
James Ford (C)............. 273
*Henry Charles Harford (C).......................... 273
William Lewton Clarke (C).......................... 267
William Singer Jacques (L)........................... 222
William Knowles (L) ... 208
James Poole, sen. (L) ... 202
William Johnson (L) ... 171

*Mr. Harford was elected to fill a vacancy caused by the death of Mr. Goldney in the preceding February.

1838. March 30 (*vice* Ford, deceased).
Peter Freeland Aiken (C)

1838.
Charles Payne, J.P. (C) 283
James Norroway Franklyn (C) 272
Henry Charles Harford (C) 251
William Singer Jacques (L) 188
William Johnson (L)... 157
John Naish Sanders, J.P. (L) 151

CLIFTON WARD.—Continued.

1839.
Robert Edward Case (C) 237
Edward Frampton (C) 235
William Oliver Bigg (C) 227
Thomas Royall (L) 37
Thomas Lane Coulson (C) 33
John Beames Burroughes (C) 16

1840.
Joseph Cookson, J.P.(C) 240
William Goldney (C) ... 240
William Lewton Clarke (C) 235
John Jacques (L) 88

1841.
James Norroway Franklyn (C)
Thomas Lane Coulson (C)
Charles Blisset (C)

1842, Aug. 13 (*vice* Franklyn, resigned).
William Kay (C) 133
Joseph Coates (L) 43

1842.
Robert Edward Case (C) 159
William Oliver Bigg (C) 159
John Gray (C) 146
John Fowler (C) 53
John Jacques (L) 34
Joseph Coates (L) 33

1843.
William Goldney (C) ... 141
William Lewton Clarke (C) 139
Charles Edward Bernard (C) 135
John Fowler (C) 61
Thomas Burbidge (C)... 55
John Mintorn (C) 54

1844, May 11 (*vice* Case, deceased)
Charles Wait (C) 85
John Fowler (C) 63

1844.
James Gibbs (C) 240
George Woodroffe Franklyn (C) 233
Charles Blisset (C) 219
Joseph Coates (L) 165
Wm. Henry Gore Langton (L) 139
Gabriel Goldney (C) 131

1845.
John Gray (C) 176
John Beames Burroughes (C)............... 170
Charles Wait (C) 123
William Oliver Bigg (C) 65

1846.
William Hautenville (C) 292
William Goldney (C) ... 286
Charles Edward Bernard (C) 283
Joseph Coates (L) 240
Thomas White (C) 131

1847.
James Gibbs (C)
George Woodroffe Franklyn (C)
Thomas Porter Jose (C)

1848.
Charles Wait (C)
William Henry Gore Langton, J.P. (L)
*Charles Warde, K.H. (C)
*Captain, R.N.; became Rear-Admiral, March, 1851

1849.
William Goldney (C) ... 179
William Hautenville (C) 172
John Ware (C) 169
George Bush (C) 49
Charles Hill (C)............ 49
Gabriel Goldney (C)...... 42

[Messrs. Bush, Hill, and G. Goldney represented the Dock party.]

1850, Feb. 1 (*vice* Goldney, deceased).
Odiarne Coates Lane (C) 175
George Bush (C) 106

1850.
Henry Lechmere Worrall, J.P. (C) 329
John Mills Kempster (L) 236
Joseph Coates, J.P. (L) 230
James Gibbs, J.P. (C) ... 219
John Jones (C) 212

[Col. Worrall was supported by both parties. Messrs. Kempster and Jones coalesced against Messrs. Gibbs and Coates.]

CLIFTON WARD.—*Continued.*

1851.
Wm. Henry Gore Langton, J.P. (L) 631
James Gibbs, J.P. (C)... 444
Charles Wait (C) 402
John Carter, jun. (C)... 336
John Beames Burroughes (C)............... 294

1852.
William Hautenville (C)
Odiarne Coates Lane (C)
John Beames Burroughes (C)

1852, Nov. 15 (*vice* Worrall, resigned).
John Carter, jun. (C)

1853, March 5 (*vice* Gibbs, deceased).
Henry Lechmere Worrall, J.P. (C)
[Became a Major-General in Nov., 1854.]

1853.
John Carter (C)............ 198
John Mills Kempster (L) 195
John Mintorn (C)......... 188
Joseph Coates, J.P. (L)..... 7

1854, Oct. 17 (*vice* Hautenville, deceased).
John Colthurst (C)

1854.
Michael Henry Castle, J.P. (L) 263
Isaac Allan Cooke (C)   253
Henry Lechmere Worrall, J.P. (C) 218
Charles Wait (C) 10

1855, April 14 (*vice* Carter resigned).
George Cooke (C)

1855.
Odiarne Coates Lane (C)
John Beames Burroughes (C)
John Colthurst (C)

1856.
John Mills Kempster (L)
George Cooke (C)
Joseph Coates, J.P. (L)

1857.
Henry Lechmere Worrall, J.P. (C)
Michael Henry Castle, J.P. (L)
Isaac Allan Cooke (C)

1858.
Odiarne Coates Lane, J.P. (C)
John Beames Burroughes (C)
John Colthurst (C)

1859.
John Mills Kempster (L)
George Cooke (C)
Joseph Coates, J.P. (L)

1860.
Henry Lechmere Worrall, J.P. (C)
Michael Henry Castle, J.P. (L)
Isaac Allan Cooke (C)

1861.
Odiarne Coates Lane, J.P. (C)
John Beames Burroughes (C)
John Colthurst (C)

1862, Aug. 13 (*vice* Coates, deceased).
Benj. Gustavus Burroughes (C) 417
Francis Tothill (L) 209

1862.
John Mills Kempster (L) 447
George Cooke (C)......... 413
Benj. Gustavus Burroughes (C) 404
Francis Tothill (L) 74
Peter Stewart Macliver (L) 40
Henry Browning (L) ... 8

1863.
Michael Henry Castle, J.P. (L)
Isaac Allan Cooke (C)
Richard Henry Walwyn (L)

1864.
Odiarne Coates Lane, J.P. (C)
John Beames Burroughes (C)
John Colthurst (C)

1865.
John Mills Kempster (L)
George Cooke (C)
Benj. Gustavus Burroughes (C)

1865, Dec. 1 (*vice* Lane, deceased).
James Newberry Cooper (L)

CLIFTON WARD.—Continued.

1866.
Lewis Fry (L).............. 607
Richard William Giles (C) 442
Isaac Allan Cooke (C) 421
Fredk. Nelson Watkins (L) 271
Charles Tovey (L)......... 259
John Jones (C) 31

1867, April 4 (vice Colthurst, resigned).
Joseph Haynes Nash (C) 147
George Kelson Stothert (C) 13

1867.
John Beames Burroughes (C)
James Newberry Cooper (L)
Joseph Haynes Nash (C)

1868.
George Cooke (C)......... 552
Benj. Gustavus Burroughes (C).............. 543
Joseph Dodge Weston (L) 494
John Hurn (C) 232
Thomas Clements (L) 102
Fredk. Nelson Watkins (L) 101
John Thorn (L)............. 34
Joseph Leech (C) 1

1869.
*Woodforde Ffooks (C) 760
Isaac Allan Cooke (C) 751
Henry Adams (C)......... 748
Lewis Fry (L).............. 589
*Took the name of Woodforde, October, 1871.

1870.
William Smith (C) 815
John Beames Burroughes (C).............. 795
Joseph Haynes Nash (C) 790
James Newberry Cooper (L) 419

1871.
George Cooke (C)
Benj. Gustavus Burroughes (C)
Joseph Dodge Weston (L)

1872.
Woodforde Ffooks-Woodforde (C) 614
James Inskip (C) 611
Isaac Allan Cooke (C) 541
Henry Cook (L)............ 330
John Hurn (C) 89
William Carro Pomeroy (C) 75

1873.
John Beames Burroughes (C) 390
William Smith (C) 388
Joseph Haynes Nash (C) 383
Henry Cook (L)............ 73
Richard William Giles (C) 22
John Thorn (L)............. 19
George Kelson Stothert (C) 13

1874, May 21 (vice Woodforde, resigned).
Wm. Wilberforce Jose (C) 512
Thomas Gibson (C)...... 97

1874.
Joseph Dodge Weston (L) 631
Benj. Gustavus Burroughes (C).............. 448
George Cooke (C)......... 383
Henry Cook (L)............ 266
Henry Taylor (C) 149
Benjamin White 41
Thomas Gibson (C)...... 36
Alfred Brittan (L)......... 29
William Lee (L) 20
Henry Isaac Brown (L) 18

1874, Dec. 31 (vice I. A. Cooke, deceased).
Henry Taylor (C) 276
Chas. John Collins Prichard (C) 7
William Lee (L)............ 2

1875.
James Inskip (C)
William Wilberforce Jose (C)
Henry Taylor (C)

1876.
Thomas Gibson (C)...... 732
William Smith (C) 662
Chas. John Collins Prichard (C) 660
Algernon Wm. Warren, J.P. (L) 656

1877.
*Joseph Dodge Weston, J.P. (L) 839
Alfred George de Lisle Bush (C) 688
William Baker (L)......... 621
Richard William Giles (C) 555

CLIFTON WARD.—Continued.

1878.
*James Inskip (C) 930
Henry Taylor (C) 914
Thomas Francis (C)...... 866
†Samuel Wills (L).......... 765
John Hurn (C) 38
Thomas Royall (L) 38
Roger Moore (L) 24
†Afterwards took the name Day before Wills.

1879.
*Thomas Gibson (C) ... 549
Chas. John Collins Prichard (C) 515
William Smith, J.P. (C) 449
Thomas Royall (L) 120
George Martin Carlile (L) 98
*Transferred to Westbury Ward, Oct 22, 1880, in accordance with a resolution passed Sept. 28, the number of councillors for Clifton Ward being reduced to six by the Act of that year.

1880.
Alfred George de Lisle Bush (C) 824
Uriah Alsop (C)............ 679
Alexander Thorburn Macgowan (C) 614
Roger Moore (L) 327
Thomas Royall (L) 10

1881.
Henry Joseph Williams (C) 618
Henry Taylor, J.P. (C) 595
Thomas Francis (C) ... 554
Job George Pinnigar(C) 111
Thomas Royall (L) 17
1882, Sep. 26 (vice Taylor, deceased).
Thomas Francis (C)

1882.
Thomas Gibson (C)...... 864
William Lyne Fear (C) 657
William Lee (L)............ 408
John Pavey (C) 29
Thomas Royall (L) 9

1883.
Uriah Alsop (C)............ 803
Alfred George de Lisle Bush (C) 501
Charles John Collins Prichard (C) 498
Thomas Royall (L) 21

1884.
Charles John Collins Prichard (C) 888
Thomas Francis (C) ... 742
John Thorn (L)............. 544
Thomas Royall (L) 36

1885.
William Lyne Fear (C) 959
Samuel Budgett (L)...... 736
John Thorn (L)............. 729
[Mr. Gibson had been nominated, but retired too late for another Conservative to be proposed in his place.]

1886.
John Pavey (C) 762
Alfred George de Lisle Bush (C) 697
Henry Joseph Williams (C) 569

1887.
Charles John Collins Prichard (C) 550
Thomas Francis (C) ... 538
Thomas Nimrod Simmons (L) 66

1888.
William Lyne Fear (C)
George Pearson (C)

1889.
Alfred George de Lisle Bush (C)
Edward Burrow Hill (C)

1890.
Charles John Collins Prichard (C) 1011
Thomas Winter Gibson (C) 889
Albert Essery (L).......... 381

1891.
George Pearson (C)...... 778
William Lyne Fear (C) 740
Henry Rossiter (L)...... 210
Roger Moore (L) 53

1892, April 27 (vice Gibson deceased).
Alfred Marshall (C)

1892.
Edward Burrow Hill(C)
Henry William Carter (C)

CLIFTON WARD.—Continued.

1893.
Charles John Collins Prichard (C) 775
Alfred Marshall (C)...... 732
Louis Edward de Ridder (C) 511
William Horace Brain (L) 111

1893, Nov. 23 (*vice* Prichard, elected an Alderman).
John Hancocke Wathen (C) 863
Louis Edward de Ridder (C) 853

1894.
Louis Edward de Ridder (C) 1149
George Pearson (C)...... 893
William Lyne Fear (C) 698

1895.
Commander George Cawley (C) 1114
Edward Burrow Hill (C) 742
Robert Gough (C)......... 725
William Horace Brain (L) 205

1896.
Arthur Albert Levy-Langfield (L U)......... 933
Admiral Francis Arden Close (C) 751
John Hancocke Wathen (C) 740
William Horace Brain (L) 227

1897, July 27 (*vice* Hill, deceased).
Samuel Shirley (C) 642
Charles Henry Tucker (C) 590
William Horace Brain (L) 110

1897.
George Pearson (C)......1102
Charles Peter Billing (C) 1025
Charles Henry Tucker (C) 887
William Horace Brain (L) 101

CLIFTON WARD was represented by

7 Conservatives and 2 Liberals from 1835 to 1836.
6 Conservatives and 3 Liberals from 1836 to Feb., 1837.
5 Conservatives and 3 Liberals from Feb. to Oct., 1837.
6 Conservatives and 2 Liberals from Oct. to Nov., 1837.
8 Conservatives and 1 Liberal from 1837 to 1839.
9 Conservatives from 1839 to 1848.
8 Conservatives and 1 Liberal from 1848 to 1850.
6 Conservatives and 3 Liberals from 1850 to 1853.
7 Conservatives and 2 Liberals from 1853 to 1856.
6 Conservatives and 3 Liberals from 1856 to July, 1862.
7 Conservatives and 2 Liberals from Aug., 1862, to 1863.
6 Conservatives and 3 Liberals from 1863 to Nov., 1865.
5 Conservatives and 4 Liberals from Dec., 1865, to 1866.
6 Conservatives and 3 Liberals from 1866 to 1869.
7 Conservatives and 2 Liberals from 1869 to 1870.
8 Conservatives and 1 Liberal from 1870 to 1877.
7 Conservatives and 2 Liberals from 1877 to Sept., 1880.
5 Conservatives and 1 Liberal from Oct. to Nov., 1880.
6 Conservatives from Nov., 1880, to 1885.
5 Conservatives and 1 Liberal from 1885 to 1888.
6 Conservatives from 1888 to 1896.
5 Conservatives and 1 Liberal Unionist from 1896.

76 individuals have represented Clifton Ward, of whom 62 were Conservatives, 13 Liberals, and one a Liberal Unionist.

[Of the 62 Conservatives, Messrs. Williams and De Ridder and Commander Cawley were returned as Independents, in opposition to official Conservative candidates, as also was the Liberal Unionist, Mr. Levy-Langfield.]

CLIFTON WARD.—*Continued.*

15 councillors for this ward were, or subsequently became, Justices of the Peace for the city, viz., those after whose name J.P. is appended above, and also Messrs. J. N. Franklyn, Bigg, T. P. Jose, and W. W. Jose.

1 (Mr. Prichard) was elected Alderman while serving as Councillor, and 1 (Dr. Kay) at the termination of his period of office.

5 (Messrs. Bigg, Smith, Inskip, W W. Jose. and Wathen) were also elected Aldermen after ceasing to be Councillors for Clifton Ward.

2 (Messrs. G. W. Franklyn and Gibbs) were Aldermen up to the date of their election as Councillors, and had already served the office of Mayor.

7 (Messrs. J. N. Franklyn, Clarke, W. Goldney, Langton, I. A. Cooke, Lane, and Taylor) served the office of Mayor whilst Councillors for Clifton Ward, and 2 (Mr. T. P. Jose and Sir J. D. Weston) after ceasing to represent it ; 3 (Messrs. Hillhouse, G. Goldney, and Payne) were Mayors before the Act of 1835.

1 (Mr. W. Smith) served the office of High Sheriff; 5 (Messrs. Hillhouse, G. Goldney, Payne, M. Hinton Castle, and J. N. Franklyn) had been High Sheriffs before the Act of 1835.

13 (Messrs. G. Goldney, Warne, Ford, Case, W. Goldney, Gibbs, Hautenville, Coates, Lane, I. A. Cooke, Taylor, T. W. Gibson, and Hill) died in office.

5 (Messrs. J. N. Franklyn, Worrall, Carter, Colthurst, and Woodforde) vacated their seats by resignation ; the last-named of these on appointment to a County Court Judgeship. General Worrall was re-elected a few months after his resignation.

The longest period of office was that of Mr. J. B. Burroughes, who served for 27 years (1845 to 1848 and 1852 to 1876) : the shortest that of Mr. Ford, whose two terms amounted to less than fifteen months.

The highest poll in this Ward was 1,149 for Mr. de Ridder in 1894.

REDCLIFF WARD.

1835.
Christopher George (L-C) 235
Henry Ricketts (L-C)... 236
Richard Jenkins Poole King (C) 228
George Thomas (L)...... 228
William Orchard Gwyer (C) 222
George Eddie Sanders (L) 222
John Hare, jun. (L)...... 213
William Fripp (C)......... 209
William Tothill (L)...... 206
Robert Fiske (L) 182
Nicholas Roch (C)......... 175
Henry Revell Llewellyn (L) 166

1836.
George Eddie Sanders (L) 259
William Tothill (L)...... 257
John Decimus Pountney (C) 216
William Ringer (C)...... 200

1837.
Richard Jenkins Poole King (C) 292
George Thomas (L)...... 282
Henry Fyson (L) 251
John Decimus Pountney (C) 229

1838.
Henry Ricketts, J.P. (C) 470
Christopher George (C) 270
William Day Wills (L) 251

REDCLIFF WARD.—*Continued.*

1839.
Charles Bowles Hare (C) 417
Samuel Lucas (C).......... 403
George Eddie Sanders
(L) 263
William Tothill, J.P. (L) 228

1840.
Richard Jenkins Poole King (C)
George Thomas (L)

1841.
Matthew Perkins (C)
William Thomas Poole King (C)

1842.
Charles Bowles Hare (C)
Thomas Powell (L)

1843.
Richard Jenkins Poole King, J.P. (C)
George Thomas (L)

1844.
William Thomas Poole King (C) 426
Matthew Perkins (C) ... 376
George Eddie Sanders, J.P. (L) 363

1845.
Charles Bowles Hare (C)
Thomas Powell (L)

1846.
Richard Jenkins Poole King, J.P. (C)
George Thomas (L)

1847.
Matthew Perkins (C)
William Thomas Poole King (C)

1848.
Charles Bowles Hare (C)
Thomas Powell (L)

1849.
Richard Jenkins Poole King, J.P. (C)
George Thomas (L)

1850.
Matthew Perkins (C)
William Thomas Poole King (C)

1851.
Charles Bowles Hare (C)
Thomas Powell (L)

1852.
Richard Jenkins Poole King, J.P. (C)
Samuel Pim Jackson (L)

1853.
William Thomas Poole King (C) 445
Matthew Perkins (C) ... 367
Charles Price (L)......... 345

1854.
John Hare (C)
Charles Price (L)

1855.
Richard Jenkins Poole King, J.P. (C)
Henry Prichard, J.P. (L)

1856.
Matthew Perkins (C)
William Thomas Poole King (C)

1857.
John Hare (C)
Charles Price (L)

1858.
Richard Jenkins Poole King, J.P. (C)
Algernon William Warren (L)

1859.
William Thomas Poole King (C) 367
Edward Thomas Lucas (C) 358
Mark Whitwill (C) 95
[Mr. Whitwill was nominated without his consent.]

1860.
John Hare (C)
Charles Price (L)

1861.
Richard Jenkins Poole King, J.P. (C)............ 498
William Augustus Frederick Powell (C) 435
Algernon William Warren (L) 398

1862.
William Thomas Poole King (C)
Edward Thomas Lucas (C)

1863, Aug. 14 (*vice* Lucas, deceased).
Algernon William Warren (L)

REDCLIFF WARD.—Continued.

1863.
John Hare, J.P. (C)
Charles Price (L.)

1864.
Richard Jenkins Poole King, J.P. (C)
William Augustus Fredk. Powell (C)

1865.
William Thomas Poole King (C)
Algernon William Warren (L.)

1866.
John Hare, J.P. (C)
Charles Price (L.)

1867.
Richard Jenkins Poole King, J.P. (C)
William Augustus Fredk. Powell (C)

1868.
William Thomas Poole King (C)
Algernon William Warren (L.)
1869, February 5 (vice Price, deceased).
William Priestley Sibree(L.)

1869.
John Hare, J.P. (C)
William Priestley Sibree(L.)

1870.
Richard Jenkins Poole King, J.P. (C)
William Augustus Fredk. Powell (C)

1871.
William Thomas Poole King (C).................... 896
Conrad William Curling Finzel (C)................. 893
Algernon Wm. Warren (L.) 353
1871. Nov. 17 (vice Hare, resigned).
Charles Bowles Hare (C) 80
Henry Pethick (L) 0
[Mr. Pethick's name was withdrawn before the poll.]

1872.
Charles Bowles Hare (C) 784
John Lucas (C)............ 754
Algernon Wm. Warren (L.) 483
William Priestley Sibree (L.).................. 471

1873.
Richard Jenkins Poole King, J.P. (C)............ 598
William Augustus Frederick Powell (C) 566
Henry Cook (L.)............ 57
1874, Oct 15 (vice R. P. King, deceased).
Mervyn Kersteman King (C)

1874.
Arthur Baker (C)......... 675
William Thomas Poole King (C) 627
Richard Cripps (C)...... 235

1875.
Charles Bowles Hare (C)
John Lucas (C)

1876.
Mervyn Kersteman King (C).................... 554
William Augustus Fredk. Powell, J.P.(C) 483
Roger Moore (L.) 367

1877.
Arthur Baker (C)......... 690
William Thomas Poole King (C) 664
Roger Moore (L.) 587

1878.
Charles Bowles Hare (C) 795
John Lucas (C) 725
Roger Moore (L) 505
Samuel Cashmore (L.)... 423

1879.
William Augustus Fredk. Powell, J.P. (C)
Richard Charles Ring (C)

1880.
Arthur Baker (C)......... 930
Charles Felce Hare (C) 941
Edward Payson Wills (L) 716
Robert Henry Symes (L) 678
1881, Feb. 7 (vice Lucas, deceased).
James Evan Jefferies (C) 837
Richard Cripps (C)...... 548

1881.
Charles Bowles Hare, J.P. (C)
James Evan Jefferies (C)

1882.
William Augustus Fredk. Powell (C)
Richard Charles Ring (C)

REDCLIFF WARD.—*Continued.*

1883.
Arthur Baker (C)
Charles Felce Hare (C)

1884.
Charles Bowles Hare, J.P. (C)
James Evan Jefferies (C)

1885, April 10 (*vice* Ring, resigned).
Richard Cripps (C) 858
Robert Henry Symes (L) 675

1885.
Richard Cripps (C) 877
Thomas Harding (C) ... 810
Henry Joseph Williams (C) 351

1886, Jan. 2 (*vice* C. F. Hare, deceased).
Edward Beadon Colthurst (C)

1886.
Arthur Baker (C)
Edward Beadon Colthurst (C)

1887.
Charles Bowles Hare, J.P. (C)
James Evan Jefferies (C)

1888.
Richard Cripps (C) 915
Thomas Harding (C) ... 903
Henry William Twiggs (L) 753

1889.
Arthur Baker, J.P. (C)
Edward Beadon Colthurst (C)

1890.
Charles Bowles Hare, J.P. (C) 1087
Henry William Twiggs (L) 979
James Evan Jefferies (C) 919

1891, Jan. 16 (*vice* Cripps, resigned).
Edward Burnet James (C)

1891.
Edward Burnet James (C) 1057
James Evan Jefferies (C) 1017
William Dove Willcox (L) 996

1892.
Arthur Baker, J.P. (C)
Edward Beadon Colthurst (C)

1893, March 4 (*vice* Jefferies, resigned).
James Colthurst Godwin, J.P. (LU)

1893.
Charles Bowles Hare, J.P. (C) 997
Henry William Twiggs (L) 837
Harold Brabham (Lab.) 488

1894.
James Colthurst Godwin, J.P. (LU) 995
Edward Burnet James (C) 974
Harold Brabham (Lab.) 546

1895.
Arthur Baker, J.P. (C)
Edward Beadon Colthurst, J.P. (C)

1896, May 14 (*vice* Hare, elected as Alderman).
Samuel Betty (C)

1896.
Herbert George Edwards (C)
Benjamin Perry (C)

1897.
Edward Burnet James (C)
James Colthurst Godwin (LU)

REDCLIFF WARD was represented by
4 Conservatives and 2 Liberals from 1835 to 1836
3 Conservatives and 3 Liberals from 1836 to 1839
5 Conservatives and 1 Liberal from 1839 to 1842
4 Conservatives and 2 Liberals from 1842 to 1861
5 Conservatives and 1 Liberal from 1861 to August, 1863
4 Conservatives and 2 Liberals from August, 1863, to 1871
5 Conservatives and 1 Liberal from 1871 to 1872
6 Conservatives from 1872 to 1890
5 Conservatives and 1 Liberal from 1890 to Feb., 1893.
4 Conservatives, 1 Liberal Unionist, and 1 Liberal from March, 1893, to 1895
5 Conservatives and 1 Liberal Unionist from 1896.

REDCLIFF WARD.—*Continued.*

37 individuals have represented Redcliff Ward, of whom 25 were Conservatives, 11 Liberals, and 1 a Liberal Unionist.

13 Councillors (Messrs. C. George, H. Ricketts, R. P. King, G. E. Sanders, W. Tothill, H. Prichard, J. Hare, W. A. F. Powell, A. W. Warren, C. B. Hare, A. Baker, J. C. Godwin, and E. B. Colthurst) have been Justices of the Peace for the city.

1 (Mr. C. B. Hare) was elected Alderman whilst serving as Councillor, and one (Mr. H. Ricketts) at the first meeting of the Council after ceasing to be a Councillor.

2 (Messrs. R. P. King and J. Hare) served the office of Mayor.

4 (Messrs. W. P. King, C. B. Hare, Baker, and Godwin) served the office of High Sheriff.

4 (Messrs. E. T. Lucas, R. P. King, J. Lucas, and C. F. Hare) died in office.

4 (Messrs. J. Hare, King, Cripps, and Jefferies) vacated their seats by resignation.

The longest period of office was that of Mr. W. P. King, who served for 39 years (from 1841 to 1880); the shortest that of Mr. S. Betty, who served for 5½ months (May to October, 1896).

The highest poll in this Ward was 1,087 for Mr. C. B. Hare in 1890.

ST. AUGUSTINE'S WARD.

1835.
Thomas Daniel (C) 152
Charles Hare (C) 149
Richard Smith (C) 147
James Ezekiel Nash (C) 145
Peter Maze, jun. (C) ... 134
Thomas Powell (C) 124
Charles Pinney (L-C)... 90
John Maningford (L)... 72
Joseph Reynolds (L)... 69
Richard Ricketts (L)... 68
Joseph Frankel Alexander (L) 68
James Jenkins (L) 54

1836.
Charles Vining (C) 163
Thomas Powell (C) 118
George Bengough (L)... 75

1837.
Richard Smith (C)
James Ezekiel Nash (C)

1833.
Thomas Daniel (C)
Cam Gyde Heaven (C)

1839.
Thomas Powell (C)
Charles Vining (C)

1840.
Richard Smith (C)
James Ezekiel Nash (C)

1841.
Cam Gyde Heaven (C)
Edward Joseph Staples (C)

1842.
Thomas Powell (C)
Frederick William Green (C)

1843, Feb. 2 (*vice* Smith, deceased).
John Fisher (C)

1843.
John Fisher (C)
Thomas William Hill (C)

1844.
Cam Gyde Heaven (C)
Edward Joseph Staples (C)

ST. AUGUSTINE'S WARD.—*Continued.*

1845.
Thomas Powell (C)
Frederick William Green (C)
1846, May 13 (*vice* Staples, resigned).
Charles Taylor (C) 149
Robert Bright (L) 86
Wm. Wolfe Alexander (C) 16

1846.
John Fisher (C)
Thomas William Hill (C)

1847.
Cam Gyde Heaven (C)
Charles Taylor (C)

1848.
Thomas Powell (C)
Frederick William Green (C)

1849.
John Fisher (C)
George Rogers (C)

1850.
Cam Gyde Heaven (C)
Charles Taylor (C)

1851.
Frederick Wm. Green (C) 330
Charles Nash (C) 194
Thomas Powell (C) 178

1852.
John Fisher (C)
George Rogers (C)

1853.
Cam Gyde Heaven (C)
Charles Taylor (C)

1854.
Frederick William Green (C)
Charles Nash (C)

1855.
John Fisher (C)
George Rogers (C)

1856.
Cam Gyde Heaven (C)
Charles Taylor (C)

1857.
Frederick William Green (C)
Charles Nash (C)

1858.
John Fisher (C)
Thomas Porter Jose (C)

1859.
William Jeffery (C) 220
Thomas Terrett Taylor (C) 196
Cam Gyde Heaven (C).. 159

1860.
Frederick William Green (C)
Charles Nash (C)

1861.
Henry Augustus Salmon (C) 287
Thomas Porter Jose (C) 242
James Protheroe (L) ... 200
Isaac Riddle (L) 154

1862.
William Jeffery (C)
Thomas Terrett Taylor (C)

1863.
Charles Nash (C)
William Spark (C)

1864, March 10 (*vice* Jeffery, deceased).
John Hellicar (C)

1864.
Thomas Porter Jose (C) 241
William Merrett Webb (C) 223
William Llewellyn (L) 208

1865.
Thomas Terrett Taylor (C)
John Hellicar (C)

1866.
Charles Nash (C)
William Spark (C)

1867.
Thomas Porter Jose (C)
William Merrett Webb (C)

1868.
Thomas Terrett Taylor (C)
John Hellicar (C)

1869.
Charles Nash (C)
William Spark (C)

1870.
Thomas Porter Jose, J.P. (C)
William Merrett Webb (C)

1871.
Thomas Terrett Taylor (C)
John Hellicar (C)

ST. AUGUSTINE'S WARD.—*Continued.*

1872.
Charles Nash, J.P. (C).. 477
William Spark (C) 421
William Llewellyn (L) 296

1873.
William Merrett Webb (C)
Edward Arthur Harvey (C)

1874.
Thomas Terrett Taylor
(C) 375
Richard Ridler (C) 336
Robert Henry Symes
(L) 188

1875.
Charles Nash, J.P. (C)
William Spark (C)

1876.
William Merrett Webb (C)
Edward Arthur Harvey (C)

1877.
*William Lee (L) 461
Thomas Terrett Taylor
(C) 454
Joseph Seymour
Metford (C) 381

1878.
Charles Nash, J.P. (C)
*William Spark (C)

1879.
*William Merrett Webb (C)
Edward Arthur Harvey (C)

1880, July 12 (*vice* Taylor, deceased).
John Strachan Bridges (C)
* Transferred to Bedminster Ward (East), October 22, 1880, in accordance with a resolution passed Sept. 28, the number of Councillors for St. Augustine's Ward being reduced to three by the Act of that year.

1880.
John Strachan Bridges
(C) 537
William Lee (L)............ 350

1881.
Charles Nash, J.P. (C)

1882.
Edward Arthur Harvey
(C) 466
Henry Isaac Brown (L) 28

1883.
John Strachan Bridges (C)

1884.
Charles Nash, J.P. (C)

1885.
Edward Arthur Harvey (C)

1886.
James Fuller Eberle (C)

1886, Nov. 23 (*vice* Nash, elected an Alderman).
John Walls (C) 511
Walter William Hughes
(L) 269

1887.
John Walls (C)

1888.
Edward Arthur Harvey (C)

1889.
James Fuller Eberle (C)

1890.
John Walls (C)

1891.
Edward Rogers (C)

1892.
James Fuller Eberle (C)

1893, June 23 (*vice* Rogers, resigned).
Charles Robert Hancock (C)

1893.
John Walls (C)

1894.
Charles Robert Hancock (C)

1895.
James Fuller Eberle (C)

1896.
John Walls (C)

1897.
Charles Robert Hancock (C)

St. Augustine's Ward was represented by

6 Conservatives from 1835 to 1877
5 Conservatives and 1 Liberal from 1877 to Oct., 1880
3 Conservatives since Oct., 1880

ST. AUGUSTINE'S WARD.—*Continued.*

30 individuals have represented St. Augustine's Ward, of whom 29 were Conservatives and 1 a Liberal (Mr. W. Lee).

5 (Messrs. Daniel, Fisher, Jose, C. Nash, and Spark) were, or subsequently became, Justices of the Peace for the city.

1 (Mr. C. Nash) was elected Alderman whilst serving as Councillor; one (Mr. Heaven) at the first meeting of the Council after ceasing to be a Councillor; one (Mr. Spark) at the first vacancy after ceasing to represent Bedminster (East), to which he had been transferred from St. Augustine's.

2 (Messrs. Daniel and Jose) were elected to the Mayoralty, the former of whom declined to serve, having already filled the office in 1797-98.

2 (Messrs. Maze and Fisher) served the office of High Sheriff after retiring from the Council. Mr. Maze had also filled the office before the Act of 1835, and Mr. Daniel as far back as 1786-7.

3 (Messrs. Smith, Jeffery, and T. T. Taylor) died in office; two (Messrs. Staples and E. Rogers) vacated their seats by resignation.

The longest period of office was that of Mr. C. Nash, who served for 35 years (1851 to 1886); the shortest that of Mr. Maze, 10 months (December, 1835, to October 31, 1836).

The highest poll in this Ward was 537 for Mr. Strachan Bridges in 1880.

ST. PHILIP'S WARD.

1835.
Thomas Harris (L) ... 302
William Herapath (L).. 242
Edward Bowles Fripp (L) 236
Samuel Gayner Flook (C) 107
John Winwood (C)...... 92

[Mr. Harris was supported by both parties.]

1836.
Edward Bowles Fripp (L) 182
Thomas Edwards (C).. 59

1837.
William Herapath, J.P. (L) 166
Robert Trapp Lilly (C) 150

1838.
Thomas Harris (L) ... 159
Robert Trapp Lilly (C) 146

1839.
Edward Bowles Fripp (L).

1840.
William Done Bushell (C) 300
William Herapath, J.P. (L) 248

1841.
Michael Hinton Castle (L).

1842.
Harman Visger (L)

1843.
William Done Bushell (C).

1844.
Michael Hinton Castle (L).

1845, Jan. 31 (*vice* Castle, deceased).
Christopher James Thomas (L).

ST. PHILIP'S WARD.—*Continued.*

1845.
Harman Visger (L).

1846.
William Done Bushell (C).

1847.
Christopher James Thomas (L).

1848.
Harman Visger (L).

1849.
Henry Brown Jordan (C).

1850.
Christopher James Thomas (L).

1851.
Harman Visger (L).

1852.
Isaac Riddle (L) 513
Henry Brown Jordan (C) 252

1853.
Christopher James Thomas (L)

1854.
Harman Visger (L).

1855.
Robert Leonard, jun. (L).

1856.
Christopher James Thomas, J.P. (L)...... 330
Thomas Bush (C) 119

1857.
Harman Visger (L).

1858.
Henry William Green (L).

1859.
Christopher James Thomas, J.P. (L).

1860.
Henry Duffett (L) 445
Isaac Riddle (L) 341
William Augustus Frederick Powell (C) 275

1861.
Henry William Green (L)

1862.
Christopher James Thomas, J.P. (L).

1863.
Joseph Wethered (L.)

1864.
Henry William Green (L)

1865.
Christopher James Thomas, J.P. (L)

1866.
Joseph Wethered (L).

1867.
Henry William Green (C)
[Mr. Green, who had previously been a Liberal, supported the Conservative candidate, Mr. J. W. Miles, at the Parliamentary election in the following April.]

1868.
Christopher James Thomas, J.P. (L)

1869.
David Parker Evans (L)

1870.
Mark Whitwill (L)...... 1922
Henry Naish (L)......... 269
[Mr. Naish was proposed without his consent.]

1871.
Christopher James Thomas, J.P. (L)

1872.
Lewis Fry (L)

1873.
Mark Whitwill (L)

1874.
Christopher James Thomas, J.P. (L)

1875.
Lewis Fry (L)

1876.
Mark Whitwill, J.P. (L)

1877.
Christopher James Thomas, J.P. (L)...... 1616
William Count (Lab.).. 502

1878.
Lewis Fry (L) 1195
William Count (Lab.).. 287

1879.
Mark Whitwill, J.P. (L)
[The three sitting Councillors were assigned to the Southern Division of the Ward Oct. 22, 1880, by a resolution passed Sept. 28.]

ST. PHILIP'S WARD.—*Continued.*

St. Philip's Ward was represented by

3 Liberals from 1835 to 1840
2 Liberals and 1 Conservative from 1840 to 1852
3 Liberals from 1852 to 1867
2 Liberals and 1 Conservative from 1867 to 1870
3 Liberals from 1870 to October, 1880, when it was divided into two Wards, each returning 3 Liberals.

16 individuals represented St. Philip's Ward before its sub-division, of whom 14 were Liberals and 2 (Messrs. Bushell and Jordan) Conservatives. Mr. Green, who was returned as a Liberal, also became a Conservative.

3 (Messrs. Herapath, Thomas, and Whitwill) were Justices of the Peace for the city while serving as councillors, and one (Mr. Evans) subsequently to his retirement.

1 (Mr. Jordan) was elected alderman after ceasing to be a councillor.

1 (Mr. Thomas) served the office of Mayor.

1 (Mr. Castle) had served the office of High Sheriff before the Act of 1835.

1 (Mr. Castle) died in office; no vacancies occurred by resignation.

The longest period of office was that of Mr. Thomas, who served for more than 35 years (January, 1845, to 1880), and afterwards represented the Southern Division of the Ward; five councillors (Messrs. Jordan, Riddle, Leonard, Duffett, and Evans) served for only one term of three years each.

ST. PHILIP'S WARD (SOUTH).

1880. Oct. 22.
ChristopherJamesThomas, J.P. (L), to retire in 1880.
Lewis Fry (L) to retire in 1881.
Mark Whitwill, J.P. (L), to retire in 1882.

1880.
ChristopherJamesThomas, J.P. (L)

1881.
Lewis Fry (L)

1882.
Mark Whitwill, J.P.(L) 574
Henry Isaac Brown (L) 46

1883.
James Dole (L) 1035
Thomas Dix Sibly (L) 602
JamesDuffettLucas(C) 123

1884.
Thomas Dix Sibly (L)

1885.
Mark Whitwill, J.P. (L)

1886.
James Dole (L)

1887.
William Butler (L)...... 960
George Belsten (Lab.) 617

1888.
Mark Whitwill, J.P. (L)

1889.
Hugh Holmes Gore (U, Soc.) 1293
James Dole (L U) 465
William Henry Cowlin (L) 15

1890.
John Swaish (L)

1891.
William Henry Elkins (L)

1892.
Hugh Holmes Gore (U. Soc.) 1008
William Henry Cowlin (L) 429

ST. PHILIP'S WARD (SOUTH).—*Continued.*

1893.
John Swaish (L.)

1894.
William Henry Elkins (L.)

1895.
James Smith Naish (Ind. C) 612
Albert Essery (L) 479
Richard Thomas Daniell (Lab.) 270

1896.
John Swaish (L)

1897, Oct. 2 (*vice* Naish, deceased).
Henry Frederick Cotterell (L.) 653
Harold Brabham (Lab.) 408
John William Lane (L. U) 332
Thomas Griffiths (Ind.) 167

1897.
William Henry Elkins (L)

St. Philip's Ward (South) was represented by

3 Liberals from 1880 to 1889 (one of these a Liberal Unionist from 1886 to 1887, and another from 1886 to 1889)
2 Liberals and 1 Unionist Socialist from 1889 to 1895
2 Liberals and 1 Independent Conservative from 1895 to Sept., 1897
3 Liberals since Oct., 1897.

11 individuals have represented St. Philip's Ward (South), of whom 9 were Liberals, 1 a Unionist Socialist, and 1 an Independent Conservative. (Messrs. Dole and Sibly, elected as Liberals, became Unionists in 1886.)

2 (Messrs. Thomas and Whitwill) were Justices of the Peace for the city.

1 (Mr. Thomas) had served the office of Mayor whilst representing the undivided Ward.

1 (Mr. Naish) died in office; no vacancy occurred by resignation.

The longest period of office was that of Mr. Whitwill, who served for 11 years (1880 to 1891); the shortest was that of Mr. Naish, who died in Sept., 1897—22 months after his election.

The highest poll in this ward was 1,293, for Mr. Holmes Gore, in 1889.

ST. PHILIP'S WARD (NORTH).

1880. Oct. 22.
William Henry Wills, J.P. (L.), to retire in 1880.
James Derham (L.), to retire in 1881.
George Wills, J.P. (L), to retire in 1882.
[Transferred from Bristol Ward.]

1880.
Algernon William Warren, J.P. (L.) 1021
John Henry Clifton (C) 806

1881.
James Derham

1882.
Moss Levy (L) 1037
George Wills, J.P. (L.)... 432

1883, May 7 (*vice* Warren deceased).
Charles Garton (L.) 702
Samuel Peters (Labour) 153

1883.
Charles Garton (L.) 944
Francis Gilmore Barnett (L) 422

1884.
James Derham (L) 716
Francis Gilmore Barnett (L) 659

ST. PHILIP'S WARD (NORTH).—*Continued.*

1885.
Moss Levy (L) 1449
James Britt (C) 54

1886.
FrancisGilmoreBarnett (L) 1114
Charles Garton (L) 779

1887.
Charles Garton (L U)... 995
Samuel Waltham Pritchett (Labour)......747

1888.
Moss Levy (L)

1889.
FrancisGilmoreBarnett (L)

1890.
AlbertGeorgeCunningham (L).....................1305
Philip Owen (L) 455

1891.
Moss Levy (L)

1892.
FrancisGilmoreBarnett(L)

1893.
JohnSharland(Labour)1227
George Baker (Ind.) ... 561

1894.
Moss Levy (L)

1895.
FrancisGilmoreBarnett (L) 793
George Baker (Ind.) ... 39

1896.
John Sharland (Labour)

1897.
Moss Levy (L)

St. Philip's Ward (North) was represented by

3 Liberals from 1880 to 1887.
2 Liberals and 1 Liberal Unionist from 1889 to 1890.
3 Liberals from 1890 to 1893.
2 Liberals and 1 Labour member from 1893.

9 individuals have represented St. Philip's Ward (North), of whom eight were Liberals and one a Labour member. One of the eight Liberals (Mr. Garton) was a Unionist at the date of his last election, and another (Mr. George Wills) became one after ceasing to be a councillor.

3 Councillors (Sir W. H. Wills, Messrs. G. Wills and Warren) were Justices of the Peace for the city.

1 (Sir W. H. Wills) had previously served the office of High Sheriff.

1 (Mr. Warren) died in office; no vacancies occurred by resignation.

The longest period of office has been that of Mr. Levy, who has served since 1882; the shortest term was that of Sir W. H. Wills, who served for only ten days (Oct. 22 to 31, 1880).

The highest poll in this Ward was 1,449 for Mr. Levy, in 1885.

BEDMINSTER WARD.

1835.
Robert Phippen (C) ... 93
John Drake (L)............ 92
Samuel Brown (L) 79
Henry Glascodine (C).. 58
James Bartlett (C) 56
James Powell (L).......... 46
[Mr. Powell was nominated without his consent.]

1836.
Samuel Brown (L)

1837.
John Drake, J.P. (L)

1838.
William Terrell (L)...... 91
Robert Phippen (C) ... 74

1839.
Robert Phippen (C) ... 155
Henry Fyson (L) 150

1840.
William Tothill (L)

BEDMINSTER WARD.—*Continued.*

1841.
William Terrell (L.)

1842.
Robert Phippen (C) ... 139
Harman Visger (L.) 130

1843.
William Tothill (L.)

1844.
William Terrell (L)

1845.
Robert Phippen (C)

1846.
William Tothill (L)

1847.
Frederick Terrell (L)

1848.
Robert Phippen (C)

1849.
William Tothill (L.)

1850.
Frederick Terrell (L)

1851.
Robert Phippen, J.P.
(C) 206
Henry Prichard (L) ... 91

1852.
William Tothill (L.)

1853.
Frederick Terrell (L)... 243
William Patterson (C).. 150

1854.
John Ayre, jun. (L) 405
Robert Phippen, J.P.
(C) 245

1855.
Henry Terrell (L)

1856.
Frederick Terrell (L)

1857.
John Ayre, jun. (J.) 277
Henry Bennett (L) 90
[Mr. Bennett was nominated without his consent.]

1858, July 26 (*vice* H. Terrell, deceased.)
Elisha Smith Robinson (L)

1858.
Elisha Smith Robinson (L)

1859.
Frederick Terrell (L)

1860.
John Ayre, jun. (L)

1861.
Elisha Smith Robinson
(L) 592
John Frederick Lucas
(C) 439

1862.
Frederick Terrell (L)

1863, August 21 (*vice* Ayre, deceased).
Stephen Fitchew Cox (C)

1863.
Stephen Fitchew Cox (C)

1864.
Elisha Smith Robinson (L)

1865.
Frederick Terrell (L)

1866.
William Pethick (L) ... 779
Stephen Fitchew Cox
(C) 613

1867.
Elisha Smith Robinson, J.P. (L)

1868.
Frederick Terrell, J.P. (L)

1869.
William Pethick (L)

1870.
Elisha Smith Robinson, J.P. (L)

1871.
Frederick Terrell, J.P. (L)

1872.
Stephen James (C) 1014
William Pethick, J.P.
(L) 934

1873.
Elisha Smith Robinson,
J.P. (L) 1209
Henry Isaac Brown (L) 368
Henry Beaven (C) 106
Alfred Robinson (L) ... 32
Henry Bennett (L) 10
Frank R. Robinson (L) 7
William Pethick, J.P.
(L) 4
Thomas Evans 3
Harry Robinson (L) ... 2
George Pine 2
James Jones 1
Robert John Crocker
(L) 1
Thomas Cleverdon (L) 1

BEDMINSTER WARD.—*Continued.*

1874, Jan. 2 (*vice* James, deceased).
William Pethick, J.P. (L) 1070
Charles Amesbury Whitley Deans Dundas (C) 524
[Mr. Dundas was nominated twice, once by his full name, and once as C. A. W. Dundas, omitting the name "Deans." 475 votes were polled for him under the former, and 49 under the latter appellation.]

1874.
Frederick Terrell, J.P. (L)

1875.
William Pethick, J.P. (L)

1876.
Elisha Smith Robinson, J.P. (L)

1877.
Frederick Terrell, J.P. (L)

1878.
William Pethick, J.P. (L) 1339
Albert Essery (L).......... 625

1879.
Elisha Smith Robinson, J.P. (L)
[The three sitting Councillors were assigned to the Western Division of the Ward Oct. 22, 1880, by a resolution passed September 28.]

BEDMINSTER WARD was represented by

2 Liberals and 1 Conservative from 1835 to 1838
3 Liberals from 1838 to 1839.
2 Liberals and 1 Conservative from 1839 to 1854
3 Liberals from 1854 to August, 1863
2 Liberals and 1 Conservative from August, 1863, to 1866
3 Liberals from 1866 to 1872
2 Liberals and 1 Conservative from 1872 to Dec., 1873
3 Liberals from Jan., 1874, to Oct., 1880

12 individuals represented Bedminster Ward before its subdivision, of whom 9 were Liberals and 3 Conservatives.

5 (Messrs. Phippen, Drake, F. Terrell, Robinson, and Pethick) were Justices of the Peace for the city whilst serving as Councillors, and one (Mr. Brown) after ceasing to be a Councillor.

1 (Mr. Phippen) became an Alderman and served the office of High Sheriff after ceasing to be a Councillor for the undivided Ward, and one (Mr. Pethick) after serving for the Western Division.

2 (Messrs. Phippen and Robinson) served the office of Mayor.

3 (Messrs. H. Terrell, Ayre, and James) died in office; no vacancies occurred by resignation.

The longest period of office was that of Mr. F. Terrell, who served for 33 years (from 1847 to 1880), and subsequently represented the Western Division of the Ward for three years; the shortest was that of Mr. H. Terrell, 2 years and 8 months (from 1855 to July, 1858).

The highest poll in this Ward was 1,339 for Mr. Pethick in 1878.

BEDMINSTER WARD (WEST).

1880. Oct. 22.
Frederick Terrell, J.P. (L),
to retire in 1880.
William Pethick, J.P. (L),
to retire in 1881.
Elisha Smith Robinson,
J.P. (L), to retire in
1882.

1880.
Frederick Terrell, J.P. (L)

1881.
William Pethick, J.P. (L)

1882.
Elisha Smith Robinson,
J.P. (L)

1883.
Stephen George James
(C) 1062
Edward Payson Wills
(L) 959

1884.
William Pethick, J.P. (L)
(Became a Liberal Unionist
in 1886.)

1885, Sept.22 (vice Robinson,
deceased).
Frederick Wills (L)

1885.
Frederick Wills (L)
(Became a Liberal Unionist
in 1886.)

1886.
Stephen George James
(C)

1887.
Henry Joseph Williams
(Ind. C) 676
William Pethick, J.P.
(L U) 485
Edward Colston White
(C) 82

1888.
William Mereweather (L)

1889.
Edward Parsons (L) ...1429
Stephen George James,
J.P. (C) 944

1890.
William Albina Latham (L)

1891.
Thomas Cleverdon (L)

1892.
Edward Parsons (L)

1893.
William Albina Latham
(L) 1207
William Baster (Soc.)... 904
Walter Edwin Gardner
(C) 689

1894.
Joseph Pembery, J.P.
(L) 1381
William Baster (Soc.)... 724

1895.
Edward Parsons (L)

1896.
William Albina Latham (L)

1897.
Joseph Pembery, J.P. (L)

BEDMINSTER WARD (WEST) was represented by

3 Liberals from 1880 to 1883
2 Liberals and 1 Conservative from 1883 to 1886
2 Liberal Unionists and 1 Conservative from 1886 to 1887
2 Conservatives and 1 Liberal Unionist from 1887 to 1888
2 Conservatives and 1 Liberal from 1888 to 1889
2 Liberals and 1 Conservative from 1889 to 1890
3 Liberals from 1890

11 individuals have represented Bedminster Ward (West), of whom 9 were Liberals and 2 Conserva-tives. Of the nine Liberals two (Messrs. Pethick and Wills) became Unionists during their term of office.

5 (Messrs. Terrell, Robinson, Pethick, James, and Pembery) were Justices of the Peace for the city.

1 (Mr. Pethick) became Alderman and High Sheriff after ceasing to be a Councillor.

BEDMINSTER WARD (WEST).—Continued.

1 (Mr. Robinson) had served the office of Mayor whilst representing the undivided Ward.

1 (Mr. Robinson) died in office; no vacancies occurred by resignation.

The longest period of office has been that of Mr. Parsons (since 1889); three Councillors (Messrs. Mereweather, Williams, and Cleverdon) served only for a single term of three years each.

The highest poll in this Ward was 1,429 for Mr. Parsons in 1859.

BEDMINSTER WARD (EAST).

1880, Oct. 22.
William Lee (L), to retire in 1880.
William Spark (C), to retire in 1881.
William Merrett Webb (C), to retire in 1882.
[Transferred from St. Augustine's Ward.]

1880.
Robert John Crocker (L) 650
Thomas Harding (C) ... 561

1881.
Roger Moore (L) 600
Thomas Harding (C) ... 546

1882.
William Terrett (L)...... 454
Henry Isaac Brown (L) 312

1883.
Robert John Crocker (L)

1884.
Roger Moore (L) 783
Edward James Thatcher (C) 626

1885, Jan. 1 (vice Crocker, deceased).
William Howell Davies (L)

1885.
William Terrett (L)

1886.
William Howell Davies (L).

1887.
Samuel Lloyd (L)........ 872
Alfred Froud (C) 541

1888.
William Terrett (L)

1889.
William Howell Davies (L)

1890.
Samuel Lloyd (L)

1891.
William Terrett (L)

1892.
William Howell Davies (L)

1893.
Samuel Lloyd (L)

1894.
William Terrett (L)...... 989
William Gorman (Lab) 677

1895.
William Howell Davies, J.P. (L)

1896.
Samuel Lloyd (L)

1897.
William Terrett (L)

1897, Nov. 24 (vice Davies, elected an Alderman).
Edward Horwood Chandler (L) 693
William Gorman (Lab) 674

BEDMINSTER WARD (EAST) was represented by

1 Liberal and 2 Conservatives from 1880 to 1881.
2 Liberals and 1 Conservative from 1881 to 1882.
3 Liberals since 1882.

BEDMINSTER WARD (EAST).—*Continued.*

9 individuals have represented Bedminster Ward (East), of whom 7 were Liberals and 2 Conservatives. No Conservative has yet been elected by the Ward, the two who originally represented it having been transferred to it by the Council from St. Augustine's.

2 (Messrs. Spark and Davies) became Justices of the Peace for the City.

1 (Mr. Davies) served the office of Mayor, and was elected Alderman whilst serving as Councillor.

1 (Mr. Spark) was elected an Alderman at the first vacancy after ceasing to be a Councillor.

1 (Mr. Crocker) died in office. No vacancy has been created by resignation.

The longest period of office has been that of Mr. Terrett, who has served since 1882; the shortest was that of Mr. Lee, who served for 10 days (October 22—31, 1880).

The highest poll in this ward was 989 for Mr. Terrett in 1894.

ST. MICHAEL'S WARD.

1835.
John Howell (C) 208
James George (C) 156
Charles Ludlow Walker (C) 136
John Mills (L) 115
John Irving (L) 87

1836.
John Harding (C) 110
John Mills (L) 85

1837.
James George (C)

1838.
John Howell (C)

1839.
John Harding (C)

1840.
James George, J.P. (C)

1841.
John Howell, J.P. (C)

1842.
Oliver Coathupe (C)

1843.
James George, J.P. (C)

1844.
John Howell, J.P. (C)

1845.
Oliver Coathupe (C)

1846.
Francis Kentucky Barnes (L) 171
James George, J.P. (C) 162
[Mr. Barnes, who voted for Berkeley at the Parliamentary elections in 1837 and 1841, and for Berkeley and Fripp in 1847, was now supported by the Liberals, but he afterwards became a Conservative.]

1847.
James Poole, jun. (C)

1848.
Oliver Coathupe (C)

1849.
John Smith (C) 116
Francis Kentucky Barnes (L) 76

1850.
James Poole, jun. (C)

1851.
Charles Thornton Coathupe (L)

1852.
John Smith (C) 179
Robert Goss (L) 126

1853.
James Poole, jun. (C)

ST MICHAEL'S WARD.—*Continued.*

1854.
John Wetherman, jun. (L) 188
Hattil Foll (C) 143

1855.
John Smith (C)

1856.
James Poole, jun. (C)

1857.
John Wetherman, jun. (L)

1858.
Thomas Waterman (L) 230
William Sweet (C) 156

1859.
James Poole, J.P. (C)

1860.
John Wetherman, jun. (L)

1861.
Thomas Waterman (L)

1862.
James Poole, J.P. (C)

1863.
John Wetherman, jun. (L)

1864.
Thomas Waterman (L) 299
William Herapath, J.P. (L) 179

1865.
James Poole, J.P. (C)

1866.
John Wetherman, jun. (L)

1867.
Thomas Waterman (L)

1868.
James Poole, J.P. (C)

1869.
John Wetherman, jun. (L)

1870.
Thomas Gibson (C) 548
Thomas Waterman (L) 507

1871.
James Poole, J.P. (C)... 515
Robert Henry Symes (L) 320

1872.
John Wetherman (L)

1873, Jan. 10 (*vice* Poole, deceased).
Charles Hoskins Low (C) 622
Matthew Dunlop (L) ... 575

1873.
Frederick James (L) ... 714
Thomas Gibson (C)...... 663

1874.
Charles Hoskins Low (C)

1875.
John Wetherman (L)

1876.
Robert Iles Hewett (C) 714
Frederick James (L) ... 686

1877, Oct. 19 (*vice* Wetherman, deceased).
Matthew Dunlop (L)

1877.
Charles Hoskins Low (C)

1878.
Matthew Dunlop (L)

1879.
Robert Iles Hewett (C)

1880.
Charles Hoskins Low (C) 430
William Lane (L)......... 430
Henry Joseph Williams (C) 62

[The presiding alderman (Mr. G. W. Edwards) gave his casting vote for Mr. Low.]

1881.
William Lane (L) 534
Richard Court Stephens (C) 281

1882.
Henry Daniel (L)......... 503
Robert Iles Hewett (C) 463

1883.
Charles Hoskins Low (C)

1884.
William Lane (L) 575
Ernest George Lorymer (C) 535

1885.
Henry Daniel (L)......... 623
Ernest George Lorymer (C) 529

1886.
Charles Hoskins Low (C) 466
Ernest George Lorymer (C) 377

1887.
William Lane (L)

ST MICHAEL S WARD.—*Continued*

1888.
Henry Daniel (L.)

1889.
Charles Hoskins Low, J.P. (C)

1890.
Walter William Hughes (L) 611
Ernest George Lorymer (C) 72

1891. May 27 (*vice* Low, elected an alderman).
Fenwick Richards (C)

1891.
Fairfax Spofforth (C)... 639
James Thierry Broad (L) 417

1892.
Fenwick Richards (C) 624
Herbert Parker (L)...... 417

1893.
Walter William Hughes (L)

1894.
Fairfax Spofforth (C)

1895.
Henry Anstey (C)

1896.
Walter William Hughes (L)

1897.
Fairfax Spofforth (C)

St. Michael's Ward was represented by

3 Conservatives from 1835 to 1846
2 Conservatives and 1 Liberal from 1843 to 1849.
3 Conservatives from 1849 to 1851.
2 Conservatives and 1 Liberal from 1851 to 1858.
1 Conservative and 2 Liberals from 1858 to 1870.
2 Conservatives and 1 Liberal from 1870 to 1873.
1 Conservative and 2 Liberals from 1873 to 1876.
2 Conservatives and 1 Liberal from 1876 to 1882.
1 Conservative and 2 Liberals from 1882 to 1891.
2 Conservatives and 1 Liberal since 1891.

22 individuals have represented St. Michael's Ward, of whom 13 were Conservatives and 9 Liberals.

5 (Messrs. George, Howell, Walker, Poole, and Low) were Justices of the Peace for the city whilst serving as Councillors, and 2 (Messrs. Daniel and Lane) were appointed after ceasing to be Councillors.

1 (Mr. Low) was elected an Alderman whilst serving as a Councillor.

2 (Messrs. George and Barnes) were elected Aldermen after ceasing to be Councillors.

2 (Messrs. George and Poole) served the office of Mayor whilst Councillors.

1 (Mr. Harding) served the office of High Sheriff. Messrs. George and Walker had held both the Mayoralty and the Shrievalty before 1835.

2 (Messrs. Poole and Wetherman) died in office; there have been no vacancies through resignation.

The longest period of office was that of Mr. Poole, who served for over 25 years (1847 to Dec., 1872); the shortest was that of Mr. Walker, 10 months (Dec., 1835, to Oct. 31, 1836).

The highest number of votes polled in this Ward was 714 for Mr. F. James in 1875 and the same number for Mr. Hewett in 1876.

ST JAMES'S WARD

1835.
James Cunningham (L) 224
Samuel Simon Wayte (L) 214
John Wesley Hall (L)... 208
Thomas Menlove (C) ... 118
James Moore (C) 111
Michael Hinton Castle (L) 54
[Mr. Castle, who was a member of the old Corporation, received Conservative votes.]

1833.
John Wesley Hall (L)

1837.
John Mills (L)

1838.
William Leonard ThomasPyle Taunton (L) 182
James Cox (L) 32
James Moore (C) 2

1839.
John Wesley Hall (L) 182
James Cox (L) 165

1840.
John Mills (L) 198
James Cox (L) 185

1841.
Francis Jarman (L) ... 183
James Cox (L) 121

1842.
William Herapath, J.P. (L) 262
James Moore (C) 148

1843.
John Mills (L)

1844.
Francis Jarman (L)

1845.
William Herapath, J.P. (L)

1846.
John Mills (L)

1847.
Francis Jarman (L)

1848.
William Herapath, J.P. (L)

1849, March 19 (vice Jarman, deceased).
Edward Halsall (L)...... 181
William Phillips (L) ... 128

1849, March 26 (vice Mills, deceased).
Thomas Rankin (L) ... 207
William Phillips (L) ... 182

1849, July 27 (vice Rankin, deceased).
John Wetherman, jun. (L)

1849.
John Wetherman, jun. (L)

1850.
Thomas Field Gilbert (L) 215
Edward Halsall (L)...... 173

1851.
William Herapath, J.P. L)

1852.
George Cole (L)............ 213
John Wetherman, jun. (L) 5

1853.
Thomas Field Gilbert (L) 197
Edward Halsall (L)...... 154

1854.
William Herapath, J.P. (L)

1855.
George Cole (L)

1856.
Richard Fry (L) 164
William Phillips (L) ... 84

1857.
William Herapath, J.P. (L)

1858.
George Cole (L)

1859.
Richard Fry (L)

1860.
William Herapath, J.P. (L) 250
Matthew Dunlop (L) ... 176

1861.
Henry Naish (L) 237
George Cole (L)............ 193

1862.
Richard Fry (L)

1863.
Thomas Pethick (L) ... 262
William Herapath, J.P. (L) 223

1864.
Henry Naish (L)

ST JAMES'S WARD.—Continued

1865.
Richard Fry (L)

1866.
Thomas Pethick (L)

1867.
Henry Naish (L)

1868.
George Cole (L)

1869.
Thomas Pethick (L)

1870.
Christopher Godwin(L.) 439
Uriah Alsop (C) 424

1871.
George Cole (L)............ 357
Uriah Alsop (C)............ 285

1872.
Henry Naish (L.) 233
Matthew Henry Hale
  (C) 191
James Derham (L) 137

1872, Nov. 19 (vice Godwin, resigned).
Charles Fisher (C) 317
William Pethick (L) ... 296
James Derham (L) 19
Henry Pethick (L) 2
Thomas Pethick (L) ... 1
Uriah Alsop (C) 0
Stephen Alsop (C) 0

[Mr. Fisher was nominated without his consent by the Liberals as a "bogus" candidate to take away votes from another Conservative who was expected to stand. The Conservatives adopted his candidature, and carried him.]

1873.
Charles Fisher (C) 383
Algernon William
  Warren (L) 358
Robert Hall Warren (L) 2

1874.
Frederick Cordeux (L) 472
Thomas Gibson (C)...... 284
Charles Cordeux (L) ... 2
John Cordeux (of
  Savile-place) 2
John Cordeux (of
  Regent-street) 2

1875.
Henry Naish (L.)

1876.
Henry Gale Gardner
  (L) 400
Charles Fisher (C) 364

1877.
Frederick Cordeux (L)

1878.
Henry Naish (L) 395
John Henry Clifton (C) 346

1879.
Henry Gale Gardner(L) 284
Richard Hunt (Lab) ... 159

1880.
Frederick Cordeux (L) 374
Charles Fisher (C) 148
Thomas Gadd Matthews
  (C) 5
[Messrs. Fisher and Matthews were nominated without their consent.]

1881.
James Henry Lockley
  (Ind. L)..................... 507
John Wesley Hall (L.)... 249

1882.
Henry Gale Gardner (L)

1883.
John Wesley Hall (L)
[Became a Unionist in 1885.]

1884.
James Henry Lockley
  (Ind. L)..................... 514
William Taylor (L) 164

1885.
Henry Gale Gardner (L)

1886.
Robert Champion (C)

1887.
James Henry Lockley (Ind.
  U)

1888.
Edwin Thomas Lewis
  (Ind. C) 366
Arthur Pottow (L) 333
Samuel Waltham Pritchett (Lab.)............... 55

1889.
Arthur Pottow (L) 403
Robert Champion (C)... 360

1890.
William Cottrell (Ind.
  C).............................. 473
Charles Newth (L) 364

ST. JAMES'S WARD.—*Continued.*

1891.
Edwin Thomas Lewis (Ind. C).................... 470
William Henry Cowlin (L) 329

1892.
Robert Champion (C)... 386
Thomas Joseph Coe (L) 384
John Butchard (L) 31

1893.
Thomas Joseph Coe (L) 487
William Cottrell (Ind. C) 455

1894.
Edwin Thomas Lewis (Ind. C)

1895 April 6 (*vice* Champion, deceased).
William Cottrell (Ind. C).............................. 365
John Valentine (L)...... 23

1895.
William Cottrell (Ind. C)

1896.
Thomas Joseph Coe (L)

1897.
Edwin Thomas Lewis (Ind. C)

ST. JAMES'S WARD was represented by—

3 Liberals from 1835 to Nov., 1872.
2 Liberals and 1 Conservative from Nov., 1872, to 1876.
3 Liberals from 1876 to 1886.
1 Liberal, 1 Conservative, and 1 Independent Unionist from 1886 to 1888.
2 Conservatives and 1 Independent Unionist from 1888 to 1889.
1 Liberal, 1 Conservative, and 1 Independent Unionist from 1889 to 1890.
1 Liberal and 2 Conservatives from 1890 to 1892.
3 Conservatives from 1892 to 1893.
2 Conservatives and 1 Liberal since 1893.

[Messrs. Lockley (Liberal Unionist) and Lewis and Cottrell (Conservatives) were returned as Independents, but were opposed by Liberals at each contested election.]

26 individuals have represented St. James's Ward, of whom 22 were Liberals and 4 Conservatives. Two of the former (Messrs. Hall and Lockley), who were Councillors in 1886, became Unionists, and Mr. Lockley is now understood to be a Conservative; of the latter, 2 were returned as Independents.

4 (Messrs. Herapath, Godwin, Hale, and Champion) were Justices of the Peace for the City.

2 (Messrs. Naish and Hall) were elected Aldermen after ceasing to be Councillors.

1 (Mr. Lockley) served the office of High Sheriff two years in succession.

4 (Messrs. Jarman, Mills, Rankin, and Champion) died in office; 1 (Mr. Godwin) vacated his seat by resignation.

The longest period of office was that of Mr. Herapath, who served for 21 years (1842 to 1863); the shortest that of Mr. Rankin, 4 months (March—July, 1849).

The highest poll in this Ward was 514 for Mr. Lockley in 1884.

ST. PAUL'S WARD.

1835.
Nehemiah Moore (L) ... 170
ThomasRichard Guppy (L) 164
William Harwood (L)... 137
Robert Trapp Lilly (C) 129
Thomas Hooper Riddle (C) 106
Edward Harley (C) 105

1836.
William Harwood (L)... 145
Robert Trapp Lilly (C) 119

1837.
William Henry Castle (L) 162
Samuel Lucas (C)......... 2

1838.
Nehemiah Moore (L)

1839.
William Harwood (L)

1840.
William Henry Castle (L)

1841.
Nehemiah Moore (L)

1842.
William Harwood (L)

1843.
James Wood, J.P. (L)

1844.
Nehemiah Moore (L)

1845.
Henry Overton Wills (L)

1846, March 26 (vice Wood, deceased).
William Day Wills (L)

1846.
William Day Wills (L)

1847, July 5 (vice Moore, deceased).
Charles Tovey (L)

1847.
Charles Tovey (L)

1848.
Henry Overton Wills (L)

1849.
William Day Wills (L)

1850.
Charles Tovey (L)

1851.
Henry Overton Wills (L)

1852.
William Day Wills (L)

1853.
Charles Tovey (L)

1854.
Henry Overton Wills (L)

1855.
William Day Wills (L)

1856.
Charles Tovey (L)

1857.
Henry Overton Wills, J.P. (L)

1858.
William Day Wills (L).. 225
Edward Follwell (L) ... 207

1859.
Charles Tovey (L)

1860.
Edward Follwell (L) ... 271
William Terrell (L)...... 240

1861.
Thomas Castle (L) 299
Thomas Wedmore (L).. 239

1862.
Thomas Wedmore (L).. 238
Charles Tovey (L) 92

1863.
Edward Follwell (L) ... 224
Henry Melsom (C) 5
[Proposed without his consent.]

1864.
Handel Cossham (L) ... 325
Henry Melsom (C) 240

1865.
Thomas Wedmore (L)

1866.
Edward Follwell (L)

1867.
Handel Cossham (L)

1868.
Thomas Wedmore (L)

1869.
Edward Follwell (L)

1870.
Henry Matthews (L)

ST. PAUL'S WARD.—*Continued.*

1871.
Thomas Wedmore (L)

1872.
Edward Follwell (L)

1873.
Henry Matthews (L)

1874.
Thomas Wedmore (L)

1875.
Edward Follwell (L)

1876.
Henry Matthews (L)

1877.
Charles Wathen (L)

1878.
Edward Follwell (L)

1879.
Henry Matthews (L)

1880.
Charles Wathen (L)

1881.
Edward Follwell (L)

1882.
Henry Matthews (L)

1883.
Charles Wathen (L)...... 601
William Henry Bennett (C) 455

1884.
Edward Follwell (L)

1885.
Henry Matthews (L)

1886.
Charles Wathen (L U).. 584
Robert Gray Tovey (Lab) 566

1887.
Robert Gray Tovey (Lab) 418
Edward Follwell (L) ... 392
Henry William Carter (C) 369

1888.
Henry Matthews (L)

1888, Nov. 5 (*vice* Wathen, elected an Alderman).
John Coulthard (L)...... 624
Albert Vincent (Lab) ... 553

1889.
John Coulthard (L)...... 793
Albert Vincent (Lab)... 362

1890.
Robert Gray Tovey (Lab) 643
Edward Follwell (L) ... 511

1890, Dec. 8 (*vice* Matthews, deceased).
Herbert Ashman (L) ... 874
John William Lane (L U) 340
William Baster (Lab)... 275
Edward Follwell (L) ... 75
Henry Edmunds (Ind) 43

1891, March 20 (*vice* Tovey, resigned).
Heber Mardon (L) 348
Edward Follwell (L) ... 24
Henry Edmunds (Ind) 6

1892.
John Coulthard (L)

1893.
Frank Sheppard (Lab)

1894.
Herbert Ashman (L)

1895.
*William Henry Cowlin (L) 909
John William Lane (L U) 308

1896, March 11 (*vice* Cowlin, deceased).
John Boyd (L)

1896.
John Curle, J.P. (Lab)

1897.
Herbert Ashman (L)

* Mr. W. H. Cowlin, builder, of Stratton-street, not to be confounded with his relative, Mr. W. H. Cowlin, bootmaker, of Brentwood, who contested St. James' and St. Philip's (South).

ST. PAUL'S WARD.—*Continued.*

St. Paul's Ward was represented by

3 Liberals from 1835 to 1886.
2 Liberals and 1 Liberal Unionist from 1886 to 1887.
1 Liberal, 1 Liberal Unionist, and 1 Labour member from 1887, to Dec., 1888.
2 Liberals and 1 Labour member from Dec., 1888, to March, 1891.
3 Liberals from March, 1891, to 1893.
2 Liberals and 1 Labour member since 1893.

22 individuals have represented this Ward, 3 (Messrs. R. G. Tovey, Sheppard, and Curle) being Labour members and the rest Liberals, of whom 1 (Sir C. Wathen) became a Liberal Unionist during his term of office. Messrs. Wedmore and Follwell also joined the Unionists after ceasing to be Councillors.

6 (Messrs. Wood, H. O. Wills, W. D. Wills, Wedmore, Wathen, and Curle) were or subsequently became Justices of the Peace for the city.

Sir C. Wathen served the office of Mayor, and was elected an Alderman whilst still a Councillor.

4 (Messrs. Wood, Moore, Matthews, and Cowlin) died in office; 1 (Mr. R. G. Tovey) vacated his seat by resignation.

The longest period of office was that of Mr. Follwell, who served for 27 years, from 1860 to 1887. The shortest was that of Mr. Cowlin, who died less than four months after his election.

The highest poll in this Ward was 909 for Mr. Cowlin, in 1895.

THE DISTRICT WARD.

1835.
John Evans Lunell (L) 221
Thomas Richard Sanders (L) 131
Richard Ash (L) 127
Robert Henry Webb (C) 124
George Shapland (C) ... 119
[Mr. Lunell was supported by both parties.]

1836.
Richard Ash (L) 133
George Shapland (C) ... 91

1837.
Thomas Richard Sanders (L)

1838.
John Evans Lunell, J.P.(L)

1839.
Robert Henry Webb (C) 154
Joseph Grace Smith(L) 144

1840.
Thomas Richard Sanders (L)

1841.
John Evans Lunell, J.P.(L)

1842.
Joseph Grace Smith (L)

1843.
Thomas Richard Sanders (L)

1844.
John Evans Lunell, J.P.(L)

1845.
Joseph Grace Smith (L)

THE DISTRICT WARD.—Continued.

1846.
Thomas Richard Sanders (L)

1847.
William Naish (L)

1848.
Henry Prichard (L)

1849.
Richard Jones (L)

1850.
William Naish (L)

1851.
Henry Prichard (L)

1852.
Richard Jones, J.P. (L)

1853.
William Naish (L)

1854.
Robert Goss (L) 236
James Candy (L) 102

1855.
John Perry (L)

1856.
William Naish, J.P. (L)

1857.
Robert Goss (L)

1858.
John Perry (L)

1859.
Thomas Powell (L) 270
William Naish, J.P. (L) 205

1860.
Robert Goss (L)

1861.
John Perry (L)

1862.
Thomas Powell (L)

1863.
Robert Goss (L)

1864.
John Perry (L)

1865.
Thomas Powell (L)

1866, July 6 (vice Goss deceased).
Henry James Mills (L)

1865.
Henry James Mills (L)

1867.
John Perry, J.P. (L)

1868.
Thomas Powell (L)

1869.
Henry James Mills (L)

1870.
John Perry, J.P. (L)

1871.
Robert Carpenter (L)... 540
Henry Naish (L) 494

1872.
Henry James Mills, J.P.(L)

1873.
Charles Townsend (L)

1874.
Robert Carpenter (L)

1875.
Henry James Mills, J.P. (L)

1876.
Charles Townsend (L)

1877.
Robert Carpenter (L)

1878.
Henry James Mills, J.P. (L)

1879.
Charles Townsend (L)

1880.
Robert Carpenter (L)

1881, April 8 (vice Mills, deceased).
Charles Edward Ley Gardner (L).............. 888
Charles Highett (C)...... 611

1881.
Charles Highett (C)...... 167
George Snow Tricks (C) 35

[Mr. Gardner, who had been nominated, was disqualified, being in France and unable to sign his nomination paper.]

1882.
Charles Townsend, J.P. (L)

1882, Nov. 4 (vice Carpenter deceased).
Charles Edward Ley Gardner (L)

1883.
Charles Edward Ley Gardner (L)

THE DISTRICT WARD.—Continued.

1884.
John Bastow (L) 919
Charles Highett (C)...... 793

1885.
Charles Townsend, J.P. (L)

1886.
Charles Edward Ley Gardner (L)

1887.
John Bastow (L) 948
George Pearson (C)...... 625

1888.
Charles Townsend, J.P. (L)

1889.
Charles Edward Ley Gardner (L)

1890.
John Bastow (L)

1891.
Charles Townsend J.P. (L)

1892.
Charles Edward Ley Gardner (L)

1893, March 20 (vice Townsend, resigned).
Charles Newth (L) 1026
Nathaniel Palmer(L.U) 782
John Butchard (L)...... 13

1893.
John Bastow (L)

1894.
Charles Newth (L)

1895.
Charles Edward Ley Gardner (L)

1896.
John Bastow (L) 1242
James O'Grady (Lab.)... 423

1897.
Charles Newth (L)

THE DISTRICT WARD was represented by

3 Liberals from 1835 to 1839.
2 Liberals and 1 Conservative from 1839 to 1842.
3 Liberals from 1842 to 1881.
2 Liberals and 1 Conservative from 1881 to 1884.
3 Liberals since 1884.

18 individuals have represented the Ward, of whom 16 were Liberals, and two (Mr. Webb and Dr. Highett) were Conservatives.

9 (Messrs. Ash, Lunell, Jones, Prichard, Naish, Goss, Perry, Mills, and Townsend) were Justices of the Peace for the city.

4 (Messrs. Webb, Naish, Highett, and Townsend) were elected Aldermen after ceasing to be Councillors.

2 (Messrs. Naish and Highett) subsequently served the office of Mayor.

1 (Mr. Lunell) had served the office of Sheriff before the Act of 1835.

3 (Messrs. Goss, Mills, and Carpenter) died in office; one (Mr. Townsend) vacated his seat by resignation.

The longest period of office was that of Mr. Townsend, who served for over nineteen years (1873 to March, 1893); the shortest were those of Messrs. Webb and Highett, who served for one term of three years each.

The highest poll in this Ward was 1,242 for Mr. Bastow in 1896.

WESTBURY WARD.

1880, Oct. 22.
Joseph Dodge Weston, J.P. (L), to retire in 1880
James Inskip (C), to retire in 1881
Thomas Gibson (C), to retire in 1882
[Transferred from Clifton Ward.]

1880.
Joseph Dodge Weston, J.P. (L)

1881.
James Inskip (C)

1882.
William Robert Barker (L) 565
William Smith, J.P. (C) 557

1883.
Joseph Dodge Weston, J.P. (L)

1884.
James Inskip (C) 650
Charles Edward Alfred George (L).................. 568

1885.
William Robert Barker (L) 693
George Pearson (C)...... 628

1886.
Joseph Dodge Weston, J.P. (L)
[Knighted Nov. 26, 1886].

1887.
James Inskip (C)

1888.
William Robert Barker (L)

1889.
Sir Joseph Dodge Weston, J.P. (L)

1890.
James Inskip (C)

1891.
William Robert Barker, J.P. (L)

1892.
John Ryan Bennett (L)

1892, Nov. 22, *vice* Inskip (elected an Alderman).
Stephen Tryon (C) 786
William Lane (L)......... 688

1893.
Stephen Tryon (C)

1894.
William Robert Barker, J.P. (L)

1895.
John Ryan Bennett (L) 616
Edmund Phillips (C)... 223

1896.
Stephen Tryon (C)

1897.
William Robert Barker, J.P. (L)

WESTBURY WARD was represented by

1 Liberal and 2 Conservatives from 1880 to 1882.
2 Liberals and 1 Conservative since 1882.

6 individuals have represented the Ward, of whom three were Liberals and three Conservatives.

2 (Sir J. D. Weston and Mr. Barker) were Justices of the Peace for the city.

1 (Mr. Inskip) was elected an Alderman whilst serving as Councillor.

2 (Sir J. D. Weston and Mr. Barker) served the office of Mayor, the former for five years in succession.

No representative of this Ward died in office or vacated his seat by resignation.

The longest period of office has been that of Mr. Barker, who was first elected in 1882.

The highest poll in the Ward was 786 for Mr. Tryon in 1892.

HORFIELD WARD.
1897.

Colston Wintle (Ind. C) 740
Charles James Lowe (L) 684
Charles Wills, J.P. (L) 610
Robert Charles Smart (C) 427
William Henry Curtis (C) 415

Alfred William Francis (C) 405
Edwin Thomas Phillips (Lab.) 265
Alfred William Gordon (L) 230

One member (Mr. C. Wills) is a Justice of the Peace for the city.

ST. GEORGE'S WARD.
1897.

William Henry Butler (L) 1336
John Coole (L) 1163
George Bryant Britton (L) 990
Robert Inkerman Weight (C) 908

Francis Hicks (Ind.) ... 845
Thomas Watkins (Ind.) 702
William Whitefield (Lab.) 594
Joseph John Ballard (Ind.) 240

STAPLETON WARD.
1897.

Alfred John Saise (C)...1010
Arthur James Harris (C) 907
John Poole (L) 619
Frederick Greenway (C) 514
William Coran (L) 503

John Cousins (Ind. L) 466
Edward Tuckett Daniell (Ind. L) 408
Edwin Cotterell (L)...... 288
George Saunders (L) ... 146

SOMERSET WARD.
1897.

Alfred John Smith (L) 594
Frank Moore (L) 550
William Baster (Soc.)... 413
William Philip Jones (L) 408
John Stroud Gwyther William Stroud (C)... 367

William Thomas Gregory (Ind.) 346
James Sinnott (C)........ 322
William Church (C)..... 300
Frederick Burris (Ind.) 241

EASTON WARD.
1897.

Alfred George Verrier (L) 1241
William Jennings (L)... 944
James O'Grady (Lab.) 926
George Winter (Ind.)... 532
George Samuel Gerrish (C) 392

Frederick Leonard (Ind.) 262
Thomas Hobbs (C) 227
Frederick Henry Jullion (C) 221
Daniel John Turner (Ind.) 159

ALDERMEN.

December 31, 1835

*William Fripp (C) \
*Charles Pinney (L-C) } To serve till 1841. \
*Thomas Hooper Riddle (C) \
Richard Ricketts (L) \
Thomas Stock (L) \
Edward Harley (C) \
John Winwood (C) \
John Vining (C)

William Bushell (C) \
Geo. Woodroffe Franklyn (C) } To serve till 1838. \
*Nicholas Roch (C) \
*William Watson (C) \
*William Killigrew Wait (C) \
John Kerle Haberfield (C) \
John Maningford (L) \
James Gibbs (C)

* Members of the old Corporation.

[At this election the names were proposed individually, instead of being voted for collectively. Mr. Fripp's name was first proposed by Mr. Cookson, seconded by Mr. H. Ricketts, whereupon an amendment was moved by Mr. Guppy that all the nominations should be handed in to the Town Clerk. 24 Conservative Councillors voted against, and the 22 Liberals, together with Messrs. C. George and H. Ricketts, for the amendment. The numbers were thus equal, and the Town Clerk ruled that the chairman had no casting vote. The deadlock was terminated by a compromise, the two parties consenting to propose names alternately until the whole sixteen had been elected. Messrs. Fripp, Pinney, Riddle, R. Ricketts, and Bushell were then proposed by the Conservatives and Liberals in turn, and elected without opposition. Then Mr. W. Tothill (L) was proposed by the Liberals, and defeated by 25 to 23. Mr. C. George voting with the Conservatives, and Mr. H. Ricketts with the Liberals. Next Mr. Watson was elected by 26 to 22; then Mr. Joseph Reynolds (L) rejected, and Messrs. Haberfield, Maningford, and Gibbs successively elected, each by 25 to 23. Then Mr. Robert Castle (L) was rejected by 27 to 21, and Mr. Roch was elected by 26 to 22. Mr. Stock (L), who had left the room, having previously declined nomination, was proposed by Messrs. C. George and Acraman from the Conservative side, and unanimously elected, as was Mr. Harley, who was nominated by Mr. F. Ricketts, from the Liberal side. Then Mr. Isaac Cooke, a Conservative, was proposed by two Liberals, and rejected by 28 to 19. Mr. G. W. Franklyn was next proposed and elected, the numbers being reversed. Then Mr. Winwood (C) was proposed by a Liberal (Mr. Herapath) and elected without a division, and Mr. Wait by 26 to 20; Mr. James Johnson (L) was rejected by 25 to 22, and Mr. Vining elected unopposed, thus completing the list. Nine aldermen had been elected without a division; eight of these were appointed to retire in 1841, and the seven opposed aldermen and Mr. Bushell to retire in 1838. During the proceedings Mr. C. George proposed 4 Liberal councillors (Messrs. Stock, Wood, F. Ricketts and Wayte),

ALDERMEN.—*Continued.*

and Mr. Cunningham (one of the Liberal leaders) 4 Conservative councillors (Messrs. Payne, Cookson. Bush and J. George), all of whom declined, though, as stated above, Mr. Stock was elected in spite of his refusal. Before this meeting a list of 16 had been prepared on both sides, Messrs. Pinney and Harley being included in each list. The names that were not put to the vote were the following :— Conservatives : Messrs. T. Cole, J. D. Pountney, and John Brent Cross ; Liberals : Messrs. John Cave. M. H. Castle, J. Addington. W. Brown, R. Bligh, W. Johnson, S. Waring, and T. Carlisle. Mr. T. Daniel occupied the chair at this meeting of the Council, the office of Mayor being vacant by the expiration of Mr. Payne's term of office with that of the old Corporation, while his successor's appointment was deferred until the completion of the new Council.]

1838, May 4 (*vice* Stock, deceased).
Thomas Cole (C)............ 32
John Hare, jun. (L) 20
John Savage, J.P. (C) ... 2
[Mr. Savage's supporters were Messrs. H. and R. Ricketts. 5 Liberals and 4 Conservatives were absent, viz : Messrs. Maningford, Wood, C. B. Fripp, Fiske, Tothill, Acraman, Phippen, Harley, and Watson.]

1838.
William Bushell (C) 30
George Woodroffe Franklyn (C) 30
William Watson (C) 30
James Gibbs (C)............ 30
Richard Brickdale Ward (C) 30
Robert Trapp Lilly (C) 30
Edmund Butcher (C) ... 30
John Decimus Pountney (C) 29
John Maningford (L) ... 25
James Wood, J.P. (L) ... 25
Frederick Ricketts (L) 24
William Day Wills (L) ... 24
Henry Prichard (L)...... 24
William Johnson (L) ... 24
Robert Leonard (L) 24
Samuel Lang (L)............ 23

[At this contest all the members of the Council voted with their respective parties, except that Alderman Harley voted for Wood instead of Pountney, Mr. Aiken for Maningford instead of Franklyn, and Mr. Prust for Franklyn instead of Lang. The only absentee was Mr. H. Ricketts.]

1841.
William Fripp, J.P. (C)
Charles Pinney (C)
Edward Harley (C)
John Vining (C)
Thomas Cole (C)
Henry Ricketts, J.P. (C)
Charles Grevile (C)
Richard Robinson (C)

1844.
Richard Brickdale Ward(C)
Edmund Butcher (C)
John Decimus Pountney(C)
William Kay (C)
Philip Vaughan (C)
Jacob Ricketts (L)
Francis Grevile Prideaux (C)
William Hopton Wyld (C)

1845, Nov. 19 (*vice* Fripp, resigned).
Thomas Lucas (C)

1846, Oct. 13 (*vice* J. Ricketts, deceased).
James Moore (C)............ 18
Robert Bright J.P. (L)...

1847.
Charles Pinney (C)
Edward Harley (C)
John Vining (C)
Henry Ricketts, J.P. (C)
Charles Grevile (C)
Richard Robinson (C)
Thomas Lucas (C)
Robert Bright, J.P. (L)

1847, Nov. 26 (*vice* Bright, declined to serve).
James George, J.P. (C)

ALDERMEN—*Continued*.

1850, April 18 (*vice* Moore, deceased).
Francis Kentucky Barnes (C)

1850.
Richard Brickdale Ward (C)
Philip Vaughan (C)
William Hopton Wyld (C)
Francis Kentucky Barnes (C)
James Gibbs, J.P. (C)
William Oliver Bigg (C)
William Plummer (C)
William Wolfe Alexander (C)

1850, Nov. 18 (*vice* Gibbs, declined to serve).
Robert Gay Barrow (C)

1851, March 17 (*vice* Harley, deceased).
Robert Leonard, J.P. (L) 17
George Percy Whittall (C) 14

1853, April 9 (*vice* Ward, deceased).
Henry Brown Jordan (C)

1853, Sept. 6 (*vice* Wyld, deceased).
Conrad William Finzel (C)

1853, Sept. 22 (*vice* Finzel, declined to serve).
John Hopton Wyld (C)

1853.
John Vining (C)
Henry Ricketts, J.P. (C)
Richard Robinson (C)
Thomas Lucas (C)
Thomas Green (C)
Charles Edwards (C)
William Charles Beloe (C)
Thomas Proctor (C)

1854, July 10 (*vice* Jordan, deceased).
Henry Abbot (C)

1855, Nov. 19 (*vice* Edwards resigned).
Robert Phippen, J.P. (C)

1856, April 19 (*vice* Lucas, deceased).
James Ford (C)

1856.
Philip Vaughan (C)
Francis Kentucky Barnes (C)
William Oliver Bigg (C)
William Wolfe Alexander (C)
Robert Gay Barrow, J.P. (C)
John Hopton Wyld (C)
Henry Abbot (C)
Sholto Vere Hare (C)

1857, Oct. 8 (*vice* Wyld, resigned).
Francis Adams (C)

1859, May 17 (*vice* Ricketts, deceased).
Robert Henry Webb (C) 31
Richard Jenkins Poole King, J.P. (C) 1

1859.
Richard Robinson (C)... 35
Robert Phippen, J.P. (C) 32
Robert Henry Webb (C) 31
Thomas Green (C) 31
William Charles Beloe J.P. (C)........................ 31
Thomas Proctor (C) 31
James Ford (C) 31
Cam Gyde Heaven (C)... 30
William Herapath, J.P. (L) 18
William Day Wills, J.P. (L) 18
Harman Visger (L) 17
Christopher James Thomas. J.P. (L).......... 17
Richard Jenkins Poole King, J.P. (C) 15
James Poole, J.P. (C) ... 13
John Fisher, J.P. (C) ... 11
John George Shaw, J.P. (C) 10
Isaac Allan Cooke (C) ... 1

1861, Sept. 9 (*vice* Beloe, deceased).
William Naish, J.P. (L)... 20
Henry Overton Wills, J.P. (L)........................ 2

ALDERMEN.—Continued.

1862.
Philip Vaughan (C)
Francis Kentucky Barnes (C)
William Oliver Bigg, J.P. (C)
William Wolfe Alexander (C)
Robert Gay Barrow, J.P. (C)
Henry Abbot (C)
Sholto Vere Hare (C)
Francis Adams (C)

1864, April 23 (*vice* Vaughan, deceased).
George Rocke Woodward (C)

1865, Sept. 13 (*vice* Heaven, deceased).
Edward Slaughter (C)

1865.
Richard Robinson (C)
Robert Phippen, J.P. (C)
Thomas Green (C)
Thomas Proctor (C)
James Ford (C)
Robert Henry Webb (C)
William Naish, J.P. (L)
Francis Frederick Fox (C)

1868.
William Wolfe Alexander (C) 28
Robert Gay Barrow, J.P. (C) 28
Henry Abbot (C) 28
Sholto Vere Hare, J.P. (C) 28
Francis Adams, J.P. (C) 28
George Rocke Woodward, J.P. (C) 28
Thomas Barnes (C) 26
John Frederick Lucas (C) 26
Christopher James Thomas, J.P. (L)......... 14
James Poole, J.P. (C) ... 14

1869, July 15 (*vice* Phippen, deceased).
William Proctor Baker, (C) 28
Christopher James Thomas, J.P. (L)......... 1

1871.
Thomas Green (C)......... 41
Thomas Proctor, J.P. (C) 41
William Proctor Baker (C) 41
Richard Robinson (C)... 40
James Ford (C) 40
Robert Henry Webb (C) 40
William Naish, J.P. (L) 40
William Hathway (C) ... 30
John Averay Jones (C) 24
Christopher James Thomas, J.P. (L)......... 2
James Poole, J.P. (C) ... 1
Frederick Terrell, J.P. (L) 1

[At this election the Liberal leaders, Messrs. E. S. Robinson, W. Terrell, W. H. Wills, and M. Whitwill voted for Mr. Jones, but at the next election they all voted against him on the ground of his not having been an elected member of the Council.]

1873, Nov. 14 (*vice* Naish, resigned.)
John Averay Jones (C) 32
Christopher James Thomas, J.P. (L)......... 17
John Perry, J.P. (L)...... 2

1874, April 11 (*vice* Abbot, deceased).
George William Edwards (C) 39
Thomas Gibson (C) 2

1874, Aug. 24 (*vice* Alexander, deceased).
George King Morgan (C)

1874.
Sholto Vere Hare, J.P. (C)
Francis Adams, J.P. (C)
George Rocke Woodward, J.P. (C)
John Frederick Lucas (C)
George William Edwards (C)
George King Morgan (C)
Henry Brittan (C)
Reginald Wyndham Butterworth (C)

1875, March 9 (*vice* Webb, deceased).
Francis Frederick Fox (C)

ALDERMEN.—Continued.

1876, May 23 (vice Proctor, deceased).
James Creswell Wall (C)

1877.
James Ford (C) 30
William Proctor Baker, J.P. (C)................... 30
William Hathway, J.P. (C) 30
James Creswell Wall (C) 30
Richard Robinson (C)... 29
John Averay Jones (C) 29
Francis Frederick Fox (C) 29
John Harvey, jun. (C)... 28
Christopher James Thomas, J.P. (L)......... 20

1878, Oct. 25 (vice Robinson, deceased).
Charles William Cope-Proctor (C)

1880, Sept. 3 (vice Adams, deceased).
Henry Adams (C)

1880.
John Frederick Lucas (C) 34
George William Edwards, J.P. (C)................... 34
George King Morgan (C) 34
George Rocke Woodward, J.P. (C) 33
Henry Brittan (C)......... 33
Reginald Wyndham Butterworth (C) 33
Henry Adams (C) 33
John Sandham Warren (C) 32
Christopher James Thomas, J.P. (L)......... 17
Frederick Terrell, J.P. (L) 17
William Spark (C)......... 1
George Wills, J.P. (L) ... 1
Elisha Smith Robinson, J.P. (L)...................... 1

1881, Nov. 16 (vice Woodward and Adams, resigned).
Henry Naish (L)............ 35
William Spark, J.P. (C) 35
Christopher James Thomas, J.P. (L)......... 1

1881, Dec. 13 (vice Brittan, deceased).
William Wilberforce Jose (C) 36
Christopher James Thomas, J.P. (L)......... 2
Frederick Terrell, J.P. (L) 1

1882, Nov. 17 (vice Ford, resigned).
William Edwards George (C) 21
Elisha Smith Robinson, J.P. (L) 16
Charles Nash, J.P. (C)... 2

1883, April 18 (vice Warren, resigned).
William Smith, J.P. (C) 24
Elisha Smith Robinson, J.P. (L) 15

1883.
William Proctor Baker, J.P. (C)................... 35
John Averay Jones, J.P. (C) 33
Francis Frederick Fox, J.P. (C)................... 33
William Hathway, J.P. (C) 32
James Creswell Wall, J.P. (C)................... 31
John Harvey (C)............ 30
Charles William Cope-Proctor (C).................. 30
William Edwards George (C) 30
Joseph Dodge Weston, J.P. (L) 19
Elisha Smith Robinson, J.P. (L) 19
William Pethick, J.P. (L) 18
Mark Whitwill, J.P. (L) 18
Charles Nash, J.P. (C)... 4
Edward Follwell (L) 2
William Killigrew Wait (C) 1

1886.
Charles Nash, J.P. (C)... 31
John Frederick Lucas, J.P. (C)................... 30
*George William Edwards, J.P. (C) 30
George King Morgan (C) 30
William Wilberforce Jose (C) 30

*Knighted Aug. 5, 1887.

ALDERMEN.—Continued

1886 (continued).
William Smith, J.P. (C) 30
Henry Naish (L.U) 29
William Killigrew Wait (C) 29
Sir Joseph Dodge Weston J.P. (L) 22
Charles Wathen (L.U) ... 22
Edward Follwell (L)...... 1

1888, Oct. 23 (*vice* Naish, resigned).
*Charles Wathen, J.P. (L.U)
*Knighted, Jan. 29, 1889.

1889.
Francis Frederick Fox, J.P. (C).......................... 32
William Proctor Baker, J.P. (C).......................... 31
William Hathway, J.P. (C) 30
John Averay Jones, J.P. (C) 30
John Creswell Wall, J.P. (C) 30
John Harvey (C)............ 30
Charles William Cope-Proctor, J.P. (C) 30
William Pethick, J.P. (L.U) 27
Sir Joseph Dodge Weston, J.P. (L)......................... 24
Mark Whitwill, J.P. (L) 23
James Inskip (C) 1

1890, July 8 (*vice* Jones, resigned.)
John Bartlett (C) 32
Mark Whitwill, J.P. (L) 14

1891, Feb. 20 (*vice* Hathway, resigned.)
John William Stone Dix (C) 30
Mark Whitwill, J.P. (L) 19

1891, May 22 (*vice* Wait, resigned).
Charles Hoskins Low, J.P. (C)........................ 24
Mark Whitwill, J.P. (L) 18

1892, Jan. 29 (*vice* Naish, deceased).
Charles Highett (C) 27
Charles Wills, J.P. (L)... 18

1892.
Sir Charles Wathen, J.P. (L.U) 33
Sir George William Edwards, J.P. (C) 30
William Wilberforce Jose J.P. (C).......................... 30
William Smith, J.P. (C) 29
Charles Hoskins Low, J.P. (C).......................... 29
John Frederick Lucas, J.P. (C).......................... 28
Charles Highett (C) 28
James Inskip (C) 28
William Robert Barker, J.P. (L) 21
Charles Wills, J.P. (L)... 20
William Howell Davies (L) 19
Mark Whitwill, J.P. (L) 19
John William Stone Dix (C) 1

1893, Feb. 24 (*vice* Wathen, deceased).
Francis James Fry, J.P. (L.U)

1893, Nov. 9 (*vice* Lucas, deceased).
Charles John Collins Prichard (C)

1895.
Charles William Cope-Proctor, J.P. (C) 39
Francis Frederick Fox, J.P. (C).......................... 37
William Proctor Baker, J.P. (C).......................... 36
John William Stone Dix (C) 34
William Pethick, J.P. (L.U.) 33
*Robert Henry Symes, J.P. (C)........................ 33
John Bartlett (C) 32
John Harvey (C)............ 28
William Robert Barker, J.P. (L) 14
William Howell Davies, J.P. (L)........................ 13
Charles Edward Ley Gardner (L) 13
Moss Levy (L) 12
Henry Napier Abbot (C) 3
Francis Gilmore Barnett (L) 3
Charles Hoskins Low, J.P. (C).......................... 2
Fenwick Richards (C) ... 1
Charles Wills, J.P. (L)... 1
*Knighted, Jan. 1, 1898.

ALDERMEN.—*Continued.*

1896, May 12 (*vice* Highett, deceased).
Charles Bowles Hare, J.P. (C)

1897, Nov. 9.

[Five additional aldermen elected on the extension of the boundaries.]

John Wesley Hall, J P. (L.U) .... 62 } To serve till 1904.
John Hancocke Wathen (C)......... 62 }

1897 (Continued).

Edward James Thatcher (C) ...... 58 }
William Howell Davies, J.P. (L) 54 } To serve till 1901.
Charles Townsend J.P. (L)............. 52 }

Edward Tuckett Daniell (L) 1

Mark Whitwill, J.P. (L) 1

THE ALDERMANIC BENCH consisted of

13 Conservatives and 3 Liberals from 1835 to April, 1838.
14 Conservatives and 2 Liberals from May to Nov., 1838.
15 Conservatives and 1 Liberal from 1838 to 1841.
16 Conservatives from 1841 to 1844.
15 Conservatives and 1 Liberal from 1844 to Oct., 1846.
16 Conservatives from October, 1846, to 1847.
15 Conservatives and 1 Liberal in November, 1847.
16 Conservatives from 1847 to March, 1851.
15 Conservatives and 1 Liberal from March, 1851, to 1853.
16 Conservatives from 1853 to September, 1861.
15 Conservatives and 1 Liberal from Sept , 1861, to Nov., 1873.
16 Conservatives from Nov., 1873, to Nov. 1881.
15 Conservatives and 1 Liberal (Unionist after 1886) from Nov., 1881, to Oct , 1888.
14 Conservatives and 2 Liberal Unionists from Oct., 1888, to 1889.
13 Conservatives and 3 Liberal Unionists from 1889 to Jan., 1892.
14 Conservatives and 2 Liberal Unionists from Jan., 1892, to 1897.
16 Conservatives, 2 Liberals, and 3 Liberal Unionists since 1897.

Ninety-four individuals have been elected Aldermen, of whom 80 were Conservatives, 10 Liberals, and 4 (Sir C Wathen, Messrs. Pethick, Fry, and Hall) Liberal Unionists at the dates of their respective elections.

Of the 10 Liberals (Messrs. Stock. R. Ricketts, Mauingford, J. Ricketts, Bright, Leonard, W. Naish, H. Naish, Davies, and Townsend), one (Mr. Bright) afterwards became a Conservative, and one (Mr. H. Naish) a Liberal Unionist.

Of the Conservatives, 8 (Messrs. Fripp, Pinney, Harley, H. Ricketts, J. George, F. K. Barnes, W.W. Alexander, and Sir R. Symes) had at an earlier period belonged to the Whig or Liberal party.

Three gentlemen who were elected Aldermen declined to serve, viz., Messrs. Bright, Gibbs, and Finzel. Of these, Mr. Gibbs had already served the office.

Three (Messrs. Fripp, Roch, and J. George) had been Aldermen, and 5 (Messrs. Pinney. Riddle, Watson. Wait, and H. Ricketts) Common Councillors before the Act of 1835.

Three (Messrs. Haberfield, Gibbs, and Franklyn) were elected Councillors on the 1st of November in the years in which their terms of office as Aldermen would have ended on the 9th of the same month.

With the exception of Mr. Stock, one of the original 16 elected in 1835, no sitting Councillor was chosen Alderman until 1886.

ALDERMEN.—*Continued.*

Since 1886, of 18 vacancies, 9 have been filled by representatives of the Wards (Sir C. Wathen, Messrs. Nash, Bartlett, Dix, Low, Inskip, Prichard, C. B. Hare, and Davies).

Twenty-four ex-Councillors have been elected, of whom 4 (Messrs. H. Ricketts, Kay, Spark, and H. Naish) had retired from the representation of their Wards, and 3 (Mr. Gibbs, who declined the office, Dr. Green, and Mr. Heaven) had been rejected by their constituents, on a 1st of November, and were chosen Aldermen during the same month.

Of the remaining 17, in whose cases a longer interval had elapsed between the termination of their services as Councillors and their elevation to the Aldermanic bench, 9 (Messrs. J. George, F. K. Barnes, Bigg, Jordan, Phippen, W. Naish, Pethick, J. H. Wathen, and Dr. Highett) had been defeated in the Wards which they formerly represented, and 1 (Mr. Smith) had retired from the representation of Clifton and unsuccessfully sought election in Westbury. 7 (Messrs. Webb, Wall, H. Adams, Jose, Wait, Hall, and Townsend) had voluntarily retired from the Council.

Of the original 16 Aldermen, one (Mr. Stock) was an elected representative of a Ward, and 11 had been defeated at the polls at the first election of Councillors; only 4 (Messrs. Haberfield, Gibbs, Wait, and Bushell) had not sought to enter the Council.

Of those subsequently elected who had never sat in the Council, 11 had been unsuccessful candidates in the Wards on one or more occasions, viz., Messrs. Lilly, Butcher, Pountney, Grevile, Moore, Bright, Plummer, W. W. Alexander, J. F. Lucas, Sir R. Symes, and Thatcher; 33, as detailed above, had served as Councillors, and 35 had never sought election.

Forty-one of the Aldermen have been Justices of the Peace, viz., those to whose names J.P. is appended above, and Sir J. K. Haberfield, Messrs. Stock, Vining, and W. E. George, who were appointed after their last elections as Aldermen.

Sixteen (Messrs. Fripp, J. George, Haberfield, Franklyn, Gibbs, Pountney, Barrow, Vining, S. V. Hare, W. Naish, F. Adams, Baker, Hathway, T. Barnes, Jones, and Sir G. Edwards) were elected to the Mayoralty while serving as Aldermen; of these, Messrs. Fripp and George had served the office before the Act of 1835, as also had Mr. Pinney.

Five (Messrs. Phippen, Wait, Davies, Sir C. Wathen, and Sir R. Symes) served the office of Mayor before being elected Aldermen. Sir C. Wathen was elected in his third year of office as Mayor, and Sir R. Symes immediately after the conclusion of his second year, and both served again after becoming Aldermen. Sir J. K. Haberfield was Mayor 5 times after ceasing to be an Alderman.

Thirteen (Messrs. Bright, Phippen, Woodward, Proctor, Smith, C. B. Hare, Fox, W. E. George, Harvey, Butterworth, Fry, Pethick, and Sir R. Symes) served the office of High Sheriff, as did Messrs. J. George, Fripp, Pinney, and Wait before the Act of 1835.

Twenty-four (Messrs. Stock, J. Ricketts, Moore, Harley, Ward, W. H. Wyld, Jordan, T. Lucas, H. Ricketts, Beloe, Vaughan, Heaven, Phippen, Abbot, Alexander, Webb, Proctor, Robinson, F. Adams, Brittan, H. Naish, Sir C. Wathen, J. F. Lucas, and Dr. Highett) died in office.

Twelve (Messrs. Fripp, Edwards, J. H. Wyld, W. Naish, Woodward, H. Adams, Ford, Warren, Nash, Jones, Hathway, and Wait) vacated their seats by resignation.

The longest period of office was that of Mr. Robinson, nearly 7 years (1841 to 1873); the shortest that of Mr. Slaughter, 7 weeks.

MAYORS.

1836, January 1.
Thomas Daniel (C), St. Augustine's 38
Thomas Stock (L), Alderman 22

[Two Liberals were absent, Aldermen R. Ricketts and Maningford. Alderman Stock voted for Daniel, as did Mr. H Ricketts and Alderman Pinney. Mr. Christopher George voted for Stock and Mr. Daniel did not vote at all. The rest went with their respective parties.]

1836, January 11 (*vice* Daniel, declined to serve).
William Fripp (C), Alderman

1836, November 9.
James George (C), St. Michael's 30
Thomas Stock (L), Alderman 29

[Alderman Herley and Messrs. C. George and H. Ricketts supported Alderman Stock; Mr. F. Ricketts did not vote; the two candidates and Mr. A. Hilhouse were absent. In other respects, a strict party vote, reckoning Alderman Pinney as a Conservative.]

1837.
John Kerle Haberfield (C), Alderman 32
Thomas Stock, J.P. (L) Alderman 29

[The two candidates did not vote; Alderman Harley and Mr. H. Ricketts voted for Stock; Mr. C. George for Haberfield; Mr. Phippen was absent.]

1838.
John Kerle Haberfield (C), Bristol 35
John Evans Lunell, J.P. (L), District 24

[Alderman R. Ricketts and Mr. C. George voted for Haberfield. Mr. H. Ricketts and Aldermen Roch and Maningford were absent. Mr. Lunell did not vote, and Mr. Haberfield voted for Mr. Lunell.]

1839
James Norroway Franklyn (C), Clifton

1840.
Robert Phippen (C), Bedminster

1841.
George Woodroffe Franklyn (C), Alderman

1842.
James Gibbs (C), Alderman

1843.
William Lewton Clarke (C), Clifton

1844.
Richard Jenkins Poole King (C), Redcliff

1845.
John Kerle Haberfield (C), Bristol

1846.
William Goldney (C), Clifton

1847.
John Decimus Pountney (C), Alderman

1848.
John Kerle Haberfield, J.P., (C), Bristol

1849.
John Kerle Haberfield, J.P., (C), Bristol

MAYORS.—Continued.

1850.
John Kerle Haberfield, J.P., (C), Bristol
Knighted March 26, 1851.

1851.
William Henry Gore-Langton, J.P. (L), Clifton

1852.
Robert Gay Barrow (C), Alderman

1853.
John George Shaw (C), Bristol

1854.
John George Shaw, J.P. (C), Bristol

1855.
John Vining (C), Alderman

1856.
John Vining, J.P. (C), Alderman

1857.
Isaac Allan Cooke (C), Clifton

1858.
James Poole (C), St. Michael's

1859.
John Bates (C), Bristol

1860.
Odiarne Coates Lane, J.P. (C), Clifton

1861.
John Hare (C), Redcliff

1862.
Sholto Vere Hare (C), Alderman

1863.
Thomas Porter Jose (C), St. Augustine's

1864.
William Naish, J.P. (L), Alderman

1865.
Joseph Abraham (C), Bristol

1866.
Elisha Smith Robinson, J.P. (L), Bedminster

1867.
Francis Adams (C), Alderman

1868.
Francis Adams, J.P. (C), Alderman

1869.
William Killigrew Wait (C), Bristol

1870.
Thomas Canning, J.P. (C), Bristol

1871.
William Proctor Baker (C), Alderman

1872.
William Hathway (C), Alderman

1873.
Thomas Barnes (C), Alderman

1874.
Christopher James Thomas, J.P. (L), St. Philip's

1875.
John Averay Jones (C), Alderman

1876.
George William Edwards (C), Alderman

1877.
George William Edwards (C), Alderman

1878.
George William Edwards, J.P. (C), Alderman

1879.
Henry Taylor (C), Clifton

1880.
Joseph Dodge Weston, J.P. (L), Westbury

1881.
Joseph Dodge Weston, J.P. (L), Westbury

1882.
Joseph Dodge Weston, J.P. (L), Westbury

1883.
Joseph Dodge Weston, J.P. (L), Westbury

MAYORS.—Continued.

1884.
Charles Wathen (L), St. Paul's

1885.
Charles Wathen (L), St. Paul's

1886.
George William Edwards J.P. (C). Alderman Knighted May 5, 1887.

1887.
Charles Wathen, J.P. (L.U.), St. Paul's
Elected Alderman Oct., 1888.

1888.
Charles Wathen, J.P. (L.U.), Alderman
Knighted Jan. 29, 1889.

1889.
Sir Charles Wathen, J.P. (L.U.), Alderman

1890.
Sir Charles Wathen, J.P. (L.U), Alderman

1891.
Charles Highett (C)

[Division: For 33, against 18. Elected Alderman Jan. 29, 1892. The majority consisted of 31 Conservatives and 2 Liberal Unionists; the minority were all Liberals. Messrs. Cottrell and Lewis (Conservatives), the Mayor (Sir C. Wathen, Unionist), and Messrs. Barker and C. Wills (Liberals) did not vote. The absentees were Aldermen Jose and Harvey, Messrs. Fear, De Lisle Bush, Pottow, Levy, Gore, and Sir J. Weston.]

1892.
William Robert Barker, J.P. (L), Westbury

1893.
Robert Henry Symes, J.P. (C)

[Division: For 35, against 9. Before the final division Alderman Smith was proposed, without his consent, by Messrs. Davies and C. Wills, and received the votes of 19 (18 Liberals and Mr. Lewis), against 37 (33 Conservatives, including Alderman Smith himself, 3 Liberal Unionists, and Mr. Gore). The Mayor and Mr. Bennett (Liberals) did not vote, and there were 5 absentees, Aldermen Wall and Inskip and Mr. Cottrell (Conservatives) and Messrs. Hughes and Gardner (Liberals), one seat being vacant by the death of Alderman Lucas. Mr. Twiggs then proposed Alderman Dix, but afterwards withdrew his proposition. At the final division the 9 irreconcilables were Messrs. Lloyd, Parsons, Bastow, Newth, Coe, Ashman, Swaish, Elkins, and Gore, the other Liberals present and Mr. Richards, who had voted with the majority at the first division, abstaining from voting.]

1894.
Robert Henry Symes, J.P. (C)

1895.
William Howell Davies, J.P. (L), Bedminster (East)

1896.
Robert Henry Symes, J.P. (C), Alderman

1897.
Robert Henry Symes, J.P. (C), Alderman
Knighted Jan. 25, 1898.

MAYORS.—*Continued.*

42 individuals have been elected to the Mayoralty, of whom one (Mr. Daniel) declined to serve.

34 were Conservatives, 8 Liberals (viz. Messrs. Langton, Naish, Robinson, Thomas, Sir J. D. Weston, Sir C. Wathen, Barker, and Davies), of whom one (Sir C. Wathen) became a Liberal Unionist.

Although only eight Liberals were elected, they held the office sixteen times.

Sir J. K. Haberfield and Sir C. Wathen were each elected 6 times: Sir G. W. Edwards, Sir J. D. Weston, and Sir R. H. Symes each four times: Mr. Shaw, Alderman Vining, and Alderman F. Adams each twice. Alderman Fripp and Mr. J. George served the office of Mayor both before and after the Act of 1835.

There are at present (February, 1898) only 7 gentlemen living who have passed the chair, including the present Mayor, viz., Messrs. S. V. Hare, Wait, W. P. Baker, Sir G. W. Edwards, Barker, Sir R. H. Symes, and Davies, of whom all, except Messrs. Hare and Wait, are still members of the Corporation.

DISTRIBUTION OF SEATS IN THE COUNCIL.

	1835-1880.	1880-1897.	1897.
Aldermen	16	16	21
Bristol Ward	9	6	6
Clifton	9	6	6
Redcliff	6	6	6
St. Augustine's	6	3	3
St. Philip's	3	{ North 3 / South 3	3 / 3
Bedminster	3	{ East 3 / West 3	3 / 3
St. Michael's	3	3	3
St. James's	3	3	3
St. Paul's	3	3	3
District	3	3	3
Westbury	—	3	3
Horfield	—	—	3
Stapleton	—	—	3
Easton	—	—	3
St. George's	—	—	3
Somerset	—	—	3
	64	64	84

From Nov. 9, 1891, to Jan. 29, 1892, and from Nov. 9, 1893, to Nov. 9, 1895, the number of members was 65, the Mayoralty being held by Messrs. Highett and Symes, who were neither Councillors nor Aldermen at those dates respectively.

POLITICAL COMPOSITION OF THE BRISTOL CORPORATION, 1835-1898.

Year	Month	Conservatives.	Liberals.	Liberal Unionists.	Labour Members.	Socialists.
*1835	December	39	24	—	—	—
*1836	November	35	28	—	—	—
†1837	February	34	28	—	—	—
†1837	October	35	27	—	—	—
1837	November	36	28	—	—	—
1838	May	37	27	—	—	—
1838	November	39	25	—	—	—
1839	November	46	18	—	—	—
1840	November	50	14	—	—	—
1841	November	51	13	—	—	—
1842	November	49	15	—	—	—
1843	November	46	18	—	—	—
1844	November	45	19	—	—	—
1846	October	46	18	—	—	—
1846	November	45	19	—	—	—
1847	November 9th	44	20	—	—	—
1847	November 26th	45	19	—	—	—
1848	November	43	21	—	—	—
1849	November	44	20	—	—	—
1850	November	42	22	—	—	—
1851	March	41	23	—	—	—
1851	November	40	24	—	—	—
1852	November	41	23	—	—	—
1853	November	42	22	—	—	—
1856	November	41	23	—	—	—
1861	September	40	24	—	—	—
1861	November	41	23	—	—	—
1862	August	42	22	—	—	—
1863	November	40	24	—	—	—
1865	December	39	25	—	—	—
1866	March	38	26	—	—	—
1866	November	39	25	—	—	—
1867	November	40	24	—	—	—
1870	November	41	23	—	—	—
1871	November	42	22	—	—	—
1872	November 1st	44	20	—	—	—
1872	November 19th	45	19	—	—	—
1873	November 1st	44	20	—	—	—
1873	November 14th	45	19	—	—	—
1874	January	44	20	—	—	—
1877	November	42	22	—	—	—
1880	November	43	21	—	—	—
1881	November	42	22	—	—	—
1882	November	39	25	—	—	—
1884	November	38	26	—	—	—
1885	November	37	27	—	—	—
1886	May	37	18	9	—	—
1886	November	38	19	7	—	—

POLITICAL COMPOSITION OF THE BRISTOL CORPORATION.
1835-1898.—Continued.

		Conservatives.	Liberals.	Liberal Unionists.	Labour Members.	Socialists.
1887	November	39	18	6	1	—
1888	November	40	18	5	1	—
1889	November	37	20	5	1	1
1890	November	35	23	3	1	1
1891	March	35	24	3	—	1
1891	November	33	23	3	—	1
1892	January	38	23	2	—	1
1892	November	31	21	3	—	1
1893	March	33	22	3	—	1
1893	November	38	21	3	2	1
1895	November	39	20	3	2	—
1896	November	39	19	4	2	—
1897	October	33	20	4	2	—
1897	November	43	32	5	3	1

* One seat vacant in Bristol Ward.
† One seat vacant in Bristol and Clifton Wards.

[The Municipal Corporations Act had provided that casual vacancies should not be filled up until the whole Council was reduced to less than two-thirds of its full number, but this was repealed by the amending Act passed in July, 1837.]

In this estimate Messrs. Pinney, C. George, and H. Ricketts are reckoned as Conservatives. Mr. Richard Ricketts as a Liberal, and Mr. F. K. Barnes as a Liberal while a Councillor for St. Michael's (1846-1849). Messrs. H. J. Williams, De Ridder, Lewis, W. Cottrell, J. S. Naish, and Wintle are also included amongst Conservatives, and Mr. Lockley is classed as a Liberal up to 1886 and afterwards as a Liberal Unionist, to which division Mr. Levy-Langfield is assigned, but these gentlemen were returned as Independents and always acted without regard to political parties in municipal matters.

The poll books show that the votes of the members of the Council in the general elections of 1837, 1841, 1847, and 1852 were—

1837. Fripp, 54 ; Miles, 30 ; Berkeley, 28.
[29 voted for Miles and Fripp, 23 plumped for Berkeley, 4 (Alderman R. Ricketts, Messrs. Wood, F. Ricketts, and H. Ricketts) voted for Berkeley and Fripp, 1 (Alderman Harley) plumped for Fripp, and 1 (Mr. Jacques) voted for Berkeley and Miles. Alderman Fripp, Messrs. Hilhouse, Case, and Drake did not vote.]

1841. Fripp, 46 ; Miles, 45 ; Berkeley, 13.
[43 voted for Miles and Fripp, 11 plumped for Berkeley, 3 (Alderman Harley, Messrs. H. Ricketts and W. D. Bushell) plumped for Fripp, and 2 (Alderman R. Ricketts and Mr. E. B. Fripp) voted for Miles and Berkeley. Aldermen Fripp, Butcher, Watson, and Messrs. Bayly and Taunton did not vote.]

1847. Miles, 28 ; Fripp, 21 ; Berkeley, 19.

POLITICAL COMPOSITION OF THE BRISTOL CORPORATION,
1835-1898.—*Continued.*

1852. McGeachy, 37 ; Berkeley, 23 ; Langton, 19.
[35 plumped for McGeachy, 19 voted for Berkeley and Langton, 2 (Alderman Leonard and Sir J. K. Haberfield) for Berkeley and McGeachy, and 2 (Messrs. Langton and A. H. Palmer) plumped for Berkeley. Aldermen Alexander and Lucas and Messrs. Kempster, A. Alexander, C. T. Coathupe, and Shaw did not vote.]

In the election of 1847, when the Conservative party was divided, 6 members of the Council voted for both Miles and Fripp (Aldermen Prideaux and W. H. Wyld, Messrs. R. P. King, W. P. King, J. B. Burroughs, and J. Fisher) ; 21 plumped for Miles (Aldermen Cole, Pinney, Grevile, Robinson, Ward, Pountney, Kay, Vaughan, Dr. Green, Messrs. J. W. Miles, G. W. Franklyn, C. Blisset, Gray, C. Wait, Hautenville. W. Goldney, T. Powell, F. W. Green, Howell, C. J. Vining, and O. Coathupe); 11 plumped for Fripp (Aldermen H. Ricketts. Moore. Messrs. Shaw, Phippen, Gibbs, Perkins, C. B. Hare, Heaven, C. Taylor, T. W. Hill, and W. D. Bushell). Alderman Butcher voted for Berkeley and Miles, Aldermen Harley and Lucas and Mr. F. K. Barnes for Berkeley and Fripp, as also did Mr. R. Castle. There were 14 plumpers for Berkeley. Alderman Vining and Messrs. Haberfield, A. Alexander, Bernard, G. Thomas, J. Mills, and H. O. Wills did not vote.

The total number of individuals elected to the Council from the passing of the Municipal Corporations Act of 1835 to the present time (January, 1898) is 404, including two (Messrs. R. Bright and C. W. Finzel) who declined to serve. Of these, 233 may be regarded as having been at the dates of their respective first elections Conservatives in Imperial politics, 161 Liberals, 3 (Alderman Fry, Messrs. J. C. Godwin, and Levy Langfield) Liberal Unionists, 5 (Messrs. R. G. Tovey, Sheppard, Sharland, Curle, and O'Grady) Labour members, and 2 (Messrs. Gore and Baster) Socialists.

Of those classed as Liberals, Mr. F. K. Barnes, who was a Liberal Councillor, became a Conservative Alderman. Mr. H. W. Green had been a Conservative before entering, and rejoined that party before leaving the Council. Mr. J. Perry, though remaining nominally a Liberal, voted for Mr. J. W. Miles at the Parliamentary election of 1868, and with the Conservative members of the Council in December, 1869, against Mr. C. J. Thomas's motion for a redistribution of the Wards (on which occasion Mr. Woodforde Ffooks, a Conservative, voted with the Liberals). Mr. Cunningham, one of the prominent Liberal leaders (whose name stands second in the list of 57 who signed the address to the electors on behalf of Sir John Hobhouse in 1835, and who seconded Mr. Berkeley in 1837) was a Conservative in his later years, and Mr. S. S. Wayte also voted on that side in 1868.

Of the 27 Liberals who were members of the Council at the date of the introduction of the Home Rule Bill in 1886, nine (Messrs. W. Pethick, J. W. Hall, H. Naish, F. Wills, C. Wathen, Garton, Lockley, Dole, and Sibly) adhered to the Unionist section, and Mr. Follwell joined the Unionists later ; Messrs. G. Wills, L. Fry, M. Castle, Wedmore, Halsall, T. Castle. C. Tovey, and Dunlop, who had formerly sat in the Council as Liberals, also declined to follow Mr. Gladstone's lead on the Irish question.

POLITICAL COMPOSITION OF THE BRISTOL CORPORATION,
1335-1898.—*Continued.*

Of those classed as Conservatives, Aldermen W. Fripp, Pinney, J. George, H. Ricketts, Harley, W. W. Alexander, Sir R. Symes, and Messrs. Lean, C. George, and Ffooks-Woodforde entered on public life as members of the Whig or Liberal party.

Many of the contested elections in the wards have been fought on matters of local, rather than Imperial, concern, the Docks question having for many years been the battle-ground of parties. It may be interesting to notice some of the chief divisions, as showing how political connection was entirely disregarded in this matter.

On October 25, 1847, the motion approving of the transfer of the Bristol Docks to the Corporation was carried by 42 to 4, the dissentients being two Conservatives (Alderman Harley and Mr. J. B. Burroughes) and two Liberals (Messrs. Prust and G. E. Sanders).

In the division of October 7, 1858, when Mr. Shaw's amendment, refusing to appoint a committee to confer with representatives of other public bodies for the promotion of increased dock accommodation, was carried by 25 votes to 24, the majority was made up of 15 Conservatives (Aldermen Ford, Robinson, Phippen, Barrow, Vaughan, Alexander, Beloe, Bigg, Messrs. Shaw, Canning, O. C. Lane, Poole, J. B. Burroughes, J. Colthurst, and General Worrall) and 10 Liberals (Messrs. Herapath, F. Terrell, Goss, M. Castle, Lang, Kempster, Coates, Ayre, W. Naish, and Wetherman). The minority was composed of 14 Conservatives (Aldermen S. V. Hare, Abbot, F. Adams, F. K. Barnes, and Dr. Green, Messrs. I. A. Cooke [Mayor], R. P. King, W. P. King, J. Hare, G. Cooke, Hassell, C. Nash, Heaven, Dr. Rogers) and 10 Liberals (Messrs. E. S. Robinson, C. J. Thomas, Visger, W. D. Wills, H. O. Wills, Perry, Cole, Price, C. Tovey, and Leonard). Two Conservatives (Messrs. Fuidge and Bates) paired respectively for and against the amendment. Ten Conservatives (Aldermen Vining, Proctor, and Webb, Messrs. J. W. Miles, A. Alexander, Perkins, C. Taylor, J. Fisher, F. W. Green, and J. Smith) and three Liberals (Messrs. A. H. Palmer, H. Prichard, and R. Fry) were absent unpaired.

On June 18, 1872, Mr. Perry's resolution, declaring it inexpedient for the Council to subscribe to either of the competing Dock undertakings at the mouth of the river, was rejected by 37 to 18, the minority consisting of 13 Conservatives (Aldermen Proctor Baker [Mayor], Robinson, S. V. Hare, J. F. Lucas, Barrow, Alexander, Messrs. Ffooks-Woodforde, R. P. King, W. P. King, J. B. Burroughes, B. G. Burroughes, Gibson, and Poole) and 5 Liberals (Alderman W. Naish, Messrs. Perry, H. J. Mills, F. Terrell, and Wetherman). The majority was made up of 22 Conservatives (Aldermen Abbot, T. Barnes, Ford, Dr. Green, Hathway, Proctor, Woodward, Messrs. R. Bush, Bartlett, Canning, I. A. Cooke, W. Smith, G. Cooke, J. H. Nash, Finzel, C. B. Hare, W. A. F. Powell, C. Nash, Spark, W. M. Webb, T. T. Taylor, and J. Hellicar) and 15 Liberals (Messrs. W. Terrell, W. H. Wills, G. Wills, W. Pethick, E. S. Robinson, Weston, Carpenter, Sibree, T. Pethick, G. Cole, Follwell, Matthews, C. J. Thomas, Whitwill, and Evans, the absentees being seven Conservatives (Aldermen F. Adams, Webb, Messrs. Wait, W. H. Miles, W. H. Harford, H. Adams, and T. P. Jose) and two Liberals (Messrs. C. Godwin and Wedmore).

POLITICAL COMPOSITION OF THE BRISTOL CORPORATION,
1835-1898.—*Continued.*

On July 1, 1872, Alderman Hathway's proposal to subscribe £100,000 to the Portishead Dock was carried by 36 to 19, the majority including 15 of the 18 gentlemen who voted with Mr. Perry in the preceding month, the three exceptions being Aldermen Lucas and Naish, and Mr. Wetherman. The remaining 21 who voted for the subscription were Aldermen Hathway, Woodward, Ford, F. Adams, and Abbot, Messrs. Canning, Bartlett, H. Adams, I. A. Cooke, C. B. Hare, Finzel, T. P. Jose, J. Hellicar, W. A. F. Powell, and G. Cooke (Conservatives), and Messrs. W. Pethick, Weston, Sibree, Follwell, Wedmore, and Cole (Liberals), making a total of 27 Conservatives and 9 Liberals. The minority of 19 was made up of 12 Conservatives (Aldermen Lucas, Proctor, T. Barnes, and Dr. Green, Messrs. C. Nash, W. K. Wait, R. Bush, W. M. Webb, W. Smith, J. H. Nash, Spark, and T. T. Taylor) and 7 Liberals (Messrs. E. S. Robinson, T. Pethick, G. Wills, Carpenter, Whitwill, Matthews, and Evans).

On the same day Mr. E. S. Robinson had moved to appoint a committee for the purpose of arranging for the acquisition by the Council of an interest by purchase, or otherwise, in the Avonmouth Docks, but was defeated by 33 to 22, the names being the same as on Alderman Hathway's motion, with the exception that four Liberals (Messrs. W. Pethick, Sibree, Cole, and Wedmore) and one Conservative (Mr. Wait) changed sides in the two divisions. The voting was thus—For Avonmouth, 11 Conservatives and 11 Liberals; against, 28 Conservatives and 5 Liberals. Mr. W. Terrell and Alderman W. Naish paired for Avonmouth and Portishead respectively. The absentees were Alderman Webb and Messrs. W. H. Harford and W. H. Miles (Conservatives), and Messrs. C. J. Thomas, W. H. Wills, Wetherman, and C. Godwin (Liberals).

MISCELLANEOUS NOTES ON THE COMPOSITION OF THE BRISTOL CORPORATION, 1835-1898.

Of the original 63 members of the Council elected in 1835 (the full number of 64 was not completed till 1837, when the seat for Bristol Ward, vacated by Mr. Stock's election as an alderman, was filled), 20 had been members of the Corporation before the passing of the Act of that year, viz., Aldermen Fripp, Pinney, Riddle, Roch, Watson, Wait; Messrs. Daniel, Hillhouse, J. George, C. George, G. Goldney, Savage, Payne. J. N. Franklyn, Walker, Lunell, Lean, M. H. Castle, H. Ricketts, and P. Maze, jun. Of these, Messrs. Daniel, Fripp, Hillhouse, J. George, Goldney, Savage, and Roch were aldermen under the old *régime*.

The following (25 in all) represented more than one Ward at various periods of their service as Councillors, viz., Messrs. M. Hinton Castle, Herapath, Visger, Tothill, T. Powell (of Montpelier), J. Wood, T. R. Sanders, G. E. Sanders, A. W. Warren, Wetherman, H. Prichard, Derham, L. Fry, Lee, G. Wills, C. Wills. Sir J. D. Weston, Sir W. H. Wills, T. Gibson, Aiken, T. P. Jose, Inskip, Spark, W. M. Webb, and H. J. Williams, the first 18 of these being Liberals.

MISCELLANEOUS NOTES —*Continued.*

Five of these (Messrs. Lee, Spark, Webb, Gibson, and Sir W. H. Wills), who had been transferred from the Wards for which they had been elected, by vote of the Council at the redistribution of 1880, did not offer themselves for re-election in the Wards to which they had been thus assigned, and one of them (Mr. Gibson) returned, at the expiration of his term of office, to the Ward he had previously represented.

The last survivor of the original body, as elected in 1835, was Mr. T. R. Guppy, Councillor for St. Paul's Ward, who died June 28, 1882, aged 84, at Naples, having resided abroad for many years. The last survivor of the Aldermen elected in 1835 was Mr. William Fripp, who died Dec. 24, 1894, aged 86. Of the original members of the Council, the last to vacate his seat was Mr. Richard Poole King, who continued to represent Redcliff Ward till his death, at the age of 75, on Sept. 26, 1874.

The senior member of the Council at the present time (Feb., 1898), by continuity of service, is Alderman Proctor Baker (first elected July 15, 1869), Alderman Bartlett being his junior by a few weeks (first elected Aug. 30, 1869). Those next in order are Aldermen Hare (1871), Inskip (1872), Low (1873), Sir G. Edwards (1874). Councillor Arthur Baker (1874), Alderman Fox (1875), Councillor Abbot (1877), and Alderman Harvey (1877), all of whom have served continuously for more than 20 years.

If, however, seniority be reckoned by priority of entrance into the Council, without regard to continuity, Alderman Fox, who was first elected in 1865, is the Father of the Council, the next to him in order of time being Alderman Pethick (1866); Aldermen Smith (1870). Townsend (1873), and Jose (1874) take precedence of some of those named in the preceding paragraph.

The Fathers of the Council by *continuity of service* have been—	If *priority of entrance* to the Council be preferred to continuity of service, the succession of Fathers of the Council runs thus—
Dec. 1835, Mr. T. Daniel	Dec. 1835, Mr. Thomas Daniel
Nov. 1841, Alderman Fripp	
Nov. 1845, Mr. James George	Nov. 1841, Alderman Fripp
Nov. 1846, Alderman Pinney	Nov. 1845, Mr. James George
Nov. 1853, Alderman H. Ricketts	Nov. 1846, Alderman Pinney
May 1859, Mr. Richard Poole King	Nov. 1847, Alderman James George
Sep. 1874, Mr. William Poole King	Nov. 1853, Alderman H. Ricketts
Nov. 1880, Mr. Christopher Thomas	May 1859, Mr. Richard Poole King
Nov. 1883, Mr. Charles Nash	Sep. 1874, Alderman Webb
Nov. 1888, Sir Joseph Weston	Feb. 1875, Mr. William Poole King
Nov. 1892, Alderman J. F. Lucas	Nov. 1880, Mr. Christopher Thomas
Oct. 1893, Alderman Proctor Baker	Nov. 1883, Mr. Charles Nash
	Nov. 1888, Alderman Fox

MISCELLANEOUS NOTES.—*Continued.*

The senior surviving ex-member of the Council is Mr. Edward Halsall, who was elected for St. James's Ward in March, 1849, the next to him being Mr. Charles Nash, who was returned for St. Augustine's in March, 1851, and served as Councillor and Alderman for 37 years.

The longest period of service since the Act of 1835 was that of Mr. William Poole King, who sat for Redcliff Ward exactly 39 years (Nov. 1, 1841, to Oct. 31, 1880). Mr. Richard Poole King and Mr. Christopher Thomas each served for 38 years and 9 months, the former from Dec. 26, 1835, to Sept. 26, 1874, and the latter from Jan. 31, 1845, to Oct. 31, 1883. Mr. T. Daniel was a member of the unreformed and reformed Councils continuously for more than 56 years (June 29, 1785, to Oct., 31, 1841).

The shortest period of office was that of Mr. T. S. Butterworth, who was elected as Councillor Aug. 12, 1842, and died Sept. 5, in the same year, only 24 days afterwards.

Of well known Bristol families, that of Hare has contributed 6 members to the Council; those of Castle and Lucas 5 each; those of Bush, Ricketts, Terrell, and Wills (of the tobacco firm), 4 each; those of Fripp, Fry, George, King, Miles, Nash, Vining, and Wait, 3 each.

Of the 404 members elected to the Council, 74 (24 Aldermen and 50 Councillors) have died in office, and 188 after ceasing to be Councillors, leaving 142 survivors, of whom 84 are present members and 58 have retired.

Of the 246 members whose connection with the Council was not terminated by death, 206 members withdrew at the close, and 15 in the course, of a term of office; 23 were rejected by their constituents, and either did not seek, or were unsuccessful in the attempt, to obtain re-admission. These were Alderman Maningford, Messrs. Savage, C. B. Fripp, J. Cox, and W. H. Harford (Bristol); S. F. Cox, S. G. James (Bedminster). Jacques, C. Wait, Cooper, and Fear (Clifton); Sibree (Redcliff), T. Powell, of Charlotte-street (St. Augustine's), Halsall, Herapath, and C. Fisher (St. James'); Waterman, F. James, and Hewett (St. Michael's); C. Tovey and Follwell (St. Paul's), Dole and G. Wills (St. Philip's). Besides these, Mr. J. Cunningham gave up his seat for St. James' in 1838 to stand for Bristol, and Mr. Lee retired from Bedminster to contest his old seat in St Augustine's in 1880, and in each case failed to obtain election. Three Councillors, Messrs. I. Riddle, Guppy, and Giles, who had voluntarily retired at the end of a term of office, made unsuccessful attempts to recover a seat in later years.

118 have been Justices of the Peace for the city, 41 served the office of Mayor, and 25 that of High Sheriff during the period since 1835. Nine (Messrs. T. Daniel, W. Fripp, J. George, Hillhouse, G. Goldney, Savage, Payne, Pinney, and Walker) filled both offices, and eight others (Messrs. J. N. Franklyn, W. K. Wait, T. H. Riddle, Lunell, Lean, Maze, jun., Roch, and M. Hinton Castle) that of Sheriff before the passing of the Act.

43 have been Masters of the Society of Merchant Venturers, whose names will be found in the supplementary lists; three (Messrs. W. W. Davies, C. George, and E. T. Lucas), of whom the

MISCELLANEOUS NOTES.—*Continued.*

last died in office, attained to the Wardenship of the Society without reaching the chair. Mr. John Hellicar was Treasurer of the Society for four years.

38 have been Presidents of the Dolphin Society, 35 of the Anchor, 42 of the Grateful, and 34 of the Colston or Parent Society.

12 have been members of the School Board, the chairmanship of which was held in succession by Messrs. Whitwill and L. Fry; 6 have been unsuccessful in attempts to gain seats upon the Board.

19 have been Governors of the Incorporation of the Poor; six (Messrs. J. Wood, Herapath, Wedmore, Gilbert, Levy, and Coulthard) have been Deputy-Governors, but have not gone on to occupy the chair. Mr. T. Daniel was Treasurer 1810-1818, and Alderman Maningford 1827 till his death in 1854.

11 have been Presidents, and 10 Chairmen, of the Chamber of Commerce since its resuscitation in 1853; 3 had held the presidency of the earlier Chamber.

45 have been Charity Trustees, three of whom (Messrs. J. Cunningham, G. Thomas, and F. Terrell) have presided over that body.

24 have presided over the Society of St. Stephen's Ringers.

Two members of the Council (Messrs. W. H. Wills and F. Wills) have been made Baronets: a Baronetcy has also been conferred on Mr. C. D. Cave, who was never a member of the Council, but served as High Sheriff in 1862. Five (Messrs. Haberfield, G. Edwards, Weston, C. Wathen, and Symes) were knighted, as was also Mr. John Hare, who was an unsuccessful candidate for Redcliff Ward in 1835, and for a seat on the Aldermanic bench in 1838, but never effected an entrance to the Council.

The following have held seats in the House of Commons :—

    G. W. Franklyn, M.P. for Poole 1852-1865.
    W. H. Gore-Langton, M.P. for Bristol 1852-1865.
    J. W. Miles, M.P. for Bristol April—June, 1868 (unsuccessful candidate Nov., 1868).
    E. S. Robinson, M.P. for Bristol March—June, 1870 (unsuccessful candidate 1880).
    W. K. Wait, M.P. for Gloucester May, 1873-1880 (unsuccessful candidate 1880, 1885).
    L. Fry, M.P. for Bristol Dec. 1878-1885, North Bristol 1885-1892, and since 1895 (unsuccessful candidate 1892).
    Sir W. H. Wills, Bart, M.P. for Coventry 1880-1885; East Bristol since March, 1895 (contested South-East Essex 1885, 1886, South Bristol 1892).
    H. Cossham, M.P. for East Bristol 1885—April, 1890 (contested Nottingham May, 1866, Dewsbury 1868, Chippenham 1874).
    Sir J. D. Weston, M.P. for South Bristol 1885-1895; East Bristol May, 1890—March, 1895 (contested South Bristol 1886).
    C. Townsend, M.P. for North Bristol, 1892-1895 (unsuccessful candidate 1895).

MISCELLANEOUS NOTES.—*Continued.*

The following, who have not obtained seats in Parliament, have unsuccessfully contested constituencies :—

W. Fripp, Bristol, 1837, 1841, 1847.

S. V. Hare, Bristol, March, 1870, June, 1870, 1874.

W. Pethick, Launceston borough, July, 1885.

J. Inskip, East Bristol, 1886, May, 1890.

H. Holmes Gore, East Bristol, March, 1895.

Sir F. Wills, Bart., Launceston Division of Cornwall, 1895.

One member of the Council, Mr. C. W. C. Finzel, took Holy Orders after retiring from municipal public life. Four (Messrs. Grace Smith, Ffooks-Woodforde, Taunton, and T. W. Gibson) were barristers ; the two former of these became County Court judges, and Mr. Taunton was the editor of a well-known volume of Law Reports.

The other branch of the legal profession has always been represented in the Council. The original 63 included three attorneys, viz., Alderman Haberfield, Messrs. Phippen and Wayte ; in the present 84 are numbered 8 solicitors (Aldermen Dix, Inskip, and Prichard, Messrs. Pearson, Abbot, Hancock, Barnett, and Spofforth), and there have been at various periods 20 others (Aldermen Ward, Heaven, Greville, Abbot, and Brittan, Messrs. L. Fry, A. H. Palmer, Jarman, Frampton, Clarke, B. G. Burroughs, I. A. Cooke, G. Cooke, Perkins, R. Leonard, jun., Salmon, Ayre, Sibly, Gore, and Pottow), making 31 in all, of whom only 10 were Liberals, and of these three belong to the Unionist wing of that party.

There have been 12 medical practitioners (Aldermen Kay, Green, Highett, and J. H. Wathen, Messrs. Staples, G. Rogers, F. Terrell, R. Smith, J. B. Burroughes, J. Colthurst, A. G. Cunningham, and Wintle), of whom only two were Liberals. Mr. Coates, who was the proprietor of the Sion spring, was also a qualified surgeon, and Mr. Ware had at one time been in practice after he came to Clifton.

The fighting services contributed General Worrall, Admirals Warde and Close, and Commander Cawley (all of them representing Clifton Ward), to whom may be added Alderman Warren, formerly a Captain in the 91st Foot, and Colonel Bush, who had attained the rank of Major in the Regulars before becoming a Volunteer officer. All these were Conservatives.

The banking interest sent Alderman Maningford, Messrs. Lean, Bayly, Aiken, J. W. Miles, W. H. Miles, R. F. Miles, Cave, Bates, and W. H. Harford, all of whom, except Alderman Maningford, were councillors for Bristol Ward and Conservatives.

The West India merchants included Mr. T. Daniel, Captain Strachan Bridges, Alderman Pinney, and R. Robinson, Messrs. J. Cunningham, Payne, Bruce, Lunell, Case, Bernard, and R. Bright ; and African trade has been represented by the families of King the Lucas, which between them contributed six councillors for Redcliff Ward and two aldermen, all Tories ; the American by Alderman Jose and his father, Mr. T. P. Jose.

The liquor and kindred interests have been almost as strongly represented as the law ; there have been twelve brewers (Aldermen

MISCELLANEOUS NOTES.—*Continued.*

J. George, W. E. George, and Vaughan, Messrs. Wetherman, W. H. Castle, Dunlop, Lockley, Garton, S. James, S. G. James, J. Carter, and Hewett); the distillers include four members of the Castle family and Messrs. T. Harris and Board, and twelve wine merchants figure in the lists of the Council, viz., Aldermen Watson, W. H. Wyld, J. H. Wyld, Harvey, and Moore; Messrs. E. A. Harvey, J. Fisher, C. Fisher, C. Tovey, Fear, Rankin, and Abraham. Mr. G. Wills was also in the wine trade at one time, and Mr. F. Ricketts had been a partner in George's Porter Brewery. Mr. A. J. Harris is secretary to a licensed victuallers' association. Alderman Lilly, Messrs. I. Riddle and H. W. Green were maltsters.

Three Bristol firms of world-wide fame have contributed to the Council—Alderman F.J. Fry and Mr. R. Fry from the great chocolate manufactory, six Hares from the floorcloth works, and four Willses representing the celebrated "Bristol Bird's Eye"; several other members also having been associated with the tobacco trade, viz., Aldermen Sir G. W. Edwards, G. W. Franklyn, Bigg, R. Ricketts, J. Ricketts and Morgan, Messrs. J. N. Franklyn, E. B. James, H. G. Edwards, and Richards.

Other industries which have been conspicuously represented in the Bristol Corporation are—

Sugar by Aldermen Stock and Vining, Messrs. Finzel, Savage, Fiske, C. Vining, C. J. Vining, T. S. Butterworth, Wedmore, and Guppy (of whom the last-named afterwards forsook commerce for civil engineering, a profession which at present has its representative in Mr. Saise).

Iron by Aldermen Harley, Winwood, Butterworth, and Slaughter; Sir J. D. Weston, Messrs. P. Maze (sen. and jun.), W. W. Davies, C. Godwin, J. Colthurst Godwin, J. H. Nash, Lang, Jackson, and Sibree.

Soap by Alderman Fripp, Messrs. C. B. Fripp, E. B. Fripp, C. J. Thomas, J. Harding, Shaw, and R. Moore.

Timber by Aldermen F. K. and T. Barnes, C. Nash, J. Averay Jones, and Low; Messrs. Howell and H. Taylor (all Conservatives).

Corn by Aldermen Baker, Adams, and W. K. Wait (sen. and jun.); Messrs. A. Baker, H. W. K. Wait, Marshall, and W. Lane, of whom the last-named is the only Liberal.

Leather manufacture by Alderman Davies, Messrs. Hassell, N. Moore, Latham, Ashman, and Boyd; the kindred industry of boots and shoes by Messrs. Derham, Waterman, Kempster, Coe, and Britton; and the tanneries by Messrs. Brown, Drake, J. Cox, S. F. Cox, and Evans. Only two of these 15 gentlemen, viz., Messrs. Hassell and S. F. Cox, were Conservatives, there being apparently some occult connection between leather and advanced Liberalism, and, similarly, between timber and Toryism.

To these may be added the various firms in the glass industry represented by Messrs. Cookson, T. Powell (of Charlotte-street), W. A. F. Powell, O. Coathupe, C. T. Coathupe, J. W. Hall, sen., and Aldermen H. Ricketts and Hall; the oil and colour trade and drysalting by Aldermen Bushell, Fox, R. Leonard, and Thatcher, Messrs. E. B. Colthurst, T. Harding, H. Prichard, and J. E. Nash; pottery

MISCELLANEOUS NOTES.—*Continued.*

by Alderman Pountney and Mr. Price; coach-building by Messrs. J. Perry, Eberle, E. Rogers, and Cleverdon; building and contracting by Messrs. W. Baker, Bastow, Crocker, Mereweather, Cowlin, Lloyd, Coole, and F. Moore (all Radicals); the provision trade by Sir R. H. Symes, Alderman Webb, Messrs. Dole and Shirley; wholesale grocery by Alderman Butcher, Messrs. Budgett, W. Harwood, J. B. Harwood, G. Thomas, Fuidge, F. James, H. G. Gardner, C. E. L. Gardner, and Jennings (eight Liberals and only two Conservatives); the wholesale drug trade by Alderman Townsend, Messrs. A. Warren and Matthews (all Liberals); cabinet making by Messrs. Alsop and Newth; linen, drapery, and silk mercery by Aldermen Cole, Plummer, Prideaux, and Spark, Messrs. Carlisle, Cordeux, J. Smith, and Francis; woollen drapery by Alderman Hathway, Messrs. Carpenter, Coulthard, Levy, and Levy-Langfield; wholesale clothing by Messrs. Todd, C. Wills, and Sir C. Wathen; the hemp, rope, and sailcloth manufactures by Messrs. W. Terrell (sen. and jun.), H. Terrell, Gwyer, and C. Wait.

The coal trade has contributed three colliery proprietors (Messrs. Cossham, Wethered, and Bennett) and three merchants (Messrs. James Poole, Ring, and A. J. Smith). Mr. Pembery was a coal agent.

The patent shot, lead, and brass manufactures were represented respectively by Mr. Christopher George, Alderman Riddle, and Mr. C. L. Walker (all Conservatives and members of the old Corporation); Messrs. G. E. Sanders, T. R. Sanders, T. Powell (of Montpelier), and Parsons (all Liberals) were seed merchants; Alderman Woodward and Mr. W. M. Webb, vinegar merchants; Alderman Ford, Mr. James Ford, sen., Mr. Canning,and the various members of the Bush family were bonded warehousemen; Mr. Cripps, a wharfinger and marble merchant; Mr. Lee was also a marble merchant, having formerly been in the building trade; Aldermen Beloe and W. Smith were Colonial produce brokers; Aldermen Proctor and Cope-Proctor, chemical manure manufacturers; Messrs. W. and W. H. Butler, resin and turpentine importers; Messrs. F. W. Green, Acraman, and E. B. Hill, shipbuilders; Alderman Alexander, Messrs. Whitwill and A. Alexander, ship brokers; Messrs. V. and J. Hellicar, general merchants and agents in oil and foreign produce; Alderman Barrow, an insurance broker; Mr. Ridler, a Manchester warehouseman; Messrs. Tothill and Visger, manufacturers of Roman cement and vegetable dyes respectively; Mr. T. Pethick and Alderman Pethick, hide and tallow merchants; Messrs. E. S. Robinson, Mardon, O. C. Lane,and Jefferies, stationers; Messrs. T. Gibson and Betty, hat manufacturers; Messrs. C. and T. T. Taylor, goldsmiths, the latter of whom was afterwards a sugar refiner; Mr. Champion represented the wholesale confectionery trade, and Mr. H. W. Carter the aerated water manufacture; Alderman W. Naish hosiery, Alderman H. Naish the cotton manufacture, Alderman Gibbs that of vitriol, and Alderman Jordan that of alkali. The last-named gentleman, who was borough auditor before becoming a councillor, had been an accountant—a profession which has also contributed to the Council Messrs. Anstey and Tryon, all three being Conservatives. Messrs. H. Daniel and Lewis are auctioneers, Alderman Bartlett is a weighing machine manufacturer; Messrs. H. F. Cotterell and W. Cottrell deal in wall paper and china respectively; Mr. Follwell is a fly proprietor; Mr. Duffett was a brick manufacturer; the sartorial art has been represented by Messrs. Jeffery and Walls (both Conservatives and both councillors for St. Augustine's), and by Mr. Verrier; pawnbroking by Messrs. G. Cole, Swaish, and

MISCELLANEOUS NOTES.—*Continued.*

Chandler (all Liberals); the profession of land surveying and estate agency by Messrs. Hughes, Pavey, and De Ridder; stockbroking by Messrs. Goss, White, and Lowe, of whom the first-named had been previously a haberdasher; Mr. Herapath was an analytical chemist of considerable eminence; Mr. Halsall was a watchmaker, Mr. H. J. Williams an architect, Messrs. Cooper, Giles, and J. Wood, retail chemists and druggists; Messrs. Billing and John Poole are undertakers; Alderman Wall and Messrs. B. Perry and Stephens were hauliers and railway carriers; Mr. J. S. Naish was a bacon curer; Mr. Terrett a purveyor of meat; Messrs. J. and H. J. Mills were printers and proprietors of the now defunct *Bristol Gazette*; and Mr. Field Gilbert, originally a dyer, was for several years the secretary of the old Liberal Association for the undivided city; Mr. Elkins, who was formerly a carpenter, discharges those duties now in the Western Division; and Messrs. Swaish and Twiggs, the latter of whom is a maker of perambulators, are honorary secretaries for the Radical party in the Eastern and Southern Divisions.

Of the Labour and Socialist members, Mr. Easter is agent for the carriers, Messrs. Sutton and Co.; Mr. Curle is a carpenter, Mr. O'Grady a chairmaker, Mr. Sharland an engine fitter, Mr. Sheppard a bootmaker, and Mr. R. G. Tovey was a clothier's cutter.

It will be seen from the foregoing that the Council has, especially of late years, comprised representatives of almost every variety of professional, commercial, and industrial occupation.

ALPHABETICAL INDEX OF MAYORS, ALDERMEN & TOWN COUNCILLORS OF BRISTOL FROM THE MUNICIPAL CORPORATION ACT, 1835, TO 1898.

Abbot, Henry, Alderman July, 1854—April, 1874; died April 3, 1874, aged 62. Charity Trustee 1865-1874; President Grateful 1850; President Colston (Parent) 1864.

Abbot, Henry Napier, Bristol, August, 1877. Charity Trustee 1875.

Abraham, Joseph, Bristol, 1861—January, 1867; Mayor 1865-1866; died January 30, 1867, aged 52.

Acraman, William Edward, Bristol, 1835—August, 1842; died November 27, 1874, aged 75.

Adams, Francis, Alderman, October, 1857 — August, 1880; Mayor 1857-1859; died August 24, 1880, aged 74. J.P., 1868; President Grateful, 1859.

Adams, Henry, Clifton, 1869-1872; Alderman September, 1880—November, 1881.

Aiken, Peter Freeland, Clifton, March, 1839-1840; Bristol, 1840 1843; died March 3, 1877, aged 78. Contested Bristol 1837; President Dolphin 1859.

Alexander, Abraham, Bristol, 1845-1866; died July 22, 1870, aged 80.

Alexander, William Wolfe, Alderman 1850—August, 1874; died August 15, 1874, aged 76. Contested St. Augustine's May, 1846.

ALPHABETICAL INDEX.—Continued.

Alsop, Uriah, Clifton, 1880-1886. Contested St. James' 1870, 1871; member of School Board 1871-1874.

Anstey, Henry, St. Michael's, 1895. Candidate for School Board 1895.

Ash, Richard, District, 1835-1839; died February 11, 1866, aged 85. J.P. 1836; Charity Trustee 1836-1850; President Anchor 1841.

Ashman, Herbert, St. Paul's, December 1890. J.P. 1898; President Anchor 1898.

Ayre, John, Bedminster, 1854 — August, 1863; died August 6, 1863, aged 46. Assessor 1853.

Baker, Arthur, Redcliff, 1874. J.P. 1887; Sheriff 1891-1892; Master Merchant Venturers 1875-1876; Charity Trustee 1891; President Colston (Parent) 1889.

Baker, William, Clifton, 1877-1880; died August 16, 1884.

Baker, William Proctor, Alderman July, 1869; Mayor 1871-1872. J.P. 1875; Master Merchant Venturers 1869-1870; member of School Board 1871-1880; President Colston (Parent) 1881.

Barker, William Robert, Westbury, 1882; Mayor 1892-1893. J.P. 1889.

Barnes, Francis Kentucky, St. Michael's, 1843-1849; Alderman April, 1850-1858; died July 13, 1876, aged 83. Contested St. Michael's 1849; Master Merchant Venturers 1860-1861; President Grateful 1829; Mayor's Auditor 1852-1868.

Barnes, Thomas, Alderman 1868-1874; Mayor 1873-1874; died April 11, 1892. Master Merchant Venturers 1865-1866; President Grateful 1835; Mayor's Auditor 1869-1874.

Barnett, Francis Gilmore, St. Philip's (North), 1886. Contested St. Philip's (North) 1883, 1884.

Barrow, Robert Gay, Alderman November, 1850-1874; Mayor 1852-1853; died July 4, 1880, aged 73. J.P. 1854; Master Merchant Venturers 1839-1840, 1867-1868; acting President Grateful 1834.

Bartlett, John, Bristol, August, 1869—July, 1890; Alderman July, 1890. Governor Incorporation of Poor 1858-1870.

Baster, William, Somerset, 1897. Contested St. Paul's December, 1890, Bedminster (West) 1893, 1894.

Bastow, John, District, 1884.

Bates, John, Bristol, 1854—July, 1869; Mayor 1859-1860; died July 2, 1869. J.P. 1854; President Grateful 1856.

Bayly, Thomas Kington, Bristol, 1839-1845; died June 19, 1846, aged 45. Sheriff 1837-1838.

Beloe, William Charles, Alderman 1853—August, 1861; died August 31, 1861, aged 52. J.P. 1858.

Bennett, John Ryan, Westbury, 1892. President Chamber of Commerce 1891-1893.

Bernard, Charles Edward, Clifton, 1843-1849; died February 25, 1854, aged 48.

Betty, Samuel, Redcliff, May—October, 1896.

Bigg, William Oliver, Clifton, 1839-1845; Alderman, 1850-1868; died November 7, 1874, aged 74. Contested Clifton 1836, 1845; J.P. 1858; Master Merchant Venturers 1857-1858.

ALPHABETICAL INDEX.—*Continued.*

Billing, Charles Peter, Clifton, 1897.

Blisset, Charles, Clifton, 1841-1847; died March 16, 18 9, aged 46.

Board, Joseph Thomas, Bristol, 1885.

Boyd, John, St. Paul's, March, 1896.

Bridges, John Strachan, St. Augustine's, July, 1880-1886. President Grateful 1883.

Bright, Robert, elected Alderman 1847, but declined to serve; died September 19, 1869 aged 74. Contested St. Augustine's May, 1846; J.P. 1836; Sheriff 1852-1853; President Anchor 1830; President Chamber of Commerce, 1858—1859.

Brittan, Henry, Alderman, 1874—December, 1881; died December 6, 1881, aged 79.

Britton, George Bryant, St. George's, 1897.

Brown, Samuel, Bedminster, 1835-1839; died June 28, 1850, aged 49. J.P. 1847; Charity Trustee 1836-1850.

Bruce, Robert, Bristol, 1849-1852; died December 26, 1874, aged 82. Contested Bristol, 1839; Master Merchant Venturers, 1830-1831; President Anchor 1836.

Budgett, Samuel, Clifton, 1885-1888.

Burroughes, Benjamin Gustavus, Clifton, August, 1862-1877.

Burroughes, John Beames, Clifton, 1845-1848, 1852-1876; died September 16, 1878, aged 72. Contested Clifton 1839, 1851.

Bush, Alfred George De Lisle, Clifton, 1877-1892. Master Merchant Venturers 1882-1883; President Dolphin 1891; President Chamber of Commerce 1878-1880; Master St. Stephen's Ringers 1877.

Bush, Henry, Bristol, 1835-1842; died February 23, 1857, aged 61. Master Merchant Venturers 1848-1849; President Dolphin 1835.

Bush, James, Bristol, 1858—March, 1866; died March 13, 1866, aged 61. Contested Bristol 1849, 1852; Master Merchant Venturers 1859-1860; President Dolphin 1862; Chairman Chamber of Commerce 1853-1854; Master St. Stephen's Ringers 1846.

Bush, Robert, Bristol, 1866—August 1877; died August 5, 1877, aged 68. J.P. 1871; President Dolphin 1866.

Bushell, William, Alderman, 1835-1844; died December 19, 1849, aged 81.

Bushell, William Done, St. Philip's, 1840-1849; died February 8, 1883, aged 75. President Grateful 1838, and (acting) 1841.

Butcher, Edmund, Alderman 1838-1850; died July 11, 1872, aged 81. Contested Bristol 1837.

Butler, William, St. Philip's (South), 1887-1890.

Butler, William Henry, St. George's, 1897. President Anchor 1896.

Butterworth, Reginald Wyndham, Alderman 1874-1886. Sheriff 1885-1886; Master Merchant Venturers 1884-1885; member of School Board 1874-1877; President Dolphin 1884.

Butterworth, Thomas Stock, Bristol, August—September, 1842; died September 5, 1842, aged 25.

ALPHABETICAL INDEX.—Continued.

Canning, Thomas, Bristol, 1852-1876 ; Mayor 1870-1871 ; died December 21, 1888, aged 72. J.P. 1863 ; Charity Trustee 1865-1888 ; President Dolphin 1872.

Carlisle, Thomas, Bristol, 1836-1839, 1843-1846 ; died January 23, 1865, aged 75. Contested Bristol 1835 ; Charity Trustee 1836-1865.

Carpenter, Robert, District, 1871—October, 1882 ; died October 25, 1882, aged 63.

Carter, Henry William, Clifton, 1872-1895. Contested St. Paul's 1887. Candidate for School Board 1892.

Carter, John, Clifton, November, 1852-1855; died March 8, 1872, aged 45. Contested Clifton 1851.

Case, Robert Edward, Clifton, 1835—May, 1844 ; died May 3, 1844, aged 62.

Castle, Michael Henry, Clifton, 1854—1866 ; died October 7, 1891, aged 82. J.P. 1851 ; Charity Trustee, 1836-1891.

Castle, Michael Hinton, Clifton, 1835-1839 ; St. Philip's, 1841—January, 1845 ; died January 23, 1845, aged 60. Contested St. James' 1835, Bristol 1839, 1840. Common Councillor 1831—1832 ; Sheriff 1832-1833 ; President Anchor 1820.

Castle, Robert, Bristol, 1843-1849 ; died July 3, 1866, aged 59. J.P. 1856.

Castle, Thomas, St. Paul's, 1861-1864.

Castle, William Henry, St. Paul's, 1837-1843 ; died March 10, 1865, aged 54.

Cave, Charles Henry, Bristol, 1894. President Dolphin 1896.

Cawley, George, Clifton, 1895. Commander R.N.

Champion, Robert, St. James', 1886-1889, 1892—March, 1895 ; died March 24, 1895, aged 50. Contested St. James' 1889 ; J.P. 1894.

Chandler, Edward Horwood, Bedminster (East), November, 1897.

Clarke, William Lewton, Clifton, 1837-1846 ; Mayor 1843-1844 ; died April 30, 1867, aged 90. President Dolphin 1826.

Cleverdon, Thomas, Bedminster (West), 1891-1894.

Close, Francis Arden, Clifton, 1896. Admiral.

Coates, Joseph, Clifton, 1850-1853, 1856—July, 1862 ; died July 24, 1862, aged 65. Contested Clifton August, 1842, November, 1842, 1844, 1846, 1853 ; J.P. 1848 ; President Anchor 1845.

Coathupe, Charles Thornton, St. Michael's, 1851-1854 ; died February 26, 1857, aged 56. Charity Trustee 1852-1857.

Coathupe, Oliver, St. Michael's, 1842-1851 ; died February 11, 1886, aged 82. President Dolphin 1852.

Coe, Thomas Joseph, St. James', 1893. Contested St. James' 1892.

Cole, George, St. James', 1852-1861, 1868-1874 ; died October 27, 1878, aged 66. Contested St. James' 1851.

Cole, Thomas, Alderman May, 1838-1847 ; died May 6, 1861 aged 91. President Colston (Parent) 1809.

Colthurst, Edward Beadon, Redcliff, January, 1886. J.P. 1894; Master Merchant Venturers 1888-1889 ; President Colston (Parent) 1893.

ALPHABETICAL INDEX.—*Continued.*

Colthurst, John, Clifton, October, 1854—March, 1867 ; died October 18, 1895, aged 85. President Dolphin 1864.

Cooke, George, Clifton, April, 1855-1877 ; died April 11, 1894, aged 89.

Cooke, Isaac Allan, Clifton, 1854—December, 1874. Mayor 1857-1858 ; died December 11, 1874, aged 68.

Cookson, Joseph, Clifton. 1855-1843 ; died October 26. 1865, aged 82. J.P. 1836. President Chamber of Commerce 1829-1831.

Coole, John, St. George's, 1897.

Cooper, James Newberry, Clifton, December, 1865-1870 ; died December 3, 1892, aged 80. Contested Clifton 1870.

Cope-Proctor, Charles William, Alderman October, 1878. J.P. 1887 ; Master St. Stephen's Ringers 1894 ; President Colston (Parent) 1895.

Cordeux, Frederick, St. James', 1874-1883.

Cossham, Handel, St. Paul's, 1864-1870 ; died April 23, 1890, aged 65.

Cotterell, Henry Frederick, St Philip's (South), October, 1897.

Cottrell, William, St. James', 1890-1893, April, 1895. Contested St. James' 1893.

Coulson, Thomas Lane, Clifton, 1841-1844 ; died December 31, 1877, aged 68. Nominated for Clifton 1839. President Grateful 1853.

Coulthard, John, St. Paul's, November, 1888-1895. Deputy-Governor Incorporation of the Poor 1893-1895.

Cowlin, William Henry, St. Paul's, 1895—February, 1896 ; died February 26, 1896, aged 28.

Cox, John, Bristol, 1851-1852 ; died December 19, 1878 aged 73. Contested Bristol 1852. J.P. 1854.

Cox, Stephen Fitchew, Bedminster, August, 1853-1866 ; died January 3, 1889, aged 73. Contested Bedminster 1866.

Cripps, Richard, Redcliff, April, 1885—January, 1891. Contested Redcliff 1874, February, 1881 ; Chairman Chamber of Commerce 1868-1869 ; Master St. Stephen's Ringers 1870 ; President Colston (Parent) 1892.

Crocker, Robert John, Bedminster (East), 1880—December, 1884 ; died December 12, 1884, aged 51.

Cunningham, Albert George, St. Philip's (North), 1890- 1893 ; died January 17. 1897, aged 36.

Cunningham, James, St. James', 1835-1838 ; died March 12, 1863, aged 83. Contested Bristol 1838. Charity Trustee 1836-1863 (Chairman 1836-1852).

Curle, John, St. Paul's, 1896. J.P. 1894.

Daniel, Henry, St. Michael's, 1882-1891. J.P. 1894 ; President Anchor 1886 ; Charity Trustee 1891.

Daniel, Thomas, St. Augustine's, 1835-1841. Elected Mayor, but declined, January, 1836 ; died April 6. 1854, aged 91. Common Councillor 1795-1798 ; Alderman 1798-1835 ; Sheriff 1786-1787 ; Mayor 1797-1798 ; J.P. 1841 ; Master Merchant Venturers 1805-1806 ; President Dolphin 1816 ; President Colston (Parent) 1807 ; Governor Incorporation of Poor 1803-1808 ; Treasurer Incorporation of Poor 1810-1818.

ALPHABETICAL INDEX.—Continued.

Davies, William Howell, Bedminster (East), January, 1885—November, 1897. Alderman 1897; Mayor 1895-1896; nominated for Alderman, 1892, 1895 ; J.P. 1894 ; President Anchor 1892 ; President Chamber of Commerce 1884-1885.

Davies, William Weaver, Bristol, 1840-1843; died Jan. 25, 1862, aged 75. Warden Merchant Venturers 1841-1842.

Derham, James, Bristol, 1878—October, 1880; St. Philip's (North), October, 1880-1887; died February 24, 1890, aged 70. Contested St. James' 1872.

De Ridder, Louis Edward, Clifton, 1894-1897. Contested Clifton 1893, November, 1893.

De Winton, Cann, Clifton, October, 1837-1839; died November 19, 1852, aged 72.

Dix, John William Stone, Bristol, 1876—February, 1891. Alderman February, 1891; J.P. 1898.

Dole, James, St. Philip's (South), 1883-1889.

Drake, John, Bedminster, 1835-1840; died January 17, 1874, aged 69. J.P. 1836.

Duffett, Henry, St. Philip's, 1860-1863 ; died Oct. 9, 1879, aged 67.

Dunlop, Matthew, St. Michael's, October, 1877-1881. Contested St. James' 1860, St. Michael's January, 1873.

Eberle, James Fuller, St. Augustine's, 1886. Master St. Stephen's Ringers 1888.

Edwards, Charles, Alderman 1853—November, 1855 ; died June 12, 1883, aged 63. President Grateful 1858; Chairman Chamber of Commerce 1855-1856.

Edwards, Sir George William, Alderman April, 1874; Mayor, 1876-1879, 1886-1887. J.P. 1878; Master Merchant Venturers 1879-1880; President Dolphin 1886 ; President Grateful 1879 ; President Colston (Parent) 1868 ; member School Board, 1880-1883.

Edwards, Herbert George, Redcliff, 1896. Warden Merchant Venturers 1896.

Elkins, William Henry, St. Philip's (South), 1891. J.P. 1898; member School Board 1889-1892.

Evans, David Parker, St. Philip's, 1869-1872; died November 13, 1880, aged 64. J.P. 1878 ; Charity Trustee 1875-1880.

Fear, William Lyne, Clifton, 1882-1894. Contested Clifton 1894.

Ffooks-Woodforde Woodforde, Clifton, 1869—May, 1874 ; died August 11, 1896, aged 80.

Finzel, Conrad William, elected Alderman, but declined to serve, September, 1853 ; died October 21, 1859, aged 69.

Finzel, Conrad William Curling, Redcliff, 1871-1874.

Fisher, Charles, St. James', November, 1872-1876 ; died March 2, 1893. Contested St. James' 1876, 1880.

Fisher, John, St. Augustine's, February, 1843-1861 ; died February 25, 1877, aged 77. Nominated for Alderman 1859 ; J.P. 1858 ; Sheriff 1870-1871 ; Charity Trustee 1852-1877; Governor Incorporation of Poor 1845-1847.

ALPHABETICAL INDEX.—*Continued.*

Fiske, Robert, Bristol, 1837-1840; died May 21, 1859, aged 63. Contested Redcliff 1835; Charity Trustee 1836-1859; President Grateful 1832.

Follwell, Edward, St. Paul's, 1860-1887. Contested St. Paul's 1858, 1887, 1890, December 1890, March 1891; nominated for Alderman 1893, 1893.

Ford, James, Clifton, 1835-1836, 1837—March, 1838; died March 21, 1838, aged 47. Contested Clifton 1836.

Ford, James, Alderman April, 1856—November 1882; died Dec. 18, 1889, aged 7-. Member School Board 1871-1874.

Fox, Francis Frederick, Alderman 1865-1871 and March, 1875. J.P. 1878; Sheriff 1880-1881; Master Merchant Venturers 1877-1879; Charity Trustee 1875; President Grateful 1869; President Colston (Parent) 1879.

Frampton, Edward, Clifton, 1839-1842.

Francis, Thomas, Clifton, 1878-1881, September 1882-1890; died May 27, 1893, aged 76. Contested Clifton 1881.

Franklyn, George Woodroffe, Alderman 1835-1844; Clifton 1844-1850; Mayor 1841-1842; died November 5, 1870, aged 74. Contested Bristol 1835; Master Merchant Venturers 1847-1848; President Dolphin 1854.

Franklyn, James Norroway, Clifton, 1835—August, 1842; Mayor 1839-1840; died December 15, 1852; Common Councillor 1831-1835; Sheriff 1832-1833, 1834-1835, J.P. 1841; Master St. Stephen's Ringers 1841.

Fripp, Charles Bowles, Bristol, 1835-1840; died August 6, 1849, aged 43. Contested Bristol, 1840; Charity Trustee 1836-1849; President Anchor 1839.

Fripp, Edward Bowles, St. Philip's, 1835-1842; died September 1, 1870, aged 83.

Fripp, William, Alderman 1835—November, 1845; Mayor January—November, 1836; died December 24, 1871, aged 86. Contested Redcliff 1835; Common Councillor 1814-1821; Alderman 1821-1835; Sheriff 1814-1815; Mayor 1819-1820; J.P. 1836; Charity Trustee, 1852-1865; President Dolphin 1834; President Colston (Parent) 1842; Mayor's Auditor 1839-1841.

Fry, Francis James, Alderman February, 1893, J.P. 1878; Sheriff 1886-1887; Charity Trustee 1891; President Grateful 1885; President Anchor 1881.

Fry, Lewis, Clifton, 1866-1869; St. Philip's, 1872—October, 1880; St. Philip's (South), October, 1880-1884. Contested Clifton 1869; chairman of School Board 1871-1880; President Anchor 1868.

Fry, Richard, St. James', 1856-1868; died Dec. 1, 1878, aged 71.

Fuidge, Richard, Bristol, 1852-1861; died May 11, 1878, aged 60; J.P. 1866; Charity Trustee 1865-1878; Master St. Stephen's Ringers 1859.

Gardner, Charles Edward Lev. District, April—October, 1881, and November 1882; nominated for Alderman 1895, J.P. 1898.

Gardner, Henry Gale, St. James', 1876-1888; died September 27, 1894, aged 77.

ALPHABETICAL INDEX.—Continued.

Garton, Charles, St. Philip's (North), May, 1883-1886, 1887-1890 ; died Jan. 26, 1892, aged 66. Contested St. Philip's (North) 1886.

George, Christopher, Redcliff, 1835-1841 ; died May 30, 1866, aged 80. Common Councillor 1833-1835 ; J.P. 1841 ; Warden Merchant Venturers 1843-1844.

George, James, St. Michael's, 1835-1846 ; Alderman November 1847-1853 ; Mayor 1836 1837 ; died June 27, 1858, aged 69. Contested St. Michael's 1846 ; Common Councillor 1814-1827 ; Alderman 1827-1835 ; Sheriff 1814- 1815, 1819-1820 ; Mayor 1822-1823 ; J.P. 1841 ; Master Merchant Venturers 1827-1828 ; President Dolphin 1842.

George, William Edwards, Alderman November 1882-1889. J.P. 1887 ; Sheriff 1881-1882 ; President Grateful 1882 ; candidate for School Board 1880.

Gibbs, James, Alderman 1835-1844 ; re-elected, but declined, 1850 ; Clifton 1844-1850, 1851—February, 1853 ; Mayor 1842-1843 ; died February 24, 1853, aged 62. Contested Clifton 1850 ; J.P. 1848 ; President Dolphin 1846 ; Master St. Stephen's Ringers 1842.

Gibson, Thomas, St. Michael's, 1870-1873 ; Clifton 1876—October, 1880, 1882-1885 ; Westbury October, 1880-1882 ; died February 20, 1887, aged 79. Contested St. Michael's 1873 ; St. James' 1874 ; nominated for Clifton May, 1874, November, 1874 ; nominated for Alderman April, 1874

Gibson, Thomas Winter, Clifton, 1890—April, 1892 ; died April 12, 1892, aged 32. President-elect Grateful at his death.

Gilbert, Thomas Field, St James', 1850-1856 ; died Jan. 31, 1870, aged 73. Deputy-Governor Incorporation of Poor 1850-1852.

Giles, Richard William, Clifton, 1866-1869 ; died Dec. 25, 1897, aged 73. Contested Clifton 1873, 1877.

Godwin, Christopher, St James', 1870—November, 1872 ; died February 18, 1887, aged 77. J.P. 1871.

Godwin, James Colthurst, Redcliff, March, 1893. J.P. 1889 ; Sheriff 1893-1897 ; President Anchor 1885 ; President Chamber of Commerce 1885 1887.

Goldney, Gabriel, Clifton, 1835—February, 1837 ; died February 9, 1837, aged 71. Common Councillor 1822-1829 ; Alderman 1829-1835 ; Sheriff 1822-1823, 1825-1826 ; Mayor 1827-1828.

Goldney, William, Clifton, 1840—January, 1850 ; Mayor 1846-1847 ; died January 24, 1850.

Gore, Hugh Holmes, St. Philip's (South), 1889-1895. Member of School Board 1889.

Goss, Robert, District, 1854—June, 1866 ; died June 25, 1866, aged 72. Contested St. Michael's 1852, Bristol 1853 ; J.P. 1864.

Gray, John, Clifton, 1842-1843 ; died November 21, 1892, aged 90.

Green, Frederick William, St. Augustine's, 1842-1863 ; died Dec. 27, 1871. Master Merchant Venturers 18 1-1832.

Green, Henry William, St. Philip's, 1858-1870 ; died May 27, 1885, aged 67. President Grateful 1871.

Green, Thomas, Bristol, September, 1842-1853 ; Alderman 1853-1877 ; died October 31st, 1878, aged 75. Contested Bristol 1853 President Dolphin 1853.

Grevile, Charles, Alderman 1841-1853 ; died Sept. 19, 1862, aged 74 Contested Bristol 1837.

ALPHABETICAL INDEX.—*Continued.*

Guppy,Thomas Richard, St Paul's, 1835-1837 ; died June 28, 1882, aged 84. Contested Bristol 1838.

Gwyer. William Orchard, Redcliff, 1835-1836; died April 20, 1843, aged 61. President Grateful 1828.

Haberfield, Sir John Kerle, Alderman 1835-1838; Bristol 1838—Dec. 1857 ; Mayor 1837-1839, 1845-1846, 1848-1851 ; died December 27, 1857, aged 72. J.P. 1848; Charity Trustee 1836-1857 ; Governor Incorporation of Poor 1838-1845 ; President Dolphin 1838 ; President Grateful 1840 ; Master St. Stephen's Ringers 1837.

Hall, John Wesley, St. James', 1835-1842 ; died March 3, 1875, aged 85.

Hall, John Wesley, St. James', 1883-1883 ; Alderman 1897. Contested St. James' 1881 ; J.P. 1881 ; President Anchor 1879.

Halsall, Edward, St. James', March 1849-1830. Contested St James' 1850, 1853 ; Auditor 1846-1849.

Hancock, Charles Robert, St. Augustine's, June, 1893. President Dolphin 1894 ; Master St. Stephen's Ringers 1891.

Harding, John, St. Michael's, 1833-1842; died June 18, 1851, aged 44. Sheriff 1844-1845 ; Master Merchant Venturers 1843-1844 ; President Grateful 1839 ; Master St. Stephen's Ringers 1843.

Harding, Thomas, Redcliff, 1885-1891. Contested Bedminster (East) 188 , 1831.

Hare, Charles, St. Augustine's, 1835-1838 ; died March 13, 1840, aged 56. President Colston (Parent) 1830.

Hare, Charles Bowles, Redcliff, 1839-1854 ; died August 3, 1855, aged 45. President Colston (Parent) 1850.

Hare, Charles Bowles, Redcliff, Nov., 1871—May, 1896 ; Alderman May, 1893. J.P. 1881 ; Sheriff 1878-1879 ; Master Merchant Venturers 1876-1877 ; Mayor's Auditor 1878 ; President Colston (Parent) 1887.

Hare, Charles Felce, Redcliff, 1880—December, 1885 ; died December 18, 1835, aged 34. President Chamber of Commerce 1882-1883.

Hare, John, Redcliff, 1854—November, 1871 ; Mayor 1861-1862 ; died September 25, 1897, aged 84. J.P. 1863 ; President Colston (Parent) 1854.

Hare, Sholto Vere, Alderman 1856-1880 ; Mayor 1862-1863. J.P. 1863 ; Master Merchant Venturers 1866-1867 ; President Dolphin 1871 ; President Colston (Parent) 1863 ; member of School Board 1871-1874.

Harford, Henry Charles, Clifton, 1837-1841 ; died February 15, 1879, aged 81.

Harford, William Henry, Bristol, January 1862-1883. Contested Bristol 1883 ; J.P. 1866 ; Sheriff 1858-1859 ; Charity Trustee 1865 ; President Dolphin 1835.

Harley, Edward, Alderman 1835 — March, 1851 ; died March 8, 1851, aged 77. Contested St. Paul's 1835 ; Mayor's Auditor 1842-1844, 1846.

Harris, Arthur James, Stapleton, 1897.

Harris, Thomas, St. Philip's, 1835-1841 ; died Mar. 4, 1847, aged 72.

Harvey, Edward Arthur, St. Augustine's 1873-1891 ; President Grateful 1890.

ALPHABETICAL INDEX.—Continued.

Harvey, John, Alderman 1877. Sheriff 1884-1885; Charity Trustee 1875; President Grateful 1875.

Harwood, John Ballard, Bristol, 1837-1838; died January 16, 1844, aged 45.

Harwood, William, St. Paul's, 1835-1845; died February 11, 1848, aged 74. Charity Trustee 1836-1848.

Hassell, James, Bristol, January, 1858 — December, 1861; died December 25, 1851, aged 43. Master Merchant Venturers 1855-1856; President Chamber of Commerce 1855-1856.

Hathway, William, Alderman 1871—February, 1891; Mayor 1872-1873; died January 3, 1895, aged 87. J.P. 1875; President Grateful 1864.

Hautenville, William, Clifton, 1848—October, 1854; died October 6, 1854, aged 62.

Heaven, Cam Gyde, St. Augustine's, 1838-1859; Alderman 1859—September, 1865; died September 4, 1865, aged 68. Contested St. Augustine's 1859; President Dolphin 1845.

Hellicar, John, St. Augustine's March, 1864-1874; died June 4, 1877, aged 69. Master Merchant Venturers 1840-1841; President Grateful 1870.

Hellicar, Valentine, Bristol, 1840-1843; died February 27, 1864, aged 58. Master Merchant Venturers 1838-1839; Governor Incorporation of Poor 1836-1838.

Herapath, William, St. Philip's, 1835-1840; St. James' 1842-1863; died February 13, 1868, aged 71. Contested St. Philip's 1840, St. James' 1863, St. Michael's 1864. Nominated for Alderman 1859; J.P. 1836; Charity Trustee 1836-1868; Deputy-Governor Incorporation of Poor 1828-1830.

Hewett, Robert Iles, St. Michael's, 1876-1882; died July 10, 1897, aged 53. Contested St. Michael's, 1882.

Highett, Charles, District 1881-1884; Alderman January 1892—April, 1896; Mayor 1891-1892; died April 20, 1896. Contested District April, 1881, 1884.

Hilhouse, Abraham, Clifton, 1835-1837; died March 16, 1867, aged 80. Common Councillor 1812-1822; Alderman 1832-1835; Sheriff 1812-1813, 1817-1818; Mayor 1821-1822; Master Merchant Venturers 1825-1826.

Hill, Edward Burrow, Clifton, 1889—June, 1897; died June 29, 1897, aged 37. Master Merchant Venturers 1894-1895.

Hill, Thomas William, St. Augustine's, 1843-1849; died January 21, 1874, aged 85.

Howell, John, St. Michael's, 1835-1847; died November 29, 1854, aged 77. J.P. 1841; Master St. Stephen's Ringers 1824; President Colston (Parent) 1843.

Hughes, Walter William, St. Michael's 1890. Contested St. Augustine's November, 1866.

Inskip, James, Clifton, 1872—October, 1880; Westbury, October, 1880—November, 1892; Alderman 1892; nominated for Alderman 1889. Charity Trustee 1891; member of School Board 1877—June, 1885; President Grateful 1877; candidate for School Board 1871.

ALPHABETICAL INDEX.—Continued.

Jackson, Samuel Pim, Redcliff, 1852-1855; died February 6, 1883, aged 72. Contested Bristol 1847.

Jacques, William Singer, Clifton, 1835-1837; died February 23, 1845, aged 77. Contested Clifton 1837, 1838; President Chamber of Commerce 1832-1834.

James, Edward Burnet, Redcliff, January, 1891. Master Merchant Venturers 1895-1896.

James, Frederick, St. Michael's, 1873-1876; died April 22, 1880, aged 42. Contested St. Michael's 1876; Master St. Stephen's Ringers 1866.

James, Stephen, Bedminster, 1872—December, 1873; died December 16, 1873, aged 61.

James, Stephen George, Bedminster (West), 1883-1889. Contested Bedminster (West) 1889; J.P. 1887; President Colston (Parent) 1894.

Jarman, Francis, St. James', 1841—March, 1849; died March 10, 1849 aged 53. Assessor 1838, 1839.

Jefferies, James Evan, Redcliff, February, 1881-1890, 1891—March, 1893. Contested Redcliff 1890.

Jeffery, William, St. Augustine's, 1859—February, 1864; died February 24, 1864, aged 50.

Jennings, William, Easton, 1897. Contested Bristol 1881, 1883; candidate for School Board, 1874.

Jones, Richard, District, 1849-1855; died January 16, 1857, aged 67. J.P. 1850.

Jones, John Averay, Alderman November, 1873—June, 1890; Mayor 1875-1876; died February 8, 1896, aged 82. Nominated for Alderman 1871; J.P. 1878; Master Merchant Venturers 1862-1864; President Grateful 1867.

Jordan, Henry Brown, St. Philip's, 1849-1852; Alderman April, 1853—June, 1854; died June 30, 1854, aged 52. Contested St. Philip's 1852; President Grateful 1848; Burgesses' Auditor 1839-1840.

Jose, Thomas Porter, Clifton, 1847-1850; St. Augustine's, 1858-1873; Mayor 1863-1864; died January 19, 1875, aged 73. J.P. 1868; Master Merchant Venturers 1856-1857; President Dolphin 1861; President Chamber of Commerce 1856-1858.

Jose, William Wilberforce, Clifton, May, 1874-1878; Alderman December, 1881. J.P. 1889; Master Merchant Venturers 1870-1871; candidate for School Board 1871.

Kay, William, Clifton, August, 1842-1844; Alderman 1844-1850; died January 12, 1861, aged 54.

Kempster, John Mills, Clifton, 1850-1868; died March 26, 1872, aged 80.

King, Mervyn Kersteman, Redcliff, October, 1874-1879. J.P. 1898; Master Merchant Venturers 1874-1875; President Colston (Parent) 1885; Master St. Stephen's Ringers 1868, 1869.

King, Richard Jenkins Poole, Redcliff, 1835—September, 1874; Mayor 1844-1845; died September 26, 1874, aged 75. Nominated for Alderman May and November, 1859; J.P. 1847; Master Merchant Venturers 1851-1852; President Colston (Parent) 1841; President Chamber of Commerce 1839-1842.

ALPHABETICAL INDEX.—Continued.

King, William Thomas Poole, Redcliff, 1841-1880; died September 13, 1887, aged 81. Sheriff 1871-1872; Master Merchant Venturers 1850-1851; President Colston (Parent) 1853.

Lane, Odiarne Coates, Clifton, February, 1850—November, 1865; Mayor, 1860-1861; died November 16, 1865, aged 72. J.P. 1856; Master Merchant Venturers 1864-1865; President Grateful 1857.

Lane, William, St. Michael's, 1881-1890. Contested St. Michael's 1880; Westbury November, 1892; J.P. 1894.

Lang, Robert, Bristol, 1853-1852. President Anchor 1860.

Langton, William Henry Gore, Clifton, 1848-1854; Mayor 1851-1852; died May 16, 1875, aged 73. Contested Clifton 1844; J.P. 1848; President Anchor 1848, 1856.

Latham, William Albina, Bedminster (West), 1890. J.P. 1898.

Lean, James, Bristol, 1835-1836, 1839-1845; died July 9, 1849, aged 75. Contested Bristol 1836; Common Councillor 1832-1835; Sheriff 1833-1834; J.P. 1841; President Anchor 1824; Master St. Stephen's Ringers 1821.

Lee, William, St. Augustine's, 1877—October, 1880; Bedminster (East), October 22-31, 1880; died February 12, 1886, aged 59. Nominated for Clifton November and December, 1874; contested St. Augustine's 1880, Clifton 1882.

Leonard, Robert, Alderman March, 1851-1853; died May 21, 1863, aged 75. Nominated for Alderman 1838; J.P. 1850.

Leonard, Robert, St. Philip's, 1855-1858; died October 10, 1861, aged 44. President Anchor 1858; Assessor 1847.

Levy, Moss, St. Philip's (North), 1882. Nominated for Alderman 1895; contested Bristol 1879, 1881; Deputy-Governor Incorporation of Poor 1886-1887.

Levy-Langfield, Arthur Albert, Clifton, 1896.

Lewis, Edwin Thomas, St. James', 1888.

Lilly, Robert Trapp, Alderman 1838-1844; died November 27, 1870, aged 85. Contested St. Paul's 1835, 1836; St. Philip's 1837, 1838.

Lloyd, Samuel, Bedminster (East), 1887.

Lockley, James Henry, St. James', 1881-1890. Sheriff 1889-1891; President Grateful 1892.

Low, Charles Hoskins, St. Michael's, January, 1873—May, 1891; Alderman May, 1891. J.P. 1887; President Grateful 1887; Chairman Chamber of Commerce 1865-1866.

Lowe, Charles James, Horfield, 1897. Member of School Board September, 1894.

Lucas, Edward Thomas, Redcliff, 1859—July, 1863; died July 24, 1863, aged 39. Warden Merchant Venturers 1861—July, 1863.

Lucas, John, Redcliff, 1872—January, 1881; died January 13, 1881, aged 75. Chairman Chamber of Commerce 1867-1868; President Colston (Parent) 1856.

Lucas, John Frederick, Alderman, 1868—October, 1893; died October 12, 1893, aged 62. Contested Bedminster 1861; J.P. 1881; Master Merchant Venturers 1868-1869; President Colston (Parent) 1877.

ALPHABETICAL INDEX.—*Continued.*

Lucas, Samuel, Redcliff, 1839-1842; died January 15, 1853, aged 83. Contested St. Paul's 1837; President Colston (Parent) 1835.

Lucas, Thomas, Alderman November, 1845—April, 1856; died April 12, 1856, aged 60. President Colston (Parent) 1846.

Lunell, John Evans, District, 1835-1847; died June 21, 1870, aged 80. Nominated for Mayor 1838. Common Councillor 1829 1835; Sheriff 1829-1830; J.P. 1836; Master Merchant Venturers 1835-1836; President Anchor, 1823, 1842.

Maningford, John, Alderman 1835-1838; died October 22, 1854, aged 77. Contested St. Augustine's 1835; nominated for Alderman 1838; Treasurer Incorporation of Poor 1827-1851.

Mardon, Heber, St. Paul's, March, 1891-1893.

Marshall, Alfred, Clifton, April, 1892-1893.

Matthews, Henry, St. Paul's, 1870—November, 1890; died November 12, 1890.

Maze, Peter, Bristol, 1835-1837, 1833-1844; died June 14, 1849, aged 80. Contested Bristol 1837; Master Merchant Venturers 1831-1832.

Maze, Peter, St. Augustine's, 1835-1836; died May 14, 1869, aged 63. Common Councillor 1833-1835; Sheriff 1833-1834, 1848-1849; Master Merchant Venturers 1837-1838; Master St. Stephen's Ringers 1838.

Mereweather, William, Bedminster (West), 1888-1891.

Miles, John William, Bristol, 1844-1868; died November 5, 1878, aged 61. President Dolphin 1853.

Miles, William Henry, Bristol, 1868-1886; died January 15, 1888, aged 57. Sheriff 1866-1867; President Dolphin 1874.

Miles, Robert Fenton, Bristol, February 1891-1894.

Mills, Henry James, District, July, 1866—March, 1881; died March 15, 1881, aged 69. J.P. 1871; Charity Trustee, 1865-1881; President Anchor 1852.

Mills, John, St. James', 1837—March, 1849; died March 17, 1849, aged 73. Contested St. Michael's 1835, 1836; President Anchor 1833; Master St. Stephen's Ringers 1828.

Mintorn, John, Clifton, 1853-1856; died April 26, 1870, aged 96. Contested Clifton 1843.

Moore, Frank, Somerset, 1897.

Moore, James, Alderman October 1846—April, 1850; died April 9, 1850, aged 70. Contested St. James' 1835, 1838, 1842.

Moore, Nehemiah, St. Paul's, 1835—June, 1847; died June 28, 1847, aged 55.

Moore, Roger, Bedminster (East), 1881-1887. Contested Redcliff 1876, 1877, 1878; Clifton 1878, 1880, 1891.

Morgan, George King, Alderman August, 1874-1892; died November 13, 1892, aged 80.

ALPHABETICAL INDEX.—*Continued.*

Naish, Henry, St. James', 1861-1870, 1872-1881; Alderman November 1881—December, 1891; died December 23, 1891, aged 79. Contested District 1871; nominated for St. Philip's 1870. Governor Incorporation of Poor 1870-1874, 1875-1877.

Naish, James Smith, St. Philip's (South), 1895—September, 1897; died September 16, 1897, aged 40.

Naish, William, District, 1847-1859; Alderman September 1861—November, 1873; Mayor 1864-1865; died July 29, 1875, aged 69. Contested District 1859; J.P. 1856; President Grateful 1866.

Nash, Charles, St. Augustine's, 1851—November, 1886; Alderman 1886—October, 1888. Nominated for Alderman November, 1882, 1883; J.P. 1871; President Dolphin 1869; President Chamber of Commerce 1874-1875.

Nash, James Ezekiel, St. Augustine's, 1835-1843; died January 2, 1845, aged 67.

Nash, Joseph Haynes, Clifton, April, 1867-1876; died September 20, 1892, aged 76.

Newth, Charles, District, March, 1893. Contested St. James' 1890.

O'Grady, James, Easton, 1897. Contested District 1896.

Palmer, Arthur Hare, Bristol, 1848-1854. 1855-1858; died January 28, 1868. Contested Bristol 1854; Governor Incorporation of Poor 1853-1854; President Anchor 1850.

Parsons, Edward, Bedminster (West), 1889. J.P. 1898.

Pavey, John, Clifton, 1886-1889; died August 15, 1891, aged 68. Nominated for Clifton 1892.

Payne, Charles, Clifton, 1835-1841; died December 4, 1846. Common Councillor 1827-1835; Sheriff 1827-1828; Mayor 1834-1835; J.P. 1835; President Dolphin 1833.

Pearson, George, Clifton, 1888. Contested Westbury 1885, District 1887; Governor Incorporation of Poor 1886-1889; Master St. Stephen's Ringers, 1880.

Pembery, Joseph, Bedminster (West), 1894. J.P. 1894.

Perkins, Matthew, Redcliff, 1841-1859; died June 6, 1871, aged 73. Assessor 1838, 1839; President Colston (Parent) 1847.

Perry, Benjamin, Redcliff, 1896.

Perry, John, District, 1855-1873; died April 2, 1879, aged 78. Nominated for Alderman November, 1873; J.P. 1866; Governor Incorporation of Poor, 1860-1864; President Anchor, 1864.

Pethick, Thomas, St. James', 1863-1872; died February 23, 1884, aged 78.

Pethick, William, Bedminster, 1866-1872. January, 1874—October, 1880; Bedminster (West), October, 1880-1887; Alderman, 1889. Nominated for Alderman 1883; contested Bedminster 1872, St. James' November, 1872, Bedminster (West) 1887; J.P. 1871; Sheriff 1894-1895; President Anchor 1873.

ALPHABETICAL INDEX.—Continued.

Phippen, Robert. Bedminster, 1835-1838, 1839-1854 ; Alderman November, 1855—July, 1869; Mayor 1840-1841 ; died July 5, 1869, aged 68. Contested Bedminster 1838, 1854 ; J.P. 1850 ; Sheriff 1854-1855, 1868—July, 1869 ; Charity Trustee 1852-1869 ; President Colston (Parent) 1851.

Pinney, Charles, Alderman 1835-1853; died July 17, 1867, aged 74. Contested St. Augustine's 1835 ; Common Councillor 1822-1835 ; Sheriff 1823-1824 ; Mayor 1831-1832 ; Master Merchant Venturers 1844-1845 ; President Anchor 1822.

Plummer, William, Alderman 1850-1856; died September 14, 1857, aged 52. Contested Bristol 1835.

Poole, James, St. Michael's, 1847—December, 1872 ; Mayor 1858-1859 ; died December 24, 1872, aged 75. Nominated for Alderman, 1859, 1868, 1871 ; J.P. 1858 ; President Grateful 1842 ; Master St. Stephen's Ringers 1847.

Poole, John, Stapleton, 1897.

Pottow, Arthur, St. James', 1889-1892. Contested St. James' 1888.

Pountney, John Decimus, Alderman 1838-1850 ; Mayor 1847-1848 ; died December 30, 1852, aged 65. Contested Redcliff 1836, 1837 ; President Dolphin 1848.

Powell Thomas (of Charlotte-street), St. Augustine's, 1835-1851 ; died February 21, 1874, aged 86. Contested St. Augustine's 1851.

Powell, Thomas (of Montpelier), Redcliff, 1842-1854 ; District, 1859-1871 ; died February 15, 1872, aged 76. Charity Trustee 1836-1872.

Powell, William Augustus Frederick, Redcliff, 1861-1885. Contested St. Philip's 1860 ; J.P. 1875 ; Master Merchant Venturers 1873-1874 ; President Colston (Parent) 1866.

Price, Charles, Redcliff, 1854—January, 1869; died January 22, 1869, aged 70. Contested Redcliff 1853.

Prichard, Charles John Collins, Clifton, 1876-1882, 1884—November, 1893 ; Alderman November, 1893. Nominated for Clifton December, 1874 ; Contested Clifton 1883.

Prichard, Henry, District, 1848-1854 ; Redcliff, 1855-1858 ; died June 4, 1864, aged 69. Contested Bedminster 1851 ; nominated for Alderman 1833 ; J.P. 1854.

Prideaux, Francis Grevile, Alderman 1844-1850 ; died October 27, 1855, aged 75. Sword-bearer 1850-1855 ; President Dolphin 1841.

Proctor, Thomas, Alderman 1853—May, 1876 ; died May 15, 1876) aged 64. J.P. 1858 ; Sheriff 1859-1870 ; President Colston (Parent, 1861.

Prust, Stephen, Bristol, 1837-1840, 1843-1849; died November 13) 1850, aged 79.

Rankin, Thomas, St. James', March — July, 1849 ; died July 22, 1849, aged 71. Governor Incorporation of Poor 1832-1833.

Richards, Fenwick, St. Michael's, May, 1891-1895. Nominated fo Alderman 1895 ; J.P. 1898.

Ricketts, Frederick, Bristol, 1835-1837 ; died July 8, 1871, aged 81. Nominated for Alderman 1833 ; President Anchor 1840.

ALPHABETICAL INDEX.—*Continued.*

Ricketts, Henry, Redcliff, 1835-1841 ; Alderman 1841—May, 1859; died May 7, 1859, aged 76. Common Councillor 1832-1835 ; J.P. 1836.

Ricketts, Jacob, Alderman, 1844—October, 1846 ; died October 4, 1846.

Ricketts, Richard, Alderman 1835-1841; died March 31, 1851. Contested St. Augustine's 1835.

Riddle, Isaac, St. Philip's, 1852-1855; died June 27, 1878, aged 78. Contested St. Philip's 1860 ; St. Augustine's 1861.

Riddle, Thomas Hooper, Alderman 1835-1841 ; died September 19, 1848, aged 54. Contested St. Paul's 1835 ; Common Councillor, 1828-1835 ; Sheriff 1828-1829.

Ridler, Richard, St. Augustine's, 1874-1877 ; died July 12, 1878, aged 61.

Ring, Richard Charles, Redcliff, 1879—April, 1885.

Robinson, Elisha Smith, Bedminster, July, 1858—October, 1880 ; Bedminster (West), October, 1880—August, 1885 ; Mayor 1866-1867 ; died August 29, 1835, aged 68. Nominated for Alderman 1880, November, 1882, April, 1883, November, 1883 ; J.P. 1864 ; Governor Incorporation of Poor 1857-1860 ; President Grateful 1880 ; President Anchor 1859.

Robinson, Richard, Alderman 1841—October, 1878 ; died October 17, 1878, aged 76. Master Merchant Venturers 1846-1847 ; Master St. Stephen's Ringers 1839.

Roch, Nicholas, Alderman 1835-1838; died April 6, 1866, aged 80. Contested Redcliff 1835 ; Common Councillor 1818-1834 ; Alderman 1834-1835 ; Sheriff 1818-1819, 1821-1822.

Rogers, Edward, St. Augustine's, 1891—June, 1893.

Rogers, George, St. Augustine's, 1849-1858 ; died February 4, 1891, aged 82. Governor Incorporation of Poor 1855-1857.

Saise, Alfred John, Stapleton, 1897.

Salmon, Henry Augustus, St. Augustine's, 1861-1864.

Sanders, George Eddie, Redcliff, 1835-1839; Bristol, 1846—April, 1851 ; died April 2, 1851, aged 70. Contested Redcliff 1839, 1844 ; J.P. 1836 ; Charity Trustee 1836-1851.

Sanders, Thomas Richard, District, 1835-1849 ; Bristol, 1849-1855 ; died October 14, 1876, aged 84.

Savage, John, Bristol, 1835-1836 ; died January 9, 1870, aged 85. Contested Bristol 1836 ; nominated for Alderman May, 1838 ; Common Councillor 1822-1831 ; Alderman 1831-1835 ; Sheriff 1823-1824, 1825-1826 ; Mayor 1829-1831 ; J.P. 1836 ; Charity Trustee 1836-1865 ; Master Merchant Venturers 1842-1843.

Sharland, John, St. Philip's (North) 1893.

Shaw, John George, Bristol, 1842-1863 ; Mayor, 1853-1855 ; died Oct. 22, 1876, aged 71. Nominated for Alderman 1859 ; J.P. 1854 ; Governor Incorporation of Poor 1847-1850 ; President Grateful 1837, 1860 ; Master St. Stephen's Ringers 1848.

Sheppard, Frank, St. Paul's, 1893-1896.

Shirley, Samuel, Clifton, July, 1897.

ALPHABETICAL INDEX.—Continued.

Sibly, Thomas Dix, St. Philip's (South), 1884-1887. Contested St. Philip's (South), 1883.

Sibree, William Priestley, Redcliff. February, 1869-1872; died Jan 12. 1889, aged 75. Contested Redcliff 1872.

Slaughter, Edward, Alderman September—November, 1865; died May 13, 1891, aged 75.

Smith, Alfred John, Somerset, 1897.

Smith, John, St. Michael's, 1849-1858; died Nov. 6, 1860, aged 66.

Smith, Joseph Grace, District, 1842-1848; died March 26, 1859, aged 71. Contested District 1839; President Anchor, 1831, 1837.

Smith, Richard. St. Augustine's, 1835—January, 1843; died January 24, 1843, aged 70. Charity Trustee 1836-1843; President Dolphin 1822; Master St. Stephen's Ringers 1826.

Smith, William, Clifton, 1870-1882; Alderman April, 1883. Contested Westbury, 1882; J.P. 1878; Sheriff 1876-1877; member of School Board June, 1882-1883. President Colston (Parent) 1830.

Spark, William, St. Augustine's, 1863—October, 1880; Bedminster (East) October, 1880-1881; Alderman November, 1881-1886; died December 4, 1887, aged 75. Nominated for Alderman 1880; J.P. 1881.

Spofforth, Fairfax, St. Michael's, 1891.

Staples, Edward Joseph, St. Augustine's, 1841—May, 1845; died July 12, 1853, aged 39. President Grateful 1844.

Stephens, Richard Court, Bristol, 1895. Contested St. Michael's, 1881; Governor Incorporation of Poor 1883-1885, 1895-1897.

Stock, Thomas, Bristol, December 26-31, 1835; Alderman December, 1835—April, 1838; died April 27, 1838, aged 70. Nominated for Mayor January 1836, November 1836, 1837. J.P. 1835; Governor Incorporation of Poor 1815-1817, 1827-1832. President Chamber of Commerce 1825-1829, 1830-1831.

Swaish, John, St. Philip's (South), 1890. J.P. 1898.

Symes, Sir Robert Henry, Alderman 1895; Mayor 1893-1895, 1896. Contested St. Michael's 1871, St. Augustine's 1874, Redcliff 1880, April, 1885, Bristol 1886. J.P. 1889; Sheriff 1887-1888.

Taunton, William Leonard Thomas Pyle, St. James', 1833-1841; died October 13, 1850, aged 71. Charity Trustee, 1836-1850.

Taylor Charles, St. Augustine's, May, 1846-1859; died November 17, 1861, aged 80. President Dolphin 1849.

Taylor, Henry, Clifton, December, 1874—September, 1882; Mayor 1879-1880; died September 12, 1882, aged 55. Nominated for Clifton 1874; J.P.1881; Chairman Chamber of Commerce 1874.

Taylor, Thomas Terrett, St. Augustine's, 1859—June, 1880; died June 27, 1880, aged 66. Master Merchant Venturers 1872-1873; Charity Trustee 1855-1880; President Dolphin 1873.

Terrell, Frederick, Bedminster, 1847—October, 1880; Bedminster (West), October, 1880-1883; died Aug. 14, 1889, aged 85. Nominated for Alderman 1871, 1880, December, 1881; J.P. 1866; Charity Trustee 1852-1875 (Chairman 1869-1875).

Terrell, Henry, Bedminster, 1855—July, 1858; died July 14, 1858, aged 48.

ALPHABETICAL INDEX.—*Continued.*

Terrell, William, Bedminster, 1838-1847 ; died July 25, 1851, aged 82. Contested Bristol 1835.

Terrell, William, Bristol, 1863-1863, 1869-1878 ; died May 1, 1887, aged 66. Contested Bristol 1858, 1866, St. Paul's 1860 ; J.P. 1863 ; Charity Trustee 1865-1887; President Anchor 1862 ; Chairman Chamber of Commerce 1858-1859.

Terrett, William, Bedminster (East) 1882.

Thatcher, Edward James, Alderman 1897. Contested Bedminster (East) 1884 ; President-elect Colston (Parent) 1898.

Thomas, Christopher James. St. Philip's, January, 1845—October, 1880 ; St. Philip's (South), October, 1880-1883 ; Mayor 1874-1875 ; died January 2, 1894, aged 86. Nominated for Alderman 1859, 1868, 1871, November, 1873, 1877, 1880, November, 1881, December, 1881 ; J.P. 1854 ; President Anchor 1853.

Thomas, George, Redcliff, 1835-1852 ; died December 7, 1869, aged 78. Charity Trustee, 1836-1869 (Chairman 1852-1869.)

Todd, William Ansell, Bristol, 1886. J.P. 1894 ; Sheriff 1895-1896.

Tothill, William, Redcliff, 1836-1839 ; Bedminster 1840-1855 ; died December 2, 1875, aged 91. Contested Redcliff 1835, 1839 ; nominated for Alderman 1835 ; Charity Trustee, 1836-1875 ; Governor Incorporation of Poor 1833-1834.

Tovey, Charles, St. Paul's, July, 1847-1862 ; died June 1, 1888, aged 76. Contested St. Paul's 1862, Clifton 1866 ; Governor Incorporation of Poor 1854-1855.

Tovey, Robert Gray, St. Paul's, 1887—March 1891 ; died October 28, 1896, aged 63. Contested St. Paul's 1886.

Townsend, Charles. District, 1873—March, 1893 ; Alderman, 1897. J.P. 1881 ; President Anchor 1883 ; President Chamber of Commerce 1875-1876.

Tryon, Stephen, Westbury, Nov., 1892. President Grateful 1897.

Twiggs, Henry William, Redcliff, 1830-1896. Contested Redcliff 1888.

Vaughan, Philip, Alderman, 1844—April, 1864 ; died April 14, 1864, aged 64.

Verrier, Albert George, Easton, 1897. J.P. 1898.

Vining, Charles, St. Augustine's, 1836-1842 ; died November 26, 1848, aged 72.

Vining, Charles Joseph, Bristol, 1845-1848 ; died July 3, 1869, aged 60. Master St. Stephen's Ringers 1849.

Vining, John, Alderman 1835-1859 ; Mayor 1855-1857 ; died September 26, 1866, aged 80. Contested Clifton 1835 ; J.P. 1856 ; Charity Trustee 1852-1865 ; President Dolphin 1847.

Visger, Harman, Bristol, 1836-1839 ; St. Philip's, 1842-1860 ; died January 4, 1867, aged 65. Contested Bristol 1839, 1840, Bedminster 1842 ; nominated for Alderman 1859 ; Charity Trustee 1836-1867.

Wait, Charles, Clifton, May, 1844-1854 ; died August 25, 1868, aged 75. Contested Clifton 1854.

ALPHABETICAL INDEX.—*Continued.*

Wait, Hamilton Wilfrid Killigrew, Bristol, 1893.

Wait, William Killigrew, Alderman 1835-1838 ; died March 22, 1852, aged 55. Common Councillor 1834-1835 ; Sheriff 1834-1835.

Wait, William Killigrew, Bristol, February, 1867-1885 ; Alderman 1886—May, 1891 ; Mayor 1869-1870 ; nominated for Alderman 1883. J.P. 1871-1881 ; President Dolphin 1867.

Walker, Charles Ludlow, St. Michael's, 1835-1836 ; died February 21, 1856, aged 68. Common Councillor 1822-1835 ; Sheriff 1824-1825, 1828-1829 ; Mayor 1833-1834 ; J.P. 1841 ; President Dolphin 1844 ; Master St. Stephen's Ringers 1836.

Wall, James Creswell, Bristol, 1866-1869 ; Alderman May, 1876-1895 ; died February 21, 1897, aged 72. J.P. 1878 ; President Grateful 1865 ; Master St. Stephen's Ringers 1864.

Walls, John, St. Augustine's, November, 1886.

Walwyn, Richard Henry, Clifton 1863-1866 ; died June 5, 1866, aged 81.

Ward, Richard Brickdale, Alderman 1838—April, 1853 ; died April 1, 1853, aged 76. President Dolphin 1821.

Warde, Charles (K.H. and Admiral), Clifton 1848-1851 ; died January 5, 1869, aged 82.

Ware, John, Clifton, 1849-1852 ; died February 27, 1885, aged 89.

Warne, John, Clifton, 1836—October, 1837 ; died October 14, 1837, aged 71. Contested Clifton 1835.

Warren, Algernon William, Redcliff, 1858-1861, August, 1863-1871 ; St. Philip's (North) 1880—April, 1883 ; died April 15, 1883, aged 62. Contested Redcliff 1861, 1871, 1872, St. James' 1873, Clifton 1876 ; J.P. 1875 ; President Anchor 1869.

Warren, John Sandham, Alderman 1880—April, 1883 ; died November 27, 1889, aged 69.

Waterman, Thomas, St. Michael's, 1858-1870 ; died June 1, 1873, aged 74. Contested St. Michael's 1870.

Wathen, Sir Charles, St. Paul's 1877—October, 1888 ; Alderman October, 1888—February, 1893 ; Mayor 1884-1885, 1887-1891 ; died February 14, 1893, aged 60. Nominated for Alderman 1886 ; J.P. 1887 ; Charity Trustee 1891-1893 ; President Grateful 1888.

Wathen, John Hancocke, Clifton, November 1893-1895 ; Alderman 1897. Contested Clifton 1895 ; President Grateful 1895.

Watson, William, Alderman, 1835-1844 ; died February 3, 1870, aged 82. Contested Bristol 1835 ; Common Councillor 1833-1835 ; President Dolphin 1836.

Wayte, Samuel Simon, St. James', 1835-1837 ; died April 9, 1880, aged 84.

Webb, Robert Henry, District, 1839-1842 ; Alderman May, 1859—February, 1875 ; died February 28, 1875, aged 81. Contested District 1835.

Webb, William Merrett, St. Augustine's, 1864—October 1880 ; Bedminster (East), October, 1880-1882 ; died March 12, 1892, aged 69. President Colston (Parent) 1882.

Wedmore, Thomas, St. Paul's, 1862-1877 ; died February 5, 1897, aged 88. Contested St. Paul's 1861 ; J.P. 1881 ; Deputy-Governor Incorporation of Poor 1847-1848 ; Mayor's Auditor 1875-1877.

ALPHABETICAL INDEX.—*Continued.*

Weston, Sir Joseph Dodge, Clifton. 1868—October, 1880; Westbury. October, 1880-1892; Mayor 1880-1884; died March 5. 1895, aged 72. Contested Bristol 1866; nominated for Alderman 1883, 1886, 1889; J.P. 1875; Charity Trustee 1865-1895; President Grateful 1878; President Anchor 1870.

Wethered, Joseph, St. Philip's, 1863-1869.

Wetherman, John, St. James', July, 1849-1852; St. Michael's, 1854—October, 1877; died October 14, 1877, aged 71. Contested St. James' 1852; Governor Incorporation of Poor December, 1850-1853; President Grateful 1851.

White, George, Bristol, July, 1890-1893.

Whitwill, Mark, St. Philip's, 1870—October, 1880; St. Philip's (South), October, 1880-1891. Contested Bristol 1858, 1860; nominated for Redcliff 1859; nominated for Alderman 1883, 1889, July, 1890, February, 1891, May, 1891, 1892, 1897; J.P. 1875; member of School Board 1871-1892 (Vice-Chairman 1871-1880, Chairman 1880-1892); President Anchor, 1874; Chairman Chamber of Commerce 1857-1858.

Williams, Henry Joseph, Clifton 1881-1884; Bedminster (West) 1887-1890. Contested St. Michael's 1880, Red-cliff 1885, Clifton 1886.

Wills, Charles, Bristol, 1883-1895; Horfield 1897. Contested Bristol 1895; nominated for Alderman January, 1892, November, 1892, 1895; J.P. 1889; President Chamber of Commerce 1880-1882, 1883-1884.

Wills, Sir Frederick, Bart., Bedminster (West), September, 1885-1888. President Anchor 1882.

Wills, George, Bristol. March. 1866—October, 1880; St. Philip's (North) October, 1880-1882; died December 18, 1888, aged 75. Contested St. Philip's (North) 1882; nominated for Alderman 1880; J.P. 1871; Charity Trustee 1875-1888; President Anchor 1867; Chairman Chamber of Commerce 1864-1865.

Wills, Henry Overton, St. Paul's, 1845-1860; died November 23, 1871, aged 71. Nominated for Alderman September, 1861; J.P. 1856.

Wills, William Day, St. Paul's. March, 1846-1861; died May 13, 1865, aged 68. Contested Redcliff 1838; nominated for Alderman 1838, 1859; J.P. 1858; Charity Trustee 1852-1865.

Wills, Sir William Henry, Bart., Bristol, 1862—October, 1880; St. Philip's (North) October, 22—31, 1880. J.P. 1866; Sheriff 1877-1878; Charity Trustee 1865; President Anchor 1866; Chairman Chamber of Commerce 1863-1864.

Wintle, Colston, Horfield, 1897.

Winwood, John, Alderman 1835-1841; died February 4, 1843, aged 60. Contested St. Philip's 1835.

Wood, James, Bristol, 1835-1838; St. Paul's 1843—March, 1846; died March 19, 1846, aged 65. Contested Bristol 1838, August 1842; nominated for Alderman 1838; J.P. 1836; Charity Trustee 1836-1846; Deputy-Governor Incorporation of Poor 1823-1824; Mayor's Auditor 1836-1838, 1845.

Woodward, George Rocke, Alderman April, 1864—November, 1881; died November 18, 1885, aged 76. J.P. 1866; Sheriff 1861-1862; President Grateful 1861.

Worrall, Henry Lechmere (General), Clifton. 1850—November, 1852; March, 1853-1863; died December 8, 1872, aged 74. J.P. 1850.

ALPHABETICAL INDEX.—*Continued.*

Wyld, John Hopton, Alderman September, 1853—September, 1857; died August 12, 1875, aged 76. President Colston (Parent) 1848.

Wyld, William Hopton, Alderman 1844—August, 1853; died August 28, 1853, aged 57. President Colston (Parent) 1845; Mayor's Auditor 1847-1851.

ALPHABETICAL INDEX OF CANDIDATES WHO HAVE NOT OBTAINED SEATS IN THE COUNCIL SINCE 1835

[N.B.—In several cases candidates were nominated without their consent.]

Alexander, Joseph Frankel, St. Augustine's, 1835; died November 23, 1848, aged 60.

Alsop, Stephen, St. James', November, 1872.

Baker, George, St. Philip's (North), 1893, 1895.

Baker, Thomas, Bristol, 1885; died March 20, 1893, aged 63.

Ballard, Joseph John, St. George's, 1897.

Bartlett, James, Bedminster, 1835; died March 29, 1851, aged 56.

Beaven, Henry, Bedminster, 1873.

Belsten, George, St. Philip's (South), 1887.

Bengough, George, St. Augustine's, 1836; died December 25, 1856, aged 63. J.P. 1836; Charity Trustee 1836-1850; nominated for Sheriff 1836; Common Councillor 1829-1835; Sheriff 1831-1832.

Bennett, Henry, Bedminster, 1857, 1873; died February 6, 1895, aged 83.

Bennett, William Henry, St. Paul's, 1883.

Bligh, Richard, Bristol, 1835; died August 18, 1869, aged 73.

Brabham, Harold, Redcliff, 1893, 1894; St. Philip's (South), October, 1897.

Brain, William Horace, Clifton, 1893, 1895, 1896, July, 1897, 1897. Candidate for School Board 1895, 1898.

Britt, James, St. Philip's (North), 1885; died November 2, 1889.

Brittan, Alfred, Clifton, 1874; died June 22, 1894, aged 71. Assessor 1852.

Broad, James Thierry, St. Michael's, 1891.

Brown, Henry Isaac, Bedminster, 1873; Clifton, 1874; St. Augustine's, 1882; St. Philip's (South), 1882; Bedminster (East), 1882; died February 2, 1888, aged 72.

Browning, Henry, Clifton, 1862.

ALPHABETICAL INDEX.—*Continued.*

Burbidge, Thomas, Clifton, 1843; died February 17, 1856, aged 63.
Burris, Frederick, Somerset, 1897.
Bush, George, Clifton, 1849, February, 1850; died January 11, 1895, aged 87.
Bush, Thomas, St. Philip's, 1853.
Butchard, John, St. James', 1892; District, March, 1893. Candidate for School Board, 1892, 1895.

Candy, James, District, 1854; died December 6, 1870, aged 57.
Carlile, George Martin, Clifton, 1879.
Cashmore, Samuel, Redcliff, 1878.
Church, William, Somerset, 1897.
Clarke, Edward Gustavus, Bristol, 1882. President Anchor 1877.
Clements, Thomas, Clifton, 1868.
Clifton, John Henry, St. James', 1878; St. Philip's (North) 1880; died March 29, 1894, aged 62. Candidate for School Board 1871.
Cook, Henry, Clifton, 1872, 1873, 1874; Redcliff, 1873. Candidate for School Board 1874.
Cooke, Isaac, Alderman 1835; died July 4, 1852, aged 80.
Coram, William, Stapleton, 1897.
Cordeux, Charles, St. James', 1874.
Cordeux, John, St. James', 1874.
Cottrell, Edwin, Stapleton, 1897.
Count, William, St. Philip's, 1877, 1878. Candidate for School Board 1877, 1880.
Cousins, John, Stapleton, 1897.
Cowlin, William Henry, St. Philip's (South), 1889, 1892; St. James', 1891.
Cox, James, St. James', 1838, 1839, 1840, 1841; died Nov. 8, 1842.
Curtis, William Henry, Horfield, 1897.

Daniell, Edward Tuckett, Stapleton, 1897. Nominated for Alderman 1897.
Daniell, Richard Thomas, St. Philip's (South), 1895.
Drewe, Aurelius John, Bristol, 1835; died October 22, 1875, aged 83.
Dundas, Charles Amesbury Whitley Deans, Bedminster, January 1874; died September 9, 1874, aged 28.

Edmunds, Henry, St. Paul's, December, 1890, March, 1891.
Edwards, Thomas, St. Philip's, 1836.
Essery, Albert, Bedminster, 1878; Clifton, 1890; St. Philip's (South), 1895.
Evans, Thomas, Bedminster, 1873.

ALPHABETICAL INDEX —*Continued*.

Flook, Samuel Gayner, St. Philip's, 1835; died January 28, 1839, aged 38.

Foll, Hattil, St. Michael's, 1854 ; died October 10, 1881, aged 72

Fowler, John, Clifton, 1842, 1843, May, 1844: died August 6, 1879, aged 83.

Francis, Alfred Williams, Horfield, 1897.

Froud, Alfred, Bedminster (East), 1887. Member of School Board 1883.

Fyson, Henry, Redcliff, 1837; Bedminster, 1839 ; died August 27, 1859, aged 80. Deputy Governor Incorporation of Poor May 1830-1832.

Gardner, Walter Edwin, Bedminster (West), 1893.

George, Charles Edward Alfred, Westbury, 1884.

Gerrish, George Samuel, Easton, 1897.

Giles, Richard Bobbett, Clifton, 1853; died January 5, 1870, aged 77.

Glascodine, Henry, Bedminster, 1835 ; died June 6, 1876, aged 88.

Goldney, Gabriel, Clifton, 1844, 1849; died December 3, 1859, aged 53. Governor Incorporation of Poor April—December, 1850.

Gordon, Alfred William, Horfield, 1897.

Gorman, William, Bedminster (East), 1894, November, 1897.

Gough, Robert, Clifton, 1895.

Greenway, Frederick, Stapleton, 1897.

Gregory, William Thomas, Somerset, 1897.

Griffiths, Thomas, St. Philip's (South), October, 1897.

Hale, Matthew Henry, St. James', 1872; died March 2, 1890, aged 56.

Hare, Sir John, Redcliff, 1835 ; Alderman May, 1858 ; died February 2, 1865, aged 80. President Anchor 1829.

Hare, Solomon, Bristol, 1896. Burgesses' Auditor 1898.

Hayman, Richard Manning, Bristol, 1853 ; died May 24, 1867, aged 52. President Anchor 1857 ; Chairman Chamber of Commerce 1854-1855; Master St. Stephens Ringers 1853.

Hicks, Francis, St. George's, 1897.

Hill, Charles, Clifton, 1849; died June 25, 1867, aged 75.

Hobbs, Thomas, Easton, 1897.

Hunt, Richard, St. James', 1879. Candidate for School Board 1880.

Hurn, John, Clifton, 1868, 1872, 1878; died April 25, 1891, aged 58.

Husenbeth, Frederick Charles, Bristol, 1844; died March 15, 1848, aged 83.

Irving, John, St. Michael's, 1835; died November 2, 1865, aged 86.

ALPHABETICAL INDEX.—*Continued.*

Jacques, John, Clifton, 1840, 1842 ; died July 8, 1853.

Jenkins, James, St. Augustine's, 1835 ; died April 29, 1853, aged 64.

Johnson, James, Clifton, 1835, 1836, October, 1837 ; Alderman, 1835 ; died August 14, 1844, aged 80. Governor Incorporation of Poor 1820-1823.

Johnson, William, Clifton, 1837, 1838 ; Alderman 1838 ; died January 2, 1849, aged 58.

Jones, George, Bristol, 1844, 1847 ; died July 30, 1859, aged 87.

Jones, James, Bedminster, 1873.

Jones, John, Clifton, 1850, 1866 ; died December 30, 1873.

Jones, William Philip, Somerset, 1897.

Jullion, Frederick Henry, Easton, 1897.

Knowles, William, Clifton, 1837 ; died February 23, 1871, aged 70.

Lane, John William, St. Paul's, December, 1890, 1895 ; St. Philip's (South), October, 1897. Governor Incorporation of Poor 1893-1895.

Lang, Samuel, Alderman 1838 ; died February 20, 1849, aged 65.

Lax, Joseph, Clifton, 1835 ; died January 23, 1845. Common Councillor 1831-1835 ; Sheriff 1831-1832.

Leech, Joseph, Clifton, 1868 ; died August 13, 1893, aged 78. President Grateful 1849.

Leonard, Frederick, Easton, 1897.

Llewellyn, Henry Revell, Redcliff, 1835 ; died April 23, 1844, aged 75.

Llewellyn, William, St. Augustine's, 1864, 1872 ; died August 22, 1876, aged 71.

Lorymer, Ernest George, St. Michael's, 1884, 1885, 1886, 1890. Governor Incorporation of Poor 1891-1893.

Lucas, James Duffett, St. Philip's (South), 1883 ; died June 21, 1895, aged 63.

McBayne, Lachlan, Clifton, 1835 ; died February 21, 1848, aged 70. J.P. 1836.

MacGowan, Alexander Thorburn, Clifton, 1880.

Macliver, Peter Stewart, Clifton, 1862 ; died April 19, 1891, aged 71.

Matthews, Thomas Gadd, St. James', 1880. President Grateful 1872 ; Master Merchant Venturers 1892-1893.

Menlove, Thomas, St. James', 1835 ; died August 11, 1843, aged 57. Deputy-Governor Incorporation of Poor 1824-1825.

Melsom, Henry, St. Paul's, 1863, 1864 ; died March 22, 1866, aged 54.

Metford, Joseph Seymour, St. Augustine's, 1877 ; died April 25, 1895, aged 70.

Morgan, Samuel, Bristol, 1835 ; died September 20, 1849, aged 55. Deputy-Governor Incorporation of Poor 1836-1838.

ALPHABETICAL INDEX—Continued.

Owen, Philip, St. Philip's (North), 1890.

Palmer, Nathaniel, District, March, 1893.

Parker, Herbert, St. Michael's, 1892.

Patterson, William, Bedminster, 1853 ; died March 8. 1869, aged 74.

Peters, Samuel, St. Philip's (North), May, 1883; died December, 1891.

Pethick, Henry, Redcliff, November, 1871; St. James', November, 1872.

Phillips, Edmund, Westbury, 1895.

Phillips, Edwin Thomas, Horfield, 1897.

Phillips, William, St. James', March 19 and 26, 1849, 1856.

Pine, George, Bedminster, 1873.

Pinnigar, Job George, Clifton, 1881.

Pomeroy, William Carro, Clifton. 1872 ; died Feb. 15, 1892, aged 78.

Poole, James, Clifton, 1837 ; died August 28, 1857, aged 84.

Powell, James, Bedminster, 1835.

Pritchett, Samuel Waltham, St. Philip's (North), 1887 ; St. James', 1888.

Protheroe, James, Bristol. 1849; St. Augustine's, 1861; died Jan. 1, 1867. Deputy-Governor Incorporation of Poor 1855-1857.

Rankin, Thomas Wright, Bristol, 1854, 1860; died June 28, 1885, aged 71. President Anchor 1854 ; Chairman Chamber of Commerce 1856-1857.

Reynolds, Joseph, St. Augustine's, 1835 ; Alderman 1835 ; died January 31, 1859, aged 90. Treasurer Incorporation of Poor 1820-1823 ; President Chamber of Commerce 1823-1825.

Ringer, William, Redcliff, 1833 ; died January 20, 1858

Robinson, Alfred, Bedminster, 1873. J.P. 1887.

Robinson, Frank R., Bedminster, 1873.

Robinson, Harry, Bedminster, 1873.

Rossiter, Henry, Clifton, 1891.

Royall, Thomas, Clifton, 1839, 1878, 1879, 1880, 1881, 1882, 1883, 1884 ; died September 2, 1890, aged 82.

Sanders, John Naish, Clifton, 1838; died January 20, 1870, aged 93. J.P. 1836.

Saunders, George, Stapleton, 1897.

Shapland, George, District, 1835, 1833; died Nov. 9, 1870, aged 77.

Short, Francis, Bristol, 1852; died February 12, 1853, aged 57 President Anchor 1844 ; Assessor 1841, 1851.

Simmons, Thomas Nimrod, Clifton, 1887.

ALPHABETICAL INDEX.—*Continued.*

Sinnott, James, Somerset, 1897.
Smart, Robert Charles, Horfield, 1897.
Stevens, William, Bristol, 1881. Governor Incorporation of Poor 1835-1883.
Stothert, George Kelson, Clifton, April, 1867, 1873.
Stroud, John Stroud George William, Somerset, 1897.
Sweet, William, St. Michael's, 1858.

Tanner, Daniel John, Easton, 1897.
Taylor, William, St. James', 1884.
Thorne, John, Clifton, 1868, 1873, 1884, 1895.
Tothill, Francis, Clifton, August and November, 1862.
Tricks, George Snow, District, 1881; died October 14, 1883, aged 49. Governor Incorporation of Poor 1881-1883; Auditor 1870-1883.
Tucker, Charles Henry, Clifton, July and November, 1897.
Tuckett, Francis, Bristol, 1858; died May 2, 1868, aged 65.

Valentine, John, St. James', April, 1895.
Vincent, Albert, St. Paul's, November, 1888, 1889. Candidate for School Board, 1892.

Waring, Samuel, Bristol, 1835, 1836; died June 27, 1839, aged 44.
Warren, Robert Hall, St. James', 1873.
Watkins, Frederick Nelson, Clifton, 1866, 1868; died March 31, 1872, aged 73.
Watkins, Thomas, St. George's, 1897.
Weight, Robert Inkerman, St. George's, 1897.
White, Edward Colston, Bedminster (West), 1887; died November 8, 1889.
White, Benjamin, Clifton, 1874; died August, 1890, aged 71.
White, Thomas, Clifton, 1846; died September 29, 1857, aged 77.
Whitefield, William, St. George's, 1897. Member of School Board 1892 –October, 1893.
Whittall, George Piercy, Alderman March, 1851; died February 4, 1859, aged 63.
Willcox, William Dove, Redcliff, 1891. J.P. 1894. President Chamber of Commerce 1889-1891.
Wills, Edward Payson, Redcliff, 1880; Bedminster (West), 1883. President Anchor 1880.
Wills, Henry Overton, Bristol, 1866. J.P. 1878.
Wills, Samuel Day, Clifton, 1878. J.P. 1881; President Anchor 1878.
Winter, George, Easton, 1897.

THE OLD CORPORATION AT THE DATE OF THE PASSING OF THE MUNICIPAL CORPORATIONS ACT, 1835.

The unreformed Corporation consisted of 42 persons, including 12 Aldermen, the Recorder being, in virtue of his office, senior Alderman. At the date of the passing of the Act of 1835, the Corporation was composed as follows :—

MAYOR AND SHERIFFS

*Charles Payne ; Mayor ; Sheriff 1827-8. Elected Common Councillor July 11, 1827.

*James Norroway Franklyn ; Sheriff. Elected Common Councillor July 20, 1831.

*William Killigrew Wait ; Sheriff. Elected Common Councillor September 6, 1834.

ALDERMEN.

Trinity Ward, Sir Charles Wetherell (Recorder). Elected July 28, 1827; died August 17, 1846, aged 76.

St. Michael's, *Thomas Daniel ; Sheriff 1786-7 ; Mayor 1797-8. Elected Common Councillor June 29, 1785 ; Alderman October 27, 1798 (Redcliff, transferred to St. James' September 24, 1806 : St. Michael's March 23, 1814).

All Saints', John Haythorne ; Sheriff 1803-4, 1807-8 ; Mayor 1808-9, 1816-18, 1825-6. Elected Common Councillor September 15, 1803 ; Alderman March 23, 1814 (St. Nicholas, transferred to All Saints' November 3, 1822); died July 16, 1845, aged 78.

Redcliff, *William Fripp ; Sheriff 1814-15 ; Mayor 1819-20. Elected Common Councillor June 8, 1814 ; Alderman January 3, 1821 (Maryleport, transferred to Redcliff November 3, 1822).

St. Nicholas', *Abraham Hillhouse ; Sheriff 1812-13, 1817-1818. Elected Common Councillor August 15, 1812 ; Alderman November 3,1822 ; Mayor 1821-2.

St. James', *James George ; Sheriff 1814-15, 1819-20 ; Mayor 1822-3. Elected Common Councillor June 8, 1814 ; Alderman May 16, 1827.

St. Stephen's, Thomas Camplin ; Sheriff 1821-2 ; Mayor 1826-7. Elected Common Councillor June 13, 1821 ; Alderman July 21, 1829 ; died December 8, 1856, aged 75.

Temple, *Gabriel Goldney ; Sheriff 1822-3, 1825-6 ; Mayor 1827-8. Elected Common Councillor June 12, 1822 ; Alderman July 21, 1829.

Maryleport, *John Savage ; Sheriff 1823-4, 1825-6 ; Mayor 1829-31. Elected Common Councillor June 12, 1822 ; Alderman September 10, 1831.

St. Thomas', *Nicholas Roch ; Sheriff 1818-19, 1821-22. Elected Common Councillor August 13, 1818 ; Alderman March 4, 1834.

St. Ewen, Vacant by the resignation of John Bunn.

Castle Precincts, Vacant by the resignation of George Hilbrough.

THE OLD CORPORATION.—*Continued.*

COMMON COUNCILLORS.

Philip Protheroe; Sheriff 1804-5; Mayor 1810-11. Elected June 13, 1804; died June 4, 1846, aged 65.

James Fowler; Sheriff 1810-11; Mayor 1813-14. Elected September 12, 1810 (Alderman St. Thomas January 3, 1821—November 28, 1833).

George Hillhouse; Sheriff 1812-13, 1817-18; Mayor 1820-1. Elected July 18, 1812 (Alderman Castle Precincts November 3, 1822—Feb. 12, 1835); died December 24, 1848, aged 70.

John Cave; Sheriff 1822-3; Mayor 1828-9. Elected June 12, 1822; died March 27, 1842, aged 77.

*Charles Pinney; Sheriff 1823-4; Mayor 1831-2. Elected June 12, 1822.

*Charles Ludlow Walker; Sheriff 1824-5, 1828-9; Mayor 1833-4. Elected August 24, 1822.

William Weare. Elected May 17, 1782; died Dec. 24, 1836, aged 84.

Richard Bright. Elected Dec. 10, 1783; died Jan. 25, 1840, aged 84.

Sir Henry Protheroe; Sheriff 1802-3, 1807-8. Elected June 9, 1802; died June 18, 1840, aged 63.

Levi Ames; Sheriff 1804-5. Elected June 13, 1804; died December 26, 1846, aged 68.

Benjamin Bickley; Sheriff 1808-9, 1811-12, 1813-14, 1815-16. Elected September 2, 1807; died October 15, 1846, aged 83.

Robert Jenkins; Sheriff 1820-1. Elected August 16, 1820; died August 4, 1837, aged 61.

Francis Savage. Elected September 13, 1825; died Oct. 21, 1845.

Henry Wenman Newman; Sheriff 1827-8. Elected September 11, 1827; died July 24, 1865, aged 77.

*Thomas Hooper Riddle; Sheriff 1828-9. Elected September 13, 1828.

Hugh William Danson; Sheriff 1829-30. Elected September 13, 1828; died February 15, 1840.

*John Evans Lunell; Sheriff 1829-30. Elected September 12, 1829.

George Protheroe; Sheriff 1830-1. Elected Dec. 9, 1829; died 1860.

William Claxton; Sheriff 1830-1. Elected December 9, 1829; died June 24, 1873, aged 75.

George Bengough; Sheriff 1831-2. Elected December 9, 1829; died December 25, 1856, aged 63.

Joseph Lax; Sheriff 1831-2. Elected June 8, 1831; died January 23, 1845.

*Michael Hinton Castle; Sheriff 1832-3. Elected July 20, 1831.

*James Lean; Sheriff 1833-4. Elected September 19, 1832.

*Henry Ricketts. Elected September 19, 1832, but did not act.

*Christopher George. Elected March 18, 1833.

*Peter Maze, jun.; Sheriff 1833-4. Elected March 18, 1833.

*William Watson. Elected June 12, 1833.

Richard Hunt. Elected September 6, 1834; died November 18, 1866, aged 91.

Those marked * became members of the Reformed Corporation'
One vacancy in place of Evan Baillie, who died June 28, 1835.

OFFICERS APPOINTED BY THE CORPORATION.

HIGH STEWARDS.

(Appointed by the old Corporation.)

1834, February 8, Henry Charles, Duke of Beaufort : died Nov. 23, 1835.

(Appointed by the Town Council.)

1836, February 5, Henry, Duke of Beaufort ; died November 17, 1853.

1854, January 2, Henry Charles FitzRoy, Duke of Beaufort

HIGH SHERIFFS.

1836, Jan.
Daniel Cave 35
George Bengough 25

1836, Nov.
Thomas Kington, J.P. ... 32
Michael Hinton Castle... 27

The voting was the same as at the election of Mayor, except that Aldermen Maningford and Harley supported Kington, Mr. F. Ricketts voted for Castle, and Mr. C. George did not vote.

1837.
Thomas Kington Bayly 33
Michael Hinton Castle... 27

The voting was the same as at the election of Mayor, except that Alderman Harley voted for Bayly, and Mr. Castle did not vote.

1838.
Francis Savage

1839.
Richard Vaughan

1840.
Hugh Vaughan

1841.
Thomas Jones

1842.
Jeremiah Hill

1843.
Thomas Wadham

1844.
John Harding

1845.
Thomas Hill

1846.
Abraham Gray Harford Battersby

1847.
Edward Sampson, jun.

1848.
Peter Maze, jun.

1849.
John Jasper Leigh Bayly

1850.
Joseph Walters Daubeny

1851.
John Battersby Harford

1852.
Robert Bright, J.P.

1853.
Philip John William Miles

1854.
Robert Phippen, J.P.

1855.
Albany Bourchier Savile

1856.
George Oldham Edwards

HIGH SHERIFFS.—*Continued.*

1857.
John Henry Grevile Smyth
Declined to serve ; his predecessor performed the duties during his year of office.

1858.
William Henry Harford, jun.

1859.
William Montague Baillie

1860.
Joshua Saunders

1861.
George Rocke Woodward

1862.
Charles Daniel Cave

1863.
William Wright

1864.
Henry Cruger William Miles

1865.
Joseph Cooke Hurle

1866.
William Henry Miles

1867.
William Gale Coles

1868.
Robert Phippen, J.P. (Alderman)
Died during his year of office, July 5, 1869.

1869.
Thomas Proctor, J.P. (Alderman)

1870.
John Fisher, J.P.

1871.
William Thomas Poole King (Councillor for Redcliff)

1872.
Thomas Todd Walton

1873.
Thomas Todd Walton

1874.
Charles Hill

1875.
George Bright

1876.
William Smith (Councillor for Clifton)

1877.
William Henry Wills, J.P. (Councillor for Bristol)

1878.
Charles Bowles Hare (Councillor for Redcliff)

1879.
Robert Lowe Grant Vassall

1880.
Francis Frederick Fox, J.P. (Alderman)

1881.
William Edwards George

1882.
John Lysaght, J.P.

1883.
Henry Bourchier Osborne Savile

1884.
John Harvey (Alderman)

1885.
Reginald Wyndham Butterworth (Alderman)

1886.
Francis James Fry, J.P.

1887.
Robert Henry Symes

1888.
George Henry Pope

1889.
James Henry Lockley (Councillor for St. James')

1890.
James Henry Lockley

1891.
Arthur Baker, J.P. (Councillor for Redcliff)

1892.
Alfred Deedes, J.P.

1893.
Charles Coates

1894.
William Pethick, J.P. (Alderman)

1895.
William Ansell Todd, J.P. (Councillor for Bristol)

1896.
James Colthurst Godwin, J.P. (Councillor for Redcliff)

1897.
Francis Richardson Cross

HIGH SHERIFFS.—*Continued.*

60 individuals have been elected to the office of High Sheriff since the Act of 1835, of whom one (Mr. Maze) had held it under the old *régime*, when 2 Sheriffs were elected annually.

Three (Messrs. Phippen, Walton, and Lockley) held the office twice, of whom the first-named died before the expiration of his second term. Mr. Edwards also acted for a second year, his elected successor declining to serve.

14, as indicated above, were members of the Council at the dates of their respective elections.

Three (Messrs. Harding, Maze, and Fisher) had ceased to be, and 7 (Messrs. T. K. Bayly, Harford, Woodward, W. H. Miles, George, Fry, and Sir R. Symes) subsequently became, members of the Council.

Mr. Phippen's first election took place in the interval between his ceasing to be a Councillor and his appointment as Alderman, and Mr. Lockley ceased to be a Councillor at the end of his first Shrievalty. Only two of the Sheriffs since 1835 (Alderman Phippen and Sir R. Symes) also served as Mayor.

There are at present (March, 1898) 27 living who have been elected to the office of High Sheriff, of whom 10 (Sir R. Symes, Aldermen Smith, Hare, Fox, Harvey, Fry, and Pethick, Messrs. Baker, Todd, and Godwin) are present members of the Council.

TOWN CLERKS.

1836, February 23, Daniel Burges (*vice* Serjt. Ebenezer Ludlow, resigned); died April 16, 1864, aged 88.
1849, March 29, Daniel Burges, jun. (*vice* Burges, resigned); died November 10, 1874, aged 64.
1874, November 20, William Brice (*vice* Burges, deceased); died March 14, 1887, aged 74.
1880, September 28, Daniel Travers Burges (*vice* Brice, resigned).

BOROUGH TREASURERS

*1836, January 1, Thomas Garrard, resigned March, 1856; died December 18, 1859, aged 73.
1856, March 15, John Harford; died March 7, 1881, aged 78.
1881, March 15, John Tremayne Lane.

*Mr. Garrard had been Chamberlain under the old Corporation from April 6, 1822, till the abolition of that office by the Municipal Corporations Act.

CLERKS OF THE PEACE.

1836, May 16, William Ody Hare; died October 17, 1868, aged 82.
1868, December 27, James Davison Wadham; died July 20, 1871, aged 45.
1871, August 1, Thomas Danger; died August 20, 1878, aged 67.
1878, September 24, Francis Fox Cartwright.

CORONERS.

*1836, May 4, Joseph Baker Grindon, resigned September 21, 1868; died January 2. 1870, aged 80.
1868, September 29, Henry Sidney Wasbrough; died February 7, 1892, aged 79.
1892, February 13, Hugh Greenfield Doggett (elected by 28 votes to 23 for Edward Morcom Harwood).

*Mr. Grindon was one of the two Coroners under the old Corporation.

REGISTRARS OF THE TOLZEY COURT.

1838, February 28, Henry Andrews Palmer, resigned March, 1860; died December 16, 1884, aged 82.
1860, March 27, Arthur Henry Wansey.

CHIEF CONSTABLES.

1836, May 21, Joseph Bishop; died May 5, 1839.
1839, May 29, Henry Fisher; died May 23, 1858.
1856, February 20, John Sims Handcock (vice Fisher, resigned); died September 19, 1877.
1876, March 8, Edwin Weise Coathupe (vice Handcock, resigned).
1894, September 11, Harry Allbutt (vice Coathupe, resigned).

HAVEN MASTERS.

1825, November 11, Edward Robe; died May 29, 1841.
1841, August 14, John Drew; died March 6, 1874.
1874, March 31, Edward Thornborough Parsons.

MEDICAL SUPERINTENDENTS OF THE LUNATIC ASYLUM.

1860, May 9, Henry Oxley Stephens; resigned 1871; died April 12 1881.
1871, May 19, George Thompson; resigned 1890; died August 8, 1895.
1890, April 5, Harry Arthur Benham.

MEDICAL OFFICERS OF HEALTH.

1834, August 18, David Davies; resigned June, 1886; died March 9, 1894.
1886, June 29, David Samuel Davies.

SURVEYORS.

1851, September 30, John Armstrong; died March 11, 1854.
1844, March 27, Frederick Ashmead; resigned 1894.
1894, December 11, Thomas Henry Yabbicom.

INSPECTORS OF NUISANCES.

1851, October 24, Joseph Yeates; died May 15, 1887.
1877, June 24, James William Kirley.

CLERKS TO THE SANITARY AUTHORITY.

1851, August 12, James Harris; died June 19, 1855.
1855, July 14, John Gyde Heaven; resigned 1887; died May 31, 1893.
1887, June 24, Daniel Travers Burges (Town Clerk).

INSPECTORS OF WEIGHTS AND MEASURES.

1837, January 14, William James Gingell; died November 2, 1863.
1864, January 1, John Clark; died August 3, 1881.
1881, September 27, Thomas Crew; died September 19, 1888.
1889, February 12, Frederick William Vining; died Feb. 3, 1898.
1898, March 8, Fred Newton.

SWORD BEARERS.

(RE-ELECTED ANNUALLY.)

1836, *John Foy Edgar; died Nov. 5, 1850, aged 83. (Common Councillor August 13, 1793–Sept. 26, 1797; Sheriff 1793; elected Mayor 1805, but declined to serve.)
1850, November 25, Francis Greville Prideaux; died October 27, 1865, aged 75. (Alderman 1844-50.)
1865, November 9, William Spry Stock; died July 17, 1877, aged 68.
1877, August 14, Edward Stock.
1883, January 1, James Arthur Bush (elected by 18 votes to 15 for Joseph Collins Vining).

*Held the office under the old Corporation, having being first elected September 26, 1818.

CITY LIBRARIANS.

1856, April 25, George Pryce; died March 15, 1868.
1868, March 31, James Fawckner Nicholls; died Sept. 19, 1883.
1883, October 16, John Taylor; died April 9, 1893.
1893, June 14, Edward Robert Norris Mathews.

AUDITORS UNDER THE MUNICIPAL ACT, 1835.

I.—Mayor's Auditors (appointed annually by the Mayor from the Members of the Council).

1835 to 1838, inclusive,	James Wood (Councillor for Bristol), lost his seat Nov. 1838.
1839 to 1841 ,,	William Fripp (Alderman).
1842 to 1844 ,,	Edward Harley (Alderman).
1845	James Wood (Councillor for St. Paul's).
1846	Edward Harley (Alderman).
1847 to 1851, inclusive,	William Hopton Wyld (Alderman).
1852 to 1868 ,,	Francis Kentucky Barnes (Alderman), retired from the Council Nov., 1868.
1869 to 1874 ,,	Thomas Barnes (Alderman), retired from the Council Nov., 1874.
1875 to 1877 ,,	Thomas Wedmore (Councillor for St. Paul's), retired from the Council Nov., 1877.
1878 to 1898 ,,	Charles Bowles Hare (Councillor for Redcliff; elected Alderman May, 1896).

II.—Auditors elected annually by the Burgesses on March 1st (not members of the Council).

1836	Robert Fletcher, Fulke Tovey Barnard.
1837	Joshua Jones, Fulke Tovey Barnard.
1838	John Moxham, Fulke Tovey Barnard.
1839	William Mallard, Henry Brown Jordan.
1840	William Mallard, John Stroud Broad.
1841	Joshua Jones, John Stroud Broad. [Mr. Broad died July 20, 1841.]
1842 to 1844, inclusive,	William Chapman, Francis Plumley Lasbury
1845	Edward Slade, Francis Plumley Lasbury.
1846	Edward Halsall, William Chapman.
1847, 1848	Edward Halsall, John Thorner Pike.
1849, 1850	John Thorner Pike, John Mercer, jun.
1851, 1852	John Thorner Pike, William Mallard.
1853 to 1870, inclusive,	John Thorner Pike, George Thomas.
1870, Aug. 1	George Snow Tricks (*vice* Pike deceased).
1871	George Thomas, George Snow Tricks.
1872 to 1883, inclusive,	George Snow Tricks, Wilberforce Tribe. [Mr. Tricks died Oct. 14, 1883.]
1884 to 1890 ,,	Wilberforce Tribe, Frank Wood Tricks.
1891 to 1893 ,,	Wilberforce Tribe, Edwin John Richards.
1894 to 1897 ,,	Edwin John Richards, Frank Newton Tribe.
1898	Edwin John Richards, Solomon Hare.

ASSESSORS.

(Under the Municipal Corporation (General) Act, 1837.

Elected Annually by the Burgesses to revise the Burgess Lists with the Mayor.

1837	William Blackwell Cross, William Gregory.
1838, 1839	Francis Jarman, Matthew Perkins.
1840	Brooke Smith, William Gregory.
1841	Francis Short, William Gregory.
1842	Henry Wheeler King, Henry Wait Hall.
1843, 1844	Henry Wheeler King, George Pullin Hinton.
1845, 1846	Thomas Crosby, John Hopkins.
1847	Robert Leonard, jun., Francis Quick.
1848	William Powell Hartley, James Flower Fussell. [Mr. Fussell declined to serve, and Mr. George Ley King was elected in his place.]
1849, 1850	William Powell Hartley, George Ley King. [Mr. Hartley died July 10, 1850.]
1851	Francis Short, George Ley King.
1852	Alfred Brittan, George Ley King.
1853	John Ayre, jun., George Ley King.
1854 to 1869, inclusive,	Frederick Viel Jacques, George Ley King.
1870 to 1875 „	Frederick Viel Jacques, Charles Abbott Peters.
1876, 1877	Henry Fricker Lawes, jun., Charles Abbott Peters.
1878	Benjamin Bedell, Charles Abbott Peters.

By the Parliamentary and Municipal Registration Act, 1878, Assessors were no longer required to be elected in any Municipal Borough which is co-extensive with the area of a Parliamentary Borough. Assessors already elected ceased to hold office on Feb. 1, 1879.

JUDICIAL OFFICERS AND MAGISTRATES.

COMMISSIONERS IN BANKRUPTCY.

(Appointed by the Crown.)

1842, October 21, Henry JohnStephen, Serjeant-at-law; resigned January, 1854; died November 28, 1864.
    Richard Stevenson, transferred to Liverpool 1849; died June 15, 1858.
1849, Ebenezer Ludlow, Serjeant-at-law; transferred from Liverpool (formerly Town Clerk); died March 18, 1851, aged 73.
1851, March 24, Matthew Davenport Hill, Q.C.; died June 7, 1872, aged 79. [Sole Commissioner after Serjeant Stephen's resignation in 1854.]

District Courts of Bankruptcy abolished from December 31, 1869, by an Act of Parliament passed in that year.

RECORDERS.

(Appointed by the Old Corporation.)

1827, July 28, Sir Charles Wetherell, Attorney - General; died August 17, 1846.

(Appointed by the Crown.)

1846, September, Richard Budden Crowder, Q.C. (appointed a Judge of the Court of Common Pleas 1854); died December 5, 1859, aged 64.

1854, April 10, Sir Alexander James Edmund Cockburn, Attorney-General (appointed Lord Chief Justice of the Common Pleas 1856, afterwards Lord Chief Justice of the Queen's Bench); died November 20, 1880, aged 78.

1856, December, John Alexander Kinglake, Serjeant-at-law; died July 8, 1870.

1870, July, Sir Robert Porrett Collier, Attorney-General; resigned September, 1870 (created Lord Monkswell 1885); died October 27, 1886, aged 69.

1870, September 13, Montagu Bere, Q.C. (appointed a County Court Judge 1872); died October 19, 1887, aged 63.

1872, August 26, Thomas Kingdon Kingdon, Q.C.; died December 2, 1879, aged 67.

1879, December 11, Charles Grevile Prideaux, Q.C.; died June 18, 1892, aged 81.

1892, July 4, Arthur Ruscombe Poole, Q.C.; died May 22, 1897, aged 57.

1897, June 15, Edward James Castle, Q.C.

JUDGES OF THE COUNTY COURT.

1847, March, Arthur Palmer, resigned January, 1854; died Nov. 19, 1856, aged 73.

1854, January 26, Sir John Eardley Eardley-Wilmot, Bart.; transferred to Marylebone County Court January, 1863.

1863, January, William Henry Willes, transferred from Newcastle-on-Tyne; died February 2, 1863, aged 40.

1863, February 18, Edward John Lloyd, Q.C.; resigned September, 1874; died June, 1, 1879, aged 87.

1874, October 1, Robert Alexander Fisher; died September 30, 1879.

1879, October 20, William James Metcalfe, Q.C.; died December 8, 1892, aged 74.

1892, James Valentine Austin.

JUSTICES OF THE PEACE.

1836, March 21.
William Fripp (C), died December 24, 1871
Thomas Stock (L), died April 27, 1838
James Wood (L), died March 19, 1846
Richard Ash (L), died February 11, 1866
Charles Payne (C), died December 4, 1846
William Herapath (L), died February 13, 1868
Robert Bright (L), died September 19, 1869
George Bengough (L), died December 25, 1856
John Savage (C), died January 9, 1870
George Eddie Sanders (L), died April 2, 1851
Joseph Cookson (C), died October 26, 1865
Henry Ricketts (L C), died May 7, 1859
Thomas Kington (C), died February 20, 1857
John Evans Lunell (L), died June 21, 1870
Lachlan McBayne (L), died February 21, 1848
Henry Wenman Newman (C), died July 24, 1865
John Drake (L), died January 17, 1874
John Naish Sanders (L), died January 20, 1870, aged 93.

[NOTE.—The Town Council, at a meeting held on February 15, 1836, had recommended a list, consisting of 12 Liberals (including Mr. H. Ricketts, who was nominated by that party, though returned to the Council by, and generally voting with, the Conservatives), and 12 Conservatives, but the Home Secretary (Lord John Russell) struck out the names of six Conservatives, viz. Thomas Daniel, Charles L. Walker, James George, Abraham Hillhouse, James N. Franklyn, and Nicholas Roch. On March 29 the appointment of magistrates in Bristol and other boroughs was the subject of a warm debate in the House of Commons, in the course of which Sir R. R. Vyvyan, M.P. for Bristol, charged Lord John Russell with being influenced by corrupt motives in the selections he had made from the names submitted to him. On April 18 the Council carried a resolution (by 33 votes to 23) to ask the Home Secretary to state the reasons for excluding these gentlemen, but this was, of course, refused. In this division Mr. H. Ricketts and all the Liberals present voted with the minority; all the other Conservatives present, including Alderman Harley and Mr. C. George, with the majority. The four members absent were Alderman R. Ricketts and Mr. F. Ricketts (Liberals), and Alderman Wait and Mr. T. Daniel (Conservatives.)]

1841, November 18.
Thomas Daniel (C), died April 6, 1854
James Norroway Franklyn (C), died December 15, 1852
James George (C), died June 27, 1853
Christopher George (C), died May 30, 1856
John Howell (C), died November 29, 1854
James Lean (C), died July 4, 1849
Charles Ludlow Walker (C), died February 21, 1856

1847, February 23.
Richard Jenkins Poole King (C), died September 23, 1874
Samuel Brown (L), died June 28, 1850

1848, March.
William Henry Gore Langton (L), died May 16, 1875
James Gibbs (C), died February 24, 1853
Joseph Coates (L), died July 24, 1862
John Kerle Haberfield (C), died December 27, 1857

JUSTICES OF THE PEACE.—*Continura.*

1850, August.
Robert Phippen (C), died July 5, 1869
William Brown (L), died January 19, 1896, aged 91
Daniel Burges, sen. (C), died April 16, 1864, aged 88
Robert Leonard, sen. (L), died May 21, 1863
Henry Lechmere Worrall (C), died December 8, 1872
Richard Jones (L), d ed January 16, 1857
John Hughes (L), died May 2, 1859, aged 58

1851, June.
Michael Henry Castle (L), died October 7, 1891, aged 82
Thomas Drake (L), died April 3, 1856, aged 53

1854, April 4.
John George Shaw (C), died October 22, 1876
Robert Gay Barrow (C), died July 4, 1880
Henry Prichard (L), died June 4, 1864
Christopher James Thomas (L), died January 2, 1894, aged 86
John Cox (L), died December 19, 1878

1856, July.
William Naish (L), died July 29, 1875
Robert Castle (L), died July 3, 1866
John Vining (C), died September 26, 1866
Odiarne Coates Lane (C), died November 16, 1865
Henry Overton Wills (L), died November 23, 1871

1858, November 18.
William Oliver Bigge (C), died November 7, 1874
William Sanders (L), died November 12, 1875
William Charles Beloe (C), died August 31, 1861
William Day Wills (L), died May 13, 1865
James Poole (C), died December 24, 1872
John Fisher (C), died February 25, 1877

1863, January 23.
*Sholto Vere Hare (C)
Solomon Leonard (L), died July 23, 1867, aged 68
John Hare (C), died September 25, 1897, aged 84
Samuel Woolcot Brown (L), died November 7, 1881, aged 63
William Terrell (L), died May 1, 1887, aged 66
Thomas Canning (C), died December 21, 1888, aged 72

1864, November.
Robert Goss (L), died June 25, 1866
Elisha Smith Robinson (L), died August 29, 1885, aged 68
John Bates (C), died July 2, 1869

1866, August 7.
George Rocke Woodward (C), died November 18, 1835, aged 76
Frederick Terrell (L), died August 14, 1889, aged 85
*William Henry Harford, jun. (C)
*William Henry Wills (L)
Richard Fuidge (C), died May 11, 1878
John Perry (L), died April 2, 1879

1868, January 15.
Francis Adams (C), died August 24, 1880
George Miller (L), died January 23, 1881, aged 60
Thomas Porter Jose (C), died January 14, 1875
*Herbert Thomas (L)
Thomas Proctor (C), died May 15, 1876
James Godwin (L), died June 16, 1890, aged 69

1871, August 3.
Henry James Mills (L), died March 15, 1881, aged 70
Christopher Godwin (L), died February 18, 1889, aged 77
George Wills (L), died December 18, 1888, aged 75

JUSTICES OF THE PEACE.—*Continued.*

*William Pethick (L)
*Charles Nash (C)
Robert Bush (C), died August 5, 1877
William Killigrew Wait (C), resigned August, 1881

1875, January.
*William Proctor Baker (C)
William Fuidge (C), died January 31, 1887, aged 67
William Hathway (C), died January 3, 1895, aged 87
*William Augustus Frederick Powell (C)
Algernon William Warren (L), died April 15, 1883, aged 62
Joseph Dodge Weston (L), died March 5, 1895
*Mark Whitwill (L)

1878, March 1.
*George William Edwards (C)
John Averay Jones (C), died February 8, 1898, aged 82
David Parker Evans (L), died November 13, 1880
*Francis Frederick Fox (C)
*Francis James Fry (L)
*George Hare Leonard (L)
James Creswell Wall (C), died February 21, 1897, aged 72
*Samuel Wills (C)
*Henry Overton Wills (L)
*Charles Hill (C)
*William Smith (C)
*William Henry Budgett (L)

1881, June 13.
Samuel Derham (L), died June 7, 1886, aged 69
*Peter Fabyan Sparke Evans (L)
*John Wesley Hall (L)
*Charles Townsend (L)
Thomas Wedmore (L), died February 5, 1897, aged 88
*Samuel Day Wills (L)
*Charles Bowles Hare (C)
John Frederick Lucas (C), died October 12, 1893, aged 62
John Lysaght (C), died October 1, 1895

William Spark (C), died December 4, 1887
Henry Taylor (C), died September 12, 1882
David Macliver (L), died January 16, 1888, aged 45

1887, May 24.
*Henry Bourchier Osborne Savile (C)
*†Alfred Deedes (C)
*William Edwards George (C)
Charles Wathen (L U), died February 14, 1893
William Mills Baker (L), died July 6, 1890, aged 59
*Arthur Baker (C)
*Charles William Cope-Proctor (C)
*Obed Hosegood (L)
*Charles Hoskins Low (C)
*Stephen George James (C)
*Alfred Robinson (L)
*Philip John Worsley (L)

1839, October 9.
William Paul Hudden (C), died February 9, 1891, aged 58
*Robert Henry Symes (C)
*William Wilberforce Jose (C)
*Andrew Hamill Ford (C)
*William Charles Beloe (C)
John Fuller (C), died February 21, 1895, aged 75
*William Robert Barker (L)
*Edward Robinson (L)
*Alfred Newell Price (L)
*Wilberforce Tribe (L)
*Charles Wills (L)
*James Colthurst Godwin (L U)
*Albert Fry (L U)

1894, August 9.
*His Honour James Valentine Austin
*James Williams Arrowsmith (L)
*Ruscombe Washer Ashley (L)
Robert Champion (C), died March 22, 1895
*Edward Beadon Colthurst (C)
*John Curle (L)
*Henry Daniel (L)
*†Thomas Davey (C)

JUSTICES OF THE PEACE.—*Continued.*

*William Howell Davies (L)
*William James Davis (L)
*William Lane (L)
*Alfred Capper Pass (L U)
*Joseph Pembery (L)
*William Ansell Todd (C)
*William Dove Willcox (L)
Josiah Williams (L), died October 9, 1894, aged 72
*John Henry Woodward (C)

1898, January.

*Henry Charles Fitzroy, Duke of Beaufort, K.G. (C)
*Herbert Ashman (L)
*Charles Coates (C)
*George Edmund Davies (C)

*John William Stone Dix (C)
*Robert Dugdale (C)
*William Henry Elkins (L)
*Charles Edward Ley Gardner (L)
*Robert Gore Graham (L)
*James Henry Howell (C)
*Mervyn Kersteman King (C)
*William Albina Latham (L)
*Arthur Lee (L U)
*Edward Parsons (L)
*Fenwick Richards (C)
*John Edwin Shellard (L U)
*Augustus William Summers (C)
*John Swaish (L)
*Frank Newton Tribe (L)
*Albert George Verrier (L)

† These two gentlemen have never qualified.

The members of the existing bench (79 in all) are marked with a *. The senior magistrate is Mr. Sholto Hare. The last survivor of the original eighteen was Mr. John Drake, who died in 1874. The political composition of the present bench is 35 Liberals, 35 Conservatives, and 8 Liberal Unionists, Judge Austin not being classified. 177 individuals have been appointed in all, of whom 87 were Liberals, 83 Conservatives, and 6 Liberal Unionists at the date of their respective commissions. Liberal Governments have nominated 88 (53 Liberals, 33 Conservatives, 1 Liberal Unionist, and Judge Austin); Conservative Governments 89 (50 Conservatives, 34 Liberals, and 5 Liberal Unionists). 30 present members of the Corporation (15 Aldermen and 15 Councillors) and 12 retired members (3 Aldermen and 9 Councillors) now have seats on the bench.

CLERKS TO THE JUSTICES.

(Appointed by the Justices.)

1836, May 3 { William Brice; resigned April, 1875; died March 14, 1887.
Daniel Burges, jun.; resigned March 29, 1849; died November 10, 1874.

1875, April 17, Thomas Holmes Gore.

TRUSTEES OF THE BRISTOL MUNICIPAL CHARITIES.

1836, October 19.

Richard Smith (Conservative), died January 24, 1843
Thomas Carlisle (Liberal), died January 23, 1865
George Thomas (Liberal), died December 7, 1839; chairman, 1852-1869
John Savage, J.P. (Conservative), resigned 1865
George Bengough, J.P. (Liberal), resigned 1850
James Wood, J.P. (Liberal), died March 19, 1846
Thomas Powell (Liberal), died February 15. 1872
William Harwood (Liberal), died February 11, 1843
Richard Ash, J.P. (Liberal), resigned 1850
James Cunningham (Liberal), died March 12, 1863; chairman, 1836-1852
Harman Visger (Liberal), died January 4, 1867
Michael Henry Castle (Liberal), died October 7, 1891
George Eddie Sanders, J.P. (Liberal), died April 2, 1851
William Herapath, J.P. (Liberal), died February 13. 1868
John Kerle Haberfield (Conservative), died December 27, 1857
Samuel Brown (Liberal), died June 28, 1850
Robert Fiske (Liberal), died May 21, 1859
William Leonard Thomas Pyle Taunton (Liberal), died October 13, 1850
William Tothill (Liberal), resigned 1875
Thomas Davies (Liberal), died April 3, 1854
Charles Bowles Fripp (Liberal), died August 6, 1849.

[On September 6, 1836, the Town Council unanimously agreed to recommend a list of 18, consisting of an equal number from each party, the Conservatives proposing Aldermen Vining and Watson, and Councillors Daniel, Bush, Payne, Savage, Phippen, Smith, and P. Maze, jun.; the Liberals Councillors Cunningham, Herapath, Thomas, Weare, G. E. Sanders, and Ash, and Messrs. Visger, Taunton, and Tothill. The Court of Chancery, however, insisted that the number should be 21, and that not more than 12 of them should be members of the Council. This necessitated the omission of three of the names suggested, and as the Liberals had proposed six Councillors and the Conservatives nine, it was proposed to omit three from the Conservative list and retain the whole of the Liberal list, the latter party also claiming to name two of the six required to complete the number, and thereby secure the majority on the Board. The Conservatives refused to agree to this, and it was finally resolved, on September 13, by a majority of 21 to 14, that the Council should take no further steps in the matter and should decline to make any nominations at all. The result was that the Court of Chancery named a list of 18 Liberals, including the whole of their original nominees, with only three Conservatives. In the division of September 13 the majority consisted of 18 Conservatives, viz., the Mayor (Alderman Fripp), Aldermen Pinney, Harley, Gibbs, and Winwood, Messrs. Acraman, Payne, Goldney, J. N. Franklyn, King, C. George, Gwyer, Hare, Smith, Nash, Powell, Phippen, and Howell, and three Liberals (Messrs. Thomas, Drake, and L. Ricketts). The minority of 14 was composed of 11 Liberals (Messrs. Weare, G. E. Sanders, Brown, Ash, T. R. Sanders, Cunningham, Wayte, Hall, Moore, Harwood, and Herapath), and three Conservatives (Alderman Watson and Messrs. Savage and J. George). Twenty Conservatives and eight Liberals were absent from the division.]

TRUSTEES OF THE BRISTOL MUNICIPAL CHARITIES.—
Continued.

1852, June 12.

William Day Wills (Liberal), died May 13, 1865
William Sanders (Liberal) resigned 1875; died November 12, 1875
Frederick Terrell (Liberal), resigned 1875; chairman, 1869-1875
Edward Bowles Fripp, jun. (Liberal), resigned 1865; died Sept. 5, 1866, aged 75
Charles Thornton Coathupe (Liberal), died February 26, 1857
William Fripp, J.P. (Conservative), resigned 1865
Robert Phippen, J.P. (Conservative), died July 5, 1869
John Fisher (Conservative), died February 25, 1877
John Vining (Conservative), resigned 1865.

[The existing Trustees proposed a list of 8 Liberals, viz., W. D. Wills, W. Sanders, F. Terrell, E. B. Fripp, jun., H. Prichard, C. T. Coathupe, R. Jones, and R. Leonard. The Town Council, on July 9, 1851, by a majority of 27 to 14, proposed a list of eight Conservatives, viz., W. Fripp, R. Phippen, G. W. Franklyn, J. Gibbs, R. J. Poole King, J. D. Pountney, J. Fisher, and J. Vining, an amendment by Mr. Shaw, to nominate four of each party, viz., Messrs. W. Fripp, Phippen, King, Gibbs, Wills, Sanders, Terrell, and Coathupe, being rejected by 36 to 4.]

1865, September 27.

William Terrell, J.P. (Liberal), died May 1, 1887
*William Henry Harford, jun. (Conservative)
*Herbert Thomas (Liberal), appointed chairman 1875
Henry Abbot (Conservative), died April 3, 1874
Henry James Mills (Liberal), died March 15, 1881
Thomas Canning, J.P. (Conservative), died December 21, 1888
Charles Sly Godwin (Liberal), died September 10, 1896, aged 85
Thomas Terrett Taylor (Conservative), died June 27, 1880
Joseph Dodge Weston (Liberal), died March 5, 1895
Richard Fuidge (Conservative), died May 11, 1878
*William Henry Wills (Liberal).

1875, June 29.

*Henry Napier Abbot (Conservative)
William Mills Baker (Liberal), died July 6, 1890
David Parker Evans (Liberal), died November 13, 1880
*Francis Frederick Fox (Conservative)
*John Harvey, jun. (Conservative)
Samuel Lang (Liberal), died September 5, 1885
*Alfred Newell Price (Liberal)
George Wills (Liberal), died Dec. 18, 1888
*Augustine Fielding Woodward (Conservative).

1891, November 20.

*Arthur Baker (Conservative)
Thomas Baker (Liberal), died March 20, 1893
*John Henry Clarke (Conservative)
*Henry Daniel (Liberal)
*Francis James Fry (Liberal Unionist)
*Obed Hosegood (Liberal)
*James Inskip (Conservative)
*Edmund Ambrose King (Conservative)
*Frank Newton Tribe (Liberal)
Sir Charles Wathen (Liberal Unionist), died February 14, 1893
*Philip John Worsley (Liberal).

TRUSTEES OF THE BRISTOL MUNICIPAL CHARITIES.—
Continued.

The appointments in 1836 and 1852 were made by the Lord Chancellor, those since that date by the Charity Commissioners.

The original batch consisted of 18 Liberals and 3 Conservatives. Of those subsequently appointed, 21 have been Liberals, 17 Conservatives, and 2 Liberal Unionists. The existing trustees, 17 in number (marked in the list with a *), are divided thus—7 Liberals, 9 Conservatives, and 1 Liberal Unionist. The last survivor of those included in the first nominations was Mr. Michael Castle, who was a member of the board for 55 years. The three senior trustees at present are Mr. H. Thomas, Mr. Harford, and Sir W. H. Wills, who were appointed in 1865.

CHAIRMEN.

1836 November 7, James Cunningham
1852 July 2, George Thomas
[Elected by 9 votes (Messrs. Powell, Visger, Castle, Davies, Wills, Sanders, Terrell, E. B. Fripp, and Coathupe) to 6 (Sir J. K. Haberfield, Messrs. W. Fripp, Phippen, Savage, Fisher and Vining) for Mr. Cunningham.]
1869 August 17, Frederick Terrell
1875 May 28, Herbert Thomas.

SECRETARIES.

1836 November 11, Thomas John Manchee, died June 11, 1853
[Elected by 13 votes to 8 for Mr. John Harford. The minority consisted of the three Conservative Trustees and Messrs. G. Thomas, Ward, Herapath, Bengough, and C. B. Fripp.]
1853 July 22, Alfred Robertson Miller, died January 24, 1874
1870 September 23, James Hurman London, resigned September, 1870; died November 30, 1872
1873 January 10, Frederick Wentworth Newton.

APPENDIX

OF

MISCELLANEOUS BRISTOL LISTS.

BRISTOL SCHOOL BOARD.

1871, January 27.

Sholto Vere Hare (Conservative)	17,267
Mark Whitwill (Liberal)	14,433
Thomas Turner (Independent)	12,308
William Henry Budgett (Wesleyan)	11,641
Lewis Fry (Liberal)	11,081
Herbert Thomas (Liberal)	10,600
Henry Fricker Lawes (Methodist)	9,712
Rev. Samuel Dousland Waddy, D.D. (Wesleyan)	9,648
James Ford (Roman Catholic)	9,294
Uriah Alsop (Conservative)	7,937
William Proctor Baker (Conservative)	7,861
Rev. Frederick William Gotch, LL.D. (Liberal)	7,147
Rev. Henry Goldney Randall (Conservative)	6,957
Rev. John Percival (Liberal)	6,712
Rev. John Wm. Caldicott (Liberal, Independent)	6,680
Rev. Aaron Rogers (Conservative)	6,071
Rev. Samuel Abraham Walker (Protestant)	5,587
William Wilberforce Jose (Conservative)	5,476
James Inskip (Conservative)	5,444
James Lane (Conservative)	5,073
Samuel Wills (Conservative)	5,070
Rev. John Pilkington Norris (Independent)	4,295
Alfred Pole (Radical Operative)	2,849
John Henry Clifton (Independent)	2,065
Samuel Lewis (Radical Operative)	1,853
Joseph Moss (Secularist)	1,169

BRISTOL SCHOOL BOARD.—*Continued.*

[The Conservatives proposed seven official candidates—the Revs. H. G. Randall and A. Rogers, Messrs. Hare, Baker, Jose, Inskip, and Wills; the Liberals five—Messrs. Whitwill, Fry, Thomas, and the Revs. J. Percival and F. W. Gotch; Messrs. Alsop and Lane were nominated by the Conservative Working Men's Association; Dr. Waddy and Mr. Budgett represented the general Wesleyan body; Mr. Lawes the Free Methodist churches. Mr. Caldicott was originally in the official Liberal list, but withdrew from it when it was reduced to five, and his candidature was then taken up by his old pupils and personal friends. Mr. Ford, the Roman Catholic candidate, was the political leader of the Conservative party. Mr. Turner was supported as a practical schoolmaster. Messrs. Walker, Norris, and Clifton were all in favour of denominational education, and their candidature, by dividing the votes of their party, gave the majority to the Liberals.]

1874, January 22.

Mark Whitwill (Liberal)	15,465
William Proctor Baker (Conservative)	13,593
Lewis Fry (Liberal)	12,129
Rev. John William Caldicott (Liberal)	10,505
Henry Bouchier Osborne Savile (Conservative)	9,474
Rev. Urijah Rees Thomas (Liberal)	9,375
Rev. Thomas Charles Price (Conservative)	9,135
Rev. Frederick William Gotch, LL.D. (Liberal)	9,066
Reginald Wyndham Butterworth (Conservative)	9,042
Thomas Coomber (Conservative)	8,709
Rev. John Joseph Clarke (Roman Catholic)	8,483
William Henry Budgett (Wesleyan)	8,421
Henry Fricker Lawes (Liberal)	7,816
Alfred Hall (Wesleyan)	7,065
Rev. Samuel Abraham Walker (Protestant)	6,386
John Cawsey (Radical Operative)	6,294
William Jennings (Temperance Candidate)	5,604
Thomas Turner (Independent)	5,398
John Thompson Exley (Protestant)	3,273
Henry Cook (Independent)	360

[The Liberals originally nominated seven official candidates, but Mr. Herbert Thomas withdrew on the ground of ill-health. The Conservatives nominated five. Mr. Turner, who stood independently, Mr. Coomber, one of the Conservative candidates, and Mr. Exley were schoolmasters; Messrs. Walker and Exley represented the Protestant party, and Messrs. Budgett and Hall the Wesleyans. Mr. Lawes, who was elected as a representative of the Free Methodist churches at the preceding election, was now adopted as one of the official Liberal candidates.]

1877, January 22.

Mark Whitwill (Liberal)	15,310
Rev. Urijah Rees Thomas (Liberal)	11,978
Lewis Fry (Liberal)	11,237
William Proctor Baker (Conservative)	11,064
John Freeman Norris (Liberal)	10,221
Rev. John William Caldicott, D.D. (Liberal)	10,128
Rev. Frederick William Gotch, LL.D. (Liberal)	10,056
William Henry Budgett (Wesleyan)	8,800

BRISTOL SCHOOL BOARD.—*Continued.*

*Rev. Samuel Abraham Walker (Protestant) ...	8,792
Miss Helena Richardson (Temperance Candidate)	8,536
James Inskip (Conservative)	8,155
Rev. John Joseph Clarke (Roman Catholic) ...	8,036
Thomas Coomber (Conservative)	7,606
Rev. Thomas Charles Price (Conservative) ...	7,499
Henry Bouchier Osborne Savile (Conservative) ...	7,423
Alfred Hall (Wesleyan)	7,268
Thomas Hodge (Radical Operative)	7,041
William Count (Radical Operative)	6,917
William Clark Voisey (Secularist)	2,383

* Died November 30th, 1879, aged 70, and his seat remained vacant until the next e.ection.

[The Conservatives nominated five and the Liberals six official candidates, all of whom were returned. The Protestant party had no separate candidate, Mr. Inskip, who represented their views, being included in the Conservative list. Messrs. Budgett and Hall were joint candidates in the Wesleyan interest, and Messrs. Hodge and Count in that of the Radical working men.]

1880, January 24.

Mark Whitwill (Liberal)	14,274
Miss Emily Sturge (Liberal)	10,273
John Henry Woodward (Conservative)	10,203
Rev. John William Caldicott, D.D. (Liberal) ...	10,040
Rev. Cornelius Witherby (Independent Churchman)	9,982
George William Edwards (Conservative) ...	9,661
George Fowley Jones (Liberal)	9,630
John Freeman Norris (Liberal)	9,616
Peter Fabyan Sparke Evans (Liberal) ...	9,391
Rev. John Joseph Clarke (Roman Catholic)	9,283
Rev. Urijah Rees Thomas (Liberal)	9,229
Rev. Thomas Charles Price (Conservative) ...	9,010
Alfred Hall (Liberal)	8,664
James Inskip (Protestant)	8,413
Wm. Kearsey (Independent Conservative) ...	8,186
Rev. Frederic Vaughan Mather (Conservative) ...	7,461
William Edwards George (Conservative)	7,246
Miss Helena Richardson (Temperance Candidate)	7,104
Richard Hunt (Radical Operative)	5,534
Edmund Ball (Licensed Victualler)	2,580
William Count (Radical Operative)	2,134
George Powell (Radical Operative)	1,430

[The Conservatives nominated five official candidates—Messrs. Woodward, Edwards, George, and the Revs. T. C. Price and F. V. Mather. The Liberals adopted eight, including Mr. Hall, who had previously represented the Wesleyan body, and Mr. Jones, a working man. Mr. Kearsey was brought forward by the Working Men's Conservative Association, and the Rev. C. Witherby, who stood independently of party, was a Conservative Churchman. Mr. Inskip, who was one of the official Conservative cadidates in 1877, now represented the Protestant League. Mr. Powell was nominated by the Working Men's Reform Association. Messrs. Hunt and Count also stood, independently of each other and of the remaining working men candidates, in the Labour interest.]

BRISTOL SCHOOL BOARD.—Continued.

1881, April 29, vice Kearsey (resigned), Joseph Gould (Liberal), elected by 8 votes to 5 for the Rev. F. V. Mather. [The eight Liberals voted for Mr. Gould; Monsignor Clarke, Mr. Witherby, and the three Conservatives for Canon Mather. Mr. Inskip was absent.]

1882, May 26. vice Hall (deceased), Henry Charles Perry (Liberal). [Mr. Perry was a representative of the Wesleyans.]

1882, June 16. vice Witherby and Norris (resigned), Rev. William Samuel Bruce (Conservative) and William Smith (Conservative).

1883, January 18.

James Inskip (Protestant)	12,724
Rev. Edwin Gorsuch Gange (Liberal)	10,085
Rev. John Joseph Clarke (Roman Catholic)	9,924
Miss Emily Sturge (Liberal)	9,883
Mark Whitwill (Liberal)	9,859
George Fowley Jones (Liberal)	9,564
Rev. Urijah Rees Thomas (Liberal)	9,533
John Henry Woodward (Conservative)	9,433
Mrs. Alice Grenfell (Liberal)	9,374
Rev. William Samuel Bruce (Conservative)	8,455
Joseph Gould (Liberal)	8,404
Miss Elizabeth Douglas (Conservative)	8,314
Henry Charles Perry (Liberal)	8,263
Alfred Froud (Conservative)	8,091
Rev. Thomas Charles Price (Conservative)	8,015
Rev. Richard William Randall (Independent Churchman)	7,531

[The official Conservatives nominated five, and the official Liberals eight candidates. Amongst the latter, Mr. Perry was a special representative of the Wesleyan body, and Mr. Jones of the working men. Mr. Randall was brought forward by the High Church party.]

1884, May 31, vice Gange (resigned), Rev. Thomas William Harvey (Liberal).

1884, July 25, vice Jones (resigned), Thomas Thomas (Liberal). [Mr. Thomas succeeded Mr. Jones as the working men's Liberal representative.]

1885, January 30. vice Bruce (resigned), Rev. Josiah George Alford (Conservative).

1886, June 26. vice Grenfell and Inskip (resigned), Miss Eva Selina Tribe (Liberal), Augustus William Cruickshank (Protestant).

1884, August 7. vice Price (resigned), Rev. Alexander Cluny Macpherson (Conservative).

1885, October 30. vice Douglas (resigned), Miss Georgina Caroline Annie Taylor (Conservative).

BRISTOL SCHOOL BOARD.—*Continued.*

1886, January 21.

Mark Whitwill (Liberal)
Rev. Urijah Rees Thomas (Liberal)
Rev. John Joseph Clarke (Roman Catholic)
Miss Emily Sturge (Liberal)
John Henry Woodward (Conservative)
Joseph Gould (Liberal)
Henry Charles Perry (Liberal)
Alfred Froud (Conservative)
Rev. Thomas William Harvey (Liberal)
Thomas Thomas (Liberal)
Rev. Josiah George Alford (Conservative).
Rev. Alexander Cluny Macpherson (Conservative)
Miss Georgina Caroline Annie Taylor (Conservative)
Rev. Thomas Henry Clark (Conservative)
John Fox (Labour)

[No contest. 19 candidates were nominated on January 10 but 4 withdrew before the day of election.]

1887, May 27, *vice* Perry (resigned), Herbert John Jones (Liberal),

1889, January 22.

Henry John Walker (Teachers' Representative)...	16,717
Hugh Holmes Gore (Christian Socialist)	14,132
Rev. John Joseph Clarke (Roman Catholic) ...	13,047
Mark Whitwill (Liberal)	12,163
John Henry Woodward (Conservative)	11,775
Rev. John Thompson (Conservative)	11,501
Rev. Josiah George Alford (Conservative) ...	10,640
Alfred Froud (Conservative)	10,085
Miss Emily Sturge (Liberal)	9,935
Rev. Urijah Rees Thomas (Liberal)	8,705
Rev. Mordaunt Charles Crofton (Liberal)	8,564
Miss Georgina Caroline Annie Taylor (Conservative)	7,864
Francis Stanley Toplis (Protestant)	7,827
William Henry Elkins (Liberal)	7,685
Mrs. Louisa Swann (Liberal)	7,289
Thomas Davies (Liberal)	7,150
Joseph Gould (Liberal)	6,691
Thomas George Harding (Trades Unionist) ...	3,869
Rev. Alexander Cluny Macpherson (Independent)	3,670
William Pepler (Independent)	306

[The official Conservatives proposed five, and the official Liberals eight, including Mr. Davies, who represented the Wesleyans, and Mr. Elkins, the nominee of the Radical operatives. Mr. Macpherson, who had been one of the official Conservative six at the preceding election, now stood as an Independent candidate.]

1889, June 28, *vice* Crofton (resigned), Rev. Thomas William Harvey (Liberal)

1890, January 31, *vice* Thomas (resigned), Rev. Henry Wright (Liberal)

BRISTOL SCHOOL BOARD—Continued.

1892, January 21.

Rev. George Patterson (Wesleyan)	12,406
Hugh Holmes Gore (Christian Socialist)	12,370
Rev. John Joseph Clarke (Roman Catholic)	11,870
Rev. James Ormiston (Protestant)	11,593
Rev. Gabriel Estwick Ford (Conservative)	10,447
Rev. Josiah George Alford (Conservative)	10,372
Rev. John M'Ildowie (Liberal)	9,971
Miss Emily Sturge (Liberal)	9,828
John Henry Woodward (Conservative)	9,511
Mrs. Louisa Swann (Liberal)	8,352
Alfred Froud (Conservative)	8,275
William Whitefield (Labour)	7,640
Henry John Walker (Teachers' Representative)	7,542
Henry Rogers (Liberal)	7,311
Rev. Henry Wright (Liberal)	7,229
Henry William Carter (Conservative)	7,030
Henry Cabot Trapnell (Liberal)	6,634
Miss Georgina Caroline Annie Taylor (Conservative)	6,224
James Vickery (Labour)	5,249
Albert Vincent (Labour)	4,054
John Butchard (Independent)	1,098
William Pepler (Independent)	335

[The Conservatives proposed six official candidates, and the Liberals the same number. Professor Patterson stood independently as the representative of the Wesleyans. Mr. Whitefield was brought forward by the Miners' Association.]

1892. July 25, vice Sturge (deceased). Rev. Urijah Rees Thomas (Liberal).

1892, September 26, vice Wright (resigned). Miss Fanny Marion Townsend (Liberal).

1893. July 31, vice Patterson (resigned), Rev. Herbert Brook Workman (Wesleyan).

1893, October 30, vice Whitefield (resigned). Henry Jolliffe (Labour).

1893. November 27, vice Ford (resigned). Rev. Charles Samuel Taylor (Conservative).

1894, September 24, vice Workman (resigned), Charles James Lowe (Wesleyan).

1895, January 18.

Hugh Holmes Gore (Christian Socialist)	15,442
Henry John Walker (Teachers' Representative)	14,992
Rev. John Joseph Clarke (Roman Catholic)	14,280
Henry Jolliffe (Labour)	13,868
John Henry Woodward (Conservative)	13,215
Rev. James Ormiston (Protestant)	12,477
Rev. Urijah Rees Thomas (Liberal)	10,518
Ernest Henry Cook (Conservative)	9,883

BRISTOL SCHOOL BOARD.—*Continued.*

Rev. James Eustace Brenan (Conservative)	9,830
Rev. John M'Ildowie (Liberal)	9,693
Rev. Joseph James Martin (Free Methodist)	9,463
Alfred Froud (Conservative)	9,326
Miss Fanny Marion Townsend (Liberal)	8,717
Charles James Lowe (Wesleyan)	8,660
Rev. Charles Samuel Taylor (Conservative)	8,548
Henry Anstey (Ratepayers' Association)	8,471
Mrs. Louisa Swann (Liberal)	8,204
Henry Rogers (Liberal)	7,136
Rev. Henry John Wilkins (Independent)	5,651
William Horace Brain (Independent)	5,501
John Butchard (Independent)	889

[The Liberals and the Conservatives each supported five official candidates; the Methodist denominations brought forward two. The Rev. H. J. Wilkins, a Liberal Churchman, stood independently, and Mr. Anstey, a Conservative, was the nominee of the Ratepayers' Association.]

1895, November 25, *vice* Brenan (resigned), Miss Mabel Susan Killigrew Wait (Conservative).

1896, July 27, *vice* M'Ildowie (resigned), Rev. Richard Richard (Liberal).

1896, November 30, *vice* Jolliffe (resigned), Alfred Gustavus Gregory (Labour).

1897, January 25, *vice* Ormiston and Taylor (resigned), Rev. Frederick John Horsefield (Protestant), Rev. Frederick Campbell Paul (Conservative).

1897, July 26, *vice* Clarke (deceased), Rev. David O'Brien (Roman Catholic).

1897, August 30, *vice* Martin (resigned), Thomas Butler (Free Methodist).

1898, January 22.

Rev. James Trebilco (Progressive)	20,831
Hugh Holmes Gore (Christian Socialist)	20,474
Rev. Frederick John Horsefield (Protestant)	20,205
Miss Fanny Marion Townsend (Progressive)	19,972
Rev. David O'Brien (Roman Catholic)	19,944
John Henry Woodward (Conservative)	18,336
Rev. Edward Evans (Conservative)	16,713
Rev. Urijah Rees Thomas (Progressive)	16,697
Rev. George Jarman (Progressive)	15,745
Edwin Thomas Morgan (Progressive)	15,108
Henry John Walker (Educationalist)	14,493
Alfred Froud (Conservative)	14,165
James William Jones (Progressive)	13,410
Charles James Lowe (Progressive)	13,227
Miss Mabel Susan Killigrew Wait (Conservative)	12,930
George Cambridge (Progressive)	12,877
Rev. Frederick Campbell Paul (Conservative)	11,072
William Horace Brain (Independent)	9,794
Alfred Gustavus Gregory (Labour)	5,295
Alfred Henry Harvey (Independent)	4,964

[The official Liberals, now styled Progressives, proposed eight candidates, and the Conservatives five.]

BRISTOL SCHOOL BOARD.—*Continued.*

CHAIRMEN

1871, February 16, Lewis Fry ; re-elected January 30, 1874, February 2, 1877.
1880, January 30, Mark Whitwill ; re-elected February 2, 1883, January 29, 1886.
1889, February 1, Mark Whitwill, 7 ; John Henry Woodward, 6.

[All the members of the Board voted, except the candidates. Mr. Woodward was supported by Monsignor Clarke. Messrs. Alford, Froud, Thompson, Toplis, and Miss Taylor.]

1892, January 29, John Henry Woodward ; re-elected January 28, 1895.
1898, January 31, Rev. Urijah Rees Thomas, 7 ; John Henry Woodward, 6.

[All the members voted, except the candidates. The Progressives and Mr. Walker voted for Mr. Thomas ; the Conservatives, Father O'Brien, and Mr. Gore for Mr. Woodward.]

VICE-CHAIRMEN.

1871, February 16, Mark Whitwill, 8 ; Thomas Turner, 5.

[Messrs. Hare, Ford, Alsop, Baker, and Randall voted for Mr. Turner, the rest of the Board, except the candidates themselves, for Mr. Whitwill.]

1874, January 30, Mark Whitwill ; re-elected February 2, 1877.
1880, January 30, Rev. John William Caldicott.
1883, February 2, Rev. Urijah Rees Thomas ; re-elected Jan. 29, 1886.
1889, February 1, John Henry Woodward, 8 ; Rev. Urijah Rees Thomas, 3.

[Messrs. Elkins and Whitwill and Mrs. Swann voted for Mr. Thomas ; the candidates, Mr. Gore, and Miss Sturge abstained from voting.]

1892, January 29, Rev. Henry Wright, 7   Miss Emily Sturge, 6.

[All the members of the Board voted, except the candidates. Miss Sturge was supported by Messrs. Woodward, Alford, Ford, Froud, Patterson, and Walker.]

1892, September 26, *vice* Wright (resigned), Rev. Urijah Rees Thomas ; re-elected January 23, 1895.
1898, January 31, John Henry Woodward.

CLERKS.

1871, March 10, Benjamin Wilson ; died October 9, 1895
1895, October 28, William Avery Adams.

The total number of individuals hitherto elected to the School Board is 85, of whom 34 were ministers of various denominations, and 9 ladies.

Of the clerical members the Established Church contributed the following, 20 in all, viz.: Messrs. Caldicott, Percival, Randall, Price, Walker, Witherby, Bruce, Harvey, Alford, Macpherson,

BRISTOL SCHOOL BOARD.—*Continued.*

Clark, Thompson, Crofton, Ormiston, Ford, Taylor, Brenan, Horsefield, Paul, and Evans. Of these, Messrs. Caldicott, Percival, Harvey, and Crofton voted with the Liberal and undenominational party, and Messrs. Walker, Ormiston, and Horsefield were specially representative of the Protestant League.

Two (Monsignor Clarke and Father O'Brien) were Roman Catholics; 4 (Dr. Waddy, Professor Patterson, and Messrs. Workman and Martin) represented the Wesleyan and Methodist denominations; 3 (Messrs. U. R. Thomas, M'Ildowie, and Trebilco) the Congregationalists; and 5 (Dr. Gotch, Messrs. Gange, Richard, Wright, and Jarman) the Baptists.

Of the lady members 3 represented the Conservatives, 7 (including the only married ladies on the board, Mrs. Grenfell and Mrs. Swann) the Liberals, and 1 (Miss Richardson) the temperance party.

BRISTOL INCORPORATION OF THE POOR.

GOVERNORS & DEPUTY-GOVERNORS.

The list of Governors, Deputy-Governors, and Treasurers of the Incorporation of the Poor has not, so far as I know, been printed before, except that in a work by Mr. James Johnson entitled "Transactions of the Corporation of the Poor in the City of Bristol during a period of 120 years," published in 1826, the succession is given to the year 1822 inclusive. Mr. Johnson's lists are, however, exceedingly inaccurate, especially in the earlier portion. By the kindness of Mr. J. J. Simpson, the present Clerk to the Board of Guardians (who has, at a time when the pressure of his official duties was exceptionally heavy, put himself to a good deal of trouble in aiding my researches), I have been enabled to have access to the Court books of the Corporation, and thus correct Mr. Johnson's errors of omission and commission, and to bring the lists up to date with, I hope, complete accuracy.—A.B.B.

[The first name in each paragraph is that of Governor, the second that of Deputy-Governor.]

1696, May 19, and 1697, April 8, Samuel Wallis, Common Councillor; William Swymmer, Alderman.
1698, April 14, William Swymmer, Alderman; William Jackson, Alderman.
1699, April 13, William Jackson, Alderman; Sir John Duddleston, Bart.
1700, April 11, Sir John Duddleston, Bart.; Edward Martindale.
1701, April 10, Sir Thomas Day, Alderman; Thomas Callowhill.
1702, April 9, Robert Yate, Alderman; Peter Saunders, Common Councillor.
1703, April 8, John Bacheler, Alderman; George Mason.

BRISTOL INCORPORATION OF THE POOR—*Continued.*

1704, April 13, John Bacheler, Alderman ; Nathaniel Wade.
1705, April 12, Sir William Daines, Alderman ; Abraham Elton, Common Councillor.
1706, April 11, Sir John Hawkins, Alderman ; Richard Bayly, Common Councillor.
1707, April 10, Sir William Lewis, Alderman ; Henry Walter, Common Councillor.
1708, April 8, and 1709, April 14, Francis Whitchurch, Alderman ; Joseph Watkins.
1710, April 13, George Stephens, Alderman ; Henry Samson.
1710, April 27, *vice* Stephens (not qualified), Nathaniel Day, Alderman, Governor.
1711, April 12, George Stephens, Alderman ; John Cox.
1712, April 10, Robert Bound, Alderman ; Robert Bound, jun.
1713, April 9, Abraham Elton, sen., Alderman ; Arthur Taylor.
1714, April 8, Abraham Elton, sen., Alderman ; Richard Jefferis.
1715, April 4, Christopher Shuter, Alderman ; Edward Foy.
1716, April 12, Anthony Swymmer, Alderman ; John Day, Common Councillor.
1717, April 11, Thomas Edwards ; Richard Shute.
1718, April 10, Robert Smith ; Thomas Eston.
1719, April 9, William Hart ; Thomas Eston.
1720, April 14, William Hart ; Samuel Hunt.
1721, April 13, William Hart ; William Prosser.
1722, April 12, John Brickdale ; Robert Wilcox.
1723, April 11, Nicholas Hicks, Alderman ; John Fisher.
1724, April 9, Nicholas Hicks, Alderman ; Joseph Hunt.
1725, April 8, Henry Walter, Alderman ; Richard Tyler.
1726, April 14, Henry Swymmer, Alderman ; Joseph Swayne.
1727, April 13, Edmund Mountjoy, Alderman ; John Norman.
1728, April 11, John Becher, Alderman ; Thomas Warren.
1729, April 10, Joseph Jefferis, Alderman ; William Barnsdale.
1730, April 9, James Donning, Alderman ; Thomas Collins.
1731, April 8, Robert Earl, Alderman ; William Thornhill.
1732, April 13, Peter Day, Alderman ; Robert Wilcox.
1733, April 12, Henry Nash, Alderman ; Robert Wilcox.
1734, April 11, John Price, Alderman ; Robert Wilcox.
1735, April 10, Arthur Taylor, Alderman ; Robert Wilcox.
1736, April 8, John Tyler ; Robert Wilcox.
1737, April 14, and 1738, April 13, Robert Smith, Common Councillor ; Robert Wilcox.
1739, April 12, Nathaniel Day, Alderman ; Robert Wilcox.
1740, April 10, Thomas Chamberlain ; Thomas Holmes.
1741, April 9, John Rich ; John Brickdale.
1742, April 8, Paul Fisher ; Robert Farnell.
1743, April 14, William Jefferis, Alderman ; John Sampson.
1744, April 12, William Jefferis, Alderman ; Robert Wilcox. 1744, Dec. 19, Joseph Oliver, *vice* Wilcox (deceased), Deputy-Governor.
1745, April 11, Nathaniel Day, Alderman ; Stephen Cox.
1746, Feb. 10, William Berrow ; Thomas Durbin.
1747, April 9, William Berrow ; Slade Baker.
1748, April 14, William Hart, jun. ; Richard Smith.
1749, April 13, William Hart, jun. ; William Hull.
1750, April 12, Francis Browne ; Joseph Rigge.
1751, April 11, Francis Browne ; Robert Bridle.
1752, April 9, Henry Hobhouse ; Richard Camplin.
1753, April 12, Henry Hobhouse ; Christopher Viner.
1754, April 11, George Daubeny ; Simeon Cox.
1755, April 10, George Daubeny ; Oliver Jelf.

BRISTOL INCORPORATION OF THE POOR.—*Continued.*

1756, April 8, John Brickdale; Walter Perkins, jun.
1757, April 14, John Brickdale; Joseph Godwin.
1758, April 13, David Peloquin, Alderman; Roger Watts.
1759, April 12, David Peloquin, Alderman; Samuel Smith.
1760, April 10, John Hobhouse; Jacob Thrall.
1761, April 9, John Hobhouse; Edmond Gomond.
1762, April 8, Stephen Nash; William Fisher.
1763, April 14, Stephen Nash; Frederick Yeamans.
1764, April 12, Slade Baker; John Masters.
1765, April 11, Slade Baker; Joseph Flower.
1766, April 10, John Durbin, Alderman; Joseph Flower.
1767, April 9, John Durbin, Alderman; Henry Burgum.
1768, April 14, Henry Dampier, Alderman; Abraham Brown.
1769, April 13, Henry Dampier, Alderman; Jacob Player.
1770, April 12, Henry Dampier, Alderman; Richard Williams.
1771, April 11, Jeremiah Ames, Alderman; William James.
1771, April 25, *vice* Ames (declined). Morgan Smith, Alderman, Governor.
1772, April 9, Morgan Smith, Alderman; Joseph Green.
1773, April 8, Henry Muggleworth, Alderman; William Day.
1774, April 14, Richard Farr, Alderman; Samuel Thomas.
1775, April 13, Richard Farr, Alderman; William Fry.
1776, April 11, John Powell; John Woodward.
1777, April 10, John Powell; John Chivers.
1778, April 9, William Jones; Griffith Maskelyn (declined), Leighton Wood (declined), Joseph Watson, jun.

[These were successively elected on the same day. Mr. Watson afterwards refused to accept the office, and paid the fine.]

1778, July 30, Deputy-Governor, William Lucy.
1779, April 8, William Jones; George Williams.
1780, April 13, John Cave; Gabriel Rymer.
1781, April 12, John Cave; Edward Willis.
1782, April 11, Thomas Hayes; Thomas Hembury.
1783, April 10, Thomas Hayes; John Tustin. 1783, Nov. 6, James Mullowney, *vice* Tustin (deceased), Deputy-Governor.
1784, April 8, Sir John Durbin, Alderman; John Bletchly.
1785, April 14, Sir John Durbin, Alderman; Isaac Cooke.
1786, April 13, Richard Vaughan; Thomas Lyne.
1787, April 12, Richard Vaughan; Richard Webb.
1788, April 10, and 1789, April 9, George Daubeny, Alderman; William Green.
1790, April 8, Edward Brice, Alderman; Robert Hall.
1791, April 11, Edward Brice, Alderman; William Fisher.
1792, April 12, and 1793, April 11, Lowbridge Bright; Richard Webb.
1794, April 10, and 1795, April 9, James Tobin; Richard Errington.
1796, April 14, and 1797, April 13, John Pinney; Richard Webb.
1798, April 12, 1799, April 11, and 1800, April 10; John Pinney; Thomas Batchelor.
1801, April 9, Peter Baillie; Richard Hill. 1801, April 30, Josiah Thomas, *vice* Hill (declined), Deputy-Governor.
1802, April 8, Peter Baillie; James Norton.
1803, April 14, Richard Vaughan, jun., Alderman; Henry Rudhall.
1804, April 12, Richard Vaughan, jun., Alderman; John Birtill.
1805, April 11, Richard Vaughan, jun., Alderman; Richard Lambert.
1806, April 10, Thomas Daniel, Alderman; Thomas Batchelor.
1807, April 9, Thomas Daniel, Alderman; Richard Lambert.
1808, April 14, Edward Rolle Clayfield; John Birtill.
1809, April 13, Edward Rolle Clayfield; Samuel Capper.

BRISTOL INCORPORATION OF THE POOR.—*Continued.*

1810, April 12, Edward Rolle Clayfield ; John Coles.
1811, April 11, Daniel Wait, Alderman ; Christopher Shapland.
1812, April 9, Daniel Wait, Alderman ; Thomas Stock.
1813, April 8, and 1814, April 14, John Cave ; Thomas Stock.
1815, April 13, and 1816, April 16, Thomas Stock ; William Stock.
1817, April 10, John Haythorne, Alderman ; James Johnson.
1818, April 9, and 1819, April 8, Michael Castle, Common Councillor ; James Johnson.
1820, April 13, 1821, April 12, and 1822, April 11, James Johnson ; James Dunbar.
1823, April 10, James Perry ; James Wood.
1824, April 8, James Perry ; Thomas Menlove.
1825, April 14, James Perry ; Benjamin Sangar.
1826, April 13, James Perry ; Silas Dibsdall.
1827, May 3, Thomas Stock ; James Webb.
1828, April 10, and 1829, April 9, Thomas Stock ; William Herapath.
1830, April 8, Thomas Stock ; John James Beard. 1830, May 27, Henry Fyson, *vice* Beard, (deceased), Deputy-Governor.
1831, April 14, Thomas Stock ; Henry Fyson.
1832, April 12, Thomas Rankin ; John Robson. 1832, April 26, William Barrett, *vice* Robson (declined), Deputy-Governor.
1833, April 11, William Tothill ; John Righton.
1834, April 10, and 1835, April 9, Job Harrill ; Thomas John Manchee.
1836, April 14, and 1837, April 13, Valentine Hellicar ; Samuel Morgan.
1838, April 12, John Kerle Haberfield, Mayor and Alderman ; Charles Hickes.
1839, April 11, and 1840, April 9, John Kerle Haberfield, Councillor ; Gabriel Goldney.
1841, April 8, John Kerle Haberfield, Councillor ; Henry Lancaster.
1842, April 14, John Kerle Haberfield, Councillor ; James Martin.
1843, April 13, John Kerle Haberfield, Councillor ; John Fisher, Councillor.
1844, April 11, John Kerle Haberfield, Councillor ; Gabriel Goldney.
1845, April 10, John Fisher, Councillor ; Samuel Edward Taylor.
1846, April 9, John Fisher, Councillor ; Henry Lambert.
1847, April 8, John George Shaw, Councillor ; Thomas Wedmore.
1848, April 13, John George Shaw, Councillor ; William Howe.
1849, April 12, John George Shaw, Councillor ; John Wetherman, jun.
1850, April 11, Gabriel Goldney ; Thomas Field Gilbert.
1850, Dec. 20, *vice* Goldney (resigned), John Wetherman, jun., Councillor, Governor.
1851, April 10, John Wetherman, jun., Councillor ; Thomas Field Gilbert, Councillor.
1852, April 8, John Wetherman, jun., Councillor ; Andrew Nicholas Langdon.
1853, April 14, Arthur Hare Palmer, Councillor ; Andrew Nicholas Langdon.
1854, April 13, Charles Tovey, Councillor ; Andrew Nicholas Langdon.
1855, April 12, and 1856, April 10, George Rogers, M.D., Councillor ; James Protheroe.
1857, April 9, Elisha Smith Robinson ; Henry Fricker Lawes.
1858, April 8, and 1859, April 14, Elisha Smith Robinson ; Henry Hunt, jun.
1860, April 12, 1861, April 11, and 1862, April 10, John Perry, Councillor ; Henry Hunt, jun.
1863, April 9, John Perry, Councillor ; Henry Amelius Powell Robertson, M.D.

BRISTOL INCORPORATION OF THE POOR..—*Continued.*

1864, April 14, and 1865, April 13, Henry Amelius Powell Robertson, M.D.; John Linter.
1866, April 12, and 1867, April 11, Henry Amelius Powell Robertson, M.D.; Thomas Hodge Pengelly.
1868, April 9, and 1869, April 8, John Bartlett; James Bremner.
1870, April 12, 1871, April 13 and April 11, 1372, Henry Naish, Councillor; William Thomas.
1873, April 10, Henry Naish, Councillor; William Madden.
1874, April 9, William Thomas; William Madden.
1875, April 8, and 1876, April 13, Henry Naish, Councillor; James Bessell.
1877, April 12, and 1878, April 11, James Bessell; Charles Wintle.
1879, April 10, and 1880, April 8, Charles Wintle; George Snow Tricks
1881, April 14, and 1882, April 13, George Snow Tricks; Richard Court Stephens.
1883, April 12, and 1884, April 10, Richard Court Stephens; William Stevens.
1885, April 9, William Stevens; George Pearson.
1886, April 8, George Pearson; Moss Levy, Councillor.
1887, April 14, and 1888, April 12, George Pearson; William Bennett.
1889, April 11, and 1890, April 10, William Bennett; Ernest George Lorymer.
1891, April 9, and 1892, April 14, Ernest George Lorymer; John William Lane.
1893, April 13, and 1894, April 12, John William Lane; John Coulthard, Councillor.
1895, April 18, Richard Court Stephens; Thomas Protheroe.
1896, April 16, Richard Court Stephens, Councillor; William Jones.
1897, April 22, William Jones; Charles Edward Douglas Boutflower —till March 31, 1898, on which date the Incorporation of the Poor ceased to exist.

TREASURERS.

Elected annually at the same meeting as the Governor and Deputy-Governor.

1696, James Harris
1697, Thomas Callowhill
1698, Edward Martindale
1690, Peter Saunders (Common Councillor)
1700, Charles Harford
1701, Abraham Elton
1702, Thomas Winston
1703, Thomas Hungerford
1704, George Stephens (Common Councillor)
1705, James Haines (Common Councillor)
1706, Henry Walter (Common Councillor)
1707, Thomas Oade
1708, Mark Goddard
1709, James Peters
1710, William Saunders (declined)
1710, April 27th, Thomas Melton

1711, William Swymmer
1712, John Andrews
1713, Christopher Wallis
1714, Jacob Elton
1715, John Day (Common Councillor)
1716, Nathaniel Webb
1717, Edward Foy (Common Councillor)
1718, Henry Swymmer (Common Councillor)
1719, Ezekiel Longman (Common Councillor)
1720, Richard Champion
1721, Edward Garlick [Daniel Kill was elected but declined, and Mr. Garlick was then chosen on the same day.]
1722, John Bartlett
1723, Thomas Gibbs
1724, Thomas Freke

BRISTOL INCORPORATION OF THE POOR.—*Continued.*

1725, Paul Fisher
1726, John Rainstorp
1727, William Jefferis (Common Councillor)
1728, Edmund Saunders
1729, John Hawkins
1730, Edward Harford
1731, Walter Lougher
1732, Nathaniel Champion
1733, William Lyne
1734, Corsley Rogers
1735, Richard Bayly (Common Councillor)
1736, William Berrow
1737, John Newman
1738, Thomas Chamberlain
1739, Conrade Smith
1740, George Packer
1741, Richard Blake
1742, William Miller
1743, 1744, Richard Day
1745, Daniel Woodward
1746, 1747, George Daubeny
1748, 1749, Francis Browne
1750, 1751, Henry Hobhouse
1752, 1753, Thomas Daniel
1754 to 1757, John Vaughan
1758, 1759, John Hobhouse
1760, 1761, Stephen Nash
1762, 1763, Matthew Hale
1764, 1765, James Reed
1766, 1767, Daniel Tayler
1768, 1769, William Miles (Common Councillor)
1770, 1771, John Gresley, jun.
1772, William Hasell

1772, June 11, *vice* Hasell (deceased), Samuel Delpratt, re-elected 1775.
1774, 1775, Henry Burgum
1776 to 1778, James Vaughan
1780, 1781, Isaac Bence
1782, 1783, James Vaughan
1784 to 1787, Benjamin Gillam
1788 to 1797, Richard Vaughan
1798 to 1809, Benjamin Baugh
1810 to 1817, Thomas Daniel (Alderman)
1818, 1819, John Ballard
1820 to 1822, Joseph Reynolds
1823 to 1825, Thomas Reynolds
1826, John Coulsting
1827, John Maningford; died October 22, 1854. Re-elected annually till his death
1854, December 14, Charles Paul; died November 1, 1857. Re-elected annually till his death
1857, William Gale Coles; died March 23, 1890. Re-elected annually till his death.
1890 to 1896, Alfred Deedes
1897, John Chetwood Chetwood-Aiken.

CLERKS.

Messrs. Osborne and Ward, the solicitors to the Incorporation, who had acted as clerks for many years previously, were formally appointed annually from 1823 to 1856, inclusive. In 1857 a clerk was appointed as a distinct officer.

1857, January 16, Walter Benjamin Wilmot (went to Lambeth as clerk to the Guardians in January, 1867, and died February, 1897).

1867, January 25, Edward Greenfield Doggett; died February 13, 1887.

1887, March 18, Jesse James Simpson

---

104 individuals have been elected to the Governorship, of whom 50 served the office of Mayor of Bristol. Of these Mr. Wallis, the first Governor, was Mayor at the date of his first election. Mr. Haberfield also was Mayor both at his first and second elections. Mr. Haythorne was elected Mayor while serving as Governor, and Mr. John Cave several years after he had ceased to hold that office. Every Governor elected from 1697 to 1745 was an ex-Mayor, with the exception of Sir J. Duddleston. Messrs. Edwards, R. Smith, W. Hart, Brickdale, Tyler, Chamberlain, and Fisher. All the Governors from 1766 to 1775, and from 1784 to 1791 inclusive, except Mr. Vaughan, were also ex-Mayors, as were Messrs. Peloquin, Daniel, Wait, and Castle. Messrs. R. Vaughan, jun., Shaw, and Robinson attained to the Mayoralty after passing the chair of the Incorporation.

BRISTOL INCORPORATION OF THE POOR.—*Continued.*

Of the 145 who served the office of Deputy-Governor, only 24 subsequently occupied the chair of the Incorporation. Among these were the first three Deputies (Messrs. Swymmer, Jackson, and Sir J. Duddleston), five of those who held that office between 1705 and 1747 (Messrs. A. Elton, sen., Walter, Tyler, Brickdale, and Baker), and six elected between 1812 and 1872 (Messrs. T. Stock, Johnson, Goldney, Wetherman, Robinson, and Thomas). No Deputy elected between 1747 and 1812 was promoted to the chair; on the other hand, of 14 Deputy Governors elected since 1872 only four did not subsequently become Governors, viz., Messrs. Levy, Coulthard, T. Protheroe, and Boutflower.

I am indebted to Mr. Simpson for the following historical note:—In May, 1696, the Incorporation of the Poor of the City and County of Bristol was constituted by the Bristol Poor Act, 1696. This was the first Board of Guardians in England and Wales for the purpose of providing relief for the destitute poor, and establishing workhouses for their maintenance.

In 1826 the Incorporation was reconstituted, and its duties slightly varied and increased.

In 1856 the Poor Law Board compelled the Incorporation, after a long resistance, to submit to the general authority which that Board claimed, and accordingly early in January, 1857, the by-laws of the Incorporation were rescinded, and on January 16 Mr. E. S. Robinson and Mr. H. F. Lawes were elected respectively Chairman and Vice-Chairman of the Board of Guardians for Bristol Union, and Mr. Wilmot, previously Master of St. Peter's Hospital, was appointed Clerk to the Guardians. The Incorporation, however, continued to exist, and at the next annual election (April 9, 1857) Messrs. Robinson and Lawes were chosen Governor and Deputy-Governor respectively, and after that date the Chairmanship and Vice-Chairmanship of the Board of Guardians were united to the offices of Governor and Deputy-Governor of the Incorporation of the Poor. Mr. Wilmot was at the same time appointed Clerk to the Incorporation.

From 1696 to 1837 the Incorporation had exercised authority over the whole city and county of Bristol, but at the extension of the boundaries by the Municipal Corporations Act of 1835 no change was made in the area under the supervision of that body; consequently the Unions of Clifton (afterwards re-named Barton Regis) and Bedminster being established in accordance with the Poor Law Amendment Act, 1834, the city, for Poor Law purposes, formed part of three Unions. In 1897 the boundaries of the city were again extended, and the Act provided for the inclusion of the whole of the city thus extended in one Poor Law Union. This Act came into operation from March 31, 1 98, at which date the Incorporation of the Poor was dissolved, the portions of the enlarged city hitherto comprised in Barton Regis, Bedminster, and Keynsham Unions were transferred to the new Union, and a Board of Guardians for the whole city came into office on April 1, 1898, when Major George Ferris Rumsey, who had for several years presided over the Barton Regis Union, was elected Chairman. Messrs. Charles Edward Douglas Boutflower and Samuel Lloyd Vice-Chairmen, *pro. tem.*, and Mr. Jesse James Simpson was appointed Clerk. On April 12 the Chairman and Vice-Chairmen were re-elected to serve for the year 1898-9, and Messrs. Osborne, Ward, Vassall, and Co. were appointed solicitors to the Board, their firm having acted as legal advisers to the Incorporation of the Poor continuously from 1760 to its dissolution—a period of 138 years.

On April 7, 1898, Mr. Edwin Hilton Naish was appointed Treasurer.

SOCIETY OF MERCHANT VENTURERS.

1605—1897.

The following succession of Masters, Wardens, and Treasurers of the Society of Merchant Venturers is practically a reproduction of the list, carefully compiled by Mr. G. H. Pope, the present Treasurer, which was published in the *Times and Mirror* of July 21, 1885, and a portion of which was reproduced in Mr. Latimer's "Annals of Bristol in the 18th Century." I have corrected a few misprints, and brought the lists up to date, noting the names of those who were members of the Corporation. I have to acknowledge the courtesy of Mr. Pope, who has given me every assistance in preparing the record.

[The first name in each paragraph is that of Master, the second and third are those of Wardens.]

1605, John Hopkins, Alderman; William Vawer, Alderman, and John Whitson, M.P., Alderman.
1606, John Whitson, M.P., Alderman; Thomas James, M.P., Alderman, and Mathew Haviland, Common Councillor.
1607, Thomas James, M.P., Alderman; Robert Aldworth, Common Councillor, and Abell Kitchen, Common Councillor.
1608, Mathew Haviland, Common Councillor (elected Alderman 1609); John Boulton, Common Councillor, and Thomas Hopkins, Common Councillor.
1609, Robert Aldworth, Mayor and Common Councillor; William Hopkins, Common Councillor, and John Aldworth, Common Councillor.
1610, Abell Kitchen, Common Councillor; William Cole, Common Councillor, and George White, Common Councillor.
1611, John Whitson, Alderman; John Barker (elected Common Councillor and Sheriff September, 1612) and John Gonninge, Common Councillor.
1612, Robert Aldworth, Common Councillor; John Harrison, Common Councillor, and John Aldworth, Common Councillor.
1613, Mathew Haviland, Alderman; Christopher Carie, Common Councillor, and John Langton, Common Councillor.
1614, John Aldworth, Common Councillor; John Barker, Common Councillor, and Robert Haviland.
1615, Thomas James, Alderman; Arthur Hibbins and Thomas Wright (elected Common Councillor September, 1616).
1616, Mathew Haviland, Alderman; Robert Haviland and Richard Long.
1617, John Barker, Common Councillor; William Jones and Humphrey Browne (elected Common Councillors January, 1618).
1618, John Barker, Common Councillor; William Pitt, Common Councillor, and Walter Ellis.

SOCIETY OF MERCHANT VENTURERS.—*Continued.*

1619, John Gonninge, Common Councillor; Edward Coxe, Common Councillor, and William Hickes.
1620, John Langton, Common Councillor; Miles Jackson and Giles Elbridge.
1621, Humphrey Hooke, Common Councillor; Francis Derrick and Nathaniel Butcher.
1622, John Guy, Alderman; William Wyatt and John Tayler.
1623, John Doughty, Alderman; Richard Pley, Common Councillor, and Alexander James, Common Councillor.
1624, William Pitt, Alderman; Francis Creswicke and Derrick Popley.
1625, Robert Aldworth, Alderman; Martin Pring and Thomas Colston.
1626, John Barker, Common Councillor; John Gardiner and Edward Petre.
1627, John Tomlinson, Common Councillor; Gabriel Sherman and Thomas Jackson.
1628, Thomas Wright, Common Councillor; William Chetwind and William Cann.
1629, Humphrey Browne, Common Councillor; George Lane and John Gonninge, jun. (elected Common Councillor April, 1630).
1630 and 1631, Humphrey Hooke, Common Councillor (elected Alderman March, 1632); John Langton, jun. (elected Common Councillor July, 1632), and William Hobson.
1632, Humphrey Hooke, Alderman; Thomas Hooke (elected Common Councillor August, 1633) and Edward Pitt.
1633, Humphrey Hooke, Alderman; Thomas Nethway and Joseph Jackson.
1634, Humphrey Hooke, Alderman; Hugh Browne and John Drayton
1635, Richard Holworthy, Mayor and Common Councillor (elected Alderman August, 1636); Thomas Chamber and Thomas Griffeth.
1636 and 1637, Richard Longe, Mayor (till September 29, 1637) and Alderman; Edmond Arundell and Hugh Griffith.
1638, Humphrey Hooke, Alderman; Giles Elbridge, Common Councillor, and Thomas Colston, Common Councillor.
1639, Andrew Charlton, Alderman; Alexander James, Common Councillor, and Francis Creswicke, Common Councillor.
1640, John Gonninge, Alderman; John Gonninge, jun., Common Councillor, and Miles Jackson, Common Councillor
1641, William Jones, Alderman; Richard Aldworth, Common Councillor, and John Langton, Common Councillor.
1642, Alexander James, Common Councillor; Richard Vickris, Common Councillor, and Walter Deyos, Common Councillor.
1643, Francis Creswicke, Common Councillor (elected Alderman December, 1643); Henry Creswicke, Sheriff and Common Councillor, and William Colston, Sheriff and Common Councillor.
1644, Thomas Colston, Common Councillor (elected Alderman June, 1645); William Bevan, Sheriff and Common Councillor, and William Cann, Common Councillor.
1645, William Cann, Common Councillor; Joseph Jackson, Common Councillor (elected Alderman September, 1646), and Thomas Amory, Common Councillor.
1646, Hugh Browne, Alderman; William Dale, Common Councillor, and James Crofte, Common Councillor.
1647, Joseph Jackson, Alderman; Edward Tyson, Common Councillor, and George Lane, Common Councillor.
1648, Richard Vickris, Alderman; Robert Challoner, Sheriff and Common Councillor, and Robert Yate, Sheriff and Common Councillor.

SOCIETY OF MERCHANT VENTURERS.—*Continued.*

1649, Hugh Browne, Alderman (elected Mayor September, 1650); William Dale, Sheriff and Common Councillor, and William Yeamans, Sheriff and Common Councillor.
1650, Miles Jackson, Alderman; Robert Cann, Common Councillor (elected Sheriff September, 1651) and William Clare.
1651, Hugh Browne, Alderman; Thomas Speed and William Merricke
1652, Hugh Browne, Alderman; Walter Tocknell and Robert Yeamans.
1653, Joseph Jackson, Alderman; John Bowen, Common Councillor, and Robert Vickris, Common Councillor.
1654, Joseph Jackson, Alderman; John Knight, jun., and Richard Deane.
1655, Joseph Jackson, Alderman; John Knight, jun., and William Willett.
1656, Robert Yate, Common Councillor; Anthony Gay, Common Councillor, and John Willoughby, Common Councillor (elected Sheriff September, 1657).
1657, William Yeamans, Common Councillor; Walter Tocknell and Thomas Langton.
1658, Robert Cann, Common Councillor; Shershaw Cary and John Bowen, Common Councillor.
1659, John Bowen, Common Councillor; John Knight, jun., and Alexander Jackson.
1660, Henry Creswicke, Mayor and Common Councillor (elected Alderman September, 1661); Thomas Langton, Sheriff and Common Councillor, and Robert Yeamans.
1661, Henry Creswicke, Alderman; John Pope, Common Councillor, and John Knight, jun., Common Councillor.
1662, Robert Yeamans, Common Councillor and Sheriff (knighted September 7, 1663); Henry Gough, Common Councillor, and Thomas Moore.
1663, Sir John Knight, Mayor and Alderman; Alexander Jackson, Common Councillor, and William Hasell, Common Councillor.
1664, Thomas Langton, Alderman; Thomas Moore and Thomas Scrope.
1665, John Willoughby, Mayor and Alderman; John Aldworth, Common Councillor, and William Lysons.
1666, John Knight, Common Councillor; Joseph Creswicke, Sheriff and Common Councillor, and Richard Streamer, Common Councillor.
1667 and 1668, Walter Tocknell; William Willett, Common Councillor (Sheriff June-September, 1668), and William Hasell, Common Councillor.
1669, Robert Vickris, Common Councillor; Richard Hart, Common Councillor, and Gabriel Deane.
1670, William Willett, Common Councillor; Thomas Eston, Sheriff and Common Councillor, and Thomas Earle, Common Councillor.
1671, Shershaw Cary; George Lane, jun., Common Councillor, and John Knight, jun., Common Councillor (elected Alderman September, 1672).
1672, Richard Streamer, Alderman (elected Mayor September, 1673); John Cooke, Sheriff and Common Councillor, and Charles Williams, Common Councillor.
1673, Thomas Earle, Common Councillor; William Hayman, Common Councillor, and William Browne.
1674, William Lysons, Common Councillor; William Jackson, Common Councillor, and William Donning, Common Councillor.
1675 and 1676, Richard Hart, Common Councillor; Arthur Hart (elected Common Councillor 1677) and George Hart (elected Common Councillor August, 1677).

SOCIETY OF MERCHANT VENTURERS.—*Continued.*

1677, George Lane, Common Councillor; Edmond Arundell and Samuel Hale, Common Councillor.
1678, George Lane, Common Councillor; Giles Merrieke and Stephen Watts, Common Councillor.
1679, September 18 (*vice* Lane, deceased), William Hayman, Common Councillor.
1679, William Hayman, Sheriff and Common Councillor; William Swymmer, Sheriff and Common Councillor, and Edward Tocknell.
1680, William Jackson, Common Councillor; Richard Lane, Common Councillor (elected Sheriff September, 1681), and William Merrieke, Common Councillor.
1681, Thomas Eston, Common Councillor (elected Mayor September, 1682); William Clutterbuck, Common Councillor, and John Knight, Sheriff and Common Councillor (knighted March 16, 1682).
1682, William Merrieke, Common Councillor; Samuel Price and Henry Daniel.
1683, William Clutterbuck, Mayor and Common Councillor (knighted November 27, 1683; appointed Alderman June, 1684); John Cary and John Combes, Common Councillor.
1684, Richard Lane, Common Councillor; John Yeamans, sen., Common Councillor, and John Cam.
1685 and 1686, Edward Tocknel', Common Councillor; Robert Yate, Sheriff (till September, 1686) and Common Councillor, and Walter Lougher.
1687, William Donning (appointed a Common Councillor January, 1688); Peter Saunders (appointed a Common Councillor January, 1688) and Richard Champneys.
1688, Arthur Hart, Common Councillor (elected Mayor September, 1689); Thomas Cole, Sheriff and Common Councillor, and Charles Pope.
1689, Giles Merrieke, Common Councillor; John Seward and John Yeamans, jun., Common Councillor.
1690, William Swymmer, Common Councillor; Jacob Beele and Robert Kirke.
1691, John Cooke, Chamberlain Henry Gibbes and Edward Jones.;
1692 and 1693, Robert Yate, Common Councillor (elected Mayor September, 1693); Thomas Richardson and William Daines, Common Councillor (elected Sheriff September, 1694).
1694, Samuel Price; Sir Richard Crumpe, Alderman, and John Swymmer.
1695, Samuel Price; Joseph Jackson and James Hollidge (elected Common Councillor September, 1696).
1696, Peter Saunders, Common Councillor; Thomas Hort and Thomas Earle.
1697, Peter Saunders, Common Councillor; Thomas Hort and William Clarke.
1698, Sir William Daines, Common Councillor; John Bacheler, Common Councillor, and John Day, sen., Common Councillor.
1699, Sir William Daines, Common Councillor (elected Mayor September, 1700); Abraham Elton, Common Councillor, and Anthony Swymmer (elected Common Councillor March, 1700).
1700, James Hollidge, Common Councillor; Thomas Moore and Isaac Davies, Sheriff and Common Councillor.
1701, James Hollidge, Common Councillor; Thomas Moore and George Mason.
1702 and 1703, Thomas Hort, Common Councillor (Sheriff 1703-1704); Abraham Hooke, Common Councillor, and Richard Franklyn, Common Councillor.

SOCIETY OF MERCHANT VENTURERS.—*Continued.*

1704, William Clarke; Philip Freke, Common Councillor, and Henry Watts, Common Councillor.
1705, William Clarke; Sir John Duddleston, Bart., and Francis Rogers, Common Councillor.
1706, John Cacheler, Alderman; John Day, Common Councillor, and William Swymmer, Alderman.
1707, John Bacheler, Alderman; Henry Swymmer and Joseph Whitchurch.
1708, Abraham Elton, sen., Common Councillor; Abraham Elton jun., and James Donning.
1709, Anthony Swymmer, Common Councillor; Joseph Earle and William Hart.
1710, Thomas Moore; Abraham Birkin and John Becher, Common Councillor.
1711, George Mason; Robert Bound, Common Councillor (elected Alderman March, 1712), and Joshua Franklyn.
1712, Abraham Hooke; Sir John Hawkins, Alderman, and Hugh Bickham, Common Councillor.
1713, Philip Freke, Common Councillor; Thomas Longman and Samuel Hunt.
1714, Henry Watts, Common Councillor; Jeremy Innys and Joseph Browne.
1715, Sir John Duddlestone, Bart.; John Blackwell and William Attwood.
1716, August 24 (*vice* Duddlestone deceased), Henry Watts, Common Councillor.
1716, John Day, Common Councillor (elected Mayor September, 1717); John Norman and Jacob Elton.
1717, William Swymmer; Abell Grant and James Hilhouse.
1718, Henry Swymmer, Common Councillor; Christopher Shuter, Alderman, and Marmaduke Bowdler.
1719, Abraham Elton, Mayor and Common Councillor; William Freke and Edmund Baugh.
1720, James Donning, Common Councillor; Peter Day, Common Councillor, and Robert Earle, Common Councillor.
1721, Joseph Earle; John Hollidge and Edward Jones.
1722, John Becher, Common Councillor elected Alderman July, 1723); Nathaniel Wraxall, Common Councillor (elected Sheriff September, 1723), and John Hobbs.
1723, Thomas Longman; John King, Common Councillor, and James Day.
1724, Samuel Hunt; John Dukinfield and John Coysgarne
1725, Jeremy Innys; Edward Foy, Common Councillor, and Edward Curtis.
1726, John Blackwell, Common Councillor; Richard Lougher and Harrington Gibbs.
1727, John Norman; Thomas Eston and Thomas Freke.
1728, Jacob Elton, Common Councillor; John Templeman and William Challoner.
1729, Abell Grant; Lyonel Lyde, Common Councillor, and Michael Pope.
1730, James Hilhouse; John Day, Common Councillor, and Richard Henvile.
1731, Edmund Baugh; Henry Combe, Common Councillor, and Walter Lougher.
173?, Peter Day, Alderman; Michael White and Arthur Hart.
1733, Robert Earle Alderman; Robert Smith, Common Councillor, and Christopher Willoughby.
1734, John Hollidge; Henry Hart and John Foy, Common Councillor
1735, James Day; Lewis Casamajor and Thomas Chamberlayne.

SOCIETY OF MERCHANT VENTURERS.—*Continued.*

1736, John Dukinfield ; Michael Becher and Henry Dampier (elected Common Councillor May, 1737 ; Sheriff Sept., 1737).
1737, John Coysgarne; William Jefferis, Common Councillor (elected Mayor September, 1738), and James Laroche, Common Councillor.
1738, Richard Lougher; William Hare and Nathaniel Foy.
1739, Thomas Eston ; Abraham Elton, Common Councillor, and Edward Cooper, Common Councillor.
1740, William Challoner ; William Dukinfield and John Hilhouse.
1741, Lyonel Lyde, Alderman ; William Hart, jun., and Joseph Iles, Common Councillor.
1742, John Day, Common Councillor; Henry Swymmer and Cranfield Becher.
1743, Richard Henvile ; Abraham Elton, Common Councillor, and Henry Casamajor.
1744, Walter Lougher ; Isaac Baugh and James Day, jun.
1745, Arthur Hart ; Joseph Jefferis and Thomas Power.
1746, Robert Smith, Common Councillor; Joseph Daltera and John King.
1747, Christopher Willoughby, Chamberlain ; George Becher and Edward Willcocks.
1748, John Foy, Alderman ; Richard Farr, Common Councillor, and William Bowen.
1749, Michael Becher, Common Councillor ; Henry Hobhouse and Samuel Smith.
1750, Henry Dampier, Common Councillor ; Robert Bound and George Daubeny.
1751, James Laroche, Common Councillor (elected Alderman May, 1752); John Cross and Isaac Elton.
1752, William Hare ; William Reeve and James Hillhouse.
1753, Nathaniel Foy ; Ebenezer Hare and James Bonbonous.
1754, Edward Cooper, Alderman ; Abraham Isaac Elton, Town Clerk, and Francis Rogers, sen.
1755, Henry Swymmer, Common Councillor ; Samuel Munckley and William Wansey.
1756, Cranfield Becher ; John Hobhouse and Edward Charleton.
1757, Abraham Elton, Alderman ; Richard Combe and Thomas Farr, jun.
1758, Henry Casamajor ; Andrew Pope and James Daltera.
1759, Isaac Baugh, Common Councillor ; Joseph Daltera, Common Councillor, and Richard Farr, Common Councilor.
1760, Joseph Daltera, Common Councillor (elected Sheriff September, 1761) ; Thomas Willoughby and Samuel Smith.
1761, William Hart ; William Jones and Samuel Span.
1762, Richard Farr, Common Councillor (elected Mayor September, 1763) ; Nathaniel Wraxall and William Hillhouse.
1763. Samuel Smith ; Isaac Elton, jun., and Peter Hatton.
1764, Isaac Elton, Common Councillor ; Robert Smith and Paul Farr.
1765, William Reeve; Samuel Gardner and James Laroche, jun., Common Councillor
1766, James Bonbonous ; Andrews Reeve and Samuel Gardner ; 1767, August 10 (*vice* Gardner deceased), Cranfield Becher.
1767, Sir Abraham Isaac Elton, Bart., Town Clerk ; Michael Miller, jun., Common Councillor, and Henry Garnett.
1768, Samuel Munckley ; John Powell and Henry Cruger, Common Councillor.
1769, Andrew Pope, Common Councillor; George Daubeny, Common Councillor and Sheriff, and Thomas Perkins.
1770, William Jones ; George Champion and Edward Elton

SOCIETY OF MERCHANT VENTURERS.— *Continued.*

1771, Thomas Farr, Common Councillor; John Fowler and William Weare, Common Councillor.
1772, James Daltera; Richard Champion and Henry Lippincott, Common Councillor.
1773, Isaac Elton, jun., Common Councillor; John Vaughan and Jeremiah Hill.
1774, Robert Smith; Paul Farr and John Powell.
1775, Paul Farr; Edward Brice, Sheriff and Common Councillor, and John Garnett.
1776, Henry Garnett; John Champion and Henry Hobhouse.
1777, Samuel Span; John Daubeny and George Gibbs.
1778, Michael Miller, jun., Common Councillor (elected Mayor September, 1779); Henry Casamajor and John Fisher Weare, Common Councillor.
1779, John Powell; Jeremiah Hill, jun., and Richard Bright.
1780, Thomas Perkins; James Martin Hilhouse and Joshua Powell.
1781, Henry Cruger, Mayor and Common Councillor (elected Alderman July, 1782); John Fowler, jun., and Joseph Harford, Common Councillor.
1782, Sir James Laroche, Bart., Common Councillor; Charles Hill and John Scandrett Harford.
1783, John Fowler; William Weare, jun., Common Councillor, and Samuel Whitchurch.
1784, George Daubeny, Common Councillor; John Cave and Timothy Powell.
1785, Jeremiah Hill; Thomas Hungerford Powell and Joseph Bonbonous.
1786, Edward Brice, Alderman; Thomas Hill and Walter Powell.
1787, John Vaughan; John Gordon, jun., and William Randolph.
1788, Henry Hobhouse; Richard Tombs and James Rogers.
1789, John Daubeny; William Miles, Alderman, and Thomas Daniel, jun., Common Councillor.
1790, George Gibbs; William Fowler and Samuel Whitchurch.
1791, Jeremiah Hill, jun.; Charles Joseph Harford and John Cave, jun.
1792, Richard Bright, Common Councillor; Richard Vaughan, jun., and James Fowler.
1793, James Martin Hilhouse; John Blackwell and William Peter Lunell.
1794, John Garnett; James Jones and Mark Harford.
1795, Joshua Powell; Isaac Bence and Charles Hill.
1796, Joseph Harford, Common Councillor (elected Alderman June, 1797); Thomas Daniel, Common Councillor (elected Mayor September, 1797), and Charles Joseph Harford.
1797, Charles Hill; Samuel Whitchurch and Andrew Pope.
1798, John Scandrett Harford; Thomas Daniel, Alderman, and Samuel Brice.
1799, Samuel Whitchurch; Edward Protheroe, Common Councillor, and Richard Sargent Fowler.
1800, Timothy Powell; Hugh Vaughan and Edward Brice, jun.
1801, Thomas Hungerford Powell; Samuel Span, Sheriff and Common Councillor, and Hugh Vaughan.
1802, Joseph Bonbonous; Samuel Whitchurch, jun., and William Diaper Brice.
1803, Thomas Hill; George Hilhouse and Benjamin Bickley.
1804, John Gordon, Common Councillor; George Gibbs, jun., and Anthony Palmer Collings.
1805, Thomas Daniel, Alderman; William Gibbons, Common Councillor (elected Alderman September, 1806), and Robert Bruce.

SOCIETY OF MERCHANT VENTURERS.—*Continued.*

1806, Charles Joseph Harford ; John Thomson and Charles Harvey, Common Councillor.
1807, John Cave ; Thomas Hellicar and Robert Bush
1808, William Fowler ; John Barrow and James George.
1809, Richard Vaughan, jun., Councillor (elected Alderman June, 1810) ; Joseph Hellicar and Robert Vizer.
1810, James Fowler, Common Councillor ; Benjamin Bickley, Common Councillor, and Robert Bruce.
1811, John Blackwell ; William Perry and Thomas Durbin Brice.
1812, William Peter Lunell ; Abraham Hilhouse, Sheriff and Common Councillor, and James George, jun.
1813, Mark Harford ; William Danson and Philip Protheroe, Common Councillor.
1814, Andrew Pope ; Butler Thompson Claxton and James Joseph Whitchurch.
1815, Samuel Brice ; Robert Willis Vizer and James George.
1816, Richard Sargent Fowler ; Robert Hilhouse and Robert Bruce, jun.
1817, Stephen Cave ; Henry Brooke, Common Councillor (elected Mayor September, 1818), and George Lunell.
1818, Edward Brice, Common Councillor ; Peter Maze and John Barrow, Common Councillor.
1819, William Diaper Brice ; Samuel Lunell and Henry Brooke, Alderman.
1820, George Gibbs ; Hugh William Danson and John Barrow, Common Councillor.
1821, Robert Bruce ; Martin Hilhouse and Peter Maze.
1822, George Hilhouse, Alderman ; Richard Dawbney Brice and Henry George Fowler.
1823, Robert Bush ; Edmund Danson and William Bruce.
1824, John Barrow, Common Councillor ; Thomas Daniel, jun., and John Evans Lunell.
1825, Abraham Hilhouse, Alderman ; William Claxton and Peter Maze.
1826, Philip Protheroe, Common Councillor ; George Lunell and James Maze.
1827, James George, Alderman ; Richard Walker Fowler and Peter Maze, jun.
1828, James Joseph Whitchurch ; Hugh William Danson, Common Councillor, and Valentine Hellicar.
1829, Thomas Durbin Brice ; Valentine Hellicar and Danvers Hill Ward.
1830, Robert Bruce, jun. ; George Lunell and Hugh William Danson, Common Councillor.
1831, Peter Maze ; John Evans Lunell, Common Councillor, and Robert Gay Barrow.
1832, Richard Dawbney Brice ; Danvers Hill Ward and Edward Hinton.
1833, Henry George Fowler ; James Symes Barrow and John Hellicar.
1834, Thomas Daniel, jun. ; John Haythorne, Alderman, and William Claxton, Common Councillor.
1835, John Evans Lunell, Common Councillor ; Peter Maze, jun., Common Councillor, and William Brice.
1836, William Claxton ; Peter Maze, jun., and Robert Gay Barrow.
1837, Peter Maze, jun. ; Philip Protheroe and Francis Savage, jun.
1838, Valentine Hellicar ; William Claxton and George Lunell.
1839, Robert Gay Barrow ; Philip Protheroe and John Savage, J.P.
1840, John Hellicar ; John Harding, Councillor, and Charles Pinney, Alderman.

SOCIETY OF MERCHANT VENTURERS.—*Continued.*

1841, Francis Savage; William Weaver Davies, Councillor, and Edward Drew.
1842, John Savage, J.P.; George Lunell and Richard Robinson, Alderman.
1843, John Harding, Councillor; Francis Savage and Christopher George, J.P.
1844, Charles Pinney, Alderman; George Woodroffe Franklyn, Councillor, and Henry Bush.
1845, Edward Drew; John Harding and William Thomas Poole King, Councillor
1846, Richard Robinson, Alderman; Valentine Hellicar and John Hurle.
1847, George Woodroffe Franklyn; James George, J.P., Alderman, and Henry Brice.
1848, Henry Bush; John Harding and Richard Jenkins Poole King, J.P., Councillor.
1849, John Hurle; Robert Gay Barrow and Charles Pinney, Alderman.
1850, William Thomas Poole King, Councillor; James George, J.P., Alderman, and Richard Robinson, Alderman.
1851, Richard Jenkins Poole King, J.P., Councillor; Valentine Hellicar and George Pope.
1852, William Brice; James George, J.P., Alderman, and Charles Pinney, Alderman.
1853, George Pope; Robert Gay Barrow, Alderman, and John Salmon.
1854, John Salmon; Edward Drew and James Hassell.
1855, James Hassell; Thomas Porter Jose and William Oliver Bigg, Alderman.
1856, Thomas Porter Jose; William Oliver Bigg, Alderman, and Mark Davis Protheroe.
1857, William Oliver Bigg, Alderman; Alfred John Acraman and James Bush.
1858, Mark Davis Protheroe; James Bush, Councillor, and Francis Kentucky Barnes, Alderman.
1859, James Bush, Councillor; Francis Kentucky Barnes, Alderman, and Frederick William Green, Councillor.
1860, Francis Kentucky Barnes, Alderman; Frederick William Green, Councillor, and John Averay Jones.
1861, Frederick William Green, Councillor; John Averay Jones and Edward Thomas Lucas, Councillor.
1862, John Averay Jones; Edward Thomas Lucas, Councillor, and Odiarne Coates Lane, J.P., Councillor; 1863, August 8 (*vice* Lucas, deceased), Robert Gay Barrow, J.P., Alderman.
1863, John Averay Jones; Odiarne Coates Lane, J.P., Councillor, and Thomas Barnes.
1864, Odiarne Coates Lane, J.P., Councillor; Thomas Barnes and Sholto Vere Hare, J.P., Alderman.
1865, Thomas Barnes; Sholto Vere Hare, J.P., Alderman, and Charles Ringer.
1866, Sholto Vere Hare, J.P., Alderman; Charles Ringer and John Frederick Lucas.
1867, Robert Gay Barrow, J.P., Alderman; John Frederick Lucas and William Proctor Baker.
1868, John Frederick Lucas, Alderman; William Proctor Baker and William Wilberforce Jose.
1869, William Proctor Baker, Alderman; William Wilberforce Jose and Henry Cruger William Miles.
1870, William Wilberforce Jose; Henry Cruger William Miles and Thomas Terrett Taylor, Councillor.

SOCIETY OF MERCHANT VENTURERS.—*Continued.*

1871, Henry Cruger William Miles ; Thomas Terrett Taylor, Councillor, and William Augustus Frederick Powell, Councillor.
1872, Thomas Terrett Taylor, Councillor; William Augustus Frederick Powell, Councillor, and Mervyn Kersteman King.
1873, William Augustus Frederick Powell, Councillor ; Mervyn Kersteman King and Arthu Baker.
1874, Mervyn Kersteman King, Councillor; Arthur Baker and Charles Bowles Hare, Councillor.
1875, Arthur Baker, Councillor ; Charles Bowles Hare, Councillor, and Francis Frederick Fox, Alderman.
1876, Charles Bowles Hare, Councillor; Francis Frederick Fox, Alderman, and George William Edwards, Mayor and Alderman.
1877, Francis Frederick Fox, Alderman ; George William Edwards, Mayor and Alderman, and John Noble Coleman Pope.
1878, Francis Frederick Fox, J.P., Alderman ; George William Edwards, J.P., Mayor and Alderman, and John Noble Coleman Pope.
1879, George William Edwards, J.P., Alderman ; John Noble Coleman Pope and Robert Hassell.
1880, John Noble Coleman Pope ; Robert Hassell and Alfred George de Lisle Bush, Councillor.
1881, Robert Hassell ; Alfred George de Lisle Bush, Councillor, and Charles Octavius Harvey.
1882, Alfred George de Lisle Bush, Councillor ; Charles Octavius Harvey and Reginald Wyndham Butterworth, Alderman.
1883, Charles Octavius Harvey ; Reginald Wyndham Butterworth, Alderman, and Charles Paul.
1884, Reginald Wyndham Butterworth, Alderman ; Charles Paul and John Henry Woodward.
1885, Charles Paul ; John Henry Woodward and Percy Liston King.
1886, John Henry Woodward ; Percy Liston King and Edward Beadon Colthurt, Councillor.
1887, Percy Liston King ; Edward Beadon Colthurst, Councillor, and Thomas Poole King.
1888, Edward Beadon Colthurst, Councillor; Thomas Poole King and Harry Willoughby Beloe.
1889, Thomas Poole King, Harry Willoughby Beloe and Henry Frederick Tobin Bush.
1890, Harry Willoughby Beloe; Henry Frederick Tobin Bush and Thomas Gadd Matthews.
1891, Henry Frederick Tobin Bush ; Thomas Gadd Matthews and Richard Anstice Fox.
1892, Thomas Gadd Matthews; Richard Anstice Fox and John Henry Woodward.
1893, Richard Anstice Fox ; Edward Burrow Hill, Councillor, and Edward Burnet James, Councillor.
1894, Edward Burrow Hill, Councillor; Edward Burnet James, Councillor, and William Welsford Ward.
1895, Edward Burnet James, Councillor ; William Welsford Ward and John Henry Clarke.
1896, William Welsford Ward; John Henry Clarke and Herbert George Edwards, Councillor.
1897, John Henry Clarke; Herbert George Edwards, Councillor, and Averay Neville Jones.

SOCIETY OF MERCHANT VENTURERS —*Continued.*

TREASURERS.

1605, Thomas Aldworth, Common Councillor.
1606, William Hopkins, Common Councillor.
1607, William Cole, Common Councillor.
1608, John Rowberoe, Common Councillor.
1609, George White, Common Councillor.
1610, Thomas Whitehead, Sheriff and Common Councillor.
1611, *John Guy, Common Councillor.
1612, *John Barker, Sheriff and Common Councillor.
1613 and 1614, *John Gonninge, Sheriff (1613-1614) and Common Councillor.
1615, *John Langton, Common Councillor.
1616, *Humphrey Hooke, Common Councillor.
1617, *Andrew Charleton, Common Councillor.
1618, *John Tomlinson, Common Councillor.
1619, *Thomas Wright, Common Councillor.
1620. *Humphrey Browne, Common Councillor.
1621, Peter Miller, Common Councillor.
1622, *Richard Holworthie, Common Councillor.
1623. *Richard Longe, Common Councillor.
1624, *William Jones, Common Councillor.
1625, Nathaniel Butcher, Common Councillor.
1626. John Tayler, Common Councillor.
1627, John Locke, Common Councillor.
1628, Walter Ellis, Common Councillor.
1629. Richard Pley, Common Councillor.
1630. Richard Aldworth, Common Councillor.
1631, *Alexander James, Common Councillor.
1632, *Francis Creswicke, Common Councillor.
1633, Giles Elbridge, Common Councillor.
1634, *Thomas Colston, Common Councillor.
1635, Gabriel Sherman, Common Councillor.
1636 and 1637, John Gonninge, jun., Common Councillor.
1638, William Fitzherbert, Common Councillor.
1639, John Langton, Common Councillor.
1640, Thomas Hooke, Common Councillor.
1641, *William Cann, Common Councillor.
1642, William Wyatt, Common Councillor.
1643, *Hugh Browne, Common Councillor.
1644, Walter Deyos, Common Councillor.
1645, Walter Sandy, Common Councillor.
1646, Robert Challoner, Common Councillor.
1647, *Henry Creswicke.
1648, James Crofte, Common Councillor.
1649, *Robert Yate, Common Councillor.
1650, William Dale, Common Councillor.
1651, *William Yeamans, Common Councillor.
1652, George Lane, sen., Common Councillor.
1653, *Robert Cann, Common Councillor.
1654 and 1655, *John Willoughby, Common Councillor.
1656, *Robert Vickris, Sheriff and Common Councillor.
1657, William Merricke.
1658 to 1664, *Walter Tocknell.
1665 to 1672, *Robert Yate.
1673, *William Lysons, Common Councillor.
1674 to 1676, *Robert Yate.
1677 to 1683, †Richard Hart, Common Councillor (elected Alderman October, 1680 ; Mayor 1680-1681 ; Knighted October 27, 1680).

SOCIETY OF MERCHANT VENTURERS—*Continued.*

1684, †William Hayman, Mayor and Alderman (Knighted February 2, 1685).
1685 to 1687, †William Merricke, Common Councillor (Sheriff 1685-1686; Knighted May 27, 1686).
1688, †William Jackson, Common Councillor.
1689, †Arthur Hart, Mayor and Common Councillor.
1690, †Giles Merricke, Common Councillor.
1691 to 1693, †William Swymmer, Common Councillor (elected Alderman July, 1692).
1697 to 1699, Charles Jones.
1700 to 1704, †Peter Saunders, Common Councillor (Mayor 1703-1704); died October, 1705.
1705 to 1707, *Abraham Elton, sen., Common Councillor.
1708, William Hart.
1709 to 1711, *Henry Watts
1712 to 1729, *Robert Earle (elected Common Councillor April, 1715; Alderman November, 1727; Sheriff 1716-1717; Mayor 1725-1726).
1730 and 1731, William Jefferis, Common Councillor.
1732 and 1733, Henry Lloyd, Common Councillor.
1734 to 1744, Henry Combe, Common Councillor (Mayor 1740-1741).
1745 to 1750, *James Laroche, Common Councillor (Mayor 1750-1751).
1751, †Christopher Willoughby, Chamberlain (re-elected annually till his death, June 4, 1773).
1773, †James Daltera (re-elected annually till his death, April 17, 1801).
1801, May 11, †Samuel Whitchurch (re-elected annually till his death, February 23, 1816).
1816, May 3, Joseph Hellicar (re-elected annually till 1840 inclusive).
1841, †William Claxton (re-elected annually till his death, June 24, 1873).
1873, July 4, †John Hellicar, Councillor (re-elected 1874 and 1875).
1876, George Henry Pope (re-elected annually to the present time).

*Subsequently
†Previously } Served the Office of Master.

The Officers are elected annually on Charter Day, November 10, except when that day falls on a Sunday, the election then taking place on the 11th. The elections recorded in these lists took place at this time except when otherwise stated.

Since 1855 it has been usual to hold the offices of Junior Warden, Senior Warden and Master in immediate succession, the only deviations from this custom having been in the cases of (1) Mr. M. D. Protheroe, who was Junior Warden in 1856-7 and Master in 1858-9, the Senior Wardenship in the intervening year being taken by Mr. Acraman; (2) Mr. E. T. Lucas, who died when Senior Warden in 1863; (3) Mr. C. Ringer, who was unable to take the Master's chair for 1867-8 through ill-health, dying a few months after vacating the office of Warden; (4) Mr. E. B. Hill, who was elected Senior Warden in 1893, without having taken the Junior Wardenship, which in the preceding year was filled by a Past Master (Mr. Woodward).

The total number of persons who have served the office of Master from 1605 to the present time is 254, of whom 28 were elected more than once. H. Hooke was chosen seven times. Hugh Browne and J. Jackson four times each; M. Haviland, Robert Aldworth, and J. Barker three times; and J. Whitson, T. James, J. Gonninge, R. Longe, Sir W. Creswicke, W. Tocknell, Sir R. Hart, G.

SOCIETY OF MERCHANT VENTURERS.—*Continued.*

Lane, Sir W. Hayman, E. Tocknell, R. Yate, S. Price, P. Saunders, Sir W. Daines, James Hollidge, T. Hort, W. Clarke, J. Bacheler, H. Watts, J. A. Jones, R G. Barrow, and F. F. Fox twice each. It may be noticed that from 1692 to 1708 eight Masters in succession were re-elected, whereas since the latter date this has only occurred three times. In 155 years (1708-1862) there was no instance.

Ninety-nine of the Masters served the office of Mayor, of whom nine were Chief Magistrates at the date of their election to the chair of the Merchant Venturers, and nine were chosen during their Mastership. Thirty-nine had already served as Mayors, and 42 were subsequently elected. Between 1605 and 1666 only seven Masters did not attain to the Mayoralty, all of whom were Sheriffs, viz., John Aldworth, T. Wright, Humphrey Browne, T. Colston, R. Yate (1656), W. Yeamans, and J. Bowen. During the past 60 years only 12 have been elected to the Mastership who have also held the Mayoralty, viz., Messrs. Barrow, J. Savage, Pinney, G. W. Franklyn, R. J. Poole King, T. P. Jose, J. A. Jones, Lane, T. Barnes, S. V. Hare, W. Proctor Baker, and Sir G. Edwards.

CHAMBER OF COMMERCE.

The Chamber was originally established in 1823, a preliminary meeting being held on January 1st in that year, and the rules adopted at a subsequent meeting on February 25.

In 1848 it ceased to exist, having been for some years in a languishing condition, and was practically merged in the Free Port Association, but there is no extant record of its formal dissolution.

The Free Port Association, which was formed in September, 1846, dissolved itself on September 30, 1850.

In 1851 a movement was initiated for resuscitating the Chamber of Commerce, and a meeting with that object was held on September 4. It was not, however, till January 5, 1853, that the revived Chamber was fully organised. Under the rules then adopted the Master of the Society of Merchant Venturers for the time being was to be *ex-officio* President of the Chamber, and the Senior and Junior Wardens of that Society two of the four Vice Presidents, the other two being elected for two years, one to retire at each annual meeting, subject to re-election This arrangement continued till the end of 1857, and at the annual meeting in January, 1858, the rules were amended, and from that date till 1874 the President and two Vice-Presidents were chosen by the members, while the Chairman and Vice-Chairman, elected by the Committee, were the working heads of the Chamber.

In 1874 the Chamber was incorporated, being officially registered on September 16 in that year. From the annual meeting of 1875 to the present time the offices of Chairman and Vice-Chairman have been discontinued, the President and two Vice-Presidents taking the active direction, and being elected by the Council annually.

CHAMBER OF COMMERCE.—*Continued.*

(The first name in each paragraph is that of President, the second and third are those of Vice-Presidents.)

1823 to 1848.

1823, April. Joseph Reynolds ; Thomas Stock and Joseph Cookson ; re-elected February, 1824.
1825, February, Thomas Stock ; Joseph Cookson and Samuel Harford.
1826, February 5, Thomas Stock ; Henry Bush and John Matthew Gutch ; re-elected February 5, 1827, and February 4, 1828.
1829, February 2, Joseph Cookson; George Eddie Sanders and William Edward Acraman.
1830, February 1, Thomas Stock ; George Eddie Sanders and William Edward Acraman.
1831, February 7, Samuel Harford; George Eddie Sanders and William Singer Jacques.
1832, February 6, William Singer Jacques; William Tothill and Richard Jenkins Poole King; re-elected February 4, 1833.
1834, February 3, Henry Bush ; Richard Jenkins Poole King and William Edward Acraman ; re-elected February 2, 1835.
1836, February 1, Henry Bush ; William Edward Acraman, Councillor, and Edward Harley, Alderman.
1837, February 6, Edward Harley, Alderman ; Richard Jenkins Poole King, Councillor, and John Vining, Alderman ; re-elected February 5, 1838.
1839, February 4, Richard Jenkins Poole King, Councillor; Henry Bush, Councillor, and William Doue Bushell ; re-elected February 3, 1840, and February 1, 1841.
1842, February 7, John Vining, Alderman ; Edward Harley, Alderman, and Richard Robinson, Alderman.
1843, February 6, John Vining, Alderman ; Richard Jenkins Poole King, Councillor, and Francis Grevile Prideaux.
1844, February 5, John Vining, Alderman ; Richard Jenkins Poole King, Councillor, and Isaac Rouch.
1845, February 3, Isaac Rouch ; Edmund Butcher, Alderman, and John Decimus Pountney, Alderman ; re-elected February 2, 1846, and January 29, 1847.

Mr. Rouch presided at the annual meeting on January 31, 1848, and the election of officers for the year was fixed for February 7, but no record can be found of the names of those elected. The original Chamber does not appear to have met again, and had probably ceased to exist before November in that year, as it was not officially represented (as were the Corporation, the Merchant Venturers, the Incorporation of the Poor, and the Free Port Association) at the great Free Port Demonstration on November 15, to celebrate the passing of the Act by which the docks were transferred to the city.

The officers of the Free Port Association, in which the Chamber of Commerce was practically merged, were—President, Robert Bright ; Vice-Presidents, Daniel Cave, Peter Freeland Aiken, George Henry Ames, and Edward Thomas ; Secretary, Leonard Bruton.

1853 to 1857.

(The first name in each paragraph is that of President, *ex-officio*, the second and third are those of Vice-Presidents, *ex-officio*.)

1853, January, William Brice ; James George, J.P., Alderman, and Charles Pinney, Alderman.
1853, November, George Pope ; Robert Gay Barrow, Alderman, and John Salmon.

CHAMBER OF COMMERCE.—*Continued.*

1854. November, John Salmon ; Edward Drew and James Hassell.
1855. November, James Hassell ; Thomas Porter Jose and William Oliver Bigg, Alderman.
1856. November, Thomas Porter Jose ; William Oliver Bigg, Alderman, and Mark Davis Protheroe.
1857. November, William Oliver Bigg, Alderman ; Alfred John Acraman and James Bush ; till January, 1858.

(The above were Masters and Wardens of the Society of Merchant Venturers.)

Elected Presidents, 1858 to 1874

1858. January 27, Robert Bright.
1859. January 26, Philip William Skynner Miles ; re-elected annually till 1873 inclusive.
1874. April 17, Charles Nash, J.P., Councillor.

Elected Vice-Presidents, 1853 to 1874 (serving two years each).

1853. January 5, Robert Bright ; re-elected 1854 and 1856. Philip William Skynner Miles ; re-elected 1855 and 1857.
1858. January 27, Richard Jenkins Poole King, J.P., Councillor (*vice* Bright).
1859. January 26, William Montague Baillie (*vice* Miles).
1860. January 25, Peter Freeland Aiken (*vice* King).
1861. January 30, John Bates, Councillor (*vice* Baillie).
1862. January 29, Joshua Saunders (*vice* Aiken).
1863. February 11, William Gale Coles (*vice* Bates).
1864. January 27, William Henry Wills, Councillor (*vice* Saunders).
1865. January 31, James Bush, Councillor (*vice* Coles).
1866. January 31, Charles Nash, Councillor (*vice* Wills).
1867. February 1, Elisha Smith Robinson, J.P., Councillor (*vice* Bush).
1868. February 19, Joshua Saunders (*vice* Nash).
1869. March 10, Herbert Thomas, J.P., Alderman (*vice* Robinson).
1870. April 22, Francis Adams, J.P., Alderman (*vice* Saunders).
1871. March 29, Mark Whitwill, Councillor (*vice* Thomas).
1872. April 10, William Proctor Baker, Alderman (*vice* Adams).
1873. April 9, William Pethick, J.P. (*vice* Whitwill).
1874. April 17, John Lucas, Councillor (*vice* Baker).

1875 to 1898.

(The first name in each paragraph is that of President, the second and third are those of Vice-Presidents.)

1875. April 26, Charles Townsend ; John Evans and George Squier Bryant.
1876. April 21, John Evans ; George Squier Bryant and Alfred George De Lisle Bush.
1877. April 27, John Evans ; Alfred George De Lisle Bush and Henry Thomas Chamberlain.
1878. April 24, Alfred George De Lisle Bush ; Henry Thomas Chamberlain and William Middleton Gibson (Mr. Gibson died December 11, 1878).
1879. April 25, Alfred George De Lisle Bush ; Charles Wills and Francis J. de Soyres.
1880. April 28, Charles Wills ; Charles Felce Hare and Elisha Smith Robinson, J.P., ; re-elected May 25, 1881.

CHAMBER OF COMMERCE.—*Continued.*

1882, April 25, Charles Felce Hare : Elisha Smith Robinson, J.P., and Robert Henry Marten.
1883, April 25, Charles Felce Hare ; William Howell Davies and Lewis Falconer Marsh.

[Mr. Hare declined to serve a second year, and on May 7, 1883, Charles Wills was elected President in his place.]

1884, April 30, William Howell Davies ; Lewis Falconer Marsh and James Colthurst Godwin.
1885, April 22, James Colthurst Godwin ; Lewis Falconer Marsh and Charles William Allen.
1886, May 12, James Colthurst Godwin ; Charles William Allen and Arthur John Lawson.
1887, April 28. Charles William Allen ; Arthur John Lawson and Benjamin Perry.
1888. April 25, Arthur John Lawson; Benjamin Perry and William Dove Willcox.
1889, May 22, William Dove Willcox ; Benjamin Perry and John Ryan Bennett ; re-elected April 23, 1890.
1891, April 22, John Ryan Bennett ; John Weston and Edward Burrow Hill ; re-elected April 27, 1892.
1893, April 26, John Weston ; Edward Burrow Hill and George Henry Perrin.
1894, April 25, George Henry Perrin ; Edward Burrow Hill and Mark Whitwill, jun.

[Mr. Hill resigned, and Joseph Holman was elected to succeed him December 19, 1894.]

1895, May 22, George Henry Perrin ; Mark Whitwill, jun., and Joseph Holman.
1896, April 29, Mark Whitwill, jun. ; Joseph Holman and Benjamin Perry.
1897, May 26, Joseph Holman ; Benjamin Perry and Thomas Tucker Lindrea ; re-elected May 18, 1898.

CHAIRMEN AND VICE-CHAIRMEN.

1853 to 1874.

(The first name in each paragraph is that of Chairman and the second that of Vice-Chairman.)

1853, January 12, James Bush.
1853, April 22, Richard Manning Hayman, Vice-Chairman.
1854, February 6, Richard Manning Hayman ; Charles Edwards, Alderman.
1855, February, Charles Edwards, Alderman ; Thomas Wright Rankin.
1856, February, Thomas Wright Rankin ; Mark Whitwill, jun.
1857, March, Mark Whitwill, jun. ; William Terrell
1858, February, William Terrell ; George Edward Bevan.
1859, February 21, George Edward Bevan ; John Shute.
1860, February 21, John Shute ; Thomas Evans.
1861, February 18, Thomas Evans ; Herbert Thomas.
1862, February 17, Herbert Thomas ; William Henry Wills.
1863, February 16, William Henry Wills, Councillor ; George Wills.
1864, February 15, George Wills ; Charles Hoskins Low.
1865, February 20, Charles Hoskins Low ; Algernon William Warren, Councillor.

CHAMBER OF COMMERCE.—*Continued.*

1865, May 22, Augustus Phillips (*vice* Warren, resigned), Vice-Chairman.
1866, March 19, Augustus Phillips ; John Lucas.
1867, February, John Lucas ; Joseph Almond (resigned and succeeded by Richard Cripps).
1868, February, Richard Cripps ; William Turner.
1869, March, William Turner ; William Killigrew Wait, Councillor (resigned and succeeded by Richard Jefferd Crook).
1870, May 18, Richard Jefferd Crook ; Lewis Waterman.
1871, April 12, Lewis Waterman ; Richard Ridler.
1872, April 24, James Bell ; William Mills Baker.
1873, April 18, William Polglase ; Henry Taylor.
1874, April 24, Henry Taylor ; Charles Townsend, Councillor.

SECRETARIES.

1823, April 3, Gresley Hellicar (killed by a fall from his horse April 21, 1824).
1824, May 3, Lionel Oliver Bigg (Mr. Bigg retained the Secretaryship till the discontinuance of the Chamber in 1848).
1853, February 14, Leonard Bruton (late Secretary to the Free Port Association), died January 24, 1887.
1887, February 2, Henry John Spear.

[In compiling the above lists I have had the invaluable assistance of Mr. Spear, who has kindly given me unrestricted access to all the records in the office of the Chamber, supplemented by additional information from his personal knowledge.—A. B. B.]

THE COLSTON SOCIETIES.

The dates are those of the dinners held on November 13, the President being usually elected in the preceding November.

PRESIDENTS OF THE DOLPHIN SOCIETY.

		Collections.
1749	Francis Woodward	
1750	Francis Woodward	
1751	Peter Wells	£4 17 0
1752	John Averay	8 1 0
1753	Joseph Farrell	12 10 0
1754	Henry Bradburne	20 0 0
1755	Samuel Smith	26 19 0
1756	Edward Gore	34 0 9
1757	Ferdinand Penington	36 10 9
1758	Henry Morgan	26 8 3
1759	Roger Watts	25 19 3
1760	Stephen Cox	21 19 6
1761	Jeremiah Osborne	24 13 6
1762	John Powell	25 0 3
1763	Edmund Broderip	28 17 10

PRESIDENTS OF THE DOLPHIN SOCIETY.—*Continued.*

		Collections		
1764	William Yeatman	23	4	0

William Merrick, President-elect for 1765, died November 28, 1764.

Year	Name	£	s	d
1765	Fenwick Bird	27	19	3
1766	Richard Smith	26	1	0
1767	Nicholas Perry	34	5	0
1768	Nathaniel Webb	27	4	0
1769	Michael Hodgson	31	17	0
1770	Henry King	30	8	10
1771	Thomas Paty	31	10	0
1772	William Sladen	32	1	9
1773	Robert Bridle	49	4	3
1774	Nathan Windey	67	10	6
1775	George Daubeny, Common Councillor	60	0	0
1776	Thomas Berjew	72	11	6
1777	Thomas Keene	65	19	9
1778	Joseph Hinton	60	12	0

John Davies, President-elect for 1779, died December 27, 1778.

Year	Name	£	s	d
1779	Thomas Hembury	63	7	0
1780	William Jones	92	12	0
1781	James Hughes	64	15	6
1782	Michael Clayfield	83	18	6
1783	John Headington	67	14	6
1784	Charles Partridge	57	4	6
1785	Abraham Wigginton	53	11	0
1786	Richard Smith	65	12	6
1787	Henry King, jun.	63	11	0
1788	Richard Tombs	64	11	6
1789	Francis Ward	68	5	0
1790	John Hawkins	96	12	0
1791	George Daubeny, Alderman, for Edward Gore	90	16	6
1792	Edward Willis	102	7	6
1793	Simon Oliver	106	1	0
1794	Philip Crocker	116	0	6
1795	Charles Brown	120	4	6
1796	William Whittingham	124	8	6
1797	Edward Francis Colston	135	19	6
1798	Godfrey Lowe	156	9	0
1799	Thomas Sanders	169	11	6
1800	William Moncrieff, M.D.	195	16	6
1801	John Paine Berjew	172	14	6
1802	John Ward	178	10	0
1803	Anthony Palmer Collings	225	5	6
1804	Morgan Yeatman	196	16	6
1805	Joel Gardiner	203	2	6
1806	William Powell	215	0	0
1807	Edward Rolle Clayfield	231	4	6
1808	Thomas Griffiths	266	9	6
1809	Richard Hart Davis, M.P.	294	18	6
1810	Richard Vaughan, Alderman	312	16	6
1811	Charles Ridout	272	15	6
1812	Thomas Andrewes	268	2	6
1813	Richard Colston	429	10	6
1814	John Cave	339	18	6
1815	Thomas Webb Dyer, M.D.	316	11	6

PRESIDENTS OF THE DOLPHIN SOCIETY.—*Continued.*

Collections

Year	President	£	s	d
1816	Thomas Daniel, Alderman	336	3	0
1817	Rev. Charles Gore (for Wm. Gore Langton, M.P.)	283	0	6
1818	Edward Sampson	330	0	6
1819	Samuel Bowden	289	12	6
1820	Richard Lowe	307	6	0
1821	Richard Brickdale Ward	409	19	0
1822	Richard Smith	429	13	6
1823	Daniel Stanton	438	7	0
1824	John Gardiner, Sheriff and Common Councillor	400	8	0
1825	Robert Bush	421	10	0
1826	William Lewton Clarke	407	13	6
1827	John Vaughan	389	18	6
1828	Jeremiah Osborne	619	10	0
1829	John Matthew Gutch	432	14	0

Daniel Baynburn and Edward Daniel successively declined the Presidency for 1829.

1830	Walter Swayne	352	3	0
1831	Neast Grevile Prideaux (no dinner)	210	7	6
1832	William Mortimer	444	0	0
1833	Charles Payne, Common Councillor	540	0	0
1834	William Fripp, Alderman	530	2	0
1835	Henry Bush	630	6	0

The President originally elected for 1835 was John Cornish.

1836	William Watson, Alderman	545	13	0
1837	William Miles, M.P.	536	11	6

Andrew Currick, M.D., President-elect for 1837, died June 14, 1837.

1838	John Kerle Haberfield, Mayor and Councillor, for Edward Francis Colston	643	13	6
1839	Henry Wenman Newman, J.P.	500	0	6
1840	John Taylor	668	1	6
1841	Francis Grevile Prideaux	439	2	0
1842	James George, J.P., Councillor	402	9	0
1843	Philip William Skynner Miles, M.P.	552	5	0

William Weaver Davies, President-elect for 1843, resigned.

1844	Charles Ludlow Walker, J.P.	466	6	0
1845	Cam Gyde Heaven, Councillor	553	12	2
1846	James Gibbs, Councillor	517	0	6
1847	John Vining, Alderman	365	6	0
1848	John Decimus Pountney, Alderman	371	7	6
1849	Charles Taylor, Councillor	378	6	1
1850	Edward Colston	400	5	0
1851	Winchcombe Henry Howard Hartley	300	6	0
1852	Oliver Coathupe	307	3	0
1853	Thomas Green, M.D., Alderman	424	12	6
1854	George Woodroffe Franklyn, M.P.	306	1	10
1855	Francis Savage	349	6	1
1856	Thomas Daniel	342	11	8
1857	Charles Edward Ward	405	15	0
1858	John William Miles, Councillor	403	17	7
1859	Peter Freeland Aiken	529	3	8

PRESIDENTS OF THE DOLPHIN SOCIETY.—*Continued.*

Year	President	Collections £ s d
1860	Edward Sampson	476 10 11
1861	Thomas Porter Jose, Councillor	467 1 9
1862	James Bush, Councillor	514 9 10
1863	Stephen Cave, M.P.	467 15 3
1864	John Colthurst, Councillor	516 1 8
1865	William Henry Harford, jun., Councillor	549 4 8
1866	Robert Bush, Councillor	712 19 0
1867	William Killigrew Wait, Councillor	639 12 0
1868	George Fisher Prideaux	821 11 9
1869	Charles Nash, Councillor	1012 12 7
1870	Charles Stewart Clarke	899 12 9
1871	Sholto Vere Hare, J.P., Alderman	948 12 6
1872	Thomas Canning, J.P., Councillor	1138 7 0
1873	Thomas Terrett Taylor, Councillor	1030 0 4
1874	William Henry Miles, Councillor	1121 16 1
1875	Charles Daniel Cave	1049 5 6
1876	William Gale Coles	1284 15 6
1877	Richard Bright, M.P.	1013 13 0
1878	Thomas Parr	1159 10 6
1879	Sir Philip John William Miles, Bart., M.P.	1121 9 6
1880	Henry Sidney Wasbrough	1425 6 0
1881	Charles Edward Hungerford Atholl Colston	1537 12 5
1882	Charles Hill, J.P.	1619 0 1
1883	Robert Lowe Grant Vassall	1491 5 6
1884	Reginald Wyndham Butterworth, Alderman	1359 10 0
1885	John Noble Coleman Pope	1506 0 2
1886	George William Edwards, J.P., Mayor and Alderman	1706 5 8
1887	Edward Stock Hill, C.B., M.P.	1781 2 5
1888	Alfred Deedes, J.P.	1762 1 8
1889	Jeremiah Osborne	1890 12 1
1890	Rev. Richard William Randall	1602 0 7
1891	Alfred George de Lisle Bush, Councillor	1414 16 10
1892	John Henry Clarke	1607 15 0
1893	Right Hon. Sir Michael Edward Hicks Beach, Bart., M.P.	1452 17 0
1894	Charles Robert Hancock, Councillor	1324 7 4
1895	Henry O'Brien O'Donoghue	1436 19
1896	Charles Henry Cave, Councillor	1412 8 8
1897	The Duke of Beaufort, K.G.	1713 9 8

President-elect for 1898—Charles Whitchurch Wasbrough.

PRESIDENTS OF THE ANCHOR SOCIETY

Collections

Year	President	£	s	d
1769	Gilbert Davis	12	1	6
1770	Gilbert Davis	35	2	0
1771	Joseph Fowle	46	3	8
1772	John Rowand	80	16	0
1773	Andrew Paterson, M.D.	85	5	0
1774	John Wright, M.D.	120	10	0
1775	John Noble, Common Councillor	117	0	3
1776	Paul Farr	172	4	5
1777	Joseph Harford	219	14	1
1778	Samuel Span	222	2	0
1779	Benjamin Loscombe, Common Councillor	197	8	0
1780	James Kirkpatrick	231	10	8
1781	Philip Protheroe, Common Councillor	222	13	0
1782	Joseph Smith, Common Councillor	239	19	6
1783	Henry Cruger, Alderman	291	6	6
1784	John Fisher Weare, Common Councillor	304	16	0
1785	Richard Bright, Common Councillor	289	11	4
1786	Sir Stephen Nash, Common Councillor	287	19	8
1787	James Harvey, Common Councillor	289	13	0
1788	James Morgan, Common Councillor	293	11	6
1789	Robert Claxton, Common Councillor	350	13	7
1790	Levi Ames, Common Councillor	339	5	8
1791	John Harris, Common Councillor	315	12	6
1792	Charles Joseph Harford	355	14	6
1793	William Peter Lunell	317	0	0
1794	Henry Bengough, Common Councillor	318	0	0
1795	Robert Castle, Common Councillor	317	13	0
1796	Joseph Edye, Common Councillor	284	7	11
1797	Andrew Pope	277	11	5
1798	John Foy Edgar, Common Councillor	266	10	6
1799	Michael Castle	335	13	0
1800	Worthington Brice, Common Councillor (for Samuel Span, Common Councillor)	283	10	5
1801	Jacob Wilcox Ricketts	307	1	0
1802	Henry Protheroe, Sheriff and Common Councillor	278	1	2
1803	Joseph Mason Cox, M.D.	256	11	6
1804	Edward Protheroe, Mayor and Common Councillor	305	12	6
1805	Levi Ames, jun., Common Councillor	292	11	3
1806	Samuel Henderson, Common Councillor	290	9	6
1807	Hugh Duncan Baillie	304	1	6
1808	George Gibbs	311	16	6
1809	Arthur Palmer, jun.	366	2	6
1810	Peter Baillie, M.P.	339	3	6
1811	Benjamin Hobhouse, M.P.	326	4	5
1812	Philip Protheroe, Common Councillor	318	17	0
1813	John Yerbury	285	5	6
1814	Brooke Smith	359	11	6
1815	James Evan Baillie, M.P.	343	16	6
1816	John Edmund Stock, M.D.	305	0	3
1817	Brooke Smith (for Charles Abraham Elton)	283	10	0
1818	Edward Webb, M.P.	315	1	6
1819	George Henry Ames	372	2	0
1820	Michael Hinton Castle	374	3	10

PRESIDENTS OF THE ANCHOR SOCIETY—*Continued.*

		Collections
1821	Benjamin Heywood Bright..	472 9 0
1822	Charles Pinney, Common Councillor	512 4 6
1823	John Evans Lunell	511 1 3
1824	James Lean	520 0 0
1825	Henry Bright, M.P.	514 12 0
1823	Arthur Palmer	471 14 0

Henry Browne, President-elect for 1826, resigned after the failure of the Bullion Bank, in which he was the senior partner, December, 1825.

1827	William Claxton	572 1 6
1828	Edward Kentish, M.D.	414 0 0
1829	John Hare, jun.	653 5 6
1830	Robert Bright	561 17 6
1831	Joseph Grace Smith	220 8 6
1832	Charles Savery	510 4 6
1833	John Mills..	421 19 0
1834	George Gwinnett Bompas, M.D.	325 10 0
1835	Brooke Smith	367 19 6
1836	Robert Bruce, jun.	410 8 6
1837	Joseph Grace Smith	386 5 0
1838	Henry Andrews Palmer	756 13 6
1839	Charles Bowles Fripp, Councillor	533 1 0
1840	Frederick Ricketts	535 17 0
1841	Richard Ash, J.P.	440 16 0
1842	Joseph Grace Smith, for John Evans Lunell, J.P., Councillor	380 3 0
1843	Francis Henry Fitzhardinge Berkeley, M.P.	618 17 0
1844	Francis Short	613 12 6
1845	Joseph Coates	450 8 0
1846	Frederick Palmer	473 4 0
1847	Thomas Mills	400 0 0
1848	William Henry Gore Langton, J.P., Councillor	416 6 0
1849	John Mercer, jun.	383 10 6

The President-elect for 1849 was Arthur Hare Palmer, Councillor, but he resigned on account of the death of his father in August, 1849, and accepted the Presidency for the following year.

1850	Arthur Hare Palmer, Councillor	475 17 0
1851	Rev. Sir Erasmus Henry Griffies Williams, Bart.	298 10 6
1852	Henry James Mills	341 19 0
1853	Christopher James Thomas, Councillor	471 5 0
1854	Thomas Wright Rankin	526 19 0
1855	Thomas Lang	570 10 6
1856	William Henry Gore Langton, J.P., M.P.	373 1 0
1857	Richard Manning Hayman	356 6 6
1858	Robert Leonard, jun.	431 1 6
1859	Elisha Smith Robinson, Councillor	509 19 6
1860	Robert Lang, Councillor	584 7 11
1861	Arthur Henry Wansey	582 14 0
1862	William Terrell	504 0 0
1863	Herbert Thomas	610 0 0
1864	John Perry, Councillor	641 19 0
1865	John Hare Leonard	687 7 1
1866	William Henry Wills, J.P., Councillor	630 0 0

PRESIDENTS OF THE ANCHOR SOCIETY.—*Continued.*

		Collections		
1867	George Wills, Councillor	575	0	0
1868	Lewis Fry, Councillor	1000	0	0
1869	Algernon William Warren, Councillor	825	0	0
1870	Joseph Dodge Weston, Councillor	851	4	0
1871	Charles Thomas	783	12	6
1872	John Freeman Norris	920	0	0
1873	William Pethick, J.P., Councillor	950	0	0
1874	Mark Whitwill, Councillor	813	0	0
1875	Philip John Worsley	812	0	0
1876	Samuel Lang	1100	0	0
1877	Edward Gustavus Clarke	940	0	0
1878	Samuel Wills	915	0	0

Afterwards took the name Day before Wills.

		Collections		
1879	John Wesley Hall	1013	0	0
1880	Edward Payson Wills	940	16	0
1881	Francis James Fry, J.P.	1002	13	6
1882	Frederick Wills	1011	7	6
1883	Charles Townsend, J.P., Councillor	946	7	8
1884	David Macliver, J.P.	1002	0	0
1885	James Colthurst Godwin	1007	5	0
1886	Henry Daniel, Councillor	925	4	0
1887	Edward Robinson	1035	0	0
1888	Edward Stafford Howard	755	11	0
1889	Rev. Urijah Rees Thomas	903	14	0
1890	Alfred Newell Price, J.P.	856	8	6
1891	Frank William Wills	1004	0	0
1892	William Howell Davies, Councillor	1007	6	0
1893	James Williams Arrowsmith	1202	0	0
1894	Frank Newton Tribe	1005	9	0
1895	Walter Melville Wills	1020	4	0
1896	William Henry Butler	1066	18	6
1897	Joseph Weston Stevens	1033	0	6

President-elect for 1898—Herbert Ashman, J.P., Councillor.

PRESIDENTS OF THE GRATEFUL SOCIETY.

		Collections		
1759	William Fry	£20	15	6
1760	William Fry	23	3	6
1761	Samuel Curnock	28	7	6
1762	Abraham Gadd	38	0	7
1763	John Rowand	55	5	9
1764	Thomas Gadd	67	16	10
1765	Matthew Worgan	66	1	5
1766	Abraham Bernard	65	4	1
1767	Henry Burgum	70	17	6
1768	Thomas Wigan	75	1	9
1769	Henry Johns	76	9	6

The President originally elected for 1769 was Joseph Cantle.

PRESIDENTS OF THE GRATEFUL SOCIETY —*Continued.*

Collections

Year	President	£	s	d
1770	Thomas Tawman	78	7	3
1771	Charles Powell	75	12	9
1772	John Powell	84	5	3
1773	John Purrier	111	10	0
1774	Kingsmill Grove	119	13	6
1775	Henry Haskins	146	8	9
1776	James Cross	171	10	0
1777	William Vaughan	120	10	0
1778	James Hunt	125	0	0
1779	William Gant	97	4	9
1780	Thomas Nash	100	14	0

Henry Kroger was originally elected President for 1780, but resigned.

Year	President	£	s	d
1781	Edward Onion	94	14	0
1782	Josiah Greethead	98	12	0
1783	Cradock Odford	104	10	0
1784	Thomas Gadd	104	6	0
1785	Thomas Cook	82	8	0
1786	William Helps	98	11	0
1787	William Wetherill	108	8	0
1788	Benjamin Davies	121	0	0
1789	John Hobbs	100	16	6
1790	Samuel Mereweather	111	4	6
1791	William Bulgin	140	19	0
1792	John Perinton	126	10	6
1793	John Lewis	116	0	0
1794	Walter Jenkins	126	5	0
1795	John Barrow	138	12	0
1796	Preston Edgar	120	15	0
1797	Walter Vigurs	132	16	6
1798	Robert Vizer	161	14	0
1799	Henry Williams	184	5	6
1800	James Harris	193	3	4
1801	Richard Bowden	193	13	7½
1802	Samuel Robertson	201	14	0
1803	Thomas Winter	179	3	0
1804	John Rose	189	18	1
1805	Thomas Cross	181	18	6
1806	Robert Withington	203	2	0
1807	Charles Bosher	188	10	0
1808	Charles Smith	186	15	6
1809	William Vigor	176	16	6
1810	William Ball	221	8	5
1811	William Smith	224	3	6
1812	Peter Peace	235	8	7
1813	George Jones	230	3	6
1814	William Underwood	349	6	0
1815	Sir Henry Protheroe, Common Councillor	290	5	6
1816	Edward Young, junior	211	0	6
1817	Samuel Ditchett	241	10	0
1818	Peter Fry	210	0	0
1819	Robert Willis Vizer	260	0	0
1820	Thomas Gadd	240	0	0
1821	William Smith	190	0	0
1822	James Taylor Ball	230	0	0
1823	John Bowgin	209	0	0
1824	Thomas Willcox	325	8	0
1825	Preston Edgar, senior	270	0	0

PRESIDENTS OF THE GRATEFUL SOCIETY.—*Continued.*

Year	President	Collections		
1826	George Lunell	356	3	4
1827	James Lyon	321	9	1
1828	William Orchard Gwyer	388	2	9
1829	Francis Kentucky Barnes	360	0	0
1830	Thomas Gadd Matthews	441	1	3
1831	Richard Nott (no dinner)	148	7	0
1832	Robert Fiske	344	0	0
1833	Job Harrill	404	9	6
1834	John Miller (for Robert Gay Barrow)	363	9	6
1835	William Lee	450	0	0
1836	Henry Chidgey Quinton	460	18	0
1837	John George Shaw	602	18	11
1838	William Done Bushell	714	5	0
1839	John Harding, Councillor	907	15	5
1840	John Kerle Haberfield, Councillor	1144	4	0
1841	No President [(Treasurer)] William Done Bushell, Councillor	372	0	0
1842	James Poole, junior	411	6	6
1843	John Hughes	434	4	3
1844	Edward Joseph Staples, M.D., Councillor	415	4	10
1845	William Harwood, junior	452	13	2
1846	Richard Boucher Callender	502	15	2
1847	Thomas Percival Willcox	373	0	0
1848	Henry Brown Jordan	393	5	4
1849	Joseph Leech	521	15	8
1850	Henry Abbot	576	13	4
1851	John Wetherman, junior, Councillor	517	9	10
1852	Charles Paul	875	2	3
1853	Thomas Lane Coulson	504	1	6
1854	Edward Harley	812	14	9
1855	William Fripp, junior	612	12	4
1856	John Bates, Councillor	632	10	3
1857	Odiarne Coates Lane, J.P., Councillor	510	19	8
1858	Charles Edwards	634	11	0
1859	Francis Adams, Alderman	624	10	7
1860	John George Shaw, J.P., Councillor	682	18	0
1861	George Rocke Woodward, Sheriff	550	14	3
1862	James Flower Fussell	701	7	0
1863	Thomas Barnes	650	0	6
1864	William Hathway	760	0	0
1865	James Creswell Wall	941	19	0
1866	William Naish, J.P., Alderman	612	0	0
1867	John Averay Jones	670	0	0
1868	John Pomeroy Gilbert	860	1	10
1869	Francis Frederick Fox, Alderman	703	10	6
1870	John Hellicar, Councillor	645	18	8
1871	Henry William Green	733	13	3
1872	Thomas Gadd Matthews	728	3	6
1873	Charles Price	601	0	0
1874	Samuel Wills	677	16	0
1875	John Harvey, junior	908	6	0
1876	Robert Hassell	787	0	0
1877	James Inskip, Councillor	883	14	0
1878	Joseph Dodge Weston, J.P., Councillor	1035	14	3
1879	George William Edwards, J.P., Alderman	1075	0	0
1880	Elisha Smith Robinson, J.P., Councillor	715	2	0
1881	Frederick Fox Cartwright	1109	18	7
1882	William Edwards George, Alderman	1007	7	0

PRESIDENTS OF THE GRATEFUL SOCIETY.—*Continued*

		Collections
1883	John Strachan Bridges, Councillor	910 15 8
1884	Thomas Davey	930 0 0
1885	Francis James Fry, J.P.	805 0 0
1886	Thomas David Taylor	902 16 0
1887	Charles Hoskins Low, J.P., Councillor	811 7 6
1888	Charles Wathen, J.P., Mayor and Alderman	1002 0 0
1889	Francis Richardson Cross, M.D.	1032 10 0
1890	Edward Arthur Harvey, Councillor	960 3 1
1891	John Henry Woodward	840 18 8
1892	James Henry Lockley	917 8 9
	[Thomas Winter Gibson, Councillor, the President-Elect, died April 12, 1892.]	
1893	Arthur Robinson	916 12 6
1894	George Alfred Wills	1006 0 0
1895	John Hancocke Wathen, Councillor	918 4 4
1896	Herbert Cary George Batten	860 9 1
1897	Stephen Tryon, Councillor	804 11 4

President-Elect for 1898—His Honour James Valentine Austin

The sums collected at the dinners are in some reports differently stated, but in no case do they vary very materially.

From 1758 (previous to which date only the Dolphin Society collected) the largest sums have been contributed by the respective societies as follows:—

By the Dolphin—1758, 1759, 1813, 1816, 1818, 1828, 1833 to 1836 inclusive, 1845, 1846, and 1869 to 1897 inclusive.

By the Anchor—1776 to 1812 inclusive, 1814, 1815, 1817, 1819 to 1827 inclusive, 1829 to 1832 inclusive, 1838, 1841, 1843, 1844, 1847, 1848, 1861, 1866, and 1868.

By the Grateful—1760 to 1775 inclusive, 1837, 1839, 1840, 1842, 1849 to 1860 inclusive, 1862 to 1865 inclusive, and 1867.

The smallest sums have been contributed—

By the Dolphin—1760 to 1768 inclusive, 1770 to 1799 inclusive, 1801, 1802, 1829, 1831, 1838, 1839, 1847 to 1850 inclusive, 1852 to 1856 inclusive, 1858, 1860, 1861, 1863 to 1866 inclusive, and 1868.

By the Anchor—1769, 1813, 1833 to 1837 inclusive, 1840, 1842, 1845, 1846, 1851, 1857, 1859, 1862, 1867, 1875, 1878, 1879, 1881, 1888, 1889, 1890, and 1894.

By the Grateful—1758, 1759, 1800, 1803 to 1812 inclusive, 1814 to 1828 inclusive, 1830, 1832, 1841, 1843, 1844, 1869 to 1874 inclusive, 1876, 1877, 1880, 1882 to 1887 inclusive, 1891, 1892, 1893, 1895, 1896, and 1897.

THE COLSTON SOCIETIES.—*Continued*.

The largest collection made by the Dolphin was £1,890 12s. 1d.- in the year 1889, under the presidency of Mr. Jere Osborne.

The largest collection made by the Anchor was £1,204, in the year 1893, under the presidency of Mr. J. W. Arrowsmith.

The largest collection made by the Grateful was £1,144 4s., in the year 1840, under the presidency of Mr. J. K. Haberfield.

It is somewhat remarkable that five of the twelve gentlemen who filled the chair of the Anchor Society between 1819 and 1830 —Messrs. G. H. Ames, C. Pinney, J. Lean, W. Claxton, and R. Bright —subsequently became Conservatives; so also did Mr. J. F. Edgar and Col. H. D. Baillie, presidents in 1798 and 1807 respectively. Also nine of the presidents between 1866 and 1886 were included in the Unionist section of the party after the Home Rule split, viz. Messrs. G. Wills, L. Fry, C. Thomas, W. Pethick, J. W. Hall, E. P. Wills, F. J. Fry, F. Wills, and J. C. Godwin.

The ascendency of the Whig party in the Corporation at the end of the 18th and beginning of the 19th century is illustrated by the fact that of 32 presidents of the Anchor between 1775 and 1806, only 9 were not members of that body, while holding the chair of the Whig society, and of these two, Messrs. J. Harford and S. Span, were elected to the Common Council almost immediately afterwards; while another, Mr. M. Castle, had been elected to the Council, and declined to serve. Mr. Kirkpatrick, the president of 1780, was afterwards Town Clerk. Mr. P. Farr was the brother of one of the aldermen, and Mr. Pope's father had been an alderman a few years before. On the other hand, only four presidents of the Dolphin elected between 1729 and 1832 were members of the Corporation at the time, viz., Mr. G. Danbeny, Alderman Vaughan, Alderman Daniel, and Mr. Sheriff Gardiner.

PRESIDENTS OF THE COLSTON SOCIETY

(Commonly called the Parent Society).

This list, which has never appeared in print before, was originally communicated to me by Alderman Fox, and I have since been enabled, by the kindness of Alderman Thatcher, to perfect it from the minutes of the Society. I am much indebted to these gentlemen and to Alderman Cope-Proctor for facilitating my researches.

1739 Richard Warren	1745 John Pinke
1740 John Little	1746 Thomas Smith
1741 Arthur Hart	1747 William Hart, sen.
1742 Robert Smith	1748 Jarrit Smith, M.P.
1743 William Berrow	1749 Sidenham Teast
1744 Henry Gresley	1750 Joseph Lewis

PRESIDENTS OF THE COLSTON SOCIETY.—*Continued.*

1751 William Hart, jun.
1752 Right Hon. Edward Southwell, M.P.
1753 Nathaniel Day, Alderman
1754 Thomas Chester, M.P.
1755 Norborne Berkeley, M.P.
1756 Charles Bragge
1757 John Tandy
1758 Richard Blake
1759 Josiah Ross
1760 William Aleyne
1761 William Phelps
1762 Joseph Percival
1763 John Perks
1764 Samuel Smith
1765 Stephen Bagg
1766 William Gore
1767 Charles Hotchkin, Common Councillor
1768 Henry Hobhouse
1769 Francis Brown
1770 William Eagles
1771 Robert Jackson
1772 Robert Vigor
1773 Edward Sampson
1774 William Barrett
1775 John Mereweather
1776 John Cooke
1777 Joseph Wilson
1778 John Hugh Smyth
1779 John Mayo
1780 Winchcombe Henry Hartley, M.P.
1781 Michael Miller
1782 Matthew Brickdale, M.P.
1783 John Powell
1784 Henry Hobhouse
1785 Timothy Powell
1786 Richard Plaister
1787 John Vaughan
1788 Richard Symes
1789 Thomas Warren
1790 The Duke of Beaufort
1791 Thomas Eagles
1792 Richard Haynes
1793 John Cave
1794 Thomas Smyth
1795 John Tyler
1796 William Westley
1797 Robert Watkins
1798 William Hayward Winstone
1799 William Moncrieffe, M.D.
1800 Timothy Powell
1801 Peter Lilly
1802 Joshua Powell
1803 James Brown

1804 The Duke of Beaufort

[James Brown appears to have presided for him.]

1805 Samuel Edwards
1806 Thomas Hungerford Powell
1807 Thomas Daniel, Alderman
1808 Peter Clissold
1809 Thomas Cole
1810 Joseph Dyer
1811 James Leman
1812 Thomas Shute, M.D.
1813 Lord Robert Edward Henry Somerset.

[James Brown appears to have presided for him.]

1814 James Sutton
1815 William Holder

[Thomas Corser appears to have presided for him.]

1816 William Stock
1817 John Haythorne, Alderman
1818 Thomas Corser
1819 Thomas Curtis Leman

[Robert Jenkins presided for him.]

1820 William Jones
1821 Benjamin Bickley

[Thomas Corser presided for him.]

1822 Henry Overton Wills
1823 John Acraman

[William Purnell presided for him.]

1824 William Lambe Willshire
1825 William Cooke
1826 Francis Freeling

[William Purnell presided for him.]

1827 George Henry Freeling

[John Haythorne, Alderman, presided for him.]

1828 George Wyld

PRESIDENTS OF THE COLSTON SOCIETY,—*Continued.*

1829 Robert Jenkins, Common Councillor
[Thomas Curtis Leman presided for him.]
1830 Charles Hare
[William Bell, the President-elect, died before the date of the dinner.]
1831 No meeting in consequence of the riots.
1832 John Tomlinson
[William Purnell presided for him.]
1833 Jasper Westcott
1834 Samuel Crady Edwards
1835 Samuel Lucas
1836 John Rocke Panter
1837 William Purnell
[Samuel Lucas presided for him.]
1838 Henry Attwood
[William Purnell presided for him.]
1839 John Steele
1840 Benjamin Purnell
1841 Richard Jenkins Poole King, Councillor
1842 William Fripp, J.P., Alderman
1843 John Howell, J.P., Councillor
1844 Thomas Still
1845 William Hopton Wyld, Alderman
1846 Thomas Lucas, Alderman
1847 Matthew Perkins, Councillor
1848 John Hopton Wyld
1849 William Powell
1850 Charles Bowles Hare, Councillor
1851 Robert Phippen, J.P., Councillor
1852 John Warry
1853 William Thomas Poole King, Councillor
1854 John Hare, Councillor
1855 John Russ Grant
1856 John Lucas
1857 William Hellier Baily
1858 Charles Stewart Clarke
1859 Joel Gardner

1860 The Rev. Martin Henry Whish
1861 Thomas Proctor, Alderman
1862 John Warry, jun.
1863 Sholto Vere Hare, J.P., Alderman
1864 Henry Abbot, Alderman
1865 Thomas Wilson Hall
1866 William Augustus Frederick Powell, Councillor
1867 Richard Gibbs
1868 George William Edwards
1869 James Baily
[John Lucas presided for him.]
1870 George Frederick Fox
1871 The Rev. George Madan
[William H. Edwards, the President-elect, died before the date of the dinner.]
1872 Elias George Hall
1873 William Frayne
1874 William Taylor
1875 George Gardiner
1876 George William Lucas
1877 John Frederick Lucas, Alderman
1878 Charles Thornton Jefferies
1879 Francis Frederick Fox, J.P., Alderman
1880 William Smith, J.P., Councillor
1881 William Proctor Baker, J.P., Alderman
1882 William Merrett Webb
1883 John Reed Farler
1884 Henry Grace Hare
1885 Mervyn Kersteman King
1886 Sydney Gray Bees
1887 Charles Bowles Hare, J.P., Councillor
1888 Joseph Lovell Gibbs
[H. R. Gibbs presided for him.]
1889 Arthur Baker, J.P., Councillor
1890 Edmund Ambrose King
1891 Harry Willoughby Beloe
1892 Richard Cripps
1893 William Hurle Clarke

PRESIDENTS OF THE COLSTON SOCIETY.—*Continued.*

1894 Stephen George James, J.P.
[Edward Burnet James, Councillor, presided for him.]

1895 Charles William Cope-Proctor, Alderman.
1896 Edward Beadon Colthurst, Councillor
1897 Henry Kater Cripps

President-elect for 1898—Edward John Thatcher, Alderman.

The dates given above are those of the dinners, the President being annually elected in the preceding year.

According to the rules of the Society each member is liable to take the chair in succession, according to seniority of admission, subject to a fine in case of refusal.

The following is a list of members who have declined to serve in their respective turns :

For the year
1743 Edward Oliver
1757 George Randolph, M.D.
1760 Richard Rogers
1763 James Purnell
1774 Alexander Colston
1775 John Tandy, Timothy Gyde
1777 Joseph Thomas
1788 and 1789, John Ford, M.D.
1792 Robert Smith
1800 William Hicks
1801 William Miles, Alderman, Sir John Durbin, Alderman, William Delpratt, and James Vaughan
1803 John Maxse
1806 James Ireland
1807 John Tyndall Warre and Lowbridge Bright
1810 James Tobin, Robert Bush, and Sydenham Teast
1813 Thomas Sanders
1814 John Lambert
1816 Thomas Graeme
1818 Sir Henry Cann Lippincott, Bart., and George Eddie Sanders

For the year
1820 John Naish Sanders and John Elton
1822 William Clissold
1827 Isaac Cooke
1828 John Bartlett Hill
1830 James Clark and Joshua Powell, jun.
1833 Samuel Reynolds Wilmot
1836 Thomas Stock, Alderman
1841 John Clark
1844 John Fothergill and John Kerle Haberfield, Councillor
1845 Alfred B'cock
1846 Samuel Brown
1854 Thomas Drake
1855 William Cooper
1863 Thomas Tanner Harris and John Farler
1868 Samuel Lucas. the Rev. George Campbell, the Rev. John Martin Hale Whish, and George Godwin
1878 T. W. Wickham
1879 Samuel Wilfred Lucas and William Proctor
1890 Charles Phipps Lucas
1896 C. F. S. Abbot

TREASURERS.

Elected
1739 John Fisher
1742 John Little
1752 John Tandy
1755 John Pinke
1765 Joseph Wilson
1790 William Fry
1793 Richard Plaister
1799 Peter Lilly
1807 Joshua Powell
1825 William Cooke

Elected
1841 William Hopton Wyld
1853 John Hopton Wyld
1857 William Hellier Baily
1864 James Baily
1867 John Warry, jun.
1885 William H. Butt
1890 William Paul Hudden
1891 Charles Bowles Hare
1893 Edward John Thatcher

THE COLSTON SOCIETY.—*Continued.*

SECRETARIES.

1825 Samuel Lucas
1841 John Lucas

1878 Charles William Cope-Proctor

Sir G. Edwards presided over three of the four Colston Societies, viz., Parent, Dolphin, and Grateful. 14 gentlemen have occupied the chair of two of them, viz.:

Parent and Dolphin :—Messrs. S. Smith, Dr. Moncrieffe, W. Fripp, S. V. Hare, and C. S. Clarke.

Dolphin and Grateful :—Sir J. K. Haberfield.

Parent and Grateful :—Messrs. J. Powell*, H. Abbot, and F. F. Fox.

Anchor and Grateful :—Sir H. Protheroe, Sir J. D. Weston, Messrs. Rowand, E. S. Robinson, and F. J. Fry.

[* The early minutes of the Grateful Society being lost, it is impossible to identify with certainty the John Powell who was President in 1772, but he was probably the Collector of Customs, who was President of the Parent in 1783 and Master of the Merchant Venturers in 1779. The President of the Parent was not identical with the President of the Dolphin in 1762.]

SOCIETY OF ST. STEPHEN'S RINGERS.

The date of the foundation of this Society is not known. It existed in the reign of Queen Elizabeth, and its annual meeting is held, unless under exceptional circumstances, on November 17, the anniversary of her accession. The ordinances of the Society date from 1620. The early minute books are lost, the oldest now in possession of the Society beginning with 1732, at which period John Hobbs was the senior surviving, and Thomas Horwood the immediate, Past Master. The records in the existing minute books were not always made with the accuracy which has marked the entries of more recent years; there are several errors both of omission and commission ; but with the valuable co-operation of my friend, Mr. Fuller Eberle, who has given a great deal of time to the solution of the difficulties thus presented, I have been enabled to compile what I believe is a complete and accurate list of Masters and Wardens of this Antient Society from 1732 to the present time. The succession of Wardens has never before appeared

SOCIETY OF ST. STEPHEN'S RINGERS.—*Continued.*

in print, and that of Masters, which was published some years ago in the *Times and Mirror*, was very far from accurate. It may be interesting to readers of the *Times and Mirror* to notice that the first press mention of the Society's meetings is contained in the *Bristol Mirror* of December 7, 1822, and that the Father of the Society is Mr. T. D. Taylor, who was admitted to membership as far back as 1846.

[In the following lists the first date is that of election, the second that of the dinner, at which the Master presided in person or by deputy. It will be noticed that during the last 30 years it has been usual to go through the regular gradation of Junior and Senior Warden and Master in successive years, as is the case with the Society of Merchant Venturers.]

(The first name in each paragraph is that of Master, the second and third are those of Wardens.)

1732—1733, Stephen Baugh; Christopher Willoughby and Walter Middleton.
1733, Sept. 29—1738, James Laroche, Common Councillor; Michael Becher and John Gythens.

[No meeting was held between 1733 and 1738.]

1738, Sept. 29—1741, Joseph Jones; Samuel Gardner, jun., and Robert Wilcox
1741, Nov. 17—1742, Joseph Jones; John Pollard and John Beaton
1742, Sept. 29—1743, John Pollard; John Perks and Thomas Gibbs
1743, Oct. 20—1744, John Beaton; Richard Lowe and David Campbell
1744, Sept. 29—1745, Thomas Gibbs; Edward Gwatkin and Robert Bound
1745, Oct. 6—1746, Richard Lowe; Edward Gwatkin and Robert Bound
1746, Sept. 29—1747, David Campbell; John Pollard and Thomas Gibbs
1747, Sept. 29—1748, Robert Bound; Richard Seaborne and James Bowyer, jun.
1748, Sept. 29—1749, Richard Seaborne; George Escott and Henry Smith
1749, Sept. 29—1750, James Bowyer, jun.; Nathaniel Hodgson and Charles Swanton
1750, Sept. 29—1751, George Escott; John Neale and Valentine Watkins
1751, Sept. 30—1752, Henry Smith; James Bonbonous and William Clymer
1752, Sept. 29—1753, Nathaniel Hodgson; Richard Sheldon and Worthington Brice
1753, Sept. 29—1754, Valentine Watkins; William Pynn and Gilbert Davis
1754, Sept. 30—1755, James Bonbonous; Peter Wells and Richard Robinson
1755, Sept. 29—1756, William Clymer; George Welch and Joseph Shapland
1756, Sept. 29—1757, Richard Sheldon; Thomas Prankerd and Philip Jarrett
1757, Sept. 29—1758, William Pynn; Samuel Berry and Gilbert Davis
1758, Oct. 5—1759, Worthington Brice; Marmaduke Coules and William Sladen

SOCIETY OF ST. STEPHEN'S RINGERS.—*Continued*.

1759, Sept. 29—1760, Gilbert Davis; Roger Watts and Thomas Griffin
1760, Sept. 29—1761, George Welch; William Blake and Edmund Fidoe
1761, Sept. 29—1762, Joseph Shapland; William Clymer and Thomas Griffin
1762, Sept. 29—1763, Roger Watts ; Edmund Fidoe and John Powell
1763, Sept. 29—1764, Thomas Griffin; William Blake and Thomas Owen
1764, Sept. 29—1765, William Blake ; John Sinclair and Diedrich Meyerhoff
1765, Sept. 30—1766, Edmund Fidoe; James Laroche, jun., Common Councillor, and John Davis
1766, Sept. 29—1767, John Powell; Edward Davis and William James
1767, Sept. 29—1768. Diedrich Meyerhoff; Thomas Griffiths and Griffith Maskelyn
1768, Sept. 29—1769, James Laroche, jun., Common Councillor; Samuel Span and Constantine Phipps
1769, Sept. 29—1770, John Sinclair; William Gibbons and John James
1770, Sept. 29—1771. John Davis; William Stevenson and Thomas Perkins
1771, Oct. 10—1772, Edward Davis; Godfrey Lowe and Samuel Deipratt
1772, Sept. 29—1773, William James ; William Rogers Jones and Charles Harford
1773, Sept. 29—1774, Thomas Griffiths; John Mallard and Gilbert Davis, jun
1774, Sept. 29—1775, Griffith Maskelyn; William Dighton and Francis Jacques
1775. Oct. 24—1776. Samuel Span ; Francis Owen and John Evans
1776, Sept. 30—1777, William Rogers Jones ; James Norman and John Woodward
1777, Sept. 29—1778, William Gibbons; Robert Shute and Edward Rosser
1778, Oct. 9—1779, Charles Harford; Paul Farr and William Jones
1779, Nov. 12—1780, Gilbert Davis; William Broderip and Lancelot Cowper
1780, Sept. 29—1781, James Norman; Colin Drummond, M.D., and Charles Harford, jun.
1781, Nov. 9—1782, Edward Rosser; John Clark and James Taylor
1782, Oct. 29—1783, John Woodward; Joseph Wood and Thomas Aldridge
1783, Oct. 13—1784, William Broderip; George Packer McCarthy and James Williams
1784, Oct. 30—1785, Colin Drummond. M.D.; Benjamin Lawrence and Robert Howe
1785. Sept. 29, Charles Harford, jun. (declined), and 1785, Nov. 17—1786. Joseph Wood ; John Maddick and Morgan Yeatman
1786, Oct. 27- 1787, Thomas Aldridge; John Anderson, Alderman, and John Chubb
1787, Oct. 11—1788, George Packer McCarthy; William Fox and Philip Furse.
1788, Oct. 14—1789, Robert Howe ; George King and Richard Aldridge
1789, Sept. 29—1790, John Maddick; Thomas Andrewes and John James
1790, Sept. 29—1791, John Anderson, Alderman ; William Acraman and Benjamin Bickley
1791, Sept. 29—1792. John Chubb; James Ewer and John Franklyn
1792, Sept. 2 —1793. George King ; Philip George and Henry Cooke

SOCIETY OF ST. STEPHEN'S RINGERS.—*Continued.*

1793, Sept. 30—1794, William Fox; Richard Price and Joshua Springer
1794, Oct. 16—1795, Philip Furse; James Harvey, Common Councillor, and Thomas Bowdich
1795, Sept. 29—1796, William Acraman; Robert Bigg and Henry Richards
1796, Sept. 29—1797, Benjamin Bickley; Chamberlain Cox and Edward Bird
1797, Sept. 29—1798, Thomas Andrewes; Philip Jones and Richard Robinson
1798, Oct. 12—1799, John Franklyn; William Tanner and John Span, Common Councillor
1799, Nov. 12—1800, Richard Price; William Broom and Samuel Span, Common Councillor
1800, Sept. 29—1801, Joshua Springer; Worthington Brice, Common Councillor, and Richard Lambert
1801, Oct. 30—1802, James Harvey, Alderman; Charles Anderson, Common Councillor, and Daniel Wade Acraman
1802, Nov. 10—1803, Thomas Bowdich; William Priest and William Robert James
1803, Sept. 29—1804, Robert Bigg; John Barrow and William Oliver
1804, Oct. 30, Chamberlain Cox; Thomas Coates and Henry Bengough, Alderman

[Messrs. Cox and Bengough declined to serve, and on November 9 Edward Bird and Charles Harvey were elected Master and Warden respectively. Mr. Bird also declined the Master's chair, and on November 14 Philip Jones was elected, and he presided at the dinner of 1805. Mr. Coates died June 13, 1805; there is no record of his successor as Warden.]

1805, Nov. 6—1806, William Tanner; William Inman, Sheriff and Common Councillor, and Charles Harford
1806, Nov. 12—1807, Worthington Brice, Common Councillor; William Hood and Thomas Morgan Hobbs
1807, Sept. 29—1808, Richard Lambert; Norman Daunsey Southall and Richard Priest
1808, Sept. 29—1809, Charles Anderson, Common Councillor; Joseph Bonbonous and Henry Daniel
1809, Nov. 15—1810, Edward Bird; William Gibbons and John Acraman
1810, Sept. 29, John Barrow (declined), and 1810—1811, William Oliver; Lewis Fisher and William Merrick
1811, Sept. 30—1812, Charles Harvey; James Room, jun., and Charles Hodges
1812, Sept. 29—1813, Charles Harford; Joseph Bally and William Acraman
1813, Sept. 29—1814, William Hood; Thomas Corser and James Lean

[John Lane was elected November 9, 1814, to take the place of Mr. Lean, who was prevented by illness from acting at the dinner.]

1814, Nov. 9—1815, Thomas Morgan Hobbs; John Haythorne, Alderman, and Ebenezer Ludlow
1815, Nov. 17—1816, Joseph Bonbonous; William Underwood and Robert Howe

[According to the minutes, Messrs. Hobbs and Bonbonous were elected to serve for the years 1815 and 1816 respectively, but they appear to have exchanged years, as the former presided in 1816 and the latter in 1815.]

1816, Sept. 30—1817, Henry Daniel; Thomas Carter and George Edwards.

SOCIETY OF ST. STEPHEN'S RINGERS.—*Continued.*

1817, Dec. 17, William Merrick (resigned), and 1818, April 30—1818, James Room, jun.; Thomas Lewis and Lancelot Beck.
1818, Nov. 16—1819, Joseph Bally; Thomas Fuidge and Charles Granger.
[Mr. Fuidge served in place of William Scott, declined.]
1819, Nov. 16—1820, William Acraman, jun.; John Lane and Henry Revell Llewellin
[Mr. Llewellin served in place of Henry Smith, declined.]
1820, Nov. 2—1821, James Lean; Henry Smith and James Perry
1821, Nov. 13—1822, John Haythorne, Alderman; Thomas Elias Danson and Thomas Stone
1822, Nov. 25—1823, Charles Granger; Richard Fuidge and Charles Grevile
1823, Nov. 10—1824, John Howell; Thomas Lewis and Lionel Oliver Bigg
1824, Nov. 10—1825, Thomas Fuidge; Thomas Wintle and Robert Dyer
1825, Nov.—1826, Richard Smith; John Adams Ames and John Mills
1826, Oct. 30, Lionel Oliver Bigg; George Edwards and Antonio Lopez Vildosola
1826-1827, George Edwards; Philip Jones and William Pritchard
[Messrs. Bigg and Vildosola declined to serve, and Mr. Edwards was then transferred from the Wardenship to the Master's chair.]
1827, Oct. 10—1828, John Mills; John Kirby and William Lury Riddle
[The two Wardens declined, and were succeeded by Thomas Mullett Evans and John Farr.]
1828, Nov. 1—1829, Thomas Wintle; John Fargus and Richard Thomas Williams
1829, Oct. 12—1830, Thomas Camplin, Alderman; William Strong and James Gillett
1830, Oct. 30—1832, John Haythorne, Alderman; Richard Davis and Jacob Strickland
[Owing to the riots, no dinner was held in 1831, and at the meeting of 1832 Richard Smith presided for Alderman Haythorne.]
1832, Nov. 14—1833, John Miller; Charles Peter Branstrom Howell and Richard Stoate
[Mr. Stoate declined to serve, and was succeeded by Robert Mullett Evans.]
1833, Nov. 7, Thomas Mullett Evans; Charles Innes Pocock and Richard Robinson, jun.
[Mr. Evans died May 5, 1834, and there is no record of any dinner having been held in that year. Joseph Grazebrook appears to have been elected Warden in place of Mr. Pocock.]
1834, Nov. 12—1835, Edward Sampson; Robert Gould and Alfred Bleeck
[Richard Robinson, jun., served instead of Mr. Gould. The dinner for the year 1835 was not held till December 4, when Mr. Sampson, whose year of office had expired, presided.]
1835, Nov. 17—1836, Charles Ludlow Walker, Councillor; William Lury Riddle and Joseph Grazebrook
1836, Nov. 7—1837, John Kerle Haberfield, Alderman; Samuel Gustavus Clements and William Morgan
[Thomas Sheppard served instead of Mr. Morgan.]

SOCIETY OF ST. STEPHEN'S RINGERS.—*Continued.*

1837, Nov. 8—1838, Peter Maze, jun.; Henry Chidgey Quinton and Charles Bowles Hare

[Thomas Charles Cornish served instead of Mr. Hare.]

1838, Nov. 3—1839, Richard Robinson; George Piercy Whittall and James Marks Masey
1839, Nov. 11—1840, William Strong; Thomas Saunders Parnell and Thomas Doddrell

[Jarvis Holland Ash served instead of Mr. Doddrell.]

1840, Nov. 4, Henry Bush, Councillor; James Ford and James Bush

[Messrs. H. Bush and Ford declined to serve.]

1840, Nov. 14—1841, James Norroway Franklyn, Councillor; John Harding, Councillor (*vice* Ford)
1841, Nov. 6—1842, James Gibbs, Alderman; Thomas Fuidge, jun., and Francis Savage, jun.
1842, Nov. 1, Samuel Gustavus Clements; Joseph Wintle and William Bartlett James

[Messrs. Clements and Wintle declined to serve.]

1842-1843, John Harding, Councillor; Henry Robert Fargus (*vice* Wintle)
1843, Nov. 4—1844, Henry Chidgey Quinton; James Poole, jun., and Thomas Canning

[Alderman Robinson presided at the dinner for Mr. Quinton. Richard Fuidge served as Warden instead of Mr. Canning.]

1844, Nov. 6—1845, Francis Savage; Charles Joseph Vining and Charles Hassell

[Charles Blisset, Councillor, presided at the dinner for Mr. Savage.]

1845, Nov. 7—1846, James Bush; Joseph Wintle and Thomas Canning
1846, Nov. 10—1847, James Poole, jun.; William Vining, jun., and William Fuidge
1847, Nov. 10—1848, John George Shaw, Councillor; Henry Dayrell and Francis Adams
1848, Oct. 27—1849, Charles Joseph Vining; Alfred Robinson and Daniel Burges, jun.
1849, Oct. 27—1850, Thomas Saunders Parnell; Henry Sidney Wasbrough and George Gibbs
1850, Nov. 9—1851, William Fuidge; Samuel Edward Taylor and John Marsh Jones

[Richard Manning Hayman served instead of Mr. Taylor.]

1851, Nov. 5—1852, Henry Robert Fargus; George Cornish Glasson and W. H. Brown

[James Harris served instead of Mr. Brown.]

1852, Nov. 6—1853, Daniel Burges, jun.; William Butcher and Charles Stopford
1853, Nov. 6—1854, Henry Sidney Wasbrough; Richard Hathaway and Henry Ariel Clark
1854, Nov. 11—1855, George Cornish Glasson; George Cornish Glasson, jun., and Samuel Butcher
1855, Nov.—1856, Francis Savage; Frederick Fargus and John Danger

[Thomas Drummond served instead of Mr. Danger.]

1856, Nov.—1857, Charles Hassell; Cam Gyde Heaven, Councillor, and Thomas Pike

SOCIETY OF ST. STEPHEN'S RINGERS.—*Continued.*

1857, Nov. 3—1858, Richard Manning Hayman; Philip Douglas Alexander and Francis Frederick Fox.

1858, Nov. 4—1859, Richard Fuidge, Councillor; William Fripp, jun. and George Gibbs

[John Gunning served instead of Mr. Gibbs.]

1859, Nov. 2—1860, William Butcher; James Creswell Wall and Joseph Graham Guy

[Mr. Gay died before the annual dinner, and Thomas Pike was chosen Warden in his place.]

1860, Nov. 8—1861, Frederick Fargus; Charles Wintle and David Poole

1861, Nov. 6—1862, Thomas Pike; John Frost and Charles Joseph Vining

[John Gunning presided at the dinner.]

1862-3, James Creswell Wall; Edward W. Perrin and Charles F. Kemball

[The minutes for this year are lost (apparently they were never entered), and I have been unable to find the name of the Master originally elected. Messrs. Wall and Joseph Almond are put down as Wardens in a MS. list, but the newspapers in reporting the dinner of 1863 record that Mr H. R. Fargus presided in the absence of the Master, Mr. Wall, owing to a family bereavement, and that Messrs. Perrin and Kemball were the Wardens. Mr. Almond served as Warden in the following year.]

1863, Nov. 7—1864, James Creswell Wall; Joseph Almond and John Wood

1864, Nov. 7—1865, Joseph Almond; Frederick James and John Glasson

1865, Nov.—1866, Frederick James; Robert Gray Barnes and Charles Fisher

[Mr. Fisher resigned, and John Frederick Lucas was chosen in his place. Nov. 7, 1866, to act at the dinner.]

1866, Nov. 7—1867, Robert Gray Barnes; William Charles Beloe and Mervyn Kersteman King

1867, Nov. 7—1869, Mervyn Kersteman King; Ralph Henry Cole and Richard Cripps

[There was no dinner in 1868: it was originally postponed on account of the General Election taking place in November, and afterwards abandoned out of respect to the memory of Frederick Fargus and John Wood, recently deceased. On November 11, 1868, Francis Frederick Fox, Alderman, was elected Warden for the intended dinner in that year, in place of Mr. Cole, and on Dec. 3, 1868, Mr. Cripps was re-elected Warden for 1869, with Frederick John Fargus as his colleague.]

1869, Nov. 11—1870, Richard Cripps; Henry Grace Hare and Lewis Morris

[Both Wardens declined to serve, and were succeeded Nov. 11, 1870, by James Anthony Gardner and William Lemon.]

1870, Nov. 11—1871, James Anthony Gardner; William Lemon and William Lyne Fear

1871, Nov. 28—1872, William Lemon; George Nichols and James Austin Ware

SOCIETY OF ST. STEPHEN'S RINGERS.—*Continued.*

1872, Nov. 6—1873, George Nichols; James Austin Ware and Charles William Paul
1873, Nov. 7—1874, James Austin Ware; Charles William Paul and Donald McArthur
1874, Oct. 26—1875, Charles William Paul; Donald McArthur and Alfred George de Lisle Bush

[Mr. McArthur declined to serve, and was succeeded by Frederick John Fargus. The 1875 dinner was postponed till January 31, 1876.]

1875, Nov. 12—1876, Frederick John Fargus; Alfred George de Lisle Bush and John Morgan
1876, Oct. 28—1877, Alfred George de Lisle Bush; John Morgan and Thomas Watkins Baker
1877, Oct. 30—1878, John Morgan; Thomas Watkins Baker and George Pearson
1878, Nov. 4—1879, Thomas Watkins Baker; George Pearson and Samuel Lang
1879, Nov.—1880, George Pearson; Samuel Lang and Charles Octavius Harvey
1880, Oct. 13—1881, Samuel Lang; Charles Octavius Harvey and John Abraham
1881, Oct.—1882, Charles Octavius Harvey; John Abraham and Arthur James Williams Bennett
1882, Oct. 31—1883, John Abraham; Arthur James Williams Bennett and William Arthur Jones
1883, Oct. 22—1884, Arthur James Williams Bennett; William Arthur Jones and Frederick Fox Cartwright
1884, Nov. 3—1885, William Arthur Jones; Frederick Fox Cartwright and John Henry Goodenough Taylor
1885, Nov. 3—1886, Frederick Fox Cartwright; John Henry Goodenough Taylor and James Fuller Eberle, Councillor
1886, Oct. 26—1887, John Henry Goodenough Taylor; James Fuller Eberle, Councillor, and William Henderson

[Mr. A. B. James was elected Junior Warden, but declined to serve that year.]

1887, Oct. 24—1888, James Fuller Eberle, Councillor; William Henderson and Alfred Bartlett James
1888, Oct. 10—1889, William Henderson; Alfred Bartlett James and Charles William Cope Proctor, Alderman
1889, Oct. 10—1890, Alfred Bartlett James; Charles William Cope-Proctor, Alderman, and Charles Robert Hancock

[Alderman Cope-Proctor declined and Frank William Wills was elected in his place.]

1890, Oct. 15—1891, Charles Robert Hancock; Frank William Wills and Edward W. B. Villiers

[Mr. Villiers declined and was succeeded by Arthur Vivian James.]

1891, Oct. 12—1892, Frank William Wills; Arthur Vivian James and Beverley Robinson Vachell

[Mr. Vachell declined and Alderman Cope-Proctor was elected in his place, Nov. 10, 1891.]

SOCIETY OF ST. STEPHEN'S RINGERS.—*Continued.*

1892, Sept. 30—1893. Arthur Vivian James; Charles William Cope-Proctor, Alderman, and John Day Miller
1893, Oct. 20—1894. Charles William Cope-Proctor, Alderman; John Day Miller and John Nichols
1894, Oct. 12—1895. John Day Miller; John Nichols and Michael Bowring Castle
1895, Oct. 25—1896. John Nichols; Michael Bowring Castle and Allan McArthur
1896, Oct. 13—1897. Michael Bowring Castle; Allan McArthur and William Proctor
1897, Oct. 1—1898. Allan McArthur; William Proctor and Gerald Lysaght

THE GLOUCESTERSHIRE SOCIETY.

The Presidents of this ancient charitable society include a large number of Bristol citizens, whose names occur in other lists connected with the city. The following succession of Stewards (as they were originally styled) and Presidents has been furnished me by the secretary, Mr. F. A. Jenkins, and I have noted those who were members of the Bristol Corporation at the dates of their respective appointments.

The society was established on December 1, 1657. Up to 1892 the society's year ended in August; in that year it was decided that in future it should end in December, and Mr. Perceval, the President elected in 1892 for 1892-3, retained office till the close of 1893.

The annual dinner of the society was discontinued after 1890.

STEWARDS.

		Collections
1658	Thomas Bubb, Common Councillor ...	£5 4 4
1659	Jonathan Blackwell, Common Councillor	5 9 4
1660	John Lawford, Common Councillor ...	3 6 4
1661	Thomas Wickham	4 7 0
1662	Henry Gough, Common Councillor ...	3 5 5
1663	John Hicks, Common Councillor	

[No meeting, on account of the visit of the King and Queen, with the Duke and Duchess of York, to Bristol.]

| 1664 | John Hicks, Common Councillor ... | 2 17 9 |
| 1665 | Walter Tocknell | |

[No meeting, on account of the prevalence of the plague. There is no record of a meeting or of an election of Steward for 1666 and 1667.]

THE GLOUCESTERSHIRE SOCIETY.—*Continued.*

		£	s.	d.
1668	Walter Tocknell	5	1	6
1669	Richard Crumpe, Common Councillor	4	9	4
1670	Edward Hurne, Sheriff and Common Councillor	6	7	5
1671	Samuel Wharton	4	1	0
1672	Edward Feilding, Common Councillor	9	2	0
1673	John Robins	6	14	3
1674	William Brown, Common Councillor	5	5	0
1675	John Erkly	6	16	3
1676	Samuel Hale, Common Councillor	4	9	2
1677	John Lawford, Alderman	4	16	0
1678	Thomas Green	4	6	3
1679	Thomas Oldfield	3	6	11
1680	John England	3	10	0
1681	Robert Bound	3	18	10
1682	Thomas Wilcox	4	2	6
1683	Charles Wintour	2	14	0

[By a resolution of the society, August 10, 1683, it was decided to exchange the title of Steward to that of President.]

PRESIDENTS.

		£	s.	d.
1684	Sir Richard Crumpe, Alderman	2	19	0
1685	Nathaniel Driver, Common Councillor	3	10	3
1686	Thomas Hicks	3	5	3
1687	John Chesshire	2	14	0
1688	John Sandford	4	7	9
1689	Abraham Elton	3	11	3
1690	William Clark	4	5	0
1691	Edward Millard	3	6	6
1692	Robert Bound	4	6	0
1693	Nathaniel Wade	4	15	4
1694	George Bryan	5	0	0
1695	Nicholas Standfast	5	17	9
1696	Robert Kirke, Common Councillor	5	4	6
1697	Thomas Tyler	6	2	0
1698	Onesiphorus Tyndall	5	8	6
1699	Thomas Clements	7	1	6
1700	Thomas Hort, Common Councillor	5	11	6
1701	[No meeting on account of the visit of the Queen to Bristol.]			
1702	Richard Bayly, Sheriff and Common Councillor	2	12	6
1703	Nicholas Hicks	7	7	0
1704	Benjamin Turner	7	1	0
1705	William Stratton	7	0	3
1706	John Corsley	7	12	6
1707	George Packer	7	13	0
1708	Henry Fane	6	10	0
1709	Jonathan Elliott	7	16	9
1710	Morgan Smith, Common Councillor	17	19	3
1711	Samuel Jacob	11	1	9
1712	Charles Grevile	16	4	6
1713	William Bayly, Common Councillor	25	18	9
1714	John Paul	7	6	6
1715	Abraham Elton, Alderman, M.P.	11	0	0
1716	Samuel Fox	5	10	6
1717	Peter Hardwicke, M.D.	10	18	0

THE GLOUCESTERSHIRE SOCIETY.—*Continued.*

Year	Name	£	s	d
1718	George Martin	12	7	9
1719	Richard Price	10	18	0
1720	James Davie	19	4	0
1721	Abraham Alyes	6	15	6
1722	Robert Summers	17	14	6
1723	Charles Penrose	18	2	6
1724 to 1727 the records are missing.				
1728	John Russell	22	19	6
1729	William Cann	26	9	0
1730	Edmund Brown	–	–	–
1731	James Hardwicke	41	2	6
1732	Samuel Adams	49	12	6
1733	Nicholas Careless	82	5	6
1734	Rice Charlton	51	11	0
1735	John Morse	68	10	6
1736	Thomas Coster, M.P.	56	18	0
1737	Richard Tombs	58	1	6
1738	Thomas Ashmead	50	1	0
1739	Richard Warren	47	15	0
1740	Thomas Stephens	50	19	6
1741	John Taylor	50	1	0
1742	Job Gardiner	60	11	6
1743	Matthew Wayne	53	3	0
1744	John Pitman	67	5	3
1745	James Whitfield	66	9	6
1746	Richard Blake	72	1	0
1747	James Bowyer, jun.	62	1	0
1748	James Bowyer, jun.	80	10	6
1749 and 1750 the records are missing.				
1751	George Escott	69	2	0
1752	Sidenham Teast	85	0	6
1753	Nicholas Perry	101	4	0
1754	John Wade	121	11	6
1755	William Richards	109	10	9
1756	William Tombs	102	7	6
1757	Nathaniel Daniel	118	13	6
1758	Stephen Bagg	157	0	3
1759	Richard Parker	178	4	3
1760	Valentine Watkins	214	3	3
1761	Henry Cotton	164	7	3
1762	John Bush	160	16	0
1763	Webb Weston	145	4	0
1764	Thomas Sandell	117	3	0
1765	Joshua Power	143	14	0
1766	Michael Clayfield	147	6	0
1767	Robert Bush	140	15	0
1768	Richard Hayward	108	13	0
1769	Henry Burgum	178	2	0
1770	The Duke of Beaufort	285	6	0
1771	Edward Southwell, M.P.	306	12	9
1772	Winchcombe Henry Hartley	195	2	6
1773	Robert Jackson	211	0	0
1774	Edward Sampson	176	1	0
1775	Matthew Hale	226	1	0
1776	The Earl of Berkeley	312	5	0
1777	Matthew Brickdale, Common Councillor	323	17	0
1778	William Bromley Chester, M.P.	337	12	0
1779	Sir William Guise, Bart., M.P.	282	0	6
1780	Thomas Bathurst	262	10	6
1781	Thomas Estcourt	210	15	6

THE GLOUCESTERSHIRE SOCIETY.—*Continued.*

Year	Name	£	s	d
1782	James Dutton, M.P.	203	3	6
1783	Edward Andrews	180	19	6
1784	Samuel Blackwell, M.P.	139	7	6
1785	The Hon. George Cranfield Berkeley, M.P.	172	4	0
1786	Lord Apsley, M.P.	152	5	0
1787	Charles Westley Coxe	126	16	0
1788	William Hayward Winstone	141	19	0
1789	Thomas Master, M.P.	133	6	0
1790	Thomas Saunders	129	3	0
1791	Edward Loveden Loveden, M.P.	141	4	6
1792	William Hicks	140	14	0
1793	William Tyndall	130	4	0
1794	Samuel Edwards	131	15	6
1795	Lord de Clifford	159	1	6
1796	The Marquess of Worcester, M.P.	174	7	0
1797	Samuel Peach	181	9	0
1798	John Gordon, jun., Common Councillor	185	11	0
1799	Edward Andrews	157	10	0
1800	John Paul Paul	173	3	8
1801	Michael Hicks Beach, M.P.	175	10	6
1802	Lord Charles Henry Somerset, M.P.	177	7	0
1803	Anthony Palmer Collings	192	13	6
1804	Joel Gardiner	209	15	0
1805	Sir Henry Cann Lippincott, Bart.	195	6	6
1806	Isaac Elton	185	14	6
1807	The Right Hon. Charles Bathurst, M.P.	198	13	6
1808	Charles Joseph Harford	205	4	0
1809	Robert Bush	198	10	0
1810	Richard Hart Davis, M.P.	267	14	0
1811	Samuel Birch, Common Councillor	239	4	0
1812	Christopher Codrington, M.P.	205	7	0
1813	Lord Robert Edward Henry Somerset, M.P.	242	4	0
1814	Thomas Grimston Estcourt, M.P.	212	14	0
1815	Thomas Daniel, Alderman	234	17	0
1816	Rev. Charles Gore	199	11	0
1817	William Dowell	180	15	6
1818	John Ward	196	6	0
1819	Gabriel Goldney	212	0	0
1820	Samuel Webb	202	8	6
1821	Daniel Bayntun	212	15	0
1822	Henry Davis	195	8	6
1823	James Fowler, Alderman	236	10	0
1824	William Blathwayt	234	2	0
1825	The Marquess of Worcester, M.P.	259	15	9
1826	Sir Berkeley William Guise, Bart., M.P.	244	0	0
1827	Colonel William Gore Langton, M.P.	267	9	0
1828	John Vaughan, Esq.	282	8	6
1829	Rev. Robert John Charleton, D.D.	267	9	1
1830	Rev. George Cooke, D.D.	360	19	8
1831	Anniversary not celebrated in consequence of the Bristol riots. Subscriptions sent in	176	17	0
1832	Edward Sampson	389	6	6
1833	Colonel Edward Webb, M.P.	270	6	0
1834	William Miller	311	16	6
1835	Richard Brickdale Ward	374	5	6
1836	Robert Blagden Hale, M.P.	385	3	0
1837	Christopher William Codrington, M.P.	349	8	2
1838	John Savage, J.P.	407	16	8
1839	Charles Ludlow Walker	558	18	6

THE GLOUCESTERSHIRE SOCIETY.—*Continued.*

Year	Name	£	s.	d.
1840	William Miles, M.P.	473	15	0
1841	Francis Savage	415	19	0
1842	Ebenezer Ludlow, Serjeant-at-Law	445	5	0
1843	Winchcombe Henry Howard Hartley	374	6	0
1844	William Lewton Clarke, Mayor	443	15	7
1845	Robert Blagden Hale, M.P.	380	18	0
1846	Philip William Skynner Miles, M.P.	407	12	4
1847	Robert Stayner Holford	317	16	2
1848	John Decimus Pountney, Mayor and Alderman	320	0	0
1849	Henry Wenman Newman, J.P.	310	3	6
1850	Sir John Kerle Haberfield, Mayor and Councillor, J.P.	314	0	10
1851	Edward Sampson	316	8	8
1852	Henry Charles Harford	269	14	6
1853	Henry Shute	257	1	6
1854	Henry Ray	322	9	9
1855	George Woodroffe Franklyn, M.P.	250	12	6
1856	John Bolt, Q.C.	232	17	8
1857	John Vining, J.P., Mayor and Alderman	241	17	8
1858	Rev William Birkett Allen, D.C.L, Hon. Canon of Bristol	271	15	4
1859	Thomas Johnson Ward	333	15	6
1860	Rev. Charles Robert Davy, M.A.	287	10	10
1861	Stephen Cave, M.P.	307	17	4
1862	Thomas Daniel	289	5	9
1863	Sir George Samuel Jenkinson, Bart.	246	10	7
1864	William Osborne Maclaine	271	3	2
1865	The Duke of Beaufort	283	2	1
1866	Charles Daniel Cave	298	11	11
1867	John Battersby Harford	268	6	1
1868	Thomas William Chester Master	255	10	8
1869	William Henry Harford, jun., J.P., Councillor	266	19	7
1870	John William Miles	263	13	5
1871	Major-General Edward Arthur Somerset, C B.	269	3	10
1872	Rev. James Heyworth, M.A.	330	2	2
1873	Henry Cruger William Miles	282	6	0
1874	Rev. Sir Edward Harry Dutton Colt, Bart.	264	1	9
1875	Robert Gay Barrow, J.P., Alderman	253	8	7
1876	John Rolt	244	2	0
1877	John Altham Graham-Clarke	216	7	0
1878	The Hon. Randall Edward Sherborne Plunkett, M.P.	228	2	9
1879	George William Edwards, J.P., Mayor and Alderman	219	14	6
1880	Sir Gerald William Henry Codrington, Bart.	201	3	3
1881	John S. Smyth Osbourne	219	18	4
1882	Francis Frederick Fox, J.P., Alderman	224	5	1
1883	Robert Low Grant Vassall	212	17	3
1884	Henry Bourchier Osborne Savile, Sheriff	168	11	8
1885	William Edwards George, Alderman	144	11	0
1886	William Harrington Bush	162	15	10
1887	George Walters Daubeny	207	5	2
1888	Captain George Henry Bridges	166	14	1
1889	Henry Carpenter Ray	160	5	2
1890	Robert Hilhouse Bush	176	1	3

THE GLOUCESTERSHIRE SOCIETY.—*Continued.*

			£ s. d.
1891	Jeremiah Osborne	... ...	161 4 9
1892 1893	{ Ernest A. Perceval		202 6 9
1894	Philip Napier Miles		129 15 2
1895	Charles Walter Savage		120 4 10

[Mr. Savage was elected President for the year 1895, but did not enter on the office, dying on December 7, 1894, and no successor was chosen for that year.]

1896	George F. Heyworth	128 11 4
1897	Francis James Fry, J.P., Alderman ...	117 16 10
1898	Rev. John Hugh Way, M.A.	

MEMBERS OF PARLIAMENT FOR BRISTOL.

1529 — 1896.

The following list embraces a continuous series of the members elected to represent Bristol in Parliament since the year 1529, with the exceptions of the brief Parliaments of 1536 and 1545, for which no returns are extant. It is impossible to obtain a complete series for the period before 1529, as the returns for many of the earlier Parliaments are quite lost. The lists given in Barrett's and Pryce's histories are very defective, and at the same time do not indicate the Parliaments for which returns are wanting. So far as I have been able to discover, there is no extant list which is quite accurate and complete for the period since 1529, and I have therefore endeavoured to supply that want as far as possible.

For the Parliaments preceding the Revolution of 1688 I have added to the date of election that of dissolution, inasmuch as there were frequently considerable intervals between the conclusion of one and the election of a succeeding Parliament. For the Parliaments since 1688 this is not necessary, a dissolution of the old having always been followed immediately by the summoning of the new Parliament.

1529—1536, Thomas Jubbes ; Richard Abyngdon (Mayor 1525-1526).

[These names are given in the State papers 21 Henry VIII., Vol. iv., No. 6,043 (2). Barrett and Pryce give John Shipward instead of Jubbes, whom he may possibly have succeeded, or *vice versa*, during the continuance of this Parliament.]

1536 (June—July), no return found.
1539—1540. Nicholas Thorne (Mayor 1544-1545) ; Roger Cooke (Mayor 1534-1535, 1541-1542, 1551-1552).
1542—1544, David Broke, Recorder (afterwards Serjeant-at-Law and Chief Baron of the Exchequer) ; Robert Elyott (Mayor 1540-1541).

MEMBERS OF PARLIAMENT FOR BRISTOL.—Continued.

1545—1547, no return found.
1547—1552, Robert Kelway, Recorder (M.P. for Salisbury in the preceding Parliament); John Drewys.
1553 (February—March), John Walshe, Recorder; David Harris (Mayor 1550 1551).
1553 (September—December), John Walshe, Recorder; David Harris
1554 (March—May), John Walshe, Recorder; Thomas Lanseden (Sheriff 1543-1544).
1554—1555, John Walshe, Recorder. (Second name not preserved.)
1555 (October — December), John Walshe, Recorder; William Chester, sen., Alderman (Mayor 1537-1538, 1552-1553).
1558 (January—November), William Tyndall (Sheriff 1547-1548); Robert Butler.

[Mr. Tyndall died this year, but there is no record of his successor. In this Parliament Mr. Walshe sat for Somersetshire.]

1559 (January—May), John Walshe, Recorder (made Serjeant-at-Law April, 1559); William Carr (Sheriff 1546-1547; Mayor 1560-1561).
1563—1567, John Walshe, Serjeant-at-Law and Recorder; William Carr.

[Mr. Walshe was appointed a Judge of the Common Pleas in February, 1583, and succeeded by Thomas Chester (Sheriff 1560-1561; Mayor 1569-1570). Mr. Chester subsequently represented Gloucestershire.]

1571 (March — May), John Popham, Recorder; Philip Langley (Mayor 1567-1568).
1572—1583, John Popham, Recorder; Philip Langley.

[Serjeant Popham was appointed Solicitor-General in 1579, elected Speaker in January, 1581, and made Attorney-General in June, 1581. He afterwards became Lord Chief Justice of the Queen's Bench.]

1584—1585, Thomas Hannam, Recorder; Richard Cole (Sheriff 1569-1570; Mayor 1585-1586).
1586—1587, Thomas Hannam, Recorder; Thomas Aldworth (Mayor 1583-1584).
1588—1589, Thomas Hannam, Recorder (made a Serjeant-at-Law 1589); William Salterne (Sheriff 1575-1576).

[Mr. Salterne died, and was succeeded by Thomas Aldworth.]

1593 (February—April), Thomas Hannam, Serjeant-at-Law and Recorder; Richard Cole, Alderman.
1597—1598, George Snigge, Serjeant-at-Law and Recorder; Thomas James, Alderman.
1601 (September—December), George Snigge, Serjeant-at-Law and Recorder; John Hopkins, Alderman.
1604—1611, Sir George Snigge, Serjeant-at-Law and Recorder; Thomas James, Alderman.

[Sir George Snigge was appointed a Baron of the Exchequer in October, 1604; on November 9, 1605, his seat was declared vacant and a new writ issued.]

1605, November 11, John Whitson, Alderman, vice Snigge.
1614 (March — June), Thomas James, Alderman; John Whitson, Alderman.
1620—1622, John Whitson, Alderman; John Guy, Alderman.
1624—1625, John Guy, Alderman; John Barker, Common Councillor
1625 (April—August), John Whitson, Alderman; Nicholas Hyde, Recorder.

[Mr. Hyde was afterwards Lord Chief Justice of the King's Bench.]

MEMBERS OF PARLIAMENT FOR BRISTOL — *Continued.*

1626 (January—June), John Whitson, Alderman ; John Doughty, Alderman.
1628—1629, John Doughty, Alderman ; John Barker, Common Councillor.
1640 (March—May), John Glanville, Serjeant-at-Law and Recorder ; Humphrey Hooke, Alderman.
1640 (October) [the Long Parliament], Humphrey Hooke, Alderman ; Richard Longe, Alderman.

[Messrs. Hooke and Longe were expelled the House on the charge of being monopolists May 12, 1642, and new writs issued.]

1642 (June), Sir John Glanville, Serjeant-at-Law and Recorder ; John Tayler, Alderman.

[Mr. Tayler was "disabled" for adhering to the King on February 5, 1644, and was killed at the siege of Bristol September 9, 1645. Sir John Glanville was also "disabled" on September 29, 1645, on which day new writs were issued to fill both seats.]

1646 (January 26), Richard Aldworth, Alderman ; Luke Hodges, Common Councillor (elected Alderman September, 1646).

[This Parliament was forcibly removed by Cromwell April 20, 1653, but restored May, 1659, and finally dissolved in March, 1660.]

1654—1655, Robert Aldworth ; Miles Jackson, Alderman.
1656—1658, Robert Aldworth ; John Doddridge, Recorder.
1659 (January—April), Robert Aldworth ; Joseph Jackson, Alderman.
1660 (April—December), John Stephens, Recorder ; John Knight, sen. (elected Common Councillor June, 1660).

[Admiral William Penn was an unsuccessful candidate.]

1661, John Knight. sen., Common Councillor (elected Alderman April, 16 2; knighted September 5, 1663); the Earl of Ossory and Sir Humphrey Hooke, (double return)
1661. May 16, the Earl of Ossory seated, Sir H. Hooke having renounced his election.

[Lord Ossory was created an English Peer in September, 1666, and no new writ was issued to fill his place, the validity of the election of 1661 being referred to the Committee of Elections.]

1666 (October 30), Sir Humphrey Hooke, seated by the House on the report of the Committee of Elections that he had a majority of votes in 1661.

[Sir H. Hooke died October 16, 1677, and a new writ was issued January 28, 1678.]

1678 (February 11), *vice* Hooke, Sir Robert Cann, Bart., Alderman.

[This Parliament, which had sat since 1661, was dissolved January 24, 1679.]

1679 (February—July). Sir John Knight, Alderman ; Sir Robert Cann, Bart., Alderman.
1679—1681, Sir John Knight, Alderman (Tory) ; Sir Robert Cann, Bart., Alderman (Tory).

[Robert Henley (Whig) was an unsuccessful candidate, and petitioned against the return. Sir Robert Cann was expelled the House on October 28, 1680, for expressing disbelief in the Popish Plot. On December 20 Mr. Henley was declared by the Committee of Elections to have been duly elected in 1679, but the House disagreed, and voted the election of Sir R. Cann a void one, and a new writ was issued.]

MEMBERS OF PARLIAMENT FOR BRISTOL —*Continued*.

1680 (December), no official return extant. It has been stated that Sir Walter Long, Bart., was elected. The Parliament was dissolved in the following week.

1681. Thomas Earle, Common Councillor (Tory), 1,491; Sir Richard Hart, Alderman (Tory), 1,482; Sir Robert Atkyns, K.B., Recorder (Whig), 1,345; Sir John Knight, Alderman (Tory), 1,301.

[Sir John Knight, who was a Tory, being in favour of the Exclusion Bill, and a believer in the Popish Plot, was supported by the Whigs. Mr. Earle was rather a Whig than a Tory, but supported by the latter party, being opposed to the strong anti-Catholic policy of the Whig leaders. The Parliament was dissolved in the same month in which it was elected.]

1685—1687, Sir Richard Crumpe, Alderman (Tory); Sir John Churchill, Recorder and Master of the Rolls (Tory).

[Sir John Churchill died in the summer of 1685, and a new writ was issued November 9.]

1685 (December 10), *vice* Churchill, Sir Richard Hart, Alderman (Tory).

1689. Sir Richard Hart, Alderman (Tory); Sir John Knight, Common Councillor (Tory).

1690. Sir Richard Hart, Alderman (Tory); Sir John Knight, Common Councillor (Tory).

[The seats were contested by William Powlett, Serjeant-at-Law and Recorder, and Robert Yate, Common Councillor, in the Whig interest, who subsequently petitioned against the return.]

1695. Sir Thomas Day, Alderman (Whig); Robert Yate, Common Councillor (Whig).

[Although there is no extant record of the fact, it is probable that Sir R. Hart and Sir J. Knight were the Tory candidates at this election.]

1698. Robert Yate, Common Councillor (Whig), 1,136; Sir Thomas Day, Alderman (Whig), 976; Sir John Knight, Common Councillor (Tory), 785; Sir Richard Hart, Alderman (Tory), 421; John Cary, 279.

1701 (February—November). Robert Yate, Alderman (Whig); Sir William Daines, Common Councillor (Whig).

1701 (December). Robert Yate, Alderman (Whig); Sir William Daines, Common Councillor (Whig).

1702. Robert Yate, Alderman (Whig); Sir William Daines, Common Councillor (Whig).

1705. Robert Yate, Alderman (Whig); Sir William Daines, Alderman (Whig).

1708. Robert Yate, Alderman (Whig); Sir William Daines, Alderman (Whig).

1710. Edward Colston (Tory), 1,785; Joseph Earle (Tory), 1,529; Sir William Daines, Alderman (Whig), 940; Robert Yate, Alderman (Whig), 744.

1713. Joseph Earle (Tory), 653; Thomas Edwards, jun. (Tory), 474; Sir William Daines, Alderman (Whig), 189.

[Mr. Earle, whose Toryism was wavering, and who soon after was expelled from the Loyal Society and openly joined the Whigs, was supported by both parties at this election. (See Latimer's "Annals of Bristol in the 18th Century," page 102.) Sir W. Daines petitioned against the return.]

MEMBERS OF PARLIAMENT FOR BRISTOL.—*Continued.*

1715, Sir William Daines, Alderman (Whig). 1,936; Joseph Earle (Whig), 1.899; Philip Freke, Common Councillor (Tory), 1,991; Thomas Edwards, jun. (Tory), 1,976.

[Although Messrs. Freke and Edwards polled a majority, the Whig Sheriffs returned Sir W. Daines and Colonel Earle. The other candidates petitioned, but found it impossible to obtain justice from a Whig House of Commons.]

1722, Joseph Earle (Whig), 2,141; Sir Abraham Elton, Bart., Alderman (Whig), 1,869; William Hart (Tory), 1,743.

1727, John Scrope (Whig), 765; Abraham Elton, jun., (Whig), 411; William Hart (Tory), 386; Joseph Earle (Whig), 4.

[Mr. Scrope, who was Secretary to the Treasurer, was elected Recorder July, 1728. Mr. Elton succeeded to the Baronetcy on the death of his father, February 9, 1728.]

1734, Sir Abraham Elton, Bart., Alderman (Whig), 2,428; Thomas Coster (Tory), 2,071; John Scrope (Whig), 1,866.

[Mr. Coster died September 30, 1739; new writ issued Nov. 15.]

1739 (December 12), *vice* Coster, Right Hon. Edward Southwell (Whig), 2,651; Henry Combe, Common Councillor (Whig), 2,203.

[Mr. Southwell, who was Secretary of State for Ireland, was an opponent of Sir Robert Walpole's Government, and received the unanimous support of the Tories.]

1741, Sir Abraham Elton, Bart., Alderman (Whig); Right Hon. Edward Southwell (Whig).

[Sir A. Elton was, like his colleague, an opponent of Walpole in the latter years of his administration. He died Oct. 19, 1742; new writ November 16.]

1742 (November 24), *vice* Elton, Robert Hoblyn (Tory).

[Sir A. Elton, Bart., Mayor, son of the late member, was a candidate, but did not go to a poll.]

1747, Right Hon Edward Southwell (Whig); Robert Hoblyn (Tory).
1754. Robert Nugent (Whig), 2,592; Richard Beckford (Tory), 2,245; Sir John Philipps, Bart. (Tory), 2,160.

[Mr. Nugent, who was a Lord of the Treasury, was appointed a Vice-Treasurer of Ireland in December, 1759, and sworn a member of the Privy Council Dec. 15. A new writ was ordered December 19. Mr. Beckford died January 24, 1756; new writ ordered February 23.]

1756 (March 17), *vice* Beckford, Jarrit Smith (Tory), 2,418; John Spencer (Whig), 2,347.

1759 (December 26), the Right Hon. Robert Nugent (Whig), re-elected.
1761, the Right Hon. Robert Nugent (Whig); Jarrit Smith (Tory).

[Mr. Smith was created a Baronet in January, 1763. Mr. Nugent was appointed First Lord of Trade, and created Viscount Clare in the Irish peerage December, 1766. New writ ordered December 10.]

1766 (December 15), the Right Hon. Viscount Clare (Whig), re-elected.
1768. the Right Hon. Viscount Clare (Whig); Matthew Brickdale, Common Councillor (Tory).

[Lord Clare was appointed a Vice-Treasurer of Ireland in June, 1768; new writ ordered June 21.]

1768 (June 27), the Right Hon. Viscount Clare (Whig), re-elected.

[Lord Clare, though nominally a Whig, was a supporter of the King's American policy, and in effect a Tory.]

MEMBERS OF PARLIAMENT FOR BRISTOL.—*Continued.*

1774, Henry Cruger, jun., Common Councillor (Whig), 3,565; Edmund Burke (Whig), 2,707; Matthew Brickdale, Common Councillor (Tory), 2,456; the Right Hon. Viscount Clare (Tory), 283.

[Lord Clare withdrew on the second morning of the poll.]

1780, Matthew Brickdale, Common Councillor (Tory), 2,771; Sir Henry Lippincott, Bart., Common Councillor (Tory), 2,518; Henry Cruger, Common Councillor (Whig), 1,271; Samuel Peach (Whig), 788; Edmund Burke (Whig), 18.

[Mr. Richard Combe, Treasurer of the Ordnance, who had been a candidate in 1768, and retired without going to the poll, came forward as Mr. Brickdale's colleague in the Tory interest, but died on the day before the poll (September 8), and Sir H. Lippincott was then substituted for him. Mr. Burke retired on the morning of the first day's poll, and Mr. Peach was then proposed in conjunction with Mr. Cruger, who was his son-in-law. Sir H. Lippincott died January 1, 1781, and a new writ was ordered January 23.]

1781 (February 24), *vice* Lippincott, George Daubeny, Common Councillor (Tory), 3,143; Henry Cruger, Common Councillor (Whig), 2,771.

1784, Matthew Brickdale, Common Councillor (Tory), 3,458; Henry Cruger, Alderman (Whig), 3,052; George Daubeny, Common Councillor (Tory), 2,982; Samuel Peach (Whig), 373.

[Messrs. Brickdale and Daubeny, the Tory candidates, had both supported the Fox-North Coalition in the preceding Parliament, while Alderman Cruger, the Whig, was in favour of Pitt.]

1790, the Marquess of Worcester (Tory), 544; Lord Sheffield (Whig), 537; David Lewis (Whig), 12; William Cunninghame (Whig), 5.

[Lord Sheffield, though the nominee of the Whig party, gave a general support to Pitt's Government.]

1796, Charles Bragge (Tory), 714; Lord Sheffield (Whig), 679; Benjamin Hobhouse (Whig), 102; David Lewis (Whig), 4; Samuel Thomas (Whig), 2.

[Mr. Bragge was proposed by Alderman Daubeny and Councillor Baker; Lord Sheffield by the Mayor (Councillor Harvey) and Alderman Noble; Mr. Hobhouse by Messrs. Philip George and M. M. Coates. Mr. Bragge was appointed Treasurer of the Navy in Nov., 1801, and sworn a Privy Councillor on November 18, on which day a new writ was ordered.]

1801 (November 23), the Right Hon. Charles Bragge (Tory), re-elected.

1802, the Right Hon. Charles Bragge (Tory); Evan Baillie, Common Councillor (Whig).

[Sir Frederick Eden, Bart. (Whig), retired before the election. Mr. Bragge, who was proposed at this election by Aldermen Daubeny and Daniel, accepted the Chiltern Hundreds on appointment to the Secretary-ship at War in August, 1803, and a new writ was ordered August 11.]

1803 (August 16), the Right Hon. Charles Bragge (Tory), re-elected.

[Mr. Bragge changed his name to Bathurst May 11, 1804.]

1806, the Right Hon. Charles Bathurst (Tory); Evan Baillie, Alderman (Whig).

[Mr. Bathurst, who now held the office of Master of the Mint, was proposed by Alderman Daniel and R. H. Davis; Mr. Baillie by Councillor E. Protheroe and Alderman Ames.]

MEMBERS OF PARLIAMENT FOR BRISTOL.—Continued.

1807, the Right Hon. Charles Bathurst (Tory) ; Evan Baillie, Alderman (Whig).

[Sir John Jervis, Bart., was nominated by Henry Hunt, the Radical demagogue, but did not go to the poll. Mr. Bathurst was proposed by the Mayor (Councillor Vaughan) and Alderman Daniel; Mr. Baillie by Alderman Claxton and H. Bright. Mr. Bathurst was appointed Chancellor of the Duchy of Lancaster in June, 1812, and a new writ was ordered June 23.]

1812, July 15, *vice* Bathurst, Richard Hart Davis (Tory), 1,907; Henry Hunt (Radical), 235.

[Mr. Bathurst was elected for Bodmin on July 1; Mr Davis resigned his seat for Colchester to stand for Bristol, where he was nominated by T. Jones and G. Goldney, Mr. Hunt being proposed by J. Lidiard and W. Bright.]

1812, Richard Hart Davis (Tory), 2,910 ; Edward Protheroe, Common Councillor (Whig), 2,435; Sir Samuel Romilly, K.C. (Whig), 1,685 ; Henry Hunt (Radical), 456.

[Mr. Davis was proposed by T. Jones and Alderman Vaughan ; Mr. Protheroe by Councillor Fripp and A. Pope ; Sir S. Romilly by the Mayor (M. Castle) and Sir A. Elton, Bart. ; Mr. Hunt by W. Pimm and J. Lidiard. There were 2,141 split votes between Davis and Protheroe, and only 89 between the two Whigs. Mr. Protheroe, though a Whig, opposed Catholic Emancipation, and gave considerable support to the measures of the Tory Government, including the suspension of the Habeas Corpus Act in 1817.]

1818. Richard Hart Davis (Tory), 3,377 ; Edward Protheroe, Councillor (Whig), 2,259 ; Hugh Duncan Baillie (Whig), 1,684.

[Mr. Davis was proposed by Thomas Graeme and J. S. Harford ; Mr. Protheroe by Butler Claxton and A. Pope ; Colonel Baillie by R. Teast and T. Stocking. Colonel Baillie was brought out in opposition to Mr. Protheroe by the supporters of Catholic Emancipation, and many of the Tories voted for the latter with Mr. Davis.]

1820, Henry Bright (Whig), 2,997 ; Richard Hart Davis (Tory), 2,811 ; James Evan Baillie (Whig), 115.

[Mr. Davis was proposed by Councillor Hassell and R. Bush; Mr. Bright by W. P. Lunell and Levi Ames, jun. ; Mr. Baillie, who was nominated without his consent, by T. Stocking and J. Cossens.]

1826, Richard Hart Davis (Tory), 3,887 ; Henry Bright (Whig), 2,315 ; Edward Protheroe, Common Councillor (Whig), 1,873.

[Mr. Davis was proposed by Councillor Hassell and H. Bush ; Mr. Bright by Councillor Pinney and A. Palmer, sen. ; Mr. Protheroe, who was nominated without his consent, by J. Harris and J. Bowgin. The contest was between the two Whigs, Mr. Davis being practically unopposed.]

1830, Richard Hart Davis (Tory), 5,012 ; James Evan Baillie (Whig), 3,378 ; Edward Protheroe, jun. (Whig), 2,842 ; James Acland (Radical), 25.

[The contest was between the two Whigs. Mr. Baillie, who represented the West India interest, was proposed by Sir A. Elton, Bart., and Councillor Pinney ; Mr. Protheroe, the Anti-Slavery candidate, by C. George and R. Ash ; Mr. Davis by H. Bush and J. Cookson.]

MEMBERS OF PARLIAMENT FOR BRISTOL.— *Continued.*

1831, James Evan Baillie (Whig) ; Edward Protheroe, jun. (Whig).

[Mr. Baillie was proposed by A. Palmer, sen., and I. Elton ; Mr. Protheroe by C. George and R. Ash. Mr. Hart Davis, who had issued an address seeking re-election, withdrew his candidature.]

1832, Sir Richard Rawlinson Vyvyan, Bart. (Tory), 3,697 ; James Evan Baillie (Whig), 3,159 ; Edward Protheroe, jun. (Reformer), 3,030 ; John Williams, K.C. (Reformer), 2,741.

[The Tories supported Mr. Baillie, whose views were less advanced than those of the other Reformers. Sir R. Vyvyan was proposed by Alderman Daniel and J. S. Harford ; Mr. Baillie by R. Bright and A. Palmer ; Mr. Protheroe by R. Ash and G. E. Sanders ; Mr. Williams by T. Reynolds and J. Addington.]

1835, Philip John Miles (Conservative), 3,709 ; Sir Richard Rawlinson Vyvyan, Bart. (Conservative), 3,313 ; James Evan Baillie (Liberal), 2,518 ; the Right Hon. Sir John Cam Hobhouse, Bart. Liberal), 1,808.

[Sir J. C. Hobhouse was brought forward unexpectedly on the day of nomination, being proposed by C. A. Elton and R. Ash, and an address was issued on his behalf signed by 57 leading Liberals. The Conservatives had not intended to oppose Mr. Baillie, and did not anticipate a contest, but after the nomination of Sir John Hobhouse they determined to attack the second seat, and just before the opening of the poll Mr. Miles was proposed by Alderman Fripp and W. E. Acraman. Sir R. Vyvyan had been proposed on the nomination day by Alderman Daniel and J. Cookson ; Mr. Baillie by Robert Bright and Councillor M. H. Castle.]

1837, Philip William Skynner Miles (Conservative), 3,839 ; Francis Henry FitzHardinge Berkeley (Liberal), 3,212 ; William Fripp, J.P., Alderman (Conservative), 3,156.

[Mr. Miles was proposed by Councillor Daniel and J. S. Harford ; Mr. Berkeley by Alderman Stock and Councillor Cunningham ; Alderman Fripp by Councillor Cookson and I. Cooke.]

1841, Philip William Skynner Miles (Conservative), 4,193 ; Francis Henry FitzHardinge Berkeley (Liberal), 3,739 ; William Fripp, J.P., Alderman (Conservative), 3,684.

[Mr. Miles was proposed by Councillor Cookson and C. L. Walker ; Mr. Berkeley by J. Cunningham and Councillor G. Thomas ; Alderman Fripp by Councillors Haberfield and R. J. Poole King.]

1847, Francis Henry FitzHardinge Berkeley (Liberal), 4,381 ; Philip William Skynner Miles (Conservative), 2,595 ; William Fripp, J.P. (Conservative), 2,476 ; Apsley Pellatt (Radical), 171.

[The contest was a personal one between the friends of Messrs. Miles and Fripp, but the candidates also differed politically on the Corn Law question, Mr. Miles being a Protectionist, and Mr. Fripp an adherent of Sir Robert Peel's Free Trade policy. Mr. Pellatt was brought forward by the Anti-State-Church party, being proposed by J. Shoard and R. Norris. Mr. Miles was proposed by J. Cookson, J.P., and C. L. Walker, J.P. ; Mr. Berkeley by Councillors G. E. Sanders and Visger ; Mr. Fripp by Councillors Shaw and Phippen.]

1852, Francis Henry FitzHardinge Berkeley (Liberal), 4,681 ; William Henry Gore Langton, J.P., Mayor (Liberal), 4,531 ; Forster Alleyne McGeachy (Conservative), 3,632.

[Mr. Berkeley was proposed by Councillors Visger and T. R. Sanders ; Mr. Langton by Councillors M. Castle and Coates ; Mr. McGeachy by J. S. Harford and Alderman Vining.]

MEMBERS OF PARLIAMENT FOR BRISTOL.--*Continued.*

1857, Francis Henry Fitzhardinge Berkeley (Liberal); William Henry Gore Langton, J.P. (Liberal).

[Mr. Berkeley was proposed by Councillors Visger and Coates; Mr. Langton by Councillors Castle and H. O. Wills.]

1859, Francis Henry FitzHardinge Berkeley (Liberal), 4,432; William Henry Gore Langton, J.P. (Liberal), 4,285; Frederic William Slade, Q.C. (Conservative), 4,205.

[Mr. Berkeley was proposed by Councillors Visger and Coates; Mr. Langton by Councillor M. Castle and J. Cox; Mr. Slade by Councillors J. W. Miles and R. J. Poole King.]

1865, Francis Henry FitzHardinge Berkeley (Liberal), 5,296; Sir Samuel Morton Peto, Bart. (Liberal), 5,228; Thomas Francis Fremantle (Conservative), 4,269.

[Mr. Berkeley was proposed by Councillor M. Castle and H. O. Wills; Sir M. Peto by G. Thomas and Councillor F. Terrell; Mr. Fremantle by P. W. S. Miles and Councillor R. J. Poole King.]

[Sir Morton Peto retired by accepting the Stewardship of Northstead, in consequence of the bankruptcy of his firm, in April, 1868. New writ ordered April 22.]

1868, April 29, *vice* Peto, John William Miles, Councillor (Conservative), 5,173; Samuel Morley (Liberal), 4,977.

[Mr. Miles was proposed by Councillor R. J. Poole King and Alderman S. V. Hare; Mr. Morley by G. Thomas and M. Castle.]

[Mr. Miles was unseated June 25, 1868, and Mr. P. W. S. Miles issued an address offering himself as the Conservative candidate in place of his brother for the remainder of the Parliament, but no writ was issued for a fresh election. Parliament was dissolved in the November following.]

1868, Francis Henry FitzHardinge Berkeley (Liberal), 8,759; Samuel Morley (Liberal), 8,714; John William Miles (Conservative), 6,694.

[Mr. Berkeley was proposed by Councillors C. J. Thomas and E. S. Robinson; Mr. Morley by M. Castle and Councillor F. Terrell; Mr. Miles by Councillor R. J. Poole King and W. Kearsey.]

[Mr. Berkeley died March 10, 1870. New writ ordered March 12.]

1870 (March 28), *vice* Berkeley, Elisha Smith Robinson, J.P., Councillor (Liberal), 7,832; Sholto Vere Hare, J.P., Alderman (Conservative), 7,062.

[Two other Liberal candidates had offered themselves, Messrs. K. D. Hodgson, who was supported by the leaders of the Liberal organisation, and George Odger, representing the artisans. A test ballot was held on March 22, when the numbers were—Robinson, 4,502; Hodgson 7,861, Odger 1,335, whereupon the two last-named retired. Mr. Robinson was proposed at the nomination by Councillors F. Terrell and Wedmore; Alderman Hare by Councillor Ffooks and W. Kearsey. On June 9 Mr. Robinson was unseated by the Court of Common Pleas in consequence of bribery committed on his behalf in connection with the test ballot. Baron Bramwell, who originally tried the petition, found that bribery had been committed at the test ballot but not at the election, and referred the question as to the forfeiture of the seat thereby to the Court of Common Pleas for decision. A new writ was ordered June 18.]

MEMBERS OF PARLIAMENT FOR BRISTOL.—*Continued.*

1870 (June 25). *vice* Robinson, Kirkman Daniel Hodgson (Liberal), 7,816; Sholto Vere Hare, J.P., Alderman (Conservative), 7,238.

[Mr. Hodgson was proposed by Councillors C. J. Thomas and F. Terrell; and Alderman Hare by J. W. Miles and W. Kearsey. This was the last election at which there were public nominations.]

1874. Kirkman Daniel Hodgson (Liberal), 8,888; Samuel Morley (Liberal), 8,732; Sholto Vere Hare, J.P., Alderman (Conservative), 8,552; George Henry Chambers (Conservative), 7,626.

[Mr. Hodgson was proposed by Councillors F. Terrell and Lewis Fry, Mr. Morley by Councillors C. J. Thomas and E. S. Robinson; Alderman Hare and Mr. Chambers by J. W. Miles and Councillor R. J. Poole King. Mr. Hodgson retired from Parliament by acceptance of the Stewardship of the Chiltern Hundreds in December, 1878, and a new writ was ordered December 5.]

1878 (December 14). *vice* Hodgson, Lewis Fry, Councillor (Liberal), 9,342; Sir Ivor Bertie Guest, Bart. (Conservative), 7,795.

[Mr. Fry was proposed by Councillors C. J. Thomas and E. S. Robinson; Sir I. Guest by Aldermen S. V. Hare and Ford.]

1880. Samuel Morley (Liberal), 10,704; Lewis Fry, Councillor (Liberal), 10,070; Sir Ivor Bertie Guest, Bart. (Conservative), 9,325; Elisha Smith Robinson, J.P., Councillor (Liberal), 4,100.

[Mr. Robinson stood independently of the Liberal organisation, and received considerable Conservative support—he was proposed by C. Tovey and R. H. Warren; Mr. Morley by Councillors C. J. Thomas and C. Townsend; Mr. Fry by Councillor F. Terrell and M. Castle; Sir I. Guest by Aldermen Hare and Ford.]

By the Redistribution Act of 1885 Bristol was divided into four single-membered constituencies.

BRISTOL (WEST).

1885, the Right Hon. Sir Michael Edward Hicks Beach, Bart. (Conservative). 3,876; Brinsley de Courcy Nixon (Liberal), 2,463.
1886, the Right Hon. Sir Michael Edward Hicks Beach, Bart. (Conservative). 3,819; James Judd (Liberal), 1,801.

[Sir M. Hicks Beach was appointed Chief Secretary to the Lord-Lieutenant of Ireland in August, 1886. New writ ordered August 6.]

1886 (August 11), the Right Hon. Sir Michael Edward Hicks Beach, Bart. (Conservative), re-elected.

[Sir M. Hicks Beach was appointed President of the Board of Trade in February, 1888. New writ ordered February 15.]

1888 (February 20), the Right Hon. Sir Michael Edward Hicks Beach, Bart. (Conservative), re-elected.

MEMBERS OF PARLIAMENT FOR BRISTOL.—*Continued.*

1892, the Right Hon. Sir Michael Edward Hicks Beach, Bart. (Conservative).

[Sir M. Hicks Beach was appointed Chancellor of the Exchequer in June, 1895. New writ ordered June 26.]

1895 (July 1), the Right Hon. Sir Michael Edward Hicks Beach, Bart. (Conservative).

[Parliament was dissolved a few days afterwards.]

1895, the Right Hon. Sir Michael Edward Hicks Beach, Bart. (Conservative), 3,815; Henry Hamilton Lawless, (Liberal), 1,842.

BRISTOL (SOUTH).

1885, Joseph Dodge Weston, J.P., Councillor (Liberal), 4,217; Edward Stock Hill, C.B. (Conservative), 4,121.
1886, Edward Stock Hill, C.B. (Conservative), 4,447; Joseph Dodge Weston, J.P., Councillor (Liberal), 3,423.

[Colonel Hill was made a K.C.B. May 10, 1892.]

1892, Sir Edward Stock Hill, K.C.B. (Conservative), 4,990; William Henry Wills, J.P. (Liberal), 4,442.
1895, Sir Edward Stock Hill, K.C.B. (Conservative), 5,190; John O'Connor Power (Liberal), 4,431.

BRISTOL (NORTH).

1885, Lewis Fry (Liberal), 4,110; Charles Edward Hungerford Atholl Colston (Conservative), 3,046.
1886, Lewis Fry (Liberal Unionist), 3,587; Alfred Carpenter (Liberal), 2,737.
1892, Charles Townsend, J.P., Councillor (Liberal), 4,409; Lewis Fry (Liberal Unionist), 4,064.
1895, Lewis Fry (Liberal Unionist), 4,702; Charles Townsend, J.P. (Liberal), 4,434.

BRISTOL (EAST).

1885, Handel Cossham (Liberal), 4,647; James Broad Bissell (Conservative), 2,383.
1886, Handel Cossham (Liberal), 3,672; James Inskip, Councillor (Conservative), 1,936.

[Mr. Cossham died April 23, 1890. New writ ordered May 2.]

1890, May 9, Sir Joseph Dodge Weston, J.P., Councillor (Liberal), 4,775; James Inskip, Councillor (Conservative), 1,900; Joseph Havelock Wilson (Labour), 602.
1892, Sir Joseph Dodge Weston, J.P. (Liberal).

[Sir J. Weston died March 5, 1895. New writ ordered March 13.]

1895 (March 13), Sir William Henry Wills, Bart., J.P. (Liberal), 3,740; Hugh Holmes Gore (Socialist), 3,558.
1895, Sir William Henry Wills, Bart, J.P. (Liberal), 4,129; Samuel George Hobson (Labour), 1,874.

NOTES ON ELECTIONS AND MEMBERS FOR BRISTOL.

The poll books for the following years are in existence, viz., 1722, 1734, 1739, 1754, 1774, 1781, 1784, 1812, 1820, 1830, 1832, 1835, 1837, 1841, 1847, 1852. The only extant copy of that for 1722 is in the British Museum; that for 1820 has never been printed, but may be seen in MS. at the Reference Library, Queen's-road. The votes of the members of the Corporation as recorded in the poll-books were as follows:—

1722. Earle, 20; Elton, 20; Hart, 5.
[19 voted for the two Whig candidates; 1 (Sir John Hawkins) for Elton and Hart; 1 (Mr. Gravett) for Earle and Hart; and 3 (Messrs. Freke, Haynes, and Gibbs) plumped for Hart.]

1734. Elton, 35; Scrope, 33; Coster, 2.
[33 voted for Elton and Scrope, and 2 (Messrs. King and R. Smith) for Elton and Coster.]

1739. Combe, 25; Southwell, 11.
[6 Aldermen (Jefferis, Taylor, Jacob Elton, Rich. Lyde, and Blackwell) and 19 Common Councillors voted for Combe; 5 Aldermen (Becher, Donning, Nash, Day, and the Recorder, Serjeant Foster) and 6 Councillors for Southwell.]

1754. Nugent, 33; Beckford, 3; Philipps, 2.
[Alderman Day and Councillor R. Smith voted for the Tory candidates, Beckford and Philipps; Mr. J. Curtis for Nugent and Beckford; 9 Aldermen, and 23 Common Councillors plumped for Nugent.]

1774. Brickdale, 18; Cruger, 14; Burke, 12; Clare, 10.
[2 Aldermen (Weare and Deane) and 10 Common Councillors (Webb, Pignenit, T. Farr, Bull, Brice, Edgar, Ames, Noble, Anderson, and Pierce) voted for Cruger and Burke; 4 Aldermen (M. Smith, Mugleworth, Isaac Elton, and Whatley) and 6 Councillors (Hotchkin, Mayor; Harris, H. Bright, Foy, I. Elton, jun., and Miller) for Brickdale and Clare; 2 Councillors (Pope and Laroche) for Brickdale and Cruger; 2 Aldermen (Baugh and Barnes) and 4 Councillors (Miles, Lippincott, Daubeny, and Baker) plumped for Brickdale.]

1781. Cruger, 22; Daubeny, 7.
[5 Aldermen (M. Smith, R. Farr, Deane, Gordon, and Pope) and 17 Common Councillors (W. Weare, Brice, Edgar, Crofts, Merlott, Ames, Noble, Anderson, Pierce, Hill, J. Farr, Harris, J. F. Weare, Protheroe, Loscombe, Morgan, and Harford) voted for Cruger; 4 Aldermen (Mugleworth, Harris, Foy, and Hotchkin) and 3 Councillors (Miles, Mayor; J. Baker, and Sir J. Durbin) for Daubeny.]

1784, Cruger, 16; Brickdale, 9; Daubeny, 5; Peach, 1.
[2 Aldermen (Deane and Pope) and 10 Councillors (Anderson, Pierce, Hill, Harris, Morgan, Loscombe, Coleman, Collard, Williams, and Blake) plumped for Cruger; 3 Aldermen (Miles, Sir J. Durbin, and Brice) and 1 Councillor (Baker) voted for Brickdale and Daubeny; 4 Councillors (Edgar, Span, J. Smith, and Ames) for Brickdale and Cruger; Mr. Daubeny plumped for Brickdale, and Mr. Brickdale voted for Daubeny and Peach.]

1812. Davis, 16; Protheroe, 13; Romilly, 5.
[5 Aldermen (Ames, Evans, Daniel, Fripp, and Sir R. Vaughan) and 8 Councillors voted for Davis and Protheroe; 2 Councillors (Joseph Smith and Anderson) for Davis and Romilly; Councillor Bickley plumped for Davis; the Mayor (Councillor Castle) and Councillors Richard Bright and P. George plumped for Romilly.]

NOTES ON ELECTIONS AND MEMBERS FOR BRISTOL.
Continued.

1820, Bright, 10 ; Davis, 2.
[Aldermen Ames and Page and 7 Councillors plumped for Bright ; Alderman Wilcox voted for Davis and Bright, and Councillor Barrow plumped for Davis. No member of the Corporation voted for Baillie. The majority of the Corporation abstained from voting including all the prominent Tory leaders, Aldermen Daniel, Haythorne, Brooke, and Sir R. Vaughan, and Councillors Bickley, James George, Hassell, and Gardiner. Mr. Hart Davis was not supported on this occasion by the Steadfast Society, which had hitherto nominated the Tory candidates, and had intended to bring out Mr. Philip John Miles as its candidate at this election.]

1830, Baillie, 16 ; Davis, 15.
[5 Aldermen (Daniel, G. Hilhouse, A. Hilhouse, Barrow, and Goldney) and 10 Councillors voted for Davis and Baillie ; Councillor Claxton plumped for Baillie. No member of the Corporation voted for Protheroe, and of the 10 Whigs who were the only representatives of that party Messrs. Claxton and Pinney alone recorded their votes.]

1832, Baillie, 21 ; Vyvyan, 20 ; Protheroe, 3 ; Williams, 1.
[20 voted for Baillie and Vyvyan ; 1 (Mr. Bengough) plumped for Baillie ; 2 (Messrs. Philip and George Protheroe) plumped for Protheroe ; and 1 (Mr. Lunell) voted for Protheroe and Williams.]

1835, Miles, 22 ; Vyvyan, 20 ; Baillie, 8 ; Hobhouse, 3.
[9 Aldermen and 10 Councillors voted for the two Conservatives ; Messrs. Lunell and Philip and George Protheroe for Baillie and Hobhouse ; Messrs. Pinney, C. George, and Claxton for Miles and Baillie ; Mr. Lean for Vyvyan and Baillie ; Mr. M. Hinton Castle plumped for Baillie.]

*1837, Fripp, 34 ; Miles, 30 ; Berkeley, 28.
*1841, Fripp, 47 ; Miles, 46 ; Berkeley, 13.
*1847, Miles, 28 ; Fripp, 21 ; Berkeley, 21.
*1852, McGeachy, 38 ; Berkeley, 23 ; Langton, 19.

[*Particulars as to the voting of the members of the Council at these elections have already been given, at pages 54 and 55, in the notes on the political composition of the Bristol Corporation. The numbers given for Miles and Fripp in 1841, for Berkeley in 1847, and for McGeachy in 1852, on these pages are not quite accurate, but are correctly recorded above. In 1841 the split votes for Miles and Fripp were 44 (not 43), Alderman Butcher, who is erroneously described as not voting, having been omitted. In 1847 there were 20 (not 21) plumpers for Miles and 15 plumpers for Berkeley ; Mr. F. W. Green split for Miles and Berkeley, instead of plumping for the former, and Mr. George Thomas, who is stated on page 55 not to have voted, plumped for Berkeley. In 1852 Mr. McGeachy had 36 plumpers ; Alderman Lucas, who is stated at page 55 not to have voted, should be added.]

The following M.P.'s for Bristol since 1529 have represented other Parliamentary constituencies :—
R. Kelway—Salisbury, 1545
J. Walshe—Somersetshire, 1558
T. Chester—Gloucestershire, 1573
J. Popham—Lyme Regis, 1558
T. Hannam—Weymouth, 1572
G. Snigge—Cricklade, 1588
N. Hyde—Andover, 1601 ; Christchurch, 1604 ; Bath, 1614

NOTES ON ELECTIONS AND MEMBERS FOR BRISTOL.
Continued.

Sir J. Glanville—Liskeard, 1614; Plymouth, 1620, 1624, 1625, 1626, 1628; St. German's, 1659
Robert Aldworth—Devizes, 1660-1661 (probably, but not certainly, the same as the M.P. for Bristol)
Earl of Ossory—Dublin University (Parliament of Ireland) 1661-1662
T. Edwards—Wells, 1719-1735
J. Scrope—Ripon, 1722-1727; Lyme Regis, 1734-1752
Sir A. Elton, jun.—Taunton, 1724-1727
E. Southwell—Downpatrick (Parliament of Ireland) 1727-1755
Lord Clare—St. Mawes, 1741-1754 and 1774-1784
E. Burke—Wendover, 1765-1774; Malton, 1774 and 1780-1794.
Marquess of Worcester—Monmouth, 1788-1790; Gloucestershire, 1796-1803
Lord Sheffield—Coventry, February—September, 1780, and 1781-1784.
C. Bragge (Bathurst)—Monmouth, 1790-1796; Bodmin, 1812-1818; Harwich, 1818-1823
R. Hart Davis—Colchester, 1807-1812
J. E. Baillie—Tralee, 1813-1818
E. Protheroe, jun.—Evesham, 1826-1830; Halifax, 1837-1847
Sir R. R. Vyvyan—Cornwall, 1825-1831; Okehampton, 1831-1832; Helston, 1841-1857
P. J. Miles—Westbury, 1820-1826; Corfe Castle, 1829-1832
Sir S. M. Peto—Norwich, 1847-1854; Finsbury, 1859-1865
S. Morley—Nottingham, 1865-1866
K. D. Hodgson—Bridport, 1857-1868
Sir M. Hicks Beach—East Gloucestershire, 1864-1885
Sir W. H. Wills—Coventry, 1880-1885.

Of the unsuccessful candidates for Bristol, the following obtained seats for other constituencies :—

R. Henley—Lyme Regis, 1693-1701
Sir R. Atkyns—Evesham, 1659; East Looe, 1661-1672; Middlesex, 1680-1681.
Sir J. Philipps—Camarthen, 1745-1747; Petersfield, 1754-1761; Pembrokeshire, 1761-1764
J. Spencer—Warwick, 1756-1761.
R. Combe—Milborne Port, April—May, 1772; Aldeburgh, 1774-1780
B. Hobhouse—Bletchingley, 1797-1802; Grampound, 1802-1806; Hindon, 1806-1818
H. Hunt—Preston, 1830-1832
Sir S. Romilly—Queenborough, 1806-1807; Horsham, 1807-1808; Wareham, 1808-1812; Arundel, 1812-1818; Westminster, July—November, 1818
H. D. Baillie—Rye, 1830-1831; Honiton, 1835-1847
J. Williams—Lincoln, 1822-1826; Ilchester, 1826-1827; Winchelsea, 1830-1832
Sir J. C. Hobhouse—Westminster, 1820-1833; Nottingham, 1834-1847; Harwich, 1848-1851
A. Pellatt—Southwark, 1852-1857
F. A. McGeachy—Honiton, 1841-1847
T. F. Fremantle—Buckinghamshire, 1876-1885 (in succession to Lord Beaconsfield)
C. E. H. A. Colston—South Gloucestershire since 1892
J. Havelock Wilson—Middlesborough since 1892.
J. O'Connor Power—Mayo County, 1874-1885

NOTES ON ELECTIONS AND MEMBERS FOR BRISTOL.
Continued.

The following M.P.'s and candidates have also unsuccessfully contested other constituencies:—
H. Hunt—Westminster, 1818 ; Somersetshire, 1826
J. Acland—Hull, 1832
K. D. Hodgson—Penryn, 1868
F. W. Slade—Salisbury, 1852 ; Cambridge, 1854
Sir I. Guest—Glamorganshire, 1874 (general election); Poole, 1874 (bye-election).
Sir W. H. Wills—South-East Essex, 1885, 1886
J. Judd—North Suffolk, 1892
B. de C. Nixon—Dundee, 1886
A. Carpenter—Reigate Division of Surrey, 1885
H. Cossham—Nottingham, 1866 ; Dewsbury, 1868 ; Chippenham, 1874.
J. O'Connor Power—Kensington Division of Lambeth, 1885

The following either inherited Peerages or were created Peers:—
Thomas Butler, by courtesy Earl of Ossory, summoned to the Irish House of Peers by that title June, 1662; created Lord Butler of Moor Park, in the English Peerage, September, 1666
John Spencer, created Viscount Spencer April, 1761 ; Earl Spencer October, 1765
Robert Nugent, created Viscount Clare (Ireland) December, 1766 ; Earl Nugent (Ireland) June, 1776
John Baker Holroyd, created Lord Sheffield (Ireland) December, 1780 ; Lord Sheffield (United Kingdom) July, 1802; Earl of Sheffield (Ireland) January, 1816
The Marquess of Worcester succeeded to the Dukedom of Beaufort October 11, 1803
Sir John Cam Hobhouse, Bart., created Lord Broughton February, 1851
Hon. Thomas F. Fremantle succeeded to the Barony of Cottesloe December 3, 1890
Sir Ivor B. Guest, Bart., created Lord Wimborne April, 1880

The following inherited Baronetcies, or were created Baronets:—
Sir Robert Cann, created September, 1662
Sir Abraham Elton, sen., created October, 1717
Sir Abraham Elton, jun., succeeded February 9, 1728
Sir John Philipps, succeeded October, 1743
Sir Jarrit Smith, created January, 1763
Sir Henry Lippincott, created July, 1778
Sir Benjamin Hobhouse, created November, 1812
Sir Richard R. Vyvyan, succeeded January 27, 1820
Sir John Cam Hobhouse, succeeded August 15, 1831
Sir S. Morton Peto, created February, 1855
Sir Frederic W. Slade, succeeded August 13, 1859
Sir Ivor Guest, succeeded November 26, 1853
Sir Michael Hicks Beach, succeeded November 22, 1854
Sir William Henry Wills, created August, 1893

The following were Knighted:—
Sir David Broke (1553) ; Sir John Popham (June 2, 1592); Sir George Snigge (about 1603 ; Sir Nicholas Hyde (January 28, 1627) : Sir John Glanville (August 7, 1641); Sir John Knight, sen.

NOTES ON ELECTIONS AND MEMBERS FOR BRISTOL.
Continued.

(September 5, 1663); Sir Humphrey Hooke (February 21, 1661); Sir Robert Cann (April 22, 1662); Sir Thomas Earle (December 4, 1681); Sir Richard Hart (October 27, 1680); Sir John Knight, jun. (March 12, 1682); Sir John Churchill (August 18, 1670); Sir Richard Crumpe (October 18, 1681); Sir Thomas Day (November 28, 1694); Sir William Daines (November 28, 1694); Sir Samuel Romilly (February 12, 1806); Sir John Williams (April 16, 1834); Sir George Chambers (July 31, 1880); Sir Joseph D. Weston (November 26, 1886).

The above were Knights Bachelor, or ordinary Knights.

Sir Robert Atkyns was made a K.B. April 23, 1661, and Sir Edward S. Hill, K.C.B., May 10, 1892

The following were sworn members of the English Privy Council :—

The Earl of Ossory (June 13, 1666); Viscount Clare (December 15, 1759); Edmund Burke (March 27, 1782); Lord Sheffield (December 20, 1809); Charles Bragge (November 18, 1801); Sir Michael Hicks Beach (March 2, 1874). Lords Ossory and Clare and Sir M. Hicks Beach were members of the Irish Privy Council, as also was Edward Southwell.

The following held high judicial office:—

Sir David Broke—Lord Chief Baron of the Exchequer, 1553-1558
Sir John Walshe—Judge of the Common Pleas, 1563-1572
Sir John Popham—Lord Chief Justice of the Queen's (King's from 1603) Bench, 1592-1607
Sir George Snigge—Baron of the Exchequer, 1604-1617
Sir Nicholas Hyde—Lord Chief Justice of the King's Bench, 1627-1631
Sir Robert Atkyns—Judge of the Common Pleas, 1672-1680; Lord Chief Baron of the Exchequer, 1689-1694
Sir John Churchill—Master of the Rolls, 1685 till his death in the same year
John Scrope—Baron of the Exchequer in Scotland, 1708-1724
Sir John Williams—Judge of the King's Bench (Queen's from 1837), 1834-1846.

All the above held the Recordership of Bristol, as also did Robert Kelway, Thomas Hannam, Sir John Glanville, John Doddridge, John Stephens, and William Powlett.

Sir John Popham was Speaker of the House of Commons 1581-1583, and Sir John Glanville in the Short Parliament of 1640. Sir Robert Atkyns was Speaker of the House of Lords 1689-1693

The following were Serjeants-at-Law :—Sir David Broke, Robert Kelway, Sir John Walshe, Sir John Popham, Thomas Hannam, Sir George Snigge, Sir Nicholas Hyde, Sir John Glanville, and William Powlett.

The following were King's or Queen's Counsel :—Sir John Churchill, Sir Samuel Romilly, Sir John Williams, and Sir Frederic Slade

NOTES ON ELECTIONS AND MEMBERS FOR BRISTOL.
Continued.

The following held political office:—

Sir John Popham—Solicitor-General, 1579-1581; Attorney-General, 1581-1592
The Earl of Ossory—A Lord of the Bed-chamber, 1666-1680; a Lord of the Admiralty, 1675-1679; Lord Deputy of Ireland, 1664-1665 and 1668-1669
John Scrope—Secretary to the Treasury, 1724-1752
Edward Southwell—Secretary of State for Ireland, 1730-1755
Sir John Philipps—A Lord of Trade, 1744-1745
Viscount Clare—A Lord of the Treasury, 1754-1759; a Vice-Treasurer of Ireland, 1760-1765 and 1768-1782; First Lord of Trade, 1765-1768
Richard Combe—Treasurer of the Ordnance a few days in September, 1780
Edmund Burke—Paymaster-General, March—July, 1782, and April—December, 1783
Lord Sheffield—A Commissioner of the Board of Trade, 1809-1821
Sir Benjamin Hobhouse—Secretary to the Board of Control 1803-1804
Charles (Bragge) Bathurst—Treasurer of the Navy, 1801-1803; Secretary at War, 1803-1804; Master of the Mint, 1806-1807; Chancellor of the Duchy of Lancaster, 1812-1823
Sir Samuel Romilly—Solicitor-General, 1806-1807
Sir John Cam Hobhouse—Secretary at War, 1832-1833; Chief Secretary to the Lord-Lieutenant of Ireland, March—May, 1833; First Commissioner of Woods and Forests, July—November, 1834; President of the Board of Control, 1835-1841, and 1846-1852
Sir Michael Hicks Beach—Secretary to the Poor Law Board, March—September, 1868; Under Home Secretary, September—December, 1868; Chief Secretary to the Lord-Lieutenant of Ireland, 1874-1878 and 1886-1887; Colonial Secretary, 1878-1880; Chancellor of the Exchequer, 1885-1886 and since 1895; President of the Board of Trade, 1888-1892.

The following M.P.'s were Mayors of Bristol:—

R. Abyngdon, R. Elyott, R. Coke, N. Thorne, D. Harris, W. Chester, W. Carr, T. Chester, P. Langley, R. Cole, T. Aldworth, J. Hopkins, J. Whitson, T. James, J. Barker, J. Guy, J. Doughty, H. Hooke, sen., R. Longe, J. Tayler, Richard Aldworth, M. Jackson, J. Jackson, Sir J. Knight, sen., Sir R. Cann, Sir R. Hart, Sir T. Earle, Sir R. Crumpe, Sir J. Knight, jun., Sir T. Day, R. Yate, Sir W. Daines, Sir A. Elton, sen., Sir A. Elton, jun., H. Cruger, G. Daubeny, E. Protheroe, sen., W. H. G. Langton, E. S. Robinson, Sir J. D. Weston. Mr. Brickdale also was elected Mayor, but declined the office
H. Combe, W. Fripp, and S. V. Hare, who were unsuccessful candidates for the Parliamentary representation, also served the office of Mayor
The following held the Shrievalty without attaining to the Chief Magistracy:—T. Lauseden, W. Tyndall, W. Salterne, L. Hodges, P. Freke, Sir H. Lippincott, E. Baillie, and Sir W. H. Wills

NOTES ON ELECTIONS AND MEMBERS FOR BRISTOL.
Continued.

The following M.P.'s and candidates were also members of the Corporation:—The Recorders named above, Sir H. Hooke, J. W. Miles, H. Cossham, L. Fry, C. Townsend, J. Inskip, and H. Holmes Gore.

The following sat for Bristol in more than four Parliaments:—

F. H. F. Berkeley, 8; Sir J. Walshe, 7; R. Yate, 7; Sir W. Daines, 6; R. Hart Davis, 6; J. Whitson, 5; L. Fry, 5. The longest periods of representation have been those of Mr. Berkeley, nearly 33 years; Sir John Knight, sen., 21 years; Mr. Hart Davis, 19 years; Mr. Lewis Fry, 17 years; and Sir W. Daines, 6 years.

Mr. Fry is the only survivor of those who represented Bristol before its division into separate constituencies by the Redistribution Act of 1885. In addition to the four sitting members (Sir Michael Hicks Beach, Sir W. H. Wills, Sir E. S. Hill, and Mr. Fry), there is only one surviving ex-member for the divisions, Alderman Townsend.

Of defeated candidates for the undivided city there are still living Lord Cottesloe, Lord Wimborne, Mr. Sholto Hare, and Sir George Chambers, and of those who have contested any of the four separate constituencies, and are not now in Parliament, there remain Messrs. Judd, Nixon, Lawless, Bissell, Inskip, Gore, Hobson, and O'Connor Power.

The highest number of votes polled for any candidate for the whole city was 10,704 for Mr. Morley, in 1830; the highest in one of the divisional constituencies being 5,190 for Sir E. S. Hill in 1895.

Since the Redistribution Act it has been usual to present a large number of nomination papers for each candidate. Amongst the proposers and seconders have been the following:—

WEST.

1885. Sir M. Hicks Beach, proposed by C. D. Cave; seconded by J. Ford. Mr. Nixon, proposed by W. H. Elkins and F. J. Fry; seconded by Herbert Thomas.

1886. Sir M. Hicks Beach, proposed by C. D. Cave, Councillor Dix, and Alderman Smith; seconded by Councillor Bridges, Alderman Morgan, and Councillor Bartlett. Mr. Judd, proposed by Herbert Thomas and W. H. Elkins; seconded by the Rev. U. R. Thomas.

1892. Sir M. Hicks Beach, proposed by C. D. Cave, Councillors Eberle, Prichard, Walls, and Spofforth; seconded by E. A. Harley, Councillor Marshall, and Steuart Fripp.

1895. Sir M. Hicks Beach, proposed by C. D. Cave, Councillors Eberle and Wathen, E. A. Harvey, and R. H. Warren; seconded by Alderman Prichard, C. W. Paul, and Councillor Walls. Mr. Lawless, proposed by Councillor Hughes; seconded by Kossuth Robinson.

NOTES ON ELECTIONS AND MEMBERS FOR BRISTOL.
Continued.

EAST.

1885, Mr. Cossham, proposed by W. Sommerville and J. Swaish; seconded by W. H. Butler. Mr. Bissell, proposed by T. S. Bush, J. D. Lucas, and the Rev. T. H. Barnett

1886, Mr. Cossham, proposed by W. Sommerville and J. Swaish; seconded by W. Butler and J. Pembery. Mr. Inskip, proposed by Alderman Fox, T. S. Bush, and J. D. Lucas

1890, Sir J. Weston, proposed by Herbert Thomas, J. Pembery, and Councillor W. Butler; seconded by P. J. Worsley, W. Sommerville, jun., and G. Cambridge. Mr. Inskip, proposed by W. Bonner; seconded by R. I. Weight. Mr. Havelock Wilson, proposed by S. W. Pritchett

1892, Sir J. Weston, proposed by Herbert Thomas, W. H. Butler, and A. G. Verrier; seconded by M. Whitwill, J. Pembery, and G. Cambridge

1895 (bye-election), Sir W. H. Wills, proposed by Councillors Swaish and Pembery; Mr. Gore by H. Brabham and W. Whitefield

1895 (general election), Sir W. H. Wills, proposed by Councillors Swaish and Pembery, and A. G. Verrier

SOUTH.

1885, Mr. Weston, proposed by J. C. Godwin, Councillor Pethick, T. Cleverdon, and A. N. Price; seconded by W. H. Budgett, C. W. Allen, and W. D. Willcox. Colonel Hill, proposed by Alderman Edwards and R. C. Stephens; seconded by Alderman Baker

1886, Colonel Hill, proposed by Alderman Edwards; seconded by Councillor W. H. Miles and R. Dugdale. Mr. Weston, proposed by Councillor C. Wills; seconded by C. W. Allen and W. A. Latham

1892, Sir E. S. Hill, proposed by Sir G. Edwards, J. C. Godwin, W. E. Gardner, E. J. Thatcher, Councillors Hill and James; seconded by Councillor Todd and Arthur Robinson. Sir W. H. Wills, proposed by Sir J. D. Weston, Councillors Davies, Lloyd, and Parsons, A. N. Price, and J. W. Arrowsmith; seconded by E. H. Chandler, W. Jennings, W. D. Willcox, Edward Robinson, W. Lane, and Councillors Latham and Cleverdon.

1895, Sir E. S. Hill, proposed by Sir G. Edwards, E. J. Thatcher, J. N. C. Pope, and H. W. Beloe; seconded by Councillors Abbot and James. Mr. O'Connor Power, proposed by Councillors Davies, Parsons, and Lloyd, and A. N. Price; seconded by Councillor Latham, E. Robinson, and F. Moore

NORTH.

1885, Mr. Fry, proposed by Councillor C. E. L. Gardner and J. Coulthard; seconded by Councillor J. W. Hall. Mr. Colston, proposed by Dr. Highett

1886, Mr. Fry, proposed by N. Palmer and R. Champion; seconded by G. E. Davies. Dr. Carpenter, proposed by J. Coulthard

1892, Mr. Townsend, proposed by Councillors Cunningham and Ashman, the Rev. J. R. Graham, C. Newth, and R. W. Ashley. Mr. Fry, proposed by J. W. Hall, N. Palmer, and A. Brittan; seconded by R. Champion and A. Lee

1895. Mr. Fry, proposed by J. W. Hall, N. Palmer, A. Lee, J. W. Lane, and Councillor Cottrell; seconded by Alderman Fox and G. E. Davies. Mr. Townsend, proposed by Councillors Ashman and Elkins, and R. W. Ashley; seconded by Councillor Newth.

THE OLD CORPORATION OF BRISTOL FROM 1599 TO THE PASSING OF THE MUNICIPAL CORPORATIONS ACT OF 1835.

I was enabled, some years ago, by the kindness and with the active assistance of the Town Clerk, Mr. Travers Burges, and the City Treasurer, Mr. Tremayne Lane, to compile a practically complete record of the succession of Aldermen and Common Councillors of Bristol from the date of the earliest existing Minute Books (1599) to the Municipal Reform Act of 1835. I have frequently been urged to publish my collections, no such list having ever been printed, and I have, therefore, determined to include them in the present compilation.

ALDERMEN.

The number of Aldermen under the Charter of Henry VII. (December 17, 1499) was six, including the Recorder; this was increased to twelve by the Charter of Elizabeth (July 28, 1581). Three Aldermen (Thomas Chester, Thomas Kelke, and William Tucker) died in the same week in September, 1583. In 1591 nine of the twelve Aldermen were William Hopkins, Mayor; Thomas Hannam, Recorder; John Browne, Philip Langley, Thomas Aldworth, Thomas Colston, Richard Cole, William Hickes, and John Barnes.

The Minute Book under date January 13, 1598-9, gives the following list, from which time the succession is continuous. When the cause of a vacancy is not otherwise stated, it was created by the death of the Alderman whose place was filled:—

William Ellys, Mayor; George Snigge, Recorder; Thomas Aldworth, Richard Cole, William Hickes, Francis Knight, William Parfrey, William Yate, John Webbe, John Horte, John Hopkins, and William Vawer

[Mr. Ellys' place, according to seniority, was between Messrs. Webbe and Horte.]

March, 1598-9—Ralph Hurte, *vice* Aldworth
October, 1599—Rice Jones, *vice* Cole
June, 1600—John Whitson, *vice* Horte
March, 1601-2—Christopher Kedgwin, *vice* Jones
Early in 1604—Thomas James, *vice* Yate
September 25, 1605—Lawrence Hyde, Recorder, *vice* Snigge
January 8, 1607-8—Richard Smyth, *vice* Parfrey
September, 1609—Matthew Haviland, *vice* Smyth
March 4, 1610-11—John Butcher, *vice* Ellys
January 8, 1613-4—Robert Aldworth, *vice* Webbe
August 10, 1615—John Eglesfield, *vice* Hurte

THE OLD CORPORATION OF BRISTOL.—*Continued.*

August 13, 1615—Nicholas Hyde, Recorder, *vice* L. Hyde, resigned
December 13, 1615—William Cary, *vice* Hopkins
August 27, 1616—Abel Kitchin, *vice* Knight
August 8, 1618—Thomas Farmer, *vice* Cary, resigned on being appointed Master of the Back Hall; George Harrington, *vice* Hickes
February 9, 1618-19—John Guy, *vice* James
February 24, 1619-20—Thomas Packer, *vice* Vawer; John Doughty, *vice* Kedgwin
March 14, 1619 20—Robert Rogers, *vice* Haviland
July 15, 1623—William Young, *vice* Butcher
September 1, 1624—William Pitt, *vice* Packer
December 24, 1624—Henry Gibbes, *vice* Farmer
March 15, 1628-9—John Barker, *vice* Guy; Christopher Whitson, *vice* Whitson
February 15, 1629-30—John Gonninge, *vice* Doughty
August 5, 1630—John Glanville, Recorder, *vice* Hyde
March 20, 1631-2—John Langton, *vice* Eglesfield; Humphrey Hooke, *vice* Pitt
May, 1633—John Tomlinson, *vice* Rogers
July 25, 1634—Henry Yate, *vice* Young
July 15, 1635—Henry Hobson, *vice* Aldworth
April 12, 1636—Andrew Charleton, *vice* Hobson
August 13, 1636—Richard Holworthie, *vice* Barker; Richard Longe *vice* Gibbes
January 9, 1636-7—William Jones, *vice* Langton
January 23, 1636-7—Ezekiel Wallis, *vice* Yate
June 6, 1638—George Knight, *vice* Whitson
January 13, 1639-40—John Tayler, *vice* Harrington
August 4, 1640—John Lock, *vice* Kitchin
December 9, 1643—Alexander James, *vice* Holworthie; Francis Creswicke, *vice* Charleton
June 5, 1645—Thomas Colston, *vice* Gonninge
October 20, 1645—Richard Aldworth, *vice* Tayler
January 5, 1645-6—Edmund Prideaux, Recorder, *vice* Glanville, removed
September 14, 1646—John Gonninge, *vice* Jones
[In December, 1645, in accordance with an Ordinance of the Parliament, dated October 28 of that year, the Royalist Aldermen (Hooke, Longe, Wallis, James, Creswicke, and Colston) were removed, and their successors, all of whom were, of course, Parliamentarians, were elected at the meeting of the Council on September 15, 1646.]
September 15, 1646—Richard Vickris, Gabriel Sherman, Luke Hodges, Henry Gibbes, Joseph Jackson, and Hugh Browne
March 9, 1647-8—William Cann, *vice* Tomlinson
August 6, 1650—Miles Jackson, *vice* Gibbes, resigned
November 11, 1651—Bulstrode Whitelocke, Recorder, *vice* Prideaux, resigned
July 16, 1652—Henry Gibbes, *vice* Hodges, resigned
September 30, 1654—George Hellier, *vice* Browne
May 4, 1655—John Doddridge, Recorder, *vice* Whitelocke, resigned
August 29, 1655—Walter Deyos, *vice* Aldworth
[On February 18, 1655-6, Aldermen Knight, Lock, and Sherman resigned, nominally on the plea of age and infirmity, but really under compulsion, being suspected of favouring the Royalists, and, Alderman Hellier having died on April 21, the four vacancies were filled on September 5 following.]
September 5, 1656—Richard Balman, Arthur Farmer, Walter Sandy and Edward Tyson
June 8, 1658—George White, *vice* Cann

THE OLD CORPORATION OF BRISTOL.—*Continued.*

October 16, 1658—Robert Chaloner, *vice* Deyos
 [Alderman Chaloner resigned nine days afterwards, October 25, on appointment to the Mastership of the Back Hall.]
December 31, 1658—Robert Yate, *vice* Chaloner
March 29, 1659—John Stephens, Recorder, *vice* Doddridge
June 19, 1660—By *mandamus* of this date it was ordered that John Lock and Gabriel Sherman be restored to their seats as Aldermen; the Council demurred at first, on the ground that they had voluntarily resigned; but on November 6, 1660, Lock resumed his place, and on August 23, 1661, Sherman and Alexander James, who had been removed in 1645, were also restored, bringing the total number of Aldermen to 15. Sherman does not appear in the list after October 31, 1661; James did not resume his seat; he was re-elected March 1, 1663-4, but not sworn, and was finally discharged September 12, 1665
September 27, 1661—Henry Creswicke, *vice* White, resigned
 [On October 4, 1661, an order was made for displacing all those who had been "unduly brought in" during the Commonwealth period, and restoring the Aldermen and Councillors who had been removed. In accordance with this order, Aldermen Vickris and Gibbes, who had been elected in 1646 in place of the Royalist Aldermen then removed, and also Aldermen Tyson and Yate, ceased to attend the Council. The other Aldermen elected during the Commonwealth period, with the exception of Alderman Sherman, whose name disappears from the list after October 31, seems to have retained their seats. Alderman Farmer appears to have been removed under the provisions of the Corporation Act about December, 1662, having ceased to attend at the end of the preceding year.]
October, 1661—William Colston and Richard Gregson
April, 1662—John Knight
May 27, 1662—Sir Robert Atkyns, Recorder, *vice* Stephens, resigned
August 25, 1662—Nathaniel Cale, *vice* J. Jackson
December, 1662—Sir Humphrey Hooke, *vice* Farmer
July 25, 1663—Sir Robert Cann, Bart., *vice* Gonninge; John Pope, *vice* M. Jackson; John Lawford, *vice* Gregson
 [Mr. Pope was removed September 29, 1663, for refusing to take the Mayoralty. His place was not filled, and the normal number of 12 Aldermen was resumed.]
August 24, 1664—John Willoughby, *vice* Colston; Edward Morgan, *vice* Hooke
 [Aldermen Colston and Sir H. Hooke had resigned on June 7; Mr. Morgan declined to serve.]
September 16, 1664—Thomas Langton, *vice* Morgan
September 12, 1665—Edward Morgan, *vice* James, resigned
August 31, 1667—Thomas Stevens and John Hickes, *vice* Lock and Balman
August 17, 1669—John Wright, *vice* Creswicke
September 5, 1672—Sir Robert Yeamans, Bart., John Knight, jun., and Richard Streamer, *vice* Sandy, Morgan, and Cale
September 2, 1673—Ralph Olliffe and William Crabb, *vice* Willoughby and Wright
 [Mr. Olliffe died September 30, 1683, and his place was not filled up before the revocation of the Charter.]
August 2, 1675—Richard Crumpe, *vice* Langton
August 21, 1679—Sir John Lloyd, Tory, *vice* Stevens; Joseph Creswicke, Tory, *vice* Knight, jun.
October 11, 1680—Richard Hart, Tory, *vice* Streamer
March 8, 1680-1—Thomas Day, Whig, *vice* Lloyd, resigned
September 28, 1681—Thomas Earle, Tory, *vice* Day, unseated

THE OLD CORPORATION OF BRISTOL.—*Continued.*

December 19, 1682—Sir John Churchill, Tory, Recorder, *vice* Atkyns, resigned
August 22, 1683—Thomas Eston, Tory, *vice* Earle, unseated
In 1683, a writ of *quo warranto* having been issued against the Corporation, the Charter was surrendered on December 9 in that year, and on June 2, 1684, a new Charter was granted, the King nominating the whole of the Council. The surviving old Aldermen, all of whom were Tories, were re-appointed. The names were:—Sir John Churchill, Recorder; Sir Robert Cann, Bart., John Lawford, Sir Robert Yeamans, Bart., John Hickes, William Crabb, Sir Richard Crumpe, Joseph Creswicke, Sir Richard Hart, Thomas Eston, Sir William Clutterbuck, and William Hayman, the two last named taking the places vacant by the deaths of Sir J. Knight and R. Olliffe.
November, 1685—The Hon. Roger North, Recorder, Tory, *vice* Churchill
June 21, 1686—John Moore, *vice* Hart, removed
August 28, 1686—Abraham Saunders, *vice* Cann
March 23, 1686-7—William Swymmer, Whig, *vice* Yeamans; John Coombes, *vice* Moore, resigned
On January 13, 1687-8, Aldermen Hickes, Eston, Sir W. Clutterbuck, Saunders, Swymmer, and Coombes were removed on account of their opposition to the Declaration of Indulgence; their successors were nominated by the King on January 14, and admitted February 4.
February 4, 1687-8—Michael Pope, Whig, Walter Stephens, William Jackson, Whig, William Brown, Humphrey Corsley, Tory, and Thomas Scrope
April 11, 1688—Simon Hurle, *vice* Stephens, removed
September 15, 1688—Henry Gibbes, *vice* Hurle, removed
On October 17, 1688, the old Charter was restored, when six of the old Aldermen who survived resumed their offices, viz.:—
John Hickes, Tory; William Crabb, Tory; Sir Richard Crumpe, Tory; Joseph Creswicke, Tory; Sir Richard Hart, Tory; Thomas Eston, Tory
October 27, 1688—William Powlett, Recorder, Whig, *vice* North, resigned
August 5, 1689—Sir William Clutterbuck, Tory; Thomas Day, Whig
August 8, 1689—Alderman Eston's election in 1683 declared void, and Sir Thomas Earle restored to his seat with the presidency of 1681
On the same day the number of Aldermen was completed by the election of
William Jackson, Whig; Edward Feilding, Whig; William Donning, Whig
[October 21, 1690—Sir Thomas Earle was removed, but was restored by writ of the King's Bench February 27, 1690-1.]
February 23, 1690-1—Sir William Hayman, Tory, *vice* Feilding
July 12, 1692—William Swymmer, Whig, *vice* Donning
June 29, 1696—Richard Lane, Whig, *vice* Earle
February 3, 1699-1700—Robert Yate, Whig, *vice* Crumpe
March 20, 1699-1700—Samuel Wallis, Whig, *vice* Hickes
February 19, 1701-2—John Blackwell, Whig, *vice* Harte
July 14, 1702—John Bacheler, *vice* Clutterbuck, resigned
August 13, 1702—Sir William Daines, Whig, *vice* Hayman
October 26, 1702—Sir John Hawkins, Tory, *vice* Crabb
March 24, 1702-3—William Lewis, Tory, *vice* Blackwell
July 19, 1704—Robert Eyre, Recorder, Whig, *vice* Powlett
June 30, 1705—Peter Saunders, *vice* Lane
October 27, 1705—Francis Whitchurch, *vice* Saunders
April 21, 1708—Nathaniel Day, *vice* Creswicke
January 21, 1709-10—George Stephens, *vice* Sir T. Day.

THE OLD CORPORATION OF BRISTOL —*Continued*.

November 9, 1711—William Whitehead, Whig, *vice* Bacheler
March 7, 1711-12—Robert Bound, *vice* Whitehead
May 26, 1712—Abraham Elton, Whig, *vice* Lewis (created a Baronet October 1717)
February 7, 1714-15—Christopher Shuter, Whig, *vice* Swymmer
December 29, 1715—Anthony Swymmer, Whig, *vice* Bound
April 21, 1716—Henry Whitehead, Whig, *vice* Jackson
June 18, 1718—Henry Walter, Whig, *vice* Whitchurch
December 6, 1718—Nicholas Hickes, Whig, *vice* Stephens
August 29, 1719—Thomas Clement, Whig, *vice* Swymmer
December 2, 1719—Edmund Mountjoy, Whig, *vice* N. Day
January 10, 1722-3—Abraham Elton, Whig, *vice* Clements (succeeded to the Baronetcy February 9, 1727-8)
July 15, 1723—John Becher, Whig, *vice* Hawkins
October 7, 1723—Henry Swymmer, Whig, *vice* Whitehead
September 23, 1724—James Donning, Whig, *vice* Daines
September 25, 1725—Joseph Jefferis, Whig, *vice* Wallis
November 29, 1727—Robert Earle, Whig, *vice* Hickes
February 21, 1727-8—Peter Day, Whig, *vice* Sir A. Elton
July 22, 1728—John Scrope, Whig, Recorder, *vice* Eyre
June 15, 1730—Henry Nash, Whig, *vice* Shuter
October 3, 1732—John Price, Whig, *vice* Swymmer
February 21, 1734-5—Arthur Taylor, Whig, *vice* P. Day
August 6, 1735—Michael Foster, Whig, Recorder, *vice* Scrope, resigned
September 4, 1735—Jacob Elton, Whig, *vice* Mountjoy
February 3, 1736-7—John Rich, Whig, *vice* Earle
November 9, 1737—Lionel Lyde, Whig, *vice* Yate; John Blackwell, Whig, *vice* Walter
February 12, 1738-9—Nathaniel Day, Whig, *vice* Price
   [Mr. Day voted for the Tory candidates in 1754.]
June 1, 1742—William Jefferis, Whig, *vice* Nash, resigned
November 1, 1742—Stephen Clutterbuck, Whig, *vice* Sir A. Elton
July 20, 1743—Henry Combe, Whig, *vice* Becher
January 9, 1745-6—John Day, Whig, *vice* Lyde; William Barnes, Whig, *vice* Taylor
October 8, 1747—Edward Cooper, Whig, *vice* Donning; John Foy, Whig, *vice* Clutterbuck
November 30, 1749—Buckler Weekes, Whig, *vice* J. Day
October 3, 1750—Thomas Curtis, Whig, *vice* Blackwell
May 9, 1752—James Laroche, Whig, *vice* W. Jefferis
October 4, 1752—David Peloquin, Whig, *vice* Combe
November 3, 1753—John Clements, Whig, *vice* J. Jefferis
September 30, 1754—Abraham Elton, Whig, *vice* Curtis
September 30, 1755—Morgan Smith, Whig, *vice* Rich
   [Mr. Smith voted for the Tory candidates in 1774, but for the Whigs in 1781, as he had done at all contests before 1774.]
October 13, 1760—Henry Dampier, Whig, *vice* Clements
February 8, 1762—Giles Baily, Whig, *vice* Cooper
August 30, 1762—William Martin, Whig, *vice* A. Elton
March 16, 1763—The Hon. Daines Barrington, Whig, Recorder, *vice* Foster
February 11, 1765—Henry Mugleworth, Tory, *vice* Martin
June 27, 1765—Jeremiah Ames, Whig, *vice* J. Elton
August 31, 1765—John Durbin, Whig, *vice* N. Day
February 5, 1766—John Dunning, Whig, Recorder, *vice* Burrington, resigned; created Lord Ashburton April, 1782
March 27, 1766—Isaac Elton, Whig, *vice* Peloquin
   [Mr. Elton voted for the Tory candidates in 1774.]
February 8, 1767—John Noble, Whig, *vice* Baily
August 8, 1767—Richard Farr, Whig, *vice* Barnes
March 31, 1768—Isaac Baugh, Whig, *vice* Noble
   [Mr. Baugh plumped for Brickdale (Tory) in 1774.]

THE OLD CORPORATION OF BRISTOL.—*Continued.*

October 15, 1770—William Barnes, Whig, *vice* Laroche, resigned
 [Mr. Barnes plumped for Brickdale in 1774.]
February 6, 1771—George Weare, Whig, *vice* Foy
October 28, 1771—Edward Whatley, Tory, *vice* Dampier
April 15, 1772—Thomas Deane, Whig, *vice* Weekes
April 18, 1776—Thomas Harris, Tory, *vice* Ames
June 17, 1776—Nathaniel Foy, Tory, *vice* Elton
November 12, 1777—Robert Gordon, Whig, *vice* Barnes
December 19, 1778—Charles Hotchkin, Tory, *vice* Weare
December 4, 1779—Andrew Pope, Whig, *vice* Whatley
August 29, 1781—Sir John Durbin, Tory, *vice* Smith
June 1, 1782—William Miles, Tory, *vice* Farr
July 25, 1782—Henry Cruger, Whig, *vice* Mugleworth
August 14, 1782—Edward Brice, Tory, *vice* Hotchkin
May 8, 1783—John Merlott, Whig, *vice* Foy
December 10, 1783—Richard Burke, Whig, Recorder, *vice* Ashburton
August 23, 1784—John Anderson, Whig, *vice* Pope
February 9, 1785—John Farr, Whig, *vice* Gordon
January 16, 1786—John Crofts, Whig, *vice* Merlott
January 15, 1787—George Daubeny, Tory, *vice* Baugh
December 8, 1788—Alexander Edgar, Whig, *vice* Crofts, resigned
February 25, 1792—Levi Ames, Whig, *vice* Edgar; Jeremy Baker, Tory,
 vice Durbin, sen. [Mr. Baker declined to serve.]
September 26, 1792—John Harris, Whig, *vice* Baker
December 1, 1792—John Noble, Whig, *vice* Cruger, resigned
March 12, 1794—Vicary Gibbs, Tory, Recorder, *vice* Burke—knighted
 February 20, 1805
March 4, 1797—Henry Bengough, Whig, *vice* T. Harris
June 12, 1797—Joseph Harford, Whig, *vice* Farr
January 17, 1798—James Harvey, Whig, *vice* Anderson
October 27, 1798—*Thomas Daniel, jun., Tory, *vice* Deane
July 11, 1801—Robert Claxton, Whig, *vice* J. Harris
December 23, 1802—Evan Baillie, Whig, *vice* Harford
April 16, 1803—John Morgan, Whig, *vice* Miles
September 24, 1806—William Gibbons, Tory, *vice* Daubeny
May 13, 1807—David Evans, Whig, *vice* Gibbons
December 21, 1807—John Page, Whig, *vice* Harvey
February 22, 1808—Daniel Wait, Tory, *vice* Morgan
June 16, 1810—Richard Vaughan, jun., Tory, *vice* Brice—knighted
 April 20, 1815
October 24, 1812—William Fripp, Whig, *vice* Claxton
March 3, 1814—Samuel Birch, Tory, *vice* Wait; *John Haythorne,
 Tory, *vice* Durbin
September 16, 1816—John Hilhouse Wilcox, Whig, *vice* Evans
January 14, 1818—Sir Robert Gifford, Tory, Recorder, *vice* Gibbs,
 resigned; created Lord Gifford January, 1824
September 29, 1819—Henry Brooke, Tory, *vice* Bengough
January 3, 1821—James Fowler, Tory, *vice* Birch, resigned; *William
 Fripp, jun., Whig, *vice* Ames
 [Mr. Fripp afterwards left the Whigs and became one of the Conservative leaders, and a candidate for the Parliamentary representation in that interest.]
November 3, 1822—George Hilhouse, Tory, *vice* Page; *Abraham
 Hilhouse, Tory, *vice* Baillie, resigned; Stephen Cave, Tory,
 vice Wilcox, resigned on appointment to the Registrarship of
 the Court of Conscience
September 28, 1826—Sir John Singleton Copley, Tory, Recorder
May 16, 1827—*James George, Tory, *vice* Cave, resigned
July 28, 1827—*Sir Charles Wetherell, Tory, Recorder, *vice* Copley,
 resigned
February 2, 1828—John Barrow, Tory, *vice* Noble
December 24, 1828—Thomas Hassell, Tory, *vice* Vaughan, resigned

THE OLD CORPORATION OF BRISTOL.—*Continued.*

July 4, 1829—*Gabriel Goldney, Tory, *vice* Fripp, sen.; *Thomas Camplin, Tory, *vice* Brooke
September 10, 1831—*John Savage, Tory, *vice* Hassell
March 4, 1834—*Nicholas Roch, Tory, *vice* Fowler, resigned

Those marked (*) were Aldermen at the date of the passing of the Municipal Corporation Act, 1835. Alderman Barrow had resigned on October 25, 1834, and Alderman G. Hillhouse in May, 1835, and the vacancies thereby created were not filled up. The latter remained a member of the Common Council, but the former withdrew entirely from the Corporation. Messrs. Cruger, Baillie, and Fowler had retained their seats in the Common Council after resigning their Aldermancies, the two former till their deaths, and the last till the passing of the Act of 1835.

The ancient city was divided into eleven wards, viz., those of Trinity, St. Michael, Redcliff, St. Nicholas, St. James, St. Ewen, St. Stephen, Temple, St. Maryleport, and St. Thomas. To these, on the destruction of the Castle in the time of the Commonwealth, was added the Ward of Castle Precincts. Each of the twelve Aldermen was assigned to one of these wards, and on the occurrence of a vacancy each Alderman in turn, in order of seniority, had, in accordance with an order dated March 29, 1614, and confirmed August 23, 1636, the option of transferring himself to the ward then vacant. After the passing of the Municipal Corporation Act of 1835, the ancient wards were still retained for purposes of Poor-law administration, two guardians being chosen to represent each of them in the Incorporation of the Poor, at a ward mote presided over by the Alderman of the ward. Accordingly, on February 19, 1836, twelve of the sixteen Aldermen elected under the provisions of the new Act were assigned to the ancient wards, and similar nominations were made annually until 1894. This system was abolished by the Poor Law Amendment Act of 1894, and the ancient wards and their Aldermen then ceased to exist. The following is the succession of the Aldermen in their respective wards as far as can be ascertained from the Minute Books. There is preserved a list of the division of the wards amongst the Aldermen on March 6, 1620-1, and occasional notes of appointments to vacancies up to 1689, since which date the succession is practically complete:—

TRINITY.

Mar. 6, 1620-1, J. Butcher
Oct. 3, 1623, W. Young
1634, A. Kitchin
Aug. 4, 1640, J. Tayler
Oct. 20, 1645, R. Aldworth
Aug. 29, 1655, W. Deyos
Dec. 31, 1658, R. Yate
July 25, 1663, N. Cale
Sept. 5, 1672, T. Stevens
Aug. 21, 1679, R. Olliffe
1680, R. Hart
1686, J. Shore
1687, J. Coombes
Aug. 9, 1688, H. Corsley
Sept. 6, 1689, W. Donning
July 12, 1692, Sir W. Hayman
July 2, 1700, W. Swymmer
1715, C. Shuter
Oct. 5, 1716, R. Yate
Nov. 9, 1737, J. Blackwell
July 20, 1743, H. Combe

Jan. 11, 1745-6, J. Day
Sept. 30, 1748, J. Foy
Feb. 8, 1762, J. Bailey
June 27, 1765, H. Mugleworth
Oct. 28, 1771, E. Whatley
Nov. 20, 1771, J. Dunning, Recorder
Feb. 16, 1784, R. Burke, Recorder
Mar. 15, 1794, V. Gibbs, Recorder
Mar. 2, 1818, Sir R. Gifford, Recorder
Jan. 4, 1827, Sir J. S. Copley, Recorder
July 28, 1827, Sir C. Wetherell, Recorder
Feb. 19, 1836, C. Pinney
Jan. 2, 1854, P. Vaughan
Jan. 1, 1865, G. R. Woodward
Jan. 2, 1882, F. F. Fox

THE OLD CORPORATION OF BRISTOL.—*Continued.*

ST. MICHAEL.

Mar. 6, 1620-1, T. Packer
1624, G. Harrington
Jan., 1639-40, J. Tayler
Aug. 4, 1640. J. Lock
Sept. 15, 1646, J. Jackson
Aug., 1662, N. Cale
July 25, 1663, J. Pope
Oct. 15, 1664, T. Langton, till 1673
1675, R. Streamer
1680, J. Lawford
1688, H. Gibbes
Sept. 6, 1689, Sir W. Clutterbuck
July 18, 1702, R. Lane
Aug. 13, 1705, P. Saunders
Sept. 30, 1706, F. Whitchurch

Oct. 5, 1716, A. Swymmer
Aug., 1719, P. Clements
Oct. 3, 1732, J. Becher
July 20, 1743, J. Blackwell
Sept. 30, 1748, J. Cooper
Feb. 8, 1762, J. Foy
Feb. 6, 1771, H. Dampier
Oct. 28, 1771, H. Mugleworth
July 25, 1782, Sir J. Durbin
Mar. 3, 1814, T. Daniel
Feb. 19, 1836, J. Vining
Jan. 1, 1859, S. V. Hare
Jan. 1, 1881, H. Adams
Jan. 2, 1832, W. Spark
Jan. 1, 1887, C. Nash
Jan. 1, 1839, W. W. Jose

ALL SAINTS.

Mar. 6, 1620-1, J. Whitson
1628-9, J. Barker
Aug. 23, 1636, R. Holworthie
Dec. 9, 1643, A. James
Sept. 15, 1646, J. Lock
Sept., 1656, R. Vickris
1661, J. Lock, till Oct., 1666
Aug., 1667, J. Wickes
Aug. 9, 1688, T. Scrope
Sept. 6, 1689, Sir R. Hart
July 18, 1702, J. Blackwell
Oct. 13, 1702, J. Bacheler
Mar., 1712, R. Bound
Dec. 16, 1712, G. Stephens
Feb. 25, 1718-9, H. Walter
1725, H. Swymmer
Oct., 1732. J. Price
Nov. 9, 1736, A. Taylor

Feb. 12, 1738-9, J. Elton
Mar. 18, 1742, L. Lyde
Jan. 11, 1745-6, H. Combe
May 21, 1752, J. Laroche
Oct. 15, 1770, W. Barnes
Nov. 12, 1777, R. Gordon
Feb. 9, 1785, J. Farr
June 12, 1797, J. Harford
Dec. 23, 1802, E. Baillie
Nov. 3, 1822, J. Haythorne
Feb. 19, 1836, W. Watson
Jan. 1, 1839, W. Fripp
Jan. 1, 1846, T. Lucas
Jan. 1, 1857, T. Proctor
Jan. 1, 1860, R. Phippen
Jan. 1, 1870, F. F. Fox
Jan. 1, 1872, W. Hathway
Jan. 1, 1892, J. W. S. Dix

REDCLIFF.

March 6, 1620-1, A. Kitchin
1634, J. Langton
Jan. 9, 1636-7, W. Jones
Sept. 15, 1646, H. Browne
Sept. 30, 1654, G. Hellier
Sept. 5, 1656, A. Farmer
1662, W. Colston
Oct. 15, 1664, J. Willoughby
Sept., 1673, R. Olliffe
Aug. 21, 1679, Sir R. Crumpe
Aug., 1688. T. Day
Jan. 21, 1709-10, N. Day
Jan., 1729, E. Mountjoy
Nov. 9, 1736, H. Nash
June 1, 1742, W. Jefferis
Jan. 11, 1745-6, W. Barnes
Oct. 19, 1747, E Cooper
1750, T. Curtis
Oct. 4, 1752, D. Peloquin
Oct. 11, 1754, A. Elton

Aug. 30, 1762, W. Martin
Feb. 11, 1765, H. Mugleworth
June 27, 1765, J. Ames
Feb. 8, 1767, J. Noble
Mar. 31, 1768, I. Baugh
Feb. 6, 1771, G. Weare
April 15, 1772, T. Deane
June 1, 1782, W. Miles
Mar. 4, 1797, H. Bengough
Oct. 27, 1798, T. Daniel
Sept. 24, 1806, W. Gibbons
May 13, 1807, D. Evans
Sept. 16, 1816. J. H. Wilcox
Nov. 3, 1822, W. Fripp, jun.
Feb. 19, 1836, T. H. Riddle
Jan. 1, 1842, H. Ricketts
Jan. 1, 1845, J. Ricketts
Jan. 1, 1846, H. Ricketts
Jan. 1, 1860, T. Proctor
Jan. 1, 1877, G. W. Edwards

THE OLD CORPORATION OF BRISTOL.—*Continued.*

CASTLE PRECINCTS.

In the time of Charles II. the Mayor for the year, whether an Alderman or Common Councillor only, appears to have acted as the Alderman of this ward: in August, 1688, the Recorder (the Hon. Roger North); and in the reigns of William III. and Anne the Mayor again filled that post.

On November 9, 1736, the Recorder (Sir Michael Foster) was the Alderman; after him the succession was:—

Oct. 19, 1747, J. Foy
Dec. 4, 1749, B. Weekes
Nov. 3, 1753, J. Clements
Oct. 13, 1760, H. Dampier
April 5, 1766, J. Dunning, Recorder
Nov. 20, 1771, E. Whatley
Dec. 4, 1779, A. Pope
Aug. 23, 1784, J. Anderson
Jan. 17, 1798, J. Harvey
Dec. 21, 1807, J. Page
Nov. 3, 1822, G. Hillhouse

Feb. 19, 1836, J. K. Haberfield
Jan. 12, 1837, Nehemiah Moore
[Mr. Moore was not an Alderman, but Councillor for St. Paul's Ward.]
Jan. 1, 1838, E. Butcher
Jan. 1, 1851, W. W. Alexander
Jan. 1, 1875, G. K. Morgan
Jan. 2, 1893, W. Pethick
Jan. 1, 1894, J. Inskip

ST. NICHOLAS.

March 6, 1620-1, J. Doughty
1630, J. Gonninge
June, 1645, T. Colston
Sept. 15, 1646, J. Gonninge (the second)
July 25, 1663, Sir R. Cann, Bart., till 1685
1686, A. Saunders
Aug. 19, 1688, W. Browne
Sept. 6, 1689, Sir T. Earle
June 29, 1696, R. Lane
July 18, 1702, S. Wallis
1725, H. Walter
Feb. 12, 1738 9, A. Taylor
Jan. 11, 1745-6, W. Jefferis

1752, T. Curtis
Oct. 11, 1754, D. Peloquin
Mar. 27, 1766, I. Elton
June 17, 1776, T. Harris
Mar. 4, 1797, W. Miles
April 16, 1803, R. Claxton
Oct. 24, 1812, R. Vaughan
Mar. 3, 1814, J. Haythorne
Nov. 3, 1822, A. Hillhouse
Feb. 19, 1836, W. Bushell
Jan. 1, 1845, F. G. Prideaux
Jan. 2, 1848, J. George
Jan. 1, 1851, R. G. Barrow
Jan. 1, 1875, H. Brittan
Jan. 1, 1882, J. Harvey

ST. JAMES.

Mar. 6, 1620-1, R. Aldworth
Aug., 1635, H. Hobson
Aug. 23, 1636, A. Charleton
Dec. 9, 1643, F. Creswicke
Sept. 15, 1646, L. Hodges
July, 1652, H. Gibbes
(?) 1662, R. Gregson
July 25, 1663, J. Lawford, till Oct., 1664
1665, E. Morgan
Sept. 5, 1672, R. Streamer
Aug., 1675, R. Crumpe
Aug. 21, 1679, Sir J. Lloyd
Sept. 28, 1681, T. Earle
Sept. 9, 1684, T. Eston
Aug. 19, 1688, M. Pope
Sept. 6, 1689, E. Feilding
Dec. 16, 1691, Sir W. Hayman
July 12, 1692, W. Swymmer
July 2, 1700, S. Wallis
July 18, 1702, J. Bacheler
Oct. 13, 1702, Sir W. Daines
Aug. 26, 1708, N. Day
Aug. 14, 1710, G. Stephens

Dec. 16, 1712, A. Elton
Oct. 5, 1716, H. Whitehead
Feb. 25, 1718-9, N. Hickes
1728, P. Day
Nov. 9, 1736, J. Price
Feb. 12, 1738-9, Sir A. Elton, Bart.
Nov. 8, 1742, J. Elton
June 27, 1765, G. Bailey
Feb. 8, 1767, M. Smith
Aug. 29, 1781, I. Baugh
Jan. 15, 1787, G. Daubeny
Sept. 24, 1806, T. Daniel
Mar. 3, 1814, R. Vaughan
May 16, 1827, J. George
Feb. 19, 1836, T. Stock
Jan. 1, 1839, J. D. Pountney
Jan. 2, 1848, F. G. Prideaux
Jan. 1, 1849, J. D. Pountney
Jan. 1, 1851, W. Plummer
Jan. 1, 1857, R. Phippen
Jan. 1, 1860, R. H. Webb
Jan. 2, 1871, W. P. Baker

THE OLD CORPORATION OF BRISTOL.—*Continued.*

ST. EWEN.

Mar. 6, 1620-1, G. Harrington
Dec. 24, 1624, H. Gibbes
Aug. 23, 1636, R. Longe
Sept. 15, 1646, G. Sherman
Sept., 1656, R. Ballman
Aug., 1658, M. Jackson
July 25, 1663, Sir H. Creswicke till Sept, 1668
Aug., 1669, J. Wright
1673, Sir J. Knight
Sept. 9, 1684, W. Clutterbuck
Aug. 19, 1688, Sir W. Hayman
Sept. 6, 1689, J. Hickes
July 2, 1700, Sir W. Hayman
Oct. 13, 1702, J. Blackwell
Oct. 12, 1703, R. Yate
Oct. 5, 1716, F. Whitchurch
Feb. 25, 1718-9, Sir A. Elton, Bart.
1728, R. Earle
Feb. 12, 1738-9, J. Rich
Sept. 30, 1755, M. Smith
Feb. 8, 1767, J. Ames
Feb. 6, 1771, I. Baugh
Aug. 29, 1781, Sir J. Durbin
July 25, 1782, J. Durbin, sen.
Feb. 25, 1792, J. Baker
Sept. 26, 1792, J. Harris
July 11, 1801, R. Claxton
April 16, 1803, J. Morgan
Feb. 22, 1808, D. Wait
Mar. 3, 1814, W. Fripp
July 4, 1829, J. Barrow
Feb. 19, 1836, J. Winwood
Jan. 1, 1842, C. Grevile
January 2, 1854, T. Green
Jan. 1, 1878, J. A. Jones
Jan. 1, 1891, J. Bartlett

ST. STEPHEN.

Mar. 6, 1620-1, T. Farmer
1624, W. Pitt
Aug., 1632, H. Hooke
Sept. 15, 1646, R. Vickris
Sept., 1656, W. Sandy
Sept. 5, 1672, J. Knight
Aug. 21, 1679, J. Creswicke
April 21, 1708, Sir W. Daines
1725, J. Jefferis
Nov. 3, 1753, Sir M. Foster, Recorder
June 1, 1763, Hon. D. Barrington, Recorder
April 5, 1766, H. Dampier
Feb. 6, 1771, R. Farr
June 1, 1782, T. Deane
Oct. 27, 1798, H. Bengough
Sept. 29, 1819, H. Brooke
July 4, 1829, T. Camplin
Feb. 19, 1836, J. Gibbs
Jan. 2, 1843, R. T. Lilly
Jan. 1, 1844, J. Gibbs
Jan. 1, 1845, R. Robinson
Jan. 1, 1879, R. W. Butterworth
Jan. 1, 1887, W. K. Wait
Jan. 1, 1890, W. Smith

TEMPLE.

Mar. 6, 1620-1, J. Guy
1629, C. Whitson
June 6, 1638, G. Knight
Sept. 5, 1656, E. Tyson
Aug., 1662, J. Knight
1673, W. Crabb
Oct. 26, 1702, Sir J. Hawkins
July, 1723, A. Elton
Feb. 12, 1738-9, N. Day
Aug. 31, 1765, J. Durbin
July 25, 1782, H. Cruger
Dec. 1, 1792, J. Noble
Feb. 2, 1828, J. Barrow
July 4, 1829, G. Goldney
Feb. 19, 1833, E. Harley
Jan. 1, 1852, W. O. Bigg
Jan. 1, 1869, J. F. Lucas
Jan. 1, 1894, W. Pethick

ST. MARYLEPORT.

Mar. 6, 1620-1, J. Eglesfield
Aug., 1632, J. Langton
1634, H. Yate
Jan., 1636-7, E. Wallis
Sept. 15, 1646, H. Gibbes
(?) Aug., 1650, M. Jackson
Aug. 21, 1658, G. White
Sept. 27, 1661, H. Creswicke
Oct. 15, 1664, J. Lawford
1680, R. Olliffe
Sept. 9, 1684, Sir W. Hayman
Aug. 9, 1688, W. Jackson
Oct. 5, 1716, A. Elton
Feb. 25, 1718-9, H. Whitehead
Sept., 1724, J. Donning
Oct. 18, 1746, W. Barnes
Aug. 8, 1767, R. Farr
Feb. 6, 1771, J. Ames
April 18, 1776, T. Harris
June 17, 1776, N. Foy
May 8, 1783, J. Merlott
Jan. 16, 1786, J. Crofts
Dec. 8, 1788, A. Edgar
Feb. 25, 1792, L. Ames

THE OLD CORPORATION OF BRISTOL.—*Continued.*

Jan. 3, 1821, W. Fripp, jun.
Nov. 3, 1822, S. Cave
May 16, 1827, Sir R. Vaughan
Dec. 24, 1828, T. Hassell
Sept. 10, 1831, J. Savage
Feb. 19, 1836, R. Ricketts

Jan. 1, 1842, R. Robinson
Jan. 1, 1845, W. H. Wyld
Jan. 2, 1854, J. H. Wyld
Jan. 1, 1858, F. Adams
Jan. 1, 1877, J. C. Wall

ST. THOMAS.

Mar. 6, 1620-1, R. Rogers
May, 1633, J. Tomlinson
Mar., 1647-8, W. Cann
Aug., 1658, R. Ballman
Sept. 5, 1672, Sir R. Yeamans, Bart.
1667, T. Stevens
1686-7, Sir R. Crumpe
Feb. 3, 1699-1700, R. Yate
Oct. 12, 1703, W. Lewis
Dec. 16, 1712, R. Bound
Oct. 5, 1716, C. Shuter
June, 1730, H. Wash
Nov. 9, 1736, J. Elton
Feb. 12, 1738-9, L. Lyde
Nov. 18, 1742, S. Clutterbuck
Oct. 19, 1747, Sir M. Foster, Recorder
Nov. 3, 1753, B. Weekes

April 15, 1772, G. Weare
Nov. 19, 1778, C. Hotchkin
Aug. 14, 1782, E. Brice
June 16, 1810, R. Vaughan, jun.
Oct. 24, 1812, W. Fripp
Mar. 3, 1814, S. Birch
Jan. 3, 1821, J. Fowler
Mar. 4, 1834, N. Roch
Jan. 12, 1837, J. Maningford
Jan. 1, 1839, T. Cole
Jan. 1, 1845, H. Ricketts
Jan. 1, 1847, J. Moore
Jan. 1, 1851, F. K. Barnes
Jan. 1, 1869, T. Barnes
Jan. 1, 1875, R. W. Butterworth
Jan. 1, 1879, C. W. Cope-Proctor

The Senior Aldermen have been as follows:—

Jan. 13, 1598-9, Thomas Aldworth
Feb., 1598-9, Richard Cole
July, 1599, William Hickes
July, 1618, William Vawer
Jan., 1619-20, John Whitson
Feb., 1628-9, Robert Aldworth
Nov., 1634, Abel Kitchin
July, 1640, John Gonninge
May, 1645, Humphrey Hooke
Dec., 1645, John Tomlinson
Jan., 1647-8, John Knight
Feb., 1655-6, John Gonninge (the second)
Nov., 1662, John Lock
Oct., 1666, Richard Ballman
June, 1667, Walter Sandy
June, 1672, Sir John Knight
Dec., 1683, Sir Robert Cann, Bart.
Nov., 1685, John Lawford
July, 1688, William Crabb
Oct., 1702, Sir Thomas Day
Jan., 1709-10, William Jackson
April, 1716, Robert Yate

Oct., 1737, Sir Abraham Elton, Bart.
Oct., 1742, James Donning
Mar., 1745-6, Joseph Jefferis
Oct., 1752, Jacob Elton
June, 1765, Nathaniel Day
Aug., 1765, William Barnes
July, 1767, John Foy
Jan., 1771, Buckler Weekes
Feb., 1772, Morgan Smith
Aug., 1781, Henry Muglewortb
July, 1782, John Durbin, sen.
Feb., 1792, Thomas Deane
Jan., 1798, Sir John Durbin
Jan., 1814, Levi Ames
Dec., 1820, John Noble
Jan., 1828, Thomas Daniel
Jan., 1836, William Fripp
Nov., 1845, Charles Pinney
Nov., 1853, John Vining
Nov., 1859, Richard Robinson
Oct., 1878, James Ford
Nov., 1882, William Proctor Baker

[Alderman Fox was elected before Alderman Baker, but his continuity of service was broken, he being absent from the Council from 1871 to 1875.]

THE OLD CORPORATION OF BRISTOL.—*Continued.*

COMMON COUNCIL.

The Common Council originally consisted under the Charter of Edward III. (October 30, 1372) of 42 members, viz., the Mayor, the Sheriff, and 40 of "the better and more honest men of the town," chosen by them.

The Charter of Henry VII. (December 17, 1499), which created six Aldermen, increased the Common Council to 43, consisting of the Mayor, two Aldermen selected by him, and 40 others chosen by them. Until 1684 an Alderman, and therefore the Recorder, was not necessarily a member of the Council, but as vacancies among the Aldermen, other than the Recorder, were almost invariably filled by existing members of the Council, it was so in effect. The Charters of 1684 and 1710 made it legally necessary to fill vacancies amongst the Aldermen (except in the case of the Recorder) from the Common Council.

During the seventeenth century the number of 43 was frequently exceeded, and, this being done without legal sanction, a writ of *quo warranto* was issued in the reign of Charles II., calling on the Mayor and Common Council to show by what authority they exercised their powers. The Council, by a formal deed dated November 9, 1683, surrendered their existing Charters, and on June 2, 1684, a new Charter was granted, incorporating the city (which had not hitherto been 'technically a Corporation), establishing a Council of 43, all named in the first instance by the King, who reserved power to remove any of them, or of their successors, at his discretion. On October 17, 1688, the old Charters, the surrender of which had not been duly recorded and enrolled, were restored by Royal proclamation, and the Charter of 1684 was annulled. Queen Anne granted a further Charter, dated July 24, 1710, which declared the City of Bristol to be incorporate, and explicitly renounced the right of removing any of the members of the Corporation, or of its officers.

On January 13, 1598-9, the date of the earliest extant minutes, the Corporation consisted of the following 43 members, viz. :—

*Thomas Aldworth, Alderman, died February 25, 1599 ⎫
*Richard Cole, Alderman, died July, 1599 ⎪
*William Hickes, Alderman, died July, 1618 ⎪
*Francis Knight, Alderman, died August 20, 1616 ⎬ Ex-Mayors
*William Parfrey, Alderman, died September, 1606 ⎪
*William Yate, Alderman, died about December, 1603 ⎪
*John Webbe, Alderman, died December, 1613 ⎭
*William Ellys, Mayor and Alderman, died February, 1610-11
*John Horte, Alderman, died May 4, 1600
*John Hopkins, Alderman, died December, 1615
*William Vawer, Alderman, died about January, 1619-20
*Rice Jones, Alderman, October, 1599 ; died January, 1601-2
†Edward Long, removed September 15, 1604
*Ralph Hurte, Alderman, March, 1598-9 ; died about March, 1614-15
John Whitson, Alderman about July, 1600 ; died February 25, 1628-9
*Christopher Kedgwin, Alderman about March, 1601-2 ; died February 14, 1619-20
*Thomas James, Alderman, 1604 ; died January, 1618-19
†Richard May, died about the end of 1603
*John Barker, died September 13, 1607
*Richard Smyth, Alderman, January 1607-8 ; died May, 1609
*Matthew Haviland, Alderman, August, 1609 ; died March, 1619-20

THE OLD CORPORATION OF BRISTOL.—*Continued.*

†Thomas Pytcher, died about December, 1610
†Richard Rogers, died about June, 1599
†John Slye, died about April, 1599
*John Butcher, Alderman, March, 1610-11; died March, 1622-3
*Robert Aldworth, Alderman, January, 1613-14; died Nov. 6, 1634
*John Eglesfield, Alderman, August, 1615; died about Feb., 1631-2
†Richard George, died about March, 1608-9
*William Cary, Alderman, December, 1615—August, 1618; died about March, 1632-3
*Abell Kitchin, Alderman, August, 1616; died July, 1640
Thomas Salterne, died September, 1600
†John Boulton, died about June, 1619
†William Hopkins, died July, 1610
†Thomas Hopkins, died about May, 1614
†John Harrison, discharged July 2, 1616
†William Colston, died about August, 1603
†John Aldworth, died November, 1615
†John Rowbero, died about May, 1614
†William Barnes, died about February, 1616-17
*Thomas Farmer, Alderman, August, 1618; died about Nov., 1624
George White, discharged December 7, 1613
†John Fownes, died August, 1609
*Thomas Packer, Alderman, February, 1619-20; died about March 1623-4
(Those marked * served the office of Mayor and Sheriff, and those marked † that of Sheriff only.)

The succession since that date has been as follows:—

1599, April 19, *vice* Alderman Aldworth and Slye—William Gibbes, died April 3, 1603. †George Richards, died September, 1610
1599, June 16, *vice* Rogers—John Roberts, died June, 1608
1599, August 16, *vice* Alderman Cole—Andrew Yate, died August, 1602
1600, May 5, *vice* Alderman Horte—†William Cole, died about October, 1613
1600, September 9, *vice* Salterne—*Robert Rogers, Alderman, March, 1619-20; died April 13, 1633
1601-2, February 17, *vice* Alderman Jones—Hugh Murcott, died about January, 1608-9
1602, September 14, *vice* A. Yate—†Thomas Aldworth, discharged August 22, 1611
1603, May 5, *vice* Gibbes—*John Guy, Alderman, February, 1618-9; died about February, 1628-9
1603, September 15, *vice* Colston—†Thomas Moore, died Jan., 1620-1
1604, April 20, *vice* Alderman Yate and May—*William Young, Alderman, July, 1623; died February, 1633-4. Hugh Peard, discharged December 8, 1612
1604, September 15, *vice* Long—†Arthur Needes, discharged January 15, 1615-16. *George Harrington, Alderman, 1618; died January 2, 1639-40
1605, September 20, *vice* Aldermen Parfrey—*John Doughty, Alderman, February 24, 1619-20; died January 2, 1639-40
1608, September 6, *vice* Barker—†William Challoner, died July, 1620
1608-9, January 30, *vice* Roberts—†Thomas Whitehead, discharged July 6, 1613 (having been elected Chamberlain)
1609, September 5, *vice* Alderman Smyth, George, and Murcott—†William Burrus, died about December, 1613. *Henry Gibbes, Alderman, December, 1624; died May 19, 1636. †Christopher Cary, died April, 1618
1610, September 15, *vice* Fownes—*William Pitt, Alderman, September 1624; died about November, 1631
1611, April 9, *vice* W. Hopkins, Pytcher, and Richards—Thomas Tomlinson, died about March, 1621-2. *Christopher Whitson,

THE OLD CORPORATION OF BRISTOL.—*Continued*

Alderman, March. 1628-9; died May, 1638. †Thomas Clements refused to serve, discharged June 27, 1611; he was again elected in 1620.

1611, August 22, *rice* Alderman Ellys and Clements—*John Gonninge, Alderman, February, 1629-30; died May, 1645. *Henry Yate, Alderman, July 25, 1634; died November, 1636

1612, September 8, *rice* T. Aldworth—*John Barker, Alderman, March, 1628-9; died March, 1635-6

1613, July 6, *rice* Peard and Whitehead—†William Baldwin, died December, 1617. *John Langton, Alderman, March, 1631-2; died about December, 1636

1613, December 7, *rice* Cole—*Matthew Warren, died about February, 1634-5

1614, April 12, *rice* Alderman Webbe, White, and Burris—†Thomas Cecil, removed January 29, 1632-3; restored November 13, 1623; died about May. 1630. *Henry Hobson, Alderman, July 15, 1635; died March, 1635-6. †William Lyssett, died September, 1638. *Humphrey Hooke, Alderman, March, 1631-2; removed December 9, 1645. The Council now numbered 44

1614, December 20, *rice* T. Hopkins and Rowbero—*Andrew Charleton, Alderman, April, 1636; died November, 1643. *John Tomlinson, Alderman, May, 1633; died January, 1647-8

1615, August 13, *rice* Alderman Horte—Thomas Fownes, refused to serve

1615-16, January 15, *rice* Fownes and J. Aldworth—†William Turner, died about August, 1631. *Richard Holworthie, Alderman, Aug., 1636; died October, 1643

1616, July 2, *rice* Alderman Hopkins—†Edward Coxe, died July, 1627

1616, September 10, *rice* Alderman Knight and Needes—†Thomas Wright, died about June, 1632. †Oliver Snell, died about Jan., 1631-2

1617-18, January 5, *rice* Barnes and Harrison—*William Jones, Alderman, January, 1636-7; died October, 1645. †Humphrey Browne, died March 22, 1629-30

1618, September 18, *rice* Baldwin—*Richard Longe, Alderman, Aug., 1636; removed December 9, 1645

1618-19, March 2, *rice* C. Cary—†William Pitt, jun., died Oct. 25, 1624

1619, August 3, *rice* Alderman Hickes—†Peter Miller, died June, 1633

1619-20, March 14, *rice* Alderman James, Boulton, and Alderman Vawer—†Thomas Clements, died about September, 1630. *George Knight, Alderman, June, 1638; resigned February 18, 1656. *Ezekiel Wallis, Alderman, January, 1636-7; removed December 9, 1645

1620, September 5, *rice* Alderman Kedgwin—*John Lock, Alderman, August, 1640; resigned February 16, 1656; restored Nov. 6, 1660

1621, September 4, *rice* Alderman Haviland—†Richard Pley, died about November, 1638

1622, September 3, *rice* Challoner—†Nathaniel Butcher, died about February, 1627-8

1623, July 30, *rice* Alderman Butcher and T. Tomlinson—*Alexander James, Alderman, December 6, 1643; removed December 9, 1645; restored August 23, 1661. †Walter Ellis, died June, 1639

1624, November 5, *rice* Alderman Packer—*John Tayler, Alderman, January, 1639-40; killed at the siege, September 9, 1645

1625, September 8, *rice* Pitt, jun.—*Richard Aldworth, Alderman, October, 1645; died August, 1655

1627, July 25, *rice* Alderman Farmer—†Giles Elbridge, died February, 1643-4

1628, July 2, *rice* Coxe—*Francis Creswicke, Alderman, December, 1643; removed December 9, 1645

THE OLD CORPORATION OF BRISTOL.—*Continued.*

1628-9. March 1. *vice* Butcher and Alderman Guy—†Derrick Popley, died about October, 1632. †Thomas Colston, Alderman, June, 1645; removed December 9, 1645

1630. April 6. *vice* Alderman Whitson, Alderman Doughty, and Browne—*Gabriel Sherman, Alderman. Sept., 1646; resigned February 18, 1656; restored August 23, 1661. *John Gonninge, jun., Alderman, September,1646; died November, 1662; †Thomas Jackson, died March, 1634-5

1631. August or September, *vice* Cecil—*Miles Jackson, Alderman, August, 1650; died about February, 166.-3

1631, September 15. *vice* Turner—†Robert Elliott, died about March, 1642-3

1632. July 25, *vice* Clements, Alderman Pitt, and Snell—†William Fitzherbert, removed December 9, 1645; restored August 23, 1661. †John Langton, died April, 1645. †Thomas Lloyd, died about August, 1652

1632. September 11, *vice* Alderman Eglesfield—*William Cann, Alderman, March, 1647-8; died March, 1657-8

1633, August 5. *vice* Wright, Popley, W. Cary, and Alderman Rogers —*Richard Vickris, removed September 13, 1643; restored Sept. 15, 1645. †Thomas Hooke, died about August 1643. †William Hobson, discharged May 10, 1641. †Edward Peters, died April, 1638

1634. August 26, *vice* Miller—†Abraham Edwards, died about December, 1640

1635, July 7. *vice* Alderman Young, Alderman Aldworth,and Warren —†Thomas Woodward, discharged September 16, 165'. †William Wyatt, died about November, 1645. †Luke Hodges, removed September 15, 1643; restored September 15, 1645.

1636. July 6. *vice* Jackson, Alderman Barker and Alderman Hobson —*George Hellier, Alderman, September 0, 1654; died April 21, 1656. † Matthew Warren, discharged March 4, 1652-3. *Henry Gibbes, Alderman, September, 1646—August, 1650, and from July, 1652; removed October, 1661

1637, September 5. *vice* Alderman Gibbes and Alderman Yate— *Richard Ballman, Alderman, September, 1656; resigned about June, 1667. *Walter Deyos, Alderman, August, 1655; died Sept., 1658

1638. April 25. *vice* Alderman Langton—*Joseph Jackson,Alderman, September, 1646; died January 5, 1661-2

1638. August 21, *vice* Peters—*Hugh Browne, Alderman, September, 1645; died about December, 1-53

1639.June 26. *vice* Alderman Whitson and Lyssett—†Robert Yeamans, executed May, 1643. †Edward Pitt, died March, 1642-3

1639. August 19, *vice* Pley—†John Young, died March, 1658

1640. March 30. *vice* Ellis—*Walter Sandy, Alderman, September 1655; died about June, 1672

1640. July 14. *vice* Alderman Harrington—*Arthur Farmer,Alderman, September, 1656; removed November, 1662

1641. June 8, *vice* Alderman Kitchin, and Edwards—Michael Meredith, refused to serve; discharged July 26, 1641. John Bush, discharged September 11, 1643

1641. July 6. *vice* Hobson—†Walter Stephens, died about May, 1654

1643, August 22. *vice* Meredith, Elliot, and Pitt—*Henry Creswicke, removed December 9, 1645; restored June 23, 1660. *Nathaniel Cale, removed December 9, 1645; returned June 23, 1660; †Robert Challoner, Alderman, October 16, 1658; resigned October 25, 1658

1643. September 13, *vice* Yeamans, Vickris, and Hodges—†William Colston, removed December 9, 1645; restored August 23, 1661. †William Tale, discharged September 9, 1657. †Robert Yate, Alderman, December, 1658; removed October, 1661

THE OLD CORPORATION OF BRISTOL.—*Continued.*

1643-4, March 18, *vice* T. Hooke, Alderman Charleton, and Alderman Holworthie—Edmund Arundell, refused to serve, †William Bevan, removed December 9, 1645. Robert Blackborne, discharged September 3, 1650

1645, August 21, *vice* Elbridge, Langton, and Arundell—William Pinney, discharged September 10, 1650. †James Crofte, discharged August 23, 1661. †Thomas Amory, discharged August 23, 1661

1645, September 9, *vice* Alderman Gonninge—†Richard Gregson, removed December 9, 1645; restored June 23, 1660. John Tayler, not sworn. Philip Love, not sworn. †George Hart, died about May, 1658. Thomas Longman, not sworn. John Elbridge, removed December 9, 1645. John Thurston, not sworn. †John Wright, not sworn till after the Restoration (December 6, 1661); Alderman, August, 1669; died September, 1672

[Messrs Gregson, Harte, and Elbridge were sworn on the same day, making the total number of the Council who had qualified 46. On the 11th the city was taken by the Parliamentarians, and the other Councillors elected on the 9th never took their seats, and their names are erased from the lists in the minutes of October 30. Mr. Wright was restored to the Council in 1661. On December 9, an Ordinance of Parliament, dated October 28, was read, removing the Royalist members of the Council, Aldermen Creswicke (Mayor), Hooke, Longe, Wallis, James, and Colston, and Messrs. Fitzherbert, H. Creswicke, W. Colston, Cale, Bevan, Gregson, and Elbridge. Further vacancies had been created by the deaths of Aldermen Jones and Tayler, and Mr. Wyatt.]

1645, December 1, restored by Ordinance of Parliament dated November 1—*Richard Vickris, Alderman, September, 1646; removed October 1661. †Luke Hodges, Alderman, September, 1646–July, 1652; resigned September, 1654

1645, December 30—*Edward Tyson, Alderman, September, 1656; died or removed September, 1661. †George White, Alderman, June, 1658; resigned September, 1661. Josias Clutterbuck, removed September, 1652; re-elected 1654; †George Lane, removed October 1661

1646, September 1—James Powell, resigned on being appointed Chamberlain, November, 1651. *John Lawford, †William Yeamans, Thomas Wall, died September, 1650. *Christopher Griffith. William Grigg, removed September, 1652; re-elected 1654

1646, September 8, †John Pope

[The Council now consisted of the regular number of members, 43.]

1648, September 5, *vice* Alderman Tomlinson—†Thomas Bubb, died about February, 1658-9

1649, July 23, *vice* Bushe—*Robert Cann

1650, September 3, *vice* Blackburne—*John Knight, not sworn; name erased January 20, 1650-1; re-elected 1654. Giles Gough, not sworn, fined September 13, 1652. †Jonathan Blackwell, removed October, 1661.

1650, September 10, *vice* Pinney and Wall—†Robert Vickris. †Thomas Harris, removed October 1661. †John Harper, removed October, 1661

1652, September 13, *vice* Lloyd, Woodward, and Powell—*John Willoughby. John Creswicke refused to serve; fined June 7, 1653. †John Bowen

1653, August 30, *vice* J. Knight and Gough—†Henry Appleton. *John Knight, jun., refused to serve; fined September 12, 1654; re-elected 1661

THE OLD CORPORATION OF BRISTOL.—*Continued.*

1653, September 15, *vice* Grigg and Clutterbuck—Henry Roe, discharged November 19, 1656. *Edward Morgan
1654, August 26, *vice* J. Creswicke—Josias Clutterbuck refused the oaths August 22, 1656
1654, September 12, *vice* Hodges and Alderman Browne—*John Knight, sen., not sworn till the Restoration; restored June 23, 1660. William Grigg, sworn September 9, 1657, with precedure of 1646; removed October, 1661
1655, September 4, *vice* W. Stephens and Knight, jun.—†Nehemiah Collins, Jeremiah Hollway, sworn September 9, 1657. Anthony Gay. All these were removed October, 1661
1656, August 22, *vice* Alderman Knight, Alderman Lock, Alderman Aldworth, Alderman Sherman, Alderman Hellier, and Knight, sen.—†Francis Gleed, died June 1, 1661. George Attwood and †Timothy Parker, removed October, 1661. William Willett refused the oaths. Henry Rich. Richard Deane refused the oaths. Andrew Hooke, Walter Stephens, sworn August 26, 1658; removed October, 1661; re-appointed January, 1687-8
1656, September 2, *vice* Clutterbuck—*John Hickes refused the oaths till the Restoration; fined September 6, 1659; re-elected August, 1661. *Thomas Stevens, Alderman, August, 1667; died April, 1679
1658, August 26, *vice* Alderman Cann—John Doddridge, Recorder, died March, 1658-9

[There were now 42 sworn members of the Council, besides those who had not taken the oaths.]

1659, May 31, *vice* Roe, Willett, and Deane—*Thomas Langton refused the oaths till the Restoration; sworn September 19, 1660. Gabriel Deane, sworn July 19; removed October, 1661. Richard Baugh, sworn September 6; removed October, 1661
1659, September 6, *vice* Hart, Young, and Dale—Edward Bovey, Thomas Prigg, not sworn. *William Crabb
1660, June 23, a mandamus was read, dated June 19, ordering the restoration to the Council of the following:—*John Lock, Alderman, died about October, 1665. *Gabriel Sherman, Alderman, died or removed November,1661. *Henry Creswicke,Alderman, September, 1661; knighted September 5, 1663; died September 28, 1668. *Nathaniel Cale, Alderman, August, 1662; died about May, 1672. †Richard Gregson, Alderman, April, 1662; died October, 1662. *John Knight, sen., not sworn: re-elected 1661
1660, September, *vice* Doddridge—John Stephens, Recorder
1661, August 23, the following were restored:—*Alexander James, Alderman, did not serve; re-elected 1664. †William Fitzherbert, died about March, 1661-2. †William Colston, Alderman, 1662; discharged November 17, 1664. The following were elected *vice* Alderman Deyos,Croft,Amory, and Bubb:—*John Knight, jun., refused to serve. †John Bradway, died about June, 1666. *John Hickes, Alderman, August, 1667; re appointed June, 1684. William Stephens did not serve

[On October 4, 1661, an order was read, dated September 29, ordering the removal of those members of the Council who had been elected during the interregnum, the restoration of such Councillors as had been ejected, and the filling up of vacancies in the ordinary number of 43. The following appear to have

THE OLD CORPORATION OF BRISTOL.—*Continued.*

been removed in accordance with this order, or the provisions of the Corporation Act, which had just been passed, viz. :—Aldermen Gibbes, Yate, Vickris, and Tyson; Messrs. Lane, Lawford, Yeamans, Griffiths, Grigg, Pope, Cann, Blackwell, Robert Vickris, Harris, Harper, Willoughby, Bowen, Appleton, Morgan, Knight, Collins, Hollway, Gay, Attwood, Parker, Rich, Hooke, Walter Stephens, Langton, Deane, Baugh, Bovey, Crabb, and J. Stephens, Recorder. Many of these were re-elected on October 13.]

1661, October 4, the members of the Council were Aldermen Lock, James, Sherman, Gonninge, M. Jackson, Ballman, J. Jackson, Sandy, Farmer, and Creswicke, Messrs. Fitzherbert, Colston, Gregson, Cale, Bradway, Hickes, J. Wright (originally elected in 1645, and T. Stevens (originally elected in 1656, and now serving as Sheriff)

1661, October 30, the following were re-elected:—*John Knight, sen., Alderman, April, 1662; knighted September 5, 1663; died December 16, 1683. *John Lawford, Alderman, July, 1663; re-appointed June, 1684. Henry Rich, discharged March 31, 1663. †William Yeamans, not sworn. *Robert Cann, knighted April 22, 1662; created Baronet September, 1662; Alderman, July, 1663; re-appointed June, 1684. †John Pope, Alderman, July, 1663; discharged September 29, 1663. *Christopher Griffith, removed June, 1684; restored October, 1688. †John Bowen, not sworn. †Robert Vickris, died or removed Nov., 1662. *John Willoughby, Alderman, August, 1664; died February, 1672-3. †Henry Appleton, died or removed Nov., 1662. *Edward Morgan, Alderman, Sept., 1665, died September 13, 1669. *Thomas Langton, Alderman, September, 1664; knighted November 4, 1666; died June, 1673. Andrew Hooke, not sworn. Edward Bovey, died or removed April, 1662. *William Crabb, Alderman, September, 1673; re-appointed June, 1684

1661, November 2, *vice* Alderman Gibbes, Alderman Yate, Alderman Vickris, Alderman Tyson, Alderman White, G. Lane, Blackwell, Harris, and Harper—*John Knight, jun., sworn September 12, 1664; Alderman, Sept., 1672; died March, 1678-9. William Lysons, discharged Mar. 5, 1663-4; re-elected June, 1669. *Richard Streamer, Alderman, Sept., 1672; died about June, 1680. William Cole, died or removed Oct., 1662. †Henry Gough, removed June, 1684; restored October, 1688. *John Lloyd, knighted November 27, 1678; Alderman, August, 1679; resigned February, 1680-1. *Ralph Olliffe, Alderman, September, 1673; died September 30, 1683. William Elliott, died about December. 1666. †Humphrey Little, died about June, 1680. †William Willett, sworn September 12, 1664; died about December, 1678

1661, November 7, *vice* W. Yeamans and Bowen—*Robert Yeamans, knighted September 7, 1663; created a Baronet December, 1666; Alderman, September, 1672; re-appointed June, 1684. Thomas Moore, refused to serve. Michael Pitman, refused to serve; discharged August 24, 1663. *Richard Hart, sworn September 12, 1664; Alderman, October, 1680; knighted October 27, 1680; re-appointed June, 1684. †Charles Powell, died about December, 1670. Edward Langley, died about May, 1669. Alexander Jackson, sworn September 12, 1664; died about April, 1672. *Richard Crumpe, Alderman, August, 1675; knighted October 18, 1681; re-appointed June, 1684. Samuel Tippett, discharged January 9, 1669-70.

1661, November 28, *vice* Alderman Sherman—†Edward Hurne, died about August, 1678. Thomas Cale, refused to serve. *Thomas Day, sworn August 23, 1662; Alderman, March—September,

THE OLD CORPORATION OF BRISTOL.—*Continued.*

1681; removed June, 1684; re-appointed January, 1687-8. †Edward Young (ceased to attend February, 1682-3, being excommunicated). Shersha Cary, refused to serve

1662, May 26—Sir Robert Atkyns, K.B. (Recorder); resigned December 10, 1682

1662, August 31, *vice* Alderman J. Jackson, W. Fitzherbert, A. Hooke, and Bovey—Gerard Lane, discharged August 8, 1671. Thomas Godman, died December, 1668. Thomas Goldsmith, refused to serve. †Richard Stubbe, sworn September 12, 1664; died about May, 1675. Nicholas Tilly, sworn August, 1663; discharged March 4, 1672-3. †William Hasell, resigned on being appointed Chamberlain April 10, 1675. William Gibbons, died September, 1667. Joseph Yeamans, sworn August, 1663; died December, 1668. Abraham Birkin, died about January, 1668-9

1662, December, *vice* Alderman Farmer—Sir Humphrey Hooke, Alderman; never sworn; discharged June 17, 1664

[NOTE.—Sir H. Hooke was not identical with, as stated by several authorities, but the grandson of Alderman Humphrey Hooke, who was a member of the Council from 1614 to 1645.]

1663, August 18, *vice* Alderman Gonninge, Alderman M. Jackson, Alderman Gregson, Vickris, Appleton, and Cole—†John Aldworth, sworn September 12, 1664. †John Cecil, removed June, 1684; restored October, 1688. Thomas Prigg, died July, 1673. Thomas Tovey, died November, 1669. *Joseph Creswicke, election invalid, he not being a freeman.

[The sworn members of the Council now numbered 43, Messrs. Knight, Willett, Hart, Stubbe, Tilly, Yeamans, Aldworth, and Creswicke not having yet taken the oaths.]

1663-4, March 11—Alexander James, Alderman; never sworn; discharged September 12, 1665

[In September, 1664, five Councillors who had hitherto refused to be sworn took the oaths, bringing the total of the Council to 48, Alderman James and Mr. Creswicke being unsworn.]

1666, September 4 — *Joseph Creswicke (re-elected), Alderman, August, 1679; re-appointed June, 1684

1667, September 3, *vice* Alderman Lock, Alderman Ballman, Bradway, and Elliott—*Thomas Eston, Alderman, August, 1683; re-appointed June, 1684. Thomas Haines, refused to serve; discharged April 7, 1668. †Samuel Wharton, died about June, 1680

1668, July 6, *vice* Aldworth—Peter Hiley, refused to serve

1668, September 8, *vice* Alderman Sir H. Creswicke, Gibbons, and Haines—†Edward Feilding, removed June, 1684; restored October, 1688. †John Dymer, died June 7, 1674. †Charles Williams, discharged September 3, 1681

1668, June 8, *vice* Langley, Godman, Birkin, J. Yeamans, and Hiley —†George Lane, died about September, 1679. William Lysons, sworn September 15, 1674; died or resigned July, 1675. *Thomas Earle, Alderman, September, 1681—August, 1683; knighted December 4, 1681; removed June, 1684; restored October, 1688. John Jackson, refused to serve. †Henry Gleson, removed June, 1684

1669, July 6, *vice* J. Jackson—†John Cooke, resigned on being appointed Chamberlain, August 13, 1680. †William Donning, removed June, 1684; restored January 14, 1687-8

THE OLD CORPORATION OF BRISTOL.—*Continued.*

1669, September 14, *vice* Alderman Morgan—Thomas Bevan, died about July, 1675. *William Jackson, removed June, 1684; re-appointed January 14, 1687-8. Richard Holland, sworn 1671; died about February, 1677-8. †John Moore, re-appointed June, 1684

[There were now 49 sworn members, besides Messrs. Lysons, Holland, and Moore, who had not taken the oaths.]

1671, September 24, *vice* Powell, Tippett, Tovey, and Gerard Lane—†Henry Merrett, removed June, 1684; restored October, 1688. John Appleton, not sworn, discharged about August, 1673. *William Hayman, re-appointed June, 1684; knighted February 28, 1684-5. James Cade, removed June, 1684; restored October, 1688. *Abraham Saunders, re-appointed June, 1684. *William Clutterbuck, knighted November 27, 1683; re-appointed June, 1684

1674, June 13, *vice* A. Jackson—*John Knight (of the Hill), refused to serve.

1674, September 1, *vice* Alderman Cole, Alderman Sandy, and Alderman Wright—*Richard Lane, re-appointed June, 1684. †Thomas Cole, removed June, 1684; restored October, 1682. Samuel Hale, removed June, 1684

1675, September 7, *vice* Alderman Willoughby, Alderman Sir T. Langton, Tilley, and Prigg—*Arthur Hart, sworn August 18, 1677; removed June, 1684; restored October, 1688. William Browne, sworn August 4, 1677; removed June, 1684; re-appointed January, 1687-8. Richard Dawe, died about October, 1680. Francis Woodward, discharged October 19, 1682

[The Council now stood at 45, there being 2 unsworn members, and 7 vacancies from death, refusal, and resignation.]

1677, August 7, *vice* Appleton, Dymer, and Knight (of the Hill)—†George Hart re-appointed June, 1684. †George White, removed June, 1684; restored October, 1688. *William Swymmer, re-appointed June, 1684

[The members of the Council reached 50 on August 18, there being still 4 vacancies.]

1678, September 12, *vice* Hasell, Stubbe, Bevan, and Lysons—†George Morgan, re-appointed June, 1684. Stephen Watts, removed June, 1684. Humphrey Corsley, removed June, 1684; re-appointed January, 1687-8. Michael Hunt, removed June, 1684

[The number of the Council reached 52, the seats of Messrs. Hurne and Holland being unfilled.]

1679, September 11, *vice* Alderman Knight, Alderman Stevens, Hurne, and Holland—*John Knight (of the Hill), sworn August 21, 1680; knighted March, 16, 1681-2; re-appointed June, 1684. †Nathaniel Driver, re-appointed June, 1684. *Edmund Arundell, re-appointed June, 1684. Nathaniel Webb, died May, 1683

1680, August 13, *vice* Alderman Streamer, G. Lane, Little, Wharton and Willett—*John Hine, removed June, 1684; re-appointed January, 1687-8. George Morris, re-appointed June, 1684. †Giles Merrick, re-appointed June, 1684. †John Sandford, re-appointed June, 1684.

1681, May 31, *vice* Cooke and Dawe—†John Combes, re-appointed June, 1684; †James Twyford, re-appointed June, 1684

1681, September 3, *vice* Williams—Walter Gunter, re-appointed June, 1684. †Robert Dowding, re-appointed June, 1684.

THE OLD CORPORATION OF BRISTOL.—*Continued.*

1682, October 19, *vice* Woodward—Thomas Colston, jun., died about January, 1683-4

1682-3, March 12, *vice* Atkyns — Sir John Churchill, Recorder, re-appointed June, 1684

The number of Councillors was now 52, which by the deaths of Alderman Olliffe, Alderman Sir J. Knight, Messrs. Webb and Colston was reduced to 48 by the end of January, 1683-4. Meantime, in consequence of the issue of the writ of *quo warranto*, the Charters had been surrendered on November 9, 1683. The instrument of surrender was signed by the Mayor (Sir W. Clutterbuck), the Recorder (Sir J. Churchill]), Sir J. Knight, Sir R. Cann, Sir R. Crumpe, Alderman Eston, and the Town Clerk (John Romsey).

[NOTE.—The John Knights of this period are somewhat confusing, and the identification and discrimination of the various persons of the same name holding official positions in connection with Bristol, has been a problem which has exercised, not always with success, the ingenuity of a good many inquirers. The most accurate account of them that has appeared in print is, I think, that contained in volume 3 of Nicholls and Taylor's *Bristol Past and Present*, which I am now able to render more complete. Mr. Tremayne Lane has very kindly given me tracings of the signatures of the John Knights who were members of the Common Council, as they appear in the records at the Council House, and Mr. G. H. Pope has very carefully examined for me the memoranda concerning them in the books of the Merchant Venturers, and has ascertained a fact which had hitherto escaped the notice of himself, as well as of all previous writers, including the author of the article on the Knights in the *Dictionary of National Biography*, viz., the relationship between Alderman John Knight the younger, and the second Sir John Knight. The following may, I think, be relied upon as a complete and accurate identification of the various John Knights who were conspicuous in our local annals.

1. John Knight "the elder"—afterwards Sir John Knight—son of Alderman George Knight, was a wholesale grocer in Temple parish. He was elected a Common Councillor in 1650 and 1654, but not sworn till 1660, in which year he was elected Sheriff, but succeeded in getting excused from serving on account of his Parliamentary duties. He was an Alderman from 1662 till his death in 1683, and Mayor in 1663-4, was knighted in 1663, and served as M.P. for Bristol in the four Parliaments from 1660 to 1680. He was also Master of the Merchant Venturers in 1663, but never Warden.

2. John Knight "the younger"—so called to distinguish him from No. 1, until the latter's knighthood, when he dropped that affix. He was elected a Common Councillor in 1653 and 1661, but not sworn till 1664, and was an Alderman from 1672 till his death in 1679. He was Sheriff 1664-5, and Mayor 1670-71, but was never knighted, and did not serve in Parliament. He was Master of the Merchant Venturers 1666-67, having been three times Warden, 1654-55, 1655-56, 1661-62. He was a sugar refiner, and belonged to St. Michael's parish.

3. John Knight " of the Hill"—afterwards Sir John Knight. He was a son of No. 2, and was elected a Common Councillor in 1674 and 1679, retired in 1685, returned to the Council in 1688, and finally withdrew in 1702, dying in

THE OLD CORPORATION OF BRISTOL.—Continued.

1718. He was Sheriff 1681-82, and Mayor 1691-92, and M.P in the two Parliaments from 1689 to 1695, and was knighted during his Shrievalty in 1682. He was Warden of the Merchant Venturers 1681-82, but never Master.

Besides these members of the Corporation there was also
4. John Knight, "the younger," son of Sir John Knight (No. 1), was never in the Council, but was Warden of the Merchant Venturers 1671-2, and died May 29, 1684, a few months after his father. My previous identification (on page 124) of the Warden for 1671-2 with No. 2, was incorrect, having been made before Mr. Pope's examination of the minutes and signatures at Merchant's Hall.

It will be seen that of the four, Nos. 1, 2, and 3 were members of the Corporation, and served the office of Mayor; Nos. 1 and 2 were Aldermen; Nos. 1 and 3 were knighted, and also served as members of Parliament for the city. All were members of the Society of Merchant Venturers: No. 2 was both Master and Warden; No. 1 was Master, but not Warden; and Nos. 3 and 4 were Wardens, but not Masters.]

On June 2, 1668, the old Charters having been surrendered, a new Council was nominated by the King (Charles II.) as follows:—

*Sir Robert Cann, Bart., Alderman; died November, 1685
*John Lawford, Alderman; died July, 1688
*Sir Robert Yeamans, Bart., Alderman; died February, 1686-7
*John Hickes, Alderman, removed January 13, 1687-8; restored October 17, 1688
*William Crabb, Alderman
*Sir Richard Crumpe, Alderman
*Joseph Creswicke, Alderman
*Sir Richard Hart, Alderman; removed June 13, 1686; restored October 17, 1688
*Thomas Eston, Alderman; removed January 13, 1687-8; restored October 17, 1688
Sir John Churchill, Recorder; died October 11, 1685
*Sir William Clutterbuck (Mayor), Alderman; removed January 13, 1687-8; restored October 17, 1688
*William Hayman, Alderman; knighted February 28, 1684-5
John Romsey, Town Clerk, removed January 13, 1687-8
*Sir John Knight, discharged January 15, 1684-5; restored October 17, 1688
*Abraham Saunders, Alderman, August, 1686; removed January 13, 1687-8; restored October 17, 1688
†John Combes, Alderman, March, 1686-7; removed January 13, 1687-8; restored October 17, 1688
†John Moore, Alderman, June, 1686; resigned March 14, 1686-7; restored October 17, 1688
*William Swymmer, Alderman, March, 1686-7; removed January 13, 1687-8; restored October 17, 1688
*Richard Lane, removed January 13, 1687-8; restored October 17, 1688
†George Hart, removed January 13, 1687-8; restored October 17, 1688
†Nathaniel Driver, removed January 13, 1687-8; restored October 17, 1688
*Edmund Arundell, removed January 13, 1687-8; restored October 17, 1688
†William Merricke, knighted August 27, 1686; removed October 17, 1688; re-elected October 27, 1688
†George Morgan, removed January 13, 1687-8; restored October 17, 1688

THE OLD CORPORATION OF BRISTOL —*Continued.*

†Giles Merrick, removed January 13, 1687-8 ; restored October 17, 1688
†John Sandford, removed January 13, 1687-8 ; restored October 17, 1688
†James Twyford, removed January 13, 1687-8 ; restored October 17, 1688
Walter Gunter, removed March 25, 1688 ; restored October 17, 1688
†Robert Dowding, removed January 13, 1687-8 ; restored October 17, 1688
George Morris, died April, 1687
Anthony Swymmer, died September, 1688
†John Yeamans, removed January 13, 1687-8 ; re-elected September 15, 1689
†Edward Tocknell, removed January 13, 1687-8 ; re-elected October 27, 1688
John Olliffe, removed January 13, 1687-8
*Robert Yate, removed October 17, 1688 ; re-elected October 27 1688
John Whiteing, removed January 13, 1687-8 ; re-elected October 15, 1689
†James Pope, removed January 13, 1687-8 ; re-elected October 15, 1689
†Henry Combe, removed January 13, 1687-8 ; re-elected July 14, 1690
†John Bradway, removed January 13, 1687-8 ; re-elected July 14, 1690
Robert Smith, removed March 25, 1688
John Hollister, removed January 13, 1687-8
Scarborough Chapman, removed March 25, 1688
Richard Gibbons, removed January 13, 1687-8

[The whole of the late Aldermen were re-appointed, and 16 others of the old Council, those omitted being Sir T. Earle, Messrs. Griffith, Gough, Cecil, Feilding, Gleson, Donning, Jackson, Merrett, Cade, Cole, Hale, A. Hart, Browne, White, Watts, Corsley, Hunt, and Hine.]

1684-5, January 16, *vice* Knight — Robert Brookhouse, refused to serve ; discharged August 21
1685, September 8, *vice* Brookhouse—Thomas Speed, refused to serve ; discharged September 15
1685, October 15, *vice* Speed—Thomas Goldney, refused to serve ; discharged October 22
1685, November 6, *vice* Goldney—Thomas Callowhill, refused to serve ; discharged same day
1685, November 25, *vice* Alderman Sir R. Cann and Callowhill —Richard Bickham, refused to serve. John Love, refused to serve ; discharged December 3, 1685
1685-6, January 6, *vice* Love—Thomas Jordan, refused to serve ; discharged March 23, 1685-6
1685-6, March 23, *vice* Bickham and Jordan—Charles Jones, jun., and Thomas Harris, refused to serve ; discharged July 12, 1686
1686, July 12, *vice* Jones — *Samuel Wallis, removed January 13, 1687-8 ; re-elected November 6, 1688
1686, July 21, *vice* Harris—James Freeman, refused to serve
1686-7, January 18, *vice* Freeman—*John Bubb, excused by Royal order, dated April 5, 1687 ; re-elected September 15, 1689
1686-7, March 14, *vice* Alderman Sir R. Hart and Alderman Sir R. Yeamans—*John Blackwell, removed October 17, 1688 ; re-elected September 15, 1689. John Seward, removed January 13, 1687-8

THE OLD CORPORATION OF BRISTOL.—*Continued.*

1687, April 29, *vice* Bubb—†Marmaduke Bowdler, removed January 13, 1687-8 ; re-elected September 2, 1690

1687, July 29, *vice* Alderman Moore and Morris—Robert Winston, removed March 25, 1688. †William Opie, removed March 25, 1688 ; re-elected September 2, 1690

On January 14, 1687-8, the King (James II.) removed Aldermen Hickes, Eston, Sir W. Clutterbuck, Saunders, Combes, and Swymmer ; Messrs. Lane (Mayor), Romsey (Town Clerk), G. Hart, Driver, Arundell, Morgan,G. Merrick, Sandford,Twyford, Dowding. Yeamans, Tocknell, Olliffe, Whiteing, Pope, Combe, Bradway, Hollister, Gibbons, Wallis, Bowdler, and Seward, and the following day appointed their successors, who were admitted on Feb. 4.

1687-8, February 4—*Thomas Day, Mayor ; Alderman August, 1688
Michael Pope (mercer), Alderman, removed October 17, 1688
Walter Stephens, Alderman ; removed March 25, 1687-8
*William Jackson, Alderman
William Browne, Alderman
Humphrey Corsley, Alderman
Thomas Scrope, Alderman, removed October 17, 1688
Nathaniel Wade, Town Clerk ; removed October 17, 1688
*John Hine
†Thomas Saunders, removed October 17, 1688
Henry Gibbs, Alderman, September 15, 1688 ; removed Oct. 17, 1688
†William Donning
†George White
Michael Pope (grocer), removed October 17, 1688
†Joseph Jackson, removed October 17, 1688
William Weaver, removed October 17, 1688
John Grant, removed October 17, 1688
John Cary, removed October 17, 1688
Alexander Dollman, removed October 17, 1688
*Peter Saunders, removed October 17, 1688 ; re-elected March 20, 1693-4
James Thomas, removed October 17, 1688
William Burges, removed October 17, 1688
*William Whitehead, removed October 17, 1688 ; re-elected September 15, 1696
John Duddlestone, removed October 17, 1688
John Curtis, removed October 17, 1688
*Nathaniel Day, removed October 17, 1688 ; re-elected August 26, 1695
Joseph Burges, removed October 17, 1688
1687-8, February 23—Henry Parsons, removed October 17, 1688

On March 25, 1688, the King removed Alderman Stephens and Messrs. Gunter, Chapman, Smith, Winston, and Opie, nominating their successors, who were elected April 11, viz :

Simon Hurle, Alderman, removed September 7, 1688
John Jones, removed October 17, 1688
James Wallis, removed September 7, 1688
Thomas Walden, removed October 17, 1688
Samuel Clark, removed October 17, 1688
Daniel Gwilliam, removed October 17, 1688
1688, August 30, *vice* Alderman Lawford—Richard Paine, removed October 17, 1688
1688, September 15, *vice* Alderman Hurle — Peter Muggleworth, removed October 17, 1688
1688, September 29, *vice* Wallis—†Thomas Liston, removed October 17 1688

THE OLD CORPORATION OF BRISTOL.—*Continued*.

By the restoration of the old Charter on October 17, 1688, the surviving members of the Council, as it existed on June 2, 1684, were reinstated, and those appointed since that date removed.

*1688, October 17—John Hickes (Tory), Alderman ; died March, 1699—1700
*Christopher Griffith ; died about December, 1689
*William Crabb (Tory), Alderman ; died October 14, 1702
†Henry Gough, resigned November 6, 1688
*Sir Richard Hart (Tory), Alderman ; died January 16, 1701-2
*Sir Richard Crumpe (Tory), Alderman ; died January 14, 1699-1700
*Thomas Day (Whig), Alderman, August, 1689 ; knighted November 28, 1694 ; died January, 1709-10
†John Cecil, resigned September 2, 1690
*Joseph Creswicke (Tory), Alderman ; died about February, 1707-8
*Thomas Eston (Tory), Alderman till August 8, 1689 ; removed October 15, 1689
†Edward Feilding (Whig), Alderman, August, 1689 ; died February 20, 1690-1
*Sir Thomas Earle (Whig), Alderman, August, 1689 ; removed Oct. 21, 1690 ; restored February 27, 1690-1 ; died June 24, 1696
†William Donning (Whig), Alderman, August, 1689 ; died about June, 1692
*William Jackson (Whig), Alderman, August, 1689 ; died April, 1716
†John Moore, resigned October 15, 1689
†Henry Merrett (Tory), refused oaths ; discharged September 11, 1690
*Sir William Hayman (Tory), Alderman, February, 1690-1 ; died July, 1702
James Cade, resigned September 15, 1689
*Abraham Saunders, discharged April 4, 1693
*Sir William Clutterbuck (Mayor), Alderman, August, 1689 ; resigned June 30, 1702
*Richard Lane (Whig), Alderman, June, 1696 ; died about May, 1705
†Thomas Cole, removed September, 1696
*Arthur Hart (Tory), died 1705
William Browne, died or resigned September, 1690
†George Hart (Tory), died or resigned September, 1691
†George White, died about March, 1689-90
*William Swymmer (Whig), Alderman, July, 1692 ; died about January, 1714-5
†George Morgan, removed September, 1696
Humphrey Corsley (Tory), refused the oaths ; discharged September 11, 1690
*Sir John Knight (Tory), resigned August, 1702
†Nathaniel Driver, discharged September 22, 1693
*Edmund Arundell, died about January, 1693-7
*John Hine, died April 28, 1699
†Giles Merrick, died about November, 1713
†John Sandford, removed September, 1696
†John Combes, died or resigned 1689
†James Twyford, discharged April 16, 1695
Walter Gunter, discharged September 8, 1691
†Robert Dowding, removed September, 1696
1688, October 27—†Sir William Merricke, discharged August 31, 1692. *Robert Yate (Whig), Alderman, February, 1699-1700 ; died October 27, 1737. †Edward Tocknell, resigned on being appointed Chamberlain, November 22, 1698

[The Council now numbered 42, the Recordership being vacant.]

THE OLD CORPORATION OF BRISTOL.—Continued.

1688, November 6, *vice* Gough—*Samuel Wallis (Whig). Alderman, March, 1699-1700; died about March, 1725

1689, September 15, *vice* Combes and Cade—*John Bubb, died about July, 1699. †John Yeamans, died or removed Sept., 1696. *John Blackwell (Whig), Alderman. February, 1701-2; died Dec. 2, 1702

1689, October 15, *vice* Eston and Moore—John Whiteing, discharged April 1, 1691. †James Pope (Whig), died about July, 1695

1690, July 14, *vice* Griffith and White—†Henry Combe, discharged August 27, 1708. †John Bradway, removed August 8, 1702

1890, September 2, *vice* Browne and Cecil—†Marmaduke Bowdler (Tory), discharged March 31, 1699. †William Opie, died May, 1695

1690, September 11, *vice* Corsley and Merrett—*John Bacheler, Alderman, July, 1702; died October, 1711. *John Hawkins, jun. (Tory), knighted September 3, 1702; Alderman, October, 1702; died July 6. 1723

1690-1, February 27, *vice* Alderman Feilding—George Mason, died August, 1695

1691, September 8, *vice* Whiteing—*William Paines (Whig), knighted November 28, 1694; Alderman, August, 1702; died September 5, 1724

1691, September 15, *vice* Gunter—*William Lewis, Alderman, March, 1702-3; knighted August 12, 1703; died May 23, 1712

1691, October 8, *vice* G. Hart—Jedidiah Pickford, died about February, 1693-4

1692, July 11, *vice* Alderman Donning—John Horne, removed September, 1696

1693, April 4, *vice* A. Saunders—John Smyth, removed Sept., 1696

1693, August 13, *vice* Sir W. Merricke—Robert Kirke, removed September, 1696

1693, September 22, *vice* Driver—†William French, died about September, 1703

1693-4, March 20, *vice* Pickford—*Peter Saunders, Alderman, June, 1705; died October, 1705

1695, April 16, *vice* Twyford—*Francis Whitchurch, Alderman, October, 1705; died about May, 1718

1695, August 26, *vice* Opie—*Nathaniel Day, Alderman, April, 1708; died about November, 1719

1695, August 26, *vice* Pope—John Lloyd, removed September, 1696

1695, September 11, *vice* Mason—*George Stephens, Alderman, January, 1709-10; died November, 1718

1696, September 15, *vice* Alderman Sir T. Earle, Cole, Morgan, Sandford, Dowding, Yeamans, Horne, Smyth, Kirke, and Lloyd—†John Day, died 1705. †Samuel Bayly, died 1708. *William Whitehead, Alderman, November, 1711; died February 25, 1711-2. *James Hollidge (Whig), resigned on being appointed Chamberlain, March 20, 1709-10. *Robert Bound, Alderman, March, 1711-12; died December, 1715. John Sandford, refused to serve; discharged August 27, 1697. †John Swymmer, died about May, 1700. Richard Franklyn, discharged July 2, 1707. William Powlett, Recorder (Whig), died October, 1703. †Isaac Davies, died about March, 1702-3.

1696-7, February 10, *vice* Arundell—William Barnsdale, re-elected August 8, 1702

1697, August 27, *vice* Sandford—†Richard Bayly, discharged August 31, 1716

1698-9, March 9, *vice* Tocknell—*Abraham Elton (Whig), Alderman, May, 1712; created a Baronet October, 1717; died February 9, 1727-8

1699, August 29, *vice* Hine—William Rishton, re-elected August 8, 1702

THE OLD CORPORATION OF BRISTOL.—*Continued*

1699, August 29, *vice* Bubb—*Christopher Shuter (Whig), Alderman, February, 1714-5; died about April, 1730.
1699, August 29, *vice* Bowdler—Thomas Winston, discharged December 10, 1700
1699-1700, February 28, *vice* Alderman Sir R. Crumpe — *Thomas Hort, died August, 1715
1699-1700, March 17, *vice* Alderman Hickes—*Anthony Swymmer, Alderman, December, 1715; died 1719
1700, September 13, *vice* J. Swymmer—Francis Rogers, re-elected August 8, 1702
1701, August 27, *vice* Winston—*Henry Watts, re-elected (having omitted to take the oaths) September 6, 1704; discharged February 16, 1704-5 ; re-elected March 22, 1711-2
1702, August 8 (re-elected, having vacated their seats by omitting to take the oaths on the Queen's accession) —William Barnsdale, discharged July 2, 1707. William Rishton, discharged September 23, 1702. Francis Rogers, discharged July 2, 1707
1702, August 8, *vice* Alderman Sir R. Hart—Thomas Moore, refused to serve; discharged September 10, 1702
1702, August 8, *vice* Alderman Sir W. Clutterbuck—Hugh Bickham, sworn October 27, 1705; died October, 1723
1702, August 8, *vice* Bradway—*Henry Whitehead, jun. Alderman, April, 1716; died October, 1723
1702, September 10, *vice* Knight, Alderman Sir W. Hayman, and Moore—†Morgan Smith (Whig) and †Abraham Hooke (Whig), discharged on the passing of the Occasional Conformity Act, March 22, 1711-2. †Philip Freke (Tory), died December 10, 1729
1702, September 23, *vice* Rishton—*Henry Walter (Whig), Alderman, June, 1718; died October 25, 1737
1703, April 19, *vice* Alderman Crabb, Alderman Blackwell, and Davies—†Onesiphorus Tyndall (Whig), discharged on the passing of the Occasional Conformity Act, March 22, 1711-2. †Nathaniel Webb (Whig), died about April, 1709. †Thomas Tyler, died 1719
1703, October 27, *vice* French—†James Haynes, died about June, 1721
1704, September 19, *vice* Powlett—Robert Eyre (Recorder, Whig), knighted May 6, 1710; resigned 1728
1705, August 13, *vice* Alderman Lane, J. Day, A. Hart, and Watts —*Thomas Clement (Whig), Alderman, August, 1719; died about November, 1722. †William Bayly, died about March, 1717. *Nicholas Hickes, Alderman, December, 1718; died about November, 1727. Francis Plomer, sworn September 6, 1707; died about January, 1708-9
1706, August 15, *vice* Saunders—Richard Liversedge, refused to serve; re-elected May 6, 1708, and again refused
1707, August 11, *vice* Barnsdale, Franklyn, and Rogers—John Lloyd (Whig), discharged March 16, 1727-8. *Edmund Mountjoy (Whig), Alderman, December, 1719; died August, 1735. Thomas Hungerford (Tory), refused to serve; re-elected May 6, 1708, and again refused
1708, May 6, *vice* Alderman Creswicke—*John Day, died June 20, 1718
1710, August 28 (re-elected) — Richard Liversedge and Thomas Hungerford (Tory), refused to serve. Mr. Hungerford was not discharged till July 20, 1717, and Mr. Liversedge not till Sept. 15, 1721

[See Latimer's "Annals of Bristol in the 18th Century," pages 86 and 87, for an account of the proceedings against Messrs. Liversedge and Hungerford.]

1710, August 28, *vice* Alderman Sir T. Day, Combe, S. Bayly, Plomer, Webb, and Hollidge—†Richard Gravett (Whig), died about

THE OLD CORPORATION OF BRISTOL.— *Continued.*

March, 1738. *Abraham Elton, jun. (Whig), Alderman, January, 1722-3; succeeded to the Baronetcy February 9, 1727-8; died October 19. 1742. *John Becher (Whig), Alderman, July, 1723; died about June, 1742. †Poole Stokes, died about August, 1714. †William Whitehead, jun., died February 25, 1720-1. *Henry Swymmer (Whig), Alderman, October, 1723; died Sept. 1732

1711-2, March 22, *vice* Alderman Bacheler—*Henry Watts, died Sept. 19, 1721

1711-2, March 22, *vice* Alderman Whitehead—*Samuel Stokes, died January, 1745-6

1712, December 10, *vice* Smithe, Hooke, Tyndall, and Alderman Sir W. Lewis—*James Donning (Whig), Alderman, September, 1724; died March 8, 1745-6. *Joseph Jefferis (Whig), Alderman, September, 1725; died October 24. 1752. Isaac Elton (Whig), died October 23, 1714. †Richard Tayler, jun, died November, 1715

1715, April 7, *vice* P. Stokes and Merrick—*Robert Earle (Whig), Alderman, November, 1727; died January 25, 1736-7. *Peter Day (Whig), Alderman, February 1'27-8; died January, 1734-5

1715, September 23, *vice* Alderman W. Swymmer, I. Elton, and Hort—*Henry Nash (Whig), Alderman, June, 1730; resigned 1742. *Edward Foy (Whig), died July, 1737. *Arthur Taylor (Whig), Alderman February 21, 1734-5; died about April, 1745

1715-6, February 7, *vice* Alderman Bound and R. Tayler—*John King (Tory), died November 27, 1734. *John Price (Whig), Alderman, October, 1732; died about January, 1738-9

1716, August 31, *vice* Alderman Jackson — †Robert Addison, died 1729

1716, August 31, *vice* R. Bayly—William French, died September, 1720

1718, Aug. 14, *vice* W. Bayly, Hungerford, and Alderman Whitchurch —*John Rich (Whig), Alderman, February, 1736-7; died February, 1755. †Noblet Ruddock, removed May 28, 1734. John Thomas, removed September 25, 1723

1720, August 11, *vice* Alderman Stephens, J. Day, Alderman N. Day, Alderman A. Swymmer, and Tyler—†Robert Smith (Tory), died early in 1762. Harrington Gibbs (Tory), discharged July 9, 1722. *Jacob Elton (Whig), Alderman, September' 1735; died June 15, 1765. *John Blackwell (Whig), Alderman, November, 1737; died July 19, 1748. *Nathaniel Day (Whig), Alderman, February, 1738-9; died August 26, 1765

[Alderman Day became a Tory later, and voted on that side in the elections of 1739 and 1754.]

1720, October 27. *vice* French—*Lyonel Lyde (Whig), Alderman, November, 1737; died about April, 1745

1721, September 9, *vice* W. Whitehead and Haynes- †Michael Puxton, died November, 1732. †Nathaniel Wraxall, died about April, 1731

1721, December 13, *vice* Liversedge and Watts—†Ezekiel Longman (Whig), sworn September 13, 1725; died August 9, 1738. *Henry Combe, jun. (Whig), Alderman, July, 1743; died April 23, 1752

1722, July 18. *vice* Gibbs—*William Jefferis (Whig), Alderman, June 1, 1742; died about April, 1752

1724, August 8, *vice* Alderman Clements and Thomas—*Stephen Clutterbuck (Whig), Alderman, November, 1742; died about June, 1746. *Richard Bayly (Whig), died May 17. 1742

1724, November 9, *vice* Bickham, Alderman H. Whitehead and Alderman Sir J. Hawkins—Christopher Wallis (Whig), died about April, 1725. Richard Henville (Whig), refused to serve. Andrew Parsons (Whig), discharged March 16, 1727-8

THE OLD CORPORATION OF BRISTOL.—Continued.

1726, July 9, *vice* Alderman Sir W. Daines and Alderman Wallis—William Swymmer (Whig), refused to serve; discharged May 8, 1728. *John Bartlett (Whig), died August 22, 1748

1726-7, February 28, *vice* C. Wallis—†Henry Lloyd (Whig), died about November, 1736

1727-8, March 16, *vice* Alderman Hickes, Alderman Sir A. Elton, and Heuville—*Abraham Elton, jun. (Whig), succeeded to the Baronetcy October 19, 1742; discharged August 29, 1757. *John Berrow (Whig), died November 29, 1745. †Edward Buckler (Whig), died about November, 1739

1728, August 20. *vice* Eyre — John Scrope (Recorder, Whig). resigned July 28, 1735

1728, September 11, *vice* J. Lloyd and Parsons—*John Day (Whig), Alderman, January, 1745-6; died March 2, 1747-8. *Edward Cooper (Whig), Alderman, October, 1747; died about January, 1762

1729, September 24, *vice* W. Swymmer and Addison- *John Foy (Whig), Alderman, October, 1747; died January 18, 1771. †William Barnsdale (Whig), discharged (on being appointed Deputy Sword Bearer) May 28, 1734

1730, June 22, *vice* Freke and Shuter—*William Barnes (Whig), Alderman, January, 1745-6; died July 29, 1767. Samuel Nelmes (Whig), died about November, 1734

1731, July 14, *vice* Wraxall—*Buckler Weekes (Whig), Alderman, November, 1749; died February 20, 1772

[Mr. Weekes voted for Earle and Hart in 1722, and for Southwell in 1739; at other elections supported the Whigs.]

1732, October 28. *vice* Alderman H. Swymmer — †Michael Pope (Whig), died December, 1739

1732-3, January 10, *vice* Puxton—†Benjamin Glisson, died March 14, 1755

1734, May 28, *vice* Barnsdale—*Thomas Curtis (Whig), Alderman, October, 1750; died early in 1754

1734, May 28, *vice* Ruddock—*James Laroche (Whig), Alderman, May, 1752; died about September, 1770

1735, June 21, *vice* Alderman P. Day—*David Peloquin (Whig), Alderman, October, 1752; died March 21, 1766

1735, June 21, *vice* King—*John Clements (Whig), Alderman, November, 1753; died September 16, 1760

1735, June 21, *vice* Nelmes—*Morgan Smith (Whig), Alderman, September, 1755; died August 7, 1781

1735, August 6, *vice* Scrope—Michael Foster (Whig, Recorder), knighted April 21, 1745; resigned October 19, 1762

1736, June 26, *vice* Alderman Mountjoy—*Abraham Elton (Whig), Alderman, September, 1754; died August 20, 1762

[There were now three Abraham Eltons in the Corporation. This one was the son of Alderman Jacob Elton.]

1737, May 18, *vice* Alderman Earle—†Joseph Iles (Whig), died early in 1750

1737, May 18, *vice* Lloyd — *Henry Dampier (Whig), Alderman, October, 1760; died October 17, 1771

1738, April 8, *vice* Alderman Yate—John Tyndall (Whig), refused to serve; again elected February, 1739-40

1738, April 8, *vice* Alderman Walter —†John Combe (Whig), died about February, 1753

1738, June 3, *vice* E. Foy—†David Dehany, refused to serve, again elected July, 1739

1738, June 3, *vice* Gravett—*Giles Bayly (Whig), Alderman, February, 1762; died February 1, 1767

THE OLD CORPORATION OF BRISTOL.—*Continued.*

1738-9, February 10, *vice* Alderman Price—†Michael Becher (Whig), died about January, 1759

1739, May 16, *vice* Dehany — James Furney, refused to serve.

1739, June 9, *vice* Longman—†David Dehany, died about July, 1754

1739, September 22, *vice* Tyndall — Samuel Martin, discharged August 9, 1740

1739-40, February 18, *vice* Buckler—John Tyndall (Whig), discharged August 29, 1741

1739-40, March 22, *vice* Pope—|Walter Jenkins (Whig), died about May, 1758

1740, June 18, *vice* Furney—*William Martin (Whig), Alderman, August, 1762; died February 4, 1765

1740, September 70, *vice* S. Martin—†John Chamberlayne, died about February, 1752

1741, August 29, *vice* Tyndall—*Henry Mugleworth (Whig), Alderman, February, 1765; died July 9, 1782. [Became a Tory later, and voted with that party in 1774 and 1781.]

1742, June 26, *vice* R. Bayly — †William Cossley, discharged (on being appointed Deputy Swordbearer) May 18, 1708

1742, June 26, *vice* Alderman Nash—*Jeremiah Ames (Whig), Alderman, June, 1765; died April 3, 1776

1742-3, January 22, *vice* Alderman Sir A. Elton—*Isaac Elton (Whig), Alderman, March, 1766; died June 6, 1776

[Voted for the Tory candidates in 1774.]

1743, August 6, *vice* Alderman Baker—*John Durbin (Whig), Alderman, August, 1765; died February 11, 1792

1745, July 13, *vice* Alderman Taylor and Alderman Lyde—†Thomas Marsh (Tory), died December 5, 1755. *John Noble (Whig), Alderman, February, 1767; died March 11, 1768

1745-6, March 15, *vice* Berrow and Stokes—*Henry Swymmer (Whig), died August 30, 1774. *Richard Farr, jun. (Whig), Alderman, August, 1767; died May 15, 1782

1747, May 23, *vice* Alderman Donning and Alderman Clutterbuck—Thomas Power (Whig), died January 27, 1747-8. †John Berrow (Whig), discharged December 14, 1767

1748, August 13, *vice* Power and Alderman J. Day—†Joseph Daltera (Whig), discharged June 23, 1764. *Isaac Baugh (Whig), Alderman, March, 1768; died December 25, 1786.

[Voted for Brickdale in 1774.]

1749, April 19, *vice* Alderman Blackwell and Cossley — *William Barnes, jun. (Whig), discharged September 13, 1760; re-elected October 13, 1760. †John Curtis (Whig), died September 12th, 1768

1750, May 12, *vice* Alderman Bartlett—*George Weare, jun. (Whig), Alderman, February, 1771; died December 7, 1778

1750, August 11, *vice* Iles—†Joseph Love (Whig), removed July 15, 1769

[Mr. Love left the country in 1765, and remained abroad.]

1752, May 30, *vice* Chamberlayne—†Daniel Woodward (Whig), died March 14, 1755

1752, July 4, *vice* Alderman Combe—*Edward Whatley (Whig), Alderman, October, 1771; died November 7, 1779

[Became a Tory later, and voted for Brickdale and Clare in 1774.]

1753, May 19, *vice* Alderman W. Jefferis and Alderman J. Jefferis—*Henry Bright (Whig), died November 25, 1777. *Thomas Harris (Tory), Alderman, April 18, 1776; died January 28, 1797

THE OLD CORPORATION OF BRISTOL.—*Continued.*

1754, August 5, *vice* J. Combe and Alderman Curtis — †Thomas Knox, discharged May 12, 1762. *Thomas Deane (Whig), Alderman, April, 1772; died January 15, 1798

1755, July 22, *vice* Alderman Lich and Dehany—†Henry Weare (Whig), discharged April 4, 1772. †James Hillhouse (Whig), died June 8, 1762

1756, June 21, *vice* Woodward and Glisson—William Mathew (Tory) refused to serve. Samuel Peach (Whig), refused to serve

1756, July 24, *vice* Marsh, Matthew, and Peach—*Nathaniel Foy (Whig), Alderman, June, 1776; died April 10, 1783. [Became a Tory later—voted for Tory candidates in 1774 and 1781] †Austin Goodwin, jun. (Whig), died about July, 1762. *Robert Gordon (Whig), Alderman, November, 1777; died December 13, 1784

1757, September 5, *vice* Sir A. Elton—†Samuel Webb (Tory), refused to serve; again elected September, 1758

1757, September 13, *vice* Webb—†Isaac Piguenit (Whig), died January 29, 1780

1758, September 4, *vice* Jenkins—†Samuel Webb (Tory), died March 8, 1777

1759, March 24, *vice* M. Becher—*Charles Hotchkin (Tory), Alderman, November 19, 1778; died July 22, 1782

1760, September 13, *vice* Barnes—†Samuel Sedgeley, discharged September 11, 1777

1760, October 13, *vice* Alderman Clements—*William Barnes, jun. (Whig) [with his original seniority, 1749], Alderman, October, 1770; died November 3, 1777.
[Voted for Brickdale in 1774.]

1762, July 10, *vice* R. Smith and Alderman Cooper—Cranfield Becher (Whig), refused to serve. Thomas Tyndall (Whig), refused to serve

1762, August 14, *vice* Becher and Tyndall—†William Weare (Whig), died January 15, 1785. *Thomas Farr (Whig), died August 30, 1791

1763, July 20, *vice* Hillhouse and Knox—*Andrew Pope (Whig), Alderman, December, 1779; died July 29, 1784. *John Durbin, jun. (Tory), knighted January 28, 1778; Alderman, August, 1781; died January 25, 1814

1763, July 20, *vice* Foster — Hon. Daines Barrington, Recorder (Whig), resigned November 28, 1765

1764, June 23, *vice* Alderman Mountjoy — †James Laroche, jun., created a Baronet, August, 1776; died September, 1804

1764, August 18, *vice* Goodwin—*John Bull, died September 9, 1783

1765, July 6, *vice* Alderman Martin—†Isaac Elton, jun. (Whig), discharged December 20, 1783

1765, July 6, *vice* Alderman J. Elton—*Michael Miller, jun. (Tory), died August 9, 1780

1766, June 7, *vice* Barrington—John Dunning, Recorder (Whig); created Lord Ashburton, April, 1782; died August 18, 1783

1766, July 23, *vice* Daltera and Alderman N. Day—*William Miles (Tory), Alderman, June, 1782; died March 12, 1803. *Henry Cruger, jun. (Whig), Alderman, July, 1782—November, 1792; died April 24, 1827

[Mr. Cruger settled in New York in April, 1790, but though he resigned his position of Alderman in 1792, he remained a member of the Common Council till his death in 1827.]

1767, August 15, *vice* Alderman Peloquin and Alderman Bayly—Matthew Brickdale (Tory), sworn August 25, 1770; discharged January 17, 1824. *Edward Brice (Whig), Alderman, August 14, 1782; died October 16, 1809.
[Voted for Brickdale and Daubeny in 1784]

THE OLD CORPORATION OF BRISTOL.--*Continued.*

1767, August 26, *rice* Alderman Barnes—*Alexander Edgar (Whig), Alderman, December 5, 1788 ; died February 2, 1792
1768, July 23, *rice* Alderman Noble and Berrow—*John Crofts (Whig), Alderman, January, 1786—November, 1788 ; died June 9, 1793. †Henry Lippincott (Tory), created a Baronet September, 1778 ; died January 1, 1781
1769. July 29, *rice* Curtis and Love—†John Merlott (Whig), Alderman, May, 1783; died December 21 1785. *George Daubeny (Tory), Alderman, January, 1787 ; died May 26, 1806
1771, June 8, *rice* Alderman Laroche—*Levi Ames (Whig), Alderman, February, 1792 ; died December 16, 1820
1771, June 8, *rice* Alderman Foy—†Jeremy Baker (Tory), died April 29, 1798
1772, April 4, *rice* Alderman Dampier—*John Noble (Whig), Alderman, December, 1792; died January 9, 1828
1772, April 4, *rice* Alderman Weekes—*John Anderson (Whig), Alderman, August, 1784 ; died June 6, 1797
1773, August 7, *vice* H. Weare—†Thomas Pierce (Whig), died December 26, 1788
1774, September 5, *rice* Swymmer—*James Hill (Whig), died October 1, 1802
1776, August 31, *rice* Alderman J. Ames—*John Farr (Whig), Alderman, February, 1783 ; died April 15, 1797
1776, August 31, *rice* Alderman I. Elton—*John Harris (Whig), Alderman, September, 1792 ; died May 20, 1801
1777, August 16, *vice* Webb—†John Fisher Weare (Whig), died January 24, 1816
1777, September 11, *rice* Sedgeley— †Philip Protheroe (Whig), died August 29, 1803.

[Exchanged precedence with H. Bengough, March 14, 1792.]

1778, June 13, *vice* Bright—†Benjamin Loscombe (Whig), died August 19, 1796
1778, June 13, *vice* Alderman Barnes—*James Morgan, jun. (Whig), died December 14, 1794
1779, August 21, *vice* Alderman Weare—†Joseph Harford (Whig), Alderman, June, 1797; died October 11, 1802
1780, August 23, *rice* Alderman Whatley—†Samuel Span (Whig), died December 2, 1795
1780, August 23, *rice* Piguenit—*Joseph Smith (Whig), died January 17, 1815
1781, August 4, *rice* Miller—†Robert Coleman (Whig), died June 23, 1794
1781, August 4, *rice* Lippincott—†John Collard (Whig), died September 5, 1788
1782, March 23, *rice* Alderman M. Smith—†John Garnett (Whig), discharged June 13, 1792
1782, August 17, *rice* Alderman R. Farr —†Rowland Williams (Whig) ; died March 7, 1798
1782, August 17, *rice* Alderman Mugleworth—†William Blake (Whig) died November 5, 1791
1782, August 17, *rice* Alderman Hotchkin—*William Weare, jun.* (Whig)
1783, September 11, *rice* Alderman Foy—†Anthony Henderson (Whig), died January 31, 1793
1783, December 10, *rice* Bull—*Richard Bright* (Whig)
1784, July 10, *rice* I. Elton—*James Harvey (Whig), Alderman, January, 1798 ; died November 5, 1807

THE OLD CORPORATION OF BRISTOL.—*Continued.*

1785, June 29, *vice* Alderman Pope—†Evan Baillie (Whig), Alderman, December, 1802—December, 1821; died June 28, 1835

[Mr. Baillie remained a member of the Common Council after resigning his position as Alderman.]

1785, June 29, *vice* Alderman Gordon — †Stephen Nash (Whig), knighted August 18, 1786; died March 3, 1792
1785, June 29, *vice* W. Weare—*Thomas Daniel, jun. (Tory), Alderman, October, 1793
1786, May 10, *vice* Lord Ashburton — Richard Burke, Recorder (Whig); died February 5, 1794
1786, August 8, *vice* Alderman Merlott — *John Morgan (Whig), Alderman, April,1803; died January 27, 1808
1787, March 3, *vice* Alderman Baugh—*Robert Claxton (Whig), Alderman, July, 1801; died June 20, 1812
1789, March 14, *vice* Collard—*Henry Bengough (Whig), Alderman, March, 1797; died April 10, 1818

[Exchanged precedence with P. Protheroe (1777) March 15, 1792. He was for several years a local Whig leader, and dictator of the Corporation, until his influence was supplanted by that of Alderman Daniel.]

1789, April 18, *vice* Pierce — †John Gordon, jun., discharged December 14, 1825
1792, March 14, *vice* T. Farr—*William Gibbons (Tory), Alderman, September, 1806; died April 27, 1807
1792, March 14, *vice* Blake—†Joseph Gregory Harris (Whig), discharged (on being appointed Swordbearer) June 10, 1801
1792, September 15, *vice* Alderman Edgar—†Charles Young (Whig), changed his name to Anderson about July, 1797; discharged (on being appointed Receiver of Town Dues) December 11, 1822
1792, September 15, *vice* Alderman Durbin, sen.—Richard Blake (Whig), died August 6, 1829
1793, June 12, *vice* Nash—†John Page (Whig), Alderman, December, 1807; died February 23, 1821
1794, June 11,*vice* Garnett—George Gibbs (Whig), refused to serve
1794, June 11, *vice* Henderson— Stephen Cave (Tory), refused to serve
1794, June 11, *vice* Burke—Vicary Gibbs, Recorder (Tory); knighted February 20, 1805; resigned December 1, 1817
1794, September 11, *vice* Crofts—*Robert Castle (Whig); died August 4, 1803
1794, *vice* Coleman—*Joseph Edye (Whig), died September 10, 1820
1795, September 5, *vice* Gibbs—Robert Bush, jun.(Tory), declined to serve; again elected August, 1810
1795, September 5, *vice* Cave —*David Evans (Whig), Alderman, May, 1807; died April 8, 1816
1795, September 10,*vice* Bush—†John Wilcox(Whig),died Sept.'28.1806
1796, March 16, *vice* James Morgan— Benjamin Baugh (Tory), refused to serve
1796, March 16, *vice* Span—Philip John Miles (Tory), refused to serve
1796, June 8, *vice* Baugh—James Brown (Tory), refused to serve
1796, June 8, *vice* Miles—Henry King (Tory), refused to serve
1796, August 13, *vice* Brown—John Pinney (Whig), resigned September, 1796
1796, August 13, *vice* King—†John Foy Edgar (Whig), discharged (on being appointed Swordbearer) September 26, 1818
1796, September 13, *vice* Loscombe—†Azariah Pinney (Whig), died January 2, 1803

THE OLD CORPORATION OF BRISTOL.—*Continued.*

1797, June 14, *vice* J. Pinney—*Edward Protheroe (Whig), discharged December 9, 1829
1797, June 14, *vice* Alderman T. Harris—†John Span (Whig), died February 12, 1799
1798, June 13, *vice* Alderman Farr—Thomas Pierce (Whig), refused to serve
1798, June 13, *vice* Alderman Anderson—Michael Castle (Whig), refused to serve ; again elected June, 1806
1798, Aug. 22. *vice* Pierce, Samuel Edwards (Tory), refused to serve
1798, August 22, *vice* M. Castle—*Daniel Wait, jun. (Tory), Alderman, February, 1808; died September 2, 1813
1798, September 8, *vice* Edwards—†William Fripp (Whig), Alderman, October, 1812; died June 10, 1829
1799, March 13, *vice* Alderman Deane—†Samuel Span (Whig), killed in a duel in Trinidad, January 5, 1811
1799, March 13, *vice* Williams—*Henry Bright (Whig), died November 22, 1807
1799, August 28, *vice* Baker—†Worthington Brice (Whig), died Jan. 13, 1826
1800, March 13, *vice* J. Span — *Samuel Birch (Tory), Alderman, March, 1814; discharged September 29, 1819
1801, July 29, *vice* Alderman J. Harris—Benjamin Freeman Coleman (Whig), refused to serve
1801, August 12, *vice* Coleman—*Richard Vaughan, jun. (Tory), Alderman, June, 1810; knighted April 20, 1815 discharged Dec. 8, 1828
1802, June 9, *vice* J. G. Harris—†*Henry Protheroe* (Whig), knighted March 16, 1803
1803, July 2, *vice* Hill—†Samuel Henderson, jun. (Whig), died February 21, 1821
1803, July 2, *vice* Alderman Harford—Robert Bruce (Whig), refused to serve
1803, Sept. 10, *vice* Bruce—Thomas Hale (Tory), refused to serve ; again elected July, 1818
1803, Sept. 15, *vice* Hale—*John Haythorne*(Tory), Alderman, March, 1814
1804, June 13, *vice* Pinney—†*Levi Ames, jun.* (Whig)
1804, June 13, *vice* Alderman Miles—*Philip Protheroe*, jun. (Whig)
1805, March 13, *vice* R. Castle—†William Inman (Whig), died April 28, 1833
[Afterwards became a Tory.]
1805, Mar. 13, *vice* P. Protheroe, sen.—*John Hilhouse Wilcox (Whig), Alderman, September 1816; discharged (on being appointed Registrar of the Court of Conscience), June 12, 1822
1806, June 11, *vice* Laroche—Michael Castle (Whig), refused to serve ; again elected March, 1809
1806, July 12, *vice* M. Castle—George Worrall (Tory), refused to serve
1806, July 12, *vice* Alderman Daubeny—Charles Harvey (Tory), refused to serve
1806, September 6, *vice* Worrall—*Henry Brooke (Tory), Alderman, September 1819; died March 31, 1829
1806, September 6, *vice* Harvey—†Edward Brice, jun. (Tory), died July 14, 1833
1807, June 10, *vice* J. Wilcox—Ambrose Gilbert King, refused to serve
1807, September 2, *vice* King—John Eames (Tory), refused to serve
1807, September 2, *vice* Alderman Gibbons—†*Benjamin Bickley* (Tory)
1807, Sept. 12, *vice* Eames—Thomas Sanders (Whig), refused to serve
1807, Dec. 9, *vice* Sanders—†Philip George (Whig), died Mar. 24, 1828
1809, Mar. 8. *vice* H. Bright—*Michael Castle(Whig), died May 22, 1821
1809, March 8, *vice* Alderman Harvey—†George King (Whig), discharged March 9, 1825

THE OLD CORPORATION OF BRISTOL.—*Continued.*

1810, August 18, *vice* Alderman Brice—John Britten Bence (Tory), refused to serve
1810, Aug. 18, *vice* Alderman Morgan—John Thomson, refused to serve
1810, August 29, *vice* Bence—William Dowell (Tory), refused to serve
1810, Aug. 29, *vice* Thomson—Robert Bush (Tory), refused to serve
1810, September 12, *vice* Dowell—*James Fowler (Tory), Alderman, January, 1821—November, 1833
[He retained his seat in the Common Council, after resigning his position of Alderman, till the Municipal Corporations Act of 1835.]
1810, Sept. 12, *vice* Bush—John Vaughan (Tory), refused to serve
1811, June 12, *vice* J. Vaughan—Charles Hill (Tory), refused to serve
1811, June 12, *vice* Span—John Cave (Tory), refused to serve
1811, June 28, *vice* Hill, James Sutton, refused to serve
1811, June 28, *vice* J. Cave—Corsley Saunders (Tory), refused to serve
1811, July 10, *vice* Sutton—Timothy Powell (Tory), refused to serve
1811, July 10, *vice* Sanders—George Thorne (Tory), refused to serve
1811, Aug. 7, *vice* Powell—John Robert Lucas (Tory), refused to serve
1811, August 7, *vice* Thorne—John Hurle (Tory), refused to serve; again elected July, 1827
1812, March 11, vice Lucas—Joshua Powell (Tory), refused to serve
1812, March 11, vice Hurle—Thomas Stock (Whig), refused to serve
1812, June 4, vice Powell—Jeremiah Hill (Tory), refused to serve
1812, June 4, vice Stock—William Danson (Tory), refused to serve
1812, July 1, vice Hill—John Nicholas (Tory), refused to serve
1812, July 1, vice Danson—George Gibbs, jun. (Whig), refused to serve
1812, July 18, vice Nicholas—Thomas Hellicar (Tory), refused to serve
1812, July 18, vice G. Gibbs—*George Hilhouse (Tory), Alderman, November, 1822—May, 1835
1812, August 15, vice Hellicar—*Abraham Hilhouse (Tory), Alderman, November, 1822
1812, August 15, vice Alderman Claxton—*William John Struth, knighted April 20, 1815; discharged December 10, 1831
1814, March 9, vice Alderman Wait—John Winwood (Tory), refused to serve
1814, June 8, vice Winwood—*William Fripp, jun. (Whig), Alderman, January, 1821
1814, June 8, vice Alderman Sir J. Durbin—*James George, jun. (Tory), Alderman, May, 1827
1815, June 14, vice J. Smith—Thomas Ransford, refused to serve
1816, April 20, vice Ransford—Thomas Hungerford Powell (Tory), refused to serve
1816, June 12, vice Powell—†Edward Daniel (Tory), discharged December 8, 1819
1816, June 12, vice J. F. Weare—Andrew Pope (Whig), refused to serve
1816, June 26, vice Pope—*John Barrow (Tory), Alderman, February, 1828; discharged December 8, 1834
1817, June 11, vice Alderman Evans—Peter Maze (Tory), refused to serve
1817, August 27, vice Maze—John Winpenny (Tory), refused to serve
1818, March 11, vice Gibbs—Sir Robert Gifford, Recorder (Tory); created Lord Gifford January, 1824; died September 4, 1826
1818, Mar. 11, vice Winpenny—Thomas Castle (Whig), refused to serve; again elected August, 1820
1818, June 10, vice T. Castle—Samuel Hall (Tory), refused to serve
1818, July 16, vice Hall—Richard Ash (Whig), refused to serve
1818, July 16, vice Bengough—Thomas Hale (Tory), refused to serve
1818, August 13, vice Ash—†*Nicholas Roch* (Tory), Alderman, March, 1834

THE OLD CORPORATION OF BRISTOL — *Continued.*

1818, August 13, vice Hale—*Thomas Hassell (Tory), Alderman, December, 1828 ; died June 18, 1829
1819, July 24, vice Edgar—†John Gardiner (Tory), died Sept. 29, 1832
   [At the date of his election he was not a burgess; he was re-elected August 28, having qualified in the interim.]
1820, August 5, vice Alderman Birch — Henry Ricketts (Whig), refused to serve
1820, Aug. 5, vice E. Daniel—Thomas Castle (Whig), refused to serve
1820, August 16, vice Ricketts—†Robert Jenkins (Tory)
1821, June 13, vice T. Castle—James Ezekiel Nash (Tory), refused to serve
1 21, June 13, vice Edye—*Thomas Camplin (Tory), Alderman, July, 1829
1822, June 12, vice Nash—Stephen Cave (Tory), Alderman, Nov. 1822, discharged May 9, 1827
1822, June 12, vice Alderman Ames—*Gabriel Goldney (Tory), Alderman, July, 1829
1822, June 12, vice Alderman Page—*John Cave (Tory)
1822, June 12, vice Henderson—*John Savage (Tory), Alderman, September, 1831
1822, June 12, vice M. Castle—*Charles Pinney (Whig)
1822, August 24, vice Alderman Wilcox—*Charles Ludlow Walker (Tory).
1825, September 13, vice Brickdale—Charles Vaughan (Tory), discharged September 12, 1829
1825, September 13, vice Anderson—*Francis Savage (Tory)
1826, September 29, vice King—*Daniel Stanton (Tory), died January 15, 1834
1826, September 29, vice Gordon—†John Evans Lunell (Whig'(refused to serve ; again elected September, 1829
1827, March 14, vice Gifford—Sir John Singleton Copley, Recorder (Tory); created Lord Lyndhurst, April, 1827; resigned June 22, 1827
1827, July 11, vice Lunell—*Charles Payne (Tory)
1827, July 21, vice W. Brice — Michael Hinton Castle (Whig), refused to serve; again elected September, 1828
1827, July 21, vice Cruger—John Hurle (Tory), refused to serve
1827, September 11, vice Alderman S. Cave — †Henry Wenman Newman (Tory)
1827, September 11, vice Copley—Sir Charles Wetherell, Recorder (Tory)
1828, September 13, vice Alderman Noble — Daniel Cave (Tory), refused to serve ; again elected July, 1831
1828, September 13, vice P. George—†Hugh William Danson (Tory)
1828, Sept. 13, vice M. H. Castle—†Thomas Hooper Riddle (Tory)
1828, September 13, vice Hurle—Michael Hinton Castle (Whig), refused to serve; again elected July, 1831
1829, September 12, vice Alderman Sir R. Vaughan—†John Evans Lunell (Whig)
1829, December 9, vice D. Cave—†George Protheroe (Whig)
1829, December 9, vice M. H. Castle—†William Claxton (Whig)
1829, Dec. 9, vice Alderman Fripp, sen.—†George Bengough (Whig)
1831, June 8, vice Alderman Brooke—†Joseph Lax (Tory)
1831, July 20, vice Alderman Hassell—Daniel Cave (Tory), refused to serve
1831, July 20, vice Blake—†James Norroway Franklyn (Tory)
1831, July 20, vice C. Vaughan—†Michael Hinton Castle (Whig)
1831, July 20, vice E. Protheroe—William Edward Acraman (Tory), refused to serve

THE OLD CORPORATION OF BRISTOL.—*Continued.*

1832, September 19, vice D. Cave—William Watson (Tory), refused to serve; again elected June, 1833
1832, September 19, vice Acraman—†*James Lean* (Tory), sworn August 16, 1833
1832, September 19, vice Struth—*Henry Ricketts* (Whig), sworn September 28, 1835
1833, March 18, vice Watson—*Christopher George* (Whig), sworn December 23, 1833
1833, March 18, vice Gardiner—†*Peter Maze, jun.* (Tory), sworn September 12, 1833
1833, June 12, vice Inman—*William Watson* (Tory), sworn July 11, 1834
1834, September 6, vice E. Brice—†*William Killigrew Wait* (Tory), sworn September 13, 1834
1834, September 6, vice Stanton—*Richard Hunt* (Tory), sworn September 15, 1835

[Messrs. Ricketts and Hunt were not sworn until after the passing of the Municipal Corporations Act (which did not come into operation until January, 1836), and only attended one meeting of the Council. The vacancies caused by the resignation of Alderman Barrow and the death of Mr. Baillie were not filled up. Aldermen Daniel, Fripp, A. Hillhouse, George, Goldney, Savage, and Roch, and Councillors Pinney, Walker, Riddle, Lunell, Lean, Castle, C. George, Watson, Maze, and Ricketts obtained seats in the Reformed Corporation, as also did Messrs. Stock, Winwood, Hall, sen., Ash, and Nash, who had previously refused to serve.]

[It will be noticed that throughout the 18th century the Whig party predominated in, and at times almost monopolised, the Common Council. In the earlier part of George III.'s reign almost the only representatives of the Tories were Messrs. Hotchkin, Miles, Mugleworth, Baker, Miller, Brickdale, Daubeny, and Lippincott, the last three of whom became members for the city. The political complexion of the Corporation was completely transformed during the quarter of a century preceding the Municipal Reform Act, mainly through the influence of Alderman Daniel. The common notion that the old Corporation was a permanently Tory institution, and that the Tories were esponsible for the abuses which that body was credited by the Reforming party with perpetuating, is altogether a popular delusion. The supremacy of the Tories in the Bristol Corporation before the Reform Act lasted for barely 25 years out of the 150 which followed the Revolution and the restoration of the old Charter; during the rest of that period it was mainly a Whig preserve. In the agitation against the town dues in the years 1823-1828, the leaders were Tories—Henry Bush and John Mathew Gutch, editor of *Felix Farley's Journal*, who wrote the letters signed "Cosmos," which served as a sort of text-book for the Anti-Corporation party.]

The succession of "Fathers of the Corporation" was for the most part, but not invariably, coincident with that of senior Alderman. It runs as follows:—

January, 1598-9—Alderman Thomas Aldworth
February, 1598-9—Alderman Cole
July, 1599—Alderman Hickes
July, 1618—Alderman Vawer
January, 1619-20—Alderman Whitson
February, 1628-9—Alderman Robert Aldworth

THE OLD CORPORATION OF BRISTOL.—*Continued.*

November, 1634—Alderman Kitchin
July, 1640—Alderman Gonninge (I.)
May, 1645—Alderman Hooke
December, 1645—Alderman Tomlinson
January, 1647-8—Alderman George Knight
February, 1655-6—Alderman Gonninge (II.)
November, 1662—Alderman Miles Jackson
February, 1662-3—Alderman Ballman
June, 1667—Alderman Sandy
June, 1672—Alderman Wright
September, 1672—Alderman Lawford and Councillor Griffith (these entered the Council the same day; Mr. Griffith was removed in June, 1684)
July, 1688—Alderman Crabb
October, 1702—Alderman Creswicke
February, 1707-8—Alderman William Swymmer
December, 1714—Alderman Yate
October, 1737—Councillor Gravett, till 1738; Alderman Sir Abraham Elton, Bart.; Alderman Becher, till June, 1742. [These had all entered the Corporation on the same day, Sir A. Elton being the last survivor.]
October, 1742—Councillor Samuel Stokes
January, 1745-6—Alderman Donning
March, 1745-6—Alderman Joseph Jefferis
October, 1752—Alderman Rich
February, 1755—Alderman Jacob Elton
June, 1765—Alderman Nathaniel Day
August, 1765—Alderman John Foy
January, 1771—Alderman Weekes
February, 1772—Alderman Morgan Smith
August, 1781—Alderman Mugleworth
July, 1782—Alderman Durbin, sen.
February, 1792—Alderman Thomas Harris
January, 1797—Alderman Deane
January, 1798—Alderman Sir John Durbin
January, 1814—Councillor Cruger
April, 1827—Alderman Noble
January, 1828—Councillor William Weare

If no account be taken of the frequent removals and restorations from the Civil War to the Revolution of 1688, the succession from 1662 to 1700 would run thus :—

November, 1662—Alderman Lock
October, 1666—Alderman Ballman
June, 1667—Alderman Sandy
June, 1672—Alderman Wright
September, 1672—Alderman Lawford and Councillor Griffith till June, 1684
July, 1688—Alderman Crabb
October, 1688—Councillor Griffith again
December, 1689—Alderman Hickes
March, 1699-1700—Alderman Crabb again

Those marked * served the offices of Mayor and Sheriff.

Those marked † held the office of Sheriff, but not the Mayoralty.

Those in italics were members of the Council at the passing of the Municipal Act, 1835.

MAYORS AND SHERIFFS, 1598-1835.

The day of election was September 15, that of entering into office September 29. In the following list the year is that of election. There were two Sheriffs until the Municipal Corporations Act, and these were always chosen from the members of the Corporation, generally from the junior Councillors.

The first name in each paragraph is that of Mayor, the second and third are those of Sheriffs.

1598. William Ellys, Alderman ; William Cary and Abell Kitchin
1599. John Horte, Alderman ; William Colston and John Harrison

[Mr. Horte died May 4, 1600, and was succeeded by Rice Jones, Alderman.]

1600. John Hopkins, Alderman ; John Boulton and Thomas Hopkins
1601. William Vawer, Alderman ; William Hopkins and John Fownes
1602. Ralph Hurte, Alderman ; John Aldworth and Thomas Farmer
1603. John Whitson, Alderman ; William Barnes and George Richards
1604. Christopher Kedgwin, Alderman ; William Cole and George Harrington
1605. Thomas James ; John Rowbers and John Grey
1606. John Barker ; Thomas Packer and John Doughty

[Mr. Barker died September 13, 1607, and was succeeded (September 14) by Richard Smyth.]

1607. Matthew Haviland ; Robert Rogers and Arthur Needes
1608. John Butcher ; Thomas Moore and William Young
1609. Robert Aldworth ; Thomas Aldworth and William Challoner
1610. John Eglesfield ; Thomas Whitehead and William Pitt
1611. William Cary ; William Burrus and Henry Gibbes
1612. Abell Kitchin ; Christopher Cary and John Barker
1613. Francis Knight, Alderman ; Christopher Whitson and John Gonninge

[Mr. Knight had served the office of Mayor for the year 1595-6.]

1614. Thomas James, Alderman ; John Langton and Humphrey Hooke
1615. John Whitson, Alderman ; William Baldwin and John Tomlinson
1616. Thomas Farmer ; Henry Yate and Henry Hobson
1617. George Harrington (elected an Alderman August 8, 1618) ; Matthew Warren and William Turner
1618. John Guy (elected an Alderman February 9, 1618-9) ; Thomas Cecil and Thomas Wright
1619. Thomas Packer (elected an Alderman February 24, 1619-20) ; William Lyssett and Humphrey Browne
1620. John Doughty, Alderman ; Andrew Charleton and Peter Miller
1621. Robert Rogers, Alderman ; Richard Holworthie and Richard Longe
1622. William Young (elected an Alderman July 15, 1623) ; Edward Coxe and William Jones
1623. William Pitt (elected an Alderman September 1, 1624) ; Oliver Snell and Ezekiel Wallis
1624. Henry Gibbes (elected an Alderman December 24, 1624) ; William Pitt, jun., and Nathaniel Butcher

[Sheriff Pitt died in October, 1624, and was succeded (Oct. 25) by Thomas Clements.]

THE OLD CORPORATION OF BRISTOL.—*Continued.*

1625, John Barker ; George Knight and John Tayler
1626, Christopher Whitson ; John Lock and Walter Ellis
1627, John Gonninge ; Richard Pley and Richard Aldworth.
1628, John Langton ; Alexander James and Francis Creswicke
1629, Humphrey Hooke ; Giles Elbridge and Thomas Colston
1630, John Tomlinson ; Derrick Popley and Gabriel Sherman
1631, Henry Yate ; John Gonninge, jun., and Miles Jackson
1632, Henry Hobson ; Thomas Jackson and William Fitzherbert
1633, Matthew Warren ; Robert Elliot and Thomas Lloyd
1634, Andrew Charleton ; John Langton and Thomas Hooke
1635, Richard Holworthie (elected an Alderman August 13, 1636), William Cann and William Hobson
1636, Richard Longe, Alderman ; Richard Vickris and Thomas Woodward
1637, William Jones, Alderman ; Edward Peters and William Wyatt

[Sheriff Peters died in April, 1638, and was succeeded (April 25) by Abraham Edwards.]

1638, Ezekiel Wallis, Alderman ; Luke Hodges and George Hellier
1639, George Knight, Alderman ; Matthew Warren and Walter Deyos
1640, John Tayler, Alderman ; Henry Gibbes and Edward Pitt
1641, John Lock, Alderman ; Richard Ballman and Robert Yeamans
1642, Richard Aldworth ; Joseph Jackson and Hugh Browne
1643, Humphrey Hooke, Alderman ; Henry Creswicke and William Colston
1644, Alexander James, Alderman ; Nathaniel Cale and William Bevan
1645, Francis Creswicke, Alderman ; John Young and Walter Stephens

[Mr. Creswicke, who was a Royalist, was displaced by virtue of a Parliamentary Ordinance dated October 28, 1645, appointing John Gonninge to succeed him, which was read at the meeting of the Council on December 9. Mr. Gonninge was formally installed as Mayor December 20, and was elected an Alderman September 14, 1646.]

1646, Richard Vickris, Alderman ; Walter Sandy and Edward Tyson
1647, Gabriel Sherman, Alderman ; Arthur Farmer and George White
1648, William Cann, Alderman ; Robert Challoner and Robert Yate
1649, Miles Jackson (elected an Alderman August 26, 1650 ; William Dale and William Yeamans
1650, Hugh Browne, Alderman ; James Crofte and George Hart
1651, Joseph Jackson, Alderman ; George Lane and Robert Cann
1652, Henry Gibbes, Alderman ; Thomas Amory and Jonathan Blackwell
1653, George Hellier ; John Pope and Thomas Bubb
1654, John Gonninge, Alderman ; John Lawford and Christopher Griffith
1635, Walter Deyos, Alderman ; Thomas Harris and John Bowen
1656, Richard Ballman, Alderman ; Robert Vickris and John Harper

[Mr. Harper was chosen September 29 in place of Josias Clutterbuck, originally elected, who had refused to serve.]

1657, Arthur Farmer, Alderman ; John Willoughby and Henry Appleton
1658, Walter Sandy, Alderman ; Edward Morgan and Nehemiah Collins
1659, Edward Tyson, Alderman ; Francis Gleed and Timothy Parker.
1660, Henry Creswicke (elected Alderman September 27, 1661) ; Richard Gregson and Thomas Langton

THE OLD CORPORATION OF BRISTOL.—*Continued.*

[Thomas Stevens was elected second Sheriff on September 15, but refused to serve, and on the same day John Knight was chosen in his place, who also claimed exemption on the ground of his Parliamentary duties, he being M.P. for Bristol. Mr. Langton was finally chosen on September 19.]

1661. Nathaniel Cale (elected Alderman August 25, 1662); Thomas Stevens and John Hickes
1662. Sir Robert Cann, Bart. (elected Alderman July 25, 1663); John Wright and Robert Yeamans
1663. Sir John Knight, Alderman; John Bradway and Richard Streamer

[Alderman John Pope was originally chosen Mayor, but refused to serve, and Sir John Knight was then elected in his place.]

1664. John Lawford, Alderman; John Knight and Ralph Olliffe
1665. John Willoughby, Alderman; William Crabb and Richard Crumpe
1666. Thomas Langton, Alderman (knighted November 4, 1666); John Lloyd and Joseph Creswicke
1667. Edward Morgan, Alderman; Henry Gough and John Aldworth

[Sheriff Aldworth died June 12, 1668, and was succeeded (June 20) by William Willett.]

1668. Thomas Stevens, Alderman; Humphrey Little and Richard Hart
1669. Sir Robert Yeamans, Bart.; Charles Powell and Edward Hurne
1670. John Knight; Thomas Day and Thomas Eston
1671. John Hickes, Alderman; Richard Stubbe and Thomas Earle
1672. Christopher Griffith; Edward Young and John Cooke
1673. Richard Streamer, Alderman; John Cecil and John Dymer

[Sheriff Dymer died June 7, 1674, and was succeeded (June 13) by William Hasell.]

1674. Ralph Olliffe, Alderman; Samuel Wharton and Edward Feilding
1675. Sir Robert Cann, Bart., Alderman; Charles Williams and George Lane
1676. William Crabb, Alderman; Henry Gleson and Henry Merrett
1677. Richard Crumpe, Alderman; William Donning and John Moore
1678. John Lloyd (knighted November 27, 1678, elected an Alderman August 21, 1679); William Jackson and William Clutterbuck
1679. Joseph Creswicke, Alderman; William Hayman and William Swymmer
1630. Richard Hart (elected an Alderman October 11, 1680, knighted October 27, 1680); Abraham Saunders and Arthur Hart
1681. Thomas Earle (elected an Alderman September 28, 1681, knighted December 4, 1681); Richard Lane and John Knight knighted March 12, 1681-2)
1682. Thomas Eston (elected an Alderman August 22, 1683); George Hart and John Coombes
1683. Ralph Olliffe, Alderman; Nathaniel Driver and Edmund Arundell

[Mr. Olliffe died September 30, and on October 9 William Clutterbuck was elected Mayor. He was knighted November 27 following. The Mayor and Sheriffs were re-appointed in the new Charter, June 2, 1684, the former being nominated an Alderman.]

16 4. William Hayman, Alderman (knighted February 28, 1684-5); Giles Merrick and James Twyford

THE OLD CORPORATION OF BRISTOL.—*Continued.*

1685, Abraham Saunders (elected an Alderman August 28, 1686); William Merricke (knighted August 27, 1688) and Robert Yate

1686, William Swymmer (elected an Alderman March 23, 1686-7); George Morgan and Edward Tocknell

[Richard Bickham was originally elected second Sheriff, and on his refusal Mr. Tocknell was chosen September 29.]

1687, Richard Lane; John Sandford and Samuel Wallis

1687-8, February 4.—In accordance with an order from the King, dated January 13, removing the Mayor and Sheriffs, and an order dated the following day nominating the persons to be chosen to succeed them, the following elections were made:—

Thomas Day (elected an Alderman August 8, 1688); Thomas Saunders and John Hinde

1688. William Jackson, Alderman; Thomas Liston and Joseph Jackson

By the restoration of the old Charter on October 17, the Mayor and Sheriffs of 1683-4 were reinstated, viz.: Sir William Clutterbuck and Sheriffs Driver and Arundell. On October 23 the surviving members of the Corporation, as it was composed at the surrender of the Charter in 1683, met under the presidency of Sir William Clutterbuck, and elected the Mayor and Sheriffs for the year 1688-9, viz.:

1688, William Jackson (elected an Alderman August 8, 1689); Thomas Cole and William Browne

[Mr. Browne refused to serve, and on November 6 George White was chosen in his place.]

1689, Arthur Hart; John Bubb and John Blackwell
1690, Sir John Knight; Robert Dowding and John Yeamans
1691, Richard Lane; John Bradway and William Opie
1692, Edmund Arundell; James Pope and Henry Combe
1693, Robert Yate; Marmaduke Bowdler and John Bacheler
1694, Thomas Day, Alderman (knighted November 28, 1694); John Hawkins and William Daines (knighted November 28, 1694)
1695, Samuel Wallis; William Lewis and William French
1696, John Hinde; Peter Saunders and Francis Whitchurch
1697, John Bubb; Nathaniel Day and John Day
1698, John Blackwell; George Stephens and John Swymmer
1699, John Bacheler; William Whitehead and James Hollidge
1700, Sir William Daines; Robert Bound and Isaac Davies
1701, John Hawkins (knighted September 3, 1702); Samuel Bayly and Richard Bayly
1702, William Lewis (elected an Alderman March 24, 1702-3, knighted August 30, 1703); Abraham Elton and Christopher Shuter
1703, Peter Saunders; Thomas Hort and Henry Whitehead
1704, Francis Whitchurch; Anthony Swymmer and Henry Walter
1705, Nathaniel Day; Morgan Smith and Nathaniel Webb
1706, George Stephens; Abraham Hooke and Nicholas Hickes
1707 William Whitehead; Onesiphorus Tyndall and Thomas Tyler
1708, James Hollidge; Philip Freke and John Day
1709, Robert Bound; James Haynes and Thomas Clement
1710, Abraham Elton; Edmund Mountjoy and Abraham Elton, jun.
1711, Christopher Shuter; William Bayly and Poole Stokes
1712, Thomas Hort; Richard Gravett and Henry Watts
1713, Anthony Swymmer; John Becher and Henry Swymmer
1714, Henry Whitehead; William Whitehead and Richard Tayler
1715, Henry Walter; James Donning and Joseph Jefferis
1716, Nicholas Hickes; Robert Earle and Peter Day

THE OLD CORPORATION OF BRISTOL.—*Continued.*

1717, John Day ; Henry Nash and John Price

[Mr. Day died June 20, 1718, and was succeeded (June 26) by Thomas Clement.]

1718. Edmund Mountjoy ; Samuel Stokes and Edward Foy
1719. Abraham Elton, jun. ; Arthur Taylor and John King
1720, Henry Watts ; Robert Addison and Jacob Elton

[Mr. Watts died on September 19, 1721, and was succeeded (September 20) by Alderman Sir Abraham Elton, Bart, who filled the office till the 29th of the same month.]

1721, John Becher ; John Rich and Noblet Ruddock
1722, Henry Swymmer ; Robert Smith and Lionel Lyde
1723. James Donning (elected an Alderman September 23, 1724) ; John Blackwell and Nathaniel Wraxall

[Mr. Wraxall was elected September 25 in place of John Thomas, originally chosen, who refused to serve.]

1724. Joseph Jefferis (elected an Alderman September 25, 1725) ; Nathaniel Day and William Jefferis
1725. Robert Earle ; Michael Puxton and Stephen Clutterbuck
1726. Peter Day ; Ezekiel Longman and Henry Combe
1727, Henry Nash ; Richard Bayly and John Bartlett
1728, John Price ; Henry Lloyd and Abraham Elton, jun.
1729. Samuel Stokes ; John Berrow and John Day
1730, Edward Foy ; Edward Buckler and William Barnsdale
1731. Arthur Taylor ; Edward Cooper and William Barnes
1732, John King ; John Foy and Buckler Weekes
1733, Jacob Elton ; Michael Pope and Benjamin Glisson
1734, John Rich ; Thomas Curtis and James Laroche
1735, Lyonel Lyde ; David Peloquin and John Clements
1736, John Blackwell ; Morgan Smith and Abraham Elton
1737, Nathaniel Day ; Joseph Iles and Henry Dampier
1738, William Jefferis ; John Combe and Giles Baily
1739. Stephen Clutterbuck ; Michael Becher and David Dehany
1740. Henry Combe ; Walter Jenkins and William Martin
1741, Richard Bayly ; John Chamberlayne and Henry Mugleworth

[Mr. Bayly died May 17, 1742, and was succeeded (May 26) by John Bartlett.]

1742. Abraham Elton (succeeded to the Baronetcy October 19, 1742) ; William Cossley and Jeremiah Ames
1743. John Berrow ; Isaac Elton and John Durbin
1744, John Day ; John Foy and Buckler Weekes
1745. William Barnes (elected an Alderman January 9, 1745-6) ; Thomas Marsh and John Noble
1746. Edward Cooper ; Henry Swymmer and Richard Farr
1747. John Foy (elected an Alderman October 8, 1747) ; John Berrow and Giles Baily

[Mr. Baily was elected September 30, in place of Thomas Power, originally chosen, who refused to serve.]

1748. Buckler Weekes ; Joseph Daltera and Isaac Baugh
1749, Thomas Curtis ; William Barnes, jun., and John Curtis
1750, James Laroche ; George Weare, jun., and Joseph Love
1751, David Peloquin ; Henry Dampier and Isaac Baugh
1752, John Clements ; Daniel Woodward and Edward Whatley
1753, Abraham Elton ; Henry Bright and Thomas Harris
1754, Morgan Smith ; Thomas Knox and Thomas Deane
1755, Henry Dampier ; Henry Weare and James Hillhouse

THE OLD CORPORATION OF BRISTOL.—*Continued.*

1756, Giles Baily ; Nathaniel Foy and Austin Goodwin, jun.
1757, William Martin ; Robert Gordon and Isaac Piguenit
1758, Henry Mugleworth ; Samuel Webb and John Berrow
1759, Jeremiah Ames ; Charles Hotchkin and John Noble
1760, John Durbin ; Isaac Piguenit and Samuel Sedgeley
1761, Isaac Elton ; Joseph Daltera and William Barnes, jun.
1762, John Noble ; William Weare and Thomas Farr
1763, Richard Farr ; Andrew Pope and John Durbin, jun.
1764, Henry Swymmer ; James Laroche, jun., and John Bull
1765, Isaac Baugh ; Isaac Elton, jun., and Michael Miller, jun.
1766, William Barnes, jun. ; William Weare and Henry Cruger, jun.
1767, George Weare ; Edward Brice and Alexander Edgar
1768, Edward Whatley ; John Crofts and Henry Lippincott
1769, Thomas Harris ; John Merlott and George Daubeny
1770, Thomas Deane ; Isaac Elton, jun. and Henry Lippincott
1771, Henry Bright ; Levi Ames and Jeremy Baker
1772, Nathaniel Foy ; John Noble and John Anderson
1773, Robert Gordon ; Andrew Pope and Thomas Pierce
1774, Charles Hotchkin ; John Durbin, jun., and James Hill
1775, Thomas Farr ; Edward Brice and John Noble
1776, Andrew Pope ; John Farr and John Harris

[William Weare was originally elected Mayor on September 15, but refused to serve, and Mr. Pope was chosen in his place on the same day.]

1777, John Durbin, jun. (knighted January 28, 1778) ; John Fisher Weare and Philip Protheroe
778, Sir John Durbin ; Benjamin Loscombe and James Morgan, jun

[John Bull was originally elected Mayor, but was unable through illness to accept, and Sir J. Durbin continued in office for a second year.]

1773, Michael Miller, jun. ; Edward Brice and Joseph Harford

[Mr. Miller died August 9, 1780, and was succeeded August 15, by John Bull.]

1780, William Miles ; Samuel Span and Joseph Smith
1781, Henry Cruger (elected an Alderman July 25, 1782) ; Robert Coleman and John Collard
1782, Edward Brice, Alderman ; Rowland Williams and William Blake
1783, John Anderson (elected an Alderman August 23, 1784) ; John Garnett and Anthony Henderson

[Mr. Anderson was elected October 2, in place of Isaac Elton, who had been chosen on September 15, but refused to serve.]

1784, John Farr (elected an Alderman February 9, 1785) ; John Fisher Weare and James Harvey
1785, John Crofts (elected an Alderman January 16, 1786) ; Joseph Harford and Stephen Nash (knighted August 18, 1786)
1786, George Daubeny (elected an Alderman January 15, 1787) ; Evan Baillie and Thomas Daniel, jun.
1787, Alexander Edgar ; John Morgan and Robert Claxton
1788, Levi Ames ; James Hill and John Harris
1789, James Hill ; Henry Bengough and John Gordon, jun.

[Mr. Hill was elected October 3 in place of Jeremy Baker, who had been chosen on September 15, but refused to serve.]

1790, John Harris ; James Morgan and Rowland Williams
1791, John Noble ; Joseph Harford and Samuel Span

[Mr. Noble was elected October 3 in place of Matthew Brickdale who had been chosen on September 15, but refused to serve.]

THE OLD CORPORATION OF BRISTOL.—*Continued.*

1792, Henry Bengough; William Gibbons and Joseph Gregory Harris
1793, James Morgan; Charles Young and John Page
1794, Joseph Smith; Robert Castle and Joseph Edye

[John Fisher Weare was elected Mayor on September 15. On his refusing to serve Joseph Harford was chosen on October 2; he also declined, and Mr. Smith was elected October 20.]

1795, James Harvey; David Evans and John Wilcox

[Mr. Harvey was elected on October 3 in place of William Weare, who had been chosen on September 15, but refused to serve.]

1796, James Harvey; John Foy Edgar and Azariah Pinney

[Mr. Harvey continued in office for a second year, Richard Bright and Evan Bailie, who had been successively elected on September 15 and October 3. having refused to serve.]

1797, Thomas Daniel, jun.; Edward Protheroe and John Span
1798, Robert Claxton; Daniel Wait, jun., and William Fripp
1799, John Morgan; Henry Bright and Worthington Brice
1800, William Gibbons; Robert Castle and Samuel Birch

[Mr. Gibbons was elected October 23. Philip Protheroe and John Gordon, who had been successively chosen on September 15 and October 2, having refused to serve.]

1801, Joseph Edye; Samuel Span and Richard Vaughan, jun.

[Mr. Edye was elected October 17. Charles Anderson (formerly Young) and John Page, who had been successively elected on September 15 and October 1, having refused to serve.]

1802, Robert Castle; John Foy Edgar and Henry Protheroe (knighted March 16, 1803)

[Mr. Castle died August 4, 1803, and was succeeded August 13 by David Evans.]

1803, David Evans; Samuel Henderson, jun, and John Haythorne
1804, Edward Protheroe; Levi Ames. jun. and Philip Protheroe
1805, Daniel Wait, jun.; William Inman and John Hilhouse Wilcox

[Mr. Wait was elected on October 2 in place of John Foy Edgar, who had been chosen September 15, but refused to serve.]

1806, Richard Vaughan, jun.; Henry Brooke and Edward Brice, jun.

[Mr. Vaughan was elected October 2 in place of William Fripp, who had been chosen September 15, but refused to serve.]

1807, Henry Bright; Sir Henry Protheroe and John Haythorne

[The Sheriffs were elected on October 5 in place of John Hilhouse Wilcox and Benjamin Bickley, who had been chosen on September 15, but refused to serve. Mr. Bright died November 22, 1807, and was succeeded, (December 1) by Samuel Birch.]

1808, John Haythorne; Benjamin Bickley and Philip George

[Mr. Haythorne was elected on October 0 in place of Worthington Brice, who had been chosen on September 15, but refused to serve.]

1809, John Hilhouse Wilcox; Michael Castle and George King
1810, Philip Protheroe; William Inman and James Fowler

[Mr. Protheroe was elected October 3 in place of his brother, Sir Henry Protheroe, who had been elected on September 15, but refused to serve.]

THE OLD CORPORATION OF BRISTOL.—*Continued*

1811, John Hillhouse Wilcox ; Edward Brice and Benjamin Bickley

[Mr. Wilcox was elected October 24, Levi Ames, jun., and William Inman, who had been successively elected on September 15 and October 2, having refused to serve.]

1812, Michael Castle ; George Hillhouse and Abraham Hillhouse
1813, James Fowler ; Benjamin Bickley and Philip George
1814, William John Struth (knighted April 20, 1815); William Fripp. jun., and James George, jun.
1815, Sir William John Struth ; Benjamin Bickley and Philip George

[Sir W. Struth retained office a second year, Henry Brooke, who had been chosen as his successor on September 15, having refused to serve.]

1816, John Haythorne, Alderman ; Edward Daniel and John Barrow
1817, John Haythorne, Alderman ; George Hillhouse and Abraham Hillhouse

[Mr. Haythorne continued in office, Edward Brice, who had been elected as his successor on September 15, having refused to serve.]

1818, Henry Brooke; Thomas Hassell and Nicholas Roch
1819, William Fripp, jun.; James George, jun., and John Gardiner
1820, George Hillhouse ; Thomas Hassell and Robert Jenkins
1821, Abraham Hillhouse ; Nicholas Roch and Thomas Camplin
1822, James George ; Gabriel Goldney and John Cave

[Mr. Goldney was elected Sheriff in place of Stephen Cave, who was chosen on September 25, but refused to serve, and paid the fine the same day.]

1823, John Barrow ; John Savage and Charles Pinney
1824, Thomas Hassell ; John Gardiner and Charles Ludlow Walker
1825, John Haythorne, Alderman ; Gabriel Goldney and John Savage

[These served as proxies for Stephen Cave, Charles Vaughan, and Francis Savage respectively.]

1826, Thomas Camplin ; Thomas Hassell and Daniel Stanton.

[Sheriff Hassell served as proxy for John Evans Lunell.]

1827, Gabriel Goldney ; Charles Payne and Henry Wenman Newman
1828, John Cave ; Charles Ludlow Walker and Thomas Hooper Riddle
1829, John Savage ; Hugh William Danson and John Evans Lunell
1830, John Savage (elected an Alderman September 10, 1831); George Protheroe and William Claxton

[Mr. Savage served in place of his brother, Francis Savage, who was elected on September 15.]

1831, Charles Pinney ; George Pengough and Joseph Lax

[Mr. Pinney was sworn into office on September 16 instead of the usual date, September 29; a question being raised as to the legality of a Mayor serving for two years in succession. Mr. Savage's tenure of office was thus terminated before the completion of the second full year.]

1832, Daniel Stanton ; James Norroway Franklyn and Michael Hinton Castle
1833, Charles Ludlow Walker ; James Lean and Peter Maze, jun.

THE OLD CORPORATION OF BRISTOL.—*Continued*.

1834. Charles Payne; James Norroway Franklyn and William Killigrew Wait

[Under the provisions of the Municipal Corporations Act of 1835 the Mayor and Sheriffs continued in office until December 31 in that year.]

Of the Mayors in the foregoing list J. Haythorne served the office three times, and F. Knight, J. Whitson, H. Hooke, J. Gonninge (H.), Sir R. Cann, R. Olliffe, Sir T. Day, R. Lane, Sir A. Elton (I.), Sir J. Durbin, J. Harvey, D Evans, J. H. Wilcox, Sir W. J. Struth, and J. Savage served twice. Messrs W. Fripp and J. George also served a second year each after the passing of the Act of 1835.

Of the Sheriffs there was no case of the office being twice filled by the same person until Mr. John Foy's election in 1744, he having already served in the year 1732-3. Afterwards it became a not unusual practice. Those besides Mr. Foy who were elected to the Shrievalty more than once were B. Bickley, who served four years, E. Brice (I.), J. Harford, and P. George, who served each three times, and B. Weekes, H. Dampier, G. Baily, J. Noble (I.), J. Berrow, J. Daltera, I. Baugh, A. Pope, Sir J. Durbin, J. Noble (II.), J. Hill, J. Harris, J. Morgan, S. Span, R. Williams, R. Castle, J. F. Edgar, Sir H. Protheroe, J. Haythorne, E Brice (II.), G. Hilhouse, A. Hilhouse, J. George, N. Roch, J. Gardiner, G. Goldney, J. Savage, C. L. Walker and J. N. Franklyn, who each held the office a second year. P. Maze, jun., who was Sheriff 1833-4, again served the office under the reformed Corporation.

9 Mayors died in office during this period (J. Horte, J. Barker, R. Olliffe, J. Day, H. Watts, R. Bayly, M. Miller, R. Castle, and H. Bright); also 4 Sheriffs (W. Pitt, jun., E. Peters, J. Aldworth, and J. Dymer).

11 Mayors (Sir T. Langton, Sir J. Lloyd, Sir R. Hart, Sir T. Earle, Sir W. Clutterbuck, Sir W. Hayman, Sir T. Day, Sir J. Hawkins, Sir W. Lewis, Sir J. Durbin, and Sir W. J. Struth) and 5 Sheriffs (Sir J. Knight, H., Sir W. Merricke, Sir W. Daines, Sir S. Nash, and Sir H. Protheroe) were knighted whilst holding their respective offices. Three Baronets held the Mayoralty (Sir R. Cann, Sir R. Yeamans, and Sir A. Elton). The second Sir A. Elton succeeded to that dignity after filling the Mayoralty, and two ex-Sheriffs (J. Laroche, jun., and H. Lippincott) were created Baronets. The following Mayors also received knighthood, but not during their terms of office as Mayor or Sheriff: Sir H. Creswicke, Sir J. Knight (I.), Sir R. Crumpe and Sir R. Vaughan.

It is a fact worthy of notice that during the 90 years 1715—1804, only eleven Tories were elected to the Mayoralty; from 1715 to 1767 inclusive, a period of 52 years, the Whigs monopolised the chair. (Messrs. Mugleworth and I. Elton, who subsequently voted for Tory candidates at the Parliamentary elections, were Whigs at the time they filled the office of Chief Magistrate.) On the other hand Messrs. Fripp and Pinney (both of whom afterwards became Conservatives), were the only Whig Mayors from 1816 to 1835.

THE OLD CORPORATION OF BRISTOL.—Continued.

LORD HIGH STEWARDS, 1541-1835.

1541, Edward, Earl of Hertford, K.G. (created Duke of Somerset February, 1546-7)
1549, Sir William Herbert, K.G. (created Earl of Pembroke October, 1551); died March 17, 1569-70
1570, Robert, Earl of Leicester, K.G.; died September 4, 1588
1588, William, Lord Burghley, K.G.; died August 4, 1598
1598, Robert, Earl of Essex, K.G.; executed for treason, February 25, 1600-1
1600-1, February 17, Thomas, Lord Buckhurst, K.G. (created Earl of Dorset March, 1602-3); died April 19, 1608
1608, April 26, Robert, Earl of Salisbury, K.G.; died May 24, 1612
1613, August 3, William, Earl of Pembroke, K.G.; died April 10, 1630
1630, August 5, Richard, Earl of Portland, K.G.; died Mar. 12, 1634-5
1635, April 20, Philip, Earl of Pembroke and Montgomery, K.G.; died January 23, 1649-50
1650, Sir Henry Vane
1651, Oliver Cromwell, died September 3, 1658
1661, August 23, James, Duke of Ormond, K.G.; died July 21, 1688
1688, James, Duke of Ormond, K.G. (grandson of his predecessor); attainted 1715
1715, September 23, James, Earl of Berkeley (K.G. March 1718); died September 2, 1736
1738, June 3, Philip, Earl of Hardwicke; died March 6, 1764
[The office was vacant for 22 years after Lord Hardwicke's death.]
1786, November 29, William Henry, Duke of Portland (K.G. July, 1794); died October 30, 1809
1810, March 14, William Wyndham, Lord Grenville; died January 12, 1834
1834, February 8, Henry Charles, Duke of Beaufort, K.G.; died November 28, 1835

Of the above the Duke of Somerset was Protector of the kingdom at the beginning of Edward VI.'s reign. The Earls of Leicester and Essex were the well-known favourites of Queen Elizabeth. Lord Burghley, the Earl of Dorset, and the Earl of Salisbury were successively Lords High Treasurer in the reigns of Elizabeth and James I., and the Earl of Portland held the same office under Charles I. The Earl of Hardwicke, the Duke of Portland, and Lord Grenville were the leaders of the Whig party in the House of Lords at the dates of their respective appointments, the first-named holding the office of Lord Chancellor, and the two latter having each been the nominal head of a Ministry (the Coalition and "All the Talents") of which Charles James Fox was the chief member.

RECORDERS, 1541-1835.

1541.—*David Broke. (Serjeant-at-Law 1541; King's Serjeant November, 1551; Lord Chief Baron of the Exchequer September, 1553; knighted 1553.)
1549.—*Robert Kelway. (Serjeant-at-Law 1552.)
1552.—*John Walshe. (Serjeant-at-Law April, 1559; Judge of the Common Pleas February, 1563; died 1572.)

THE OLD CORPORATION OF BRISTOL.—*Continued.*

1574.—*John Popham. (Serjeant-at-Law January, 1578-9; Solicitor-General June, 1579—June, 1581; Speaker of the House of Commons 1581; Attorney-General June, 1581—June, 1592; Lord Chief Justice of the Queen's Bench June, 1592, till his death, June 10, 1607; knighted 1592.)

1585.—*Thomas Hannam. (Serjeant-at-Law 1589.)

1593.—*George Snigge (Serjeant-at-Law 1603; Baron of the Exchequer June, 1604; knighted 1604; Judge in Wales May, 1608; died November 11, 1617. He resigned the Recordership September, 1605.)

1605. September 25.—Lawrence Hyde. (Attorney-General to the Queen; knighted November 7, 1634; died January 26, 1640-1).

1615. August 13.—Nicholas Hyde. (King's Serjeant and knighted January, 1623-7; Lord Chief Justice of the King's Bench February, 1626-7, till his death, August 25, 1631. He resigned the Recordership soon after his elevation to the Bench.)

1630, August 5.—*John Glanville. (Serjeant-at-Law May, 1637; King's Serjeant, July, 1640; re-appointed June, 1660; knighted August 7, 1641; Speaker of the House of Commons, April, 1640; died October 2, 1661. He was deprived of the Recordership in 1645.)

1645-6, January 5.—Edmond Prideaux. (Commissioner of the Great Seal November, 1643—October, 1646; Solicitor-General October, 1648; Attorney-General April, 1649; created a baronet by Cromwell May, 1658; died August 19, 1659. He resigned the Recordership in 1651.)

1651, November 11.—Bulstrode Whitelocke. (Attorney-General, Duchy of Lancaster, 1644; Commissioner of the Great Seal March, 1648—June, 1655, and January—May, 1659; Keeper of the Great Seal May—December, 1659. He resigned the Recordership in 1656, and died January, 28, 1675-6.)

1655, May 4—*John Doddridge. Died February 23, 1658-9.

1659, March 29.—*John Stephens. Resigned April 1, 1662; died August, 1674.

1662, May 27.—Sir Robert Atkyns, K.B. (Solicitor-General to the Queen; Serjeant-at-Law March, 1671-2; Judge of the Common Pleas April, 1672—February, 1679—80; Lord Chief Baron of the Exchequer April, 1689—October, 1694; Speaker of the House of Lords October, 1689—March, 1692-3; died February 8, 1709-10. He resigned the Recordership December, 1682.)

1682, December 19.—*Sir John Churchill, K.C. (Attorney-General to the Duke of York; Master of the Rolls January, 1684-5, till his death, October 11, 1685.)

1685, November 23.—Hon. Roger North, K.C. (Attorney-General to the Queen January, 1685-6—October, 1688; died March, 1733-4. He resigned the Recordership in October, 1688.)

1688, October 27.—William Powlett. (Serjeant-at-Law April, 1689; afterwards a Judge of South Wales till his death, October, 1703.)

1704, July 19.—Robert Eyre. (Q.C. May, 1707; Solicitor-General October, 1708; Judge of the Queen's Bench March, 1709-10—November, 1723; Lord Chief Baron of the Exchequer November, 1723—May, 1725; Lord Chief Justice of the Common Pleas May, 1725, till his death, December 28, 1735; knighted May, 1710. He resigned the Recordership, which he held with the Chief Justiceship, in 1724.)

1728, July 22.—*John Scrope. (Baron of the Exchequer in Scotland May, 1708—February, 1723-4; Commissioner of the Great Seal September—October, 1710; Secretary to the Treasury 1724 till his death, April 9, 1752. He resigned the Recordership July, 1735.)

THE OLD CORPORATION OF BRISTOL.—*Continued*.

1735, August 6.—Michael Foster. (Serjeant-at-Law June, 1736; Judge of the King's Bench April, 1745, till his death, Nov. 7, 1763; knighted April, 1745. He held the Recordership with his judgeship until the year before his death, resigning in Oct., 1762.)

1763, March 16.—Hon. Daines Barrington. (K.C. 1777. Judge of Anglesey and Carnarvon, 1757—May, 1778; Judge of Chester May, 1778—March, 1785; died March, 1800. He resigned the Recordership November, 1765.)

1766, February 5.—John Dunning. (Solicitor-General January, 1770; Chancellor of the Duchy of Lancaster April, 1782, till his death, August 18, 1783; created Lord Ashburton. April, 1782.)

1783, December 10.—Richard Burke. (Died February 5, 1794.)

1794, March 12.—Vicary Gibbs. (K.C. 1795; Solicitor-General to the Prince of Wales 1795—1800; Attorney-General to the Prince of Wales 1800—1805; Chief Justice of Chester July, 1805—February, 1806; Solicitor-General, February, 1805—February, 1806; knighted February, 1805; Attorney-General April, 1807—May, 1812; Judge of the Common Pleas, May, 1812—November, 1813; Lord Chief Baron of the Exchequer November, 1813—February, 1814; Lord Chief Justice of the Common Pleas February, 1814—October, 1818; died February 8, 1820. He retained the Recordership after his elevation to the Bench, resigning in December, 1817.)

1818, January 14.—Sir Robert Gifford. (Solicitor-General May, 1817—July, 1819; Attorney General July, 1819—January, 1824; Lord Chief Justice of the Common Pleas January—April, 1824; Master of the Rolls April, 1824, till his death, September 4, 1826; created Lord Gifford January, 1824.)

1826, September 8.—Sir John Singleton Copley. (Serjeant-at-Law July, 1813; King's Sergeant 1819; Solicitor-General July, 1819—January, 1824; Attorney-General, January 1824—September, 1826; Master of the Rolls September, 1826—April, 1827; Lord Chancellor April, 1827—November, 1830; Lord Chief Baron of the Exchequer January, 1831—November, 1834; again Lord Chancellor November, 1834—April, 1835, and September, 1841—July, 1846; created Lord Lyndhurst April, 1827. He resigned the Recordership in June, 1827, soon after his elevation to the Lord Chancellorship.)

1827, July, 28.—Sir Charles Wetherell, K.C. (Solicitor-General January, 1824—September 1826; Attorney-General September, 1826—April, 1827, and February, 1828—June, 1829.)

The list of Recorders of Bristol contains the names of a remarkable number of persons of distinction; indeed, very few have not attained to high judicial or political office. The roll includes a Lord Chancellor (Lord Lyndhurst) and three Commissioners of the Great Seal (Messrs. Prideaux, Whitelocke, and Scrope); eight were Chief Justices of one or other of the English Courts of Law (Sir D. Broke, Sir J. Popham, Sir N. Hyde, Sir R. Atkyns, Sir R. Eyre, Sir V. Gibbs, Lord Gifford, and Lord Lyndhurst); three were Masters of the Rolls (Sir J. Churchill, Lord Gifford, and Lord Lyndhurst); 3 held puisne judgeships in England (Justice Walsh, Sir G. Snigge, and Sir M. Foster), four (Sir G. Snigge, Serjeant Powlett, the Hon. D. Barrington, and Sir V. Gibbs) were judges in Wales, and one (Baron Scrope) in Scotland. Of those who did not ultimately become judges two held the Attorney-Generalship (E. Prideaux and Sir C. Wetherell), one (J. Dunning, afterwards Lord Ashburton) the Solicitor-Generalship, and one (Serjeant

THE OLD CORPORATION OF BRISTOL —*Continued*.

Kelway) was a Master in Chancery. In addition to offices involving judicial or legal functions, two (Sir J. Popham and Sir J. Glanville) were Speakers of the House of Commons, one (Sir R. Atkyns) Speaker of the House of Lords, one (Baron Scrope) Secretary to the Treasury, and one (Lord Ashburton) Chancellor of the Duchy of Lancaster. It may be noted that of the Recorders since the Municipal Act of 1835 Mr. Crowder became a judge of the Common Pleas, and Sir A. Cockburn, who was Attorney-General when appointed, was successively Lord Chief Justice of the Common Pleas and of the Queen's Bench. Sir Robert Collier, also was Attorney-General, and afterwards a judge of the Privy Council. All the Recorders marked * represented the city of Bristol in Parliament, and Sir R. Atkyns and Serjeant Powlett were unsuccessful candidates. Besides these, the following sat for other constituencies :—

Sir Lawrence Hyde —Heytesbury. 1584—1585 and 1597—1598 ; Chippenham, 1586—1587 ; Marlborough, 1601 and 1604—1611
E. Prideaux.—Lyme Regis, 1640—1653, 1654—1655, 1656—1658, and 1658 till his death, 1659.
B. Whitelocke. — Stafford, 1626 ; Marlow, November, 1640—1653 ; Buckinghamshire, 1654—1655 and 1656—1658. (In the Parliament of 1654 he was also elected for Bedford and Oxford.)
Sir R. Eyre.—Salisbury, 1698—1710. (He was Recorder of Salisbury as well as of Bristol)
Hon. Roger North,—Dunwich, 1685—1687.
J. Dunning.—Calne, 1768—March, 1782.
Sir V. Gibbs.—Totnes, December, 1804—1806 ; Great Bedwin, April —May, 1807 ; Cambridge University, 1807—May, 1812.
Sir R. Gifford.—Eye, May, 1817—January, 1824.
Sir J. S. Copley.—Yarmouth (Isle of Wight), March—June, 1818 ; Ashburton, 1818—1826 ; Cambridge University, 1826—April, 1827.
Sir C. Wetherell.—Oxford, February, 1824—1826 ; Hastings, June —December, 1826 ; Plympton, December, 1826—1830 ; Boroughbridge, 1830—1832.

Of the Recorders since the Municipal Act. Sir R. Crowder sat for Liskeard, January, 1847—March, 1854 ; Sir A. Cockburn for Southampton, 1847—November, 1856 ; Serjeant Kinglake for Rochester, 1857 till his death, 1870 ; Sir Robert Collier for Plymouth, 1852—November, 1871.

(For the succession of Recorders after Sir C. Wetherell, see page 99.)

TOWN CLERKS—1531-1835.

1531.— Hieron Ham. Resigned 1621.
1621, March 27.—James Dyer. Died 1653.
1653, October 13. — Robert Aldworth. Died March 20, 1675—6
1676, April 15.—John Romsey. Removed January, 1687-8.
1687-8, February 4.—Nathaniel Wade.
1688, October 17 (by the restoration of the Charter).—John Romsey. Died 1720—21.
1720-1, February 27.—Henry Blaake. Died July 10, 1731. (Elected by 20 votes to 15 for Giles Earle.

THE OLD CORPORATION OF BRISTOL.—*Continued.*

1731. July 14.—William Cann. (Succeeded to the baronetcy 1748.) Died March 28, 1753.

From 1734 till his death Sir W. Cann was incapacitated by illness, which ultimately resulted in mental derangement. Mr. T. Stephens acted as Deputy Town Clerk, and at his death was succeeded by Mr. Rowles Scudamore, January 18, 1745-6.)

1753, May 19.—Abraham Isaac Elton. (Succeeded to the baronetcy November 29, 1761.) Resigned November, 1786; died February 5, 1790.
1786, November 29.—James Kirkpatrick. Died May 23, 1787.
1787, June 30.—Samuel Worrall. Resigned (on the failure of the Tolzey Bank, in which he was a partner) July, 1819; died November 6, 1821.
1819, July 22.—Ebenezer Ludlow. Serjeant-at-Law June, 1827 (afterwards a Commissioner in Bankruptcy); died March 18, 1851

The Town Clerks before the Municipal Act were barristers. Mr. Aldworth represented Bristol and Devizes in Parliament; Mr. Blaake had sat for Calne 1695—1702.

(For Town Clerks since 1835, see page 94.)

CHAMBERLAINS—1603-1835.

1603, May 8.—Thomas Pitt. Died May 4, 1613.
1613, May 8.—Thomas Whitehead. Removed September, 1613.
1613, September 7.—Nicholas Meredith. Died October 9, 1639.
1639, October 16.—William Chetwynd.
1639, November 8 (by Royal command).—Ralph Farmer.
1639, December 17.—William Chetwynd. Restored: died 1651.
1651, November 11.—James Powell. Removed April, 1662.
1662, April 22.—John Thruston. Died 1675.
1675, April 10.—William Hasell,
1680, August 13.—John Cooke. Removed November 11, 1698.
1698, November 22.—Edward Tocknell.
1709—10, March 20.—James Holledge. Resigned May, 1739.
1739, May 16.—Christopher Willoughby. Died June 4, 1773.
1773, August 7.—Richard Hawkswell. Resigned June, 1811; died September 24, 1815.
1811, July 10.—Wintour Harris. Died September 3, 1815.
1815, November 23.—John Langley. (Annual term expired March 13, 1822.)
1822, April 6.—Thomas Garrard.

The office of Chamberlain was abolished by the Municipal Act of 1835; Mr. Garrard became the first Treasurer under the new Corporation. The Chamberlains were only elected for a year at a time, being usually re-elected annually until death or voluntary resignation; the case of Mr. Langley was an exception to the general practice.

THE OLD CORPORATION OF BRISTOL.—*Continued.*

VICE OR DEPUTY - CHAMBERLAINS— 1686-1835.

(The name of Vice-Chamberlain was used up to 1773. Mr. Harris and his successors were styled Deputy-Chamberlains.)

1685—6, January 8.—Bartholomew Williams. Removed July 22, 1691
1691, September 8.—Daniel Packer.
1699, August 29.—John Curtis. Died 1712.
1712, October 29.—Ezekiel Wallis.
1724. December 9.—John Vaughan.
1735—6, January 17.—Nathaniel Goodwin. Resigned 1740.
1740, September 20.—Thomas Bladen. Died 1751.
1751, July 20.—William Cadell.
1754. December 11.—Anthony Swymmer. Resigned 1766; died October 5, 1767.
1768, December 14.—Richard Hawkswell. Elected Chamberlain August, 1773.
1775, December 13.—Wintour Harris. Elected Chamberlain July, 1811.
1811, August 21.—John Langley. Elected Chamberlain November 23, 1815.
1815, December 13.—Thomas Garrard. Elected Chamberlain April, 1822.
1822, June 12.—John Hillhouse Wilcox. Resigned on being appointed Registrar of the Court of Conscience, 1824.
1924, June 9.—John Harford.

The office was abolished by the Municipal Corporations Act, 1835. Mr. Harford became chief clerk to the Treasurer, and from January 1, 1840, was styled Deputy Treasurer: on Mr. Garrard's resignation he was elected Treasurer, and the Deputy-Treasurership was abolished.

CORONERS, 1650-1836.

(Before the Act of 1835 there were two Coroners appointed by the Corporation.)

16 .—Richard Ashe
1650, October 3—Walter Tocknell. Died 1682
1656-7, January 15, *vice* Ashe—George Lynnell. Died 1701-2
1682, November 2, *vice* Tocknell—Rowland Searchfield. Died 1694-5
1694-5, February 2?, *vice* Searchfield—Richard Deane. Died 1696-7
1696-7, March 24, *vice* Deane—Martin Nelme. Died 17 5
1701-2, March 18, *vice* Lynnell—James Millard. Died 1715
1715, December 13—Henry Fane, Samuel Fox

(These gentlemen resigned shortly after their election.)

1715-6, February 7—Robert Gibbs; died 1722. Thomas Jackson; died 1721

THE OLD CORPORATION OF BRISTOL.— *Continued.*

1721, April 19, *vice* Jackson—William Dickinson. Died 1728
1722, April 18, *vice* Gibbs—George Bradford. Resigned 1753
1728, July 22. *vice* Dickinson—Richard Daniel. Died 1731
1731, September 25, *vice* Daniel—James Purnell. Resigned July, 1750
1750, July 4, *vice* Purnell—Nathaniel Goodwin. Died June 18, 1772
1753, December 11, *vice* Bradford—Thomas Stokes. Resigned September, 1755
1755, September 6, *vice* Stokes—John Thornhill. Died 1782
1772, December 10, *vice* Goodwin—Abel Dagge. Died 1778
1778, December 9, *vice* Dagge—Joseph Safford, jun. Resigned March, 1810
1782, March 23, *vice* Thornhill—Thomas Fisher. Resigned March, 1810
1810, March. 14—Theodore Lawrance; died January 13, 1821. Joseph Langley
1821, June 13, *vice* Lawrance—Joseph Baker Grindon

(By the Municipal Corporations Act of 1835 the number of Coroners was reduced to one. Messrs. Langley and Grindon retained office until April 30, 1836. The succession of coroners since 1836 is given on page 95.)

STEWARDS OF THE SHERIFFS' OR TOLZEY COURT.

1598-9, January 15—Thomas Younge
1618, May 15—George Salterne
1643, December 6—John Smith. Resigned 1645
1645, December 30—John Haggett. Removed by the Commissioners appointed for carrying out the Corporation Act September, 1662
1662, September 8—John Robins. Resigned 1690
1690, September 15—Nathaniel Haggett. Resigned 1700
1700, May 17—Henry Davie
1705, September 29—Nathaniel Wade. Resigned 1711—2
1711-2, March 22—Henry Blaake. Resigned (on appointment as Town Clerk) February, 1720-1
1720-1, February 27—William Cann. Resigned (on appointment as Town Clerk) July, 1731
1731, July 14—Edward Browne. Died 1738

(Mr. Browne was elected by 20 votes to 18 for Michael Foster, afterwards Recorder.).

1738, April 8—Thomas Stephens. Died December 7, 1745
1745-6, January 18—Abraham Isaac Elton. Resigned (on appointment as Town Clerk) May, 1753
1753, May 19—Rowles Scudamore. Resigned September, 1795
1795, September 10—Edmund Griffith. Removed January 6, 1821

(Mr. Griffith, who had been appointed one of the Metropolitan police magistrates in 1819, ceased to attend at the sittings of this court, and, in consequence of numerous complaints of his neglect of his duties, was removed by the Corporation.)

1821, January 13—Henry Adams Mayers. Resigned August 20, 1836

On Mr. Mayers's resignation the Recorder became Steward to

THE OLD CORPORATION OF BRISTOL.—*Continued.*

the court *ex-officio*, and Serjeant Ludlow was appointed deputy-judge, after whom that office was held in succession by the Clerks of the Peace. Messrs. W. Ody Hare and J D. Wadham. On the death of the latter, in July, 1871, Mr. Woodforde Ffooks-Woodforde was appointed to succeed him, upon whose resignation in 1874 the deputy-judgeship was combined with the registrarship of the court in the person of Mr. A. H. Wansey.

COURT OF REQUESTS.
Established by Act of Parliament, 1816.

ASSESSORS.

1816, July 10—Ebenezer Ludlow. Resigned (on appointment as Town Clerk) July, 1819
1819, August 28—Edward Daniel. Resigned December, 1819
1819, December 18—Joseph Smith. Died January 24, 1839
1839 February 6—Arthur Palmer, jun.

Mr. Palmer was elected by 35 votes to 25 for Joseph Grace Smith, son of the previous assessor. Mr. Palmer, who was proposed by the Mayor (Mr. Haberfield) and seconded by Alderman W. Fripp, received the votes of the Conservative members of the Corporation with the exception of Mr. H. Ricketts, who, with all the Liberals present, voted for Mr. Smith. There were four absentees, viz., Messrs. J. E. Nash, C. George, and J. N. Franklyn (Conservatives), and Mr. G. E. Sanders (Liberal).

CLERK.

1816, July 22—William Diaper Brice

The Court of Request was abolished by the County Courts Act of 1846, and at the establishment of the Bristol County Court, in March, 1847, Mr. Palmer became the first judge, and Mr. Brice one of the joint clerks.

REGISTRARS OF THE COURT OF CONSCIENCE.

[This Court was created by Act 1 William and Mary, July 25, 1689.]

1689, July—Francis Yeamans (nominated in the Act). Died 1701
1701, August 27—Robert Yeamans. Died 1715 (son of his predecessor).
1715, April 7—Nathaniel Careless. Died 1740
1740, June 18—John Michel
1746-7, February 21—Thomas Farr. Died January 30, 1760
1760, February—Anthony Swymmer. Died October 5, 1787
1787, October 13—Henry Bengough. Died April 10, 1818
1818, May—George Webb Hall. Died February 21, 1824

THE OLD CORPORATION OF BRISTOL.—*Continued.*

1824, March 2—John Hillhouse Wilcox Died December 31, 1833
1837, January 18—George Webb Hall. Died December 3, 1843
1843, December 20—Edward Harley, jun
    This Court was abolished by the County Courts Act of 1846, and Mr. Harley became, under the Act, one of the joint clerks of the County Court, established in the following year.

CLERKS AND REGISTRARS OF THE COUNTY COURT.

1847, March—William Diaper Brice, previously Clerk of the Court of Requests; died February 18, 1849. Edward Harley, jun., previously Registrar of the Court of Conscience; died Oct-25th, 1888. James Gibbs, jun., previously Deputy-Registrar of the Court of Conscience; resigned June, 1877
[These gentlemen were appointed under the provisions of the County Court Act of 1846.]

1849, March, *vice* Brice—John Kerle Haberfield, knighted March 26, 1851; died December 27th, 1857
    By the Act 19 and 20 Vict. c. 108 (1856) the title was changed from Clerk to Registrar.
    On Sir John Haberfield's death the vacancy was not filled up, the number of Registrars being permanently reduced to two.

    By the Judicature Act of 1875 the Registrars of the County Court became District-Registrars of the Supreme Court.

1877, June, *vice* Gibbs—Edward Arthur Harley
1883, November, *vice* E. Harley—Charles Edward Wright

SWORD BEARERS.

John Magge. Resigned May, 1609
1609, May 9—John Wickham. Resigned November, 1609
1609, November 14—Thomas Wickham. Resigned December 1617
1617, December 2—Richard Marloe
16 —Thomas Whitton. Died 1643
1643, October 25—Charles Sharp
1646-7, February 25—Francis Milner. Died 1661
1661, August 6—Robert Culme. Died 1667.
1667, August 6—Nicholas Burrus. Resigned 1677
1677, August 7—John Rowe. Resigned May 31, 1681
1681, August 8—Daniel Pym. Died 1710
1710, September 29—Henry Muggleworth. Died 1718 (had acted as deputy to his predecessor since June 3, 1709).
1718, October 31—Walter Chapman. Died 1725-6
1725-6, January 22—Peter Muggleworth. Died 1735
1735, June 21—William Barnsdale. Died June 19, 1748 (had acted as deputy since May 28, 1734).
1748, August 13—William Cossley. Died June 27, 1750 (had acted as deputy since May 18, 1748
1750, August 11—John Wraxall. Died July 30, 1768
1768, December 14—William Hillhouse. Died November 19, 1778
1778, December 9, Nathaniel Wraxall. Died August 8, 1781

SWORD BEARERS.—*Continued.*

1781, December 12—Freeman Smith. Died March 29, 1801
1801, June 10—Joseph Gregory Harris. Died September 8 1818
1818, September 26—John Foy Edgar
 [Mr. Edgar retained his office under the Reformed Corporation till his death. The names of his successors are given on page 96.]

HEAD MASTERS OF THE GRAMMAR SCHOOL.

William Swift. Died May 31, 1622, aged 52
1622, June 28— — Payne. Resigned immediately
1622, August 6—Richard Cheyney. Died 1635
1635, September 23—Bartholomew Man, afterwards Rector of Wenvoe, Glamorganshire
1642-3, February 17—Walter Rainstorp. Died 1657-3
1657-8, March 8—John Stephens
1662, December 9—William Ball. Died 1670
1670, December 6—John Rainstorp. Resigned 1687.
 [Mr. Rainstorp was Rector of St. Michael's from April, 1677, and of All Saints' from 1686, and Prebendary of Bristol from September, 1684, till his death, May 1, 1693.]
1687, May 11—William Stephens. Previously rector of St. Werburgh's
1689, October 16—William Wotton. Afterwards vicar of St. Augustine's
1697, November 18—Richard Welsted
1702, December 2, Edward Pearce
1709-10, January 9—William Goldwin. Resigned on presentation to the Rectory of St. Nicholas, 1717
1717, October 7—James Taylor, jun. Resigned on presentation to the Rectory of St. Michael's, 1722
1722, April 18—Alexander Stopford Catcott. Resigned on presentation to the Rectory of St. Stephen's, 1743-4
1743-4, January 18—Samuel Seyer. Resigned on presentation to the Rectory of St. Michael's, 1764
1764, April 11—Charles Lee. Died October 6, 1811
1812, March 11—John Joseph Goodenough.

The appointment to the Head-Mastership passed from the gift of the Corporation to that of the Charity Trustees in 1836. The school had been closed since 1828, but Dr. Goodenough retained possession of the school house until September, 1844, and did not finally abandon his claim to the office until July, 1845. In that year he was presented to the rectory of Broughton Pogis, Oxfordshire, which he retained till his death, April 2?, 1855. He had held successively, in conjunction with the Head-Mastership, the rectories of Bow, Brickhill, Bucks., 1830-40, and Spernall, Warwickshire, 1840-43. The subsequent holders of the office have been—

1847, November 19—Robert Evans. Died October 14, 1854
1855, March 30—Charles Thomas Hudson. Resigned 1860
1860, July 20—John William Caldicott. Resigned on presentation to the Rectory of Shipston-on-Stour, 1883
1883, July 21—Robert Leighton Leighton.

 [Dr. Caldicott was the only clerical Head-Master appointed by the Charity Trustees; all those who held office under the Corporation were in holy orders.]

SECOND MASTERS OF THE GRAMMAR SCHOOL.

(Formerly officially styled Ushers.)

Before 1629—George Harrison. Removed 1629
1629, June 23 - James Walshe. Removed 1638-9
1638-9, February 5—Elisha Farmer
Before 1653—Jonathan Prichard
1653, September 20—William Ball. Appointed Head Master December, 1662
1662, December 9—John Miller
1665, September 15—Rowland Tucker. Removed 1681
1681, June 20—Thomas Stamp
1690, July 14—Richard Wotton. Died 1694-5
1694-5, February 25—Edmund Estcourt
1698, May 25—John Deane
1704 5. February 16—William Radford. Removed 1706
1706. June 11—Henry Margetts
1707-8—January 21—Thomas Creswicke. Died 1708
1708, November 4—Walter Rainstorp
1727-8. March 16—George Harris
1739-40 March 22—Thomas Jones
1743-4, January 18—John Price. Afterwards Vicar of Temple and Rector of St. James
1755, September 6—Jonathan Gegg. Minor Canon of the Cathedral
1756, December 8—George Hayward
1759, March 31—James Brown. Minor Canon of the Cathedral
1784, December 12—Walter Trevena (previously City Librarian). Died July 5, 1785
1785, September 15—John Cooke
1793, December 11—Israel Lewis. Afterwards Vicar of Long Ashton
1798, August 22—William Edwards. Resigned August 8, 1812

There is no official record of the appointments in Dr. Goodenough's Head Mastership, but from the payments in the Council cash books the succession appears to have been as follows:—

1813, January—George D'Arville
1816, June—Stephen Britton Dowell
1817, March—James Cockaine
1823, June—Thomas Ward Franklyn
1826, September—Thomas Hope
1829, June—Charles Frederick Williams till Dec.,1829

After December, 1829, the school was deserted, and the office of Usher became vacant.

1847, December 3—John George Gordon. Afterwards Head Master of Loughborough Grammar School
1852, July 23—Charles Thomas Hudson. Promoted to the Head Mastership 1855
1855, July 20—Henry Seymour Roberts. Afterwards Head Master of Thornbury and Alford Grammar Schools
1864, May 21—Thomas Williams Openshaw. Resigned on presentation to the Rectory of Middleton Cheney, July, 1892

The office of Second Master was abolished on the resignation of Mr. Openshaw.

CITY LIBRARIANS.

1614—Richard Williams, Vicar of St. Leonard's
1631—Richard Pownall, Rector of St. John's. Died 1670
1671, June 15—Samuel Crossman, Vicar of St. Nicholas
1673—Nicholas Penwarne, Rector of St. Stephen's
1691, December—Samuel Paine, Vicar of St. Leonard's (and from May, 1693, Rector of St. Michael's). Died January 18, 1721-2
1722—Robert Clarke, Vicar of St. Leonard's
1732—John Sutton, Vicar of St. Leonard's
1734—Samuel Jocham, Vicar of St. Leonard's and Rector of St. Michael's. Died May 30 1745
1745, September 10—William Williams
1752, March 21—Richard Moore. Died January 28, 1762
1762, May 12—Walter Trevena. Resigned on appointment as Usher of the Grammar School, December, 1764
1765—Thomas Redding. Died September, 1768
1768—Benjamin Donne
1773, March 27—Thomas Johnes. Afterwards Rector of St. John's and Archdeacon of Barnstaple
1809, June 14—James Carter. Afterwards Minor Canon of the Cathedral
1815, November 23—John Peace. Resigned 1856

[Mr. Peace, unlike his predecessors (with the exception of Mr. Donne), was a layman.]

CHAPLAINS OF ST. MARK'S CHURCH.

(Appointed by the Corporation.)

1722—Alexander Stopford Catcott (Head Master of the Grammar School). Resigned 1745
1745—James Prelleur. Died about March, 1751

[On Mr. Prelleur's death the right of appointment was transferred to the Mayor.]

MAYORS' CHAPLAINS.

1751-1753—John Price
  [Usher of the Grammar School till 1755, when he was presented to the Vicarage of Temple.]
1753-1771 Carew Reynell
  [Presented to the Vicarage of St. Philip's, January, 1759.]
1771-1775—John Berjew (Vicar of All Saints')
1776-1779—Thomas Ireland. Presented to the Rectory of Christ Church, May, 1785.
  [From 1779 to 1785 there is no record; probably Mr. Ireland remained in office.]

MAYOR'S CHAPLAINS.—Continued.

1785 (to Mr. Farr)—John Audain
1785-1786 (to Mr. Crofts)—William Blake
1786-1787 (to Mr. Daubeny) William Embury Edwards
1787-1789 (to Messrs Edgar and Ames)—Robert Wilson
1789-1791 (to Messrs. Hill and Harris)—John Bull
1791-1792 (to Mr. Noble)—Edward Colston Grevile
1792-1793 (to Mr. Bengough)—John Cooke (Usher of the Grammar School)
1793-1798 (to Messrs. Morgan, Smith, Harvey, and Daniel)—Charles Pierce
1798-1799 (to Mr. Claxton)—John Emra
1799-1800 (to Mr. Morgan)—Charles Pierce
1800-1801 (to Mr. Gibbons)—Edward Colston Grevile (Rector of St. Stephen's)
1801-1802 (to Mr. Edye)—Robert Foster (Precentor of the Cathedral)
1802-1803 (to Mr. R. Castle)—Robert Watson (Vicar of Temple)
1803-1805 (to Messrs. Evans and E. Protheroe)—John Eden (Vicar of St. Nicholas')
1805-1806 (to Mr. Wait—William Wait
1806-1807 (to Mr. Vaughan)—Robert Foster (Precentor of the Cathedral)
1807-1808 (to Messrs. Bright and Birch)—Charles Pierce
1808-1809 (to Mr. Haythorne)—Charles Penry Bullock
1809-1810 (to Mr. Wilcox)—Henry Green
1810-1811 (to Mr. Protheroe)—Fountain Elwin (afterwards Vicar of Temple)
1811-1812 (to Mr. Wilcox)—Henry Green (Minor Canon of the Cathedral)
1812-1813 (to Mr. M. Castle)—Robert Watson (Vicar of Temple)
1813-1814 (to Mr. Fowler)—George Downing Bowles
1814-1818 (to Sir W. Struth and Mr. Haythorne)—Charles Penry Bullock
1818-1819 (to Mr. Brooke)—Nathaniel Struth
1819-1821 (to Messrs. Fripp and G. Hilhouse)—Charles Penry Bullock (afterwards Vicar of St. Paul's)
1821-1822 (to Mr. A. Hilhouse)—John Swete
1822-1823 (to Mr. J. George)—Thomas Tregenna Biddulph (Rector of St. James')
1823-1824 (to Mr. J. Barrow)—Joseph Porter (afterwards Rector of St. John's)
1824-1825 (to Mr. Hassell)—Edward Cowell Brice
1825-1826 (to Mr. Haythorne)—William Knight (Rector of St. Michael's)
1826-1827 (to Mr. Camplin)—Charles Gray
1827-1828 (to Mr. G. Goldney)—Ames Hellicar (Minor Canon of the Cathedral)
1828-1829 (to Mr. Cave)—Oliver Cave
1829-1831 (to Mr. Savage)—John Maynard
1831-1832 (to Mr. Pinney)—Thomas Curme
1832-1833 (to Mr. Stanton)—George Neale Barrow (Minor Canon of the Cathedral)
1833-1834 (to Mr. Walker)—Francis Thomas New
1834-1835 (to Mr. Payne)—Robert Allwood (Minor Canon of the Cathedral)
January-November, 1836 (to Mr. Fripp)—Thomas Hope
1836-1837 (to Mr. J. George)—John Bryant Clifford (presented to the Incumbency of St. Matthew's, 1837)
1837-1838 (to Mr. Haberfield)—Durbin Brice. Mr. Brice died January 14, 1839, having vacated the chaplaincy at the end of December, 1838

MAYORS' CHAPLAINS.—*Continued.*

1839-1840 (to Mr. J. N. Franklyn)—Robert Forsayth. Died January 18, 1840 ; succeeded by Robert Askwith Taylor
1840-1841 (to Mr. Phippen)—Henry George Eland (Vicar of St. Paul's, Bedminster)
1841-1842 (to Mr. G. W. Franklyn)—Robert Abercombie Johnstone
1842-1843 (to Mr. Gibbs)—James Nash (afterwards Incumbent of St. Peter's, Clifton Wood)
1843-1844 (to Mr. Clarke)—George Neale Barrow (Rector of St. John's)
1844-1845 (to Mr. R. P. King)—William Seaton
1845-1846 (to Mr Haberfield)—Samuel Emery Day (Vicar of St. Philip's)
1846-1847 (to Mr. W. Goldney)—John Durbin Gray
1847-1848 (to Mr. Pountney)—John Joseph Ebsworth
1848-1851 (to Sir J. K. Haberfield)—Samuel Emery Day (Vicar of St. Philip's)
1851-1852 (to Mr. Langton)—Arthur Rainey Ludlow
1852-1853 (to Mr. R. G. Barrow)—George Neale Barrow (Rector of St. John's)
1853-1855 (to Mr. Shaw)—Samuel Emery Day (Rector of St. Philip's)
1855-1856 (to Mr. Vining)—Robert Askwith Taylor
1856-1860 (to Messrs. Vining, Cooke, Poole, and Bates)—John Hutton Crowder
1860-1861 (to Mr. Lane)—Joseph Birch
1861-1862 (to Mr J. Hare)—Thomas Bowman (Principal of the Bishop's College)
1862-1863 (to Mr. S. V. Hare)—James Charles Norman
1863-1864 (to Mr. Jose)—Stephen Trust Jose (afterwards Minister of Dowry Chapel)
1864-1866 (to Messrs. Naish and Abraham)—John Hutton Crowder
1866-1867 (to Mr. E. S Robinson)—John William Caldicott (Head Master of the Grammar School)
1867-1869 (to Mr. Adams)—James William Lyon Bowley (Rector of St. Philip's)
1869-1871 (to Messrs. Wait and Canning)—John Hutton Crowder
1871-1872 (to Mr. Proctor Baker)—Nicholas Pocock
1872-1874 (to Messrs. Hathway and Barnes)—John Henry Bright
1874-1875 (to Mr. C. J. Thomes)—John William Caldicott (Head Master of the Grammar School)
1875-1876 (to Mr. Jones)—Philip Ashby Phelps (Assistant Master of Clifton College ; afterwards Rector of St. John's)
1876-1877 (to Mr. Edwards)—David Wright (Vicar of St Mary Magdalen, Stoke Bishop)
1877-1893 (to Sir George Edwards, Mr. Taylor, Sir J. Weston, Sir Charles Wathen, and Messrs. Highett and Barker)—John Henry Bright
1893-1894 (to Mr. Symes) — Josiah George Alford (Vicar of St. Nicholas)
1894-1895 (to Mr. Symes)—Arthur May Dewing (Vicar of St. George's, Brandon Hill)
1895-1896 (to Mr. Davies)—John Henry Bright
1896-1897 (to Mr. Symes)—Walter Cross Prideaux (Vicar of St. Saviour's)
1897-1898 (to Sir R. Symes)—Henry William Pate (Head Master of the Cathedral School)
1898-1899 (to Mr. Ashman) John Henry Bright

UNDER SHERIFFS.

Anthony Swymmer
1760, September 29—Henry Bengough
1789, October 7—Arthur Palmer, jun.
1819, September 30—William Ody Hare
1834, November—James Davison Wadham; died July 20, 1871
1871, August—George Wadham
1880, February—George Horace David Chilton

CITY SOLICITORS

John Lewis, resigned June, 1801
1801, June 10—George Webb Hall; resigned June, 1812
1812, June 10—George Merrick; resigned December, 1820. William Diaper Brice

[Mr. Brice acted alone from December, 1820, to July, 1822.]

1822, July 20—William Diaper Brice. Daniel Burges, appointed Town Clerk February, 1836
1836, February 28—William Diaper Brice; died February 18, 1849. Daniel Burges, jun., appointed Town Clerk March 29, 1849

[On Mr. Burges' resignation in March, 1849, the office was abolished.]

CLERKS OF ARRAIGNS.

1783, December 15—Daniel Burges; died April 13, 1791
1791, May 2—John Lewis; resigned June, 1807
1807, June—George Merrick; resigned June, 1820
1820, June 14—William Diaper Brice, till the passing of the Municipal Corporations Act.

MAYOR'S CLERKS.

[This office was created in 1787, and ceased at the passing of the Municipal Corporations Act, when its place was taken by that of Clerk to the Justices of the Peace.]

1787, December 12—George Merrick, appointed Clerk of Arraigns 1807
1807, September 12—William Diaper Brice; appointed Clerk of Arraigns 1820
1820, July 19—Henry Day; resigned 1823
1823, March 12—Daniel Burges; appointed Town Clerk February, 1836

QUAY WARDENS.

William Sparkes; died 1671
1671-2, February 13—John Bowrey; died 1674
1674, June 16—Samuel Warne
1694, October 31—Thomas Smyth; died 1698
1698, May 25—Robert Turpin; died 1706
1706, December 2—Charles Ansford; resigned 1711
1711-12, March 7—Richard Budge; died 1735
1735, December 10—William Lloyd; died 1739
1739, September 22—Christopher Curwen; died 1749
1749, December 24—Thomas Buckler; resigned 1758
1758, February 6—Simon Punter; resigned March 16, 1775
1758, December 13—William Bennett; died April 9, 1773
1773, August 7—John Watkins

[From December, 1758, to March, 1775, there were two Quay Wardens.]

1794, December 10—Thomas Powell; died November 2, 1809
1809, December 13—Joseph Perkins; removed 1812
1812, March 11—Thomas Etheridge; resigned 1833
1833, December 11—Christopher Claxton; resigned January, 1847
1847, January 15—Edward Robe

[Mr. Robe, who was son of the late Haven Master, received 26 votes to 20 for James Pike and 4 for William Henry Kemball.]

1861, February 12—Samuel Baker (Water Bailiff); resigned December, 1894
1895, January 1—James Turner

WATER BAILIFFS.

John Towgood; died 1668
1668, June 2—Matthew Stephens
About 1670—Leonard Hancock; removed September, 1676
1676, September 29—Alexander Morgan
1683, April 11—Henry Backwell; died 1708
1708, May 6—Joseph Baugh; died 1724
1724, October 7—Andrew Blackwell; removed December, 1726
1726-7, February 8—Joshua Franklyn; died 1727
1727, May 16—Thomas Whitchurch; died 1752
1752, December 13—Edward Bourne; died May 8, 1774
1774, August 11—John Thompson; died September 25, 1774
1774, December 14—Isaac Wheeler; died November 12, 1786
1786, November 29—Isaac Matthews; died February 7, 1798
1798, March 14—Cornelius Bryan; resigned June, 1820
1820, July 19—Christopher Deake; died April 17, 1840
1840, May 16—William Gittens Wilson; resigned December, 1848
1849, January 1—James Pike; resigned 1853
1853, February 8—Samuel Baker

[The office was united to that of Quay Warden February 12, 1861, by a vote of the Council, 31 voting for it and 26 against it.]

HAVEN MASTERS.

1752, September 29—Thomas Hollister
1759, December 15—Henry West
1767, December 14—William Jeferis; died 1773
1773, August 7—Jacob Hollister; died 1773
1773, December 8—John Baker; died 1782
1782, August 17—John Shaw; died 1797
1798, December 12—William Tomlinson; resigned 1810
1810, June 13—James Jolly
1825, March 3—Edward Robe; died May 29, 1841
1841, August 4—John Drew; died March 6, 1874
1874, March 31—Edward Thornborough Parsons

CORN MEASURERS.

1672, May 7—John Roberts; died 1674
1674, September 1—John Little; died 1674
1674, October 20—Richard Deane; died 1696-7
1696-7, March 24—Nicholas Meredith; died 1710
1710, June 27—Thomas Rogerson; died 1711
1711, December 4—Thomas Hawkins; died 1718
1718, March 25—Benjamin Darby; died 1734
1734, December 11—Samuel Jones; died 1741
1748, August 22—Thomas Buckler; resigned, on appointment as Quay Warden, 1749
1749-50, February 24—Matthew Foy; died 1757
1757, July 23—Benjamin Newport; resigned 1772
1772, April 4—Josiah Thomas
1776, December 11—William Ariel
1793, December 11—John Edwards; died 1798
1798, March 14—Robert Cottle; died March 25, 1800
1801, March 11—John Stephens; died 1810
1810, December 12—John Bryant; resigned 1825
1825, July 9—George King; died December 29, 1831
1832, March 14—Christopher Claxton; resigned, on appointment as Quay Warden, December, 1833
1833, December 11—Charles Gresley; died May 18, 1862
(On Mr. Gresley's death the office was abolished by a vote of the Council, June 24, 1862.)

RECEIVERS OF TOWN DUES.

[Previous to 1773 this office had been held for some years by the Deputy Comptroller of the Customs. On the resignation of Nathaniel Stephens in 1773 the offices were separated, and Mr. Jones was appointed Receiver by the Corporation.]

1773, March 27—Charles Jones; died 1781
1781, December 12—Charles Harford; died February 14, 1809
1809, March 8—Joseph Smith, Councillor; died January 17, 1815
1815, March 8—Charles Anderson, Councillor; died January 29, 1836
1836, February 3—James Hamilton; died May 19, 1852
[Elected by 37 votes to 20 for Jacob William Attwood.]

1852, August 10—Henry Glascodine; died June 6, 1876

[On Mr. Glascodine's death the office was united to that of Secretary to the Docks Estate.]

SECRETARIES TO THE DOCKS ESTATE.

1847, March 8—Edward Hinton ; died January 19, 1875
1875, April 30—Francis Brooke Girdlestone ; appointed also General Manager of the Bristol, Avonmouth, and Portishead Docks, October 7, 1884

SUPERINTENDENTS OF WORKS AT THE BRISTOL DOCKS.

1843, September 23—Joseph David Green
1852, March 1—Thomas Evans Blackwell

RESIDENT ENGINEERS TO THE BRISTOL DOCKS

1855, October 6—Thomas Howard
1882, August 8—John Ward Girdlestone
1890, October 14—John Martin McCurrich ; died January 13, 1899, aged 48.

LAND STEWARDS.

[This office was established in 1810, and has been continuously held by members of the Sturge family.]

1810, March 14—Young Sturge ; died February 2, 1844
1844, May 10—Jacob Player Sturge ; died October 19, 1857
1857, November 9—William Sturge

DISTRICT SURVEYORS.

[Originally appointed under the Surveyors Act, 28 George III., 1788.]

1789, April 22—William Daniel ; died January 21, 1804
    James Allen ; resigned 1792
    William Paty ; died December 12, 1800
1792, December 12, *vice* Allen—Robert Gay. Resigned 1803
1801, March 11, *vice* Paty—Thomas Pope (till his death in 1805)
1803, July 2, *vice* Gay—Joseph Glascodine. Died December, 1817
1804, March 14, *vice* Daniel—Luke Henwood. Died March 19, 1830

[In 1805 the number was reduced to two, the vacancy created by Mr. Pope's death not being filled up.]

DISTRICT SURVEYORS.—*Continued.*

1818, March 11, *vice* Glascodine—Richard Glascodine. Died May 8, 1819

1819, December 8, *vice* Glascodine—James Foster, jun. Died January 5, 1836

[From the death of Mr. Henwood till December, 1831, Mr. Foster was sole surveyor.]

1831, December 14, *vice* Henwood—Richard Shackleton Pope

1836, February 3, *vice* Foster—William Armstrong. Died October 28, 1858

[Elected by 24 votes to 22 for S. C. Fripp, and 11 for Thomas Foster.]

On the passing of the Bristol Buildings and Improvements Act, in 1840, the number of district surveyors was increased to four.

1840, September 8 (additional)—Samuel Charles Fripp
William Harris. Resigned November, 1847

[The votes were—Fripp 30, Harris 20, Charles Dyer 16.]

On the resignation of Mr. Harris, in 1849, the number of surveyors was reduced to three.

1859, January 1, *vice* Armstrong—Josiah Thomas

In 1872 it was determined to appoint a single surveyor for the whole city from January 1, 1873.

CITY SURVEYORS.

1872, September 24—Josiah Thomas. Died July 5, 1897
1897, December 14—Thomas Henry Yabbicom (city engineer).

CITY ESTATES SURVEYOR.

1897, November 12—Peter Addie.

APPENDIX

OF

MISCELLANEOUS LISTS.

LORDS-LIEUTENANT OF BRISTOL.

1602, May—Edward, Earl of Hertford ; died April 6, 1621
1621, April—William, Earl of Pembroke, K.G. ; died April 10, 1630
1630, August—Philip, Earl of Pembroke and Montgomery, K.G.
1639, March—William, Earl of Hertford, K B. ; created Marquis of Hertford June, 1640 (jointly with the Earl of Pembroke)
1640, July—William, Lord Herbert (jointly with his father, the Earl of Pembroke)

FOR THE PARLIAMENT.

1642, March—William, Earl of Bedford
1643, September—Philip, Earl of Pembroke and Montgomery, K.G. Died January 13, 1649-50

1660, July 10—William, Marquis of Hertford, K.G. (restored to the Dukedom of Somerset, September, 1649) ; died October 4, 1660
1660, December 22—James, Marquis of Ormonde, K.G. (created Duke of Ormonde, March, 1660-1)

All the above were Lords-Lieutenant of the county of *Somerset*. The Duke of Ormonde, who died July 21, 1688, resigned the Lord-Lieutenancy of Somerset in 1672, and was succeeded by Henry, Marquis of Worcester, who had been Lord-Lieutenant of Gloucestershire since July, 1660, and was created Duke of Beaufort in December, 1682. Since this period the office has been invariably annexed to the Lord-Lieutenancy of *Gloucestershire*. The Duke resigned December 31, 1688. The subsequent Lords-Lieutenant have been—

1689, April 29—Charles, Earl of Macclesfield ; died January 7, 1693-4
1694, May 25—James, Viscount Dursley, K.B. [succeeded to the Earldom of Berkeley, October 10, 1698) ; died September 24, 1710
1710, October 20—James, Earl of Berkeley ; removed March, 1711-12 ; restored 1714
1711-12, March 6—Henry, Duke of Beaufort (K.G. October, 1712); died May 24, 1714

LORDS-LIEUTENANT OF BRISTOL.—Continued.

1714, September 27—James, Earl of Berkeley (K.G. March, 1718); died September 2, 1736
1737, April 21—Augustus, Earl of Berkeley (K.T. June, 1739); died January 9, 1755
1755, February 14—Matthew, Lord Ducie; resigned 1758
1758, November 14—John Thynne, Lord Chedworth, died May 8, 1762
1762, May 29—Norborne Berkeley (confirmed in the Barony of Bottetourt); resigned 1766
1766, June 26—Frederick Augustus, Earl of Berkeley; died August 8, 1810
1810, August 22—Henry Charles, Duke of Beaufort, K.G.; died November 23, 1835
1836, February 3—William, Lord Segrave (created Earl Fitzhardinge August, 1841); died October 10, 1857
1857, November 4—Henry John, Earl of Ducie

POSTMASTERS.

1678—Thomas Cale
1690—William Dickinson
1693—Daniel Packer
1694, September—Henry Pine
1740—Thomas Pine
1760, January 16—Thomas Pine, jun ; died April 7, 1777
1777—William Fenn ; died June 11, 1788
1788—The widow of William Fenn
 [James Frye managed the Post Office for Mrs. Fenn till his death, December 2, 1805.. Mrs. Fenn retired on a pension in March, 1806.]
1806, March—Thomas Cole ; died June 1, 1825
1825, June 9—John Gardiner ; resigned 1832
1832, February 21—Thomas Todd Walton ; resigned 1842
1842, May 23—Thomas Todd Walton, jun ; resigned 1871
1871, June 21—Edward Chaddock Sampson ; resigned December, 1891
1892, April 19—Robert Charles Tombs

COLLECTORS OF CUSTOMS.

Jeremiah Burroughs ; resigned 1758
1758, May 1—Daniel Harson ; died May 23, 1779
 [Mr. Harson, who had been a Nonconformist minister, was his predecessor's son-in-law.]
1779, June—John Powell ; died July 10, 1799
1800—Anthony Palmer Collings ; died May 28, 1809
1809— Thomas Eagles ; died October 28, .812
1813, July 6—John Gordon
1832, April 27—Thomas Morris
1843, August 23—John Ker
1855, October 4—Ambrose Foote ; died February 12, 1870
1870, March 16—William James Redpath
1877, July 10—Elgar Pagden
1882, November 1—Thomas Walker Clarke
1886, October 18—Robert Thomas Dolan
1889, September 18—Edward Titt Bisshopp Smith
1895, October 1—Edward Francis Evans

REGISTRARS OF THE DISTRICT COURT OF BANKRUPTCY.

1842, October—Richard George Shum Tuckett ; died January 7, 1854
  John Henry Pollock ; transferred to London, December, 1845
1845, December—Charles Orme (vice Pollock) ; resigned 1862

  (Sole Registrar from January, 1854.)

1862—Hon. Thomas Montague Carrington Wilde
  (Till the abolition of the District Court by the Act of 1869).

OFFICIAL ASSIGNEES OF THE DISTRICT COURT OF BANKRUPTCY.

1842, October—Thomas Rennie Hutton ; removed May, 1855
  George Morgan ; transferred to Liverpool, December, 1843
  Alfred John Acraman (sole Assignee from 1863 till the abolition of the District Court by the Act of 1869)
  Edward Mant Miller ; resigned 1863
1843, December (vice Morgan)—Roger Kynaston till 1845, after which date there were three Official Assignees till 1855, and two from 1855 to 1863.

OFFICIAL RECEIVER IN BANKRUPTCY.

1884—Edward Gustavus Clarke

SUPERINTENDENT REGISTRARS OF BIRTHS, DEATHS AND MARRIAGES.

BRISTOL UNION.

1836—William Powell Hartley ; died July 10, 1850
1850—Thomas Field Gilbert ; resigned 1861
1861—John Crowther Gwynne ; died 1893
1893—Humphrey Thomas Martin Crowther Gwynne

SUPERINTENDENT REGISTRARS.

CLIFTON UNION (BARTON REGIS from March 14, 1877).

1836, Charles Arthur Latcham
1857, October, Robert Mercer
1881, June, Charles Henry Hunt
1897, May 1, Hubert Thomas Henley Lancaster

BOARD OF GUARDIANS—CLIFTON UNION.

[The name of the Union was changed to BARTON REGIS, March 14, 1877.]

CHAIRMEN.

April, 1836—William Miles, M.P.
March, 1837—Rev. William Squire Mirehouse
April 23, 1859—Odiarne Coates Lane, Councillor
May 13, 1859—George Dix
April, 1867—Henry William Green, Councillor
April, 1876—Thomas Pease
April, 1881—John Yalland
April, 1887—Charles Garton
April, 1889—George Ferris Rumsey
  In 1897 about nine-tenths of the Barton Regis Union was transferred to the Bristol Union.
April, 1898, Alfred Shipley

VICE-CHAIRMEN.

April, 1836, Abraham Gray Harford-Battersby.
March 31, 1837, Thomas White
April, 1840, Joseph Davies
April, 1848, Captain Charles Warde, K.H.
April, 1851, Thomas White
April, 1854, Odiarne Coates Lane
April 23, 1859, George Dix
May 15, 1859, Thomas Pease
April, 1863, Thomas Bowsher
April, 1866, Henry William Green
April, 1867, Rev. Frank Burges

	First Vice-Chairman.	Second Vice-Chairman.
April, 1872,	Rev. Frank Burges	Rev. Henry Richards
April, 1871,	Rev. Frank Burges	William Tanner
April, 1869,	Rev. Frank Burges	John Yalland

(Mr. Burges died July 17, 1875, and was succeeded, September by Edwin Parry.)

April, 1876,	John Yalland	Edwin Parry
April, 1881,	Edwin Parry	John Pavey
April, 1882,	John Pavey	Charles Garton
April, 1883,	Charles Garton	George Lewis
April, 1884,	Charles Garton	William Perry
April, 1886,	Charles Garton	Alfred Shipley
April, 1887,	Alfred Shipley	Rev. Samuel William Wayte
April, 1889,	Alfred Shipley	John Thomas Iles
April, 1891,	Alfred Shipley	Rev. Samuel William Wayte
April, 1893,	Alfred Shipley	Edmund Armitage Hardy
April, 1895,	William Bryant	Alfred Shipley

(Mr. Bryant died June 23, 1895, and was succeeded, July 5, by the Rev. Thomas Henry Trickey Dening.)

April, 1896, Rev. Thomas Henry Trickey Dening   Alfred Shipley
April, 1896, John Barton Tanner.

CLERKS.

April 29, 1836—Isaac Dighton
July 8, 1836—Robert Mercer
February 11, 1870—Charles Henry Hunt
May, 1897—Hubert Thomas Henley Lancaster

PROVINCIAL GRAND MASTERS OF THE SOCIETY OF FREEMASONS.

1764, Thomas Dunckerley. Died November, 1798
1799, Henry Jenner
1806, May, William Henry Goldwyer. Died March 7, 1820.
1821, Feb., John Hodder Moggridge. Resigned 1829
1830, Hugh Duncan Baillie. Resigned 1845
1845, December, Henry Shute. Died Mar. 24, 1865
1867, Jan. 29, William, Earl of Limerick. Resigned 1889
1889, Mar. 27, William Augustus Frederick Powell

PRINCIPALS AND VICE-PRINCIPALS OF BRISTOL COLLEGE (PARK ROW).

1831, Joseph Henry Jerrard (resigned 1838), Principal
    George Ash Butterton, Vice-Principal
1834, John Edward Bromby, Vice-Principal

    (Mr. Bromby was Acting Principal from 1838 to 1840, in conjunction with Francis William Newman.)

1840, James Booth, Principal
    John Thompson Exley, Vice-Principal
        (The College was closed December, 1841.)

PRINCIPALS OF THE BISHOP'S COLLEGE.

1840, Henry Dale
1846, James Robertson. Afterwards rector of Christ Church
1855, Thomas Bowman
        (The College was closed December, 1861.)

HEADMASTERS OF CLIFTON COLLEGE.

1861, Charles Evans; resigned on appointment to the Head Mastership of King Edward's School, Birmingham
1862, John Percival; resigned on election to the office of President of Trinity College, Oxford
1879, James Matthias Wilson; resigned on presentation to the vicarage of Rochdale
1891, Michael George Glazebrook

CHAIRMEN OF THE BRISTOL WATER WORKS COMPANY.

1846—George Eddie Sanders ; died April 2, 1851
1851, April 5—Sir John Kerle Haberfield ; died Dec. 27, 1857
1858, January 9—George Thomas ; died Dec. 7, 1869
1869, December 15—Henry Abbot ; died April 3, 1874
1874, April 17—Francis Fry ; died November 12, 1886
1886, November 20—Edward Bush

BRISTOL ROYAL INFIRMARY.

[The first general meeting of subscribers was held January 7, 1736-7, and the building was opened December 13. 1737.]

TREASURERS.

1736-7, January 7—John Elbridge. Died February 22, 1738-9
1738-9—John Andrews. Resigned 1740
1740, December 9—Richard Champion. Died February 23, 1747-8
1747-8, March 8—Nehemiah Champion (son of his predecessor). Died December 13, 1753
1753, December 20—Richard Champion (brother of his predecessor). Died January 9, 1766
1766, February 11—Abraham Richard Hawkesworth. Died October 29, 1768
1768, December 6—Richard Champion. Resigned December, 1778
1778, December 24—Joseph Harford. Resigned 1791
1791, December 20—Edward Ash. Resigned 1808
1808, December 20—Samuel Birch. Resigned 1811
1811, October 30—William Fripp. Resigned March, 1829
1829, March 19—Daniel Cave. Resigned March, 1844

PRESIDENTS AND TREASURERS.

1844, March 15—John Scandrett Harford. Resigned 1859
1859—March 15—John Battersby Harford. Resigned 1869
1869—April 27—Robert Phippen. Died July 5, 1869
1869, July 27—The Rev. James Heyworth. Died December 22, 1879
1880, March 23—Charles Daniel Cave. [Created a baronet July,1896]

SECRETARIES.

1736-7—Morgan Smith
1739—Richard Lathrop
1752—Joseph Beech. Died February 2, 1771
1771—Thomas Bawn. Died December 18, 1790
1791, January 8—John Jordan Palmer. Resigned 1818
1818, October 29—William Weir

[There were eight candidates. The numbers were: Weir, 223 ; George Wills, 196 ; James Williams, jun., 66 ; Thomas Hooper, jun., 44 ; R. V. Wreford, 29 ; White, 15 ; James Hill. 13 ; H. P. Edgell, 5.]

1823, October 16—Samuel Johnson. Resigned May, 1840
1840, June—Robert Johnston. Died February 11, 1849
1849, January 21—W. H. Bosworth. Resigned April 18, 1849
1849, May 4—William Trenerry. Died October 14, 1884
1884, December 19—Lieutenant-Colonel Charles Senhouse Graham. Resigned 1887
1887, December 13—Joseph Furlonge Shekleton, M.D. Resigned 1895
1895, April 9—Edward Albert Leonard

BRISTOL ROYAL INFIRMARY.—*Continued.*

CHAPLAINS.

1740—William Davies. Died 1772
1772, November—Thomas Johnes
1817, January 22—John Swete
1825—John Mais
1856, October 7—William Hood Sage
1860, April 24—John Mackie
1876, August 8—Oswald Harrison
1877, February 13—Oliver Sumner
1878, December 10—Octavius Maunsell Grindon
1885, November 24—Fairfax Goodall

PHYSICIANS.

1737, May 20—John Bonython; died November 13, 1761. William Logan; died December 14, 1757.—Hardwicke; died September 1, 1747. John Middleton; declined to serve
1737, June 3, *vice* Middleton—Etwall. Resigned 1743

[The vacancy caused by Dr. Etwall's resignation was not filled till 1747.]

1747., December 15, *vice* Hardwicke and Etwall—Archibald Drummond; resigned October, 1771. William Cadogan; resigned March, 1752

[Dr. Francis Randolph was a candidate. At the first division the numbers were: Drummond, 98 : Randolph, 78 ; Cadogan, 7. At the second division Dr. Cadogan was elected by 87 votes against 84 for Randolph. On Dr. Cadogan's resignation the vacancy remained unfilled for more than five years.]

1757, December 23, *vice* Logan and Cadogan—Francis Woodward; resigned December, 1769. Edward Lyne ; resigned October, 1763

[The vacancy cased by Dr. Lyne's resignation remained unfilled for more than three years.]

1761, December 8, *vice* Bonython—James Plomer. Resigned April, 1798.

[Dr. Plomer defeated Dr. Gordon by 19 votes.]

1767, January 13, *vice* Lyne—Samuel Farr ; resigned April, 1780. [Dr. Corryn was an unsuccessful candidate.] (Additional) John England; resigned March, 1767

[The number of physicians was thus temporarily increased to five ; but at the resignation of Dr. Woodward, in 1769, the vacancy was not filled, and the original number was restored.]

1767, March 3, *vice* England—Thomas Rigge. Resigned Feb., 1778

[Dr. Rigge, in later life, abandoned the medical profession, and was called to the Bar.]

1771, November 4, *vice* Drummond—John Wright. Died December 23, 1794
1772, September 5 (additional)—John Paul

[Dr. Robert Robertson was an unsuccessful candidate. The number of physicians was again raised to five ; but was finally reduced to four on the resignation of Dr. Collyns in 1779.]

1775, July 18, *vice* Paul—William Moncrieffe. Died Feb. 13, 1816
1778, March 17, *vice* Rigge—Benjamin Collyns. Resigned 1779

[Dr. Collyns left England about four months after his election and died a few years later in Barbados.]

BRISTOL ROYAL INFIRMARY.—*Continued.*

1780, May 14, *vice* Farr—Arthur Broughton. Resigned 1786

[Dr. Broughton went to Jamaica, with leave of absence, in December, 1783, and his place was not filled till 1786.]

1786, April 3, *vice* Broughton—Edward Long Fox. Resigned October, 1816

[Dr. Fox, who was originat'y elected for a year only, in view of the possible return of Dr. Broughton, defeated Dr. Samuel Cave by 157 to 137.]

1795, January 7, *vice* Wright—Robert Lovell. Resigned 1810

[The votes were: Lovell, 292; Dr. Andrew Carrick, 107.]

1798, April 18, *vice* Plomer—John New. Resigned October, 1802

[The votes were: New, 377; Dr, John Heathfield Hickes, 216.]

1802, November 18, *vice* New—Walter Kennedy Craufuird. Resigned March, 1811

1810, September 20, *vice* Lovell—Andrew Carrick. Resigned 1834

[This electon was vigorously contested, an element of political feeling being imported into it. Dr. Carrick, who was a Tory, was proposed by the Tory leader, Alderman Daniel, and seconded by a prominent member of the party, Councillor James Fowler. Dr. J. E. Stock, a leading Unitarian and Whig, was proposed and seconded by Sir Abraham Elton and Mr. Sheriff Castle, who were amongst the foremost of local Whig politicians. There was a third candidate, Dr. J. C. Prichard, who was proposed by Alderman Wait. The poll stood: Carrick, 448; Stock, 216; Prichard, 81.]

1811, March 28, *vice* Craufuird—John Edmonds Stock. Resigned 1828

[Dr. Stock had, in his student days, been a very vehement Reformer and an associate of the Edinburgh Republicans, Watt and Downie. He was indicted with them for high treason in 1798. He made his escape to America ; on his return to England afterwards the prosecution was abandoned in consideration of his youth. At this election there was again a keen contest, Dr. Thomas Webb Dyer, a Tory and subsequent President of the Dolphin, receiving a good deal of political support. The numbers were: Stock, 384 ; Dyer, 356.]

1816, February 29, *vice* Fox and Moncrieffe—Henry Hawes Fox ; resigned 1829. James Cowles Prichard; resigned June, 1843

[Dr. Dyer was again a candidate. The votes were: Fox, 968; Prichard, 670; Dyer, 515. Dr. Fox was a son of his predecessor.]

1828, February 21, *vice* Stock—George Wallis. Resigned January 1855

[This election was contested with great vigour, Dr. Wallis defeating his opponent, Dr. John Howell, by five votes only—361 to 356. Dr. Wallis was proposed and seconded by Councillor Hassell and Mr. Joseph Metford, formerly one of the surgeons to the Infirmary; Dr. Howell by Alderman Fripp, jun., and Mr. A. G. Harford Battersby. The contest was purely, personal, there being no political undercurrent, as in the elections of 1810 and 1811.]

1829, June 4, *vice* Fox—John Howell. Resigned June, 1843
1834, August 28, *vice* Carrick—Henry Riley. Resigned October, 1847
1843, June 29., *vice* Prichard and Howell—James Fogo Bernard; resigned May, 1856. Gilbert Lyon ; resigned August, 1857

BRISTOL ROYAL INFIRMARY.—*Continued*.

1847, October 28, *vice* Riley—William Budd. Resigned February, 1862
1855, February 15, *vice* Wallis — Frederick Brittan. Resigned October, 1873

[Dr. Fairbrother was a candidate, and there was a vigorous canvass until a few days before the election, when on a comparison of promises showing an assured majority for Dr. Brittan, his opponent withdrew.]

1856, June 5, *vice* Bernard—Alexander Fairbrother. Retired after 20 years' service, June, 1876
1857, September 3, *vice* Lyon—Edward Long Fox. Retired after 20 years' service, August, 1877

[Dr. Long Fox represents the third generation of his family on the Infirmary medical staff, being a grandson of Dr. E. L. Fox (Physician 1796-1816) and nephew of Dr. H. H. Fox (Physician 1816-1829).]

1862, March 20, *vice* Budd—John Beddoe. Resigned October, 1873
1873, November 20, *vice* Brittan and Beddoe—*William Henry Spencer, resigned March, 1888; Robert Shingleton Smith
1876, July 28, *vice* Fairbrother—*Henry Waldo
1877, September 11, *vice* Fox—*John Edward Shaw
1888, March 27, *vice* Spencer—*Arthur Bancks Prowse

[*These gentlemen formerly held the office of Assistant Physicians.]

OBSTETRIC PHYSICIANS.

1887, December 13—Ernest Wedmore. Resigned May, 1891
1891, December 8—Walter Swayne

SURGEONS.

1737, May 20 — William Thornhill; resigned December, 1754. Thomas Page; died May 5, 1741

[There were three other candidates— John Deverell, Abraham Ludlow, and James Ford.]

1741, June 5, *vice* Page—John Page. Resigned 1777

[Mr. Page, who was a son of his predecessor, defeated Mr. Ludlow.]

1743, June 13 (additional)—James Ford; resigned 1759
1754, December 20 (election of three Surgeons)—John Castelman; resigned July, 1779. John Norman; died April 29, 1763. John Townsend; resigned November, 1781

[There was one vacancy, owing to the resignation of M⁻. Thornhill; but it was decided to elect three new surgeons, thus increasing the staff to five. 139 subscribers voted for electing 3, 60 for 2, 12 for 1, 2 for 4, and 1 for none. There were three unsuccessful candidates, the numbers being: Castelman, 157; Norman, 145; Townsend, 145; Thomas Hellier, 62; William Barrett, 59; James Grace, 28.]

1759, June 12, *vice* Ford—John Ford. Resigned August, 1775

[Mr. Ford, who was the brother of his predecessor, defeated Messrs. Abraham Ludlow (son of the candidate in 1737 and 1741) and William Barrett, the historian of Bristol.]

BRISTOL ROYAL INFIRMARY.—*Continued.*

1767, January 20, *vice* Norman—Abraham Ludlow; resigned December, 1774; Thomas Skone; resigned June, 1770

[The vacancy caused by Mr. Norman's death in 1763 had remained unfilled for nearly four years. The elect on now resulted in a tie, each candidate polling 147 votes, and it was then decided to increase the staff to six, and retain the services of both gentlemen. Mr. Skone subsequently emigrated to Tobago, and was killed by a fall from his horse about the year 1779. The vacancy caused by his resignation in 1773 was not filled, and the number of surgeons remained from this date fixed at five until 1892.]

1774, December 15, *vice* Linden—Richard Smith; died June 21, 1791

[The votes were: Smith, 211; Thomas Davies, 81; J. Rawlins, 47]

1775, August 15, *vice* Ford—Godfrey Lowe. Died April 8, 1806
1777, May 6, *vice* Page—John Padmore Noble. Died June 22, 1812

[Mr. Noble obtained 211 votes against 148 for James Norman.]

1779, August 9, *vice* Castelman—James Norman. Resigned 1783

[Mr. Norman defeated Joseph Metford by a majority of three.]

1781, November 27, *vice* Townsend—Morgan Yeatman. Resigned 1807

[The votes were: Yeatman, 211; Metford, 150]

1783, April 2. *vice* Norman—Joseph Metford. Resigned June, 1793
1791, July 7, *vice* Smith—Robert Jones Allard. Resigned July, 1810

[Mr. Allard, who defeated Danvers Ward by 230 votes to 96, took the additional name of Kemeys on inheriting the estate of Ynisarwed, in Glamorganshire, July 28, 1810, when he retired from practice. He was knighted (when serving the office of High Sheriff of that county) March 6, 1817, and died January 10, 1832.]

1796, June 23, *vice* Metford—Richard Smith. Died January 24, 1843
1806, April 24, *vice* Lowe—Francis Cheyne Bowles. Died May 18, 1807

[The votes were: Bowles, 237; William Hetling, 235; Richard Lowe, 166. Mr. Bowles won his election by the votes of the lady subscribers, who for the first time took part in a contest. Ten of these voted, of whom eight were for Mr. Bowles and two for Mr. Hetling.]

1807, June 2, *vice* Bowles—William Hetling. Died November 11, 1837

[The votes were: Hetling, 395; Richard Lowe, 167; Nathaniel Smith, 74.]

1807, July 9, *vice* Yeatman—Richard Lowe. Died February 9, 1850

[Mr. Lowe, who was a son of Mr. Godfrey Lowe, a member of the surgical staff from 1775 till his death in 1806, himself retained his post to the end of his life—a period of nearly 43 years. There were five candidates at the election, the votes polled being: Lowe, 346; Henry Daniel, 121; Nathaniel Smith, 88; Richard Edgell, 66; John King, 36.]

1810, September 27, *vice* Allard—Henry Daniel; resigned 1836

[The votes were: Daniel, 383; Thomas Shute, jun., 224; Nathaniel Smith, 100.]

1812, July 9, *vice* Noble—Thomas Shute jun. Died September 2, 1816

[The votes were: Shute, 404; Nathaniel Smith, 293; John Bishop Estlin, 97; John King, 9.]

BRISTOL ROYAL INFIRMARY.—*Continued*.

1816, September 19, *vice* Shute—Nathaniel Smith. Resigned August, 1844

[Mr. Smith, who had been four times an unsuccessful candidate, was now elected without a contest. Nearly 20 years elapsed before the occurrence of another vacancy.]

1836, July 21, *vice* Daniel—John Harrison. Resigned December, 1859
1837, November 23, *vice* Hetling — William Francis Morgan. Resigned April, 1854
1843, February 23, *vice* R. Smith—Henry Clark. Resigned August, 1857

[Mr. Clark defeated Councillor Thomas Green by 521 to 283.]

1844, August 29, *vice* N. Smith—Thomas Green. Retired, after 20 years' service, August, 1864
1850, February 28, *vice* Lowe—Augustin Prichard. Retired, after 20 years' service, February, 1870

[Mr. Prichard received 410 votes, against 304 for Charles Greig and 276 for Ralph Mountague Bernard.]

1854, May 4, *vice* Morgan—Ralph Mountague Bernard. Killed by an accidental fall over the cliffs near Lampeter, August 18, 1871
1857, September 3, *vice* Clark—Henry Augustus Hore. Resigned April, 1868
1860, January 5, *vice* Harrison—Crosby Leonard. Resigned August, 1878
1864, September 15, *vice* Green—Thomas Edward Clark. Resigned September, 1873 [being elected physician to the General Hospital]
1868, April 28, *vice* Hore—Robert William Tibbits. Died November 23, 1878
1870, March 11, *vice* Prichard—Charles Steele. Resigned December, 1878
1871, September 21— *vice* Bernard — *Edmund Comer Board. Resigned May, 1892
1873, October 9, *vice* Clark—*Christopher Henry Dowson. Died January 14, 1889
1878, August 27, *vice* Leonard—*Arthur William Prichard

[Mr. Prichard represents the third generation of his family on the Infirmary staff. His father, Mr. Augustin Prichard, was Surgeon 1850—1870, and his grandfather, Dr. J. C. Prichard, Physician 1816—1843].

1879, January 7, *vice* Tibbits and Steele—*Francis Richardson Cross (resigned on appointment as ophthalmic surgeon October 26, 1885), James Greig Smith, died May 25, 1897
1885, November 10, *vice* Cross—*William Henry Harsant
1889, February 12, *vice* Dowson—*James Paul Bush

1892, May—On Mr. Board's resignation the vacancy was not filled, the number of surgeons being reduced to four.

1897, June 17, *vice* Smith—*George Munro Smith

*These gentlemen had previously served the office of assistant surgeon.

OPHTHALMIC SURGEON.

1885, October 26—Francis Richardson Cross

BRISTOL ROYAL INFIRMARY.—*Continued.*

ASSISTANT PHYSICIANS.

1871, January 28—Ebenezer Ludlow. Resigned 1872
1872, May 30—William Henry Spencer. Elected physician November, 1873
1873, November 20—Henry Waldo. Elected physician June. 1876
1876, July 28—John Edward Shaw. Elected physician September, 1877

[From 1877 to 1883 the office was not filled.]

1883, September 25—Arthur Bancks Prowse. Elected physician March, 1888
1888, March 27—Patrick Watson Williams
1893, June 13—Francis Henry Edgeworth

[The number of assistant physicians was now raised to two.]

ASSISTANT SURGEONS.

1871, January 28—Edmund Comer Board. Elected surgeon September, 1871
1871, September 21—Christopher Henry Dowson. Elected surgeon October, 1873
1873, October 9—David Edward Bernard. Resigned July, 1876
1876, August 10—Arthur William Prichard. Elected surgeon August, 1878
1878, September 10—Francis Richardson Cross. Elected surgeon January, 1879
1879, January 7—William Henry Harsant. Elected surgeon November, 1885
1885, November 10—James Paul Bush. Elected surgeon February, 1889
1889, February 12—George Munro Smith. Elected surgeon June, 1897
1892, June 7—James Swain

[The number of assistant surgeons was now raised to two.]

1897, June 17, *vice* Smith—Thomas Carwardine

APOTHECARIES.

1737, March 25—Nathaniel Rumsey
1739, October 13—Nicholas Simpson. Resigned 1744
1744, June 5—Samuel Stone. Resigned 1746
1746, March 11—Joseph Shepherd. Resigned 1752
1752, April 7—Edward Bridges. Died November 27, 1774
1775, March 6—Thomas Elme. Died October 18, 1777
1777, November 12—John Ellis. Died January, 1778
1778, June 10—John Bingham Borlase. Resigned March, 1779
1779, April 28—Benjamin Mason. Died March, 1783
1783, April 1—Charlton Yeatman. Resigned October, 1783
1783, December 2—Thomas Griffiths Resigned April, 1789
1789, April 30—Thomas Webb Dyer. Resigned August, 1810

[Dr. Dyer was elected by 210 votes to 50 for Thomas Yeld.]

1810, December 6—James Bedingfield. Resigned 1816

[Dr. Bedingfield was elected by 140 to 41 for Alfred Collett Bartley.]

1816, February 22—William Swayne. Died June 15, 1825
1825, July 7—William Francis Morgan. Resigned 1833

[On Mr. Morgan's resignation the title was changed to house surgeon and apothecary.]

BRISTOL ROYAL INFIRMARY,—*Continued.*

HOUSE SURGEONS AND APOTHECARIES.

1833, April 18—Frederick Lemon. Resigned June, 1837
1837, July 20—Charles Redwood Vachell. Resigned October, 1840
1840, November 5—Charles Greig

[Elected by 414 votes to 163 for James Barrington Prowse.]

In 1843 the office of apothecary was separated from that of house surgeon, Mr. Greig retaining the latter title.

APOTHECARIES.

1843, November 23—Richard Davis. Resigned June, 1844
1844, July 4—Henry Augustus Hore. Elected house surgeon December, 1846
1847, January 7—Joseph Seymour Metford. Resigned March, 1850

[Mr. Metford was elected by 468 votes to 282 for William Richard Bridges.]

1850, May 2—Robert Powell. Resigned April, 1851

[On Mr. Powell's resignation the title of apothecary was changed to that of assistant house surgeon.]

HOUSE SURGEONS.

1843, November—Charles Greig (previously, from November, 1840, house surgeon and apothecary)
1846, December 24—Henry Augustus Hore. Resigned January, 1856
1856, January 17—Nathaniel Crisp; resigned 1858
1858, October 7—Thomas Joseph Cookson Powell. Died February 23, 1860
1860, March 12—Geoffrey Viel Cooper. Resigned November, 1863
1863, November 19—Edmund Comer Board. Resigned 1870
1870, January 22—Ebenezer Ludlow. Elected assistant physician January, 1871
1871, January 24—Robert Shingleton Smith. Resigned 1873. Elected physician the same year
1873, March 25—Henry Macready Chute. Resigned 1877
1877, August 28—James Greig Smith. Resigned June, 1878, and elected medical superintendent
1878, June 11—George Herbert Lilley. Resigned 1879
1879, December 5—Alfred Austen Lendon. Resigned 1883
1883, February 13—James Paul Bush. Resigned 1884. Elected assistant surgeon, 1885
1884, October 28—John Fenton Evans. Resigned 1886
1886, March 16—John Dacre. Resigned 1887
1887, May 24—James Swain. Elected assistant surgeon June, 1892
1892, June 28—Walter James Hill. Resigned 1895
1895, May 14—Thomas Carwardine. Elected assistant surgeon June, 1897
1897, June 17—Harold Frederick Mole.

MEDICAL SUPERINTENDENTS.

[This office, established in 1878, was abolished in 1883.]

1878, June 25—James Greig Smith (previously house surgeon) elected surgeon January, 1879
1879, February 7—John Henry Lee Macintire. Resigned July, 1883.

BRISTOL ROYAL INFIRMARY.— *Continued.*

ASSISTANT HOUSE SURGEONS.

1851, May 22—Nathaniel Crisp. Elected house surgeon January, 1856
1856, January 17—Thomas Joseph Cookson Powell. Elected house surgeon October, 1858
1858, October 7—Geoffrey Viel Cooper. Elected house surgeon March, 1860
1860, May 17—Edmund Comer Board. Elected house surgeon November, 1863
1863, November 19—Herbert Cooper. Resigned November, 1864
1865, January 4—Ebenezer Ludlow. Elected house surgeon January, 1870
1870, March 1—Robert Shingleton Smith. Elected house surgeon January, 1871
1870, November 22—Henry Macready Chute. Elected house surgeon March, 1873
1873, December 16—John Edward Shaw. Resigned June, 1876
1876, June 27—James Greig Smith. Elected house surgeon August, 1877
1877, October 2—James Scott.

[This office was abolished in June, 1878, the new post of house physician being created in its place.]

HOUSE PHYSICIANS.

1878, June 25—James Scott. Resigned 1880
1880, February 17—Charles Scott Watson. Resigned 1882
1882, September 12—James Paul Bush. Elected house surgeon February, 1883
1883, March 13—John Fenton Evans. Elected house surgeon October, 1884
1884, October 28—John Dacre. Elected house surgeon March, 1886
1886, March 22—James Swain. Elected house surgeon May, 1887
1887, May 24—Patrick Watson Williams. Elected assistant physician March 1888
1888, May 25—Walter James Hill. Elected house surgeon June, 1892
1892, June 28—Henry Lawrence Ormerod. Resigned March, 1895
1895, May 14—Harold Frederick Mole. Elected house surgeon June, 1897
1897, July 27—Edward Hugh Edwards Stack.

BRISTOL GENERAL HOSPITAL.

Opened November 1, 1832.

PRESIDENTS.

1832—William Wyndham, Lord Grenville; died January 12, 1834
1834—Henry Duke of Beaufort; died November 23, 1835

[From 1835 to 1849 the office was vacant.]

1849—George Thomas (also treasurer); died December 7, 1869
1872—William Proctor Baker

BRISTOL GENERAL HOSPITAL.—*Continued.*

SECRETARIES.

1831, James Norton
1835, John Thorner Pike
1858, Richard Seymour Underwood
1860, William John Burgess
1869, Charles John Thompson
1872, Henry Fox, Lieutenant R.N.

(Appointed Secretary to Birmingham General Hospital, 1885.)

1885, William Thwaites

CHAPLAINS.

1834, Charles Buck. Rector of St. Stephen
1849, George Campbell
1855, William Marriott. Died October 8, 1859
1859, Adam Clarke Rowley. Vicar of St. Matthias
1860, Charles Brittan
1870, William Johnson
1870, Edmund Day
1872, Thomas William Boyce. Rector of St. Werburgh
1874, Feb. 11, Delasaux Egginton Mount Simmonds
1878, Charles Wellington Hickson. Vicar of St. Bartholomew
1891, January 27, Charles Griffiths. Vicar of St. Paul, Bedminster

PHYSICIANS.

1831, December 16—John Addington Symonds, 319; re-elected November 28, 1842, resigned 1844. James Fripp, 306; resigned 1838. Adam Chadwick, 217; refused to accept the office

[The number of physicians was originally fixed at three, and there were only three candidates, but a poll was taken to determine the order of seniority and retirement. The ordinary period of service was to be ten years, but of those chosen at the first election the highest on the poll was to serve eleven, the next ten, and the third nine years. Dr. Chadwick, who was senior in professional standing to his competitors, was so annoyed at being placed third on the list, especially below Dr. Symonds, whom he described as a "comparative stranger," that he issued an address declining to accept the office. His place was not filled, and there were only two physicians until 1856, when the original number of three was restored. Viewed in the light of Dr. Symonds' subsequent professional eminence, Dr. Chadwick's petulant address is a curiosity.]

1833, December, 13, *vice* Fripp—Alexander Fairbrother; re-elected September 25, 1848, resigned 1853

[The votes were: Fairbrother, 117; John Roche O'Bryen, 74; John Henry Cutting, 56. Dr. Fairbrother was afterwards one of the Physicians to the Infirmary.]

1845, October 6, *vice* Symonds—William Alleyne Nicholson; resigned July, 1848
1848, August 3, *vice* Nicholson—George Downing Fripp; resigned January, 1849

[Dr. Fripp had been one of the original Surgeons to the Hospital.]

1849, January 18, *vice* Fripp—William Crofton Beatty; resigned November, 1849
1849, December 10, *vice* Beatty—Charles Radclyffe Hall; resigned 1851

BRISTOL GENERAL HOSPITAL.—*Continued.*

1851, October 16, *vice* Hall—George Rogers, Councillor; resigned 1854
1853, July 7, *vice* Fairbrother—Samuel Martyn; re-elected 1863 and July 9, 1873. died July 27, 1876
1854, March 27, *vice* Rogers—John Stanton; resigned 1856
1856, June 23, *vice* Stanton—Joseph Savory Tylor; resigned 1859. George Forster Burder; re-elected 1866 and 1876, resigned July, 1884

[The number of Physicians was now restored to three.]

1859, July 14, *vice* Tylor—Henry Edward Fripp; re-elected November 10, 1869, resigned September, 1873

[Dr. Fripp was the third member of his family on the Medical Staff of the Hospital.]

1873, September 30, *vice* Fripp—Thomas Edward Clark; resigned March, 1874

[Dr. Clark, who had previously been one of the Surgeons to the Infirmary, afterwards abandoned the Medical Profession and took Holy Orders in 1885. The vacancy was not filled for more than a year.]

1875, April 20, *vice* Clark—Edward Markham Skerritt; re-elected March 9, 1885, and March 12, 1895
1876, September 11, *vice* Martyn—Joseph Bower Siddall; resigned 1879
1879, November 20, *vice* Siddall—Alfred James Harrison; re-elected November, 1889
1884, July 30, *vice* Burder—Barclay Josiah Baron

[Resigned on appointment as Specialist Physician for the Throat and Nose Department, December, 1892.]

1892, December 21, *vice* Baron—John Michell Clarke

PHYSICIAN ACCOUCHEURS.

1854, March 27—Joseph Griffiths Swayne; re-elected 1864 and 1874, resigned February, 1875
1875, February 17—Alfred Edward Aust Lawrence; re-elected March 9, 1885, and March 12, 1895; resigned March 1897
1897, March 8—William Harry Christopher Newnham

SURGEONS.

1831, December 16—George Downing Fripp; resigned January, 1840.
Henry Brigstocke; re-elected November 1, 1841, resigned 1843.
John Grant Wilson; re-elected October 29, 1840, resigned 1849.
Samuel Millard; resigned July, 1832

[The votes were—Fripp, 296; Brigstocke, 276; Wilson, 270; Millard, 258; J. G. Lansdown, 176; Thomas Fryer, 50.]

1832, August 1, *vice* Millard—Joseph Goodall Lansdown; re-elected October 24, 1839, December 10, 1849, December 15, 1859, resigned April, 1861

[Mr. Lansdown was elected by 246 votes to 103 for Edward Humpage.]

1840, January 23, *vice* Fripp—William Lang; re-elected January 21, 1850, resigned December, 1857
1843, October 12, *vice* Brigstocke—James Godfrey; re-elected October 3, 1853, died September 27, 1861

[Elected by 136 votes to 129 for Charles Smith Bompas.]

BRISTOL GENERAL HOSPITAL.—*Continued.*

1849, August 19, *vice* Wilson—John Cash Neild ; resigned January, 1853, being about to emigrate to New South Wales

[Elected by 282 votes to 53 for William Smith.]

1853, February 10, *vice* Neild—Robert William Coe ; re-elected 1863 and March 26, 1873, resigned February, 1875

[Elected by 183 votes to 178 for Robert Trout Hawley Bartley.]

1858, January 14, *vice* Lang—William Michell Clarke ; re-elected 1868, resigned July 1868

1861, May 9, *vice* Lansdown—Francis Poole Lansdown ; re-elected 1871, March 14, 1881, and March 9, 1891, resigned 1893

[Son of his predecessor.]

1861, October 31, *vice* Godfrey—Henry Marshall ; resigned 1871
1868—July 31, *vice* Clarke—George Frederick Atchley ; re-elected 1878, resigned December, 1881
1871, December 1, *vice* Marshall—Nelson Congreve Dobson ; re-elected December 14, 1881, and March 14, 1892, resigned January, 1893
1875, March 8, *vice* Coe—William Powell Keall ; re-elected March 9, 1885, died March 17, 1889
1882, January 11, *vice* Atchley—Charles Frederick Pickering ; re-elected March 14, 1892
1889, April 18, *vice* Keall—William John Penny ; resigned February, 1896
1893, February 22, *vice* Dobson—Wilfrid Martin Barclay
1893, April 22, *vice* Lansdown—Charles Alexander Morton
1896, February 26, *vice* Penny—Robert Guthrie Poole Lansdown

[Son of Mr. F. P. Lansdown. The office of surgeon to the General Hospital has been held by three successive generations of the Lansdown family, and Mr. F. P. Lansdown having been one of the honorary consulting staff since his retirement in 1893, there has been an uninterrupted period of more than 66 years, during which the family has been officially connected with the institution. Mr. J. G. Lansdown was a candidate at the first election, and became a member of the staff at the first vacancy in 1832].

OPHTHALMIC SURGEON.

1890, Cyril Hutchinson Walker

ASSISTANT PHYSICIANS.

1886, June 9, John Michell Clarke
    (Elected Physician December, 1892.)
1892, December 21, George Parker

ASSISTANT SURGEONS.

1886, June 9—William John Penny ; resigned 1888
1888, July 25—Wilfrid Martin Barclay ; elected Surgeon, February, 1893
1893, May—Robert Guthrie Poole Lansdown ; elected Surgeon, January, 1896
1896, August 1—John Lacy Firth

BRISTOL GENERAL HOSPITAL.—*Continued.*
HOUSE SURGEONS.

1832, William Lang
1836, Robert Norton
1840, John Delaroche Bragge
1841, Charles Smith Bompas
1843, Frederick Williams
1845, John Mason; died December 30, 1847
1848, John Edward Ellerton
1849, Joseph Rogers
1851, William Michell Clarke
1854, William Marrack
1856, Francis Poole Lansdown
1859, Francis Joseph Dowling
1860, Robert Carr Brackenbury Holland
1864, Walter Harris
1865, Thomas John Coleman
1866, Joseph Bower Siddall
1868, Nelson Congreve Dobson
1871, Henry William Saunders
1873, March 10, Thomas Elliott
1874, September 29, William Henry Harsant
1879, January 8, Charles Frederick Pickering
1881, November 7, William John Penny
1884, October 29, Lockhart Edward Walker Stephens
1885, Dec. 9, William Harry Christopher Newnham
1890, June 25, Reginald Vaughan Solly
1893, May 31, John Lacy Firth
1896, March 25, Martin Randall
1897, November 30, Albert Paling

ANTIENT SOCIETY OF ST. STEPHEN'S RINGERS.
MASTERS, 1681 - 1708.

Since the list of Masters and Wardens of this Antient Society, which I have given on pages 153-160, was printed, I have discovered, among the manuscripts of the late Richard Smith, at the Infirmary, a paper containing the names of the Masters from 1681 to 1708, which I at once communicated to Mr. Fuller Eberle, the Treasurer of the Society, and which in consequence appeared for the first time in print on the toast-card at the dinner of 1898. This list I now subjoin.

1681-1682, Thomas Atkins
1682-1683, John Neads
1683-1684, John Blanch
1684-1685, Francis Price
1685-1686, James Hulbert
1686-1687, Robert Bound
1687-1688, Richard Adams
1688-1689, David Potter
1689-1690, William Pugsley
1690-1691, John Thompson
1691-1692, Joseph Baugh
1692-1693, Charles Ansford
1693-1694, William Nichols
1694-1695, Robert Sergeant

(Mr. Sergeant died during his year of office, as did also his successor, Hugh Williams.)

ANTIENT SOCIETY OF ST. STEPHEN'S RINGERS.—
Continued.

1695-1696, George Novis
1696-1697, John Hobbs
1697-1698, Thomas Martin
1698-1699, William Turton
1699-1700, John Ivey
1700-1701, James Jocham
1701-1702, John Day
1702-1703, Charles Nicholls
1703-1704, Francis Cadogan
1704-1705, Henry Seaborne
1705-1706, Robert Dunning
1706-1707, James Hollidge
1707-1708, Robert Tunbridge

There is no record from 1708 to 1731, when Thomas Horwood was elected. In Mr. Smith's time the names for those years had evidently been lost, as he appends to his list the words, "hiatus valde deflendus!" John Hobbs (Master 1696-1697) was the "Father" of the Society at the date of the earliest minute book now known to exist, which begins with the year 1732.

ALPHABETICAL INDEXES.

Index I.—Mayors, Aldermen, and Town Councillors since the Municipal Corporations Act (1835-1899).

See Pages 64-84, with the following additions.

Page 64. — Abbot, H.—Add Chairman Water Works Company, 1869-1874.

,, Acraman, W. E.—Add President Chamber of Commerce, 1829-1830, 1834-1837.

,, Adams, F.—Add Vice-President Chamber of Commerce, 1870-1872; Warden St. Stephen's Ringers, 1848.

,, Aiken, P. F.—Add Vice-President Chamber of Commerce, 1860-1862; Vice-President Free Port Association, 1846-1850.

Page 66. — Ashman, H.—Add Mayor, 1898-1899.

,, Baker, W. P.—Add Vice-President Chamber of Commerce, 1874; President General Hospital, 1872.

,, Barrow, R. G.—Add Vice-President Chamber of Commerce, 1853-1854-; President Gloucestershire Society, 1875 ; dele. " acting " before " President Grateful."

,, Bates, J.—Add Vice-President Chamber of Commerce, 1861-1863.

Page 66. — Brown, S.—Add President Colston (Parent) for 1846 (declined)

,, Burroughes, J. B. and B. G.—Read Burroughs

,, Bush, H.—Add President Chamber of Commerce, 1834-1837.

,, Bush, J.—Add Vice-President Chamber of Commerce, 1857-1858, 1865-1867.

,, Bushell, W. D.—Add Vice-President Chamber of Commerce, 1839-1842.

,, Butcher, E.—Add Vice-President Chamber of Commerce, 1845-1848.

Page 67. — Canning, T. — Add Warden St. Stephen's Ringers, 1846.

,, Carter, H. William—Read H. Williams.

,, Cawley, G.—Read " Clifton 1895-1898; contested Clifton 1898; District November, 1898 (Commander R.N.)"

ALPHABETICAL INDEX (I.)—*Continued.*

Page 67. — Clarke. W. L. — Add President Gloucestershire Society, 1844.

,, Cleverdon. T.—Add nominated for Bedminster, 1873.

,, Cole, T.—Dele. President Colston (Parent), 1809.

Page 68. — Cookson, J.—For "President Chamber of Commerce, 1829-1831," read "President Chamber of Commerce, 1829-1830."

,, Cossham, H.—Add M.P. East Bristol, 1885—April, 1890 (contested Nottingham 1866, Dewsbury 1868, Chippenham 1874).

,, Crocker, R.-J.—Add nominated for Bedminster, 1873

,, Daniel, T.—Add President Gloucestershire Society, 1815.

Page 69. — Dole, J.—Add contested St. Philip's (South), 1889.

,, Edwards, Sir G. W.—Add President Gloucestershire Society, 1879; knighted 1887.

,, Edwards, H. G.—For "Warden Merchant Venturers 1896," read "Master Merchant Venturers, 1898-1899."

,, Fear, W. L.—Add Warden St. Stephen's Ringers, 1871.

,, Ffooks-Woodforde, W.—Add Deputy-Judge Tolzey Court, 1871-1874 (Judge Derbyshire County Court 1874-1889).

Page 70. — Fox, F. F.—Add President Gloucestershire Society, 1882; Warden St. Stephen's Ringers, 1858, 1868.

,, Franklyn, G. W.—Add President Gloucestershire Society, 1855 (M.P. Poole, 1852-1868).

,, Fripp, W.—Add Parliamentary candidate, 1837, 1841, 1847.

,, Fry, F. J.—Add President Gloucestershire Society, 1897; Treasurer General Hospital.

,, Fry, L.—M.P. Bristol, 1878-1885; North Bristol, 1885-1892, 1895; contested North Bristol 1892.

,, Gardner, C. E. L.—Read "District April-October, 1881; November, 1882-November, 1898; Alderman, 1898; J.P., 1898; nominated for Alderman, 1895."

Page 71. — Garton, C.—Add Chairman Barton Regis Guardians, 1887-1889.

,, George. J.—Add Vice-President Chamber of Commerce, January-November, 1853.

,, George, W. E. — Add President Gloucestershire Society, 1885.

,, Gilbert, T. F.—Add Superintendent Registrar Bristol 1850-1861.

,, Godwin, C.—For "Died February 18, 1887," read " 1889."

ALPHABETICAL INDEX (I.)—*Continued.*

Page 71. Goldney, G.—Add President Gloucestershire Society 1819.

,, Gore, H. H.—Add Parliamentary candidate, East Bristol, March, 1895.

,, Green, H. W.—Add Chairman Clifton Guardians, 1867-1876.

,, Green, T.—Add Surgeon Infirmary, 1844-1864.

,, Grevile, C.—Add Assessor, 1836; Warden St. Stephen's Ringers, 1823.

Page 72. — Haberfield, Sir J. K.—Add President Gloucestershire Society, 1850; Clerk County Court, 1847-1856; Registrar County Court, 1856-1857; Chairman Water Works Company, 1851-1857; President Colston (Parent) Society for 1844 (declined); President Stock Exchange, 1845-1857; knighted 1851.

,, Hare, C.B. (i)—Add Warden St. Stephen's Ringers, 1838.

,, Hare, C. B. (ii)—Add Treasurer Colston (Parent) 1891-1893.

,, Hare, S. V.—Add Parliamentary candidate, March, 1870; June, 1870; 1874.

,, Harford, H. C.—Add President Gloucestershire Society, 1852.

,, Harford, W. H.—Add President Gloucestershire Society, 1869.

,, Harley, E.—Add President Chamber of Commerce, 1837-1839.

Page 73. — Heaven, C. G.—Add Warden St. Stephen's Ringers, 1857.

,, Hellicar, J.—Add Treasurer Merchant Venturers, 1873-1876.

,, Hill, E. B.—Add Vice-President Chamber of Commerce, 1893-1894.

,, (Add) Holman, Joseph—District, November, 1898; President Chamber of Commerce, 1897; President Anchor, 1899.

,, Inskip, J.—Add Parliamentary candidate East Bristol, 1886, 1890.

Page 74. — Jefferies, J. E.—For "March, 1893," read "February, 1893."

,, Jennings, W.—For "1883" read "1893."

,, Jose, T. P.—For "President Chamber of Commerce 1856-1858," read "1856-1857."

Page 75. — Lane, O. C.—Add Chairman Clifton Guardians, April-May, 1859.

,, Lane, W.—Add died August 30, 1898, aged 59.

,, Lang, R.—Add died April 22, 1898, aged 82.

Langton, W. H. G.—Add M.P., 1852-1865.

ALPHABETICAL INDEX (I.)—*Continued.*

Page 75. — Lloyd, S.—Add Vice-Chairman Bristol Guardians, 1898,

,, Lucas, J.—Add Vice-President Chamber of Commerce, 1874-1875.

,, Lucas, J. F.—Add Warden St. Stephen's Ringers, 1866.

Page 76. — (Add) McIlroy, Isaac—Horfield, 1898.

,, Maningford, J.—For " 1827-1857" read " 1827-1854."

,, Miles, J. W.—Add M.P. April-June, 1868 (candidate November, 1868) ; President Gloucestershire Society, 1870.

Page 77. — Pavey, J.—For " 1892" read " 1882"; add Vice-Chairman Barton Regis Guardians, 1882-1883.

,, Perry, B.—Add Vice-President Chamber of Commerce, 1887-1891, 1896.

,, Pethick, W.—Add nominated for Bedminster, 1873; Vice-President Chamber of Commerce, 1873-1875; contested Launceston borough, 1885.

Page 78. — Phippen, R.—Add President Infirmary, April-July, 1869.

,, Pinney, C.—Add Vice-President Chamber of Commerce, January-November, 1853.

,, Pountney, J. D.—Add Vice-President Chamber of Commerce, 1845-1848; President Gloucestershire Society, 1848.

,, Powell, W. A. F.—Add Provincial Grand Master Freemasons, 1889.

,, Prideaux, F. G.—Add Vice-President Chamber of Commerce, 1843-1844.

Page 79. — Ridler, R. — Add Vice-Chairman Chamber of Commerce, 1871-1872.

,, Robinson, E. S.—Add Vice-President Chamber of Commerce, 1867-1869; M.P. March-June, 1870 ; candidate 1880.

,, Robinson R. — Add Vice-President Chamber of Commerce, 1842-1843.

,, Rogers, G.—Add Physician General Hospital, 1851-1854.

,, Sanders, G. E.—Add Vice-President Chamber of Commerce, 1846-1851; President Colston (Parent) 1818 (declined).

,, Savage, J.—Add President Gloucestershire Society, 1858.

Page 80. — Smith, J. G.—Add candidate Assessor Court of Requests, 1839; County Court Judge, Bath, 1847-1859.

,, Smith, R.—Add Surgeon Infirmary, 1796-1843.

,, Stock, T. — Add President Colston (Parent) for 1836 (declined)

ALPHABETICAL INDEX (I.)—*Continued.*

Page 80. — Symes, Sir R. H.—Add knighted 1898.

,, Taylor, H.—For "Chairman Chamber of Commerce, 1874," read "1874-1875."

Page 81. — Thatcher, E. J.—Add Treasurer Colston (Parent), 1893.

,, Thomas, G.—Add Treasurer General Hospital, 1832-1869; President General Hospital, 1849-1869; Chairman Water Works Company, 1858-1869.

,, Tothill, W.—Add Vice-President Chamber of Commerce, 1832-1834.

,, Townsend, C.—Add Vice-Chairman Chamber of Commerce, 1874-1875; M.P. North Bristol, 1892-1895; candidate 1895.

,, (Add) Tucker, Charles Henry—Clifton, 1898; contested Clifton, July, 1897, November, 1897.

,, Vining, J.—Add President Chamber of Commerce, 1842-1845; President Gloucestershire Society, 1857.

Page 82. — Wait, W. K. (ii)—Add Vice-Chairman Chamber of Commerce, 1869.

,, Walker, C. L.—Add President Gloucestershire Society 1839.

,, Ward, R. B.—Add President Gloucestershire Society, 1835.

,, Warde, C.—Add Vice-Chairman Clifton Guardians, 1848-1851.

,, Warren, A. W.—Add Vice-Chairman Chamber of Commerce, February-May, 1865.

,, Wathen, Sir C.—Add knighted 1889.

Page 83. — Weston, Sir J. D.—Add M.P. South Bristol, 1885-1886; East Bristol, 1890-1895; knighted 1886.

,, Whitwill, M.—Add Vice-President Chamber of Commerce, 1871-1873.

,, Wills, C.—For "Horfield, 1897," read "1897-1898;" add Sheriff, 1898-1899.

,, Wills, Sir F., Bart.—Add created Baronet, 1897; contested Launceston Division of Cornwall, 1895, 1898.

,, Wills, Sir W. H., Bart.—Add Vice-President Chamber of Commerce, 1864-1866; created Baronet, 1892; M.P. Coventry, 1880-1885; East Bristol, 1895; contested South-East Essex, 1885, 1886, South Bristol, 1892.

,, Wyld, J. H.—Add Treasurer Colston (Parent), 1841-1853.

,, Wyld, W. H.—Add Treasurer Colston (Parent), 1853-1857.

Index II.—Candidates for Seats in the Town Council who have not obtained Seats (1835-1899).

See pages 84-89, with the following additions.

Page 84. — Baker, T.—Add Charity Trustee, 1893-1895.
,, Brain, W. H.—Clifton, add 1898.
Page 85. — Cashmore, S.—Add died May 20, 1898, aged 58.
,, Clarke, E. G.—Add Official Receiver, 1884.
,, Clements, T.—Add died February 17, 1885, aged 78.
Cook, H.—Add died December 26, 1889, aged 70.
Cooke, I.—Add President Colston (Parent) for 1827 (declined).
Page 86. — Glascodine, H.—Add Receiver Town Dues, 1852-1876.
Page 87. — Jones, James—Add died May 6, 1874, aged 44.
,, Jones, John—For " Clifton, 1850, 1866," read " 1850, 1854, 1866."
,, (Add) Jones, William Edwin—Bedminster (East) 1898
Llewellyn, H. R.—Read Llewellin; add Warden St. Stephen's Ringers, 1820.
,, Metford, J. S.—Add Apothecary Infirmary, 1847-1850
Page 88. — Phillips, W.—Add died March 12, 1862.
,, Pine, G.—Add died December 13 1898, aged 72.
,, Powell, J.—Add died January 13, 1847, aged 67.
(Add) Robinson, Kossuth—Contested Horfield, 1898.
,, Sanders, J. N—Add President Colston (Parent) for 1820 (declined).
,, Short, F. — For Assessor. " 1841, 1851," read " 1841, 1850, 1851."
Page 89. — Thorne, J.—Read " Thorn."
,, Weight, R. 1.—Add 1898.
,, White, T.—Add Vice-Chairman Clifton Guardians, 1837-1840.
,, Whittall, G. P.—Add Warden St. Stephen's Ringers, 1859.

Index III.—Members of the Corporation, 1599-1835.

(N.B.—The first date after each name indicates the period during which the person named was a member of the Common Council.)

Acraman, William Edward—1831 (declined). (See also pages 64 and 269.)

Addison, Robert—1716-1729; Sheriff, 1720-1721.

Aldworth, John — (1599)-1625; Sheriff, 1602 - 1603 ; Master Merchant Venturers, 1614-1615; died November or December, 1615, aged 51.

Aldworth, John—1663-1668; Sheriff, 1667-1668; Warden Merchant Venturers, 1665-1666; died June 12, 1668.

Aldworth, Richard—1625-1655; Alderman, 1645-1655 (Trinity); Sheriff, 1627-1628; Mayor, 1642-1643; M.P 1646-1653; Warden Merchant Venturers, 1641-1642; Treasurer Merchant Venturers, 1630-1631; died August 2, 1655.

Aldworth, Robert — (1599)-1634 ; Alderman, 1614-1634 (St. James); Sheriff, 1596-1597; Mayor, 1609-1610 ; Master Merchant Venturers, 1609-1610, 1612-1613, 1625-1626; died November 6, 1634, aged 73.

Aldworth, Thomas—(1566)-1599; Alderman (1591)-1599; Sheriff, 1566-1567; Mayor, 1582-1583, 1589, 1592-1593; M.P., 1586-1587, 1589; died February 25, 1598-9.

Aldworth, Thomas — 1602-1611 ; Sheriff, 1609 - 1610 ; Treasurer Merchant Venturers, 1605-1606.

Ames, Jeremiah—1742-1776; Alderman, 1765-1776 (Redcliff 1765-1767, St. Ewen 1767-1771, Maryleport 1771-1776); Sheriff, 1742-1743; Mayor, 1759-1760; Governor Incorporation of Poor (declined), 1771; died April 3, 1776.

Ames, Levi—1771-1820; Alderman, 1792-1820 (Maryleport); Sheriff, 1771-1772; Mayor, 1788-1789; President Anchor, 1790; died December 16, 1820.

Ames, Levi—1804-1835; Sheriff, 1804-1805; Mayor (declined), 1811; President Anchor, 1805; died Dec. 26, 1846, aged 68.

Amory, Thomas—1645-1661; Sheriff, 1652-1653; Warden Merchant Venturers, 1645-1646.

Anderson, Charles — 1792-1822; Sheriff, 1793-1794 ; Mayor (declined), 1801; Receiver of Town Dues, 1815-1836; Master St. Stephen's Ringers, 1809; died January 19, 1836, aged 70 (took the name of Anderson in lieu of Young, 1797).

ALPHABETICAL INDEX (III.)—*Continued.*

Anderson, John—1772-1797; Alderman, 1784-1797 (Castle); Sheriff, 1772-1773; Mayor, 1783-1784; Master St. Stephen's Ringers, 1791; died June 6, 1797.

Appleton, Henry—1653-1692; Sheriff, 1657-1658.

Appleton, John—1671-1673 (not sworn).

Arundell, Edmund—1644 (declined); Warden Merchant Venturers, 1636-1638.

Arundell, Edmund—1679-January, 1688, and October, 1688-1697; Sheriff, 1683-1684, and October, 1688; Mayor, 1692-1693; Warden Merchant Venturers, 1677-1678; died 1696-7.

Ash, Richard—1818 (declined). (See also page 65.)

Ashburton, Lord (John Dunning)—1766-1783; Recorder and Alderman, 1766-1783 (Castle 1766-1771, Trinity 1771-1783); died August 16, 1783. (M.P. Calne, 1768 - 1782 · Solicitor-General, 1768 - 1770; Privy Councillor, 1782; Chancellor Duchy of Lancaster, 1782-1783; created peer, 1782.)

Atkyns, Sir Robert—1662-1682; Recorder and Alderman, 1662-1682; Parliamentary candidate, 1681; died February 8, 1709-10. (M.P. Evesham, 1639; East Looe, 1661-1672; Middlesex, 1680-1681; K.B., 1661; Judge Common Pleas, 1672-1680; Chief Baron of the Exchequer, 1683-1694; Speaker House of Lords, 1689-1693.)

Attwood, George—1656-1661.

Bacheler, John—1690-1711; Alderman, 1702-1711 (St. James 1702, All Saints 1702-1711); Sheriff, 1693-1694; Mayor, 1699-1700; Governor Incorporation of Poor, 1703-1705; Master Merchant Venturers, 1706-1708; died October, 1711.

Bailey, Giles—1738-1767; Alderman, 1762-1767 (Trinity 1762-1765, St. James 1765-1767); Sheriff, 1738-1739, and 1747-1748; Mayor, 1755-1757; died February 1, 1767.

Baillie, Evan—1785-1835; Alderman, 1802-1821 (All Saints); Sheriff, 1786-1787; Mayor (declined), 1795; M.P., 1802-1812; died June 28, 1835, aged 95.

Baker, Jeremy—1771-1798; Alderman (declined), 1792; Sheriff, 1771-1772; Mayor (declined), 1789; died April 29, 1798.

Baldwin, William—1613-1617; Sheriff, 1615-1616; died December, 1617.

Ballman, Richard—1637-1667; Alderman, 1656-1657 (St. Ewen 1656-1658, St. Thomas 1658-1657); Sheriff, 1641-1642; Mayor, 1656-1657.

Barker, John—(1593)-1607; Sheriff, 1593-1594; Mayor, 1606-1607; died September 13, 1607.

ALPHABETICAL INDEX (III.)—*Continued*.

Barker, John — 1612-1636; Alderman, 1629-1636 (All Saints); Sheriff, 1612-1613; Mayor, 1625-1626; M.P., 1624-1625, 1628-1629; Master Merchant Venturers, 1617-1619, 1626-1627; Treasurer Merchant Venturers 1612-1613; died March, 1635-6.

Barnes, William—(1599)-1617; Sheriff, 1603-1604; died about February, 1616-7.

Barnes, William—1730-1767; Alderman, 1746-1767 (Redcliff, July - October, 1746, Maryleport 1746 - 1767); Sheriff, 1731-1732; Mayor, 1745-1746; died July 29, 1767.

Barnes, William—1749-September, 1760, and October, 1760-1777; Alderman, 1770-1777 (All Saints); Sheriff, 1749-1750 and 1761-1762 ; Mayor, 1766-1767; died November 3, 1777.

Barnsdale, William—1697-1707.

Barnsdale, William—1729-1734; Sheriff, 1730-1731; Sword Bearer, 1735-1748 (deputy, 1734-1735); Deputy Governor Incorporation of Poor, 1729-1730; died June 19, 1748.

Barrington, Hon. Daines—1763-1765; Recorder and Alderman, 1763-1765 (St. Stephen); died March 14, 1800, aged 72. (Marshal Admiralty, 1751-1753 ; Secretary Greenwich Hospital, 1753-1758; Judge, North Wales, 1756-1778; K.G., 1777; Judge, Chester, 1778-1788.)

Barrow, John—1816-1834; Alderman, 1828-1834 (Temple 1828-1829, St. Ewen 1829-1834); Sheriff, 1816-1817 ; Mayor, 1823-1824 ; Master Merchant Venturers, 1824-1825; President Grateful, 1795; Master St. Stephen's Ringers (declined) for 1811; died July 3, 1841, aged 78.

Bartlett, John—1726-1748; Sheriff, 1727-1728; Mayor, May-September, 1742; Treasurer Incorporation Poor, 1722-1723; died August 22, 1748.

Baugh, Benjamin—1796 (declined); Treasurer Incorporation of Poor, 1798-1810; died December 1, 1819, aged 61.

Baugh, Isaac—1748-1786; Alderman, 1768-1786 (Redcliff 1768-1771, St. Ewen 1771-1781, St. James 1781-1786); Sheriff, 1748-1749 and 1751-1752; Mayor, 1765-1766 ; Master Merchant Venturers, 1759-1760; died Dec. 25, 1786.

Baugh, Richard—1659-1661.

Bayly, Richard—1697-1716; Sheriff, 1701-1702; President Gloucestershire Society, 1702; Deputy Governor Incorporation of Poor, 1706-1707.

Bayly, Richard—1724-1742; Sheriff, 1727-1728; Mayor, 1741-May, 1742; Treasurer Incorporation of Poor, 1735-1736; died May 17, 1742.

Bayly, Samuel—1696-1708; Sheriff, 1701-1702; died August, 1708.

ALPHABETICAL INDEX (III.)—*Continued.*

Bayly, William—1705-1717; Sheriff, 1711-1712; **President Gloucestershire Society**, 1713; died 1717.

Becher, Cranfield—1762 (declined); Master Merchant Venturers, 1756-1757; died May 10, 1799, aged 85.

Becher, John—1710-1743; Alderman, 1725-1743 (St. Michael); Sheriff, 1713-1714; Mayor, 1721-1722; Governor Incorporation of Poor, 1728-1729; Master Merchant Venturers, 1722-1723; died July 9, 1743.

Becher, Michael—1739-1758; Sheriff, 1739-1740; Master Merchant Venturers, 1749-1750; Warden St. Stephen's Ringers, 1733-1738; died December 19, 1758.

Bence, John Britton—1810 (declined); died June 25, 1820.

Bengough, George—1829-1835; Sheriff, 1831-1832. (See also page 84.)

Bengough, Henry—1789-1818; Alderman, 1797-1818 (Redcliff 1797-1798, St. Stephen 1798-1818); Sheriff, 1789-1790; Mayor, 1792-1793; Under Sheriff, 1760-1789; Registrar Court of Conscience, 1787-1818; President Anchor, 1794; Warden St. Stephen's Ringers (declined) for 1805; died April 10, 1818, aged 79.

Berrow, John—1728-1745; Sheriff, 1729-1730; Mayor, 1743-1744; died November 29, 1745, aged 60.

Berrow, John—1747-1767; Sheriff, 1747-1748 and 1758-1759; died March 10, 1776.

Bevan, Thomas—1669-1675; died 1675.

Bevan, William—1644-1645; Sheriff, 1644-1645; Warden Merchant Venturers, 1644-1645.

Bickham, Hugh—1702-1723; Warden Merchant Venturers, 1712-1713; died about October, 1723.

Bickham, Richard — 1685 (not sworn); Sheriff, (declined) 1685.

Bickley, Benjamin—1807-1835; Sheriff, 1807 (declined), 1808-1809, 1811-1812, 1813-1814, and 1815-1816; President Colston (Parent), 1821; Warden Merchant Venturers, 1803-1804, 1810-1811 ; Master St. Stephen's Ringers, 1797 ; died October 15, 1846, aged 83.

Birch, Samuel — 1800-1819 ; Alderman, 1814-1819 (St. Thomas); Sheriff, 1800-1801; Mayor, 1807-1808 ; President Gloucestershire Society, 1811; Treasurer Infirmary, 1808-1811; died August 5, 1851, aged 86.

Birkin, Abraham—1662-1669; Warden Merchant Venturers, 1710-1711.

Blackborne, Robert—1644-1650.

Blackwell, John—1687-1688 and 1689-1702; Alderman 1702 (All Saints, July-October, 1702, St. Ewen, October - December, 1702 ; Sheriff, 1689-1690 ; Mayor, 1698-1699; died December 2, 1702, aged 65.

ALPHABETICAL INDEX (III.)—*Continued.*

Blackwell, John—1720-1748; Alderman, 1737-1748 (All Saints, 1737-1739, Trinity 1739-1743, St. Michael 1743-1748); Sheriff, 1723-1724; Mayor, 1736-1737; Master Merchant Venturers, 1726-1727; died July 19, 1748.

Blackwell, Jonathan—1653-1661; Sheriff, 1652-1653 : Steward Gloucestershire Society, 1659; died 1671 (Alderman, London, Candlewick Ward, 1668).

Blake, Richard—1792-1829; died August 6, 1829, aged 69.

Blake, William—1782-1791; Sheriff, 1782-1783; Master St. Stephen's Ringers, 1765; died November 5, 1791.

Boulton, John—(1599)-1619; Sheriff, 1600-1601 ; Warden Merchant Venturers, 1608-1609; died about June, 1619.

Bound, Robert — 1696-1715; Alderman, 1712-1715 (St. James, March-December, 1712, St. Thomas, 1712-1715); Sheriff, 1700-1701; Mayor, 1709-1710; Governor Incorporation of Poor, 1712-1713; Warden Merchant Venturers, 1711-1712; Master St. Stephen's Ringers, 1687; Steward Gloucestershire Society, 1681; President Gloucestershire Society, 1692; died December, 1715.

Bovey, Edward—1659-1662.

Bowdler, Marmaduke — 1687 - 1688 and 1690 - 1699 ; Sheriff, 1693-1694; Warden Merchant Venturers, 1718-1719.

Bowen, John—1652-1661; Sheriff, 1655-1656; Master Merchant Venturers, 1659-1660.

Bradway, John—1661-1666; Sheriff, 1663-1664; died 1666.

Bradway, John—1684-1688 and 1690-1702; Sheriff, 1691-1692.

Brice, Edward—1767-1809; Alderman, 1782-1809 (St. (Thomas); Sheriff, 1767-1768, 1775-1776 and 1779-1780; Mayor, 1782-1783; Governor Incorporation of Poor, 1790-1792; Master Merchant Venturers, 1786-1787; died October 16, 1809, aged 72.

Brice, Edward—1806-1833; Sheriff, 1806-1807 and 1811-1812; Mayor (declined), 1817; Master Merchant Venturers, 1818-1819; died July 14, 1833, aged 66.

Brice, Worthington—1799-1826; Sheriff, 1799-1800 ; Mayor (declined), 1808; Acting President Anchor 1800; Master St. Stephen's Ringers, 1807; died January 13, 1826.

Brickdale, Matthew—1767-1824; Mayor (declined), 1791; M.P., 1768-1774 and 1780-1790; candidate 1774; President Colston (Parent), 1782; President Gloucestershire Society, 1777; died September 3, 1831, aged 97.

Bright, Henry—1753-1777; Sheriff, 1753-1754; Mayor, 1771-1772; died November 25, 1777, aged 62.

ALPHABETICAL INDEX (III.)—Continued.

Bright, Henry—1799-1807; Sheriff, 1799-1800; Mayor, September-November, 1807; died November 22, 1807, aged 45.

Bright, Richard—1783-1835; Mayor (declined), 1795; Master Merchant Venturers, 1792-1795; President Anchor, 1781; died January 25, 1840, aged 81.

Brooke, Henry—1806-1820; Alderman, 1813-1820 (St. Stephen); Sheriff, 1806-1807; Mayor, 1813 (declined) and 1818-1819; Warden Merchant Venturers, 1819-1820; died March 31, 1820, aged 66.

Brookhouse, Robert—1685 (not sworn).

Brown, James—1796 (declined); President Colston (Parent), 1805; died February 15, 1810, aged 79.

Browne, Hugh—1638-1673; Alderman, 1646-1653 (Redcliff); Sheriff, 1642-1643; Mayor, 1650-1651; Master Merchant Venturers, 1646-1647, 1649-1650, 1651-1653, Treasurer Merchant Venturers, 1643-1644; died about December, 1653.

Browne, Humphrey—1618-1630; Sheriff, 1619-1620; Master Merchant Venturers, 1620-1630; Treasurer Merchant Venturers, 1620-1621; died March 22, 1629-30.

Browne, William—1673-1684 and 1689-1690; Alderman January-October 1688 (St. Nicholas); Sheriff, (declined), 1688; Warden Merchant Venturers, 1673-1674; Steward Gloucestershire Society, 1674.

Bruce, Robert—1803 (declined); Master Merchant Venturers, 1821-1822; died November 21, 1838, aged 70.

Bubb, John—January-April, 1687, and 1689-1699; Sheriff, 1689-1690; Mayor, 1697-1698; died 1699.

Bubb, Thomas—1648-1659; Sheriff, 1653-1654; Steward Gloucestershire Society, 1656; died about February, 1658-1659.

Buckler, Edward—1720-1759; Sheriff, 1730-1731; died 1759.

Bull, John—1764-1785; Sheriff, 1764-1765; Mayor (declined), 1778, and August-September, 1780; died September 9, 1785.

Burges, Joseph—February-October, 1688.

Burges, William—February-October, 1688.

Burke, Richard—1786-1794; Recorder and Alderman, 1785-1794 (Trinity); died February 5, 1794.

Burrus, William—1603-1613; Sheriff, 1611-1612; died 1613.

Bush, Robert—1795 and 1810 (declined); Master Merchant Venturers, 1823-1824; President Dolphin, 1825; President Colston (Parent) for 1810 (declined); President Gloucestershire Society, 1809; died March 4, 1829, aged 67.

Bushe, John—1641-1648.

ALPHABETICAL INDEX (III.)—*Continued.*

Butcher, John—(1599)-1623; Aderman, 1611-1623 (Trinity); Sheriff, 1596-1597; Mayor, 1608-1609; died about March, 1622-3.

Butcher, Nathaniel — 1622-1628 ; Sheriff, 1624-1625; Warden Merchant Venturers, 1621-1622; Treasurer Merchant Venturers, 1625-1626; died 1628.

Cade, James—1671-1684 and 1688-1689.

Cale, Nathaniel—1643-1645 and 1660-1672; Alderman, 1662-1672 (Trinity); Sheriff, 1644-1645; Mayor, 1661-1662; died about June, 1672.

Cale, Thomas—1661 (declined); Postmaster, 1678-1690.

Callowhill, Thomas—1685 (declined); Deputy Governor Incorporation of Poor, 1701-1702; Treasurer Incorporation of Poor, 1697-1698.

Camplin, Thomas—1821-1835; Alderman, 1829-1835 (St. Stephen); Sheriff, 1821-1822; Mayor, 1826-1827, Master St. Stephen's Ringers, 1830; died December 8, 1856, aged 75.

Cann, Sir Robert, Bart.—1649-1685; Alderman, 1663-1685 (St. Nicholas); Sheriff, 1651-1652; Mayor, 1662-1663, 1675-1676; M.P., 1678-1680; Master Merchant Venturers, 1658-1659; Treasurer Merchant Venturers, 1653-1654; knighted 1662; created Baronet, 1662; died November, 1685.

Cann, William—1632-1658; Alderman, 1648-1658 (St. Thomas); Sheriff, 1635-1636; Mayor, 1648-1649 ; Master Merchant Venturers, 1645-1646; Treasurer Merchant Venturers, 1641-1642; died March, 1657-8.

Carie (or Cary), Christopher—1609-1618; Sheriff, 1612-1613; Warden Merchant Venturers, 1613-1614 ; died April, 1618.

Cary, John—February-October, 1688; Parliamentary candidate, 1698; Warden Merchant Venturers, 1683-1684.

Cary, Shersha—1661 (declined); Master Merchant Venturers, 1671-1672.

Cary, William—(1599)-1633; Alderman, 1615-1618; Sheriff, 1598-1599; Mayor, 1611-1612; died 1632-3.

Castle, Michael—1798 and 1806 (declined), 1809-1821; Sheriff, 1809-1810; Mayor, 1812-1813; Governor Incorporation of Poor, 1818-1820; President Anchor 1799; died May 22, 1821, aged 58.

Castle, Michael Hinton—1827 and 1828 (declined) and 1831-1835; Sheriff, 1832-1833. (See also page 67.)

Castle, Robert—1794-1803; Sheriff, 1794-1795 and 1800-1801; Mayor, 1802-1803; President Anchor, 1795; died August 4, 1803.

Castle, Thomas—1818 and 1820 (declined); died June 12, 1827, aged 60.

ALPHABETICAL INDEX (III.)—*Continued.*

Cave, Daniel—1828 and 1831 (declined); Sheriff, 1836; Treasurer Infirmary 1829-1844; Vice-President Free Port Association, 1846-1850; died March 9, 1872, aged 82.

Cave, John—1811 (declined) and 1822-1835; Sheriff, 1822-1823; Mayor, 1828-1829; Master Merchant Venturers, 1807-1808; President Dolphin, 1814; Governor Incorporation of Poor, 1813-1815; died March 27, 1842, aged 77.

Cave, Stephen—1794 (declined) and 1822-1827; Alderman, 1822-1827 (Maryleport); Sheriff (declined), 1822; Master Merchant Venturers, 1817-1818; died February 18, 1838, aged 74.

Cecil, John—1663-1684 and 1688-1690; Sheriff, 1673-1674.

Cecil, Thomas—1614-January, 1623, and November, 1623-1630; Sheriff, 1618-1619; died about May, 1630.

Challoner, Robert—1643-1658; Alderman, 1658 (Trinity); Sheriff, 1648-1649; Warden Merchant Venturers, 1648-1649; Treasurer Merchant Venturers 1646-1647; died 1687-8.

Challoner, William—1608-1620; Sheriff, 1609-1610; died about June, 1620.

Chamberlayne, John—1740-1752; Sheriff, 1741-1742; died 1752.

Chapman, Scarborough—1684-1688.

Charleton, Andrew—1614-1643; Alderman, 1636-1643 (St. James); Sheriff, 1620-1621; Mayor, 1634-1635; Master Merchant Venturers, 1639-1640; Treasurer Merchant Venturers, 1617-1618; died November, 1643.

Churchill, Sir John—Recorder and Alderman, 1682-1685 (Castle); M.P., March-October, 1685; died October 11, 1685 (Knighted 1670; K.C., 1673; M.P. Dorchester, 1661-1679; Newtown, 1679; Master of the Rolls, 1685; Privy Councillor, 1685.

Clark, Samuel—March-October, 1688.

Claxton, Robert—1737-1812; Alderman, 1801-1812 (St. Ewen 1801-1805, St. Nicholas 1805-1812); Sheriff, 1787-1788; Mayor, 1793-1799; President Anchor, 1789; died June 20, 1812, aged 59.

Claxton, William—1829-1835; Sheriff, 1830-1831; Master Merchant Venturers, 1836-1837; Treasurer Merchant Venturers, 1841-1873; President Anchor 1827; died June 24, 1873, aged 75.

Clement, Thomas—1705-1722; Alderman, 1719-1722 (St. Michael); Sheriff, 1709-1710; Mayor, June-September, 1718; President Gloucestershire Society, 1699; died 1722.

Clements, John 1755-1760; Alderman, 1755-1760; (Castle); Sheriff, 1735-1736; Mayor, 1752-1753; died September 16, 1760.

ALPHABETICAL INDEX (III.)—*Continued*.

Clements, Thomas—1611 (declined) and 1620-1630 ; Sheriff, 1624-1625; died 1630.

Clutterbuck, Josias—1645-1652 and 1654-1656; Sheriff, (declined), 1656; died January 6, 1659-60, aged 75.

Clutterbuck, Stephen—1724-1746; Alderman, 1742-1746 (St. Thomas); Sheriff, 1725-1726; Mayor, 1739-1740; died 1746.

Clutterbuck, Sir William—1671-January, 1688, and October, 1688-1702; Alderman, 1684-1688 (St. Ewen) and 1689-1702 (St. Michael); Sheriff, 1678-1679; Mayor, 1683-1684 and 1688; Master Merchant Venturers, 1683-1684; died March, 1707-8.

Cole, Richard—(1569)-1599; Alderman, (1591)-1599; Sheriff, 1569-1570; Mayor, 1585-1586; M.P., 1584-1585, 1593; died July, 1599.

Cole, Thomas—1674-1684 and 1688-1696; Sheriff, 1688-1689; Warden Merchant Venturers, 1688-1689.

Cole, William—1600-1613; Sheriff, 1604-1605; Warden Merchant Venturers, 1610-1611; Treasurer Merchant Venturers, 1607-1608; died 1613.

Cole, William—1661-1662.

Coleman, Benjamin Freeman—1801 (declined); died February, 1838, aged 79.

Coleman, Robert—1781-1794; Sheriff, 1781-1782; died June 23, 1794.

Collard, John—1781-1788; Sheriff, 1781-1782; died September 5, 1788.

Collins, Nehemiah—1655-1661; Sheriff, 1658-1659.

Colston, Thomas—1629-1645; Alderman June-December, 1645 (St. Nicholas); Sheriff, 1629-1630; Master Merchant Venturers, 1644-1645; Treasurer Merchant Venturers, 1634-1635.

Colston, Thomas—1632-1684; died January, 1683-4.

Colston, William—(1599)-1603; Sheriff, 1599-1600; died 1603.

Colston, William—1643-1645 and 1661-1664; Alderman, 1662-1664; Sheriff, 1643-1644; Warden Merchant Venturers, 1643-1644; died November 21, 1681, aged 73.

Combe, Henry—1684-1688 and 1690-1708; Sheriff, 1692-1693.

Combe, Henry—1721-1752; Alderman, 1743-1752 (Trinity 1743-1746, All Saints 1746-1752; Sheriff, 1726-1727; Mayor, 1740-1741; Parliamentary candidate 1739; Warden Merchant Venturers, 1731-1732 ; Treasurer Merchant Venturers, 1734-1745; died April 23, 1752.

Combe, John—1738-1753; Sheriff, 1738-1739; died 1753.

Combes, John—1681-January, 1688, and October, 1688 1689; Alderman, 1687-1688 (Trinity); Sheriff, 1682-1683; Warden Merchant Venturers, 1683-1684.

ALPHABETICAL INDEX (III.)—*Continued.*

Cooke, John—1669-1680; Sheriff, 1672-1673; Chamberlain, 1680-1698; Master Merchant Venturers, 1691-1692.

Cooper, Edward—1728-1762; Alderman, 1747-1762 (Redcliff 1747-1748, St. Michael's 1748-1762); Sheriff, 1731-1732; Mayor, 1746-1747; Master Merchant Venturers, 1754-1755; died January 20, 1762.

Copley, Sir John Singleton—See Lyndhurst.

Corsley, Humphrey—1678-1684 and 1688-1690; Alderman, January-October, 1688 (Trinity).

Cossley, William—1742-1748; Sheriff, 1742-1743; Sword Bearer, 1748-1750; died June 27, 1750.

Coxe, Edward—1616-1627; Sheriff, 1622-1623; Warden Merchant Venturers, 1619-1620; died August 3, 1627.

Crabb, William—1659-1702; Alderman, 1673-1702 (Temple); Sheriff, 1665-1666; Mayor, 1676-1677; died October 14, 1702, aged 87.

Creswicke, Francis — 1628-1645 ; Alderman, 1643-1645 (St. James); Sheriff, 1628-1629; Mayor, September-December, 1645; Master Merchant Venturers, 1643-1644; Treasurer Merchant Venturers, 1632-1633.

Creswicke, Sir Henry—1643-1645 and 1660-1668; Alderman, 1661-1668 (Maryleport 1661-1663, St. Ewen 1663-1668); Sheriff, 1643-1644; Mayor, 1660-1661 ; Master Merchant Venturers, 1660-1662; Treasurer Merchant Venturers, 1647-1648; knighted, 1663; died September 28, 1668.

Creswicke, John—1652-1653 (not sworn).

Creswicke, Joseph—1663-1708; Alderman, 1679-1708 (St. Stephen); Sheriff, 1666-1667; Mayor, 1679-1680; Warden Merchant Venturers, 1666-1667; died about February, 1707-8.

Crofte, James—1645-1661; Sheriff, 1650-1651; Warden Merchant Venturers, 1646-1647; Treasurer Merchant Venturers, 1648-1649.

Crofts, John—1768-1793; Alderman, 1786-1788 (Maryleport); Sheriff, 1768-1769; Mayor, 1785-1786; died June 9, 1793.

Cruger, Henry—1766-1827; Alderman, 1782-1792 (Temple); Sheriff, 1766-1767; Mayor, 1781-1782; M.P., 1774-1780 and 1784-1790; candidate, 1780 and 1781; Master Merchant Venturers, 1781-1782; President Anchor, 1783; died April 24, 1827, aged 88.

Crumpe, Sir Richard—1661-1700; Alderman, 1675-1700 (St. James 1675-1679, Redcliff 1679-1687, St. Thomas 1687-1700); Sheriff, 1665-1666; Mayor, 1677-1678; M.P., 1685-1687; Warden Merchant Venturers, 1694-1695; Steward Gloucestershire Society, 1669 (President 1684); knighted, 1681; died January 14, 1699-1700.

Curtis, John—February-October, 1683; Vice-Chamberlain, 1699-1712; died 1712.

ALPHABETICAL INDEX (III.)—*Continued*.

Curtis, John—1749-1768; Sheriff, 1749-1750; died September 12, 1768.

Curtis, Thomas—1734-1754; Alderman, 1750-1754 (Redcliff 1750-1752, St. Nicholas 1752-1754); Sheriff, 1734-1735; Mayor, 1749-1750; died 1754.

Daines, Sir William—1691-1724; Alderman, 1702-1724 (St. James 1702-1708, St. Stephen 1708-1724); Sheriff, 1694-1695; Mayor, 1700-1701; M.P. 1701-1710 and 1715-1722 (candidate, 1710, 1713); Governor Incorporation of Poor, 1705-1706; Master Merchant Venturers, 1698-1700: knighted, 1694: died September 5, 1724, aged 68.

Dale, William—1643-1657; Sheriff, 1649-1650; Warden Merchant Venturers, 1646-1647, 1649-1650; Treasurer Merchant Venturers, 1650-1651.

Daltera, Joseph—1748-1764; Sheriff, 1748-1749 and 1761-1762; Master Merchant Venturers, 1760-1761; died September 26, 1774.

Dampier, Henry—1737-1771; Alderman, 1760-1771 (Castle 1760-1766, St. Stephen 1766-1771, St. Michael 1771); Sheriff, 1737-1738 and 1751-1752; Mayor, 1755-1756; Governor Incorporation of Poor, 1768-1771; Master Merchant Venturers, 1750-1751; died October 17, 1771.

Daniel, Edward—1816-1819; Sheriff, 1816-1817; Assessor Court of Requests, August-December, 1819; President Dolphin for 1829 (declined); died April 14, 1847, aged 69.

Daniel, Thomas—1785-1835; Alderman, 1798-1835 (Redcliff 1798-1805, St. James 1806-1814, St. Michael 1814-1835); Sheriff, 1786-1787; Mayor, 1797-1798. (See also pages 68 and 270.)

Danson, Hugh William—1828-1835; Sheriff, 1829-1830; Warden Merchant Venturers, 1820-1821, 1828-1829, 1830-1831; died February 15, 1840.

Danson, William — 1812 (declined); Warden Merchant Venturers, 1813-1814; died March 21, 1825, aged 70.

Daubeny, George—1769-1806; Alderman, 1787-1806 (St. James); Sheriff, 1769-1770; Mayor, 1786-1787; M.P. 1781-1784 (candidate 1784); Governor Incorporation of Poor, 1788-1790; Master Merchant Venturers, 1784-1785; President Dolphin, 1775 and (acting) 1791; died May 26, 1806.

Davies, Isaac—1696-1703; Sheriff, 1700-1701; Warden Merchant Venturers, 1700-1701; died 1703.

Dawe, Richard—1675-1680; died about October, 1680.

Day, John—1696-1705; Sheriff, 1697-1698; Warden Merchant Venturers, 1698-1699; Master St. Stephen's Ringers, 1702; died 1705.

Day, John—1708-1718; Sheriff, 1708-1709; Mayor, 1717-1718; Deputy Governor Incorporation of Poor, 1716-1717; Treasurer Incorporation of Poor, 1715-1716; Master Merchant Venturers, 1716-1717; died June 20, 1718, aged 44.

ALPHABETICAL INDEX (III.)—*Continued.*

Day, John—1728-1748; Alderman, 1746-1748 (Trinity); Sheriff, 1729-1730; Mayor, 1744-1745; Master Merchant Venturers, 1742-1743; died March 2, 1747-8.

Day, Nathaniel—February-October, 1688, and 1695-1719; Alderman, 1708-1719 (St. James 1708-1710; Redcliff 1710-1719); Sheriff, 1697-1698; Mayor, 1705-1705; Governor Incorporation of Poor, 1710-1711; died November 10, 1719.

Day, Nathaniel—1720-1765; Alderman, 1739-1765 (Temple); Sheriff, 1724-1725; Mayor, 1737-1738; Governor Incorporation of Poor, 1739-1740, 1745-1746; President Colston (Parent), 1755; died Aug. 26, 1765.

Day, Peter—1715-1735; Alderman, 1728-1735 (St. James); Sheriff, 1716-1717; Mayor, 1726-1727; Governor Incorporation of Poor, 1732-1733; Master Merchant Venturers, 1732-1733; died 1734-5.

Day, Sir Thomas—1661-1684 and 1688-1710; Alderman, March-September, 1681 (St. James), August-October, 1688, and 1689-1710 (Redcliff); Sheriff, 1670-1671; Mayor, February-September, 1688, and 1694-1695; M.P., 1695-1701; Governor Incorporation of Poor, 1701-1702; knighted 1694; died Jan., 1709-10.

Deane, Gabriel — 1659-1661; Warden Merchant Venturers, 1669-1670.

Deane, Richard—1656 (declined); Warden Merchant Venturers, 1654-1655.

Deane, Thomas—1754-1798; Alderman, 1772-1798 (Redcliff 1772-1782, St. Stephen 1782-1798); Sheriff, 1754-1755; Mayor, 1770-1771; died January 15, 1798, aged 81.

Dehany, David—1738 (declined) and 1739-1754; Sheriff 1739-1740; died 1754.

Deyos, Walter — 1637-1658; Alderman, 1655-1658 (Trinity); Sheriff, 1639-1640; Mayor, 1655-1656; Warden Merchant Venturers, 1642-1643; Treasurer Merchant Venturers, 1644-1645; died Sept., 1658.

Doddridge, John—1658-1659; Recorder and Alderman, 1658-1659; M.P., 1656; died February 23, 1658-9. (M.P., Barnstaple, 1646-1653 and 1654; Devon, 1656-1658.)

Dolman, Alexander—February-October, 1688.

Donning, James—1712-1746; Alderman, 1724-1746 (Maryleport); Sheriff, 1715-1716; Mayor, 1723-1724; Governor Incorporation of Poor, 1730-1731; Master Merchant Venturers, 1720-1721; died March 8, 1745-6.

Donning, William — 1669-1684 and 1689-1692; Alderman, 1689-1692 (Trinity); Sheriff, 1677-1678; Master Merchant Venturers, 1687-1688; died 1692.

ALPHABETICAL INDEX (III.)—*Continued.*

Doughty, John—1606-1630; Alderman, 1620-1630 (St. Nicholas); Sheriff, 1606-1607; Mayor, 1620-1621; M.P., 1626 and 1628-1629; Master Merchant Venturers 1623-1624; died January 2, 1629-30, aged 67.

Dowding, Robert—1681-January, 1688, and October, 1688-1696; Sheriff, 1690-1691.

Dowell, William—1810 (declined); President Dolphin 1806; President Gloucestershire Society, 1817; died December 31, 1835, aged 80.

Driver, Nathaniel—1679-January, 1688, and October, 1688-1693; Sheriff, 1683-1684 and October, 1688; President Gloucestershire Society, 1685.

Duddlestone, Sir John, Bart.—February-October, 1688; Master Merchant Venturers, 1715-1716; Governor Incorporation of Poor, 1700-1701; knighted, 1690; created Baronet, 1692; died August, 1716.

Dunning, John—See Ashburton.

Durbin, John—1743-1792; Alderman, 1765-1792 (Temple 1765-1782, St. Ewen 1782-1792); Sheriff, 1743-1744; Mayor, 1760-1761; Governor Incorporation of Poor, 1766-1768; died February 11, 1792, aged 83.

Durbin, Sir John—1763-1814; Alderman, 1781-1814 (St. Ewen 1781-1782, St. Michael 1782-1814); Sheriff, 1763-1764 and 1774-1775; Mayor, 1777-1779; Governor Incorporation of Poor, 1784-1786; President Colston (Parent) for 1801 (declined); knighted 1778; died January 25, 1814, aged 79.

Dymer, John — 1668-1674; Sheriff, 1673-1674; died June 7, 1674.

Eames, John—1807 (declined).

Earle, Robert—1715-1737; Alderman, 1727-1737 (St. James 1727-1728, St. Ewen 1728-1737); Sheriff, 1716-1717; Mayor, 1725-1726; Governor Incorporation of Poor, 1731-1732; Master Merchant Venturers, 1733-1734; Treasurer Merchant Venturers, 1712-1730; died January 25, 1736-7, aged 68.

Earle, Sir Thomas—1669-1684, 1688-1690, and 1691-1696; Alderman, 1681-1683 (St. James), 1689-1690, and 1691-1696 (St. Nicholas); Master Merchant Venturers, 1673-1674; Sheriff, 1671-1672; Mayor, 1681-1682; M.P., 1681; knighted 1681; died June 24, 1696, aged 67.

Edgar, Alexander — 1767-1792; Alderman, 1788-1792 (Maryleport); Sheriff, 1767-1768; Mayor, 1787-1788; died February 2, 1792, aged 58.

Edgar, John Foy—1796-1818; Sheriff, 1796-1797 and 1802-1803; Mayor (declined), 1805; Sword Bearer, 1818-1850; President Anchor, 1798; died November 5, 1850, aged 83.

Edwards, Abraham — 1634-1640; Sheriff, April-Sept., 1638; died about December, 1640.

ALPHABETICAL INDEX (III.)—*Continued.*

Edwards, Samuel—1798 (declined); President Colston (Parent) 1805; President Gloucestershire Society, 1794; died January 21, 1815, aged 68.

Edye, Joseph—1794-1820; Sheriff, 1794-1795; Mayor, 1801-1802; President Anchor, 1796; died September 10, 1820.

Eglesfield, John—(1597)-1632; Alderman, 1615-1632 (Maryleport); Sheriff, 1597-1598; Mayor, 1610-1611; died 1631-2.

Elbridge, Giles — 1627-1644; Sheriff, 1629-1630; Warden Merchant Venturers, 1620-1621, 1638-1639; Treasurer Merchant Venturers, 1633-1634; died February, 1643-4.

Elbridge, John—September-December, 1645.

Elliot, Robert—1631-1643; Sheriff, 1633-1634; died March, 1642-3.

Elliott, William—1661-1666; died about December, 1666.

Ellis, Walter—1623-1639; Sheriff, 1626-1627; Warden Merchant Venturers, 1618-1619; Treasurer Merchant Venturers, 1628-1629; died about June, 1639.

Ellys, William — (1583)-1611; Alderman, (1599)-1611; Sheriff, 1583-1584; Mayor, 1598-1599; died about February, 1610-1.

Elton, Sir Abraham, Bart.—1699-1728; Alderman, 1712-1728 (St. James 1712-1716, Maryleport 1716-1719, St. Ewen 1719-1728); Sheriff, 1702-1703; Mayor, 1710-1711, and September, 1720; M.P., 1722-1727; Governor Incorporation of Poor, 1713-1715; Treasurer Incorporation of Poor, 1701-1702; Master Merchant Venturers, 1708-1709; Treasurer Merchant Venturers, 1705-1708; President Gloucestershire Society, 1689, 1715; created Baronet, 1717; died February 9, 1727-8.

Elton, Sir Abraham, Bart.—1710-1742; Alderman, 1723-1742 (Temple 1723-1739, St. James 1739-1742); Sheriff, 1710-1711; Mayor, 1719-1720; M.P., 1727-1742; Master Merchant Venturers, 1719-1720; died October 19, 1742.

Elton, Sir Abraham, Bart.—1728-1757; Sheriff, 1728-1729; Mayor, 1742-1743; died November 29, 1761.

Elton, Abraham—1736-1762; Alderman, 1754-1762 (Redcliff); Sheriff, 1736-1737; Mayor, 1753-1754; Master Merchant Venturers, 1757-1758; died August 20, 1762.

Elton, Isaac—1712-1714; died October 23, 1714, aged 54.

Elton, Isaac—1743-1776; Alderman, 1766-1776 (St. Nicholas); Sheriff, 1743-1744; Mayor, 1761-1762; Master Merchant Venturers, 1764-1765; died June 6, 1776.

ALPHABETICAL INDEX (III.)—*Continued.*

Elton, Isaac—1765-1783; Sheriff, 1765-1766 and 1770-1771; Mayor (declined), 1783; Master Merchant Venturers, 1773-1774; died March 31, 1790.

Elton, Jacob—1720-1765; Alderman, 1735-1765 (St. Thomas 1735-1737, St. Nicholas 1737-1739, All Saints 1739-1742, St. James 1742-1765); Sheriff, 1720-1721; Mayor, 1733-1734; Treasurer Incorporation of Poor, 1714-1715; Master Merchant Venturers, 1728-1729; died June 15, 1765, aged 80.

Eston, Thomas—1667-January, 1688, and October, 1688-1689; Alderman, 1683-1688 and 1688-1689 (St. James); Sheriff, 1670-1671; Mayor, 1682-1683; Master Merchant Venturers, 1681-1682.

Evans, David—1795-1816; Alderman, 1807-1816 (Redcliff); Sheriff, 1795-1796; Mayor, August, 1803-1804; died April 8, 1816, aged 74.

Eyre, Sir Robert—1704-1728; Recorder and Alderman, 1704-1728; died December 28, 1735. (M.P. Salisbury, 1698-1710; Q.C., 1707; Solicitor-General 1708-1710; knighted 1710; Privy Councillor, 1725; Judge Queen's Bench, 1710-1723; Chief Baron Exchequer, 1723-1725; Chief Justice Common Pleas, 1725-1735.)

Farmer, Arthur—1640-1662; Alderman, 1656 - 1662 (Redcliff); Sheriff, 1647-1648; Mayor, 1657-1658; died about 1668.

Farmer, Thomas—(1599)-1624; Alderman, 1618-1624 (St. Stephen); Sheriff, 1602-1603; Mayor, 1616-1617; died November, 1624, aged 83.

Farr, John—1776-1797; Alderman, 1785-1797 (All Saints); Sheriff, 1776-1777; Mayor, 1784-1785; died April 15, 1797.

Farr, Richard—1746-1782; Alderman, 1767-1782 (Maryleport 1767-1771, St. Stephen 1771-1782); Sheriff, 1746-1747; Mayor, 1763-1764; Governor Incorporation of Poor, 1774-1776; Master Merchant Venturers, 1762-1763; died May 15, 1782.

Farr, Thomas—1762-1791; Sheriff, 1762-1763; Mayor, 1775-1776; Master Merchant Venturers, 1771-1772; died August 30, 1791.

Feilding, Edward—1668-1684 and 1688-1691; Alderman, 1689-1691 (St. James); Sheriff, 1674-1675; Steward Gloucestershire Society, 1672; died February 20, 1690-1.

Fitzherbert, William—1632-1645 and 1661-1662; Sheriff, 1632-1633; Treasurer Merchant Venturers, 1638-1639; died 1662.

Foster, Sir Michael—1735-1762; Recorder and Alderman, 1735-1762 (Castle 1736-1747, St. Thomas 1747-1753, St. Stephen 1753-1762); candidate for Steward Sheriff's Court, 1731; died November 7, 1763. (Serjeant, 1736; knighted, 1745; Judge King's Bench, 1745-1763.)

ALPHABETICAL INDEX (III.)—*Continued*.

Fowler, James—1810-1835; Alderman, 1821-1833 (St. Thomas); Sheriff, 1810-1811; Mayor, 1813-1814; Master Merchant Venturers, 1810-1811; President Gloucestershire Society, 1823; died May 23, 1838, aged 73.

Fownes, John—(1599)-1609; Sheriff, 1601-1602; died August, 1609.

Fownes, Thomas—1615 (declined).

Foy, Edward—1715-1737; Sheriff, 1718-1719; Mayor, 1730-1731; Deputy Governor Incorporation of Poor, 1715-1716; Treasurer Incorporation of Poor, 1717-1718; Warden Merchant Venturers, 1725-1726; died July, 1737.

Foy, John—1729-1771; Alderman, 1747-1771 (Castle 1747-1748, Trinity 1748-1762, St. Michael 1762-1771); Sheriff, 1732-1733 and 1744-1745; Mayor, 1747-1748; Master Merchant Venturers, 1748-1749; died January 18, 1771.

Foy, Nathaniel — 1756-1783; Alderman, 1776-1783 (Maryleport); Sheriff, 1756-1757; Mayor, 1772-1773; Master Merchant Venturers, 1753-1754; died April 10, 1783.

Franklyn, Richard—1696-1707; Master Merchant Venturers, 1702-1704.

Franklyn, James Norrway—1831-1835; Sheriff, 1832-1833 and 1834-1835. (See also page 70.)

Freeman, James—1686 (declined).

Freke, Philip—1702-1729; Sheriff, 1708-1709; Parliamentary candidate, 1715; Master Merchant Venturers, 1713-1714; died December 10, 1729, aged 68.

French, William—1695-1703; Sheriff, 1695-1696.

French, William—1716-1720; died September, 1720.

Fripp, William—1798-1829; Alderman, 1812-1829 (St. Thomas 1812-1814, St. Ewen 1814-1829); Sheriff, 1798-1799; Mayor (declined), 1806; Treasurer Infirmary, 1811-1829; died June 10, 1829, aged 68.

Fripp, William — 1814-1835; Alderman, 1821-1835 (Maryleport 1821-1822, Redcliff 1822-1835); Sheriff, 1814-1815; Mayor, 1819-1820. (See also pages 70 and 270.)

Furney, James—1739 (declined).

Gardiner, John—1819-1832; Sheriff, 1819-1820, 1824-1825; Postmaster, 1825-1832; President Dolphin, 1824; died September 29, 1832, aged 54.

Garnett, John—1782-1792; Sheriff, 1783-1784; Master Merchant Venturers, 1794-1795.

Gay, Anthony—1655-1661; Warden Merchant Venturers, 1656-1657.

George, Christopher—1833-1835. (See also page 71.)

ALPHABETICAL INDEX (III.)—*Continued.*

George, James—1814-1835; Alderman, 1827-1835 (St. James); Sheriff, 1814-1815, 1819-1820; Mayor, 1822-1823. (See also pages 71 and 270.)

George, Philip—1807-1828; Sheriff, 1808-1809, 1813-1914, 1815-1816; Warden St. Stephen's Ringers, 1793; died March 24, 1828, aged 77.

George, Richard—(1599)-1609; Sheriff, 1597-1598; died 1609.

Gibbes, Henry—1609-1636; Alderman, 1624-1636 (St. Ewen); Sheriff, 1611-1612; Mayor, 1624-1625; died May 19, 1636, aged 73.

Gibbes, Henry—1636-1661; Alderman, 1645-1650 (Maryleport), and 1652-1661 (St. James); Sheriff, 1640-1641; Mayor, 1652-1653.

Gibbes, Henry—February-October, 1688; Alderman, February-October, 1688; Warden Merchant Venturers, 1691-1692.

Gibbes, William—1599-1603; died April 3, 1603.

Gibbons, Richard—1684-1688.

Gibbons, William—1662-1667; died 1667.

Gibbons, William—1792-1807; Alderman, 1806-1807 (Redcliff); Sheriff, 1792-1793; Mayor, 1800-1801; Warden Merchant Venturers, 1805-1806; died April 27, 1807, aged 75.

Gibbs, George—1794 (declined); Master Merchant Venturers, 1790-1791; President Anchor, 1808; died August 15, 1818, aged 65.

Gibbs, George—1812 (declined); Master Merchant Venturers, 1820-1821; died March 28, 1863.

Gibbs, Harrington—1720-1722; Warden Merchant Venturers, 1726-1727.

Gibbs, Sir Vicary—1794-1817; Recorder and Alderman, 1794-1817 (Trinity); died February 8, 1820. (M.P. Totnes, 1804-1806; Great Bedwin, 1807; Cambridge University, 1807-1812; K.C., 1795; knighted, 1805; Solicitor-General to Prince of Wales, 1795-1800; Attorney-General to Prince of Wales, 1800-1805; Chief Justice, Chester, 1805-1806; Solicitor-General, 1805-1806; Attorney-General, 1807-1812; Judge Common Pleas, 1812-1813; Chief Baron Exchequer, 1813-1814; Chief Justice Common Pleas, 1814-1818; Privy Councillor, 1813.)

Gifford, Lord (Sir Robert Gifford)—1818-1826; Recorder and Alderman, 1818-1826 (Trinity); died September 4, 1826. (M.P., Eye, 1817-1824; knighted, 1817; Solicitor-General, 1817-1819; Attorney-General, 1819-1824; Chief Justice Common Pleas, 1824; Master of the Rolls, 1824-1826; Privy Councillor, 1824; created a Peer, 1824.)

ALPHABETICAL INDEX (III.)—*Continued.*

Glanville, Sir John—Recorder and Alderman, 1630-1645; M.P., March-May, 1640, and 1642-1645; died October 2, 1661. (M.P., Liskeard, 1614; Plymouth, 1620-1622, 1624-1625, 1626, 1628-1629; St. Germans, 1659; knighted, 1641; Serjeant, 1637; King's Serjeant, 1640-1645 and 1660-1661; Speaker, 1640.)

Gleed, Francis—1656-1661; Sheriff, 1659-1660; died June 1, 1661, aged 67.

Gleson, Henry—1669-1684; Sheriff, 1676-1677.

Glisson, Benjamin—1733-1755; Sheriff, 1733-1734; died March 14, 1755.

Godman, Thomas — 1662-1668; died about December, 1668.

Goldney, Gabriel—1822-1835; Alderman, 1829-1835 (Temple); Sheriff, 1822-1823, 1825-1826; Mayor, 1827-1828. (See also pages 71 and 271.)

Goldney, Thomas—1685 (declined); died about 1694.

Goldsmith, Thomas—1662 (declined).

Gonninge, John—1611-1645; Alderman, 1630-1645 (St Nicholas); Sheriff, 1613-1614; Mayor, 1627-1628; Master Merchant Venturers, 1619-1620, 1640-1641; Treasurer Merchant Venturers, 1613-1615; died May, 1645.

Gonninge, John—1630-1662; Alderman, 1646-1662 (St. Nicholas); Sheriff, 1631-1632; Mayor, 1645-1646 and 1654-1655; Warden Merchant Venturers, 1629, 1630, 1640-1641; Treasurer Merchant Venturers, 1636-1638; died November, 1662.

Goodwin, Austin—1756-1762; Sheriff, 1756-1757; died August 8, 1762.

Gordon, John—1789-1825; Sheriff, 1789-1790; Mayor, (declined), 1800; Master Merchant Venturers, 1804-1805; Collector of Customs, 1813-1832; President Gloucestershire Society, 1798; died Dec. 26, 1839, aged 81.

Gordon, Robert—1756-1784; Alderman, 1777-1784 (All Saints); Sheriff, 1757-1758; Mayor, 1773-1774; died December 14, 1784.

Gough, Giles—1650-1652 (not sworn).

Gough, Henry—1661-1684 and October-November, 1688; Sheriff, 1667-1668; Warden Merchant Venturers, 1662-1663; Steward Gloucestershire Society, 1662.

Grant, John—February-October, 1688.

Gravett, Richard—1710-1738; Sheriff, 1712-1713; died 1738.

Gregson, Richard—September-December, 1645, and 1660-1662; Alderman, April-October, 1662; Sheriff 1660-1661; died about October, 1662

Griffith, Christopher—1646-1684 and 1688-1689; Sheriff, 1654-1655; Mayor, 1672-1673; died 1689.

ALPHABETICAL INDEX (III.)—*Continued.*

Grigg, William—1646-1652 and 1654-1661.

Gunter, Walter—1681-March, 1688, and 1688-1691.

Guy, John—1603-1629; Alderman, 1619-1629 (Temple); Sheriff, 1605-1606; Mayor, 1618-1619; M.P., 1620-1622, 1624-1625; Master Merchant Venturers, 1622-1623; Treasurer Merchant Venturers, 1611-1612; died about February, 1628-9.

Gwilliam, Daniel—April-October, 1668.

Haynes, James—1703-1721; Sheriff, 1709-1710; Treasurer Incorporation of Poor, 1705-1706; died 1721.

Haines, Thomas—1667-1668 (not sworn).

Hale, Samuel—1674-1684; Warden Merchant Venturers, 1677-1678; Steward Gloucestershire Society, 1676.

Hale, Thomas—1803 and 1818 (declined).

Hall, Samuel—1818 (declined).

Harford, Joseph—1779-1802; Alderman, 1797-1802 (All Saints); Sheriff, 1779-1780, 1785-1786, 1791-1792; Mayor (declined), 1794; Master Merchant Venturers, 1796-1797; President Anchor, 1777; Treasurer Infirmary, 1778-1791; died October 11, 1802.

Harper, John—1650-1661; Sheriff, 1656-1657.

Harrington, George—1604-1640; Alderman, 1618-1640 (St. Ewen 1618-1624, St. Michael 1624-1640); Sheriff, 1604-1605; Mayor, 1617-1618; died January 2, 1639-1640.

Harris, John—1776-1801; Alderman, 1792-1801 (St. Ewen); Sheriff, 1776-1777, 1788-1789; Mayor, 1790-1791; President Anchor, 1791; died May 20, 1801, aged 75.

Harris, Joseph Gregory—1792-1801; Sheriff, 1792-1793; Sword Bearer, 1801-1818; died September 8, 1818.

Harris, Thomas—1650-1661; Sheriff, 1655-1656.

Harris, Thomas—March-July, 1686 (not sworn).

Harris, Thomas—1753-1797; Alderman, 1776-1797 (Maryleport 1776, St. Nicholas 1776-1797); Sheriff, 1753-1754; Mayor, 1769-1770; died January 28, 1797, aged 86.

Harrison, John—(1599)-1616; Sheriff, 1599-1600; Warden Merchant Venturers, 1612-1613.

Hart, Arthur—1675-1684 and 1688-1705; Sheriff, 1680-1681; Mayor, 1689-1690; Master Merchant Venturers, 1688-1689; Treasurer Merchant Venturers, 1689-1690; died 1705.

Hart, George—1645-1658; Sheriff, 1650-1651; died 1658.

Hart, George—1677-January, 1688, and October, 1688-1691; Sheriff, 1682-1683; Warden Merchant Venturers, 1675-1677; died 1691.

ALPHABETICAL INDEX (III.)—*Continued.*

Hart, Sir Richard—1661-1686 and 1688-1702; Alderman, 1680-1686 and 1688-1702 (All Saints); Sheriff, 1668-1669; Mayor, 1680-1681; M.P., 1681, 1685-1687, 1689-1695; candidate, 1695, 1698; Master Merchant Venturers, 1675-1677; Treasurer Merchant Venturers, 1677-1684; knighted, 1680; died January 16, 1701-2.

Harvey, Charles—1805 (declined); Warden Merchant Venturers, 1806-1807; Master St. Stephen's Ringers, 1812; died February 11, 1829.

Harvey, James—1784-1807; Alderman, 1798-1807 (Castle); Sheriff, -784-1785; Mayor, 1795-1797; President Anchor, 1787; Master St. Stephen's Ringers, 1802; died November 5, 1807.

Hasell, William—1662-1675; Sheriff, June-September, 1674; Chamberlain, 1675-1680; Warden Merchant Venturers, 1663-1664, 1667-1669.

Hassell, Thomas — 1818-1829; Alderman, 1828-1829 (Maryleport); Sheriff, 1818-1819, 1820-1821, 1826-1827; Mayor, 1824-1825; died June 18, 1829, aged 66.

Haviland, Mathew—(1599)-1620; Alderman, 1609-1620; Sheriff, 1594-1595; Mayor, 1607-1608; Master Merchant Venturers, 1608-1609, 1613-1614, 1616-1617; died about February, 1619-20.

Hawkins, Sir John—1690-1723; Alderman, 1702 - 1723 (Temple); Sheriff, 1694-1695; Mayor, 1701-1702; Governor Incorporation of Poor, 1706-1707; Warden Merchant Venturers, 1712-1713; knighted, 1702; died July 6, 1723, aged 74.

Hayman, Sir William—1671-1702; Alderman, 1684-1688 and 1691-1702 (Maryleport 1684-1688, St. Ewen 1688, St. James 1691-1692, Trinity 1692-1700, St. Ewen 1700-1702); Sheriff, 1679-1680; Mayor, 1684-1685; Master Merchant Venturers, 1679-1680; Treasurer Merchant Venturers, 1684-1685; knighted, 1685; died July, 1702.

Haythorne, John—1803-1835; Alderman, 1814-1835 (St. Nicholas 1814-1822, All Saints 1822-1835); Sheriff, 1803-1804, 1807-1708; Mayor, 1808-1809, 1816-1818, 1825-1826; Governor Incorporation of Poor, 1817-1818; Master St. Stephen's Ringers, 1822, 1832; President Colston (Parent), 1817; Warden Merchant Venturers, 1834-1835; died July 16, 1845, aged 78.

Hellicar, Thomas—1812 (declined); Warden Merchant Venturers, 1807-1808; died February 7, 1835, aged 79.

Hellier, George—1636-1656; Alderman, 1654-1656 (Redcliff); Sheriff, 1638-1639; Mayor, 1653-1654; died April 21, 1656.

Henderson, Anthony—1785-1793; Sheriff, 1783-1784; died January 31, 1793.

Henderson, Samuel—1803-1821; Sheriff, 1803-1804; President Anchor, 1806; died February 21, 1821.

ALPHABETICAL INDEX (III.)—*Continued.*

Henville, Richard—1724 (declined); Master Merchant Venturers, 1743-1744; died April 26, 1756.

Hickes, John—1656 1659 (not sworn), 1661-January, 1688, and October, 1688-1700; Alderman, 1667-1688 (All Saints), and 1688-1700 (St. Ewen); Sheriff, 1661-1662; Mayor, 1671-1672; Steward Gloucestershire Society, 1663, 1664; died March, 1699-1700.

Hickes, Nicholas—1705-1727; Alderman, 1718-1727 (St. James); Sheriff, 1706-1707; Mayor, 1716-1717; Governor Incorporation of Poor, 1723-1725; President Gloucestershire Society, 1703; died October or November, 1727.

Hickes, William—(1591)-1618; Alderman, (1591)-1618; Sheriff, 1570-1571; Mayor, 1586-1587; died July, 1618.

Hiley, Peter—1668 (declined).

Hilhouse, Abraham—1812-1835; Alderman, 1822-1835 (St. Nicholas); Sheriff, 1812-1813, 1817-1818; Mayor 1821-1822. (See also page 73.)

Hilhouse, George — 1812-1835; Alderman, 1822-1835 (Castle); Sheriff, 1812-1813, 1817-1818; Mayor, 1820-1821; Master Merchant Venturers, 1822-1823; died December 24, 1848, aged 70.

Hilhouse, James—1755-1762; Sheriff, 1755-1756; Warden Merchant Venturers, 1752-1753; died June 8, 1761.

Hill, Charles—1811 (declined); Master Merchant Venturers, 1797-1798; died July 21, 1829.

Hill, James—1774-1802; Sheriff, 1774-1775, 1788-1789; Mayor, 1789-1790; died October 1, 1802.

Hill, Jeremiah—1812 (declined); Master Merchant Venturers, 1791-1792; died July 13, 1831, aged 78.

Hinde, John — 1680-1684 and 1688-1689; Sheriff, February-September, 1688; Mayor, 1696-1697; died April 28, 1699, aged 68.

Hobson, Henry—1614-1636; Alderman, 1635-1636 (St. James); Sheriff, 1616-1617; Mayor, 1632-1633; died March, 1635-6.

Hobson, William—1633-1641; Sheriff, 1635-1636; Warden Merchant Venturers, 1630-1632; died 1654, aged 57.

Hodges, Luke—1635-1643, 1645-1654; Alderman, 1646-1652 (St. James); Sheriff, 1638-1639; M.P., 1646-1653.

Holland, Richard—1669-1678; died about February, 1677-8.

Hollidge, James—1696-1710; Sheriff, 1699-1700; Mayor, 1708-1709; Chamberlain, 1710-1739; Master Merchant Venturers, 1700-1702; Master St. Stephen's Ringers, 1707.

Hollister, John—1684-1688.

Hollway, Jeremiah—1655-1661.

ALPHABETICAL INDEX (III.)—*Continued.*

Holworthie, Richard—1616-1643; Alderman, 1636-1643 (All Saints); Sheriff, 1621-1622; Mayor, 1635-1636; Master Merchant Venturers, 1635-1636; Treasurer Merchant Venturers, 1622-1623; died October, 1643.

Hooke, Abraham—1702-1712; Sheriff, 1706-1707; Master Merchant Venturers, 1712-1713.

Hooke, Andrew—1656-1661; died February 20, 1687, aged 72.

Hooke, Humphrey—1164-1645; Alderman, 1632-1645 (St. Stephen); Sheriff, 1614-1615; Mayor, 1629-1630, 1643-1644; M.P., March-May, 1640, and 1640-1642; Master Merchant Venturers, 1621-1622, 1630-1635, 1638-1639; Treasurer Merchant Venturers, 1616-1617; died March, 1659.

Hooke, Sir Humphrey—Alderman, 1662-1664 (not sworn); M.P., April-May, 1661, and 1666-1677; died October 16, 1677, aged 45.

Hooke, Thomas—1633-1645; Sheriff, 1634-1635; Warden Merchant Venturers, 1632-1633; Treasurer Merchant Venturers, 1640-1641; died February, 1658-9.

Hopkins, John—(1599)-1615; Alderman, (1599)-1615; Sheriff, 1586-1587; Mayor, 1600-1601; M.P., 1601; Master Merchant Venturers, 1605-1606; died December, 1615.

Hopkins, Thomas—(1599)-1614; Sheriff, 1600-1601; Warden Merchant Venturers, 1608-1609; died 1614.

Hopkins, William—(1599)-1610; Sheriff, 1601-1602; Warden Merchant Venturers, 1609-1610; Treasurer Merchant Venturers, 1606-1607; died July, 1610.

Horne, John—1692-1696.

Hort, Thomas—1700-1715; Sheriff, 1703-1704; Mayor, 1712-1713; Master Merchant Venturers, 1702-1704; President Gloucestershire Society, 1700; died 1715.

Horte, John—(1585)-1600; Alderman, (1599)-1500; Sheriff, 1585-1586; Mayor, 1599-1600; died May 4, 1600.

Hotchkin, Charles—1759-1782; Alderman, 1778-1782 (St. Thomas); Sheriff, 1759-1760; Mayor, 1774-1775; President Colston (Parent), 1767; died July 22, 1782.

Hungerford, Thomas—1707-1717 (not sworn); Treasurer Incorporation of Poor, 1703-1704.

Hunt, Michael—1578-1684.

Hunt, Richard—1834-1835; died November 18, 1866, aged 91.

Hurle, John—1811 (declined); died March 31, 1824, aged 69.

ALPHABETICAL INDEX (III.)—*Continued.*

Hurle, John—1827 (declined); Master Merchant Venturers, 1849-1850; died August 27, 1855, aged 69.

Hurle, Simon—April-September, 1688; Alderman, April-September, 1688.

Hurne, Edward — 1661 - 1678; Sheriff, 1669 - 1670; Steward Gloucestershire Society, 1670; died about August, 1678.

Hurte, Ralph — (1587)-1615; Alderman, (1599)-1615; Sheriff, 1587-1588; Mayor, 1602-1603; died 1615.

Hyde, Sir Lawrence — Recorder and Alderman, 1605-1615; died January 26, 1640-1. (Attorney-General to the Queen; knighted 1614; M.P., Heytesbury, 1584-1585, 1597-1598 ; Chippenham, 1586-1587; Marlborough, 1601, 1604-1611.)

Hyde, Sir Nicholas—Recorder and Alderman, 1615-1627; M.P., 1625; died August 25, 1631. (M.P., Andover, 1601; Christchurch, 1604-1611; Bath, 1614; King's Serjeant, 1627; knighted 1627; Chief Justice King's Bench, 1627-1631.)

Iles, Joseph—1737-1750; Sheriff, 1737-1738; Warden Merchant Venturers, 1741-1742; died 1750.

Inman, William—1805-1833; Sheriff, 1805-1806, 1810-1811; Mayor (declined), 1811; Warden St. Stephen's Ringers, 1806; died April 28, 1833, aged 77.

Jackson, Alexander—1661-1672; Warden Merchant Venturers, 1659-1660, 1663-1664; died 1672.

Jackson, John—1669 (declined).

Jackson, Joseph—1638-1662; Alderman, 1646-1662 (St. Michael); Sheriff, 1642-1643; Mayor, 1651 - 1652 ; M.P., 1659; Master Merchant Venturers, 1647-1648, 1653-1656; died January 5, 1661-2, aged 57.

Jackson, Joseph—February-October, 1688; Sheriff, September-October, 1688; Warden Merchant Venturers, 1695-1696.

Jackson, Miles—1631-1663; Alderman, 1650-1663 (Maryleport 1650-1658, St. Ewen 1658-1663); Sheriff, 1631-1632; Mayor, 1649-1650; M.P., 1654-1655; Master Merchant Venturers, 1650-1651; died February or March, 1662-3.

Jackson, Thomas—1630-1635; Sheriff, 1632-1633; Warden Merchant Venturers, 1627-1628; died March 4, 1634-5.

Jackson, William—1669-1684 and 1688-1716; Alderman, January-October, 1688, and 1689-1716 (Maryleport); Sheriff, 1678-1679; Mayor, 1688-1689; Master Merchant Venturers, 1680-1681; Treasurer Merchant Venturers, 1688-1689; Governor Incorporation of Poor, 1699-1700; died about April, 1716.

ALPHABETICAL INDEX (III.)—*Continued*.

James, Alexander—1623-1645, 1651-1662, and 1664-1665;
Alderman, 1643-1645 (All Saints), 1661-1662, 1664-1665 (not sworn); Sheriff, 1628-1629; Mayor, 1644-1645; Master Merchant Venturers, 1642-1643;
Treasurer Merchant Venturers, 1631-1632.

James, Thomas—(1591)-1619; Alderman, 1604-1619;
Sheriff, 1591-1592; Mayor, 1605-1606, 1614-1615;
M.P., 1597-1598, 1604-1611, 1614; Master Merchant Venturers, 1607-1608, 1615-1616; died about January, 1618--9.

Jefferis, Joseph—1712-1752; Alderman, 1725-1752 (All Saints 1725-1732, St. Stephen 1732-1752); Sheriff, 1715-1716; Mayor, 1724-1725; Governor Incorporation of Poor 1729-1730; Warden Merchant Venturers, 1745-1746; died October 24, 1752.

Jefferis, William—1722-1752; Alderman, 1742-1752 (Redcliff 1742-1746, St. Nicholas 1746-1752); Sheriff, 1724-1725; Mayor, 1738-1739; Governor Incorporation of Poor, 1743-1745; Treasurer Incorporation of Poor, 1727-1728; Warden Merchant Venturers, 1737-1738; Treasurer Merchant Venturers 1730-1732; died April or May, 1752.

Jenkins, Robert—1820-1835; Sheriff, 1820-1821; President Colston (Parent), 1829; died August 4, 1837, aged 61.

Jenkins, Walter—1740-1758; Sheriff, 1740-1741; died June 20, 1758.

Jones, Charles—1686 (declined); Treasurer Merchant Venturers. 1697-1700.

Jones, John—April-October, 1688.

Jones, Rice—(1584)-1602; Alderman, 1599-1602; Sheriff, 1584-1585; Mayor, May-September, 1600; died January, 1601-2.

Jones, William—1618-1645; Alderman, 1637-1645 (Redcliff); Sheriff, 1622-1623; Mayor, 1637-1638; Master Merchant Venturers, 1641-1642; Treasurer Merchant Venturers, 1624-1625; died October, 1645.

Jordan, Thomas—1686 (declined).

Kedgwin, Christopher—(1589)-1620; Alderman, 1602-1620; Sheriff, 1589-1590; Mayor, 1604-1605; died February 14, 1619-20.

King, Ambrose Gilbert—1807 (declined); died January 11, 1825, aged 61.

King, George—1809-1825; Sheriff, 1809-1810; Corn Measurer, 1825-1831; Master St. Stephen's Ringers, 1793; died December 29, 1831, aged 75.

King, Henry—1796 (declined); President Dolphin, 1787; died December 11, 1812.

King, John—1716-1734; Sheriff, 1719-1720; Mayor, 1732-1733; Warden Merchant Venturers, 1723-1724; died November 27, 1734.

ALPHABETICAL INDEX (III.)—*Continued.*

Kirke, Robert—1693-1696; Warden Merchant Venturers, 1690-1691; President Gloucestershire Society, 1696.

Kitchin, Abell—(1598)-1640; Alderman, 1616-1640 (Redcliff (1620)-1634, Trinity 1634-1640); Sheriff, 1598-1599; Mayor, 1612-1613; Master Merchant Venturers, 1610-1611; died July, 1640.

Knight, Francis—(1579)-1616; Alderman, (1599)-1616; Sheriff, 1579-1580; Mayor, 1594-1595, 1613-1614; died August 20, 1616.

Knight, George—1620-1656; Alderman, 1638-1656 (Temple); Sheriff, 1625-1626; Mayor, 1639-1640; died December 13, 1659, aged 89.

Knight, Sir John—1650-1651 and 1654 (not sworn), 1660-1683; Alderman, 1662-1683 (Temple 1662-1673, St. Ewen 1673-1683); Sheriff, 1660 (declined); Mayor, 1663-1664; M.P., 1660-1681; candidate, 1681; Master Merchant Venturers, 1663-1664; knighted, 1663; died December 16, 1683, aged 71.

Knight, John—1653-1654 and August, 1661 (not sworn), November, 1661-1679; Alderman, 1672-1679 (St. Stephen); Sheriff, 1664-1665; Mayor, 1670-1671; Master Merchant Venturers, 1666-1667; died 1679.

Knight, Sir John—1674 (not sworn), 1679-1685, 1688-1702; Sheriff, 1681-1682; Mayor, 1690-1691; M.P., 1689-1695; candidate, 1695, 1698; Warden Merchant Venturers, 1681-1682; knighted, 1682; died February, 1718.

Knox, Thomas—1754-1762; Sheriff, 1754-1755; died June 2, 1762.

Lane, Gerard—1662-1671.

Lane, George—1645-1661; Sheriff, 1651-1652; Warden Merchant Venturers, 1629-1630, 1647-1648; Treasurer Merchant Venturers, 1652-1653.

Lane, George—1669-1679; Sheriff, 1675-1676; Master Merchant Venturers, 1677-1679; died September 10, 1679.

Lane, Richard—1674-January, 1688, and October, 1688-1705; Alderman, 1696-1705 (St. Nicholas 1696-1702, St. Michael 1702-1705); Sheriff, 1681-1682; Mayor, 1687-February, 1688, 1691-1692; Master Merchant Venturers, 1684-1685; died about March, 1704-5.

Langley, Edward—1661-1669; died 1669.

Langton, John—1613-1636; Alderman, 1632-1636 (Maryleport 1632-1634, Redcliff 1634-1636); Sheriff, 1614-1615; Mayor, 1628-1629; Master Merchant Venturers, 1620-1621; Treasurer Merchant Venturers 1615-1616; died 1636.

Langton, John—1632-1645; Sheriff, 1634-1635; Warden Merchant Venturers, 1630-1632, 1641-1642; Treasurer Merchant Venturers, 1639-1640; died April, 1645.

ALPHABETICAL INDEX (III.)—Continued.

Langton, Sir Thomas—1659-1673; Alderman, 1664-1673 (St. Michael); Sheriff, 1660-1661; Mayor, 1666-1667; Master Merchant Venturers, 1664-1665; knighted, 1666; died about June, 1673.

Laroche, James—1734-1770; Alderman, 1752-1770 (All Saints); Sheriff, 1734-1735; Mayor, 1750-1751; Master Merchant Venturers, 1751-1752; Treasurer Merchant Venturers, 1745-1751; Master St. Stephen's Ringers, 1733-1738; died about September, 1770.

Laroche, Sir James, Bart.—1764-1804; Sheriff, 1764-1765; Master Merchant Venturers, 1782-1783; Master St. Stephen's Ringers, 1769; created Baronet, 1776; died September, 1804. (M.P., Bodmin, 1768-1680.)

Lawford, John—1646-1688; Alderman, 1663-1688 (St. James 1663-1664, Maryleport 1664-1680, St. Michael 1680-1688); Sheriff, 1654-1655; Mayor, 1664-1665; Steward Gloucestershire Society, 1660, 1677; died July, 1688.

Lax, Joseph—1831-1835; Sheriff, 1831-1832. (See also page 87.)

Lean, James—1832-1835; Sheriff, 1833-1834. (See also page 75.)

Lewis, Sir William—1691-1712; Alderman, 1703-1712 (St. Thomas); Sheriff, 1695-1696; Mayor, 1702-1703; Governor Incorporation of Poor, 1707-1708; knighted, 1703; died May 23, 1712.

Lippincott, Sir Henry, Bart.—1761-1781; Sheriff, 1768-1769, 1770-1771; M.P., 1780-1781; Warden Merchant Venturers, 1772-1773; created Baronet, 1778; died January 1, 1781.

Liston, Thomas—September-October, 1688; Sheriff, September-October, 1688.

Little, Humphrey—1661-1680; Sheriff, 1668-1669; died 1680.

Liveredge, Richard—1706-1721 (not sworn).

Lloyd, Henry—1727-1736; Sheriff, 1728-1729; Treasurer Merchant Venturers, 1732-1734; died 1736.

Lloyd, Sir John—1661-1681; Alderman, 1679-1681 (St. James); Sheriff, 1666-1667; Mayor, 1678-1679; knighted 1678.

Lloyd, John—1695-1696 and 1707-1728.

Lloyd, Thomas—1632-1652; Sheriff, 1633-1634; died 1652.

Lock, John—1620-1656 and 1660-1666; Alderman, 1640-1656 and 1660-1666 (St. Michael 1640-1646, All Saints 1645-1656 and 1660-1666); Sheriff, 1626-1627; Mayor, 1641-1642; Treasurer Merchant Venturers 1627-1628; died October or November, 1666.

Longe, Edward—(1586)-1604; Sheriff, 1586-1587.

Longe, Richard—1618-1645; Alderman, 1636-1645 (St. Ewen); Sheriff, 1621-1622; Mayor, 1636-1637; M.P., 1640-1642; Master Merchant Venturers, 1636-1638; Treasurer Merchant Venturers, 1623-1624; died 1650.

ALPHABETICAL INDEX (III.)—*Continued*,

Longman, Ezekiel—1721-1738; Sheriff, 1726-1727; Treasurer Incorporation of Poor, 1719-1720; died August 9, 1738.

Longman, Thomas—1645 (not sworn).

Loscombe, Benjamin—1778-1796; Sheriff, 1778-1779; President Anchor, 1779; died August 19, 1796.

Love, John—1685 (declined).

Love, Joseph—1750-1769; Sheriff, 1750-1751.

Love, Philip—1645 (not sworn).

Lucas, John Robert—1811 (declined); died July 15, 1828.

Lunell, John Evans—1826 (declined) and 1829-1835; Sheriff, 1829-1830. (See also page 76.)

Lyde, Lionel—1720-1745; Alderman, 1737-1745 (St. Thomas 1737-1742, All Saints 1742-1745); Sheriff, 1722-1723; Mayor, 1735-1736; Master Merchant Venturers, 1741-1742; died March or April, 1745.

Lyndhurst, Lord (Sir John Singleton Copley—March-June, 1827; Recorder and Alderman, 1826-1827 (Trinity); died October 12, 1863, aged 91. M.P., Yarmouth, Isle of Wight, 1818; Ashburton, 1818-1826; Cambridge University, 1826-1827; Serjeant, 1813; King's Serjeant, 1819; knighted, 1819; Solicitor-General, 1819-1824; Attorney-General, 1824-1826; Privy Councillor, 1826; Master of the Rolls, 1826-1827; Lord Chancellor, 1827-1830, 1834-1835, 1841-1846; Chief Baron of the Exchequer, 1831-1834; created Peer, 1827.)

Lysons, William—1661-1664, 1669-1675; Master Merchant Venturers, 1674-1675; Treasurer Merchant Venturers, 1673-1674.

Lyssett, William—1614-1638; Sheriff, 1619-1620; died September, 1638.

Marsh, Thomas—1745-1755; Sheriff, 1745-1746; died December 5, 1755.

Martin, Samuel—1739-1740.

Martin, William—1740-1765; Alderman, 1762-1765 (Redcliff); Sheriff, 1740-1741; Mayor, 1757-1758; died February 4, 1765.

Mason, George—1691-1695; Master Merchant Venturers, 1711-1712; Deputy-Governor Incorporation of Poor, 1703-1704.

Mathew, William—1756 (declined).

May, Richard—(1592)-1603; Sheriff, 1592-1593.

Maze, Peter—1817 (declined). (See also page 76.)

Maze, Peter—1833-1835; Sheriff, 1833-1834. (See also page 76.)

Meredith, Michael—1641 (declined).

ALPHABETICAL INDEX (III.)—Continued.

Merlott, John—1769-1785; Alderman, 1783-1785 (Maryleport); Sheriff, 1769-1770; died December 21, 1785.

Merrett, Henry—1671-1684, 1688-1690; Sheriff, 1676-1677; died September 11, 1692, aged 70.

Merrick, Giles — 1680-January, 1688, October, 1688-1713; Sheriff, 1684-1685; Master Merchant Venturers, 1689-1690; Treasurer Merchant Venturers, 1690-1691; died 1713.

Merricke, Sir William—1684-1692; Sheriff, 1685-1686; Master Merchant Venturers, 1682-1683; Treasurer Merchant Venturers, 1685-1688; knighted, 1686; died 1704-5.

Miles, Philip John—1796 (declined); M.P., 1835-1837; died March 24, 1845, aged 72. (M.P., Westbury, 1820-1826; Corfe Castle, 1829-1832.)

Miles, William—1766-1803; Alderman, 1782-1803 (Redcliff 1782-1797, St. Nicholas 1797-1803); Sheriff, 1766-1767; Mayor, 1780-1781; Treasurer Incorporation of Poor, 1768-1770; Warden Merchant Venturers, 1789-1790; President Colston (Parent) for 1801 (declined); died March 12, 1803, aged 74.

Miller, Peter—1619-1633; Sheriff, 1620-1621; Treasurer Merchant Venturers, 1621-1622; died June or July, 1633.

Miller, Michael—1765-1780; Sheriff, 1765-1766; Mayor, 1779-1780; Master Merchant Venturers, 1778-1779; died August 9, 1780.

Moore, John—1669-1687, 1688-1689; Alderman, 1686-1687 (Trinity); Sheriff, 1677-1678.

Moore, Thomas—1603-1621; Sheriff, 1608-1609; died January, 1620-1.

Moore, Thomas—1661 (declined); Warden Merchant Venturers, 1662-1663, 1664-1665; died September 16, 1675.

Moore, Thomas—1702 (declined); Master Merchant Venturers, 1710-1711.

Morgan, Edward—1653-1669; Alderman, 1665-1669 (St. James); Sheriff, 1658-1659; Mayor, 1667-1668; died September 11, 1669.

Morgan, George—1678-January, 1688, October, 1688-1696; Sheriff, 1686-1687.

Morgan, James—1778-1794; Sheriff, 1778-1779, 1790-1791; Mayor, 1793-1794; President Anchor, 1788; died December 14, 1794, aged 49.

Morgan, John—1786-1808; Alderman, 1803-1808 (St. Ewen); Sheriff, 1787-1788; Mayor, 1799-1800; died January 27, 1808.

Morris, George—1680-1687; died April, 1687.

Mountjoy, Edmund—1707-1735; Alderman, 1719-1735 (Redcliff); Sheriff, 1710-1711; Mayor, 1718-1719; Governor Incorporation of Poor, 1727-1728; died August, 1735.

ALPHABETICAL INDEX (III.)—*Continued.*

Mugleworth, Henry—1741-1782; Alderman, 1765-1782 (Redcliff February-June, 1765, Trinity 1765-1771, St. Michael 1771-1782); Sheriff, 1741-1742; Mayor, 1758-1759; Governor Incorporation of Poor, 1773-1774; died July 9, 1782.

Muggleworth, Peter—September-October, 1688; Sword Bearer, 1726-1735; died 1735.

Murcott, Hugh—1602-1609; died January, 1608-9.

Nash, Henry — 1715-1742; Alderman, 1730-1742 (St. Thomas 1730-1735, Redcliff 1735-1742); Sheriff, 1717-1718; Mayor, 1727-1728; Governor Incorporation of Poor, 1733-1734; died 1756.

Nash, James Ezekiel—1821 (declined). (See also page 77.)

Nash, Sir Stephen—1785-1792; Sheriff, 1785-1786; President Anchor, 1786; knighted, 1786; died March 3, 1792.

Needes, Arthur—1604-1616; Sheriff, 1607-1608.

Nelmes, Samuel—1730-1734; died 1734.

Newman, Henry Wenman—1827-1835; Sheriff, 1827-1828; President Dolphin, 1839; President Gloucestershire Society, 1849; J.P., 1836; died July 24, 1865.

Nicholas, John—1812 (declined); died November 30, 1837, aged 78.

Noble, John—1745-1768; Alderman. 1767-1768 (Redcliff); Sheriff, 1745-1746, 1759-1760; Mayor, 1762-1763; died March 11, 1768.

Noble, John — 1772 - 1828; Alderman, 1792 - 1828 (Temple); Sheriff, 1772-1773, 1775-1776; Mayor, 1791-1792; President Anchor, 1775; died January 9, 1828.

North, Hon. Roger—Recorder and Alderman, 1685-1688 (Castle); died March 1, 1733-4, aged 80. (K.C., 1683; Attorney-General to the Queen, 1686-1688; M.P., Dunwich, 1685-1687.)

Olliffe, John—1684-1688.

Olliffe, Ralph—1661-1683; Alderman, 1673-1683 (Redcliff 1673-1679, Trinity 1679-1680, Maryleport 1680-1683); Sheriff, 1664-1665; Mayor, 1674-1675, 1683; died September 30, 1683.

Opie, William—1687-1688, 1690-1695; Sheriff, 1691-1692; died May, 1695.

Packer, Thomas—(1599)-1624; Alderman, 1620-1624 (St. Michael); Sheriff, 1606-1607; Mayor, 1619-1620; died 1624.

ALPHABETICAL INDEX (III.)—*Continued.*

Page, John—1793-1821; Alderman, 1607-1821 (Castle); Sheriff, 1793-1794; Mayor (declined), 1801; died February 23, 1821.

Paine, Richard—August-October, 1638.

Parfrey, William—(1580)-1606; Alderman, (1599)-1605; Sheriff, 1580-1581; Mayor, 1595-1596; died September or October, 1606.

Parker, Timothy—1656-1661; Sheriff, 1659-1660.

Parsons, Andrew—1724-1728.

Parsons, Henry—February-October, 1688.

Payne, Charles—1827-1835; Sheriff, 1827-1828; Mayor, 1834-1835. (See also page 77.)

Peach, Samuel—1756 (declined); Parliamentary candidate, 1780, 1784; died May 13, 1785.

Peard, Hugh—1604-1612.

Peloquin, David—1735-1766; Alderman, 1752-1766 (Redcliff 1752-1754, St. Nicholas 1754-1766); Sheriff, 1735-1736; Mayor, 1751-1752; Governor Incorporation of Poor, 1758-1760; died March 21, 1766.

Peters, or Petre, Edward—1633-1638; Sheriff, 1637-1638; Warden Merchant Venturers, 1626-1627; died April, 1638.

Pickford, Jedidiah—1691-1694; died February or March, 1693-4.

Pierce, Thomas—1773-1788; Sheriff, 1773-1774; died December 26, 1788.

Pierce, Thomas—1798 (declined); died October 20, 1812.

Piguenit, Isaac—1757-1780; Sheriff, 1757-1758, 1760-1761; died January 29, 1780.

Pinney, Azariah—1796-1803; Sheriff, 1773-1774; died January 2, 1803.

Pinney, Charles—1822-1835; Sheriff, 1823-1824; Mayor, 1831-1832. (See also pages 78 and 272.)

Pinney, John—August-September, 1796; Governor Incorporation of Poor, 1796-1801; died January 23, 1818.

Pinney, William—1645-1650.

Pitman, Michael—1661-1663 (not sworn).

Pitt, Edward—1639-1643; Sheriff, 1640-1641; Warden Merchant Venturers, 1632-1633; died March or April, 1643.

Pitt, William—1610-1631; Alderman, 1624-1631 (St. Stephen); Sheriff, 1610-1611; Mayor, 1623-1624; Master Merchant Venturers, 1624-1625; died November or December, 1631.

Pitt, William—1619-1624; Sheriff, September-October, 1624; died October 25, 1624.

Pley, Richard—1621-1638; Sheriff, 1627-1628; Warden Merchant Venturers, 1623-1624; Treasurer Merchant Venturers, 1629-1630; died 1638.

ALPHABETICAL INDEX (III.)—*Continued.*

Plomer, Francis — 1705-1708; died about December, 1708.

Pope, Andrew—1763-1784; Alderman, 1779-1784 (Castle); Sheriff, 1763-1764, 1773-1774; Mayor, 1776-1777; Master Merchant Venturers, 1769-1770; died July 29, 1784.

Pope, Andrew—1816 (declined); Master Merchant Venturers, 1814-1815; President Anchor, 1797; died December 16, 1832, aged 58.

Pope, James—1684-1688, 1639-1695; Sheriff, 1692-1693; died about July, 1695.

Pope, John—1646-1663; Alderman, July-September, 1663 (St. Michael); Sheriff, 1653-1654; Mayor (declined), 1663; Warden Merchant Venturers, 1661-1662.

Pope, Michael—February-October, 1688; Alderman, February-October, 1688 (St. James).

Pope, Michael—February-October, 1688.

Pope, Michael—1732-1739; Sheriff, 1733-1734; Warden Merchant Venturers, 1729-1730; died December, 1739.

Popley, Derrick—1629-1632; Sheriff, 1630-1631; Warden Merchant Venturers, 1624-1625; died September or October, 1632.

Powell, Charles—1661-1670-1; Sheriff, 1669-1670; died about January, 1670-1.

Powell, James—1646-1651; Chamberlain, 1651-1662.

Powell, Joshua—1812 (declined); Master Merchant Venturers, 1795-1796; President Colston (Parent), 1802 (Treasurer, 1807-1825); died September 3, 1834.

Powell, Thomas Hungerford—1816 (declined); Master Merchant Venturers, 1801-1802; President Colston (Parent), 1806; died September 17, 1836, aged 79.

Powell, Timothy—1811 (declined); Master Merchant Venturers, 1800-1801; President Colston (Parent), 1800; died February 26, 1835, aged 80.

Power, Thomas—1747-1748; Sheriff (declined), 1747; Warden Merchant Venturers, 1745-1746; died January 26, 1747-8.

Powlett, William—1696-1703; Recorder and Alderman, 1688-1703; (Parliamentary candidate, 1690; died October, 1703; Serjeant, 1689; Judge, South Wales, till 1703.)

Price, John—1716-1738; Alderman, 1732-1738 (All Saints 1732-1735, St. James 1735-1738); Sheriff, 1717-1718; Mayor, 1728-1729; Governor Incorporation of Poor, 1734-1735; died about December, 1738.

Prideaux, Edmund—Recorder and Alderman, 1646-1651; died August 19, 1659. (M.P., Lyme Regis, 1640-1653, 1654-1655, 1656-1658, 1658-1659; Commissioner Great Seal, 1643-1646; Solicitor-General, 1648-1649; Attorney-General, 1649-1659; created Baronet (by Cromwell), 1658.)

ALPHABETICAL INDEX (III.)—Continued.

Prigg, Thomas—1659 (not sworn) and 1663-1673; died about July, 1673.

Protheroe, Edward—Councillor, 1797-1829; Sheriff, 1797-1798; Mayor, 1804 1805; M.P., 1812-1820 (candidate 1826); President Anchor, 1804; Warden Merchant Venturers, 1799-1800; died August 24, 1856, aged 81.

Protheroe, George—1829-1835; Sheriff, 1830-1831; died April 19, 1860.

Protheroe, Sir Henry — 1802-1835; Sheriff, 1802-1803, 1807-1808; Mayor (declined), 1810; President Anchor, 1802; President Grateful, 1815; knighted, 1803; died June 18, 1840, aged 63.

Protheroe, Philip—1777-1803; Sheriff, 1777-1778; Mayor, (declined), 1800; President Anchor, 1781; died August 30, 1805, aged 56.

Protheroe, Philip—1804-1835; Sheriff, 1804-1805; Mayor, 1810-1811; Master Merchant Venturers, 1826-1827; President Anchor, 1812; died June 4, 1846, aged 65.

Puxton, Michael—1721-1732; Sheriff, 1725-1726; died about November, 1732.

Pytcher, Thomas—(1594)-1610; Sheriff, 1594-1595; died about December, 1610.

Ransford, Thomas—1815 (declined) died February 14, 1843, aged 78.

Rich, Henry—1656-1663.

Rich, John—1718-1756; Alderman, 1737-1755 (St. Ewen); Sheriff, 1721-1722; Mayor, 1734-1735; Governor Incorporation of Poor, 1741-1742; died February, 1755.

Richards, George—1599-1610; Sheriff, 1603-1604; died about September, 1610.

Ricketts, Henry—1820 (declined), 1832-1835. (See also page 79.)

Riddle, Thomas Hooper—1828-1835; Sheriff, 1828-1829. (See also page 79.)

Rishton, William—1699-1702.

Roberts, John—1599-1608; died about June, 1608.

Roch, Nicholas — 1818-1835; Alderman, 1834-1835 (St. Thomas); Sheriff, 1818-1819, 1821-1822. (See also page 79.)

Roe, Henry—1653-1656.

Rogers, Francis—1700-1707; Warden Merchant Venturers, 1705-1706.

Rogers, Richard—(1595)-1599; Sheriff, 1595-1596; died about May, 1599.

Rogers, Robert—1600-1633; Alderman, 1620-1633 (St. Thomas); Sheriff, 1607-1608; Mayor, 1621-1622; died April 11, 1633, aged 80.

ALPHABETICAL INDEX (III.)—*Continued.*

Romsey, John—1684-1688; Town Clerk, 1676-January, 1688, October, 1688-1721; died February, 1720-1.

Rowbero, John—(1599)-1614; Sheriff, 1605-1606; Treasurer Merchant Venturers, 1608-1609; died 1614.

Ruddock, Noblett—1718-1734; Sheriff, 1721-1722.

Salterne, Thomas—(1599)-1600; died September, 1600.

Sanders, Thomas—1807 (declined); President Colston (Parent) for 1813 (declined); died August 30, 1854, aged 85.

Sandford, John—1680-January, 1688, October, 1688-1696; Sheriff, 1687-1688; President Gloucestershire Society, 1688.

Sandy, Walter—1640-1672; Alderman, 1656-1672 (St. Stephen); Sheriff, 1646-1647; Mayor, 1658-1659; Treasurer Merchant Venturers, 1645-1646; died May or June, 1672.

Saunders, Abraham—1671-January, 1688, October, 1688-1693; Alderman, 1686-1688 (St. Nicholas); Sheriff, 1630-1631; Mayor, 1685-1686.

Saunders, Corsley—1811 (declined); died April 27, 1814, aged 69.

Saunders, Peter—February-October, 1688, 1694-1705; Alderman, June-October, 1705 (St. Michael); Sheriff, 1696-1697; Mayor, 1703-1704; Deputy Governor Incorporation of Poor, 1702-1703; Treasurer Incorporation of Poor, 1699-1700; Master Merchant Venturers, 1696-1698; Treasurer Merchant Venturers, 1700-1705; died October, 1705.

Saunders, Thomas—February-October, 1688; Sheriff, February-September, 1688.

Savage, Francis—1825-1835; Sheriff, 1838-1839; Mayor (declined), 1830; Master Merchant Venturers, 1841-1842; President Gloucestershire Society, 1841; died October 21, 1845.

Savage, John—1822-1835; Alderman, 1831-1835 (Maryleport); Sheriff, 1823-1824, 1825-1826; Mayor, 1829-1831. (See also pages 79 and 272.)

Scrope, John — 1728-1735; Recorder and Alderman, 1728-1735; M.P., 1727-1734 (candidate, 1734); died April 9, 1752. (M.P., Ripon, 1722-1727, Lyme Regis, 1734-1752; Baron of the Exchequer, Scotland, 1708-1724; Commissioner of the Great Seal, 1710; Secretary to the Treasury, 1724-1752.)

Scrope, Thomas—February-October, 1688; Alderman, February-October, 1688 (All Saints); Warden Merchant Venturers, 1664-1665.

Sedgeley, Samuel—1760-1777; Sheriff, 1760-1761; died February 11, 1802.

Seward, John—1687-1688; Warden Merchant Venturers, 1689-1690.

ALPHABETICAL INDEX (III.)—*Continued.*

Sherman, Gabriel—1630-1655, August-November, 1661; Alderman, 1646-1656, August-November, 1661 (St. Ewen); Sheriff, 1630-1631; Mayor. 1647-1648; Warden Merchant Venturers, 1627-1628; Treasurer Merchant Venturers, 1635-1636.

Shuter, Christopher—1699-1730; Alderman, 1715-1730 (St. Michael 1715-1716, St. Thomas 1716-1730); Sheriff, 1702-1703; Mayor, 1711-1712; Governor Incorporation of Poor, 1715-1716; Warden Merchant Venturers, 1718-1719; died 1730.

Slye, John—(1595)-1599; Sheriff, 1595-1596; died 1599.

Smith, Joseph—1780-1815; Sheriff, 1780-1781; Mayor, 1794-1795; Receiver of Town Dues, 1809-1815; President Anchor, 1782; died January 17, 1815, aged 70.

Smith, Morgan—1702-1712; Sheriff, 1705-1706; President Gloucestershire Society, 1710.

Smith, Morgan—1735-1781; Alderman, 1755-1781 (St. Ewen 1755-1767, St. James 1767-1781); Sheriff, 1736-1737; Mayor, 1754-1755; Secretary Infirmary, 1737-1739; Governor Incorporation of Poor, 1771-1773; died August 7, 1781.

Smith, Robert—1684-1688.

Smith, Robert—1720-1762; Sheriff, 1722-1723; Governor Incorporation of Poor, 1718-1719, 1737-1739; Master Merchant Venturers, 1746-1747; President Colston (Parent), 1742; died January 1, 1762.

Smyth, John—1693-1696.

Smyth, Richard—(1595)-1609; Alderman, 1608-1609; Sheriff, 1593-1594; Mayor, September, 1607; died May, 1609.

Snell, Oliver—1616-1632; Sheriff, 1623-1624; died 1632.

Snigge, Sir George—Recorder and Alderman, 1593-1603; M.P., 1597-1598, 1601, 1604-1605; died Nov. 11, 1617. (M.P., Cricklade, 1588-1589; Serjeant, 1605; Baron of the Exchequer, 1604-1617; Judge in Wales, 1608-1617; knighted, 1604.)

Span, John — 1797-1799; Sheriff, 1797-1798; Warden-Elect St. Stephen's Ringers for 1799; died February 12, 1799.

Span, Samuel—1780-1795; Sheriff, 1780-1781, 1791-1792; Master Merchant Venturers, 1777-1778; President Anchor, 1778; Master St. Stephen's Ringers, 1776; died December 2, 1795.

Span, Samuel—1799-1811; Sheriff, 1801-1802; Warden Merchant Venturers, 1801-1802; President Anchor, 1800; Warden St. Stephen's Ringers, 1800; killed in a duel, January 5, 1811.

Speed, Thomas—1685 (declined).

Stanton, Daniel—1826-1834; Sheriff, 1826-1827; Mayor, 1832-1833; President Dolphin, 1823; died January 15, 1834, aged 56.

ALPHABETICAL INDEX (III.)—*Continued.*

Stephens, George—1695-1718; Alderman, 1710-1718 (St. James 1710-1711, All Saints, 1711-1718); Sheriff, 1698-1699; Mayor, 1706-1707; Governor Incorporation of Poor, 1711-1712; Treasurer Incorporation of Poor, 1704-1705; died November, 1718.

Stephens, John—1660-1662; Alderman and Recorder, 1659-1662; M.P., 1660; died August 4, 1679, aged 76. (M.P., Tewkesbury, 1645-1648; Gloucestershire 1659.)

Stephens, Walter—1641-1654; Sheriff, 1645-1646.

Stephens, Walter—1656-1661, January-October, 1688; Alderman, 1688.

Stephens, William—1661 (not sworn).

Stevens, Thomas—1656-1679; Alderman, 1667-1679 (St. Thomas 1667-1672, Trinity 1672-1679); Sheriff (declined), 1660, 1661-1662; Mayor, 1668-1669; died March or April, 1679.

Stock, Thomas—1812 (declined). (See also pages 80 and 272.)

Stokes, Poole—1710-1714; Sheriff, 1711-1712; died 1714.

Stokes, Samuel—1712-1746; Sheriff, 1718-1719; Mayor, 1729-1730; died January, 1745-6.

Streamer, Richard—1661-1680; Alderman, 1672-1680 (St. James 1672-1675, St. Michael 1675-1680); Sheriff, 1663-1664; Mayor, 1673-1674; Master Merchant Venturers, 1672-1673; died 1680.

Struth, Sir William John—1812-1831; Mayor, 1814-1816; knighted, 1815; died February 1, 1850, aged 87.

Stubbe, Richard—1662-1675; Sheriff, 1671-1672; died 1675.

Sutton, James — 1811 (declined); President Colston (Parent), 1814; died June 8, 1824, aged 74.

Swymmer, Anthony—1684-1688, 1700-1719; Alderman, 1715-1719 (St. Michael); Sheriff, 1704-1705; Mayor, 1713-1714; Governor Incorporation of Poor, 1716-1717; Master Merchant Venturers, 1709-1710; died June 18, 1719.

Swymmer, Henry—1710-1732; Alderman, 1723-1732 (Maryleport 1723-1724, St. Stephen 1724-1732); Sheriff, 1713-1714; Mayor, 1722-1723; Governor Incorporation of Poor, 1726-1727; Treasurer Incorporation of Poor, 1718-1719; Master Merchant Venturers, 1718-1719; died September, 1732.

Swymmer, Henry—1746-1774; Sheriff, 1746-1747; Mayor, 1764-1765; Master Merchant Venturers, 1755-1756; died August 30, 1774.

Swymmer, John—1696-1700; Sheriff, 1698-1699; Warden Merchant Venturers, 1694-1695; died May or June, 1700.

ALPHABETICAL INDEX (III.)—*Continued.*

Swymmer, William—1677-January, 1688, October, 1688-1714; Alderman, 1687-1688, 1692-1714 (St. James 1692-1700, Trinity 1700-1714); Sheriff, 1679-1680; Mayor, 1686-1687; Governor Incorporation of Poor, 1698-1699; Treasurer Incorporation of Poor 1711-1712; Master Merchant Venturers, 1690-1691; Treasurer Merchant Venturers, 1691-1697; died about December, 1714.

Swymmer, William — 1726-1728 (not sworn); Master Merchant Venturers, 1717-1718.

Tayler, John—1624-1645; Alderman, 1640-1645 (St. Michael January-August, 1640, Trinity, 1640-1645); Sheriff, 1625-1626; Mayor, 1640-1641; M.P., 1642-1644; Warden Merchant Venturers, 1622-1623; Treasurer Merchant Venturers, 1626-1627; killed at siege of Bristol, September 9, 1645.

Tayler, John—1645 (not sworn).

Tayler, Richard—1712-1715; Sheriff, 1714-1715; died about November, 1715.

Taylor, Arthur—1715-1745; Alderman, 1735-1745 (All Saints 1735-1737, Trinity 1737-1739, St. Nicholas 1739-1745); Sheriff, 1719-1720; Mayor, 1731-1732; Governor Incorporation of Poor, 1735-1736; died March or April, 1745.

Thomas, James—February-October, 1688.

Thomas, John—1718-1723; Sheriff, 1723 (declined).

Thomson, John—1810 (declined); Warden Merchant Venturers, 1805-1807, died July 27, 1818.

Thorne, George—1611 (declined).

Thruston, John—1645 (not sworn); Chamberlain, 1662-1675; died 1675.

Tilly, Nicholas—1662-1673.

Tippett, Samuel—1661-1670.

Tocknell, Edward—1684-January, 1688, October, 1688-1698; Sheriff, 1686-1687; Chamberlain, 1698-1710; Master Merchant Venturers, 1685-1687.

Tomlinson, John—1614-1648; Alderman, 1635-1648 (St. Thomas); Sheriff, 1615-1616; Mayor, 1630-1631; Master Merchant Venturers, 1627-1628; Treasurer Merchant Venturers, 1618-1619; died January, 1647-8.

Tomlinson, Thomas—1611-1622; died early in 1621-2.

Tovey, Thomas—1663-1669; died about November, 1669.

Turner, William—1616-1631; Sheriff, 1617-1618; died about August, 1631.

Twyford, James—1681-January, 1688, October, 1688-1695; Sheriff, 1684-1685.

Tyler, Thomas—1703-1719; Sheriff, 1707-1708; President Gloucestershire Society, 1697; died 1719.

ALPHABETICAL INDEX (III.)—*Continued.*

Tyndall, John—1738 (not sworn), 1740-1741.

Tyndall, Onesiphorus—1703-1712; Sheriff, 1707-1708; President Gloucestershire Society, 1698; died August 27, 1748, aged 91.

Tyndall, Thomas—1762 (declined); died April 17, 1794.

Tyson, Edward—1645-1661; Alderman, 1656-1661 (Temple); Sheriff, 1646-1647; Mayor, 1659-1660 · Warden Merchant Venturers, 1647-1648.

Vaughan, Charles—1825-1829; died March 27, 1850, aged 67.

Vaughan, John—1810 (declined); President Dolphin, 1827; President Gloucestershire Society, 1828; died July 16, 1834.

Vaughan, Sir Richard—1801-1828; Alderman, 1810-1828 (St. Thomas 1810-1812, St. Nicholas 1812-1814, St. James 1814-1827, Maryleport 1827-1828); Sheriff, 1801-1802; Mayor, 1806-1807; Governor Incorporation of Poor, 1803-1806; Master Merchant Venturers, 1809-1810; President Dolphin, 1810; knighted, 1815; died October 16, 1833, aged 66.

Vawer, William—(1587)-1620; Alderman, (1599)-1620; Sheriff, 1587-1588; Mayor, 1601-1602; Warden Merchant Venturers, 1605-1606; died about January, 1619-20.

Vickris, Richard—1633-1643, 1645-1661; Alderman, 1646-1661 (St. Stephen 1646-1656, All Saints 1656-1661); Sheriff, 1636-1637; Mayor, 1646-1647; Master Merchant Venturers, 1648-1649.

Vickris, Robert—1650-1662; Sheriff, 1656-1657; Master Merchant Venturers, 1669-1670; Treasurer Merchant Venturers, 1656-1657.

Wade, Nathaniel—January-October, 1688; Town Clerk, January-October, 1688; Steward Sheriff's Court, 1705-1712; Deputy Governor Incorporation of Poor, 1704-1705; President Gloucestershire Society, 1693; died March, 1717-8.

Wait, Daniel—1798-1813; Alderman, 1808-1813 (St. Ewen); Sheriff, 1798-1799; Mayor, 1805-1806; Governor Incorporation of Poor, 1811-1813; died September 2, 1813.

Wait, William Killigrew—1834-1835; Sheriff, 1834-1835. (See also page 82.)

Walden, Thomas—April-October, 1688.

Walker, Charles Ludlow—1822-1835; Sheriff, 1824-1825, 1828-1829; Mayor, 1833-1834. (See also pages 82 and 273.)

Wall, Thomas—1646-1650; died September, 1650.

Wallis, Christopher—1724-1725; Treasurer Incorporation of Poor, 1713-1714.

Wallis, Ezekial—1620-1645; Alderman, 1637-1645 (Maryleport); Sheriff, 1623-1624; Mayor, 1638-1639.

ALPHABETICAL INDEX (III.)—*Continued.*

Wallis, James—April-October, 1688.

Wallis, Samuel—1686-January, 1688, November, 1688-1724; Alderman, 1700-1724 (St. Ewen, April-July, 1700, St. James 1700-1702, St. Nicholas 1702-1724); Sheriff, 1687-1688; Mayor, 1695-1696; Governor Incorporation of Poor, 1696-1698; died 1724.

Walter, Henry—1702-1737; Alderman, 1718-1737 (All Saints 1719-1725, St. Nicholas 1725-1737); Sheriff, 1704-1705; Mayor, 1715-1716; Governor Incorporation of Poor, 1725-1726; Treasurer Incorporation of Poor, 1706-1707; died October 25, 1737, aged 76.

Warren, Matthew—1613-1635; Sheriff, 1617-1618; Mayor, 1633-1634.

Warren, Matthew—1636-1655; Sheriff, 1639-1640.

Watson, William—1832 (declined), 1833-1835. (See also page 82.)

Watts, Henry—1701-1705, 1712-1721; Sheriff, 1712-1713; Mayor, 1720-1721; Master Merchant Venturers, 1714-1715 and August-November, 1716; Treasurer Merchant Venturers, 1709-1712; died September 13, 1721.

Watts, Stephen—1678-1684; Warden Merchant Venturers, 1678-1679.

Weare, George—1750-1778; Alderman, 1771-1778 (Redcliff 1771-1772, St. Thomas 1772-1778); Sheriff, 1750-1751; Mayor, 1767-1768; died November 7, 1778.

Weare, Henry—1755-1772; Sheriff, 1755-1756; died June 5, 1773.

Weare, John Fisher—1777-1816; Sheriff, 1777-1778, 1784-1785; Mayor (declined), 1794; Warden Merchant Venturers, 1778-1779; President Anchor, 1784; died January 24, 1816.

Weare, William—1762-1785; Sheriff, 1762-1763; Mayor, (declined), 1776; Warden Merchant Venturers, 1771-1772; died January 15, 1785.

Weare, William—1782-1835; Mayor (declined), 1795; Warden Merchant Venturers, 1783-1784; died December 24, 1836, aged 84.

Weaver, William—February-October, 1688.

Webb, Nathaniel—1679-1683; died about May, 1683.

Webb, Nathaniel—1703-1709; Sheriff, 1705-1706; Treasurer Incorporation of Poor, 1716-1717.

Webb, Samuel—1757 (not sworn), 1758-1777; Sheriff, 1758-1759; died March 8, 1777.

Webbe, John—(1582)-1613; Alderman, (1593)-1613; Sheriff, 1582-1583; Mayor, 1597-1598; died December, 1613.

Weekes, Buckler—1731-1772; Alderman, 1749-1772 (Castle 1749-1753, St. Thomas 1753-1772); Sheriff, 1732-1733, 1744-1745; Mayor, 1748-1749; died February 20, 1772.

ALPHABETICAL INDEX (III.)—*Continued.*

Wetherell, Sir Charles—1827-1835; Recorder, 1827-1846; Alderman, 1827-1835 (Trinity); died August 17, 1846, aged 76. (K.C., 1816; M.P., Oxford, 1824-1826; Hastings, 1826; Plympton, 1826-1830; Boroughbridge, 1830-1832; knighted, 1824; Solicitor-General, 1824-1826; Attorney-General, 1826-1827, 1828-1829.)

Wharton, Samuel—1667-1680; Sheriff, 1674-1675; Steward Gloucestershire Society, 1671; died 1680.

Whatley, Edward—1752-1779; Alderman. 1771-1779 (Trinity, October-November, 1771, Castle 1771-1779); Sheriff, 1752-1753; Mayor, 1768-1769; died November 7, 1779.

Whitchurch, Francis—1695-1718; Alderman, 1705-1718 (St. Michael 1705-1715, Trinity 1715-1716, St. Ewen 1716-1718); Sheriff, 1696-1697; Mayor, 1704-1705; Governor Incorporation of Poor, 1708-1710; died June 10, 1718.

White, George—(1599)-1613; Treasurer Merchant Venturers, 1609-1610; Warden Merchant Venturers, 1610-1611.

White, George—1645-1661; Alderman, 1658-1661 (Maryleport); Sheriff, 1647-1648.

White, George—1677-1684, 1688-1690; Sheriff, 1688-1689; died March 1689-90.

Whitehead, Henry—1702-1723; Alderman, 1716-1723 (St. James 1716-1719, Maryleport 1719-1723); Sheriff, 1703-1704; Mayor, 1714-1715; died October, 1723.

Whitehead, Thomas—1609-1613; Sheriff, 1610-1611; Chamberlain, May-September, 1613; Treasurer Merchant Venturers, 1610-1611.

Whitehead, William—February-October, 1688, 1696-1712; Alderman, 1711-1712 (St. James); Sheriff, 1699-1700; Mayor, 1707-1708; died February 25, 1711-12, aged 40.

Whitehead, William—1710-1721; Sheriff, 1714-1715; died February 25, 1720-1, aged 40.

Whiteing, John—1684-1688, 1689-1691.

Whitelocke, Bulstrode—Recorder and Alderman, 1651-1655: died January 28, 1675-6. (M.P. Stafford, 1626; Marlow, 1640-1653; Bucks, 1654-1655, 1656-1658; Attorney-General Duchy of Lancaster, 1644; Commissioner of Great Seal, 1648-1655, 1659; Keeper of Great Seal, 1659.)

Whitson, Christopher—1611-1638; Alderman, 1629-1638 (Temple); Sheriff, 1613-1614; Mayor, 1626-1627; died May, 1638.

Whitson, John—(1589)-1629; Alderman, 1600-1629 (All Saints); Sheriff, 1589-1590; Mayor, 1603-1604, 1615-1616; M.P., 1605-1611, 1614, 1620-1622, 1625, 1626; Master Merchant Venturers, 1606-1607, 1611-1612; died February 25, 1628-9, aged 71.

Wilcox, John—1795-1806; Sheriff, 1795-1796; died September 28, 1806.

ALPHABETICAL INDEX (III.)—*Continued.*

Wilcox, John Hillhouse—18051822; Alderman, 1816-1822 (Redcliff); Sheriff, 1805-1806, 1807 (declined); Mayor, 1809-1810, 1811-1812; Deputy Chamberlain, 1822-1824; Registrar Court of Conscience, 1824-1836; died December 31, 1836.

Willett, William—1656 (not sworn), 1661-1679; Sheriff, June-September, 1668; Master Merchant Venturers, 1670-1671; died about December, 1679.

Williams, Charles—1668-1681; Sheriff, 1675-1676; Warden Merchant Venturers, 1672-1673.

Williams, Rowland—1782-1798; Sheriff, 1782-1783, 1790-1791; Deputy Governor Incorporation of Poor, 1770-1771; died March 7, 1798.

Willoughby, John—1652-1673; Alderman, 1664-1673 (Redcliff); Sheriff, 1657-1658; Mayor, 1665-1666; Master Merchant Venturers, 1665-1666; Treasurer Merchant Venturers, 1654-1656; died about February, 1672-3.

Winpenny, John—1817 (declined); died August 12, 1824, aged 74.

Winstone, Robert—1687-1688.

Winstone, Thomas—1699-1700; Treasurer Incorporation of Poor, 1702-1703.

Winwood, John—1814 (declined). (See also page 83.)

Woodward, Daniel—1752-1755; Sheriff, 1752-1753; Treasurer Incorporation of Poor, 1745-1746; died March 14, 1755.

Woodward, Francis—1675-1682.

Woodward, Thomas—1635-1650; Sheriff, 1636-1637.

Worrall, George—1806 (declined); died May 6, 1840, aged 72.

Wraxall, Nathaniel—1721-1731; Sheriff, 1723-1724; Warden Merchant Venturers, 1722-1723; died 1731, aged 44.

Wright, John—September-October, 1645 (not sworn), 1661-1672; Alderman, 1669-1672 (St. Ewen); Sheriff, 1662-1663; died September, 1672.

Wright, Thomas—1616-1632; Sheriff, 1618-1619; Master Merchant Venturers, 1628-1629; Treasurer Merchant Venturers, 1619-1620; died 1632.

Wyatt, William—1635-1645; Sheriff, 1637-1638; Warden Merchant Venturers, 1622-1623; Treasurer Merchant Venturers, 1642-1643.

Yate, Andrew—1599-1602; died about August, 1602.

Yate, Henry—1611-1636; Alderman, 1634-1636 (Marylport); Sheriff, 1616-1617; Mayor, 1631-1632; died 1636.

Yate, Robert—1645-1661; Alderman, 1658-1661 (Trinity); Sheriff, 1648-1649; Master Merchant Venturers, 1656-1657; Treasurer Merchant Venturers, 1649-1650; died December 31, 1682, aged 67.

ALPHABETICAL INDEX (III.)—*Continued.*

Yate, Robert—1684-1737; Alderman, 1700-1737 (St. Thomas 1700-1703, St. Ewen 1703-1716, Trinity 1716-1737); Sheriff, 1685-1686; Mayor, 1693-1694; M.P., 1695-1710 (candidate 1690, 1710); Governor Incorporation of Poor, 1702-1703; Master Merchant Venturers, 1692-1694; Treasurer Merchant Venturers, 1665-1673, 1674-1677; died October 27, 1737.

Yate, William—(1580)-1603; Alderman, (1599)-1603; Sheriff, 1580-1581; Mayor, 1596-1597; died 1603.

Yeamans, John—1684-1688, 1689-1696; Sheriff, 1690-1691; Warden Merchant Venturers, 1684-1685.

Yeamans, Joseph—1662-1668.

Yeamans, Robert—1639-1643; Sheriff, 1641-1642; executed May 30, 1643, aged 37.

Yeamans, Sir Robert, Bart.—1661-1687; Alderman, 1672-1687 (St. Thomas); Sheriff, 1662-1663; Mayor, 1669-1670; Master Merchant Venturers, 1662-1663; knighted, 1663; created Baronet, 1666; died about February, 1686-7.

Yeamans, William—1646-1661; Sheriff, 1649-1650; Master Merchant Venturers, 1657-1658; Treasurer Merchant Venturers, 1651-1652.

Young, Charles—See Anderson.

Young, Edward—1661-1683; Sheriff, 1672-1673.

Young, John—1639-1658; Sheriff, 1645-1646; died about March, 1657-8.

Younge, William — 1604-1634; Alderman, 1623-1634 (Trinity); Sheriff, 1608-1609; Mayor, 1622-1623; died about February, 1633-4.

Index IV.— Persons not elected to, or Candidates for, Seats in the Corporation, 1599-1899.

Abbot, Lucas Charles Fudge—President Colston (Parent) for 1896 (declined).

Abraham, John—Master St. Stephen's Ringers, 1883.

Abyngdon, Richard—Mayor, 1525-1526, 1536-1537; M.P., 1529-1536; died July 17, 1543.

Acland, James—Parliamentary candidate, 1830; died June 21, 1876, aged 77. (Contested Hull, 1832.)

Acraman, Alfred John—Warden Merchant Venturers, 1857-1858; Official Assignee in Bankruptcy, 1842-1869; Vice-chairman Chamber of Commerce, 1857-1858; died July 18, 1880, aged 71.

Acraman, Daniel Wade—Warden St. Stephen's Ringers, 1802; died August 3, 1847, aged 72.

Acraman, John—President Colston (Parent), 1823; Warden St. Stephen's Ringers, 1813; died May 23, 1836, aged 64.

Acraman, William—Master St. Stephen's Ringers, 1796; died June 11, 1825, aged 85.

Acraman, William—Master St. Stephen's Ringers, 1820; died October 10, 1830, aged 61.

Adams, Richard—Master St. Stephen's Ringers, 1688.

Adams, Samuel—President Gloucestershire Society, 1752.

Adams, William Avery—Clerk to School Board, 1895.

Addie, Peter—City Estates Surveyor, 1897.

Addington, John—Proposed for nomination as J.P., 1856; died March 9, 1939, aged 78.

Aiken—See Chetwood-Aiken.

Aldridge, Richard—Warden St. Stephen's Ringers, 1789; died December 9, 1815, aged 72.

Aldridge, Thomas—Master St. Stephen's Ringers, 1787; died November, 1807, aged 82.

Aldworth, Robert—M.P., 1654-1659; Town Clerk, 1655-1676; died March 20, 1675-6. (M.P., Devizes, 1660-1661.)

Alexander, Philip Douglas—Warden St. Stephen's Ringers, 1858; died July 17, 1885, aged 54.

Aleyne, William—President Colston (Parent), 1760.

ALPHABETICAL INDEX (IV.)—*Continued.*

Alford, Rev. Josiah George—Member School Board, 1885-1895; Mayor's Chaplain, 1893-1894. (Minor Canon, 1873-1881; Vicar St. Nicholas, 1880-1895 · Vicar Stoke Bishop, 1895.)

Allard-Kemeys, Sir Robert Jones—Surgeon Infirmary, 1791-1810; died January 10, 1832. (Took the name of Kemeys, 1810; knighted, 1817.)

Allbut, Henry—Chief Constable, 1894.

Allen, Charles William—President Chamber of Commerce, 1887-1888.

Allen, James—District Surveyor, 1789-1792.

Allen, Rev. William Birkett—President Gloucestershire Society, 1858; died November 15, 1862. (Rector Winterbourne, 1835-1862.)

Allwood, Rev. Robert—Mayor's Chaplain, 1854-1855; died October 27, 1891, aged 89. (Minor Canon, 1826-1839; Rector St. James, Sydney, 1840-1884; Chancellor, Sydney, 1876-1884.)

Almond, Joseph—Master St. Stephen's Ringers, 1865; Vice-chairman Chamber of Commerce, 1867.

Ayles, Abraham—President Gloucestershire Society, 1721.

Ames, George Henry—President Anchor, 1819; died July 20, 1873, aged 86.

Ames, John Adams—Warden St. Stephen's Ringers, 1826; died March 6, 1841, aged 44.

Andrewes, Thomas—President Dolphin, 1812; Master St. Stephen's Ringers, 1798; died September 27, 1819, aged 70.

Andrews, Edward — President Gloucestershire Society, 1783; died September 14, 1786, aged 40.

Andrews, Edward — President Gloucestershire Society, 1799.

Andrews, John—Treasurer Incorporation of Poor, 1712-1713; Treasurer Infirmary, 1739-1740.

Ansford, Charles—Quay Warden, 1706-1711; Master St. Stephen's Ringers, 1693.

Apsley, Lord (Henry Bathurst)—President Gloucestershire Society, 1786; died July 26, 1834, aged 72. (M.P., Cirencester, 1783-1794; succeeded as Earl Bathurst, 1794; Lord of the Admiralty, 1783-1789; Lord of the Treasury, 1789-1791; Teller of the Exchequer, 1790-1834; Commissioner Board of Control, 1793-1802; Master of the Mint, 1804-1806; President of the Board of Trade, 1807-1812; Foreign Secretary, 1809; Colonial Secretary, 1812-1827; President of the Council, 1828-1830; Privy Councillor, 1790; K.G., 1817.)

Ariel, William—Corn Measurer, 1776-1793.

Armstrong, John—Surveyor Board of Health, 1851-1854; died March 17, 1854, aged 78.

ALPHABETICAL INDEX (IV.)—*Continued.*

Armstrong, William—District Surveyor, 1856-1858; died October 28, 1858.

Arrowsmith, James Williams—President Anchor, 1893; J.P., 1894.

Ash, Edward—Treasurer Infirmary, 1791-1808; died May 13, 1808.

Ash, Jarvis Holland—Warden St. Stephen's Ringers, 1840.

Ashe, Richard—Coroner, 1647-1666; died August 21, 1666, aged 70.

Ashley, Ruscombe Washer—J.P., 1894.

Ashmead, Frederick—Surveyor Board of Health, 1854-1894; died August 23, 1898.

Ashmead, Thomas — President Gloucestershire Society, 1738.

Atchley, George Frederick—Surgeon General Hospital, 1668-1881.

Atkins, Thomas—Master St. Stephen's Ringers, 1682.

Attwood, Henry—President Colston (Parent), 1838; died October 8, 1841.

Attwood, Jacob William—Candidate for Receiver of Town Dues, 1852.

Attwood, William—Warden Merchant Venturers, 1715-1716.

Audain, Rev. John—Mayor's Chaplain, 1785.

Austin, James Valentine—Judge County Court, 1892; President Grateful, 1898; J.P., 1894.

Averay, John—President Dolphin, 1752; died February 26, 1774.

Backwell, Henry—Water Bailiff, 1685-1703; died 1703.

Bagg, Stephen—President Colston (Parent), 1765; President Gloucestershire Society, 1758; died February 16, 1776.

Bailey, James—President Colston (Parent), 1869 (Treasurer, 1862-1867); died March 22, 1877, aged 63.

Bailey, William Hillier—President Colston (Parent), 1857 (Treasurer, 1857-1862); died February 28, 1862, aged 57.

Baillie, Hugh Duncan—President Anchor, 1807; Parliamentary candidate, 1818; Provincial Grand Master Freemasons, 1830-1845; died June 21, 1866, aged 89. (M.P., Rye, 1830-1831; Honiton, 1835-1847.)

Baillie, James Evan—M.P., 1830-1835 (candidate, 1820, 1835); President Anchor, 1815; died June 14, 1863, aged 81. (M.P., Tralee, 1813-1818.)

Baillie, Peter—President Anchor, 1810; Governor Incorporation of Poor, 1801-1803; died September 1, 1811. (M.P., Inverness, 1807-1811.)

ALPHABETICAL INDEX (IV.)—*Continued.*

Baillie, William Montague—Sheriff, 1859-1860; Vice-President Chamber of Commerce, 1859-1861.
Baker, John—Haven Master, 1773-1782; died 1782.
Baker, Samuel—Water Bailiff, 1853-1894; Quay Warden, 1861-1894; died October 20, 1896, aged 78.
Baker, Slade—Governor Incorporation of Poor, 1764-1766; died October 26, 1784.
Baker, Thomas Watkins—Master St. Stephen's Ringers, 1879.
Baker, William Mills—Charity Trustee, 1875-1890; Vice-chairman Chamber of Commerce, 1872-1873; J.P., 1887; died July 6, 1890, aged 59.
Ball, Edmund—Candidate for School Board, 1880; died October 7, 1888, aged 62.
Ball, James Taylor—President Grateful, 1822; died January 13, 1859, aged 73.
Ball, Rev. William—Master Grammar School, 1662-1670 (Usher, 1655-1662); died 1670.
Ball, William—President Grateful, 1810; died April 7, 1845, aged 78.
Ballard, John—Treasurer Incorporation of Poor, 1818-1820; died July 1, 1828.
Bally, Joseph—Master St. Stephen's Ringers, 1819; died July 27, 1836.
Barclay, Wilfrid Martin—Assistant Surgeon General Hospital, 1888-1893; Surgeon, 1893.
Barnard, Fulko Tovey—Auditor, 1836-1839; died November 25, 1867, aged 70.
Barnes, Robert Gray — Master St. Stephen's Ringers, 1867; died October 18, 1897.
Baron, Barclay Josiah—Physician General Hospital, 1884-1892 (Specialist for throat and nose diseases, 1892).
*Barrett, William—President Colston (Parent), 1774; candidate for Surgeon Infirmary, 1754, 1759; died October 13, 1789.
Barrett, William—Deputy Governor Incorporation of Poor, 1832-1833.
Barrow, James Syms—Warden Merchant Venturers, 1833-1834; died August 14, 1843, aged 54.
Barrow, Rev. George Neale—Mayor's Chaplain, 1832-1833, 1843-1844, 1852-1853; died February 16, 1872, aged 63. (Minor Canon, 1832-1841; Rector of St. John's, 1834-1835; Vicar St. Nicholas, 1841-1855; Rector West Kington, 1855-1872.)
Bartley, Alfred Collett—Candidate for Apothecary, Infirmary, 1810.
Bartley, Robert Trout Hawley—Candidate for Surgeon, General Hospital, 1853; died July 21, 1882, aged 62.
Batchelor, Thomas—Deputy Governor Incorporation of Poor, 1798-1801, 1806-1807.

*The Historian of Bristol.

ALPHABETICAL INDEX (IV.)—*Continued.*

Bathurst, Earl—See Apsley.

Bathurst, Right Hon. Charles—M.P., 1796-1812; President Gloucestershire Society, 1807; died August 13, 1831, aged 78. (M.P., Monmouth, 1790-1796; Bodmin, 1812-1818; Harwich, 1818-1823; Privy Councillor, 1801; Treasurer of the Navy, 1801-1803; Secretary at War, 1803-1804; Master of the Mint, 1806-1807; Chancellor of the Duchy of Lancaster, 1812-1823; changed name from Bragge to Bathurst, 1804.)

Bathurst, Thomas—President Gloucestershire Society, 1780; died November 9, 1791.

Batten, Herbert Cary George—President Grateful, 1896. (Contested West Dorset, 1885, 1886.)

Battersby—See Harford-Battersby.

Baugh, Edmund—Master Merchant Venturers, 1731-1732.

Baugh, Joseph—Master St. Stephen's Ringers, 1692; Water Bailiff, 1708-1724; died 1724.

Baugh, Stephen—Master St. Stephen's Ringers, 1755.

Bawn, Thomas—Secretary Infirmary, 1771-1790; died December 18, 1790.

Bayly, John Jasper Leigh — Sheriff, 1849-1850; died November 20, 1860, aged 56.

Bayntun, Daniel—President Gloucestershire Society, 1821; President Dolphin for 1829 (declined); died May 29, 1835, aged 86.

Beach—See Hicks-Beach.

Beard, John James—Deputy Governor Incorporation of Poor, April-May, 1830; died May 26, 1830, aged 51.

Beaton, John—Master St. Stephen's Ringers, 1744; died 1767.

Beatty, William Crofton — Physician, General Hospital, January-November, 1849; died about 1891.

Beaufort (1st), Duke of (Henry Somerset)—Lord-Lieutenant, 1672-1688; died January 21, 1700. (M.P., Monmouthshire, 1660, 1661-1667; succeeded as Marquis of Worcester, 1667; created Duke, 1682; Lord-Lieutenant of Gloucester, Hereford, and Monmouthshires, 1660-1688; Lord-President of Wales, 1672-1688; Privy Councillor, 1672; K.G., 1672.)

Beaufort (2nd), Duke of (Henry Somerset)—Lord-Lieutenant, 1712-1714; died May 24, 1714, aged 30. (Privy Councillor, 1710; Lord-Lieutenant Hants, 1710-1714; K.G., 1712; Captain Gentlemen Pensioners, 1712-1714.)

Beaufort (5th), Duke of (Henry Somerset)—President Colston (Parent), 1790; President Gloucestershire Society, 1770; died October 11, 1803, aged 59. (Master of Horse to the Queen, 1768-1770; Lord-Lieutenant of Monmouthshire, 1771-1803; Lord-Lieutenant of Brecknock, 1787-1803; Lord-Lieutenant of Leicestershire, 1787-1799; K.G., 1786.)

ALPHABETICAL INDEX (IV.)—Continued.

Beaufort, (6th) Duke of (Henry Charles Somerset)—M.P. (as Marquis of Worcester), 1790-1796; High Steward, 1834-1835; President Colston (Parent), 1804; President Gloucestershire Society, 1796; President General Hospital, 1834-1835; died Nov. 23, 1835, aged 69. (M.P., Monmouth, 1788-1790; Gloucestershire, 1796-1803; succeeded to Dukedom, 1803; Lord-Lieutenant Brecknock and Monmouthshire, 1803-1835; K.G., 1805.)

Beaufort (7th), Duke of (Henry Somerset) — High Steward, 1836-1853; President Gloucestershire Society, 1825; died November 17, 1853, aged 61. (M.P., Monmouth, 1813-1331, 1831-1832; West Gloucestershire, 1835; succeeded to Dukedom, 1835; K.G., 1842; Lord of the Admiralty, 1816-1819.)

Beaufort, (8th) Duke of (Henry Somerset) — High Steward, 1854; President Dolphin, 1897; President Gloucestershire Society, 1865; J.P., 1898; died April 30, 1899, aged 75. (M.P., East Gloucestershire, 1846-1853; succeeded to Dukedom, 1853; Master of the Horse, 1858-1859, 1866-1868; Lord-Lieutenant of Monmouthshire, 1867; K.G., 1867; Privy Councillor, 1858.)

Becher, George—Warden Merchant Venturers, 1747-1748.

Beck, Lancelot—Warden St. Stephen's Ringers, 1818; died September 1, 1849, aged 80.

Beckford, Richard—M.P., 1754-1756; died January 24, 1756.

Beddoe, John—Physician Infirmary, 1862-1873.

Bedell, Benjamin—Assessor, 1878.

Bedford, Earl of (William Russell)—Lord-Lieutenant, 1642-1643; died September 7, 1700, aged 87. (K.B., 1626; K.G., 1672; M.P., Tavistock, 1640-1641; created Duke of Bedford, 1694.)

Bedingfield, James—Apothecary, Infirmary, 1810-1816; died April 22, 1860, aged 72.

Beech, Joseph—Secretary Infirmary, 1752-1771; died February 2, 1771.

Beele, Jacob—Warden Merchant Venturers, 1690-1691

Bees, Sidney Gray—President Colston (Parent), 1886.

Bell, James—Chairman Chamber of Commerce, 1872-1873; died July 13, 1878, aged 56.

Bell, William — President-Elect Colston (Parent) for 1830; died 1830.

Beloe, Henry Willoughby—Master Merchant Venturers, 1890-1891.

Beloe, William Charles—J.P., 1889.

Bence, Isaac—Treasurer Incorporation of Poor, 1782-1784; Warden Merchant Venturers, 1795-1796; died May 20, 1797.

Benham, Henry Arthur—Medical Superintendent Lunatic Asylum, 1890.

ALPHABETICAL INDEX (IV.)—*Continued.*

Bennett, Arthur James Williams — Master St. Stephen's Ringers, 1884; died January 7, 1891, aged 41.

Bennett, William—Quay Warden, 1758-1773; died April 9, 1773.

Bennett, William—Governor Incorporation of Poor, 1889-1891.

Bere, Montagu—Recorder, 1870-1872; died October 19, 1887, aged 85. (Q.C., 1869; County Court Judge, Cornwall, 1872-1887.)

Berjew, Rev. John—Mayor's Chaplain, 1771-1775; died January 17, 1790. (Vicar St. Leonard's, 1750-1755; All Saints, 1755-1790.)

Berjew, John Paul—President Dolphin, 1801; died November 16, 1833, aged 85.

Berjew, Thomas—President Dolphin, 1776; died Oct. 22, 1782.

Berkeley, (2nd) Earl of (George Berkeley)—Lord-Lieutenant, 1694-1710; died September 24, 1710, aged 61. (M.P., Gloucester, 1679-1681; K.B., 1661; summoned to House of Peers, 1689; succeeded to Earldom, 1698; Privy Councillor, 1694; Envoy to The Hague, 1689-1695; Lord Justice of Ireland, 1699-1700.)

Berkeley, (3rd) Earl of (James Berkeley)—Lord-Lieutenant, 1710-1711, 1714-1736; High Steward, 1715-1736; died September 2, 1736. (M.P., Gloucester, 1701-1702; summoned to House of Peers, 1705; succeeded to Earldom, 1710; Privy Councillor, 1717; K.G., 1718; Lord of the Bedchamber, 1714-1727; Vice Admiral of Great Britain, 1718-1736; First Lord of the Admiralty, 1717-1727.)

Berkeley, (4th) Earl of (Augustus Berkeley) — Lord-Lieutenant, 1737-1755; died January 9, 1755, aged 39. (K.G., 1739.)

Berkeley, (5th) Earl of (Frederick Augustus Berkeley)—Lord-Lieutenant, 1766-1810; President Gloucestershire Society, 1776; died August 8, 1810, aged 65.

Berkeley, Francis Henry Fitzhardinge—M.P., 1837-1870; President Anchor, 1843; died March 10, 1870, aged 75.

Berkeley, Hon. Sir George Cranfield—President Gloucestershire Society, 1785; died February 25, 1818, aged 64. (Admiral; K.B., 1813; G.C.B., 1815; M.P., Gloucestershire, 1783-1810; Surveyor-General of Ordnance, 1789-1795.)

Berkeley, Norborne—Lord-Lieutenant, 1764-1766; President Colston (Parent), 1755; died October 15, 1770, aged 52. (M.P., Gloucestershire, 1741-1763; confirmed in Barony of Bottetourt, 1764; Governor of Virginia, 1768-1770.)

Bernard, Abraham—President Grateful, 1766.

Bernard, David Edward—Assistant Surgeon Infirmary, 1873-1876.

ALPHABETICAL INDEX (IV.)—*Continued.*

Berrard, James Fogo—Physician Infirmary, 1843-1856; died May 6, 1878.

Berrard, Ralph Mountague—Surgeon Infirmary, 1854-1871; died August 8, 1871.

Berrow, William—President Colston (Parent), 1743; Governor Incorporation of Poor, 1746-1748; Treasurer Incorporation of Poor, 1736-1737; died June 2, 1765.

Berry, Samuel—Warden St. Stephen's Ringers, 1758.

Bessell, James—Governor Incorporation of Poor, 1877-1879; died August 30, 1889.

Bevan, George Edward—Chairman Chamber of Commerce 1859-1860.

Biddulph, Rev. Thomas Tregenna—Mayor's Chaplain, 1822-1823; died May 19, 1838, aged 75. (Vicar St. James, 1799-1838.)

Bigg, Lionel Oliver—Secretary Chamber of Commerce, 1824-1848; Master St. Stephen's Ringers (declined) for 1827; died August 30, 1870, aged 77.

Bigg, Robert—Master St. Stephen's Ringers, 1804; died January 7, 1819.

Birch, Rev. Joseph—Mayor's Chaplain, 1860-1861; died May 4, 1871. (Perpetual Curate Brighouse, 1842-1862; Vicar West Teignmouth, 1862-1871.)

Bird, Edward—Master St. Stephen's Ringers, 1810; died August 21, 1838, aged 75.

Bird, Fenwick—President Dolphin, 1765; died June 2, 1813, aged 86.

Birtill, John—Deputy Governor Incorporation of Poor, 1804-1805, 1808-1809; died October 9, 1809.

Bishop, George—Parliamentary candidate, 1654.

Bishop, Joseph—Chief Constable, 1836-1839; died May 5, 1839, aged 40.

Bissell, James Broad—Contested East Bristol, 1885.

Blaake, Henry—Steward of Sheriff's Court, 1712-1721; Town Clerk, 1721-1731; died July 10, 1731. (M.P., Calne, 1695-1702.)

Blackwell, Andrew—Water Bailiff, 1724-1726.

Blackwell, John—Master Merchant Venturers, 1801-1802; died January 19, 1815.

Blackwell, Samuel — President Gloucestershire Society, 1784; died April 30, 1785. (M.P., Cirencester, 1774-1785.)

Blackwell, Thomas Evans—Superintendent of Dock Works, 1852-1855; died June, 1863, aged 43.

Blagden, Thomas—Vice-Chamberlain, 1740-1751; died 1751.

Blake, Richard—Treasurer Incorporation of Poor, 1741-1742; President Colston (Parent), 1758; President Gloucestershire Society, 1746; died January 3, 1771, aged 70.

ALPHABETICAL INDEX (IV.)—*Continued.*

Blake, Rev. William—Mayor's Chaplain, 1785-1786.

Blanch, John—Master St. Stephen's Ringers, 1684.

Blathwayt, William—President Gloucestershire Society, 1824; died February 25, 1839.

Bleeck, Alfred—Warden St. Stephen's Ringers, 1835; President Colston (Parent) for 1845 (declined); died April 13, 1870, aged 71.

Bletchley, John—Deputy Governor Incorporation of Poor, 1784-1785; died October, 1805.

Board, Edmund Comer—Infirmary, Assistant House Surgeon, 1860-1863; House Surgeon, 1863-1870; Assistant Surgeon, January-September, 1871; Surgeon, 1871-1892.

Bompas, Charles Smith—Candidate for Surgeon, General Hospital, 1843 (House Surgeon, 1840-1841.)

Bompas, George Gwinnett—President Anchor, 1834; died February 25, 1847, aged 58.

Bonbonous, James—Master Merchant Venturers, 1766-1767; Master St. Stephen's Ringers, 1755; died April 8, 1797.

Bonbonous, Joseph—Master Merchant Venturers, 1802-1803; Master St. Stephen's Ringers, 1815; died December 11, 1822.

Bonython, John—Physician Infirmary, 1757-1761; died November 15, 1761, aged 66.

Booth, Rev. James—Principal Bishop's College, 1840-1841; died April 15, 1878, aged 71. (Chairman Society of Arts, 1855-1857.)

Borlase, John Bingham—Apothecary Infirmary, 1779-1779.

Bosher, Charles—President Grateful, 1807; died July 1, 1812.

Bosworth, W. H.—Secretary Infirmary, January-April, 1849.

Bottetourt, Lord—See Berkeley, Norborne.

Bound, Robert—Deputy Governor Incorporation of Poor, 1712-1715.

Bound, Robert—Warden Merchant Venturers, 1750-1751; Master St. Stephen's Ringers, 1748; died April 22, 1752.

Bourne, Edward—Water Bailiff, 1752-1774; died May 8, 1774.

Boutflower, Charles Edward Douglas—Deputy Governor Incorporation of Poor, 1898; Chairman Bristol Guardians, 1899.

Bowden, Richard—President Grateful, 1801; died July 11, 1808.

Bowden, Samuel—President Dolphin, 1819; died January 1, 1834, aged 75.

ALPHABETICAL INDEX (IV.)—*Continued.*

Bowdich, Thomas—Master St. Stephen's Ringers, 1803.

Bowen, William—Warden Merchant Venturers, 1748-1749.

Bowgin, John—President Grateful, 1823; died October 7, 1830, aged 55.

Bowles, Rev. George Downing—Mayor's Chaplain, 1813-1814.

Bowles, Francis Cheyne—Surgeon Infirmary, 1806-1807; died May 18, 1807.

Bowley, Rev. James William Lyon—Mayor's Chaplain, 1867-1869; died January 1, 1871, aged 44. (Vicar St. Philip, 1864-1871.)

Bowman, Rev. Thomas—Mayor's Chaplain, 1861-1862; Principal Bishop's College, 1860-1861; died January 26, 1881, aged 61.

Bowrey, John—Quay Warden, 1672-1674; died 1674.

Bowsher, James—Vice-Chairman Clifton Guardians, 1863-1866.

Bowyer, James—President Gloucestershire Society, 1747-1748; Master St. Stephen's Ringers, 1750.

Boyce, Rev. Thomas White—Chaplain General Hospital, 1871-1874; died June, 1890. (Rector St. Werburgh, 1872-1879.)

Bradburn, Henry—President Dolphin, 1754; died September 24, 1768.

Bradford, George—Coroner, 1722-1753; died June 25, 1755.

Bragge, Charles—President Colston (Parent), 1756; died November 20, 1777.

Bragge, Right Hon. Charles—See Bathurst.

Bragge, John Delaroche—House Surgeon General Hospital, 1840-1841; died May 9, 1875, aged 58.

Bremner, James—Deputy Governor Incorporation of Poor, 1868-1870; died February 10, 1890, aged 86.

Brenan, Rev. James Eustace—Member of School Board, January-November, 1895. (Vicar Emmanuel, Clifton, 1892.)

Brice, Rev. Durbin—Mayor's Chaplain, 1837-1838; died January 14, 1839, aged 25.

Brice, Rev. Edward Cowell—Mayor's Chaplain, 1824-1825; died May 29, 1881, aged 86. (Vicar Great Newnham, 1847-1881.)

Brice, Henry—Warden Merchant Venturers, 1847-1848; died March 28, 1882, aged 67.

Brice, Richard Dawbney—Master Merchant Venturers, 1832-1833; died December 16, 1838.

Brice, Samuel—Master Merchant Venturers, 1815-1816; died February 28, 1842.

ALPHABETICAL INDEX (IV.)—*Continued.*

Brice, Thomas Durbin—Master Merchant Venturers, 1829-1830; died February 25, 1855, aged 70.

Brice, William—Clerk to Justices of the Peace, 1836-1875; Town Clerk, 1874-1880; Master Merchant Venturers, 1852-1853; President Chamber of Commerce, 1853; died March 14, 1887, aged 74.

Brice, William Diaper—Mayor's Clerk, 1807-1810; City Solicitor, 1812-1849; Clerk of Arraigns, 1820-1835; Clerk of Requests, 1816-1847; died February 18, 1849.

Brice, Worthington—Master St. Stephen's Ringers, 1759; died October 4, 1765.

Brickdale, John—Governor Incorporation of Poor, 1722-1725; died October 25, 1766, aged 89.

Brickdale, John—Governor Incorporation of Poor, 1756-1758; died November 2, 1765.

Bridges, Edward—Apothecary Infirmary, 1752-1774; died March, 1774.

Bridges, George Henry—President Gloucestershire Society, 1888.

Bridges, William Richard—Candidate for Apothecary Infirmary, 1847; died January 29, 1856, aged 31.

Bridle, Robert—Deputy Governor Incorporation of Poor, 1751-1752; President Dolphin, 1773; died August 25, 1780.

Bright, Benjamin Heywood—President Anchor, 1821; died August 4, 1843, aged 55. (Contested Oldham, 1832.)

Bright, George—Sheriff, 1875-1876.

Bright, Henry—M.P., 1820-1826; President Anchor, 1825; died March 26, 1869, aged 83.

Bright, Rev. John Henry—Mayor's Chaplain, 1872-1874, 1877-1893, 1895-1896, 1898.

Bright, Lowbridge—Governor Incorporation of Poor, 1792-1794; President Colston (Parent) for 1807 (declined); died July 30, 1818, aged 78.

Bright, Richard—President Dolphin, 1877; died February 28, 1878, aged 56. (M.P., East Somerset, 1868-1878.)

Brigstocke, Henry—Surgeon General Hospital, 1831-1845; died October 4, 1868, aged 69.

Brittan, Rev. Charles—Chaplain General Hospital, 1860-1869; died April 18, 1897. (Vicar St. Peter, Clifton, 1872-1876; Vicar Darley Abbey, 1876-1897.)

Brittan, Frederick—Physician Infirmary, 1855-1875; died February 15, 1891, aged 67.

Broad, John Stroud—Auditor, 1840-July, 1841; died July 20, 1841.

ALPHABETICAL INDEX (IV.)—*Continued.*

Broderip, Edmund—President Dolphin, 1763; died September 9, 1779.

Broderip, William—Master St. Stephen's Ringers, 1784; died October 19, 1826, aged 79.

Broke, Sir David—Recorder, 1541-1549; M.P., 1542-1544; died 1558. (Knighted, 1553; Serjeant, 1541; King's Serjeant, 1551; Chief Baron Exchequer, 1553-1558.)

Bromby, Rev. John Edward—Acting Principal Bristol College, 1839-1840; died Mar. 5, 1889, aged 80. (Principal Elizabeth College, Guernsey, 1847-1855; Head Master Melbourne Grammar School, 1858-1875.)

Broom, William—Warden St. Stephen's Ringers, 1800.

Broughton, Arthur—Physician Infirmary, 1780-1786; died May 29, 1796.

Broughton, Lord—See Hobhouse, Sir John Cam.

Brown, Abraham—Deputy Governor Incorporation of Poor, 1768-1769; died March 9, 1786.

Brown, Charles—President Dolphin, 1795; died June 26, 1802.

Brown, Edmund—Steward Sheriff's Court, 1731-1738; President Gloucestershire Society, 1730; died 1738.

Brown, Francis—Governor Incorporation of Poor, 1750-1752; Treasurer Incorporation of Poor, 1748-1750; President Colston (Parent), 1769; died Jan. 24, 1770, aged 67.

Brown, Rev. James—Usher Grammar School, 1759-1764; died June 6, 1798. (Minor Canon, 1756-1798; Precentor, 1793-1798.)

Brown, Samuel Woolcott—J.P., 1863; died November 7, 1881, aged 63.

Brown, William—J.P., 1850; died January 19, 1896, aged 91.

Brown, William Henry—Warden-Elect St. Stephen's Ringers, 1852; died June 11, 1852, aged 44.

Browne, Henry—President-Elect Anchor for 1826 (resigned); died October 16, 1834.

Browne, Joseph—Warden Merchant Venturers, 1714-1715.

Bruce, William—Warden Merchant Venturers, 1823-1824.

Bruce, Rev. William Samuel—Member School Board, 1882-1885. (Rector St. John's, 1871-1885; Vicar South Petherton, 1885-1892.)

Bruton, Leonard—Secretary Chamber of Commerce, 1853-1887; Secretary Free Port Association, 1846-1850; died January 24, 1887, aged 75.

ALPHABETICAL INDEX (IV.)—*Continued*.

Bryan, Cornelius—Water Bailiff, 1798-1820; died April 15, 1822.

Bryan, George—President Gloucestershire Society, 1794.

Bryant, George Squier—Vice-President Chamber of Commerce 1875-1877; died December 6, 1877.

Bryant, John—Corn Measurer, 1810-1825.

Bryant, William—Vice-Chairman Barton Regis Guardians, April-June, 1895; died June 23, 1895.

Buck, Rev. Charles—Chaplain General Hospital, 1834-1849; died October 20, 1858. (Rector St. Stephen, 1830-1858.)

Buckhurst, Lord—See Dorset.

Buckler, Thomas—Corn Measurer, 1748-1749; Quay Warden, 1749-1758.

Budd, William—Physician Infirmary, 1847-1862; died January 9, 1880, aged 68.

Budge, Richard—Quay Warden, 1712-1735; died 1735.

Budgett, William Henry—Member School Board, 1871-1880; J.P., 1878.

Bulgin, William—President Grateful, 1791; died September 27, 1831, aged 73.

Bull, Rev. John—Mayor's Chaplain, 1789-1791.

Bullock, Rev. Charles Penry — Mayor's Chaplain, 1808-1809, 1814-1818, 1819-1821; died September 9, 1849. Perpetual Curate St. Paul, 1822-1849.)

Burder, George Forster—Physician General Hospital 1856-1884; died February 6, 1892, aged 67.

Burges, Daniel — Clerk of Arraigns, 1788-1791; died April 10, 1791.

Burges, Daniel—City Solicitor, 1822-1836; Mayor's Clerk, 1823-1836; Town Clerk, 1836-1849; J.P., 1850; died April 16, 1864, aged 88.

Burges, Daniel—City Solicitor, 1836-1849; Clerk to Justices of the Peace, 1836-1849; Town Clerk, 1849-1874; Master St. Stephen's Ringers, 1853; died November 10, 1874, aged 64.

Burges, Daniel Travers—Town Clerk, 1880; Clerk to Sanitary Authority, 1887.

Burges, Rev. Frank—Vice-Chairman Clifton Guardians, 1867-1875; died July 17, 1875, aged 62.

Burgess, William John—Secretary General Hospital, 1860-1869.

Burghley, Lord (William Cecil)—High Steward, 1588-1598; died August 4, 1598. (Secretary of State, 1549-1553, 1558-1572; Lord High Treasurer, 1572-1598; created Peer, 1572; K.G., 1572.)

ALPHABETICAL INDEX (IV.)—*Continued.*

Burgum, Henry—Treasurer Incorporation of Poor, 1774-1776; President Grateful, 1767; President Gloucestershire Society, 1769; died June 5, 1789.

Burke, Right Hon. Edmund—M.P., 1774-1780; died July 9, 1797, aged 68. (M.P., Wendover, 1765-1774; Malton, 1774, 1780-1794; Paymaster-General, March-July, 1782, April-December, 1783; Privy Councillor, 1782.)

Burroughs, Jeremiah—Collector of Customs till 1758; died October 23, 1759.

Burrus, Nicholas—Sword Bearer, 1667-1677.

Bush, Edward—Chairman Water Works Company, 1886.

Bush, Henry Frederick Tobin—Master Merchant Venturers, 1891-1892.

Bush, James Arthur—Sword Bearer, 1883.

Bush, James Paul—Infirmary House Physician, 1882-1883; House Surgeon, 1883-1884 Assistant Surgeon, 1885-1889; Surgeon, 1889.

Bush, John—President Gloucestershire Society, 1762; died November 11, 1766.

Bush, Robert—President Gloucestershire Society, 1767; died January 31, 1800.

Bush, Robert Hilhouse—President Gloucestershire Society, 1890; died April 5, 1895, aged 65.

Bush, William Harrington—President Gloucestershire Society, 1886.

Butcher, Samuel—Warden St. Stephen's Ringers, 1855.

Butcher, William—Master St. Stephen's Ringers, 1860.

Butler, Robert—M.P., 1558.

Butler, Thomas—Member School Board, 1897-1898.

Butt, William Henry—Treasurer Colston (Parent), 1885-1890; died February 1, 1892, aged 54.

Butterton, Rev. George Ash—Vice-Principal Bristol College, 1831-1834; died August 3, 1891, aged 86. Head Master Uppingham, 1639-1646; Giggleswick, 1846-1859; Rector North Cleobury, 1859-1866.)

Cadell, William—Vice-Chamberlain, 1751-1754.

Cadogan, Francis—Master St. Stephen's Ringers, 1704.

Cadogan, William—Physician Infirmary, 1747-1752; died February 26, 1797, aged 86.

Caldicott, Rev. John William—Member School Board 1871-1883 (vice-chairman 1880-1883); Mayor's Chaplain, 1866-1867, 1874-1875; Head Master Grammar School, 1860-1883; died November 6, 1895, aged 66. (Rector Shipston-on-Stour, 1883-1895.)

ALPHABETICAL INDEX (IV.)—Continued.

Callender, Richard Boucher—President Grateful, 1846; died June 4, 1853, aged 53.

Cambridge, George—Candidate School Board, 1898, 1899.

Campbell, David—Master St. Stephen's Ringers, 1747; died September 16, 1768.

Campbell, Rev. George—President Colston (Parent) for 1868 (declined); Chaplain General Hospital, 1849-1855; died July 6, 1879. (Vicar St. Mark, New Swindon, 1852-1879.)

Camplin, Richard—Deputy Governor Incorporation of Poor, 1752-1753.

Cann, John—Warden Merchant Venturers, 1684-1685.

Cann, Sir William, Bart.—Steward Sheriff's Court, 1721-1731; Town Clerk, 1731-1755; President Gloucestershire Society, 1729; died March 28, 1755. (Succeeded to Baronetcy, 1748.)

Cantle, Joseph—President Grateful, 1769.

Capper, Samuel—Deputy Governor Incorporation of Poor, 1809-1810.

Careless, Nathaniel—Registrar Court of Conscience, 1715-1740; President Gloucestershire Society, 1733; died 1740.

Carpenter, Alfred—Contested North Bristol, 1886; died January 27, 1892, aged 68. (Contested Reigate Division of Surrey, 1885.)

Carr, William—Sheriff, 1545-1546; Mayor, 1560-1561; M.P., 1559, 1563-1567; died 1575.

Carrick, Andrew—Physician Infirmary, 1810-1834; President-Elect Dolphin for 1837; died June 14, 1837.

Carter, Rev. James—City Librarian, 1809-1815; died October 24, 1854, aged 75. (Minor Canon, 1811-1824; Vicar Bathford, 1824-1854.)

Carter, Thomas—Warden St. Stephen's Ringers, 1817.

Cartwright, Frederick Fox—Clerk of the Peace, 1878; President Grateful, 1881; Master St. Stephen's Ringers, 1886.

Carwardine, Thomas—Infirmary House Surgeon, 1895-1897; Assistant Surgeon, 1897.

Casamajor, Henry—Master Merchant Venturers, 1758-1759; died December, 1775.

Casamajor, Henry—Warden Merchant Venturers, 1778-1779; died January, 1824, aged 75.

Casamajor, Lewis—Warden Merchant Venturers, 1735-1736; died April, 1743.

Cassin, Henry—Auditor, August, 1841-1842.

Castelman, John—Surgeon Infirmary, 1754-1799; died March 31, 1801.

Castle, Edward James—Recorder, 1897. (Q.C., 1888.)

ALPHABETICAL INDEX (IV.)—*Continued.*

Castle, Michael Bowring—Master St. Stephen's Ringers, 1897.

Catcott, Rev. Alexander Stopford—Master Grammar School, 1722-1744; Chaplain St. Mark's, 1722-1745; died November 23, 1749. (Rector St. Stephen, 1744-1749.)

Cave, Sir Charles Daniel, Bart.—Sheriff, 1862-1863; President Dolphin, 1895; President Gloucestershire Society, 1866; President Infirmary, 1880. (Created Baronet, 1896.)

Cave, John—Governor Incorporation of Poor, 1780-1782; President Colston (Parent), 1793; Warden Merchant Venturers, 1784-1785; died March 6, 1800, aged 63.

Cave, Rev. Oliver—Mayor's Chaplain, 1828-1829; died February 27, 1864, aged 69.

Cave, Samuel—Candidate for Physician Infirmary, 1786.

Cave, Right Hon. Sir Stephen—President Dolphin, 1863; President Gloucestershire Society, 1861; died June 6, 1880, aged 59. (M.P., Shoreham, 1859-1880; Privy Councillor, 1866; G.C.B., 1880; Vice-President Board of Trade, 1866-1868; Judge Advocate General, 1874-1875; Paymaster-General, 1874-1880.)

Cawsey, John—Candidate School Board, 1874.

Chadwick, Andrew—Physician General Hospital (declined), 1831.

Challoner, William—Vice-Chamberlain, 1661-1686.

Challoner, William—Master Merchant Venturers, 1740-1741; died April 21, 1743, aged 67.

Chamber, Thomas—Warden Merchant Venturers, 1635-1636; died October, 1647.

Chamberlain, Henry Taylor—Vice-President Chamber of Commerce, 1877-1879; died January 22, 1881.

Chamberlain, Thomas—Governor Incorporation of Poor, 1740-1741; Treasurer Incorporation of Poor, 1738-1739; Warden Merchant Venturers, 1735-1736.

Chambers, Sir George Henry—Parliamentary candidate, 1874. (Knighted 1880.)

Champion, George—Warden Merchant Venturers, 1770-1771; died January 7, 1817.

Champion, John—Warden Merchant Venturers, 1776-1777.

Champion, Nehemiah—Treasurer Incorporation of Poor, 1732-1733; died August 5, 1747.

Champion, Nehemiah—Treasurer Infirmary, 1748-1753; died December 13, 1753.

ALPHABETICAL INDEX (IV.)—*Continued.*

Champion, Richard—Treasurer Incorporation of Poor, 1720-1721; Treasurer Infirmary, 1740-1748; died February 23, 1747-8, aged 71.

Champion, Richard—Treasurer Infirmary, 1753-1766; died January 9, 1766.

Champion, Richard—Warden Merchant Venturers, 1772-1773; Treasurer Infirmary, 1768-1778; died October 7, 1791. (Deputy Paymaster-General, 1782-1784.)

Champneys, Richard—Warden Merchant Venturers, 1687-1688.

Chapman, Walter—Sword Bearer, 1718-1726.

Chapman, William—Auditor, 1842-1845, 1846-1847; died February 28, 1855, aged 90.

Charleton, Edward—Warden Merchant Venturers, 1756-1757; died October 20, 1764.

Charleton, Rice—President Gloucestershire Society, 1734; died November 16, 1765.

Charleton, Rev. Robert John—President Gloucestershire Society, 1829; died December 24, 1844, aged 45. (Vicar Olveston, 1825-1844.)

Chedworth, Lord (John Thynne Howe)—Lord-Lieutenant, 1758-1762; died May 8, 1762.

Chester, Thomas—Sheriff, 1559-1560; Mayor, 1569-1570; M.P., 1563-1567; died August 29, 1583. (M.P., Gloucestershire, 1573.)

Chester, Thomas—President Colston (Parent), 1754; died October 1, 1763, aged 56. (M.P., Gloucester, 1727-1728; Gloucestershire, 1734-1763.)

Chester, William—Sheriff, 1522-1523; Mayor, 1537-1538, 1552-1553; M.P., 1555; 'died September 4, 1558.

Chester, William Bromley—President Gloucestershire Society, 1778; died December 12, 1780, aged 42. (M.P., Gloucestershire, 1776-1780.)

Chetwood-Aiken, John Chetwood—Treasurer Incorporation of Poor, 1897.

Chetwynd, William—Chamberlain, 1639-1651; Warden Merchant Venturers, 1628-1629.

Cheyney, Rev. Richard—Master Grammar School, 1622-1635; died 1635.

Chilton, George Horace David—Under Sheriff, 1880.

Chivers, John—Deputy Governor Incorporation of Poor, 1777-1778; died January 8, 1808.

Chubb, John—Master St. Stephen's Ringers, 1792; died November 12, 1824, aged 81.

Chute, Henry Macready—Infirmary Assistant House Surgeon, 1870-1873; House Surgeon, 1873-1877.

ALPHABETICAL INDEX (IV.)—*Continued.*

Clare, Viscount (Robert Nugent)—M.P., 1754-1774 (candidate, 1774); died October 13, 1788, aged 86. (M.P., St. Mawes, 1741-1754, 1774-1784; created Viscount Clare, 1766; Earl Nugent, 1776; Lord of the Treasury, 1754-1759; Vice-Treasurer Ireland, 1760-1765, 1768-1782; First Lord of Trade, 1765-1768; Privy Councillor, 1759.)

Clare, William—Warden Merchant Venturers, 1650-1651.

Clark, James—President Colston (Parent) for 1830 (declined).

Clark, John—Warden St. Stephen's Ringers, 1782; died March 10, 1817.

Clark, John—President Colston (Parent) for 1841 (declined).

Clark, John—Inspector Weights and Measures, 1864-1881; died August 3, 1881, aged 73.

Clark, Thomas Edward—Surgeon Infirmary, 1864-1873; Physician General Hospital, 1873-1874; died December 24, 1897, aged 62. (Ordained, 1885; Vicar St. Peter, Clifton, 1890-1893.)

Clark, Rev. Thomas Henry—Member School Board, 1886-1889.

Clark, William—President Gloucestershire Society, 1690.

Clarke, J. A. Graham—See Graham-Clarke.

Clarke, Charles Stewart—President Dolphin, 1870; President Colston (Parent), 1858; died September 15, 1877, aged 69.

Clarke, Edward Gustavus—President Anchor, 1897; Official Receiver in Bankruptcy, 1884.

Clarke, John Henry—Charity Trustee, 1891; President Dolphin, 1892; Master Merchant Venturers, 1897-1898.

Clarke, Rev. John Joseph—Member School Board, 1874-1897; died May 28, 1897.

Clarke, John Michell—Assistant Physician General Hospital, 1881-1892; Physician, 1892.

Clarke, Rev. Robert—City Librarian, 1722-1732. (Vicar St. Leonard, 1721-1732; Precentor, 1730-1731.)

Clarke, Thomas Walker—Collector of Customs, 1882-1886; died April 8, 1896.

Clarke, William—Master Merchant Venturers, 1704-1706.

Clarke, William Hurle—President Colston (Parent), 1893.

Clarke, William Michell—House Surgeon, General Hospital, 1850-1854; Surgeon General Hospital, 1858-1868; died October 2, 1885, aged 56.

Claxton, Butler Thompson—Warden Merchant Venturers, 1814-1815; died March 18, 1842, aged 56.

ALPHABETICAL INDEX (IV.)—*Continued.*

Claxton, Christopher—Corn Measurer, 1832-1833; Quay Warden, 1833-1847; died March 27, 1868, aged 78.

Clayfield, Edward Rolle—Governor Incorporation of Poor, 1808-1811; President Dolphin, 1807; died April 13, 1825, aged 58.

Clayfield, Michael—President Dolphin, 1782; President Gloucestershire Society, 1766; died October 7, 1787.

Clements, Samuel Gustavus—Master St. Stephen's Ringers for 1842 (declined); died May 17, 1874, aged 86.

Clifford, Rev. John Bryant—Mayor's Chaplain, 1836-1837; died May 15, 1886, aged 82. (Vicar St. Matthew, 1837-1879.)

Clissold, Peter—President Colston (Parent), 1803; died July 25, 1821.

Clissold, William—President Colston (Parent) for 1822 (declined).

Clymer, William—Master St. Stephen's Ringers, 1756; died March 2, 1771.

Coates, Charles—Sheriff, 1893-1894; J.P., 1898.

Coates, Thomas—Warden-Elect St. Stephen's Ringers, 1805; died June 13, 1805.

Coathupe, Edwin Weise—Chief Constable, 1876-1894.

Cockaine, Rev. James—Usher Grammar School, 1817-1825.

Cockburn, Right Hon. Sir Alexander James Edmund, Bart.—Recorder, 1854-1856; died November 20, 1880, aged 78. (M.P., Southampton, 1847-1856; knighted, 1850; succeeded to Baronetcy, 1858; G.C.B., 1873; Privy Councillor, 1857; Q.C., 1841; Solicitor-General, 1850-1851; Attorney-General, 1851-1852, 1852-1856; Chief Justice Common Pleas, 1856-1859; Chief Justice Queen's Bench, 1859-1880.)

Codrington, (Sir) Christopher Bethell Bart.)—President Gloucestershire Society, 1812; died February 4, 1843. (M.P., Tewkesbury, 1797-1812; succeeded to disputed Baronetcy, 1816.)

Codrington, (Sir) Christopher William (Bart.)—President Gloucestershire Society, 1857; died June 24, 1864, aged 59. (M.P., East Gloucestershire, 1834-1864; succeeded to disputed Baronetcy, 1843.)

Codrington, Sir Gerald William Henry, Bart.—President Gloucestershire Society, 1880.

Coe, Robert William—Surgeon General Hospital, 1853-1875.

Cole, Ralph Henry—Elected Warden St. Stephen's Ringers for 1868.

Cole, Thomas—Postmaster, 1806-1825; President Colston (Parent), 1809; died June 1, 1825.

Coleman, Thomas John—House Surgeon General Hospital, 1865-1866.

ALPHABETICAL INDEX (IV.)—*Continued.*

Coles, John—Deputy Governor Incorporation of Poor, 1810-1811; died June, 1815.

Coles, William Gale—Sheriff, 1867-1868; President Dolphin, 1876; Treasurer Incorporation of Poor, 1858-1890; Vice-President Chamber of Commerce, 1863-1865; died March 28, 1890.

Collings, Anthony Palmer—Collector of Customs, 1800-1809; President Dolphin, 1803; Warden Merchant Venturers, 1804-1805; President Gloucestershire Society, 1803; died May 28, 1809.

Collier, Right Hon. Sir Robert Porrett—Recorder, July-September, 1870; died October 27, 1885, aged 69. (M.P., Plymouth, 1852-1870; knighted, 1863; created Lord Monkswell, 1885; Q.C., 1854; Solicitor-General, 1863-1866; Attorney-General, 1868-1871; Privy Council Judge, 1871-1885.)

Collins, Thomas—Deputy Governor Incorporation of Poor, 1730-1731.

Collyns, Benjamin—Physician Infirmary, 1778-1779.

Colston, Alexander—President Colston (Parent) for 1774 (declined).

Colston, Charles Edward Hungerford Athole—President Dolphin, 1881; contested North Bristol, 1885. (M.P., South Gloucestershire, 1892.)

Colston, Edward—M.P., 1710-1713; died October 11, 1721, aged 85.

Colston, Edward—President Dolphin, 1850; died December 20, 1864, aged 42.

Colston, Edward Francis—President Dolphin, 1797; died October 28, 1825.

Colston, Edward Francis—President Dolphin, 1838; died April 9, 1847, aged 52.

Colston, Richard—President Dolphin, 1813; died October 15, 1817, aged 68.

Colt, Rev. Sir Edward Harry Vaughan, Bart.—President Gloucestershire Society, 1874; died October 15, 1882, aged 74. (Vicar Hill, 1839-1882.)

Combe, Richard—Warden Merchant Venturers, 1757-1758; Parliamentary candidate, 1780; died September 8, 1780. (M.P., Milborne Port, April-May, 1772; Aldeburgh, 1774-1780; Treasurer Ordnance, 1780.)

Cook, Ernest Henry—Member School Board, 1895-1898, 1899.

Cook, Thomas—President Grateful, 1785.

Cooke, Rev. George—President Gloucestershire Society, 1830; died September 17, 1840, aged 80. (Rector Oldbury, 1803-1840.)

Cooke, Henry—Warden St. Stephen's Ringers, 1793.

Cooke, Isaac—Deputy Governor Incorporation of Poor, 1785-1786; died September 13, 1788, aged 49.

Cooke, John—President Colston (Parent), 1776; died March 29, 1789, aged 83.

ALPHABETICAL INDEX (IV.)—*Continued.*

Cooke, Rev. John—Usher Grammar School, 1785-1793; Mayor's Chaplain, 1792-1793.

Cooke, Roger—Mayor, 1534-1535, 1541-1542, 1551-1552; M.P., 1539-1540.

Cooke, William—President Colston (Parent), 1825 (Treasurer, 1825-1841); died February 16, 1864, aged 81.

Cooke-Hurle, Joseph—Sheriff, 1865-1866; died February 27, 1894, aged 80.

Coomber, Thomas—Member School Board, 1874-1880.

Cooper, Geoffrey Viel—Infirmary, Assistant House Surgeon, 1858-1860; House Surgeon, 1860-1863; died August, 1871.

Cooper, Herbert—Assistant House Surgeon Infirmary, 1863-1864.

Cooper, William—President Colston (Parent) for 1855 (declined).

Cornish, John—President-Elect Dolphin for 1855; died July 7, 1835, aged 70.

Cornish, Thomas Charles—Warden St. Stephen's Ringers, 1838; died April 15, 1861, aged 48.

Corryn, ———Candidate Physician Infirmary, 1767.

Corser, Thomas—President Colston (Parent), 1818; Warden St. Stephen's Ringers, 1814; died April 4, 1837, aged 81.

Corsley, John—President Gloucestershire Society, 1706.

Coster, Thomas—M.P., 1734-1739; President Gloucestershire Society, 1736; died September 30, 1739, aged 55.

Cottesloe, Lord—See Fremantle.

Cottle, Robert—Corn Measurer, 1798-1800; died Nov. 25, 1800.

Cotton, Henry—President Gloucestershire Society, 1761.

Coules, Marmaduke—Warden St. Stephen's Ringers, 1759.

Coulsting, John—Treasurer Incorporation of Poor, 1826-1827; died March 31, 1848, aged 72.

Cowper, Lancelot—Warden St. Stephen's Ringers, 1780; died July 29, 1794.

Cox, Chamberlain—Master St. Stephen's Ringers for 1804 (declined).

Cox, John—Deputy Governor Incorporation of Poor, 1711-1712.

Cox, Joseph Mason—President Anchor, 1805; died July 11, 1818.

Cox, Simeon—Deputy Governor Incorporation of Poor, 1754-1755; Master St. Peter's Hospital, 1774-1778; died August 16, 1778.

ALPHABETICAL INDEX (IV.)—*Continued.*

Cox, Stephen—Deputy Governor Incorporation of Poor, 1745-1746; President Dolphin, 1760; died June, 1761.

Coxe, Charles Westley — President Gloucestershire Society, 1787; died March 10, 1806. (M.P., Cricklade, 1784-1785.)

Coysgarne, John—Master Merchant Venturers, 1737-1738.

Craufuird, Walter Kennedy—Physician Infirmary, 1802-1811; died July 24, 1817.

Creswicke, Thomas—Usher Grammar School, 1708; died 1708, aged 22.

Crew, Thomas—Inspector of Weights and Measures, 1881-1888; died September 19, 1888, aged 62.

Cripps, Henry Kater—President Colston (Parent), 1897.

Crisp, Nathaniel—Infirmary Assistant House Surgeon, 1851-1856; House Surgeon, 1856-1858; died July 17, 1888.

Crocker, Philip—President Dolphin, 1794; died February 7, 1822, aged 74.

Crofton, Rev. Mordaunt Charles—Member School Board, January-June, 1889. (Rector St. Stephen, 1885-1891; Vicar Christ Church, West Bromwich, 1891-1894; Vicar St. George, Tombland, Norwich, 1894-1898.)

Cromwell, Oliver—High Steward, 1651-1658; died September 3, 1658. (Lord Protector, 1653-1658.)

Crook, Richard Jefferd — Chairman Chamber of Commerce, 1870-1871; died February 19, 1879.

Crosby, Thomas—Assessor, 1845-1846; died October 17, 1872, aged 71.

Cross, Francis Richardson—Sheriff, 1897-1898; President Grateful, 1889; Surgeon Infirmary, 1879-1885; Ophthalmic Surgeon, 1885.

Cross, James—President Grateful, 1776; died June 27, 1791.

Cross, John—Warden Merchant Venturers, 1751-1752.

Cross, Thomas—President Grateful, 1805; died October, 1833.

Cross, William Blackwell—Assessor, 1837; died September 14, 1854, aged 63.

Crossman, Rev. Samuel—City Librarian, 1671-1676; died February 4, 1683-4, aged 59. (Vicar St. Nicholas, 1667-1683; Prebendary of Bristol, 1667-1683; Dean, 1683-1684.)

Crowder, Rev. John Hutton—Mayor's Chaplain, 1856-1860, 1864-1866, 1869-1871; died October 27, 1883.

Crowder, Sir Richard Budden—Recorder, 1846-1854; died December 5, 1859, aged 64. (M.P., Liskeard, 1849-1854; knighted, 1854; Q.C., 1837; Judge Common Pleas, 1854-1859.)

ALPHABETICAL INDEX (IV.)—*Continued.*

Cruickshank, Augustus William—Member School Board, 1885-1886.

Culme, Robert—Sword Bearer, 1661-1667; died 1667.

Cuninghame, William—Parliamentary candidate, 1790; died February, 1837.

Curme, Rev. Thomas—Mayor's Chaplain, 1831-1832 ; died June 23, 1884. (Vicar Sandford, 1841-1884.)

Curnock, Samuel—President Grateful, 1761.

Curtis, Edward—Warden Merchant Venturers, 1725-1726.

Curwen, Christopher—Quay Warden, 1739-1749; died 1749.

Cutting, John Henry — Candidate for Physician, General Hospital, 1858.

Dacre, John—Infirmary House Physician, 1884-1886; House Surgeon, 1886-1887.

Dagge, Abel—Coroner, 1772-1778; died 1778.

Dale, Rev. Henry—Principal Bishop's College, 1840-1846; died March 28, 1894, aged 81. (Rector Wilby, 1853-1891.)

Daltera, James—Master Merchant Venturers, 1772-1773; Treasurer Merchant Venturers, 1773-1801 ; died April 17, 1801, aged 72.

Danger, John—Elected Warden St. Stephen's Ringers for 1856.

Danger, Thomas—Clerk of the Peace, 1871-1878; died August 20, 1878, aged 66.

Daniel, Henry—Warden Merchant Venturers, 1682-1683.

Daniel, Henry—Surgeon Infirmary, 1810-1856; Master St. Stephen's Ringers, 1817; died April 19, 1859, aged 75.

Daniel, Nathaniel—President Gloucestershire Society, 1757.

Daniel, Richard—Coroner, 1728-1731; died 1731.

Daniel, Thomas—Treasurer Incorporation of Poor, 1752-1754; died October 29, 1761.

Daniel, Thomas—President Dolphin, 1856; Master Merchant Venturers, 1834-1835; President Gloucestershire Society, 1862; died April 22, 1872, aged 74.

Daniel, William—District Surveyor, 1789-1804; died January 21, 1804.

Danson, Edmund—Warden Merchant Venturers, 1823-1824.

Danson, Thomas Elias—Warden St. Stephen's Ringers, 1822; died May 15, 1840, aged 50.

Darby, Benjamin — Corn Measurer, 1718-1734; died 1734.

D'Arville, Rev. George—Usher Grammar School, 1813-1816. (Perpetual Curate Rangeworthy, 1825.)

ALPHABETICAL INDEX (IV.)—*Continued.*

Daubeny, George—Governor Incorporation of Poor, 1754-1756; Treasurer Incorporation of Poor, 1746-1748; Warden Merchant Venturers, 1750-1751; died January 20, 1760.

Daubeny, George Walters—President Gloucestershire Society, 1887.

Daubeny, John—Master Merchant Venturers, 1789-1790; died December 11, 1794.

Daubeny, Joseph Walters—Sheriff, 1850-1851; died January 28, 1863, aged 52.

Davey, Thomas—J.P., 1894; President Grateful, 1884.

David, John—President-Elect Dolphin for 1779; died December 27, 1778.

Davie, Henry—Steward Sheriff's Court, 1700-1705.

Davie, James—President Gloucestershire Society, 1720.

Davies, Benjamin—President Grateful, 1788; died April 10, 1792.

Davies, David—Inspector of Health, 1865-1872; Medical Officer of Health, 1872-1836; died March 9, 1894, aged 72.

Davies, David Samuel—Medical Officer of Health, 1886.

Davies, George Edmund—J.P., 1898.

Davies, Thomas—Candidate Surgeon Infirmary, 1774.

Davies, Thomas—Charity Trustee, 1836-1854; died April 3, 1854.

Davies, Thomas—Candidate School Board, 1889.

Davies, Rev. William—Chaplain Infirmary, 1740-1772; died 1772.

Davis, Edward—Master St. Stephen's Ringers, 1772; died September 21, 1796.

Davis, Gilbert—President Anchor, 1769, 1770; Master St. Stephen's Ringers, 1760; died May 2, 1778.

Davis, Gilbert—Master St. Stephen's Ringers, 1780; died September 12, 1793, aged 44.

Davis, Henry—President Gloucestershire Society, 1822; died January 31, 1837.

Davis, John—Master St. Stephen's Ringers, 1771; died July 4, 1795.

Davis, Joseph—Vice-Chairman Clifton Guardians, 1840-1848.

Davis, Richard—Warden St. Stephen's Ringers, 1832; died November 12, 1843, aged 59.

Davis, Richard—Apothecary Infirmary, 1843-1844; died September 5, 1853, aged 42.

Davis, Richard Hart—President Dolphin, 1809; M.P., 1812-1831; President Gloucestershire Society, 1810; died February 21, 1842, aged 75. (M.P., Colchester, 1807-1812.)

ALPHABETICAL INDEX (IV.)—*Continued.*

Davis, William James—J.P., 1894.

Davy, Rev. Charles Raikes—President Gloucestershire Society, 1860; died December 25, 1885, aged 67.

Day, Rev. Edmund—Chaplain General Hospital, 1870-1871.

Day, Henry—Mayor's Clerk, 1820-1822; died April 2, 1860, aged 66.

Day, James—Master Merchant Venturers, 1735-1736; died September 7, 1754.

Day, James—Warden Merchant Venturers, 1744-1745.

Day, Richmond—Treasurer Incorporation of Poor, 1743-1745.

Day, Rev. Samuel Emery—Mayor's Chaplain, 1845-1846, 1848-1851, 1853-1855; died January 24, 1864, aged 66. (Vicar St. Philip's, 1832-1864.)

Day, William—Deputy Governor Incorporation of Poor, 1773-1774; died August 22, 1794.

Dayrell, Henry—Warden St. Stephen's Ringers, 1848.

Deake, Christopher—Water Bailiff, 1820-1840; died April 17, 1840.

Dean, Rev. John—Usher Grammar School, 1698-1705. (Vicar Kempsey, 1707; Rector St. Swithin, Worcester, 1711.)

Deane, Richard—Coroner, 1695-1697; Corn Measurer, 1674-1697; died 1697.

De Clifford, Lord—See Southwell.

De Clifford, Lord—President Gloucestershire Society, 1795; died September 30, 1832, aged 65.

Deedes, Alfred—Sheriff, 1892-1893; President Dolphin, 1888; Treasurer Incorporation of Poor, 1890-1897; J.P., 1887.

Delpratt, Samuel—Treasurer Incorporation of Poor, 1772-1774; Warden St. Stephen's Ringers, 1772.

Delpratt, William—President Colston (Parent), 1801 (declined).

Dening, Rev. Thomas Henry Trickey—Vice-Chairman Barton Regis Guardians, 1895-1898; Vice-Chairman Bristol Guardians, 1899. (Rector St. Werburgh, 1888.)

Derham, Samuel—J.P., 1881; died June 7, 1886, aged 69.

Derrick, Francis—Warden Merchant Venturers, 1621-1622.

De Soyres, Francis John—Vice-President Chamber of Commerce, 1879-1880.

Dester, John Bates—Warden-Elect St. Stephen's Ringers, 1899.

Deverell, John—Candidate for Surgeon Infirmary, 1747.

Dewing, Rev. Arthur May—Mayor's Chaplain, 1894-1895. (Vicar St. George, Brandon Hill, 1892-1898.)

ALPHABETICAL INDEX (IV.)—*Continued.*

Dibsdall, Silas—Deputy Governor Incorporation of Poor, 1826-1827; died October 14, 1839, aged 52.

Dickinson, William—Postmaster, 1690-1693.

Dickinson, William—Coroner, 1721-1728.

Dighton, Isaac—Clerk Clifton Guardians, April-July, 1836.

Dighton, William—Warden St. Stephen's Ringers, 1775; died May 25, 1821.

Ditchett, Samuel—President Grateful, 1817; died February 9, 1861, aged 88.

Dix, George—Chairman Clifton Guardians, 1859-1867.

Dobson, Nelson Congreve—House Surgeon General Hospital, 1867-1870; Surgeon, 1871-1893.

Doddrell, Thomas—Warden-Elect St. Stephen's Ringers for 1840; died September 4, 1840, aged 52.

Doggett, Edward Greenfield—Clerk Incorporation of Poor, 1867-1887; died February 18, 1887, aged 69.

Doggett, Hugh Greenfield—Coroner, 1892.

Dolan, Robert Thomas—Collector of Customs, 1886-1889.

Donne, Benjamin—City Librarian, 1768-1773.

Dorset, Earl of (Thomas Sackville)—High Steward, 1601-1608; died April 19, 1608. (M.P., East Grinstead, 1558, 1559, 1563; Aylesbury, 1563-1567; knighted, 1567; created Lord Buckhurst, 1567; Earl of Dorset, 1604; K.G., 1589; Chancellor of Oxford University, 1591-1608; Lord High Treasurer, 1598-1608.)

Douglas, Elizabeth—Member School Board, 1883-1885.

Dowell, Rev. Stephen Britton—Usher Grammar School, 1816-1817; died 1864.

Dowling, Francis Joseph—House Surgeon General Hospital, 1859-1860.

Dowson, Christopher Henry—Infirmary, Assistant Surgeon, 1871-1873; Surgeon, 1873-1889; died January 14, 1889, aged 43.

Drake, Thomas—President Colston (Parent) for 1854 (declined); J.P., 1851; died April 3, 1856, aged 53.

Drayton, John—Warden Merchant Venturers, 1634-1635.

Drew, Edward—Master Merchant Venturers, 1845-1846; died June 4, 1878, aged 76.

Drew, John—Haven Master, 1841-1874; died March 6, 1874, aged 76.

Drewys, John—M.P., 1547-1552.

Drummond, Archibald—Physician Infirmary, 1747-1771.

Drummond, Colin—Master St. Stephen's Ringers, 1785; died December, 1795.

Drummond, Thomas Darling—Warden St. Stephen's Ringers, 1856; died March 20, 1860, aged 44.

ALPHABETICAL INDEX (IV.)—*Continued.*

Ducie, Lord (Matthew Ducie Moreton)—Lord-Lieutenant, 1755-1758; died December 25, 1770. (M.P., Cricklade, 1721-1722; Calne, 1725-1727; Tregony, 1727-1734; succeeded to Peerage, 1735.)

Ducie, Earl of (Henry John Reynolds-Moreton)—Lord-Lieutenant, 1857. (M.P., Stroud, 1852-1853; succeeded to Peerage, 1853; Privy Councillor, 1859; Captain Yeomen of the Guard, 1859-1866.)

Dugdale, Robert—J.P., 1898.

Dukinfield, John—Master Merchant Venturers, 1736-1737.

Dukinfield, William—Warden Merchant Venturers, 1740-1741; died March 22, 1743-4.

Dunbar, James—Deputy Governor Incorporation of Poor, 1820-1823; died July 13, 1843, aged 70.

Dunckerley, Thomas—Provincial Grand Master of Freemasons, 1764-1798; died November, 1798.

Dunning, Robert—Master St. Stephen's Ringers, 1705.

Durbin, Thomas—Deputy Governor Incorporation of Poor, 1746-1747; died March 22, 1748-9.

Dursley, Viscount—See Berkeley (2nd) Earl of.

Dutton, James—President Gloucestershire Society, 1782; died May 22, 1820, aged 75. (M.P., Gloucestershire, 1781-1784; created Lord Sherborne, 1784.)

Dyer, James—Town Clerk, 1621-1631.

Dyer, Joseph — President Colston (Parent), 1810; died January 11, 1821.

Dyer, Robert—Warden St. Stephen's Ringers, 1825; died February 25, 1856, aged 65.

Dyer, Thomas Webb—President Dolphin, 1815; Apothecary Infirmary, 1789-1810 (candidate Physician, 1811, 1816); died July 13, 1833.

Eagles, Thomas—Collector of Customs, 1809-1812; President Colston (Parent), 1791; died October 28, 1812.

Eagles, William—President Colston (Parent), 1770.

Eardley-Wilmot, Sir John Eardley, Bart. — Judge County Court, 1854-1863; died February 1, 1892, aged 81. (County Court Judge, Marylebone, 1865-1871; M.P., South Warwickshire, 1874-1885.)

Earle, Giles—candidate Town Clerk, 1721.

Earle, Joseph—Master Merchant Venturers, 1721-1722; M.P., 1710-1727; died March 13, 1729-30, aged 72.

Earle, Thomas—Warden Merchant Venturers, 1696-1697; died 1705.

ALPHABETICAL INDEX (IV.)—*Continued.*

Ebsworth, Rev. John Joseph—Mayor's Chaplain, 1847-1848; died July, 1896, aged 84. (Vicar St. Paul, Forest of Dean, 1858-1896.)

Edens, Rev. John—Mayor's Chaplain, 1803-1805; died December 25, 1840, aged 74. (Precentor, 1798-1799; Vicar St. Nicholas, 1799-1840.)

Edgar, Preston—President Grateful, 1795, 1825; died May 29, 1835, aged 80.

Edgell, Richard—Candidate for Surgeon Infirmary, 1807.

Edgeworth, Francis Henry—Assistant Physician Infirmary, 1893.

Edwards, George—Master St. Stephen's Ringers, 1827; died May 31, 1853, aged 75.

Edwards, George Oldham—Sheriff, 1856-1853; died February 18, 1883, aged 75.

Edwards, John—Corn Measurer, 1793-1798; died 1798.

Edwards, Samuel Crady — President Colston (Parent), 1834; died May 15, 1838, aged 47.

Edwards, Thomas—Governor Incorporation of Poor, 1717-1718; died July 7, 1727, aged 83.

Edwards, Thomas—M.P., 1713-1715 (candidate, 1715); died April 12, 1735. (M.P., Wells, 1719-1735.)

Edwards, Rev. William—Usher Grammar School, 1799-1812; died July 3, 1836, aged 67.

Edwards, Rev. William Embury—Mayor's Chaplain, 1786-1787; died June 11, 1797.

Edwards, William Henry—President-Elect Colston (Parent) for 1871; died 1871.

Edwards, William Henry Greville—President Gloucestershire Society, 1899.

Eland, Rev. Henry George—Mayor's Chaplain, 1840-1841; died November 28, 1882. (Vicar St. Paul, Bedminster, 1839-1852; Vicar St. John, Bedminster, 1852-1882.)

Elbridge, John—Treasurer Infirmary, 1737-1739; died February 22, 1738-9.

Ellerton, John Edward—House Surgeon General Hospital, 1848-1850; died May 30, 1893, aged 69.

Elliott, Jonathan — President Gloucestershire Society, 1709.

Elliott, Thomas—House Surgeon General Hospital, 1873-1874.

Ellis, John—Apothecary Infirmary, 1777-1778; died January, 1778.

Elme, Thomas — Apothecary Infirmary, 1775-1777; died October 18, 1777.

ALPHABETICAL INDEX (IV.)—*Continued.*

Elton, Sir Abraham Isaac, Bart.—Steward Sheriff's Court, 1746-1753; Town Clerk 1753-1786; Master Merchant Venturers, 1767-1768; died February 5, 1790. (Succeeded to Baronetcy, 1761.)

Elton, Sir Charles Abraham, Bart.—President Anchor, 1817; died June 1, 1853, aged 74. (Succeeded to Baronetcy, 1842.)

Elton, Edward—Warden Merchant Venturers, 1770-1771; died September 20, 1811, aged 68.

Elton, Isaac—President Gloucestershire Society, 1806; died April 19, 1857, aged 66.

Elton, John—President Colston (Parent) for 1820 (declined).

Elwin, Rev. Fountain—Mayor's Chaplain, 1810-1811; died May 22, 1869, aged 85. (Vicar Temple, 1816-1869.

Elyott, Robert—Mayor, 1540-1541; M.P., 1542-1554.

Emra, Rev. John—Mayor's Chaplain, 1798-1799; died September 19, 1842, aged 73. (Vicar St. George, Gloucestershire, 1808-1842.)

England, John—Steward Gloucestershire Society, 1680.

England, John—Physician Infirmary, January-March, 1767; died March, 1767.

Erkly, John—Steward Gloucestershire Society, 1675.

Errington, Richard—Deputy Governor Incorporation of Poor, 1794-1796; died July 9, 1796.

Escott, George—President Gloucestershire Society, 1751; Master St. Stephen's Ringers, 1751; died March 13, 1771.

Essex, Earl of (Robert Devereux)—High Steward, 1598-1601; executed February 25, 1600-1. (Master of the Horse, 1587-1601; Earl Marshal, 1597-1601; Master-General of Ordnance, 1598-1601; Chancellor Cambridge University, 1598-1601; Lord-Lieutenant of Ireland, 1599; K.G., 1588.)

Estcourt, Rev. Edmund—Usher Grammar School, 1695-1698; died June, 1711. (Vicar Wraxall, 1698-1711.)

Estcourt, Thomas — President Gloucestershire Society, 1781; died December 2, 1818. (M.P., Cricklade, 1790-1818.)

Estcourt, Thomas Grimston—President Gloucestershire Society, 1814; died July 26, 1853, aged 77. (M.P., Devizes, 1805-1826; Oxford University, 1826-1847; changed name to Bucknall-Estcourt, 1823.)

Estlin, John Bishop—Candidate for Surgeonn Infirmary, 1812; died June 10, 1855, aged 69.

Eston, Thomas—Deputy Governor Incorporation of Poor, 1718-1720; Master Merchant Venturers, 1739-1740.

ALPHABETICAL INDEX (IV.)—*Continued.*

Etheridge, Thomas—Quay Warden, 1812-1833.

Etwall, — —Physician Infirmary, 1737-1743.

Evans, Rev. Charles—Head Master Clifton College, 1861-1862. (Head Master King Edward's School, Birmingham, 1862-1872; Rector Solihull, 1872-1894.)

Evans, Rev. Edward—Member School Board, 1898.

Evans, Edward Francis—Collector of Customs, 1895.

Evans, John—Warden St. Stephen's Ringers, 1776.

Evans, John—President Chamber of Commerce, 1877-1878.

Evans, John Fenton—Infirmary House Physician, 1883-1884; House Surgeon, 1884-1886; died March 13, 1899, aged 41. (Professor of Pathology, Calcutta Medical College, till his death.)

Evans, Peter Fabyan Sparke—Member School Board 1880-1883; J.P., 1881.

Evans, Robert—Head Master Grammar School, 1847-1854; died October 14, 1854.

Evans, Robert Mullett—Warden St. Stephen's Ringers, 1833.

Evans, Thomas—Chairman Chamber of Commerce, 1861-1862.

Evans, Thomas Mullett—Warden-Elect St. Stephen's Ringers for 1834; died May 5, 1834, aged 34.

Ewer, James—Warden St. Stephen's Ringers, 1792; died February 3, 1815.

Exley, John Thompson—Candidate for School Board 1874; Vice-Principal Bristol College, 1840-1841.

Fairbrother, Alexander—Physician General Hospital, 1838-1853; Physician Infirmary, 1856-1876; died May 13, 1889 aged 79.

Fane, Henry—Coroner, 1715-1716; President Gloucestershire Society, 1708; died December 19, 1726.

Fargus, Frederick Charles—Master St. Stephen's Ringers, 1861; died April 14, 1868, aged 45.

*Fargus, Frederick John—Master St. Stephen's Ringers, 1876; died May 18, 1885, aged 37.

Fargus, Henry Robert—Master St. Stephen's Ringers, 1852; died April 12, 1885, aged 69.

Fargus, John—Warden St. Stephen's Ringers, 1829; died July 21, 1854, aged 77.

Farler, John—President Colston (Parent) for 1863 (declined); died February 20, 1870, aged 77.

Farler, John Reed—President Colston (Parent), 1883; died April 2, 1898.

Farmer, Rev. Elisha—Usher Grammar School, 1639.

Farmer, Ralph—Chamberlain, November-December, 1639.

---

*"Hugh Conway," author of "Called Back."

ALPHABETICAL INDEX (IV.)—*Continued.*

Farnell, Robert—Deputy Governor Incorporation of Poor, 1742-1743.

Farr, John—Warden St. Stephen's Ringers, 1828.

Farr, Paul—Master Merchant Venturers, 1775-1776 ; President Anchor, 1776; Warden St. Stephen's Ringers, 1779; died December 27, 1794.

Farr, Samuel—Physician Infirmary, 1767-1780; died March 19, 1795.

Farr, Thomas—Registrar Court of Conscience, 1747-1760; died January 30, 1760.

Farrell, Joseph—President Dolphin, 1755.

Fenn, William—Postmaster, 1777-1778; died June 11, 1788.

Fenn (widow of William Fenn)—Postmistress, 1788-1806; died August 18, 1835, aged 94.

Fidoe, Edmund—Master Merchant Venturers, 1766; died December 18, 1790.

Firth, John Lacy—House Surgeon General Hospital, 1893-1896; Assistant Surgeon, 1896.

Fisher, Henry—Chief Constable, 1839-1868; died May 23, 1868.

Fisher, John—Deputy Governor Incorporation of Poor, 1723-1724; Treasurer Colston (Parent), 1739-1742.

Fisher, Lewis—Warden St. Stephen's Ringers, 1811; died 1813.

Fisher, Paul—Governor Incorporation of Poor, 1742-1743; Treasurer Incorporation of Poor, 1725-1726; died December 4, 1762.

Fisher, Robert Alexander—Judge County Court, 1874-1879; died September 30, 1879.

Fisher, Thomas—Coroner, 1784-1810; died February 19, 1812.

Fisher, William—Deputy Governor Incorporation of Poor, 1762-1763.

Fisher, William—Deputy Governor Incorporation of Poor, 1791-1792.

Fitz-Hardinge, Earl (William Fitz-Hardinge Berkeley)—Lord-Lieutenant, 1836-1857; died October 10, 1857, aged 70. (M.P., Gloucestershire, 1810-1811; created Lord Segrave, 1831; Earl Fitzhardinge, 1841.)

Fletcher, Robert—Auditor, 1836-1837; died December 22, 1870, aged 89.

Flower, Joseph—Deputy Governor Incorporation of Poor, 1765-1767; died December 5, 1785.

Foster, Ambrose—Collector of Customs, 1855-1870 ; died February 12, 1870, aged 69.

Ford, Andrew Hamill—J.P., 1889.

Ford, Rev. Gabriel Estwick—Member School Board, 1892-1893. (Vicar Trinity, St. Philip's, 1885-1899.

ALPHABETICAL INDEX (IV.)—*Continued.*

Ford, James—Surgeon Infirmary, 1743-1759; died December 18, 1795, aged 77.

Ford, John—Surgeon Infirmary, 1759-1775; President Colston (Parent), 1788, 1789 (declined); died October 9, 1807, aged 76.

Forsayth, Rev. Robert—Mayor's Chaplain, 1839-1840; died January 18, 1840.

Foster, James—District Surveyor, 1819-1836; died January 5, 1836.

Foster, Rev. Robert—Mayor's Chaplain, 1801-1802; 1806-1807; died September 26, 1836, aged 70. (Precentor, 1799-1810; Prebendary of Wells, 1820-1836.)

Fothergill, John—President Colston (Parent) for 1844 (declined); died March 9, 1846.

Fowle, Joseph—President Anchor, 1771.

Fowler, Henry George—Master Merchant Venturers, 1833-1834; died July 20, 1870.

Fowler, John — Master Merchant Venturers, 1783-1784; died December 22, 1789.

Fowler, John—Warden Merchant Venturers, 1781-1782; died about February, 1785.

Fowler, Richard Sargent—Master Merchant Venturers, 1816-1817; died November 28, 1820.

Fowler, Richard Walker—Warden Merchant Venturers, 1827-1828; died November 10, 1860, aged 63.

Fowler, William—Master Merchant Venturers, 1808-1809; died February 13, 1839, aged 75.

Fox, Edward Long—Physician Infirmary, 1786-1816; died May 2, 1835, aged 74.

Fox, Edward Long—Physician Infirmary, 1857-1877.

Fox, George Frederick—President Colston (Parent), 1870.

Fox, Henry—Secretary General Hospital, 1872-1885.

Fox, Henry Hawes—Physician Infirmary, 1816-1829; died October 12, 1851, aged 63.

Fox, John—Member School Board, 1886-1889.

Fox, Richard Anstice—Master Merchant Venturers, 1893-1894.

Fox, Samuel—Coroner, 1715-1716; President Gloucestershire Society, 1716; died June 14, 1755.

Fox, William—Master St. Stephen's Ringers, 1794 ; died February 11, 1818.

Foy, Matthew—Corn Measurer, 1750-1757; died 1757.

Franklyn, John—Master St. Stephen's Ringers, 1799; died March 13, 1808, aged 45.

Franklyn, Joshua—Warden Merchant Venturers, 1711-1712; Water Bailiff, February-May, 1727; died May, 1727.

ALPHABETICAL INDEX (IV.)—*Continued*.

Franklyn, Rev. Thomas Ward—Usher Grammar School. 1823-1826; died May, 1876.

Frayne, William—President Colston (Parent), 1873; died March 19, 1893, aged 73.

Freeling, Sir Francis, Bart.—President Colston (Parent). 1829; died July 10, 1836, aged 72. (Secretary General Post Office, 1797-1836; created Baronet, 1828.)

Freeling, Sir George Henry, Bart.—President Colston (Parent), 1827; died November 29, 1841, aged 52. (Succeeded to Baronetcy, 1836; Commissioner of Customs, 1836-1841.)

Freke, Thomas—Treasurer Incorporation of Poor, 1724-1725; Warden Merchant Venturers, 1727-1728; died July 12, 1732, aged 38.

Freke, William—Warden Merchant Venturers, 1719-1720.

Fremantle, Hon. Thomas Francis—Parliamentary candidate, 1865. (M.P., Bucks, 1876-1885; succeeded as Lord Cottesloe, 1890.)

Fripp, Edward Bowles—Charity Trustee, 1852-1865; died September 5, 1866, aged 75.

Fripp, George Downing—Surgeon General Hospital, 1831-1840; Physician General Hospital, 1848-1849; died September 27, 1892, aged 85.

Fripp, Henry Edward—Physician General Hospital, 1859-1875; died March 23, 1880, aged 63.

Fripp, James—Physician General Hospital, 1831-1858; died March 15, 1861, aged 60.

Fripp, Samuel Charles—District Surveyor, 1840-1872; died February 9, 1882, aged 69.

Fripp, William—President Grateful, 1855; Warden St. Stephen's Ringers, 1859; died April 2, 1883.

Frost, John—Warden St. Stephen's Ringers, 1862; died January 27, 1875, aged 49.

Fry, Albert—J.P., 1889.

Fry, Francis—Chairman Water Works Company, 1874-1886; died November 12, 1886, aged 83.

Fry, Peter—President Grateful, 1818; died February 4, 1822, aged 70.

Fry, William—President Grateful, 1759, 1760; died May 9, 1776.

Fry, William—Deputy Governor Incorporation of Poor, 1775-1776; died January 4, 1788.

Fry, William—Treasurer Colston (Parent), 1790-1793; died December 12, 1812.

Frye, James—Acting Postmaster, 1797-1805; died December 2, 1805.

Fryer, Thomas—Candidate Surgeon General Hospital, 1831; died March 27, 1875, aged 79.

ALPHABETICAL INDEX (IV.)—*Continued.*

Fuidge, Richard—Warden St. Stephen's Ringers, 1823; died March 12, 1836, aged 58.

Fuidge, Thomas—Master St. Stephen's Ringers, 1825; died September 22, 1854.

Fuidge, Thomas—Warden St. Stephen's Ringers, 1842; died October 16, 1885, aged 68.

Fuidge, William—Master St. Stephen's Ringers, 1851; J.P., 1875; died January 31, 1887, aged 67.

Fuller, John—J.P., 1889; died February 21, 1896, aged 75.

Furse, Philip—Master St. Stephen's Ringers, 1795.

Fussell, James Flower—President Grateful, 1862; Auditor, 1848 (declined); died September 25, 1880, aged 62.

Gadd, Abraham—President Grateful, 1762; died March, 1808.

Gadd, Thomas—President Grateful, 1764; died October 2, 1782.

Gadd, Thomas—President Grateful, 1784; died April 2, 1798.

Gadd, Thomas — President Grateful, 1820; died September 11, 1830, aged 77.

Gange, Rev. Edwin Gorsuch—Member School Board, 1883-1884.

Gant, William—President Grateful, 1779; died May 5, 1781, aged 43.

Gardiner, George—President Colston (Parent), 1875; died February 14, 1892, aged 72.

Gardiner, Job—President Gloucestershire Society, 1742.

Gardiner, Joel—President Dolphin, 1805; President Gloucestershire Society, 1804; died January 23, 1823, aged 77.

Gardiner, Joel—President Colston (Parent), 1859; died May 29, 1869, aged 75.

Gardiner, John—Warden Merchant Venturers, 1626-1627.

Gardner, James Anthony—Master St. Stephen's Ringers, 1871; died January 14, 1882, aged 74.

Gardner, Samuel—Warden Merchant Venturers, 1765-1767; Warden St. Stephen's Ringers, 1738-1741; died 1767.

Garlick, Edward—Treasurer Incorporation of Poor, 1721-1722.

Garnett, Henry—Master Merchant Venturers, 1776-1777; died November 7, 1785.

Garrard, Thomas—Deputy Chamberlain, 1815-1822; Chamberlain, 1822-1835; Treasurer, 1836-1856; died December 18, 1859, aged 73.

ALPHABETICAL INDEX (IV.)—*Continued.*

Gay, Joseph Graham—Warden-Elect St. Stephen's Ringers for 1860; accidentally drowned September 24, 1860, aged 37.

Gay, Robert—District Surveyor, 1792-1803; died Aug. 18, 1803.

Gegg, Rev. Jonathan—Usher Grammar School, 1755-1756; died 1789. (Minor Canon, 1755-1756; Vicar Weare, 1756-1789.)

George, James—Warden Merchant Venturers, 1808-1809, 1815-1816; died March 10, 1822.

Gibbes, Henry—Warden Merchant Venturers, 1691-1692.

Gibbons, William—Master St. Stephen's Ringers, 1778; died February 4, 1785.

Gibbons, William—Warden St. Stephen's Ringers, 1810.

Gibbs, George—Warden St. Stephen's Ringers, 1850; died June 9, 1884.

Gibbs, James—Clerk County Court, 1847-1856; Registrar County Court, 1856-1877; died July 26, 1887, aged 62.

Gibbs, Joseph Lovell—President Colston (Parent), 1888.

Gibbs, Richard—President Colston (Parent), 1867; died April 29, 1874, aged 76.

Gibbs, Robert—Coroner, 1716-1722; died 1722.

Gibbs, Thomas—Treasurer Incorporation of Poor, 1723-1724.

Gibbs, Thomas—Master St. Stephen's Ringers, 1745.

Gibson, William Middleton—Vice-President Chamber of Commerce, April-December, 1878; died December 11, 1878.

Gilbert, John Pomeroy—President Grateful, 1868; died April 28, 1881, aged 67.

Gillam, Benjamin—Treasurer Incorporation of Poor 1734-1788; died May 31, 1789.

Gillett, James—Warden St. Stephen's Ringers, 1830; died November 18, 1845, aged 67.

Gingell, William James—Inspector of Weights and Measures, 1837-1863; died November 2, 1863, aged 76.

Girdlestone, Francis Brooke—Secretary Docks, 1875; Receiver of Town Dues, 1876; General Manager of Docks, 1884.

Girdlestone, John Ward—Docks Engineer, 1882-1890.

Glascodine, Joseph—District Surveyor, 1803-1818; died 1818.

Glascodine, Richard—District Surveyor, 1818-1819; died May 8, 1819.

Glasson, George Cornish—Master St. Stephen's Ringers, 1855.

ALPHABETICAL INDEX (IV.)—Continued.

Glasson, George C. B.—Warden St. Stephen's Ringers, 1855.

Glasson, John—Warden St. Stephen's Ringers, 1865.

Glazebrook, Rev. Michael George—Head Master Clifton College, 1891. (High Master Manchester Grammar School, 1886-1890.)

Goddard, Mark—Treasurer Incorporation of Poor, 1708-1709.

Godfrey, James—Surgeon General Hospital, 1843-1861; died September 27, 1861.

Godwin, Charles Sly—Charity Trustee, 1865-1896; died September 10, 1896, aged 85.

Godwin, George—President Colston (Parent) for 1268 (declined).

Godwin, James—J.P., 1888; died June 16, 1890, aged 69.

Godwin, Joseph—Deputy Governor Incorporation of Poor, 1757-1758; died January 27, 1786.

Goldwin, Rev. William—Master Grammar School, 1710-1717; died June, 1747. (Vicar St. Nicholas, 1717-1747.)

Goldwyer, William Henry—Provincial Grand Master Freemasons, 1808-1820; died March 7, 1820.

Gomond, Edmund—Deputy Governor Incorporation of Poor, 1761-1762; died February 29, 1784.

Goodall, Rev. Fairfax—Chaplain Infirmary, 1885.

Goodenough, Rev. John Joseph—Master Grammar School, 1812-1843; died April 22, 1855. (Rector Broughton Pogis, 1845-1855.)

Goodwin, Nathaniel—Coroner, 1750-1772; Vice-Chamberlain, 1736-1740; died June 18, 1772.

Gordon, —— —Candidate Physician Infirmary, 1761.

Gordon, Rev. John George—Second Master Grammar School, 1847-1852; died December 30, 1862.

Gore, Rev. Charles—Acting President Dolphin, 1817; President Gloucestershire Society, 1816; died April 21, 1841, aged 76.

Gore, Edward—President Dolphin, 1756, 1791; died March 27, 1801.

Gore, Thomas Holmes—Clerk to Justices of the Peace, 1875.

Gore, William—President Colston (Parent), 1766.

Gore-Langton, William—President Dolphin, 1817; President Gloucestershire Society, 1827; died March 14, 1847, aged 87. (M.P., Somerset, 1795-1806, 1812-1820, 1831-1832; Tregony, 1808-1812; East Somerset, 1832-1847.)

ALPHABETICAL INDEX (IV.)—*Continued.*

Gotch, Rev. Frederic William—Member of School Board, 1871-1880; died May 17, 1890, aged 82.

Gould, Joseph—Member School Board, 1881-1889 (candidate, 1889); died January 12, 1896, aged 73.

Gould, Robert—Elected Warden St. Stephen's Ringers for 1835; died October 12, 1853, aged 70.

Grace, James—Candidate for Surgeon Infirmary, 1754.

Graeme, Thomas—President Colston (Parent), 1816 (declined); died September 22, 1820, aged 62

Graham, Charles Senhouse—Secretary Infirmary, 1884-1887.

Graham, Robert Gore—J.P., 1898.

Graham-Clarke, John Altham—President Gloucestershire Society, 1877; died April 29, 1897.

Granger, Charles—Master St. Stephen's Ringers, 1825.

Grant, Abell—Master Merchant Venturers, 1729-1730.

Grant, John Russ—President Colston (Parent), 1855; died February 6, 1875, aged 63.

Gray, Rev. Charles—Mayor's Chaplain, 1826-1827; died December 30, 1854.

Gray, Rev. John Durbin—Mayor's Chaplain, 1846-1847; died February 18, 1887, aged 65. (Vicar Abbotsley, 1856-1876; Rector Market Weston, 1876-1884.)

Grazebrook, Joseph—Warden St. Stephen's Ringers, 1836; died January 29, 1888, aged 90.

Green, Rev. Henry—Mayor's Chaplain, 1809-1810, 1811-1812; died April 7, 1841, aged 63. (Minor Canon, 1810-1824; Vicar All Saints, 1816 1841.)

Green, Joseph—Deputy Governor Incorporation of Poor, 1772-1773.

Green, Joseph David—Superintendent Dock Works, 1843-1852.

Green, Thomas—Steward Gloucestershire Society, 1678.

Green, William—Deputy Governor Incorporation of Poor, 1788-1790.

Greethead, Josiah—President Grateful, 1782; died March 23, 1792.

Gregory, Alfred Gustavus—Member School Board, 1895-1898 (candidate, 1898).

Gregory, William—Assessor, 1837, 1840, 1841; died June 7, 1882, aged 92.

Greig, Charles — Infirmary House Surgeon and Apothecary, 1840-1843; House Surgeon, 1843-1846; (candidate Surgeon, 1850); died February 27, 1884.

ALPHABETICAL INDEX (IV.)—*Continued.*

Grenfell, Alice—Member School Board, 1883-1885.

Grenville, Lord (William Wyndham Grenville)—High Steward, 1810-1834; President General Hospital, 1831-1834; died January 12, 1834, aged 74. (M.P., Buckingham, 1782-1784; Bucks, 1784-1790; Secretary for Ireland, 1782-1783; Privy Councillor, 1783; Paymaster-General, 1783-1789; Vice-President Board of Trade, 1786-1789; Speaker, 1789; created Peer, 1790; Home Secretary, 1789-1791; Foreign Secretary, 1791-1801; President Board of Control, 1790-1793 First Lord of the Treasury, 1806-1807; Auditor of the Exchequer, 1794-1834.)

Gresley, Charles—Corn Measurer, 1833-1862; died May 18, 1862.

Gresley, Henry—President Colston (Parent), 1744.

Gresley, John—Treasurer Incorporation of Poor, 1770-1772; died June 4, 1796.

Grevile, Charles—President Gloucestershire Society, 1712.

Grevile, Rev. Edward Colston—Mayor's Chaplain, 1791-1792, 1800-1801; died October 28, 1830, aged 83. (Rector St. Stephen, 1793-1830.)

Griffeth, Thomas—Warden Merchant Venturers, 1635-1636.

Griffies-Williams, Rev. Sir Erasmus Henry, Bart.—President Anchor, 1851; died November 30, 1870, aged 76.

Griffin, Thomas—Master St. Stephen's Ringers, 1764.

Griffith, Hugh—Warden Merchant Venturers, 1636-1638.

Griffiths, Rev. Charles—Chaplain General Hospital, 1891. (Vicar St. Paul, Bedminster, 1888.)

Griffiths, Edmund—Steward Sheriff's Court, 1795-1811; died June 25, 1835. (Metropolitan Police Magistrate, 1819-1834.)

Griffiths, Thomas—Master St. Stephen's Ringers, 1774; died August 14, 1777.

Griffiths, Thomas—Apothecary, Infirmary, 1783-1789; President Dolphin, 1808; died May 22, 1838, aged 75.

Grindon, Joseph Baker—Coroner, 1821-1868; Assessor 1836; died January 2, 1870, aged 80.

Grindon, Rev. Octavius Maunsell—Chaplain Infirmary, 1878-1885. (Vicar South Wraxall, 1885-1896.)

Grove, Kingsmill—President Grateful, 1774; died February 19, 1814.

Guest, Sir Ivor Bertie, Bart.—Parliamentary candidate, 1878, 1880. (Contested Glamorganshire, 1874; Poole, 1874; created Lord Wimborne, 1880.)

ALPHABETICAL INDEX (IV.)—*Continued.*

Guise, Sir Berkeley William, Bart.—President Gloucestershire Society, 1826; died July 23, 1834, aged 59. (M.P., Gloucestershire, 1811-1832; East Gloucestershire, 1832-1834.)

Guise, Sir William, Bart.—President Gloucestershire Society, 1779; died April 6, 1783. (M.P., Gloucestershire, 1770-1783.)

Gunning, John—Master St. Stephen's Ringers, 1862; died January 5, 1875, aged 56.

Gutch, John Mathew—President Dolphin, 1829; Vice-President Chamber of Commerce, 1826-1829; died September 20, 1861, aged 84.

Gwatkin, Edward—Warden St. Stephen's Ringers, 1745, 1746; died October 30, 1764.

Gwynne, Humphrey Thomas Martin Crowther—Superintendent Registrar of Bristol, 1883.

Gwynne, John Crowther—Superintendent Registrar of Bristol, 1861-1883; died March 15, 1883.

Gyde, Timothy—President Colston (Parent) for 1775 (declined).

Gythens, John—Warden St. Stephen's Ringers, 1733-1738.

Haggerston, William John—Candidate for City Librarian, 1883.

Haggett, John—Steward Sheriff's Court, 1645-1662; Parliamentary candidate, 1654. (Judge, South Wales, 1653-1660.)

Haggett, Nathaniel—Steward Sheriff's Court, 1690-1700.

Halbert, James—Master St. Stephen's Ringers, 1686.

Hale, John Blagden—President (Colston) Parent 1806 (declined).

Hale, Matthew—Treasurer Incorporation of Poor, 1761-1764; died April 13, 1764.

Hale, Matthew—President Gloucestershire Society, 1775-1776; died August 27, 1784.

Hale, Thomas Blagden—President Gloucestershire Society, 1836, 1845; died July 22, 1883, aged 75. (M.P., West Gloucestershire, 1836-1857.)

Hall, Alfred—Member School Board, 1874-1877, 1880-1882 (candidate, 1877); died April 8, 1882, aged 38.

Hall, Charles Radclyffe—Physician General Hospital, 1849-1851; died March 21, 1879, aged 59.

Hall, Elias George—President Colston (Parent), 1872

Hall, George Webb—City Solicitor, 1801-1812; Registrar Court of Conscience, 1818-1824; died February 21, 1824.

Hall, George Webb—Registrar Court of Conscience, 1837-1843; died December 3, 1843.

Hall, Henry Wait—Assessor, 1842.

ALPHABETICAL INDEX (IV.)—*Continued.*

Hall, Robert—Deputy Governor Incorporation of Poor, 1790-1791; died February 5, 1800.

Hall, Thomas Wilson—President Colston (Parent), 1865; died April 14, 1874.

Ham, Hierom—Town Clerk, 1581-1621.

Hamilton, James—Receiver of Town Dues, 1836-1852; died May 19, 1852.

Hancock, Leonard—Water Bailiff till 1676.

Handcock, John Sims—Chief Constable, 1856-1876. died September 19, 1877.

Hannan, Thomas—Recorder, 1585-1593; M.P., 1584-1589, 1593; died 1593. (Serjeant, 1589; M.P., Weymouth, 1572.)

Harding, Thomas George—Candidate for School Board, 1889.

Hardwicke, Earl of (Philip Yorke)—High Steward, 1738-1764; died March 6, 1764, aged 73. (M.P., Lewes, 1719-1722; Seaford, 1722-1727; knighted, 1720; Privy Councillor, 1733; created Lord Hardwicke, 1733; Earl, 1754; Solicitor-General, 1720-1724; Attorney-General, 1724-1733; Chief Justice King's Bench, 1733-1737; Lord Chancellor, 1737-1756.)

Hardwicke, —— —Physician Infirmary, 1737-1747; died September 1, 1747.

Hardwicke, James—President Gloucestershire Society, 1731.

Hardwicke, Peter—President Gloucestershire Society 1717.

Hardy, Edmund Armitage—Vice-Chairman Barton Regis Guardians, 1893-1895.

Hare, Ebenezer—Warden Merchant Venturers, 1753-1754.

Hare, Henry Grace—President Colston (Parent). 1884; died February 7, 1892, aged 49.

Hare, William—Master Merchant Venturers, 1752-1753; died September 15, 1754.

Hare, William Ody—Under Sheriff, 1819-1864; Clerk of the Peace, 1836-1868; Deputy Judge of Tolzey Court, 1836-1864; died October 17, 1868, aged 82.

Harford, Charles—Treasurer Incorporation of Poor, 1700-1701; died April, 1723.

Harford, Charles—Master St. Stephen's Ringers, 1779; died August 17, 1801.

Harford, Charles—Receiver of Town Dues, 1781-1809; Master St. Stephen's Ringers for 1786 (declined); died February 14, 1809.

Harford, Charles—Master St. Stephen's Ringers, 1813; died September 6, 1821.

ALPHABETICAL INDEX (IV.)—*Continued*.

Harford, Charles Joseph—President Anchor, 1792; Master Merchant Venturers, 1806-1807; President Gloucestershire Society, 1808; died March 2, 1830, aged 65.

Harford, Edward—Treasurer Incorporation of Poor, 1730-1731; died 1788.

Harford, John—Deputy Chamberlain, 1824-1835; Deputy Treasurer, 1840-1856; Treasurer, 1856-1881; died March 7, 1881, aged 78.

Harford, John Battersby—Sheriff, 1851-1852; President Gloucestershire Society, 1867; President Infirmary, 1859-1869; died February 11, 1875, aged 56.

Harford, John Scandrett—Master Merchant Venturers, 1798-1799; died January 23, 1815.

Harford, John Scandrett—President Infirmary, 1844-1859; died April 16, 1866, aged 81. (Contested Cardigan Boroughs, 1841, 1849.)

Harford, Mark—Master Merchant Venturers, 1613-1814; died November 22, 1835.

Harford, Samuel—President Chamber of Commerce, 1831-1832; died August 1, 1838, aged 72.

Harford-Battersby, Abraham Gray—Sheriff, 1846-1847; Vice-Chairman Clifton Guardians, 1836-1837; died May 7, 1851, aged 64.

Harley, Edward—Registrar Court of Conscience, 1843-1847; Clerk County Court, 1847-1856; Registrar County Court, 1856-1888 (District Registrar Supreme Court, 1875-1888); President Grateful, 1854; candidate for Clerk of the Peace, 1836; died October 25, 1888, aged 81.

Harley, Edward Arthur—District Registrar Supreme Court, 1877.

Harrill, Job—Governor Incorporation of Poor, 1834-1836; President Grateful, 1833; died May 26, 1843, aged 70.

Harris, David—Mayor, 1550-1551; M.P., 1553; died October 14, 1552.

Harris, Rev. George—Usher Grammar School, 1728-1740.

Harris, James—Treasurer Incorporation of Poor, 1696-1697.

Harris, James—President Grateful, 1800; died October 24, 1819, aged 62.

Harris, James—Clerk Board of Health, 1851-1855; died June 19, 1855.

Harris, Thomas Tanner—President Colston (Parent) for 1863 (declined); died November 1, 1875, aged 64.

Harris, Walter—House Surgeon General Hospital, 1854-1865.

Harris, William—District Surveyor, 1840-1849.

ALPHABETICAL INDEX (IV.)--*Continued.*

Harris, Wintour—Deputy Chamberlain, 1775-1811; Chamberlain, 1811-1815; died September 3, 1815.

Harrison, Alfred James—Physician General Hospital, 1879.

Harrison, Rev. George—Usher Grammar School, till 1628.

Harrison, John—Surgeon Infirmary, 1836-1859; died June 6, 1892.

Harrison, Rev. Oswald—Chaplain Infirmary, 1876-1877; died July 24, 1877, aged 31.

Harsant, William Henry—House Surgeon General Hospital, 1874-1879; Infirmary Assistant Surgeon, 1879-1885; Surgeon, 1885.

Harson, Daniel—Collector of Customs, 1758-1779; died May 23, 1779.

Hart, Arthur—Master Merchant Venturers, 1745-1746; President Colston (Parent), 1741; died about January, 1779.

Hart, Henry—Warden Merchant Venturers, 1734-1735.

Hart, William—Governor Incorporation of Poor, 1719-1722; Warden Merchant Venturers, 1709-1710; Treasurer Merchant Venturers 1708-1709; President Colston (Parent), 1747; Parliamentary candidate, 1722, 1727; died June 10, 1755.

Hart, William—Governor Incorporation of Poor, 1748-1750; Master Merchant Venturers, 1761-1762; President Colston (Parent), 1751; died January 13, 1785.

Hartley, William Powell—Assessor, 1848-1850; Superintendent Registrar of Bristol, 1836-1850; candidate for Clerk of the Peace and Clerk to the Justices, 1836; died July 10, 1850.

Hartley, Winchcombe Henry—President Colston (Parent), 1780; President Gloucestershire Society, 1772; died August 12, 1794. (M.P., Berks, 1776-1734, 1790-1794; contested Berks and Gloucestershire, 1784.)

Hartley, Winchcombe Henry Howard—President 1851; President Gloucestershire Society, 1845; died October 31, 1881.

Harvey, Alfred Henry—Candidate School Board, 1898.

Harvey, Charles Octavius—Master Merchant Venturers, 1883-1884; Master St. Stephen's Ringers, 1882.

Harvey, Rev. Thomas William—Member School Board, 1884-January, 1889, June, 1889-1892. (Vicar St. Agnes, 1883.)

Harwood, Edward Morcom—Candidate Coroner, 1892; died January 10, 1897, aged 71.

Harwood, William—President Grateful, 1845; died August 15, 1862, aged 52.

ALPHABETICAL INDEX (IV.)—*Continued.*

Hazle, William — Treasurer Incorporation of Poor, 1772 (declined).

Haskins, Henry—President Grateful, 1775.

Hassell, Charles—Master St. Stephen's Ringers, 1857; died December 10, 1859, aged 45.

Hassell, Robert—Master Merchant Venturers, 1881-1882; President Grateful, 1876.

Hatton, Peter—Warden Merchant Venturers, 1763-1764; died May 10, 1781.

Hathaway, Richard Isaac—Warden St. Stephen's Ringers, 1854.

Haviland, Robert—Warden Merchant Venturers, 1614-1615, 1616-1617.

Hawkesworth, Abraham Richard—Treasurer Infirmary, 1766-1768; died October 29, 1768.

Hawkins, John—Treasurer Incorporation of Poor, 1729-1730; died March 27, 1738, aged 57.

Hawkins, John—President Dolphin, 1790; died Dec. 31, 1791.

Hawkins, Thomas—Corn Measurer, 1711-1718; died 1718.

Hawkswell, Richard—Deputy Chamberlain, 1758-1773; Chamberlain, 1773-1811; died September 24, 1815, aged 81.

Hayes, Thomas—Governor Incorporation of Poor, 1782-1784; died January 27, 1814.

Haynes, Richard—President Colston (Parent), 1792; died June 18, 1816, aged 79.

Hayward, Rev. George—Usher Grammar School, 1756-1759; died 1814. (Rector Nympsfield and Vicar of Frocester.)

Hayward, Richard — President Gloucestershire Society, 1768.

Hayward-Winston, Thomas—President Colston (Parent), 1798; President Gloucestershire Society 1788; died October 20, 1818, aged 75.

Headington, John—President Dolphin, 1783; died December 28, 1786.

Heaven, John Gyde—Clerk Board of Health (Urban Sanitary Authority), 1835-1887; died May 3, 1893, aged 73.

Hellicar, Rev. Ames—Mayor's Chaplain, 1827-1828; died September 17, 1839, aged 42. (Minor Canon, 1824-1832; Vicar Fifehead-cum-Swill, 1832-1839.)

Hellicar, Gresley—Secretary Chamber of Commerce, 1823-1824; died April 21, 1824.

Hellicar, Joseph—Warden Merchant Venturers, 1809-1810; Treasurer Merchant Venturers, 1816-1840; died November 4, 1844, aged 77.

ALPHABETICAL INDEX (IV.)—Continued.

Hellicar, Thomas—Warden Merchant Venturers, 1807-1808; died February 7, 1835, aged 79.

Hellier, Thomas—Candidate Surgeon Infirmary, 1754.

Helps, William—President Grateful, 1786.

Hembury, Thomas—Deputy Governor Incorporation of Poor, 1782-1783; President Dolphin, 1779; died December 24, 1791.

Henderson, William—Master St. Stephen's Ringers, 1889.

Henley, Robert—Parliamentary candidate, 1679; died 1709. (M.P., Lyme Regis, 1693-1701.)

Henwood, Luke—District Surveyor, 1804-1830; died March 19, 1830.

Herbert, Sir William—See Pembroke.

Herbert, Lord (Philip Herbert)—Joint Lord-Lieutenant, 1640-1642; died December 11, 1669. (M.P., Wilts, 1640; Glamorganshire, 1640-1649; succeeded as Earl of Pembroke, 1650.)

Hereford, Bishop of—See Percival.

Hertford, Earl of—See Somerset, Duke of.

Hertford, Earl of—Lord-Lieutenant, 1602-1621; died April 6, 1621.

Hertford, Marquis of (William Seymour)—Lord-Lieutenant, 1639-1643, July-October, 1660; died October 4, 1660, aged 74. (M.P., Marlborough, 1621; K.B., 1616; succeeded to Earldom, 1621; created Marquis, 1640; restored Duke of Somerset, 1660; Privy Councillor, 1641; Chancellor Oxford University, 1643-1647, May-October, 1660; K.G., 1650)

Hetling, William—Surgeon Infirmary, 1807-1837; died November 11, 1837, aged 66.

Heyworth, George Frederick—President Gloucestershire Society, 1896.

Heyworth, Rev. James—President Gloucestershire Society, 1872; President Infirmary, 1869-1879; died December 22, 1879.

Hibbins, Arthur—Warden Merchant Venturers, 1615-1616.

Hickes, Charles—Deputy Governor Incorporation of Poor, 1838-1839.

Hickes, John Heathfield—Candidate Physician Infirmary, 1798.

Hickes, Thomas—Coroner, 1641-1647.

Hickes, William—Warden Merchant Venturers, 1619-1620.

Hicks, Thomas—President Gloucestershire Society, 1686.

Hicks, William—President Gloucestershire Society, 1792; President Colston (Parent) for 1810 (declined).

Hicks-Beach, Michael—President Gloucestershire Society, 1801; died January 5, 1830, aged 59. (M.P., Cirencester, 1794-1818.)

ALPHABETICAL INDEX (IV.)—*Continued*.

Hicks-Beach, Right Hon. Sir Michael Edward, Bart.—M.P., West Bristol, 1885; President Dolphin, 1893. (M.P., East Gloucestershire, 1864-1885 ; Privy Councillor, 1874; Secretary Poor Law Board, March-September, 1868; Under Home Secretary, September-December, 1868; Secretary for Ireland, 1874-1878, 1886-1887; Colonial Secretary, 1878-1880; Chancellor of the Exchequer, 1885-1886, 1895; President Board of Trade, 1886-1892.)

Hickson, Rev. Charles Wellington—Chaplain General Hospital, 1877-1890. (Vicar St. Bartholomew, 1873-1891.)

Hilhouse, James—Warden Merchant Venturers, 1730-1731; died January 7, 1754.

Hilhouse, James Martin—Master Merchant Venturers, 1793-1794; died June 24, 1822, aged 74.

Hilhouse, John—Warden Merchant Venturers, 1740-1741.

Hilhouse, Martin—Warden Merchant Venturers, 1821-1822; died November 22, 1858, aged 75.

Hilhouse, Robert—Warden Merchant Venturers, 1816-1817; died March 11, 1822.

Hilhouse, William—Sword Bearer, 1768-1778; Warden Merchant Venturers, 1762-1765; died November 19, 1778.

Hill, Charles—Sheriff, 1874-1875; President Dolphin, 1982; J.P., 1878.

Hill, Sir Edward Stock—M.P., South Bristol, 1886 (candidate, 1885); President Dolphin, 1887. (K.C.B., 1892.)

Hill, Jeremiah—Master Merchant Venturers, 1785-1786; died July 23. 1810, aged 90.

Hill, Jeremiah—Sheriff, 1842-1843; died April 1, 1857.

Hill, John Bartlett—President Colston (Parent) for 1828 (declined); died August 23, 1833, aged 59.

Hill, Matthew Davenport—Commissioner in Bankruptcy, 1851-1869; died June 7, 1872, aged 79. (M.P., Hull, 1832-1835; K.C., 1934.)

Hill, Richard—Deputy Governor Incorporation of Poor, 1801 (declined).

Hill, Thomas—Master Merchant Venturers, 1803-1804; died March 3, 1808.

Hill, Thomas—Sheriff, 1845-1846; died February 2, 1870, aged 75.

Hill, Walter James—Infirmary House Physician, 1888-1892; House Surgeon, 1892-1895.

Hinton, Edward—Secretary of Docks, 1847-1875; Warden Merchant Venturers, 1832-1833; died January 19, 1875, aged 85.

Hinton, George Pullin—Assessor, 1843; died September 30, 1864, aged 75.

ALPHABETICAL INDEX (IV.)—*Continued.*

Hinton, James Pullin—Assessor, 1844; died September 6, 1857, aged 71.

Hinton, Joseph—President Dolphin, 1778; died September 2, 1807, aged 80.

Hippisley, Robert Townsend—President Colston (Parent) for 1372 (declined).

Hobbs, John—Master St. Stephen's Ringers, 1697; Warden Merchant Venturers, 1722-1723.

Hobbs, John—President Grateful, 1789; died June 22, 1794.

Hobbs, Thomas Morgan—Master St. Stephen's Ringers, 1816; died December 24, 1851, aged 71.

Hobhouse, Sir Benjamin, Bart.—President Anchor, 1811; Parliamentary candidate, 1796; died Aug. 15, 1831, aged 74. (M.P., Bletchingley, 1797-1802; Grampound, 1802-1806; Lindon, 1805-1818; Chairman of Committees House of Commons, 1806; Secretary Board of Control, 1803-1804; created Baronet, 1812.)

Hobhouse, Henry—Governor Incorporation of Poor, 1752-1754; Treasurer Incorporation of Poor, 1750-1752; Warden Merchant Venturers, 1756-1757; died May 21, 1737.

Hobhouse, Henry—Master Merchant Venturers, 1788-1789; President Colston (Parent), 1784; died April 2, 1792.

Hobhouse, John—Governor Incorporation of Poor, 1760-1762; Treasurer Incorporation of Poor, 1758-1760; Warden Merchant Venturers, 1756-1757; died May 21, 1787.

Hobhouse, Right Hon. Sir John Cam, Bart.—Parliamentary candidate, 1835; died June 3, 1869. (M.P., Westminster, 1820-1833; Nottingham, 1834-1847; Harwich, 1848-1851; Privy Councillor, 1832; succeeded to Baronetcy, 1831; created Peer, 1851; Secretary at War, 1832-1833; Secretary for Ireland, 1833; First Commissioner of Woods and Forests, 1834; President Board of Control, 1835-1841, 1846-1852; G.C.B., 1852.)

Hoblyn, Robert—M.P., 1742-1754; died November 17, 1756.

Hobson, Samuel George—Parliamentary candidate, East Bristol, 1895.

Hodge, Thomas—Candidate School Board, 1877.

Hodges, Charles—Warden St. Stephen's Ringers, 1812; died September 12, 1844, aged 68.

Hodgson, Kirkman Daniel—M.P., 1870-1878; died September 11, 1879, aged 65. (M.P., Bridport, 1857-1868; contested Penryn, 1868; Governor Bank of England, 1863-1865.)

Hodgson, Michael—President Dolphin, 1769; died October 13, 1773.

ALPHABETICAL INDEX (IV.)—Continued.

Hodgson, Nathaniel—Master St. Stephen's Ringers, 1753.

Holder, William—President Colston (Parent), 1815; died January 3, 1828, aged 74.

Holford, Robert Stayner—President Gloucestershire Society, 1847; died February 22, 1892, aged 83. (M.P., East Gloucestershire, 1854-1872.)

Holland, Robert Carr Brackenbury—House Surgeon General Hospital, 1860-1864.

Hollidge, John—Master Merchant Venturers, 1734-1735.

Hollister, Arthur—Vice-Chamberlain till 1669.

Hollister, Jacob—Haven Master, August-November, 1773; died November, 1773.

Hollister, Thomas—Haven Master, 1752-1759.

Holmes, Thomas—Deputy Governor Incorporation of Poor, 1740-1741; died July 25, 1761.

Hood, William—Master St. Stephen's Ringers, 1814; died February, 1821.

Hope, Rev. Thomas—Usher Grammar School, 1826-1829; Mayor's Chaplain, 1836; died January 19, 1892, aged 88.

Hopkins, John—Assessor, 1845-1846.

Hore, Henry Augustus—Infirmary Apothecary, 1844-1846; House Surgeon, 1846-1856; Surgeon, 1857-1868; died May 24, 1871, aged 48.

Horsefield, Rev. Frederick John—Member School Board, 1897. (Vicar St. Silas, 1895.)

Horwood, Thomas—Master St. Stephen's Ringers, 1732; died 1753.

Hosegood, Obed—J.P., 1887; Charity Trustee, 1891.

Howard, Edward Stafford—President Anchor, 1888. (M.P., East Cumberland, 1876-1885; South Gloucestershire, 1885-1886 (candidate, 1886, 1892); Commissioner of Woods and Forests, 1893.)

Howard, Thomas — Docks Engineer, 1855-1882; died January 17, 1896, aged 79.

Howe, Robert—Master St. Stephen's Ringers, 1789; died February 15, 1809, aged 59.

Howe, Robert—Warden St. Stephen's Ringers, 1816; died April 17, 1850, aged 71.

Howe, William—Deputy Governor Incorporation of Poor, 1848-1849.

Howell, Charles Peter Branstrom—Warden Merchant Venturers, 1833; died May 12, 1884.

Howell, James Henry—J.P., 1898.

Howell, John—Physician Infirmary, 1829-1843; died May 28, 1857, aged 79.

ALPHABETICAL INDEX (IV.)—*Continued.*

Hudden, William Paul—Treasurer Colston (Parent), 1890-1891; J.P., 1889; died February 4, 1891, aged 58.

Hudson, Charles Thomas—Head Master Bristol Grammar School, 1855-1860 (Second Master, 1852-1855.

Hughes, James—President Dolphin, 1781; died Aug. 26, 1808.

Hughes, John—President Grateful, 1843; J.P., 1850; died May 2, 1859, aged 58.

Hull, William—Deputy Governor Incorporation of Poor, 1749-1750; died March 10, 1780.

Humpage, Edward—Candidate Surgeon General Hospital, 1832; died December 22, 1864, aged 61.

Hunt, Charles Henry—Clerk Clifton (Barton Regis) Guardians, 1870-1897; Superintendent Registrar, Barton Regis, 1881-1897.

Hunt, Henry—Parliamentary candidate, June, 1812, November, 1812; died February 13, 1835, aged 62. (M.P., Preston, 1830-1832; contested Westminster, 1818; Somerset, 1826.)

Hunt, Henry—Deputy Governor Incorporation of Poor, 1858-1863.

Hunt, James—President Grateful, 1778.

Hunt, Joseph—Deputy Governor Incorporation of Poor, 1724-1725.

Hunt, Samuel—Deputy Governor Incorporation of Poor, 1720-1721; Master Merchant Venturers, 1724-1725.

Hurle—See Cooke-Hurle.

Hutton, Thomas Rennie—Official Assignee Bankruptcy, 1842-1855.

Iles, John Thomas—Vice-Chairman Barton Regis Guardians, 1889-1891.

Innys, Jeremy—Master Merchant Venturers, 1725-1726; died November 22, 1764.

Ireland, James—President Colston (Parent) for 1806 (declined).

Ireland, Rev. Thomas—Mayor's Chaplain, 1776-1779; died May 22, 1816, aged 75. (Rector Christ Church, 1735-1816; Prebendary of Wells, 1780-1816.)

Ivey, John—Master St. Stephen's Ringers, 1700.

Jackson, Robert—President Colston (Parent), 1771; President Gloucestershire Society, 1773.

Jackson, Thomas—Coroner, 1706-1721; died 1721.

ALPHABETICAL INDEX (IV.)—*Continued.*

Jacob. Samuel—President Gloucestershire Society, 1711.

Jacques, Francis—Warden St. Stephen's Ringers, 1775; died October 14. 1779.

Jacques, Frederick Viel—Assessor, 1854-1875; died May 29. 1891, aged 72.

James. Alfred Bartlett—Master St. Stephen's Ringers. 1890.

James, Arthur Vyvian — Master St. Stephen's 1893; died August 14. 1894. aged 28.

James, Rev. Henry—Master Grammar School, 1635-1636.

James, John—Warden St. Stephen's Ringers, 1770; died May 16, 1778.

James, John—Warden St. Stephen's Ringers. 1790.

James, William—Deputy Governor Incorporation of Poor, 1771; Master St. Stephen's Ringers, 1775; died January 17. 1794.

James, William Bartlett—Warden St. Stephen's Ringers, 1845; died May 14, 1864, aged 58.

James. William Robert—Warden St. Stephen's Ringers, 1803; died February 23. 1805.

Jarman, Rev. George—Member School Board, 1898.

Jarret, Philip—Warden St. Stephen's Ringers, 1757; died May 11, 1765.

Jefferis. Charles Thornton—President Colston (Parent), 1878; died January 28, 1884, aged 79.

Jefferis., Richard—Deputy Governor Incorporation of Poor, 1714-1715.

Jefferis, William—Haven Master, 1767-1773; died 1773.

Jelf. Oliver—Deputy Governor Incorporation of Poor, 1755-1756; died February 18, 1778.

Jenkins, Walter—President Grateful, 1794.

Jenkinson, Sir George Samuel, Bart.—President Gloucestershire Society, 1863; died January 19. 1892, aged 74. (M.P., North Wilts, 1868-1880; contested Nottingham. 1866.)

Jenner. Henry—Provincial Grand Master of Freemasons, 1799-1808.

Jerrard, Joseph Henry—Principal Bristol College, 1831-1838; died February 26. 1853.

Jocham, James—Master St. Stephen's Ringers, 1701.

Jocham, Rev. Samuel—City Librarian, 1734-1743; died May 30, 1743, aged 50. (Rector St. Michael, 1722-1743; Vicar St. Leonard, 1734-1743.)

Johnes, Ven. Thomas—City Librarian, 1775-1809; Chaplain Infirmary, 1772-1817; died April 21, 1826. (Rector St. John, 1779-1826; Archdeacon of Barnstaple, 1807-1826; Chancellor of Exeter Cathedral and Prebendary of Exeter, 1816-1825.)

ALPHABETICAL INDEX (IV.)—Continued.

Johns, Henry—President Grateful, 1769.

Johnson, Samuel—Secretary Infirmary. 1823-1840 ; died September 26, 1849, aged 59.

Johnson, Rev. William—Chaplain General Hospital, 1870.

Johnston, Robert—Secretary Infirmary, 1840-1849 ; died February 11, 1849.

Johnstone, Rev. Robert Abercrombie—Mayor's Chaplain, 1841-1842; died September 23, 1867.

Jolliffe, Henry—Member School Board, 1893-1896.

Jolly, James—Haven Master, 1810-1825; died October 15, 1831, aged 72.

Jones, Averay Nicholas—Warden Merchant Venturers, 1897-1899.

Jones, Charles—Receiver of Town Dues, 1773-1781; died 1781.

Jones, Edward—Warden Merchant Venturers, 1691-1692.

Jones, Edward—Warden Merchant Venturers, 1721-1722.

Jones, George—President Grateful, 1813; died June 12, 1819.

Jones, George Fowley—Member School Board, 1880-1884; Clerk of Works, 1884.

Jones, Herbert John—Member School Board, 1887-1883.

Jones, James—Warden Merchant Ventrers, 1794-1795; died March 21, 1795.

Jones, James William—Member School Board, 1898.

Jones, John Marsh—Warden St. Stephen's Ringers, 1851.

Jones, Joseph—Master St. Stephen's Ringers, 1741-1742; died 1743.

Jones, Joshua—Auditor, 1837-1838, 1841-1842; died June 11, 1852, aged 53.

Jones, Philip—Master St. Stephen's Ringers, 1805; died November 21, 1814, aged 58.

Jones, Philip—Warden St. Stephen's Ringers, 1827; died October 19, 1829, aged 34.

Jones, Samuel—Corn Measurer, 1734-1741; died 1741.

Jones, Rev. Thomas—Usher Grammar School, 1740-1744; died 1755. (Vicar Temple, 1744-1755.)

Jones, Thomas—Sheriff, 1841-1842; died May 8, 1848.

Jones William—Governor Incorporation of Poor, 1778-1780; Master Merchant Venturers, 1770-1771; President Dolphin, 1780; Warden St. Stephen's Ringers, 1779; died September 8, 1792.

ALPHABETICAL INDEX (IV.)—*Continued.*

Jones, William—President Colston (Parent), 1820

Jones, William—Governor Incorporation of Poor, 1897-1898.

Jones, William Arthur—Master St. Stephen's Ringers, 1885; died May 12, 1890, aged 39.

Jones, William Rogers — Master St. Stephen's Ringers, 1777; died April 5, 1789.

Jose, Rev. Stephen Prust—Mayor's Chaplain, 1863-1864. (Minister Dowry Chapel, 1864-1871; Perpetual Curate Churchill, 1882.)

Jubbes, Thomas—M.P., 1519-1536.

Judd, James—Candidate West Bristol, 1886. (Contested North Suffolk, 1892.)

Keall, William Powell—Surgeon General Hospital, 1875-1889; died March 17, 1889.

Kearsey, William—Member School Board, 1880-1881.

Keene, Thomas—President Dolphin, 1777.

Kelway, Robert—Recorder, 1549-1552; M.P., 1547-1552; died February, 1580, aged 84. (M.P., Salisbury, 1545; Serjeant, 1552; Master in Chancery, 1552.)

Kemball, Charles Frederick—Warden St. Stephen's Ringers, 1863; died April 25, 1868.

Kemeys—See Allard-Kemeys.

Kentish, Edward—President Anchor, 1828; died December 5, 1832, aged 69.

Ker, John—Collector of Customs, 1843-1855; died October 9, 1869.

Kill, Daniel—Treasurer Incorporation of Poor, 1721 (declined).

King, Edmund Ambrose—Charity Trustee, 1891.

King, George Ley—Assessor, 1848-1869; died March 21, 1875, aged 58.

King, Henry—President Dolphin, 1770; died November 30, 1792.

King, Henry Wheeler—Assessor, 1842-1844; died Mar. 24, 1867, aged 77.

King, John—Candidate Surgeon Infirmary, 1807, 1812; died August 18, 1846, aged 81.

King, John—Warden Merchant Venturers, 1746-1747.

King, Percy Liston—Master Merchant Venturers, 1887-1888.

King, Thomas Poole—Master Merchant Venturers, 1889-1890.

Kingdon, Thomas Kingdon—Recorder, 1872-1879; died December 2, 1879, aged 67. (Q.C., 1866.)

ALPHABETICAL INDEX (IV.)—*Continued.*

Kinglake, John Alexander—Recorder, 1856-1870; died July 8, 1870. (M.P., Rochester, 1857-1870; Serjeant, 1844.)

Kington, Thomas—Sheriff, 1836-1837; J.P., 1837; died February 20, 1857.

Kirby, Joseph—Warden St. Stephen's Ringers for 1828 (declined).

Kirkpatrick, James—Town Clerk, 1785-1787; President Anchor, 1780; died May 23, 1787.

Kirley, James William—Inspector of Nuisances, 1877.

Knight, John—Warden Merchant Venturers, 1671-1672; died May 29, 1684, aged 31.

Knight, Rev. William—Mayor's Chaplain, 1825-1826; died August 5, 1878, aged 88. (Rector St. Michael, 1816-1875.)

Kroger, Henry—President Grateful, 1786 (declined); died November 14, 1784.

Kynaston, Roger—Official Assignee in Bankruptcy, 1843-1845; died May 13, 1847, aged 71. (Official Assignee in Bankruptcy, Leeds, 1845-1847.)

Lambert, Henry—Deputy Governor Incorporation of Poor, 1846-1847.

Lambert, John—President Colston (Parent) for 1814 (declined); died March 4, 1819, aged 81.

Lambert, Richard—Deputy Governor Incorporation of Poor, 1805-1806, 1807-1808; Master St. Stephen's Ringers, 1808; died June 25, 1851, aged 86.

Lancaster, Henry—Deputy Governor Incorporation of Poor, 1841-1842; died April 15, 1875, aged 71.

Lancaster, Hubert Thomas Henley—Superintendent Registrar and Clerk to Guardians, Barton Regis, 1897

Lane, James—Candidate School Board, 1871; died February 12, 1892, aged 73.

Lane, John—Warden St. Stephen's Ringers, 1820.

Lane, John Tremayne—City Treasurer, 1881.

Lang, Samuel—Charity Trustee, 1875-1885; President Anchor, 1876; Master St. Stephen's Ringers, 1881; died September 5, 1885, aged 41.

Lang, Thomas—President Anchor, 1855; died July 27, 1865, aged 67.

Lang, William—House Surgeon General Hospital, 1832-1836; Surgeon, 1840-1857; died November 26, 1870, aged 71.

Langdon, Andrew Nicholas—Deputy Governor Incorporation of Poor, 1852-1855; died December 4, 1860, aged 61.

ALPHABETICAL INDEX (IV.)—*Continued.*

Langley, John—Deputy Chamberlain, 1811-1815, Chamberlain, 1815-1822.

Langley, Joseph—Coroner, 1810-1836; died February 28, 1849, aged 76.

Langley, Philip—Sheriff, 1566-1567; Mayor, 1581-1582; M.P., 1572-1583.

Langton—See Gore-Langton.

Lansdown, Francis Poole—House Surgeon General Hospital, 1856-1859; Surgeon, 1861-1893.

Lansdown, Joseph Goodale—Surgeon General Hospital, 1832-1851; died July 6, 1871, aged 77.

Lansdown, Robert Guthrie Poole—Assistant Surgeon General Hospital, 1893-1896; Surgeon, 1896.

Lanseden, Thomas—Sheriff, 1543-1544; M.P., 1534.

Lasbury, Francis Plumley—Auditor, 1842-1846; died October 7, 1869.

Latcham, Charles Arthur—Superintendent Registrar Clifton, 1856-1857; candidate for Clerk of the Peace, 1836.

Lathrop, Richard—Secretary Infirmary, 1739-1752.

Lawes, Henry Fricker—Member School Board, 1871-1877; Deputy Governor Incorporation of Poor, 1857-1858; died April 19, 1880, aged 72.

Lawes, Henry Fricker—Assessor, 1876, 1877.

Lawless, Henry Hamilton—Parliamentary candidate, West Bristol, 1895.

Lawrance, Theodore—Coroner, 1820-1821; died Jan. 13, 1821.

Lawrence, Alfred Edward Aust—Physician-Accoucheur General Hospital, 1875-1897.

Lawrence, Benjamin—Warden St. Stephen's Ringers 1785.

Lawson, Arthur John—President Chamber of Commerce, 1888-1889.

Lee, Arthur—J.P., 1898.

Lee, Rev. Charles—Master Grammar School, 1764-1811; died October 6, 1811.

Lee, William—President Grateful, 1835; died May 28, 1877, aged 75.

Leicester, Earl of (Robert Dudley)—High Steward, 1570-1588; died September 4, 1588, aged 54. (M.P., Norfolk, 1553-1554; K.G., 1559; created Earl, 1564; Master of the Buckhounds, 1552-1553; Master of the Horse, 1559-1587; Chancellor of Oxford University, 1564-1567; Lord Steward, 1584-1587.)

Leighton, Robert Leighton—Head Master Grammar School, 1885.

Leman, Frederick—House Surgeon and Apothecary Infirmary, 1833-1837; died August 25, 1873.

Leman, James—President Colston (Parent), 1811.

Leman, Thomas Curtis—President Colston (Parent) 1819; died April 6, 1851, aged 63.

ALPHABETICAL INDEX (IV.)—*Continued.*

Lemon, William—Master St. Stephen's Ringers, 1872; died June 21, 1893, aged 79.

Lendon, Alfred Austen — House Surgeon Infirmary, 1879-1883.

Leonard, Crosby—Surgeon Infirmary, 1860-1878; died October 13, 1879, aged 51.

Leonard, Edward Albert—Secretary Infirmary, 1895.

Leonard, George Hare—J.P., 1878.

Leonard, John Hare—President Anchor, 1865; died January 18, 1895, aged 71.

Leonard, Solomon—J.P., 1863; died July 23, 1867, aged 68.

Lewis, David—Parliamentary candidate, 1790, 1796; died September 22, 1810.

Lewis, George—Vice-Chairman Barton Regis Guardians, 1883-1884; died April 9, 1884.

Lewis, Rev. Israel—Usher Grammar School, 1793-1799; died February 20, 1841, aged 79. (Vicar Long Ashton, 1794-1841.)

Lewis, John—City Solicitor till 1801; Clerk Arraigns, 1791-1807; died May 17, 1816, aged 82.

Lewis, John—President Grateful, 1793.

Lewis, Joseph—President Colston (Parent), 1750; died February 16, 1763.

Lewis, Samuel—Candidate School Board, 1871.

Lewis, Thomas—Warden St. Stephen's Ringers, 1818, 1824; died April 18, 1859, aged 77.

Lilley, George Herbert—House Surgeon Infirmary, 1878-1879.

Lilly, Peter—President Colston (Parent), 1801 (Treasurer, 1799-1807).

Limerick, Earl of (William Hale John Charles Pery) —Provincial Grand Master of Freemasons, 1867-1889; died August 8, 1896, aged 56. (Lord-in-Waiting, 1886-1889; Captain Yeomen of the Guard, 1889-1892, 1895-1896; Privy Councillor, 1889; K.P., 1892.)

Lindrea, Thomas Tucker—Vice-President Chamber of Commerce, 1897.

Linter, John—Deputy Governor Incorporation of Poor, 1864-1866; died May 5, 1878, aged 67.

Lippincott, Sir Henry Cann, Bart.—President Gloucestershire Society, 1806; President Colston (Parent) for 1818 (declined); died August 23, 1829.

Little, John—Corn Measurer, September-October, 1674; died October, 1674.

Little, John—President Colston (Parent), 1740 (Treasurer, 1742-1752); died November 30, 1758.

ALPHABETICAL INDEX (IV.)—*Continued.*

Lloyd, Edward John—Judge County Court, 1863-1874; died June 1, 1879, aged 87. (Q.C., 1849.)

Lloyd, William—Quay Warden, 1735-1739; died 1739.

Logan, William—Physician Infirmary, 1737-1757; died December 14, 1757, aged 69.

London, James Hurman—Secretary Charity Trustees, 1870-1872; died November 30, 1872.

Long, Sir Walter, Bart.—(?) M.P., 1680-1681; died May 21, 1711, aged 84.

Longman, Thomas—Master Merchant Venturers, 1723-1724; died November 29, 1753.

Lougher, Richard—Master Merchant Venturers, 1738-1739; died October 5, 1749.

Lougher, Walter—Warden Merchant Venturers, 1685-1687.

Lougher, Walter—Treasurer Incorporation of Poor, 1731-1732; Master Merchant Venturers, 1744-1745; died July 2, 1762.

Loveden, Edward Loveden—President Gloucestershire Society, 1791; died January 4, 1822, aged 71. (M.P., Abingdon, 1783-1796; Shaftesbury, 1802-1812)

Lovell, Robert—Physician Infirmary, 1795-1810; died April 11, 1823.

Lowe, Godfrey—President Dolphin, 1798; Surgeon Infirmary, 1775-1806; Warden St. Stephen's Ringers, 1772; died April 8, 1806, aged 66.

Lowe, Richard—Master St. Stephen's Ringers, 1746.

Lowe, Richard—President Dolphin, 1820; Surgeon Infirmary, 1807-1850; died February 9, 1850.

Lucas, Charles Phipps—President Colston (Parent) for 1890 (declined).

Lucas, George William—President Colston (Parent), 1876; died July 27, 1894, aged 72.

Lucas, Samuel—President Colston (Parent) for 1868 (declined); died November 27, 1868.

Lucas, Samuel Wilfrid—President Colston (Parent) for 1879 (declined); died November 21, 1883.

Lucy, William—Deputy Governor Incorporation of Poor, 1778-1779; died June 17, 1796.

Ludlow, Abraham—Candidate Surgeon Infirmary, 1737, 1741; died January 28, 1753.

Ludlow, Abraham—Surgeon Infirmary, 1767-1774; died July 5, 1807, aged 69.

Ludlow, Rev. Arthur Rainey—Mayor's Chaplain, 1851-1852; died January 9, 1890, aged 79. (Rector Littleton-on-Severn, 1855-1869.)

ALPHABETICAL INDEX (IV.)—*Continued.*

Ludlow, Ebenezer—Assessor Court of Requests, 1814-1819; Town Clerk, 1819-1836; Deputy Judge Tolzey Court, 1836-1842; Commissioner in Bankruptcy, 1849-1851; President Gloucestershire Society, 1842; Warden St. Stephen's Ringers, 1815; died March 18, 1851, aged 73. (Serjeant, 1827; Commissioner in Bankruptcy, Manchester, 1842-1844; Liverpool, 1844-1849.)

Ludlow, Ebenezer—Infirmary Assistant House Surgeon, 1865-1870; House Surgeon, 1870-1871; Assistant Physician, 1871-1872.

Lunell, George—President Grateful, 1826; Warden Merchant Venturers, 1817-1818, 1825-1827, 1830-1831, 1838-1839, 1842-1843; died January 19, 1875, aged 82.

Lunell, Samuel—Warden Merchant Venturers, 1819-1820; died September 29, 1876, aged 81.

Lunell, William Peter—President Anchor, 1793; Master Merchant Venturers, 1812-1813; died April 3, 1840.

Lyne, Edward—Physician Infirmary, 1757-1763; died November 20, 1772.

Lyne, Thomas—Deputy Governor Incorporation of Poor, 1786-1787; died April 3, 1808.

Lyne, William—Treasurer Incorporation of Poor, 1733-1734.

Lynnell, George—Coroner, 1667-1702; died 1702.

Lyon, Gilbert—Physician Infirmary, 1843-1857; died October 5, 1873, aged 70.

Lyon, James—President Grateful, 1827; died January 27, 1858, aged 67.

Lysaght, Gerald—Warden St. Stephen's Ringers, 1888, 1889.

Lysaght, John—Sheriff, 1882-1883; J.P., 1881; died October 1, 1895, aged 63.

McArthur, Allan—Master St. Stephen's Ringers, 1898.

McArthur, Donald—Warden St. Stephen's Ringers, 1874.

McCarthy, George Packer—Master St. Stephen's Ringers, 1788.

Macclesfield, Earl of (Charles Gerard)—Lord-Lieutenant, 1689-1694; died January 7, 1693-4. (Lieutenant-General; Privy Councillor, 1689; Lord-Lieutenant of Wales, 1689-1694; created Lord Gerard, 1645; Earl, 1679.)

McCurrich, John Martin—Docks Engineer, 1890-1899; died January 18, 1899, aged 46.

McGeachy, Forster Alleyne—Parliamentary candidate, 1852; died March 20, 1887, aged 77. (M.P., Honiton, 1841-1847.)

ALPHABETICAL INDEX (IV.)—*Continued*.

McIldowie, Rev. John—Member School Board, 1892-1896; died June 18, 1898.

Macintire, John Henry Lee—Medical Superintendent Infirmary, 1879-1883.

Mackie, Rev. John—Chaplain Infirmary, 1860-1876. (Rector Fylton, 1876.)

Maclaine, William Osborne—President Gloucestershire Society, 1864.

Macliver, David—President Anchor, 1884; J.P., 1881; died January 16, 1838, aged 45.

Macpherson, Rev. Alexander Cluny—Member School Board, August, 1885-1889 (candidate, 1889).

Madan, Rev. George—President Colston (Parent), 1871; died June 29, 1891, aged 83. (Vicar Redcliffe, 1852-1865.)

Madden, William—Deputy Governor Incorporation of Poor, 1873-1875.

Maddick, John—Master St. Stephen's Ringers, 1790; died February 16, 1795.

Magge, John—Sword Bearer till 1609.

Mais, Rev. John—Chaplain Infirmary, 1825-1856. (Rector Tintern, 1827.)

Mallard, John—Warden St. Stephen's Ringers, 1774; died September 15, 1817, aged 74.

Mallard, William—Auditor, 1839-1841, 1851-1853; died January 21, 1856, aged 61.

Man, Rev. Bartholomew—Master Grammar School, 1636-1643. (Rector Wenvoe, 1641.)

Manchee, Thomas John—Deputy Governor Incorporation of Poor, 1834-1836; Secretary Charity Trustees, 1836-1853; died June 11, 1853, aged 64.

Margetts, Rev. Henry—Usher Grammar School, 1705-1707.

Marloe, Richard—Sword Bearer, 1617-1628.

Marrack, William—House Surgeon General Hospital, 1854-1856.

Marriott, Rev. Walter—Chaplain General Hospital, 1855-1859; died October 8, 1859.

Marsh, Lewis Falconer—Vice-President Chamber of Commerce, 1885-1896.

Marriott, Rev. William—Chaplain General Hospital 1855-1859; died October 8, 1859.

Marshall, Henry—Surgeon General Hospital, 1861-1871; died April 24, 1898, aged 65.

Marten, Robert Henry—Vice-President Chamber of Commerce, 1882-1883.

Martin, George—President Gloucestershire Society, 1710.

ALPHABETICAL INDEX (IV.)--*Continued.*

Martin, James—Deputy Governor Incorporation of Poor, 1842-1843.

Martin, Rev. Joseph James—Member School Board, 1895-1897.

Martin, Thomas—Master St. Stephen's Ringers, 1698.

Martindale, Edward—Deputy Governor Incorporation of Poor, 1700-1701; Treasurer Incorporation of Poor, 1698-1699.

Martyn, Samuel—Physician General Hospital, 1853-1876; died July 27, 1876, aged 49.

Masey, James Marks—Warden St. Stephen's Ringers, 1839; died June 6, 1851.

Maskelyn, Griffith—Master St. Stephen's Ringers, 1775; Deputy Governor Incorporation of Poor (declined), 1778; died October 8, 1809, aged 68.

Mason, Benjamin—Apothecary Infirmary, 1779-1783; died 1783.

Mason, John—Surgeon General Hospital, 1845-1847; died December 30, 1847, aged 25.

Master, Thomas—President Gloucestershire Society, 1789; died May 12, 1823, aged 79. (M.P., Gloucestershire, 1784-1796.)

Master, Thomas William Chester—President Gloucestershire Soliety, 1868; died January 30, 1899, aged 83. (M.P., Cirencester, 1837-1844.)

Masters, John—Deputy Governor Incorporation of Poor, 1764-1765; died May 28, 1781.

Mather, Rev. Frederic Vaughan—Candidate School Board, 1880, 1881. (Vicar St. Paul, Clifton, 1853-1898.)

Mathews, Edward Robert Norris—City Librarian, 1895.

Matthews, Isaac—Water Bailiff, 1786-1798; died February 7, 1798.

Matthews, Thomas Gadd—President Grateful, 1830; died June 23, 1860, aged 58.

Maxse, John—President Colston (Parent) for 1803 (declined).

Mayers, Henry Adams—Steward Sheriff's Court, 1821-August, 1836; died October 19, 1836, aged 54.

Maynard, Rev. John—Mayor's Chaplain, 1829-1831; died September 13, 1877, aged 78. (Rector Sudbourne, 1842-1877.)

Mayo, John—President Colston (Parent), 1779; died April 7, 1791, aged 76.

Maze, James—Warden Merchant Venturers, 1826-1827; died April 5, 1831, aged 32.

Melton, Thomas—Treasurer Incorporation of Poor, 1710-1711.

ALPHABETICAL INDEX (IV.)—*Continued.*

Mercer, John—Auditor, 1849-1851; President Anchor, 1849; died January 22, 1879, aged 76.

Mercer, Robert—Clerk Clifton Guardians, 1856-1870; Superintendent Registrar Clifton, 1857-1881.

Meredith, Nicholas—Chamberlain, 1613-1639; died October 9, 1639.

Meredith, Nicholas—Corn Measurer, 1697-1710; died 1710.

Mereweather, John—President Colston (Parent). 1775; died May 16, 1778.

Mereweather, Samuel—President Grateful, 1790; died November 22, 1793.

Merrick, George—Mayor's Clerk, 1787-1807; Clerk of Arraigns, 1807-1820; City Solicitor, 1812-1820; died January 17, 1829.

Merrick, William—President-Elect Dolphin for 1765; died November 28, 1764.

Merrick, William—Master St. Stephen's Ringers, 1818 (resigned); died September 6, 1843.

Merricke, William—Warden Merchant Venturers, 1651-1652; Treasurer Merchant Venturers, 1657-1660.

Metcalfe, William James—Judge County Court, 1879-1892; died December 8, 1892, aged 74. (Q.C., 1875.)

Metford, Joseph—Surgeon Infirmary, 1783-1796; died March 25, 1835, aged 77.

Meyerhoff, Diedrich—Master St. Stephen's Ringers, 1768; died May 8, 1808.

Michel, John—Registrar Court of Conscience, 1740-1747.

Middleton, John—Physician Infirmary (declined), 1737; died December 16, 1760, aged 62.

Middleton, Walter—Warden St. Stephen's Ringers, 1733.

Miles, Henry Crager William—Sheriff, 1864-1865; Master Merchant Venturers, 1871-1872; President Gloucestershire Society, 1873; died April 5, 1888.

Miles, Sir Philip John William, Bart.—Sheriff, 1853-1854; President Dolphin, 1879; died June 5, 1888, aged 62. (M.P., East Somerset, 1878-1885; succeeded to Baronetcy, 1878.)

Miles, Philip Napier—President Gloucestershire Society, 1894.

Miles, Philip William Skynner—President Dolphin, 1843; M.P., 1837-1852; President Gloucestershire Society, 1846; President Chamber of Commerce, 1859-1874; died October 2, 1881, aged 65.

Miles, Sir William, Bart.—Chairman Clifton Guardians, 1836-1837; President Dolphin, 1837; President Gloucestershire Society, 1840; died June 17, 1878, aged 71. (M.P., Chippenham, 1818-1820; Romney, 1830-1832; East Somerset, 1834-1865; created Baronet, 1859.)

ALPHABETICAL INDEX (IV.)--*Continued.*

Millard, Edward—President Gloucestershire Society 1691.

Millard, James—Coroner, 1702-1715.

Millard, Samuel—Surgeon General Hospital, 1831-1832; died December 25, 1859, aged 60.

Miller, Alfred Robertson—Secretary Charity Trustees, 1853-1870; died January 24, 1874.

Miller, Edward Mant—Official Assignee in Bankrutcy. 1842-1863; died November 16, 1865.

Miller, George—J.P., 1868; died January 23, 1881, aged 60.

Miller, Rev. John—Usher Grammar School, 1662-1665.

Miller, John—Acting President Grateful, 1834; Master St. Stephen's Ringers, 1833; died September 1, 1857, aged 74.

Miller, John Day—Master St. Stephen's Ringers, 1895.

Miller, Michael—President Colston (Parent), 1761; died May 24, 1785.

Miller, William—Treasurer Incorporation of Poor, 1742-1743; died January 25, 1781, aged 82.

Miller, William—President Gloucestershire Society, 1834.

Mills, Thomas—President Anchor, 1847; died Juie 21, 1849, aged 42.

Milner, Francis—Sword Bearer, 1647-1661; died 1661.

Mirehouse, Rev. William Squire—Chairman Clifton Guardians, 1837-1859; died March 26, 1864, aged 73. (Rector Colsterworth and Perpetual Curate Fishponds, 1826-1864.)

Moggridge, John Hodder—Provincial Grand Master Freemasons, 1821-1829; died February 14, 1834, aged 63.

Mole, Harold Frederick—House Physician Infirmary, 1895-1897; House Surgeon, 1897.

Moncrieffe, William—President Dolphin, 1800; President Colston (Parent), 1799; Physician Infirmary, 1775-1816; died February 13, 1816.

Monkswell, Lord—See Collier.

Moore, Rev. Richard—City Librarian, 1752-1762; died January 28, 1762.

Morgan, Alexander—Water Bailiff, 1676-1683.

Morgan, Edwin Thomas—Member School Board, 1898.

Morgan, George—Official Assignee in Bankruptcy. 1842-1843. (Official Assignee, Liverpool, 1843-1869.)

Morgan, Henry—President Dolphin, 1758; died April 28, 1786.

Morgan, John—Master St. Stephen's Ringers, 1878; died September 19, 1894, aged 47.

ALPHABETICAL INDEX (IV.)—Continued.

Morgan, William—Warden St. Stephen's Ringers, 1837.

Morgan, William Francis—Apothecary Infirmary, 1825-1833; Surgeon Infirmary, 1837-1854; died December 9, 1872, aged 72.

Morley, Samuel—M.P., 1868-1885 (candidate, April, 1868); died September 5, 1886, aged 76.

Morris, Lewis—Warden St. Stephen's Ringers, 1870 (declined).

Morris, Thomas—Collector of Customs, 1832-1843; died January 13, 1848.

Morse, John—President Gloucestershire Society, 1735

Mortimer, William—President Dolphin, 1832; died December 7, 1851, aged 70.

Morton, Charles Alexander—Surgeon General Hospital, 1893.

Moss, Joseph—Candidate School Board, 1871.

Moxham, John—Auditor, 1838-1839; candidate for Secretary, Charity Trustees, 1853; died September 21, 1868, aged 80.

Muggleworth, Henry—Sword Bearer, 1710-1718 (Deputy, 1709-1710); died 1718.

Mullowney, James—Deputy Governor Incorporation of Poor, 1783-1784; died May 13, 1822.

Munckley, Samuel—Master Merchant Venturers, 1768-1769; died July 11, 1801.

Naish, Edwin Hilton—Treasurer Incorporation of Poor, 1898.

Naish, Thomas—President Grateful, 1780.

Nash, Rev. James Ezekiel—Mayor's Chaplain, 1842-1843; died May 13, 1884, aged 76. (Perpetual Curate St. Peter, Clifton Wood, 1855-1872; Vicar Elberton, 1872-1880.)

Nash, Stephen—Governor Incorporation of Poor, 1762-1764; Treasurer Incorporation of Poor, 1760-1762; died February 8, 1766.

Neale, John—Warden St. Stephen's Ringers, 1751; died 1752.

Neades (or Needes), John—Master St. Stephen's Ringers, 1683.

Neild, John Cash—Surgeon General Hospital, 1849-1853; died about 1882.

Nelme, Martin—Coroner, 1697-1715.

Nethway, Thomas—Warden Merchant Venturers, 1633-1634.

New, Rev. Francis Thomas—Mayor's Chaplain, 1833-1834.

New, John—Physician Infirmary, 1798-1802.

Newman, John—Treasurer Incorporation of Poor, 1737-1738.

ALPHABETICAL INDEX (IV.)—Continued.

Newnham, William Harry Christopher—House Surgeon General Hospital, 1885-1890; Physician Hospital, 1897.

Newport, Benjamin—Corn Measurer, 1757-1772.

Newton, Fred—Inspector of Weights and Measures, 1893.

Newton, Frederick Wentworth—Secretary Charity Trustees, 1873.

Nicholls, Charles — Master St. Stephen's Ringers, 1703.

Nicholls, James Fawkener—City Librarian, 1868-1883; died September 19, 1893, aged 65.

Nicholls, William—Master St. Stephen's Ringers, 1594.

Nichols, George—Master St. Stephen's Ringers, 1873; died February 19, 1896, aged 67.

Nichols, John—Master St. Stephen's Ringers, 1896.

Nicholson, William Alleyne—Physician General Hospital, 1845-1848.

Nixon, Brinsley De Courcy—Contested West Bristol, 1885. (Contested Dundee, 1886.)

Noble, John Padmore—Surgeon Infirmary, 1777-1812; died June 22, 1812, aged 57.

Norman, James—Surgeon Infirmary, 1779-1783; Master St. Stephen's Ringers, 1781; died February 28, 1827, aged 79.

Norman, Rev. James Charles—Mayor's Chaplain, 1862-1863; died May 1, 1893. (Rector Warehorne, 1858-1863; Vicar Highworth, 1869-1893.)

Norman, Jerome—Surgeon Infirmary, 1754-1763; died April 29, 1763.

Norman, John—Master Merchant Venturers, 1727-1728; Deputy Governor Incorporation of Poor, 1727-1728.

Norris, John Freeman—President Anchor, 1872; Member School Board, 1877-1882. (Q C., 1882; Judge, Bengal, 1882-1895.)

Norris, Ven. John Pilkington — Candidate School Board, 1871; died December 29, 1891, aged 68. (Inspector of Schools, 1849-1864; Canon Bristol, 1864-1891; Archdeacon of Bristol, 1881-1891; Dean of Chichester, 1891; Vicar St. George, Brandon Hill, 1870-1877; Vicar Redcliffe, 1877-1882.)

Norton, James—Deputy Governor Incorporation of Poor, 1802-1803; died June 13, 1820.

Norton, James—Secretary General Hospital, 1832-1835.

Norton, Robert—House Surgeon General Hospital, 1836-1840; died July 17, 1888, aged 74.

Nott, Richard—President Grateful, 1831; died May 17, 1846, aged 74.

ALPHABETICAL INDEX (IV.)—*Continued*.

Novis, George—Master St. Stephen's Ringers, 1696.

Oade, Thomas—Treasurer Incorporation of Poor, 1707-1708.

O'Brien, Rev. David—Member School Board, 1897.

O'Bryen, John Roche—Candidate for Physician General Hospital, 1838; died July 26, 1870, aged 58.

Odford, Cradock—President Grateful, 1783; died March 20, 1788.

O'Donoghue, Henry O'Brien—President Dolphin, 1895.

Oldfield, Thomas—Steward Gloucestershire Society, 1679; died June 24, 1703, aged 65.

Oliver, Edward—President Colston (Parent) for 1743 (declined).

Oliver, Joseph—Deputy Governor Incorporation of Poor, 1744-1745.

Oliver, Simon—President Dolphin, 1795; died May 26, 1814, aged 82.

Oliver, William—Master St. Stephen's Ringers, 1811; died April 18, 1830.

Onion, Edward—President Grateful, 1781; died Jan. 12, 1820, aged 83.

Openshaw, Rev. Thomas Williams—Second Master Grammar School, 1864-1892. (Rector Middleton Cheney, 1892.)

Orme, Charles—Registrar in Bankruptcy, 1846-1862; died February, 1865, aged 54.

Ormerod, Henry Lawrence—House Physician Infirmary, 1892-1895.

Ormiston, Rev. James—Member School Board, 1892-1897. (Rector Maryleport, 1880; Vicar St. David, West Holloway, 1869-1875; Vicar Old Hill, 1875-1880.)

Ormonde, Duke of (James Butler)—Lord-Lieutenant 1660-1672; High Steward, 1661-1688; died July 21, 1688, aged 77. (Succeeded to Earldom, 1632; created Marquis, 1642; Duke, 1661; K.G., 1649; Privy Councillor, 1660; Lord-Lieutenant of Ireland, 1643-1647, 1648-1650, 1662-1669, 1677-1685; Chancellor Dublin University, 1645-1650, 1660-1688; Chancellor Oxford University, 1669-1688; Lord Steward, 1660-1688.)

Ormonde, Duke of (James Butler)—High Steward, 1688-1715; attainted, 1715; died November 16, 1745, aged 80. (Succeeded to Dukedom, 1688; Chancellor Oxford and Dublin Universities, 1688-1715; Commander-in-Chief, 1712-1714; Lord of the Bedchamber, 1685-1688, 1689-1699; Privy Councillor, 1696; Lord-Lieutenant of Ireland, 1703-1707, 1710-1713; K.G., 1688.)

ALPHABETICAL INDEX (IV.)—Continued.

Osborne, Jeremiah—President Dolphin, 1761; died February 10, 1786.

Osborne, Jeremiah—President Dolphin, 1828; died November 21, 1842, aged 65.

Osborne, Jeremiah—President Dolphin, 1889; President Gloucestershire Society, 1891.

Osbourne—See Smyth-Osbourne.

Ossory, Earl of (Thomas Butler, eldest son of Duke of Ormonde, styled Earl of Ossory by courtesy)—M.P., 1661-1666; died July 30, 1680, aged 46. (Created English Peer, 1666; M.P., Dublin University, 1661-1662; Irish Peer, 1662; Privy Councillor, 1666; Lord of the Bedchamber, 1666-1680; Lord of the Admiralty, 1675-1679; Lord Deputy Ireland, 1664-1665, 1668-1669.)

Owen, Francis—Warden St. Stephen's Ringers, 1776; Collector Exchange, 1788-1807; died 1807.

Owen, Thomas—Warden St. Stephen's Ringers, 1764.

Packer, Daniel—Vice-Chamberlain, 1691-1699; Postmaster, 1693-1694.

Packer, George—President Gloucestershire Society, 1707.

Packer, George—Treasurer Incorporation of Poor, 1740-1741.

Pagden, Elgar — Collector of Customs, 1877-1882; died March 21, 1883.

Page, John—Surgeon Infirmary, 1741-1777; died June 30, 1792, aged 78.

Page, Thomas—Surgeon Infirmary, 1737-1741; died May 5, 1741, aged 53.

Paine, Rev. Samuel—City Librarian, 1691-1722; died January 18, 1721-2, aged 57. (Vicar St. Leonard, 1690-1722; Rector St. Michael, 1695-1722.)

Paling, Albert—House Surgeon General Hospital, 1897.

Palmer, Arthur—Under Sheriff, 1789-1819; President Anchor, 1809, 1826; Prothonotary Tolzey Court, 1789-1838; died August 23, 1849, aged 94.

Palmer, Arthur—Assessor Court of Requests, 1839-1847; Judge County Court, 1847-1854; died Nov. 19, 1856, aged 73.

Palmer, Frederick—President Anchor, 1846; died July 11, 1865, aged 58.

Palmer, Henry Andrewes—President Anchor, 1838; Registrar Tolzey Court, 1838-1860; died December 16, 1884, aged 82.

Palmer, John Jordan—Secretary Infirmary, 1791-1818; Clerk of the Haymarket, 1799-1828; died April 17, 1828, aged 74.

Panter, John Rocke—President Colston (Parent), 1836; died October 28, 1840, aged 60.

ALPHABETICAL INDEX (IV.)—*Continued.*

Parker, George—Assistant Physician General Hospital, 1892.

Parker, Richard—President Gloucestershire Society 1759.

Parnell, Thomas Saunders—Master St. Stephen's Ringers, 1850; died February 28, 1875, aged 62.

Parr, Thomas—President Dolphin, 1878.

Parry, Edwin—Vice-Chairman Barton Regis Guardians, 1875-1882.

Parsons, Edward Thornborough—Haven Master, 1874.

Partridge, Charles—President Dolphin, 1784; died June 20, 1805, aged 79.

Pass, Alfred Capper—J.P., 1894.

Pate, Rev. Henry Williams—Mayor's Chaplain, 1897-1898. (Head Master Cathedral School, 1876.)

Paterson, Andrew—President Anchor, 1773; died June, 1788.

Patterson, Rev. George—Member School Board, 1892-1893.

Paty, Thomas—President Dolphin, 1771; died May 4, 1789, aged 76.

Paty, William—District Surveyor, 1789-1800; died December 12, 1800.

Paul, Charles—Treasurer Incorporation of Poor, 1854-1857; President Grateful, 1852; died November 1, 1857.

Paul, Charles—Master Merchant Venturers, 1885-1886; died June 8, 1897, aged 60.

Paul, Charles William—Master St. Stephen's Ringers, 1875; died January 1, 1897.

Paul, Rev. Frederick Campbell—Member School Board, 1897-1898 (candidate, 1898). (Rector St. Peter, 1892.)

Paul, John—Steward Gloucestershire Society, 1714.

Paul, John—Physician Infirmary, 1772-1775; died June 15, 1815.

Paul, John Paul—President Gloucestershire Society 1800.

Payne, Rev. James—Master Grammar School, June-July, 1622.

Peace, John—City Librarian, 1815-1856; died March 30, 1861, aged 75.

Peace, Peter—President Grateful, 1812; died Nov. 27, 1827, aged 73.

Peach, Samuel Peach—President Gloucestershire Society, 1797; died February 25, 1845, aged 76.

Pearce, Rev. Edward—Master Grammar School, 1702-1709. (Vicar Pitminster, 1709.)

Pease, Thomas—Chairman Clifton (Barton Regis) Guardians, 1876-1881.

ALPHABETICAL INDEX (IV.)—*Continued.*

Pellatt, Apsley—Parliamentary candidate, 1847; died April 17, 1863, aged 71. (M.P., Southwark, 1852-1857.)

Pembroke, Earl of (William Herbert) — High Steward, 1550-1570; died March 17, 1570. (Created Earl, 1551; K.G., 1548; Master of the Horse, 1543-1552; Lord President of Wales, 1550-1553, 1555-1558; Lord Steward, 1568-1570.)

Pembroke, Earl of (William Herbert)—Lord - Lieutenant, 1621-1630; High Steward, 1615-1630; died April 10, 1630. (K.G., 1603; Warden Stannaries, 1604-1630; Lord Chamberlain, 1615-1626; Lord Steward, 1626-1630; Chancellor Oxford University, 1617-1630.)

Pembroke and Montgomery, Earl of (Philip Herbert)—Lord-Lieutenant, 1630-1642, 1643-1650; High Steward, 1630-1650; died January 23, 1650. (M.P., Glamorganshire, 1604-1605; created Earl of Montgomery, 1605; K.G., 1608; succeeded to Earldom of Pembroke, 1630; Lord Chamberlain, 1626-1641; Chancellor Oxford University, 1641-1643, 1647-1650.)

Pengelly, Thomas Hodge—Deputy Governor Incorporation of Poor, 1866-1868; died September 12, 1875, aged 68.

Penington, Ferdinand—President Dolphin, 1757; died October 18, 1766.

Penn, Sir William—Parliamentary candidate, 1660; died September 3, 1670, aged 49. (Admiral; M.P., Melcombe Regis, 1661-1670; knighted 1660.)

Penny, William John—House Surgeon General Hospital, 1881-1884; Assistant Surgeon, 1885-1888; Surgeon, 1888-1896.

Penrose, Charles—President Gloucestershire Society 1723.

Penwarne, Rev. Nicholas—City Librarian, 1676-1691. (Rector St. Stephen, 1671-1691.)

Pepler, William—Candidate School Board, 1889, 1892.

Perceval, Ernest Augustus—President Gloucestershire Society, 1892-1893; died January 19, 1896, aged 88.

Percival, Right Rev. John—Member School Board, 1871-1874; Head Master Clifton College, 1862-1873. (Canon of Bristol, 1882-1887; Prebendary Exeter, 1871-1882; President Trinity College, Oxford 1878-1887; Head Master Rugby, 1887-1895; Bishop of Hereford, 1895.)

Percival, Joseph—President Colston (Parent), 1762; died June 28, 1764.

Perinton, John—President Grateful, 1792; died March 16, 1818.

Perkins, Joseph—Quay Warden, 1809-1812; died September 6, 1835, aged 69.

ALPHABETICAL INDEX (IV.)--*Continued.*

Perkins, Thomas—Master Merchant Venturers, 1780-1781; Warden St. Stephen's Ringers, 1771; died April 22, 1824.

Perkins, Walter—Deputy Governor Incorporation of Poor, 1756-1757; died September 15, 1765.

Perks, John—President Colston (Parent), 1763; Warden St. Stephen's Ringers, 1745; died December 4, 1773.

Perrin, Edward Warman — Warden St. Stephen's Ringers, 1853.

Perrin, George Henry—President Chamber of Commerce, 1894-1896.

Perry, Henry Charles—Member School Board, 1882-1887.

Perry, James—Governor Incorporation of Poor, 1823-1827; Warden St. Stephen's Ringers, 1821; died August 16, 1840.

Perry, Nicholas—President Dolphin, 1767; President Gloucestershire Society, 1755.

Perry, William—Warden Merchant Venturers, 1811-1812; died February 7, 1820, aged 55.

Perry, William—Vice-Chairman Barton Regis Guardians, 1884-1886.

Peters, Charles Abbott—Assessor, 1870-1877; died November, 1891.

Peters, James—Treasurer Incorporation of Poor, 1709-1710.

Peto, Sir Samuel Morton, Bart.—M.P., 1865-1868; died November 13, 1889, aged 80. (M.P., Norwich, 1847-1854; Finsbury, 1859-1865; created Baronet, 1855.)

Phelps, Rev. Philip Ashby—Mayor's Chaplain, 1875-1876. (Rector St. John, 1885.)

Phelps, William—President Colston (Parent), 1761.

Philipps, Sir John, Bart.—Parliamentary candidate 1754; died June 23, 1764. (M.P., Carmarthen, 1745-1747; Petersfield, 1754-1761; Pembrokeshire, 1761-1764; Lord of Trade, 1744-1745.)

Phillips, Augustus—Chairman Chamber of Commerce, 1866-1867; died December 11, 1896, aged 81.

Phipps, Constantine—Warden St Stephen's Ringers 1769.

Pickering, Charles Frederick—House Surgeon General Hospital, 1879-1881; Surgeon, 1882.

Pierce, Rev. Charles—Mayor's Chaplain, 1793-1798, 1799-1300, 1807-1303; died October 17, 1809, aged 43.

Pike, James—Water Bailiff, 1849-1853; candidate Quay Warden, 1847; died November 25, 1858, aged 61.

ALPHABETICAL INDEX (IV.)—*Continued*.

Pike, John Thorner—Auditor, 1817-1870; Secretary General Hospital, 1835-1859; died July 18, 1870, aged 80.

Pike, Thomas—Master St. Stephen's Ringers, 1852.

Pine, Henry—Postmaster, 1694-1740.

Pine, Thomas—Postmaster, 1740-1760.

Pine, Thomas—Postmaster, 1760-1777; died April 7, 1777.

Pinke, John—President Colston (Parent), 1745 (Treasurer, 1755-1765.)

Pitman, John—President Gloucestershire Society, 1744.

Pitt, Thomas—Chamberlain, 1603-1613; died May 4, 1613.

Plaister, Richard—President Colston (Parent), 1786 (Treasurer, 1793-1794); died January 31, 1794.

Player, Jacob—Deputy Governor Incorporation of Poor, 1769-1770; died June 17, 1787.

Plomer, James—Physician Infirmary, 1761-1798; died October 2, 1803, aged 88.

Plunkett, Hon. Randall Edward Sherborne—President Gloucestershire Society, 1878; died December 25, 1883, aged 35. (M.P., West Gloucestershire, 1874-1880.)

Pocock, Charles Innes—Warden St. Stephen's Ringers, 1834; died January 29, 1875, aged 68.

Pocock, Rev. Nicholas—Mayor's Chaplain, 1871-1872; died March 4, 1897, aged 72.

Polglase, William—Chairman Chamber of Commerce, 1873-1874; died February 6, 1880, aged 61.

Pollard, John—Master St. Stephen's Ringers, 1743; died December 2, 1772.

Pollock, John Henry—Registrar in Bankruptcy, 1842-1845; died November 9, 1873, aged 81.

Poole, Arthur Ruscombe—Recorder, 1892-1897; died May 22, 1897, aged 57. (Q.C., 1888.)

Poole, John David—Warden St. Stephen's Ringers, 1861; died about September, 1863.

Pope, Charles—Warden Merchant Venturers, 1688-1689.

Pope, George—Master Merchant Venturers and President Chamber of Commerce, 1853-1854; died January 16, 1888.

Pope, George Henry—Sheriff, 1888-1889; Treasurer Merchant Venturers, 1876.

Pope, John Noble Coleman—President Dolphin, 1885; Master Merchant Venturers, 1880-1881.

Pope, Richard Shackleton—District Surveyor, 1831-1873; died February 10, 1884, aged 92.

ALPHABETICAL INDEX (IV.)—*Continued.*

Pope, Thomas—District Surveyor, 1801-1805.

Popham, Sir John—Recorder, 1570-1577; M.P., 1571, 1572-1583; died June 10, 1607. aged 76. (Serjeant, 1579; knighted, 1592; Solicitor-General, 1579-1581; Attorney-General, 1581-1592; M.P., Lyme Regis, 1558; Speaker, 1581; Chief Justice Queen's Bench 1592-1607.)

Pople, Alfred—Candidate School Board, 1871.

Porter, Rev. Joseph—Mayor's Chaplain, 1823-1824; died November 2, 1833, aged 58. (Rector St. John, 1826-1833.)

Portland, Earl of (Richard Weston)—High Steward, 1630-1635; died March 12, 1634-5. (M.P., Lichfield, 1621-1622; Callington, 1625; Bodmin, 1626; knighted, 1622; created Lord Weston, 1628; Earl, 1634; Privy Councillor, 1621; Chancellor of the Exchequer, 1621-1628; Lord High Treasurer, 1628-1635; K.G., 1631.)

Portland, Duke of (William Henry Cavendish Bentinck)—High Steward, 1796-1809, died October 31, 1809. (M.P., Weobley, 1761-1762; succeeded to Dukedom, 1762; Lord Chamberlain, 1765-1766; Privy Councillor, 1765; First Lord of the Treasury, 1783, 1807-1809; Home Secretary, 1794-1801; President of the Council, 1801-1805; K.G., 1801; Chancellor of Oxford University, 1792-1809; Lord Lieutenant of Notts, 1792-1809.)

Potter, David—Master St. Stephen's Ringers, 1689.

Powell, Charles—President Grateful, 1771; died March 30, 1786.

Powell, George—Candidate School Board, 1880.

Powell, John—President Dolphin, 1762.

Powell, John—Master St. Stephen's Ringers, 1767.

Powell, John—Collector of Customs, 1779-1799; Governor Incorporation of Poor, 1776-1778; Master Merchant Venturers, 1779-1780; President Colston (Parent), 1783; (?) President Grateful, 1772; died July 10, 1799.

Powell, Joshua—President Colston (Parent) for 1830 (declined); died 1864.

Powell, Robert—Apothecary Infirmary, 1850-1851; died September 15, 1856, aged 29.

Powell, Thomas—Quay Warden, 1794-1809; died Nov. 2, 1809, aged 81.

Powell, Thomas Joseph Cookson—Assistant House Surgeon Infirmary, 1856-1858; House Surgeon, 1858-1860; died February 26, 1860, aged 27.

Powell, Timothy—President Colston (Parent), 1785; died December 1, 1795.

Powell, Walter—Warden Merchant Venturers, 1786-1787.

Powell, William—President Colston (Parent), 1849; died February 3, 1854, aged 64.

ALPHABETICAL INDEX (IV.)—*Continued*

Power, John O'Connor—Contested South Bristol 1895. (M.P., Mayo County, 1874-1885; contested Kennington, 1885.)

Power, Joshua—President Gloucestershire Society, 1765.

Pownall, Rev. Richard—City Ligrarian, 1631-1670. (Rector St. John, 1632-1670.)

Prankerd, Thomas—Warden St. Stephen's Ringers, 1757; died July 24, 1761.

Prelleur, Rev. James—Chaplain St. Mark's, 1745-1751; died 1751.

Price, Alfred Newell—Charity Trustee, 1875; President Anchor, 1890; J.P., 1889.

Price, Charles—President Grateful, 1873; died Aug. 25, 1881.

Price, Francis—Master St. Stephen's Ringers, 1685.

Price, Rev. John—Usher Grammar School, 1744-1755; Mayor's Chaplain, 1751-1758; died 1771. (Vicar Temple, 1755-1765; Rector St. James, 1766-1771.)

Price, Richard—President Gloucestershire Society, 1719.

Price, Richard—Master St. Stephen's Ringers, 1800.

Price, Samuel—Master Merchant Venturers, 1694-1696.

Price, Rev. Thomas Charles—Member School Board, 1874-1885; died November 8, 1885, aged 69. (Vicar St. Augustine, 1851-1885.)

Prichard, Arthur William—Assistant Surgeon Infirmary, 1876-1878; Surgeon, 1878.

Prichard, Augustin—Surgeon Infirmary, 1850-1870; died January 6, 1898, aged 79.

Prichard, James Cowles—Physician Infirmary, 1816-1843; died December 22, 1848, aged 63.

Prichard, Rev. Jonathan—Usher Grammar School, till 1658.

Prideaux, Charles Grevile—Recorder, 1870-1892; died June 18, 1892, aged 81. (Q.C., 1886.)

Prideaux, George Fisher—President Dolphin, 1868; died November 18, 1883, aged 68.

Prideaux, Neast Grevile — President Dolphin, 1831; died December 24, 1851, aged 68.

Prideaux, Rev. Walter Cross—Mayor's Chaplain, 1896-1897. (Vicar St. Saviour, 1883.)

Priest, Richard—Warden St. Stephen's Ringers, 1808; killed in a duel by Henry Smith, March 1, 1809.

Priest, William—Warden St. Stephen's Ringers, 1803.

ALPHABETICAL INDEX (IV.)—*Continued.*

Pring, Martin—Warden Merchant Venturers, 1625-1626; died 1626.

Pritchard, William—Warden St. Stephen's Ringers, 1827; died January 24, 1837.

Proctor, William—President Colston (Parent), 1879 (declined); died November 8, 1890.

Proctor, William—Master St. Stephen's Ringers, 1899; President-Elect Colston (Parent), 1899.

Prosser, William—Deputy Governor Incorporation of Poor, 1721-1722.

Protheroe, Edward Davis—M.P., 1831-1832 (candidate 1830, 1832); died August 18, 1852, aged 54. (M.P., Evesham, 1826-1830; Halifax, 1837-1847; took name Davis before Protheroe, 1845.)

Protheroe, Mark Davis—Master Merchant Venturers, 1858-1859; died March 6, 1863, aged 50.

Protheroe, Thomas—Deputy Governor Incorporation of Poor, 1895-1896.

Prowse, Arthur Baucks—Infirmary Assistant Physician, 1883-1888; Physician, 1888.

Prowse, James Barrington—Candidate House Surgeon and Apothecary Infirmary, 1840; died April 22, 1865, aged 49.

Pryce, George—City Librarian, 1856-1868; died Mar. 15, 1868.

Pugsley, William—Master St. Stephen's Ringers, 1690.

Punter, Simon—Quay Warden, 1758-1775.

Purnell, Benjamin—President Colston (Parent), 1840; died December 13, 1860, aged 77.

Purnell, James—Coroner, 1731-1750; President Colston (Parent) for 1763 (declined); died March 14, 1772.

Purnell, William—President Colston (Parent), 1837; died March 13, 1844.

Purrier, John—President Grateful, 1773; died January 1, 1785.

Pym, Daniel—Sword Bearer, 1681-1710; died 1710.

Pynn, William—Master St. Stephen's Ringers, 1758.

Quick, Francis—Assessor, 1847; died December 4, 1881.

Quinton, Henry Chidgey—President Grateful, 1836; Master St. Stephen's Ringers, 1844; died March 15, 1874, aged 80.

Radford, Rev. William—Usher Grammar School, 1705-1706.

ALPHABETICAL INDEX (IV.)—*Continued.*

Rainstorp, Rev. John—Master Grammar School, 1670-1687; died May 1, 1693. (Rector St. Michael, 1677-1693; Vicar All Saints, 1686-1693; Prebendary of Bristol, 1634-1693.)

Rainstorp, John—Treasurer Incorporation of Poor, 1726-1727.

Rainstorp, Rev. Walter—Master Grammar School, 1643-1658; died 1658.

Rainstorp, Rev. Walter—Usher Grammar School, 1708-1728; died October 9, 1769, aged 82. (Rector Crompton Greenfield, 1724-1769.)

Randall, Ven. Henry Goldney—Member School Board, 1871-1874; died August 7, 1881, aged 72. (Perpetual Curate Bishopsworth, 1853-1865; Vicar Redcliffe, 1865-1877; Archdeacon of Bristol, 1875-1881.)

Randall, Martin—House Surgeon General Hospital, 1896-1897.

Randall, Very Rev. Richard William—President Dolphin, 1890; candidate School Board, 1883, (Rector Woolavington, 1851-1868; Vicar All Saints, Clifton, 1868-1892; Dean of Chichester, 1892.)

Randolph, Francis—Candidate Physician Infirmary 1747; died April 21, 1764.

Randolph, George—President Colston (Parent) for 1757 (declined).

Randolph, William—Warden Merchant Venturers, 1787-1788; died June 27, 1791.

Rawlins, John—Candidate Surgeon Infirmary, 1774.

Ray, Henry—President Gloucestershire Society, 1854; died April 19, 1856, aged 37.

Ray, Henry Carpenter—President Gloucestershire Society, 1889; died September 3, 1891, aged 68.

Redding, Rev. Thomas—City Librarian, 1765-1768; died September, 1768.

Redpath, William James—Collector of Customs, 1870-1877; died November 30, 1892.

Reed, James—Treasurer Incorporation of Poor, 1764-1766; died November 22, 1785.

Reeve, Andrews—Warden Merchant Venturers, 1756-1767; died July 2, 1802.

Reeve, William—Master Merchant Venturers, 1765-1766; died September 22, 1778.

Reynell, Rev. Carew—Mayor's Chaplain, 1758-1771; died April 24, 1781, aged 51. (Vicar St. Philip, 1759-1772; Perpetual Curate St. James, 1772-1781.)

Reynolds, Thomas—Treasurer Incorporation of 1823-1826; died September 28, 1867, aged 88.

Richard, Rev. Richard—Member School Board, 1896-1898.

Richards, Edwin John—Auditor, 1891.

ALPHABETICAL INDEX (IV.)—*Continued.*

Richards, Henry—Warden St. Stephen's Ringers, 1796; died January 26, 1831, aged 75.

Richards, Rev. Henry—Vice-Chairman Clifton Guardians, 1869-1870; died May 16, 1871. (Rector Horfield, 1828-1865.)

Richards, William — President Gloucestershire Society, 1755.

Richardson, Helena—Member School Board, 1877-1880 (candidate, 1880).

Richardson, Thomas—Warden Merchant Venturers, 1692-1694.

Ricketts, Jacob Wilcox—President Anchor, 1801; died August 30, 1859, aged 86.

Riddle, William Lury — Warden St. Stephen's Ringers, 1836; died July 3, 1877, aged 81.

Ridout, Charles—President Dolphin, 1811; died February 23, 1815.

Rigge, Joseph—Deputy Governor Incorporation of Poor, 1750-1751; died October 3, 1784, aged 84.

Rigge, Thomas—Physician Infirmary, 1767-1773; died May, 1794.

Righton, John—Deputy Governor Incorporation of Poor, 1833-1834; died February 8, 1836, aged 38.

Riley, Henry—Physician Infirmary, 1834-1847; died April 20, 1848, aged 51.

Ringer, Charles—Warden Merchant Venturers, 1865-1867; died March 25, 1868.

Robe, Edward—Haven Master, 1825-1841; died May 29, 1841.

Robe, Edward—Quay Warden, 1847-1860; died Dec. 31, 1860.

Roberts, Rev. Henry Seymour—Second Master Grammar School, 1855-1864. (Head Master Thornbury Grammar School, 1864-1869; Wigton, 1869-1870; Alford, 1870-1876).

Roberts, John—Corn Measurer, 1672-1674; died 1674.

Robertson, Henry Amelius Powell — Governor Incorporation of Poor, 1864-1868; died July 24, 1880, aged 65.

Robertson, Rev. James—Principal Bishop's College, 1846-1859; died April 22, 1875. (Rector Christ Church, 1859-1875.)

Robertson, Robert—Candidate Physician Infirmary 1772.

Robertson, Samuel—President Grateful, 1802; died April 10, 1842, aged 76.

Robins, John—Steward Sheriff's Court, 1662-1690; Steward Gloucestershire Society, 1673.

Robinson, Alfred—Warden St. Stephen's Ringers, 1849; died August 16, 1887, aged 78.

Robinson, Alfred—J.P., 1887.

Robinson, Arthur—President Grateful, 1893.

ALPHABETICAL INDEX (IV.)—*Continued.*

Robinson, Edward--President Anchor, 1887; Vice-President Chamber of Commerce, 1880-1883; J.P., 1889.

Robinson, Richard—Warden St. Stephen's Ringers, 1755.

Robinson, Richard—Warden St. Stephen's Ringers, 1798; died April 14, 1834, aged 77.

Robson, John—Deputy Governor Incorporation of Poor (declined), 1832; died June 11, 1864, aged 75.

Rogers, Rev. Aaron—Candidate School Board, 1871; died September 4, 1872, aged 68. (Incumbent Trinity, St. Philip's, 1841-1849; Vicar St. Paul. 1849-1867.)

Rogers, Corsley—Treasurer Incorporation of Poor, 1734-1735.

Rogers, Francis—Warden Merchant Venturers, 1754-1755; died January 27, 1760.

Rogers, Henry—Member School Board, 1892-1895 (candidate, 1895.)

Rogers, James—Warden Merchant Venturers, 1788-1789; died 1799.

Rogers, Joseph—House Surgeon General Hospital, 1849-1851.

Rogers, Richard—President Colston (Parent) for 1760 (declined).

Rogerson, Thomas—Corn Measurer, 1710-1711; died 1711.

Rolt, Right Hon. Sir John — President Gloucestershire Society, 1856; died June 6, 1871. (M.P., East Gloucestershire, 1857-1867; contested Stamford, 1847; Bridport, 1852; Q.C., 1846; knighted, 1866; Solicitor-General, 1856-1867; Lord Justice of Appeal, 1867-1868; Privy Councillor, 1867.)

Rolt, John—President Gloucestershire Society, 1876.

Romilly, Sir Samuel—Parliamentary candidate, 1812; died November 2, 1818, aged 62. (M.P., Queenborough, 1806-1807; Horsham, 1807-1808; Wareham, 1808-1812; Arundel, 1812-1818; Westminster, 1818-1819; K.C., 1810; knighted, 1806; Solicitor-General, 1806-1807.)

Room, James—Master St. Stephen's Ringers, 1818; died July 19, 1852, aged 68.

Rose, John—President Grateful, 1804; died Jan. 26, 1814.

Ross, Josiah—President Colston (Parent), 1759; died April 29, 1771.

Rosser, Edward—Master St. Stephen's Ringers, 1782; died October 22, 1791.

Rouch, Isaac—President Chamber of Commerce, 1845-1848; died January 31, 1857, aged 70.

Rowand, John—President Anchor, 1772; President Grateful, 1763; died December 5, 1778.

ALPHABETICAL INDEX (IV.)—*Continued.*

Rowe, John—Sword Bearer, 1677-1681.

Rowley, Rev. Adam Clarke—Chaplain General Hospital, 1859-1860. (Vicar St. Matthias, 1846-1875; Vicar Sutterton, 1875.)

Rudhall, Henry—Deputy Governor Incorporation of Poor, 1803-1804; died April 20, 1828.

Rumsey, George Ferris—Chairman Barton Regis Guardians, 1889-1898; Chairman Bristol Guardians, 1898-1899; J.P., 1899.

Rumsey, Nathaniel—Apothecary Infirmary, 1737-1739.

Russell, John—President Gloucestershire Society, 1728.

Rymer, Gabriel—Deputy Governor Incorporation of Poor, 1780-1781; died August 5, 1788.

Safford, Joseph—Coroner, 1778-1810; died August 11, 1812.

Sage, Rev. William Hood—Chaplain Infirmary, 1856-1860; died December 20, 1874. (Vicar St. Michael, Two Mile Hill, 1860-1874.)

Salisbury, Earl of (Robert Cecil)—High Steward, 1608-1612; died May 24, 1612. (M.P., Westminster, 1584-1585, 1586-1587; Herts, 1588-1589, 1593, 1597-1598, 1601; knighted, 1591; Privy Councillor, 1591; created Lord Cecil, 1603; Viscount Cranbourne, 1604; Earl, 1605; K.G., 1607; Secretary of State, 1590-1612; Chancellor Duchy of Lancaster, 1597-1599; Lord High Treasurer, 1608-1612; Chancellor of Cambridge and Dublin Universities, 1601-1612.)

Salmon, John—Master Merchant Venturers and President Chamber of Commerce, 1854-1855; died March 22, 1878, aged 77.

Salterne, George—Steward Sheriff's Court, 1618-1637; died 1637.

Salterne, William—Sheriff, 1574-1575; M.P., 1588-1589; died January, 1588-9.

Sampson, Edward—President Colston (Parent), 1773; President Gloucestershire Society, 1774; died March 20, 1795.

Sampson, Edward—President Dolphin, 1818; President Gloucestershire Society, 1832; Master St. Stephen's Ringers, 1835; died August 19, 1848, aged 75.

Sampson, Edward—Sheriff, 1847-1848; President Dolphin, 1860; President Gloucestershire Society, 1851; died October 13, 1897, aged 87.

Sampson, Edward Chaddock—Postmaster, 1871-1891; died December 7, 1895, aged 74.

Sampson, John—Deputy Governor Incorporation of Poor, 1743-1744.

ALPHABETICAL INDEX (IV.)—*Continued.*

Samson, Henry—Deputy Governor Incorporation of Poor, 1710-1711.

Sandell, Thomas—President Gloucestershire Society 1763.

Sanders, Thomas—President Dolphin, 1799; died October 21, 1801.

Sanders, William—Charity Trustee, 1852-1875; J.P., 1858; died November 12, 1875, aged 76.

Sangar, Benjamin—Deputy Governor Incorporation of Poor, 1825-1826; died September 24, 1852, aged 69.

Saunders, Edmund—Treasurer Incorporation of Poor, 1728-1729.

Saunders, Henry William—House Surgeon General Hospital, 1870-1873.

Saunders, Joshua—Sheriff, 1860-1861; Vice-President Chamber of Commerce, 1862-1864, 1868-1870.

Saunders, Thomas — President Gloucestershire Society, 1790.

Saunders, William—Treasurer Incorporation of Poor, 1710 (declined).

Savage, Charles Walter—President-Elect Gloucestershire Society for 1895; died December 6, 1894, aged 65.

Savage, Francis—President Dolphin, 1855; Warden Merchant Venturers, 1837-1838; Master St. Stephen's Ringers, 1845, 1856; died October 3, 1882, aged 68.

Savery, Charles—President Anchor, 1832; died July 6, 1867, aged 79.

Savile, Albany Bourchier—Sheriff, 1855-1856; died May 24, 1873, aged 57.

Savile, Henry Bourchier Osborne—Sheriff, 1883-1884; Member School Board, 1874-1877; President Gloucestershire Society, 1884; J.P., 1887.

Sayce, Samuel John — President Stock Exchange, 1882-1884; died March 4, 1899.

Scott, James—Infirmary Assistant House Surgeon, 1877-1878; House Physician, 1878-1880.

Scott, William—Warden St. Stephen's Ringers for 1819 (declined).

Scudamore, Rowles—Steward Sheriff's Court, 1753-1795; died November 15, 1802, aged 90.

Seaborne, Henry—Master St. Stephen's Ringers, 1705.

Seaborne, Richard—Master St. Stephen's Ringers, 1749; died March, 1767.

Searchfield, Rowland—Coroner, 1682-1695.

Seaton, Rev. William—Mayor's Chaplain, 1844-1845; died March 25, 1868. (Perpetual Curate Christ Church, Pennington, 1854-1862; Vicar St. Thomas, Lambeth, 1862-1868.)

ALPHABETICAL INDEX (IV.)—Continued.

Sergeant, Robert—Died Master-Elect St. Stephen's Ringers, 1694 or 1695.

Seyer, Rev. Samuel—Master Grammar School, 1744-1764; died November 2, 1776. (Rector St. Michael, 1764-1776.)

Shapland, Christopher—Deputy Governor Incorporation of Poor, 1811-1812; died January 28, 1819, aged 57.

Shapland, Joseph—Master St. Stephen's Ringers, 1762; died April 2, 1801, aged 74.

Sharp, Charles—Sword Bearer, 1643-1647.

Shaw, John—Haven Master, 1782-1797; died 1797.

Shaw, John Edward—Infirmary Assistant House Surgeon, 1873-1876; Assistant Physician, 1876-1877; Physician, 1877.

Sheffield, Lord (John Baker Holroyd)—M.P., 1790-1802; died May 30, 1821, aged 80. (M.P., Coventry, February-September, 1780, 1781-1784; created Irish Peer, 1780; British Peer, 1802; Irish Earl, 1816; Commissioner of Trade, 1809-1821.)

Shekleton, Joseph Furlonge—Secretary Infirmary, 1887-1895.

Sheldon, Richard—Master St. Stephen's Ringers, 1757; died March 2, 1765.

Shellard, John Edwin—J.P., 1898.

Shepherd, Joseph—Apothecary Infirmary, 1746-1752; died November, 1782.

Sheppard, Thomas—Warden St. Stephen's Ringers, 1837.

Sherborne, Lord—See Dutton.

Shipley, Alfred—Chairman Barton Regis Guardians 1892.

Shute, Henry — President Gloucestershire Society, 1853; Provincial Grand Master Freemasons, 1845-1865; died March 24, 1865, aged 75.

Shute, John—Chairman Chamber of Commerce, 1860-1861; died July 23, 1877.

Shute, Richard—Deputy Governor Incorporation of Poor, 1717-1718.

Shute, Robert—Warden St. Stephen's Ringers, 1778.

Shute, Thomas—President Colston (Parent), 1812; died February 23, 1818, aged 68.

Shute, Thomas—Surgeon Infirmary, 1812-1816; died September 2, 1816.

Siddall, Joseph Bower—House Surgeon General Hospital, 1866-1867; Physician General Hospital, 1876-1879.

Simmonds, Rev. Delasaux Egginton Mount—Chaplain General Hospital, 1874-1877.

Simpson, Jesse James—Clerk Incorporation of Poor 1887-1898; Clerk Bristol Guardians, 1898.

ALPHABETICAL INDEX (IV.)—Continued.

Simpson, Nicholas—Apothecary Infirmary, 1739-1744; died March 29, 1779.

Sinclair, John—Master St. Stephen's Ringers, 1770.

Skerritt, Edward Markham—Physician General Hospital, 1875.

Skone, Thomas—Surgeon Infirmary, 1767-1770; died about 1779.

Slade, Edward—Auditor, 1845-1846; died June 13, 1863.

Slade, Sir Frederic William, Bart.—Parliamentary candidate, 1859; died August 8, 1863, aged 62. (Contested Salisbury, 1852; Cambridge, 1854; Q.C., 1851; succeeded to Baronetcy, 1859.)

Sladen, William—President Dolphin, 1772; Warden St. Stephen's Ringers, 1759; died October 9, 1801, aged 84.

Smith, Brooke—President Anchor, 1814, (acting) 1817; died September 20, 1825.

Smith, Brooke—Assessor, 1810; President Anchor, 1835; died October 24, 1881, aged 78.

Smith, Charles—President Grateful, 1808.

Smith, Conrade—Treasurer Incorporation of Poor, 1739-1740.

Smith, Edward Titt Bisshopp—Collector of Customs 1889-1895.

Smith, Freeman—Sword Bearer, 1781-1801; died March 29, 1801.

Smith, George Munro—Infirmary Assistant Surgeon 1889-1897; Surgeon, 1897.

Smith, Henry—Master St. Stephen's Ringers, 1752; died September 22, 1772.

Smith, Henry—Warden St. Stephen's Ringers, 1821; died August 16, 1840.

Smith, James Greig—Infirmary Assistant House Surgeon, 1876-1877; Surgeon, 1877-1878; Medical Superintendent, 1878-1879; Surgeon, 1879-1897; died May 25, 1897, aged 43.

Smith, Sir Jarrit, Bart.—M.P., 1756-1768; President Colston (Parent), 1748; died January 25, 1783, aged 92. (Created Baronet, 1763.)

Smith, John—Steward Sheriff's Court, 1643-1645.

Smith, Joseph—Assessor Court of Requests, 1819-1839; died January 24, 1839.

Smith, Nathaniel—Surgeon Infirmary, 1816-1844; died December 20, 1869, aged 89.

Smith, Richard—Deputy Governor Incorporation of Poor, 1748-1749.

ALPHABETICAL INDEX (IV.)—*Continued.*

Smith, Richard—President Dolphin, 1766; died February 24, 1777, aged 69.

Smith, Richard—Surgeon Infirmary, 1774-1791; President Dolphin, 1786; died June 21, 1791.

Smith, Robert—Master Merchant Venturers, 1774-1775; President Colston (Parent), 1792 (declined); died December 16, 1812, aged 73.

Smith, Robert Shingleton—Infirmary Assistant House Surgeon, 1870-1871; House Surgeon, 1871-1873; Physician, 1873.

Smith, Samuel—Master Merchant Venturers, 1763-1764; Deputy Governor Incorporation of Poor, 1759-1760; President Dolphin, 1755; President Colston (Parent), 1764; died February 15, 1772

Smith, Thomas—President Colston (Parent), 1746.

Smith, William—President Grateful, 1811.

Smith, William—President Grateful, 1821.

Smith, William—Candidate Surgeon General Hospital, 1849; died November 24, 1876, aged 55.

Smyth, Sir John Henry Greville, Bart.—Sheriff, 1857 (declined). (Created Baronet, 1859.)

Smyth, Sir John Hugh, Bart.—President Colston (Parent), 1778; died March 30, 1782. (Succeeded to Baronetcy, 1783.)

Smyth, Thomas—Quay Warden, 1694-1698; died 1693.

Smyth, Thomas—President Colston (Parent), 1794; died March 11, 1800.

Smyth-Osbourne, John Smyth—President Gloucestershire Society, 1881.

Solly, Reginald Vaughan—House Surgeon General Hospital, 1890-1893.

Somerset, Duke of (Edward Seymour) — High Steward, 1541-1549; executed January 22, 1852. (Knighted, 1523; created Viscount Beauchamp, 1536; Earl of Hertford, 1537; Duke, 1547; K.G., 1541; Earl Marshal, 1547-1551; Protector of the Realm, 1547-1549; Chancellor of Cambridge University, 1547-1552.)

Somerset, Lord Charles Henry—President Gloucestershire Society, 1802; died February 20, 1831, aged 63. (M.P., Scarborough, 1796-1802; Monmouth, 1802-1813; Privy Councillor, 1797; Comptroller of the Household, 1797-1804; Paymaster-General, 1804-1806, 1807-1813; Governor Cape of Good Hope, 1813-1828; General in the Army.)

Somerset, Edward Arthur—President Gloucestershire Society, 1781; died March 12, 1886, aged 69. (M.P., Monmouthshire, 1848-1859; West Gloucestershire, 1867-1868; General in Army; C.B. 1857.)

ALPHABETICAL INDEX (IV.)—*Continued.*

Somerset, Lord Robert Edward Henry—President Colston (Parent), 1813; President Gloucestershire Society, 1813; died September 1, 1842, aged 65. (M.P., Monmouth, 1799-1802; Gloucestershire, 1803-1831; Cirencester, 1834-1837; General in Army; K.C.B., 1815; G.C.B., 1834; Lieutenant-General of Ordnance, 1829-1831; Surveyor-General of Ordnance, 1835.)

Southall, Norman Daunsey—Warden-Elect St. Stephen's Ringers, 1808; died May 20, 1808, aged 47.

Southwell, Right Hon. Edward—M.P., 1739-1754; President Colston (Parent), 1752; died March 16, 1755, aged 50. (M.P., Downpatrick, 1727-1755; Secretary of State for Ireland, 1730-1755; Privy councillor for Ireland.)

Southwell, Edward—President Gloucestershire Society, 1771; died November 7, 1777, aged 43. (M.P., Bridgwater, 1761-1763; Gloucestershire, 1763-1776; confirmed in title of Lord de Clifford, 1776.)

Spafford, George Oswald—Warden Merchant Venturers, 1898; President-Elect Grateful for 1899.

Sparkes, William—Quay Warden till 1671; died 1671.

Spear, Henry John—Secretary Chamber of Commerce, 1887.

Speed, Thomas—Warden Merchant Venturers, 1651-1652.

Spencer, John—Parliamentary candidate, 1756; died October 31, 1783. (M.P., Warwick, 1756-1761; created Viscount Spencer, 1761; Earl, 1765.)

Spencer, William Henry—Infirmary Assistant Physician, 1872-1873; Physician, 1873-1888.

Springer, Joshua—Master St. Stephen's Ringers, 1801; died August 30, 1812, aged 80.

Squire, William Wilkinson—Docks Engineer, 1899.

Stack, Edward Hugh Edwards—House Physician Infirmary, 1897.

Stampe, Rev. Thomas—Usher Grammar School, 1688-1690.

Standfast, Nicholas—President Gloucestershire Society, 1695.

Stanton, John—Physician General Hospital, 1854-1856; died August 12, 1879, aged 68.

Stedder, Stephen Horsley—Collector of Mayor's Dues, 1847-1863; died May 7, 1863.

Steele, Charles—Surgeon Infirmary, 1870-1878.

Steele, John—President Colston (Parent), 1839; died November 5, 1846, aged 86.

ALPHABETICAL INDEX (IV.)—*Continued.*

Stephen, Henry John—Commissioner in Bankruptcy, 1842-1854; died November 28, 1864, aged 77. (Serjeant, 1827.)

Stephens, Henry Oxley—Medical Superintendent Lunatic Asylum, 1860-1871; died April 12, 1881.

Stephens, Rev. John—Master Grammar School, 1658-1662.

Stephens, John—Corn Measurer, 1801-1810; died Nov. 19, 1810, aged 78.

Stephens, Lockhart Edward Walker—House Surgeon General Hospital, 1884-1885.

Stephens, Matthew—Water Bailiff after 1668.

Stephens, Thomas—Steward Sheriff's Court, 1738-1745; President Gloucestershire Society, 1740; died 1745.

Stephens, Rev. William—Master Grammar School, 1687-1539. (Rector St. Werburgh till 1686.)

Stevens—See Weston-Stevens.

Stevenson, Richard—Commissioner in Bankruptcy, 1842-1849; died June 15, 1858. (Commissioner in Bankruptcy, Liverpool, 1849-1858.)

Stevenson, William—Warden St. Stephen's Ringers, 1771.

Stiff, Thomas—President Colston (Parent), 1844; died July 10, 1855, aged 64.

Stoate, Richard—Warden St. Stephen's Ringers for 1833 (declined); died April 5, 1844, aged 68.

Stock, Benjamin Spry—President Stock Exchange, 1884-1895; died November 1, 1895.

Stock, Edward—Sword Bearer, 1877-1883.

Stock, John Edmonds—Physician Infirmary, 1811-1828; President Anchor, 1816; died October 4, 1835, aged 61.

Stock, William—Deputy Governor Incorporation of Poor, 1815-1817; President Colston (Parent), 1816; died April 7, 1825.

Stock, William Spry—Sword Bearer, 1865-1877; died July 17, 1877, aged 68.

Stokes, Thomas—Coroner, 1753-1755.

Stone, Samuel—Apothecary Infirmary, 1744-1746.

Stone, Thomas—Warden St. Stephen's Ringers, 1822.

Stopford, Charles—Warden St. Stephen's Ringers, 1853; died October, 1875, aged 72.

Stratton, William — President Gloucestershire Society, 1705.

Strickland, Jacob—Warden St. Stephen's Ringers, 1832; died November 27, 1885, aged 84.

Strong, William—Master St. Stephen's Ringers, 1840, died June 28, 1846, aged 54,

ALPHABETICAL INDEX (IV.)—*Continued.*

Struth, Rev. Nathaniel—Mayor's Chaplain, 1818-1819; died January 30, 1847, aged 54.

Sturge, Emily—Member School Board, 1880-1892; died June 3, 1892, aged 45.

Sturge, Jacob Player—Land Steward, 1844-1857; died October 19, 1857.

Sturge, William—Land Steward, 1857.

Sturge, Young—Land Steward, 1810-1844; died February 2, 1844.

Summers, Augustus William—J.P., 1898.

Summers, Robert—President Gloucestershire Society 1722.

Sumner, Rev. Oliver—Chaplain Infirmary, 1877-1878. (Vicar Buildwas, 1888-1891; Rector Pilton, 1891-1894.)

Sutton, Rev. John—City Librarian, 1732-1734; died December 30, 1745. (Vicar St. Leonard, 1732-1734; Vicar St. Augustine, 1734-1745; Prebendary of Bristol, 1723-1745.)

Swain, James—Infirmary House Physician, 1886-1887; House Surgeon, 1887-1892; Assistant Surgeon, 1892.

Swann, Louisa—Member School Board, 1889-1895 (candidate 1895).

Swanton, Charles—Warden St. Stephen's Ringers, 1750; died 1775.

Swayne, Joseph—Deputy Governor Incorporation of Poor, 1726-1727.

Swayne, Joseph Griffiths—Physician-Accoucher General Hospital, 1854-1875.

Swayne, Walter—President Dolphin, 1830; died April 16, 1842, aged 67.

Swayne, Walter—Obstetric Physician Infirmary, 1891.

Swayne, William—Apothecary Infirmary, 1816-1825; died June 15, 1825.

Swete, Rev. John—Mayor's Chaplain, 1821-1822; Chaplain Infirmary, 1817-1825; died September 17, 1869. (Rector Blagdon, 1850-1869.)

Swift, Rev. William—Master Grammar School till 1622; died May 31, 1622, aged 52.

Swymmer, Anthony—Under Sheriff till 1760; Vice-Chamberlain, 1754-1766; Registrar Court of Conscience, 1760-1787; died October 5, 1787.

Symes, Richard—President Colston (Parent), 1788; died January 4, 1814, aged 90.

Symonds, John Addington—Physician General Hospital, 1831-1844; died February 25, 1871, aged 63.

ALPHABETICAL INDEX (IV.)—*Continued.*

Tandy, John—President Colston (Parent), 1757 (Treasurer, 1752-1755).

Tandy, John—Elected President Colston (Parent), 1775 (declined); died October 18. 1822, aged 85.

Tanner, John Barton—Vice-Chairman Barton Regis Guardians, 1898.

Tanner, William—Master St. Stephen's Ringers, 1806; died August 17, 1851, aged 81.

Tanner, William—Vice-Chairman Clifton Guardians 1870-1872; died October 20, 1887, aged 85.

Tawman, Thomas—President Grateful, 1770; died May 15, 1774.

Taylor, Rev. Charles Samuel—Member School Board 1893-1897. (Vicar St. Thomas, 1877-1896; Rector Banwell, 1896.)

Taylor, Daniel—Treasurer Incorporation of Poor, 1766-1768; died December 4, 1779.

Taylor, Edmund Judkin—Deputy Town Clerk, 1899.

Taylor, Georgina Caroline Annie—Member School Board, 1885-1892 (candidate, 1892).

Taylor, Rev. James—Master Grammar School, 1717-1722; died June, 1722. (Rector St. Michael's, April-June, 1722.)

Taylor, James—Warden St. Stephen s Ringers, 1782

Taylor, John—President Gloucestershire Society, 1741.

Taylor, John—President Dolphin, 1840; died April 11, 1850, aged 70.

Taylor, John—City Librarian, 1885-1893; died April 9, 1893, aged 63.

Taylor, John Howell Goodenough—Master St. Stephen's Ringers, 1887.

Taylor, Rev. Robert Askwith—Mayor's Chaplain, January-November, 1840, 1855-1856; died June, 1876. (Vicar Norton Malreward, 1867-1876.)

Taylor, Samuel Edward—Deputy Governor Incorporation of Poor, 1845-1846; Warden St. Stephen's Ringers, 1851; died April 4, 1891, aged 75.

Taylor, Thomas David—President Grateful, 1886.

Taylor, William—President Colston (Parent), 1874; died February 4, 1883, aged 72.

Teast, Sidenham—President Colston (Parent), 1749; President Gloucestershire Society, 1752; died January 24, 1775.

Teast, Sidenham—President Colston (Parent) for 1810 (declined); died June 13, 1813.

Templeman, John—Warden Merchant Venturers, 1728-1729.

ALPHABETICAL INDEX (IV.)—*Continued.*

Thomas, Charles—President Anchor, 1871.

Thomas, Edward—Vice-President Free Port Association, 1846-1850; died December 28, 1853, aged 59.

Thomas, George—Auditor, 1853-1872; died August 17, 1878, aged 73.

Thomas, Herbert—Charity Trustee, 1865 (Chairman 1875; Member School Board, 1871-1874; President Anchor, 1853; Chairman Chamber of Commerce, 1862-1863; Vice-President Chamber of Commerce, 1869-1871; J.P., 1868.

Thomas, Joseph—President Colston (Parent) for 1777 (declined); died May 6, 1777.

Thomas, Josiah—Corn Measurer, 1772-1776; died November 3, 1786, aged 60.

Thomas, Josiah—Deputy Governor Incorporation of Poor, 1801-1802; died June 29, 1842, aged 72.

Thomas, Josiah—District Surveyor, 1859-1872; City Surveyor, 1872-1897; died July 5, 1897.

Thomas, Samuel—Deputy Governor Incorporation of Poor, 1774-1775; Parliamentary candidate, 1796; died June 17, 1799.

Thomas, Thomas—Member Sshool Board, 1884-1889.

Thomas, Rev. Urijah Rees—Member School Board, 1874-1790, 1892 (Vice-Chairman, 1883-1889, 1892-1898, Chairman, 1898); President Anchor, 1889.

Thomas William—Governor Incorporation of Poor, 1874-1875; died September 2, 1890.

Thompson, Charles J.—Secretary General Hospital, 1869-1872.

Thompson, George—Medical Superintendent Lunatic Asylum, 1871-1890; died August 8, 1895, aged 52.

Thompson, John—Master St. Stephen's Ringers, 1691.

Thompson, John—Water Bailiff, May-September, 1774; died September 25, 1774.

Thompson, Rev. John—Member School Board, 1889-1892. (Vicar St. Gabriel, Easton, 1870-1895.)

Thorne, Nicholas—Sheriff, 1528-1529; Mayor, 1544-1545; M.P., 1539-1540; died August 19, 1546.

Thorne, Nicholas—Chamberlain, 1584.

Thornhill, John—Coroner, 1755-1762; died February 21, 1782.

Thornhill, William—Deputy Governor Incorporation of Poor, 1731-1732.

Thornhill, William—Surgeon Infirmary, 1737-1754.

Thornley, Jacob—Deputy Governor Incorporation of Poor, 1760-1761; died August 22, 1814, aged 90.

Thrall, Jacob—Deputy Governor Incorporation of Poor, 1760-1761; died August 22, 1804, aged 90.

ALPHABETICAL INDEX (IV.)—*Continued.*

Thwaites, William—Secretary General Hospital, 1885.

Tibbits, Robert William—Surgeon Infirmary, 1868-1878; died November 23, 1878, aged 36.

Tobin, James—Governor Incorporation of Poor, 1794-1796; President Colston (Parent) for 1810 (declined); died October 6, 1817.

Tocknell, Walter—Master Merchant Venturers, 1667-1669; Treasurer Merchant Venturers, 1658-1665; Coroner, 1650-1682; Steward Gloucestershire Society, 1665, 1668; died 1682.

Tombs, Richard—President Gloucestershire Society 1737; died May 24, 1762.

Tombs, Richard—President Dolphin, 1788; Warden Merchant Venturers, 1788-1789; died October 23, 1803, aged 40.

Tombs, Robert Charles—Postmaster, 1892.

Tombs, William—President Gloucestershire Society, 1756; died December 8, 1768.

Tomlinson, John—President Colston (Parent), 1832; died October 14, 1849.

Tomlinson, John—Dock Master, 1883.

Tomlinson, William—Haven Master, 1798-1810.

Toplis, Francis Stanley—Member School Board, 1889-1892.

Towgood, John—Water Bailiff till 1668; died 1668.

Townsend, Fanny Marion—Member School Board, 1892.

Townsend, John—Surgeon Infirmary, 1754-1781; died November 12, 1800, aged 70.

Trapnell, Henry Caleb—Candidate School Board, 1892.

Trebilco, Rev. James—Member School Board, 1898.

Trenerry, William—Secretary Infirmary, 1849-1884; died October 14, 1884.

Trevena, Rev. Walter—City Librarian, 1762-1764; Usher Grammar School, 1764-1785; died July 5, 1785, aged 53.

Tribe, Eva Selina—Member School Board, 1885-1886.

Tribe, Frank Newton—Auditor, 1894-1898; Charity Trustee, 1891; President Anchor, 1894; J.P., 1898.

Tribe, Wilberforce—Auditor, 1872-1894; J.P., 1889.

Tricks, Frank Wood—Auditor, 1884-1891.

Tucker, Rev. Rowland—Usher Grammar School, 1665-1681.

Tuckett, Richard George Shum—Registrar in Bankruptcy, 1842-1854; died January 7, 1854, aged 59.

Tunbridge, Robert—Master St. Stephen's Ringers, 1708.

ALPHABETICAL INDEX (IV.)—*Continued.*

Turner, Benjamin — President Gloucestershire Society, 1704.

Turner, James—Quay Warden and Water Bailiff, 1895.

Turner, Thomas—Member School Board, 1871-1874 (candidate 1874); died November 3, 1893, aged 73.

Turner, William—Chairman Chamber of Commerce 1869-1870.

Turpin, Robert—Quay Warden, 1698-1706: died 1706.

Turton, William—Master St Stephen's Ringers, 1699.

Tustin, John—Deputy Governor Incorporation of Poor, April-October, 1783; died October 28, 1783.

Tyler, John—Governor Incorporation of Poor, 1736-1737.

Tyler, John—President Colston (Parent), 1795; died April 25, 1810, aged 75.

Tyler, Richard—Deputy Governor Incorporation of Poor, 1725-1726.

Tylor, Joseph Savery—Physician General Hospital, 1856-1859.

Tyndall, William—Sheriff, 1547-1548; M.P., 1553; died 1558.

Tyndall, William — President Gloucestershire Society, 1793.

Underwood, Richard Seymour—Secretary General Hospital, 1859-1860; died November 4, 1870, aged 59.

Underwood, William—President Grateful, 1814; Warden St. Stephen's Ringers, 1816; died October 22, 1850.

Vachell, Beverley Robinson—Warden St. Stephen's Ringers, 1892 (declined).

Vachell, Charles Redwood—House Surgeon and Apothecary Infirmary, 1837-1840; died May 26, 1865.

Vane, Sir Henry—High Steward, 1650-1651; executed June 14, 1662, aged 50. (M.P., Hull, 1640-1653; Whitchurch, 1659-1660.)

Vassall, Robert Lowe Grant—Sheriff, 1879-1880; President Dolphin, 1883; President Gloucestershire Society, 1883.

Vaughan, Hugh—Warden Merchant Venturers, 1800-1802; died November 10, 1813, aged 59.

ALPHABETICAL INDEX (IV.)—*Continued.*

Vaughan, Hugh—Sheriff, 1840-1841; died September 20, 1876, aged 66.

Vaughan, James—Treasurer Incorporation of Poor, 1776-1780; President Colston (Parent) for 1801 (declined); died January 6, 1821, aged 82.

Vaughan, John—Vice-Chamberlain, 1724-1736

Vaughan, John—Treasurer Incorporation of Poor, 1754-1758; died November 20, 1771.

Vaughan, John—Master Merchant Venturers, 1787-1788; President Colston (Parent), 1787; died September 10, 1795.

Vaughan, Richard—Governor Incorporation of Poor, 1786-1788; Treasurer Incorporation of Poor 1788-1798; died October 3, 1811, aged 77.

Vaughan, Richard—Sheriff, 1839-1840; died July 26, 1893, aged 89.

Vaughan, William—President Grateful, 1777; died 1798.

Vickery, James—Candidate School Board, 1892.

Vigor, Robert—President Colston (Parent), 1772; died June 4, 1784.

Vigor, William—President Grateful, 1809; died Nov. 28, 1816.

Vigurs, Walter—President Grateful, 1797; died May 4, 1801.

Villosola, Antonio Lopez — Warden St. Stephen's Ringers for 1827 (declined); died May 17, 1855, aged 67.

Villiers, Edward W. B.—Warden St. Stephen's Ringers for 1891 (declined).

Viner, Christopher—Deputy Governor Incorporation of Poor, 1753-1754; died October 19, 1761.

Vining, Frederick William—Inspector of Weights and Measures, 1889-1898; died February 5, 1898.

Vining, Joseph Collins—Warden St. Stephen's Ringers, 1852; candidate for Sword Bearer, 1855

Vining, William—Warden St. Stephen's Ringers, 1847.

Vizer, Robert — Warden Merchant Venturers, 1809-1810; President Grateful, 1798; died January 11, 1814.

Vizer, Robert Willis—Warden Merchant Venturers, 1815-1816; President Grateful, 1819.

Voisey, William Clark—Candidate for School Board 1877; died August 28, 1881, aged 43.

Vyvyan, Sir Richard Rawlinson, Bart.—M.P., 1832-1837; died August 15, 1879, aged 78. (M.P., Cornwall, 1825-1831; Okehampton, 1831-1832; Helston, 1841-1857.)

ALPHABETICAL INDEX (IV.)—*Continued.*

Waddy, Rev. Samuel Dousland—Member School Board, 1871-1674; died November 7, 1876, aged 72.

Wade, John—President Gloucestershire Society, 1754.

Wadham, George—Under Sheriff, 1871-1880.

Wadham, James Davison—Under Sheriff, 1864-1871; Clerk of the Peace, 1868-1871; Deputy Judge Tolzey Court, 1864-1871; died July 29, 1871, aged 45.

Wadham, Thomas—Sheriff, 1843-1844; died January 16, 1849, aged 52.

Wait, Mabel Susan Killigrew—Member School Board 1895.

Wait, Rev. William—Mayor's Chaplain, 1805-1806; died January 1, 1812, aged 78.

Waldo, Henry—Infirmary Assistant Assistant Physician, 1873-1876; Physician, 1876.

Walker, Cyril Hutchinson—Ophthalmic Surgeon General Hospital, 1890.

Walker, Henry John—Member School Board, 1889.

Walker, Rev. Samuel Abraham—Member School Board, 1874-1879 (candidate, 1871); died November 30, 1879, aged 70. (Rector Maryleport, 1857-1879.)

Wallis, Ezekiel—Vice-Chamberlain, 1712-1724.

Wallis, George—Physician Infirmary, 1828-1855; died June 6, 1872.

Walshe, Rev. James—Usher Grammar School, 1629-1639.

Walshe, John—Recorder, 1552-1570; M.P., 1553-1555, 1559, 1563; died 1572. (Serjeant, 1559; M.P., Somerset, 1558; Judge Common Pleas, 1563-1572.)

Walton, Thomas Todd—Postmaster, 1832-1842; died July 13, 1857, aged 85.

Walton, Thomas Todd—Sheriff, 1872-1874; Postmaster, 1842-1871; died December 25, 1885.

Wansey, Arthur Henry—Registrar Tolzey Court, 1860 (Deputy Judge, 1874); President Anchor, 1861.

Wansey, William—Warden Merchant Venturers, 1755-1756; died February 23, 1780.

Ward, Charles Edward—President Dolphin, 1857; died March 11, 1873, aged 50.

Ward, Danvers—Candidate Surgeon Infirmary, 1791; died February 20, 1839, aged 80.

Ward, Danvers Hill—Warden Merchant Venturers, 1829-1930, 1832-1833; died December 16, 1886, aged 85.

Ward, Francis—President Dolphin, 1789; died July 1797, aged 53.

ALPHABETICAL INDEX (IV.)—*Continued.*

Ward, John—President Dolphin, 1802; President Gloucestershire Society, 1818.

Ward, Thomas Johnson—President Gloucestershire Society, 1859.

Ward, William Welsford—Master Merchant Venturers, 1896-1897; President-Elect Dolphin, 1899.

Ware, James Austin—Master St. Stephen's Ringers, 1874; died January 21, 1889, aged 53.

Warne, Samuel—Quay Warden, 1674-1694.

Warre, John Tyndale—President Colston (Parent), 1807 (declined); died about May, 1819.

Warren, John—President Colston (Parent), 1739.

Warren, Richard—President Gloucestershire Society 1739; died March 3, 1767.

Warren, Thomas—Deputy Governor Incorporation of Poor, 1728-1729; died December 23, 1766.

Warren, Thomas—President Colston (Parent), 1789; died February 24, 1792.

Warry, John—President Colston (Parent), 1852; died January 5, 1868, aged 83.

Warry, John—President Colston (Parent), 1862 (Treasurer, 1867-1885); died January 19, 1886, aged 70.

Washbrough, Charles Whitchurch—President Dolphin, 1898.

Washbrough, Henry Sidney—Coroner, 1868-1892; President Dolphin, 1880; Master St. Stephen's Ringers, 1854; died February 7, 1892, aged 79.

Waterman, Lewis—Chairman Chamber of Commerce, 1871-1872.

Watkins, John—Quay Warden, 1775-1794.

Watkins, Joseph—Deputy Governor Incorporation of Poor, 1708-1710.

Watkins, Robert—President Colston (Parent), 1737; died 1815.

Watkins, Valentine—President Gloucestershire Society, 1760; Master St. Stephen's Ringers, 1754; died December 22, 1766.

Watson, Charles Scott—House Surgeon Infirmary, 1880-1882.

Watson, George—Deputy Governor Incorporation of Poor, 1778 (declined); died April, 1806, aged 77.

Watson, Rev. Robert—Mayor's Chaplain, 1787-1789, 1802-1803, 1812-1813; died August 11, 1842, aged 84. (Vicar Temple, 1791-1816; Rector Christ Church, 1816-1842.)

Watts, Roger—President Dolphin, 1759; Deputy Governor Incorporation of Poor, 1758-1759; Master St. Stephen's Ringers, 1763; died October, 1, 1776.

ALPHABETICAL INDEX (IV.)—*Continued.*

Way, Rev. John Hugh—President Gloucestershire Society, 1898. (Vicar Henbury, 1860.)

Wayne, Matthew — President Gloucestershire Society, 1743.

Wayte, Rev. Samuel William—Vice-Chairman Barton Regis Guardians, 1887-1889, 1891-1893. (President Trinity College, Oxford, 1866-1878.)

Webb, Edward—President Anchor, 1818; President Gloucestershire Society, 1833; died September 18, 1849. (M.P., Gloucester, 1816-1832.)

Webb, James—Deputy Governor Incorporation of Poor, 1827-1828; died January 16, 1865, aged 73.

Webb, Nathaniel—President Dolphin, 1768; died March 16, 1771.

Webb, Richard—Deputy Governor Incorporation of Poor, 1787-1788, 1792-1794, 1796-1798.

Webb, Samuel—President Gloucestershire Society, 1820; died May 5, 1832.

Wedmore, Ernest—Obstetric Physician Infirmary, 1887-1891.

Weir, William—Secretary Infirmary, 1818-1823.

Welch, George—Master St. Stephen's Ringers, 1761; died December 14, 1770.

Wells, Peter—President Dolphin, 1751; Warden St. Stephen's Ringers, 1755; died October 16, 1786.

Welsted, Rev. Robert—Master Grammar School, 1697-1702.

West, Henry—Haven Master, 1759-1767.

Westcott, Jasper—President Colston (Parent), 1833; died September 4, 1849, aged 62.

Westley, William—President Colston (Parent), 1796; died July 6, 1825, aged 86.

Weston, John—President Chamber of Commerce, 1893-1894.

Weston, Webb—President Gloucestershire Society, 1764.

Weston—Stevens, Joseph—President Anchor, 1897.

Wetherill, William—President Grateful, 1787.

Wheeler, Isaac—Water Bailiff, 1774-1786; died Nov. 12, 1786.

Whish, Rev. Martin Henry—President Colston (Parent), 1860. (Perpetual Curate Bishopsworth 1844-1846; Rector Alderley, 1846.)

Whish, Rev. John Martin Hale—President Colston (Parent) for 1868 (declined); died December 4, 1891, aged 69.

Whitchurch, James Joseph—Master Merchant Venturers, 1828-1829; died November 26, 1872.

ALPHABETICAL INDEX (IV.)—*Continued.*

Whitchurch, Joseph—Warden Merchant Venturers, 1707-1708.

Whitchurch, Samuel—Master Merchant Venturers, 1799-1800; Treasurer Merchant Venturers, 1801-1816; died February 23, 1816.

Whitchurch, Samuel—Warden Merchant Venturers, 1802-1803; died June 2, 1812, aged 31.

Whitchurch, Thomas—Water Bailiff, 1727-1752; died 1752.

White, Michael—Warden Merchant Venturers, 1732-1733.

Whitfield, James—President Gloucestershire Society 1745.

Whittingham, William—President Dolphin, 1796; died September 12, 1801.

Whitton, Thomas—Sward Bearer, 1628-1643; died 1643.

Whitwill, Mark, jun. — President Chamber of Commerce, 1896-1897.

Wickham, FitzWilliam—President Colston (Parent) for 1878 (declined); died October 23, 1894, aged 86.

Wickham, John—Sword Bearer, May-November, 1609.

Wickham, Thomas—Sword Bearer, 1609-1617.

Wickham, Thomas — Steward Gloucestershire Society, 1661.

Wigan, Thomas—President Grateful, 1768; died April 23, 1790.

Wigginton, Abraham—President Dolphin, 1785; died December 28, 1798, aged 79.

Wilcox, Robert—Deputy Governor Incorporation of Poor, 1722-1723, 1732-1740, April-December, 1744; Warden St. Stephen's Ringers, 1741; died Dec. 1744.

Wilcox, Thomas—Steward Gloucestershire Society, 1632.

Wilde, Hon. Thomas Montague Carrington—Registrar in Bankruptcy, 1862-1870; died March 10, 1878, aged 59. (Registrar in Bankruptcy, Manchester, 1852-1862.)

Wilkins, Rev. Henry John—Candidate School Board 1895. (Vicar St. Jude, 1894.)

Willcocks, Edward—Warden Merchant Venturers, 1747-1748.

Willcox, Thomas—President Grateful, 1824; died November 26, 1851, aged 75.

Willcox, Thomas Percival—President Grateful, 1847; died April 26, 1871, aged 58.

Willes, William Henry—Judge County Court, January-February, 1863; died February 2, 1863, aged 40. Judge Newcastle County Court, 1859-1865.)

ALPHABETICAL INDEX (IV.)—*Continued.*

Williams, Bartholomew—Vice-Chamberlain, 1686-1691.

Williams, Charles Frederick—Usher Grammar School, June-December, 1829.

Williams, Rev. Sir Erasmus H. G.—See Griffies-Williams.

Williams, Frederick—House Surgeon General Hospital, 1843-1845.

Williams, George—Deputy Governor Incorporation of Poor, 1779-1780.

Williams, Henry—President Grateful, 1799.

Williams, Hugh—Master-Elect St. Stephen's Ringers 1695.

Williams, James—Warden St. Stephen's Ringers, 1784.

Williams, Sir John—Parliamentary candidate, 1832; died September 14, 1846, aged 69. (M.P., Lincoln, 1822-1826; Ilchester, 1826-1827; Winchelsea, 1830-1832; K.C., 1827; knighted, 1834; Judge King's Bench, 1834-1846.)

Williams, Josiah—J.P., 1894; died October 9, 1894, aged 72.

Williams, Patrick Watson—Infirmary House Physician, 1887-1888; Assistant Physician, 1888.

Williams, Rev. Richard—City Librarian, 1614 (Vicar St. Leonard.)

Williams, Richard Thomas—Warden St. Stephen's Ringers, 1829; died August 17, 1847, aged 71.

Williams, Rev. William—City Librarian, 1743-1752.

Willis, Edward—Deputy Governor Incorporation of Poor, 1781-1782; President Dolphin, 1792; died November 14, 1805.

Willoughby, Christopher—Chamberlain, 1739-1773; Master Merchant Venturers, 1747-1748; Treasurer Merchant Venturers, 1751-1773; Warden St. Stephen's Ringers, 1733; died June 20, 1773.

Willoughby, Thomas—Warden Merchant Venturers, 1760-1761; died about December, 1776.

Wills, Frank William—President Anchor, 1891; Master St. Stephen's Ringers, 1892.

Wills, George Alfred—President Grateful, 1894.

Wills, Henry Overton—President Colston (Parent), 1822; died December 1, 1825, aged 65.

Wills, Samuel—President Grateful, 1874; candidate School Board, 1871; J.P., 1878.

Wills, Walter Melville—President Anchor, 1895.

Willshire, William Lamb — President Colston (Parent), 1824; died September 9, 1826.

Wilmot, Sir J. E. E.—See Eardley-Wilmot.

ALPHABETICAL INDEX (IV.)—*Continued*.

Wilmot, Samuel Reynolds—President Colston (Parent) for 1833 (declined); died November 13, 1855, aged 73.

Wilmot, Walter Benjamin—Master St. Peter's Hospital, 1855-1857; Clerk Bristol Guardians, January-April, 1857; Clerk Incorporation of Poor, 1857-1867; died February, 1897.

Wilson, Benjamin—Clerk School Board, 1871-1895 ; died October 9, 1895, aged 75.

Wilson, Ven. James Maurice—Head Master Clifton College, 1879-1890. (Vicar Rochdale, 1890; Archdeacon Manchester, 1890.)

Wilson, John Grant—Surgeon General Hospital, 1831-1849; died November 8, 1860, aged 63.

Wilson, Joseph—President Colston (Parent), 1777 (Treasurer, 1765-1790); died April 30, 1790.

Wilson, Joseph Havelock—Contested East Bristol, 1890. (M.P., Middlesborough, 1892.)

Wilson, William Gitten-—Water Bailiff, 1840 - 1849; died October 10, 1864, aged 67.

Wimborne, Lord—See Guest

Windey, Nathan — President Dolphin, 1774; died June 21, 1795, aged 66.

Winstone—See Hayward-Winstone.

Winter, Thomas—President Grateful, 1805; died February 8, 1809

Wintle, Charles—Assessor, 1878; Governor Incorporation of Poor, 1879-1881; Warden St. Stephen's Ringers, 1851.

Wintle, Joseph—Warden St. Stephen's Ringers, 1846; died March 24, 1875.

Wintle, Thomas—Master St. Stephen's Ringers, 1829; died March 19, 1868.

Wintour, Charles—Steward Gloucestershire Society, 1683.

Witherby, Rev. Cornelius—Member School Board, 1880-1882. (Vicar St. Simon, 1868-1882; Rector St. Paul, Charlton, 1885-1898.)

Withington, Robert—President Grateful, 1806; died April 2, 1842, aged 72.

Wood, John—Warden St. Stephen's Ringers, 1864; died March 8, 1863, aged 54.

Wood, Joseph—Master St. Stephen's Ringers, 1786.

Wood, Leighton—Deputy Governor Incorporation of Poor, 1778 (declined); died March 25, 1795, aged 80.

Woodward, Augustine Fielding—Charity Trustee, 1875.

Woodward, Francis—President Dolphin, 1749-1750 ; Physician Infirmary, 1757-1769; died October 12, 1785, aged 64.

ALPHABETICAL INDEX (IV.)—*Continued.*

Woodward, John—Deputy Governor Incorporation of Poor, 1776-1777; Master St. Stephen's Ringers, 1783.

Woodward, John Henry—Member School Board, 1880 (Vice-Chairman, 1889-1892, 1898; Chairman, 1892-1898); President Grateful, 1891; Master Merchant Venturers, 1886-1887; J.P., 1894.

Worcester, Marquis of—See Beaufort (1st, 6th, and 7th Dukes).

Worgan, Matthew—President Grateful, 1765; died May 3, 1790.

Workman, Rev. Herbert Brook—Member School Board, 1893-1894.

Worrall, Samuel—Town Clerk, 1787-1819; died Nov. 6, 1821, aged 65.

Worsley, Philip John—Charity Trustee, 1891; President Anchor, 1875; J.P., 1887.

Wotton, Rev. Richard—Usher Grammar School, 1690-1695; died 1695, aged 25.

Wotton, Rev. William—Master Grammar School, 1689-1697; died January 1727-8. (Vicar St. Augustine, 1694-1728; Prebendary Salisbury, 1705-1723.)

Wraxall, John—Sword Bearer, 1750-1768; died July 30, 1768.

Wraxall, Nathaniel—Sword Bearer, 1778-1781; Warden Merchant Venturers, 1762-1763; died August 3, 1781.

Wright, Charles Edward—District Registrar Supreme Court, 1888.

Wright, Rev. David—Mayor's Chaplain, 1876-1877; died February 19, 1896, aged 78. (Minor Canon, 1849-1861; Vicar Stoke Bishop, 1860-1895.)

Wright, Rev. Henry—Member School Board, 1890-1892 (Vice-Chairman, January-September, 1892.)

Wright, John—President Anchor, 1771; Physician Infirmary, 1771-1794; died December 25, 1794, aged 62.

Wright, William—Sheriff, 1863-1864; died November 21, 1883, aged 76.

Wyld, George—President Colston (Parent), 1828; died January 1, 1834, aged 73.

Yabbicom, Thomas Henry—Surveyor Sanitary Authority, 1894; City Surveyor, 1897.

Yalland, John—Chairman Barton Regis Guardians, 1881-1887; died March 26, 1897.

Yeamans, Francis—Registrar Court of Conscience, 1689-1701; died 1701.

Yeamans, Frederick—Deputy Governor Incorporation of Poor, 1763-1764; died February 12, 1784.

ALPHABETICAL INDEX (IV.)—Continued.

Yeamans, John—Warden Merchant Venturers, 1639-1693.

Yeamans, Robert—Registrar Court of Conscience, 1701-1715; died 1715.

Yeates, Joseph—Inspector of Nuisances, 1851-1877; died May 15, 1887, aged 68.

Yeatman, Charlton—Apothecary Infirmary, April-October, 1783; died November 28, 1828.

Yeatman, Morgan—Surgeon Infirmary, 1781-1807; President Dolphin, 1804; Warden St. Stephen's Ringers, 1786; died December 5, 1817, aged 66.

Yeatman, William—President Dolphin, 1764; died April 21, 1772.

Yeld, Thomas—Candidate Apothecary Infirmary, 1783.

Yerbury, John—President Anchor, 1813; died June 21, 1845, aged 74.

Young, Edward—President Grateful, 1816; died November 16, 1857, aged 65.

Young, Thomas—Steward Sheriff's Court, 1599-1618.

The following names have been accidentally omitted in their alphabetical order:—

Arnold, Luke—President Stock Exchange, 1866-1870; died July 15, 1879, aged 91.

Bisse, Peter—Coroner, 1613-1619.

Bourne, William—Coroner, 1619 (1650).

Chesshire, John—President Gloucestershire Society 1687.

Chester, Walter—Coroner, 1626-1641.

Clark, Henry—Surgeon Infirmary, 1845-1857; died May 10, 1861, aged 59.

Clark, Henry Ariel—Warden St. Stephen's Ringers, 1854.

Edye, John—Coroner, 1605-1613.

Fry, Joseph Storrs—Treasurer General Hospital, 1892.

Gillford, Thomas—President Stock Exchange, 1895-1898; died April, 1898.

Green, Sidenham—Dock Master, 1845-1883.

Greene, Thomas—Steward Sheriff's Court, 1638-1641.

Greene, William—Steward Sheriff's Court, 1641-1643; died 1643.

ALPHABETICAL INDEX (IV.)—*Continued.*

Mardon, John—Vice-President Chamber of Commerce, 1899.

Morcom, Augustus Ferris—President Stock Exchange, 1871-1882; died December 24, 1890, aged 79.

The following dates of death should be added:—

INDEX II.:
    Bennett, W. H., June 10, 1899, aged 59.
    Gough, R., June 4, 1899, aged 53.
    Jones, W. E., February 13, 1899, aged 81.

INDEX III.:
    Hall, S., July 14, 1826.
    Lloyd, Sir J., February, 1680-1.
    Thorne, G., July 7, 1833, aged 81.

INDEX IV.:
    Bell, W., July 8, 1830, aged 65.
    Bernard, A., May 6, 1795.
    Berry, S., June 25, 1778.
    Blake, Rev. W., May, 1796.
    Bridges, E., November 27, 1774 (not as printed at page 326).
    Bull, Rev. J., December 10, 1816.
    Clark, James, February 20, 1834, aged 70.
    Cockaine, Rev. J., January 5, 1826.
    Colston, A., December 1, 1775.
    Cooper, G. V., August 23, 1871, aged 36.
    Coules, M., September 17, 1795.
    Cross, T., October 8, 1833, aged 75.
    Davies, T. (iii.), April 16, 1892, aged 74.
    Davies, Rev. W., April 24, 1772.
    Davrell, H., May 23, 1862.
    Delpratt, W., July 20, 1826.
    Dix, George, January 3, 1876.
    Dowell, Rev. S. B., August 16, 1864, aged 72.
    Edwards, J., January 8, 1798.
    Ellis, J., January 6, 1778.
    Farrell, J., June 5, 1778.

ALPHABETICAL INDEX (IV.)—*Continued.*

Fisher, L., January 26, 1814.
Fisher, W. (ii), July, 1796.
Franklyn, Rev. T. W., May 17, 1876, aged 75.
Gadd, A., April 2, 1808.
Grant, A., November 21, 1753.
Glascodine, J., December, 1817.
Hare, E., June 5, 1765.
Hobhouse, H. (i), May 18, 1773 (not as printed on page 361)
Hunt, James, April 4, 1793.
Ireland, J., July 6, 1814.
Jones, W. (ii.), July 3, 1844.
Kill, D., January 28, 1761.
Latcham, C. A., October, 1857.
Mais, Rev. J., November 15, 1871, aged 82.
Martin, J., July 13, 1862.
Maxse, J., October 24, 1806.
Rolt, J., December 23, 1876.
Stephens, T., December 7, 1745.

ADDITIONS DURING PUBLICATION.

MUNICIPAL ELECTIONS.
BRISTOL WARD.

1898—William Ansell Todd, J.P. (C)
Richard Court Stephens (C)

CLIFTON WARD.

1898—Charles Henry Tucker (C) 829
Samuel Shirley (C) 702
George Cawley (C) 672
William Horace Brain (L) 127

REDCLIFF WARD.

1898—Arthur Baker, J.P. (C)
Edward Beadon Colthurst, J.P. (C)

ST. AUGUSTINE WARD.

1898—James Fuller Eberle (C)

ST. PHILIP WARD (SOUTH).

1898—Henry Frederick Cotterell (L)

ST. PHILIP WARD (NORTH).

1898—Francis Gilmore Barnett (L)

BEDMINSTER WARD (EAST).

1898—Edward Parsons, J.P. (L)

BEDMINSTER WARD (WEST).

1898—Edward Horwood Chandler (L) 671
William Edwin Jones (L) 139

ST. MICHAEL WARD.

1898—Henry Anstey (C)

ST. JAMES WARD.

1898—William Cottrell (C)

ST. PAUL WARD.

1898—John Boyd (L)

DISTRICT WARD.

1898—Charles Edward Ley Gardner, J.P. (L)

1898, November 24—Vice Gardner (elected an Alderman).
    Joseph Holman (L) 934
    George Cawley (C) 811

WESTBURY WARD.

1898—John Ryan Bennett (L)

HORFIELD WARD.

1898—Isaac McIlroy (C) 546
    Kossuth Robinson (L) 452

ST. GEORGE WARD.

1898—George Bryant Britton (L) 1383
    Robert Inkerman Weight (C) 1267

STAPLETON WARD.

1898—John Poole (L)

EASTON WARD

1898—James O'Grady (Labour)

ALDERMEN.

1898—Charles Edward Ley Gardner, J.P. (L)...... 56
    Sir George William Edwards, J.P. (C)...... 54
    Charles Hoskins Low, J.P. (C) 53
    Charles Bowles Hare, J.P. (C).................... 50
    William Wilberforce Jose, J.P. (C) 48
    James Inskip (C) 48
    Francis James Fry, J.P. (LU) 48
    William Smith, J.P. (C) 47
    John Grant 3

MAYOR.

1898—Herbert Ashman, J.P. (L), St. Paul
   The title of Lord Mayor was conferred on Mr. Ashman and his successors, June, 1899.

HIGH SHERIFF.

1898—Charles Wills, J.P.

DEPUTY TOWN CLERK.

1899, May 9—Edmund Judkin Taylor
   A newly-created office. The proposal to establish it was carried by 44 to 23.

JUSTICES OF THE PEACE.

1899, February 20—George Frederick Rumsey, Major (C)
   Two justices have died since the names on pages 101-103 were printed, viz., Mr. Lane on August 30, 1898, and the Duke of Beaufort on April 30, 1899.

BRISTOL SCHOOL BOARD.

1899, April 24—Vice Gore (vacated his seat by continued absence).—Ernest Henry Cook (Conservative)
   Mr. George Cambridge (Progressive) was at first proposed and defeated by 7 votes to 5, and Dr. Cook was then elected without a division. Mr. Lowe and Miss Townsend were absent; the five Progressives present voted for Mr. Cambridge.

BRISTOL BOARD OF GUARDIANS.

1899, April 21—Chairman, Charles Edward Douglas Boutflower
   Vice-Chairmen, Samuel Lloyd (Councillor) and Rev. Thomas Henry Trickey Dening

SOCIETY OF MERCHANT VENTURERS.

1898—Herbert George Edwards (Councillor), Master
Averay Neville Jones and George Oswald Spafford, Wardens

CHAMBER OF COMMERCE.

1899, May 30—Thomas Tucker Lindrea, President
Arthur Lee, J.P., and John Mardon, Vice-Presidents

DOLPHIN SOCIETY.

Collection for 1898 (Mr. Wasbrough, President), £2023 19s. 9d.

President-Elect for 1899, William Welsford Ward

ANCHOR SOCIETY.

Collection for 1898 (Mr. Ashman, Mayor, President) £1315

President-Elect for 1899, Joseph Holman (Councillor)

GRATEFUL SOCIETY.

Collection for 1898 (His Honour Judge Austin, President), £1012 19s. 3d.

President-Elect for 1899, George Oswald Spafford

COLSTON (PARENT) SOCIETY.

President-Elect for 1899, William Proctor

ANTIENT SOCIETY OF ST. STEPHEN'S RINGERS.

President-Elect for 1899, William Proctor
Wardens-Elect, Gerald Lysaght and John Bates Dester

GLOUCESTERSHIRE SOCIETY.

Collection for 1898 (Rev. J. H. Way, President), £135 3s. 4d.
President-Elect for 1899, William Henry Greville Edwards

RESIDENT ENGINEER TO THE BRISTOL DOCKS.

1899, May 9—William Wilkinson Squire

The following alterations in and additions to the figures given in the Statistical Notes are consequent on changes which have occurred since they were printed up to the present date (July, 1899):—

- BRISTOL WARD (pp. 5-6)—The number of J.P.'s is increased to 22 by the addition of Mr. Dix, and that of High Sheriffs to 6 by the election of Mr. C. Wills.
- CLIFTON WARD (p. 11)—The number of individual representatives is increased to 77, and of Conservatives to 63, by the election of Mr. Tucker, who was returned as an Independent, displacing Commander Cawley, one of the official Conservative candidates, who had himself originally stood as an Independent in 1895.
- REDCLIFF WARD (p. 16)—The number of J.P.'s has been increased by the addition of Mr. Mervyn King, but is 13 as stated in the text, where Mr. Tothill's name has been wrongly included.
- ST. PHILIP'S WARD, SOUTH (p. 22)—The number of J.P.'s is increased to 4 by the addition of Messrs. Elkins and Swaish.
- BEDMINSTER WARD, WEST (p. 26)—The number of J.P.'s is increased to 7 by the addition of Messrs. Parsons and Latham.

STATISTICAL NOTES—*Continued.*

ST. MICHAEL'S WARD (p. 30)—The number of J.P.'s is increased to 8 by the addition of Mr. Richards.

ST. PAUL'S WARD (p. 36)—The number of J.P.'s is increased to 7 and of Mayors to 2 by the addition of Mr. Ashman.

DISTRICT WARD (p. 38)—The number of individual representatives is increased to 19, and of Liberals to 17, by the election of Mr. Holman; that of J.P.'s to 10, and of Aldermen to 5, by the addition of Mr. Gardner.

EASTON WARD (p. 40)—Mr. Verrier has been appointed a Justice of the Peace.

ALDERMEN (pp. 47-48)—The composition of the aldermanic bench since November, 1897, has been 15 Conservatives, 3 Liberals, and 3 Liberal Unionists. The number of individuals chosen to be Aldermen is increased to 95, and that of Liberals to 11, by the addition of Mr. Gardner. The number of vacancies since 1886 is increased to 19, of which 10 have been filled by representatives of the Wards, the total number of Councillors and ex-Councillors elected since 1835 having been raised to 34. The addition of Messrs. Dix and Gardner to the bench of magistrates increases the number of Aldermen who have been J.P.'s to 43.

MAYORS (p. 52)—The election of Mr. Ashman increases the number of individuals who have been elected to the Mayoralty since the Act of 1835 to 43, of Liberals to 9, and of years in which the chief magistracy has been held by a Liberal to 17.

THE WHOLE COUNCIL (p. 59)—The total number of individuals elected to the Council is 407, the number that have died in office remains 74, as stated in the text; 191 have died after retirement, leaving 142 survivors, including the 84 existing members. The number of Conservatives is increased to 235 by the addition of Messrs. Tucker and McIlroy, and of Liberals to 162 by that of Mr. Holman. The number of members whose connection with the Council was not terminated by death is 249, of whom 208 withdrew at the close and 15 in the course of a term of office; 24 failed to obtain re-election. The name of Commander Cawley should be added to those enumerated in the text under the last head. Forty-two have served the office of Mayor, 26 that of High Sheriff since 1835; 44 have been Masters of the Society of Merchant Venturers; 38 have been Presidents of the Anchor (including the President-Elect for 1899, and 33 of the Colston (or Parent) Society. The number of those that have been Presidents of the Chamber of Commerce since 1855 is 13, and of the earlier **Chamber 7.**

COUNCIL, &c.—*Continued.*

SHERIFFS (p. 94) — The number of individuals elected to the Shrievalty is increased to 61, of those still living to 28, and of those chosen after retiring from the Council to 4, by the addition of Mr. C. Wills.

JUSTICES OF THE PEACE (p. 103)—The number of existing Justices is reduced to 78 (of whom two have not qualified) by the death of the Duke of Beaufort. The addition of Major Rumsey fills the vacancy caused by the death of Mr. Lane. The present magistrates consist of thirty-six Conservatives, thirty-two Liberals, nine Liberal Unionists, and His Honour Judge Austin. (Mr. Alfred Robinson, who is a Liberal Unionist, was wrongly described as a Liberal on page 102, and Mr. H. O. Wills, who was formerly a Liberal, is now a Conservative. Of the 178 appointments, 85 were of Liberals, and 8 of Liberal Unionists, Messrs. W. M. Baker and A. Robinson having been erroneously reckoned with the former in the numbers given on page 103. For the same reason the number appointed by Conservative Governments should be read as: 32 Liberals and 7 Liberal Unionists.) There are at present 16 Aldermen and 13 Councillors on the city bench.

SOCIETY OF MERCHANT VENTURERS (p. 133)— The number of Masters elected since 1605 is increased to 355 by the addition of Mr. Edwards.

THE COLSTON SOCIETIES (pp. 147-148)—The Dolphin Society contributed the largest and the Grateful the smallest sum at the dinners of 1898, on which occasion both the Dolphin (under the presidency of Mr. C. W. Washrough) and the Anchor (under that of the Mayor, Mr. Ashman) raised the "record" collections of their respective societies, that of the former being £2,028 19s. 9d., and of the latter £1,315.

SUPPLEMENTARY LISTS.

The following lists should have been inserted between pp. 247-248:

CHAIRMEN OF THE DOCKS COMMITTEE,
1848-1899.

1848, August 31, Richard Jenkins Poole King, J.P.
1859, November 14, James Poole; died December 24, 1872.
1873, Charles Nash, J.P.
1877, November 12, George Wills, J.P.
1880, March 15, William Proctor Baker, J.P.
1882, November 13, Charles Hoskins Low.
1893, July 31, William Proctor Baker, J.P.

COLLECTORS OF MAYOR'S DUES.

1847, January 15, Stephen Horsley Stedder; died May 7, 1863.
1863, June 30, Edward Hinton (Secretary to the Docks Estate.

Previous to 1847 the Mayor's Dues were collected by the Water Bailiff; in that year, on the recommendation of a Committee of the Corporation, a special officer was appointed. On Mr. Stedder's death the office was united to that of Secretary of the Docks Estate, and Mr. Hinton's successor, Mr. Girdlestone, was also appointed Receiver of Town Dues on the next vacancy in 1876 (see p. 247).

TRUSTEES OF DR. WHITE'S CHARITY,
1836-1899.

Before the passing of the Municipal Corporations Act of 1835 the Trustees, in accordance with the will of Dr. White, were the Vicar of Temple, the Town Clerk, the Chamberlain, and the "two antientest Aldermen"; after that Act the Vicar of Temple was retained as ex-officio Chairman, and the four other seats were filled by annual election from members of the Council.

1837, January 2, Thomas Stock, J.P., Alderman; died April 27, 1858.
Henry Ricketts, J.P.; died May 7, 1859.
Thomas Daniel; retired from Council November, 1841.
William Fripp, J.P., Alderman; retired from Council, November, 1845.

SUPPLEMENTARY LISTS—*Continued.*

1838, May 2 (vice Stock), Edward Bowles Fripp; retired from Council, November, 1842.

1842, January 1 (vice Daniel), Henry Bush; retired from Council November, 1842.

1842, January 2 (vice E. B. Fripp and Bush), George Woodroffe Franklyn, Alderman; retired from Council November, 1850.
James George, J.P.; retired from Council, November, 1846.

1846, January 1 (vice W. Fripp), Robert Phippen; retired from Council November, 1854.

1847, January 1 (vice George), James Gibbs; retired from Council November, 1850.

1851, January 1 (vice Franklyn and Gibbs), James George, J.P., Alderman; retired from Council November, 1853.
Richard Jenkins Poole King, J.P., Alderman; died September 26, 1874.

1854, January 2 (vice George), Robert Gay Barrow, Alderman; retired from Council November, 1874.

1855, January 1 (vice Phippen), John George Shaw, J.P.; retired from Council November, 1864.

1859, May 27 (vice Ricketts), Robert Phippen, J.P., Alderman; died July 5, 1869.

1864, January 1 (vice Shaw), Isaac Allan Cooke; died December 11, 1874.

1870, January 1 (vice Phippen), Francis Adams, J.P., Alderman; resigned January, 1877.

1875, January 1 (vice King, Barrow, and Cooke), Thomas Proctor, J.P., Alderman; died May 15, 1876.
Shoito Vere Hare, J.P., Alderman; retired from Council November, 1880.
William Hathway, Alderman; resigned January, 1891.

1877, January 1 (vice Adams and Proctor), William Proctor Baker, J.P., Alderman.
John Averay Jones, Alderman; retired from Council June, 1890.

1878, January 1 (vice Hare), George William Edwards, Alderman; resigned January, 1899.

1891, January 1 (vice Jones and Hathway), Sir Charles Wathen, J.P., Alderman; died February 14, 1893.
Charles Bowles Hare, J.P.

1893, April 24 (vice Wathen), William Robert Barker, J.P.

1899, January 2 (vice Edwards), Sir Robert Henry Symes, J.P., Alderman.

SUPPLEMENTARY LISTS—*Continued.*

DOCK MASTERS (BRISTOL DOCKS).

1822, Martin Hilhouse (vice Thomas Davis); resigned 1843.
1843, September 28, Sidenham Green; resigned 1883.
1883, August 15, John Tomlinson.

PRESIDENTS OF BRISTOL STOCK EXCHANGE.
1845-1899.

1845, March, John Kerle Haberfield, Councillor; died December 27, 1857.
1858, March, Robert Goss, Councillor.
1866, March, Luke Arnold.
1870, March, George William Edwards.
1871, March, Augustus Ferris Morcom.
1882, March, Samuel John Sayce.
1884, March, Benjamin Spry Stock; died November 1, 1895.
1895, November, Thomas Gillford; died April, 1898.
1898, April, George White.

ADDITIONAL NOTES.

ELECTION OF COUNCILLORS (pp. 1-40).

At the first election the first nine on the poll were returned in Bristol and Clifton Wards, the first six in Redcliff and St. Augustine's respectively, and the first three in each of the other wards, the first third of the total number elected in each ward retiring in 1836, the second third in 1837, and the rest in 1838. In all the succeeding annual elections Bristol and Clifton returned three each to 1879, and two each from 1880, Redcliff and St. Augustine two each till 1879, and one each from 1880, the remaining wards one each. Each Councillor chosen at an annual election serves for three years, those returned to fill casual vacancies till the expiration of the term for which their predecessors were serving.

Under the Act of 1835 no casual vacancies were to be filled till the total number of Councillors was reduced to two-thirds of the full complement, hence the vacancies in Bristol and Clifton caused by the election of Mr. Stock as Alderman and the death of Mr. Goldney remained unsupplied till the annual election of 1837, after the passing of the amending Act of that year by which this provision was repealed.

ELECTION OF ALDERMEN (pp. 42-47).

At the triennial elections from 1838 to 1898 eight Aldermen were elected on each occasion to serve for six years, and five additional Aldermen were chosen in 1897 after the extension of the boundaries, of whom two were to serve for seven years and three for four years. In 1901 and each succeeding sixth year eleven will be elected, and in 1904 and each succeeding sixth year ten.

To complete the record of aldermanic elections, I give here the number of votes recorded at those elections which were uncontested:—In 1841, 36 for each; 1844, 30 for each; 1845, Mr. Lucas, 33; Nov. 9, 1847, 25 for each; November 26, 1847, Mr. J. George, 25; April 18, 1850, Mr. Barnes, 22 (16 Conservatives and 6 Liberals, viz., Messrs. G. Thomas, C. J. Thomas, F. Terrell, Tovey, Palmer, and Halsall); November 9, 1850, Mr. Gibbs 45, Mr. Barnes 37, the rest 35 each; November 18, 1850, Mr. Barrow, 34; April 9, 1853, Mr. Jordan, 29; September 6, 1853, Mr. Finzel, 25; September 22, 1853, Mr. J. H. Wyld, 21; November 9, 1853, Messrs.

ELECTION OF ALDERMEN—*Continued.*

Vining and Green 31 each, the rest 30 each; 1854, Mr. Abbot, 25; 1855, Mr. Phippen, 22; April 19, 1856, Mr. Ford, 22; November 9, 1856, 28 for each; 1857, Mr. F. Adams, 25; 1862, 25 for each; 1864, Mr. Woodward, 31; September 13, 1865, Mr. Slaughter, 31; November 9, 1865, 27 for each; August 24, 1874, Mr. Morgan, 24; November 9, 1874, Messrs. F. Adams and Brittan, 33 each, the rest 32 each; 1875, Mr. Fox, 26; 1876, Mr Wall, 30; 1878, Mr. Cope-Proctor, 28; September 3, 1880, Mr. H. Adams, 27; 1888, Mr. C. Wathen, 45; February 24, 1893, Mr. Fry, 28; November 9, 1893, Mr. Prichard, 36; 1896, Mr. C. B. Hare, 25.

At the election of March 17, 1851, when Mr. Leonard (Liberal) defeated Mr. Whittall (Conservative) by 17 to 14, no less than 27 Conservatives absented themselves from the division, those who supported Mr. Whittall being Aldermen Vining, Greville, Robinson, Lucas, Bigg, Barrow, Plummer and Alexander, Councillors Hautenville, Wait, Taylor, Powell, Smith, and Phippen. Only five Liberals were absent, Messrs. G. Thomas, Herapath, Coates, Naish, and Tovey.

In September, 1861, Mr. W. Naish (Liberal) received the votes of 16 Conservatives and only 4 Liberals (Messrs. Castle, F. Terrell, Kempster, and Wetherman). Several Liberals who were present did not vote. Two Conservatives (Messrs. F. W. Green and J. Bush) voted for Mr. H. O. Wills (Liberal).

In November, 1871, Mr. Hathway was supported by 24 Conservatives and 6 Liberals, the latter being Messrs. Weston, F. Terrell, Miles, Perry, Wedmore, and Follwell; Mr. Jones by 10 Conservatives and 14 Liberals. Of those 14, no less than 8 (Messrs. E. S. Robinson, W. H. Wills, W. Terrell, Whitwill, Carpenter, G. Wills, Matthews, and Cole) voted against Mr. Jones at the next election in 1873; of the remaining 6, one (Mr. C. J. Thomas) did not vote, being himself nominated, and five (Messrs. T. Pethick, W. Pethick, Sibree, Evans, and Godwin) were no longer members of the Council.

MAYORS (pp. 49-50).

In the 64 years 1836-1899 the Mayoralty has been held by Aldermen in 26 years; Councillors for Bristol Ward, 11 years; Councillors for Clifton Ward, 6 years; Councillors for Westbury Ward, 5 years; Councillors for St. Paul Ward, 4 years; Councillors for Bedminster Ward, 3 years; Councillors for Redcliff Ward, 2 years; Councillors for St. Michael Ward, 2 years; Councillor for St. Augustine Ward, 1 year; Councillor for St. Philip Ward, 1 year; and in three years by gentlemen who were not at the date of election either Aldermen or Councillors.

LORD HIGH STEWARDS (p. 92).

In 1836 the Duke of Beaufort was elected by 31 votes to 15 for Lord Segrave, a proposal to abolish the office having been previously rejected by 34 to 20.

HIGH SHERIFFS (p. 94).

Of the 61 High Sheriffs since 1835, 55 have been Conservatives, 2 (Sir W. H. Wills and Mr. C. Wills) Liberals, and 4 (Aldermen Pethick and Fry and Messrs. Lockley and Godwin) Liberal Unionists.

CLERKS OF THE PEACE (p. 94).

In 1836 Mr. Ody Hare was elected by 22 votes to 17 for William Powell Hartley, 10 for Edward Harley, jun., and 9 for Charles Arthur Latcham. All Mr. Hartley's votes were from Liberals.

TOLZEY COURT (p. 95).

Mr. H. A. Palmer was the first Registrar under that title; his predecessor, Mr. Arthur Palmer, was styled Prothonotary, and held that office nearly 50 years.

MEDICAL OFFICERS OF HEALTH (p. 95.)

The date in the text is erroneous Dr. Davies was first appointed under the title of "Inspector of Health" February 2, 1855, which designation was exchanged for that of Medical Officer of Health after the passing of the Public Health Act in August, 1872, which rendered the appointment of such an officer compulsory

INSPECTORS OF NUISANCES (p. 96).

The officers whose names are given in the text were appointed by the Corporation, acting as the Board of Health (now the Sanitary Authority). There was besides an Inspector of Nuisances elected by the Corporation annually, two such being appointed from 1795 to 1805 and from 1822 to 1823, the succession since 1782 being:—
1782, December 11, John Tommas.
1783, December 10, William May, till December, 1794.
1795, June 10, Thomas Batty till 1805; John Frankland till 1823.
1822, February 9, William Sayer, till his death, December 13, 1856.
On Mr. Sayer's death no fresh appointment was made, Mr. Yeates, who had been Inspector under the Board of Health since 1851, becoming the sole official under that designation.

SWORD BEARERS (p. 96).

On the occurrence of the vacancy in 1850 a motion was made to abolish the office, which was rejected by 43 to 12. The minority was composed entirely of Liberals, and 7 of that party voted for retaining the office, viz., Messrs. Langton, Visger, W. D. Wills, H. O. Wills, G. E. Sanders, Prichard, and Wetherman.

CITY LIBRARIANS (p. 96).

In 1883 Mr Taylor was elected by 25 votes to 15 for Mr. William John Haggerston, Chief Librarian at Newcastle-on-Tyne. The minority consisted exclusively of Liberals, and in the majority were 21 Conservatives and 2 Liberals (Alderman H. Naish and Mr. F. Terrell).

ASSESSORS (p. 98).

Assessors were appointed in 1836 and 1837 under the Act of 1835, which was subsequently amended by the Act of 1837. The Assessors for 1837 are given in the text. Those for 1836 were Joseph Baker Grindon and Charles Grevile.

JUSTICES OF THE PEACE (p. 100).

At the meeting of the Council to select names for recommendation as fit persons to serve as magistrates, 20 of the 24 names chosen were adopted without opposition. Mr. Newman was carried by 51 to 1 (the sole dissentient wishing to substitute Mr. Gabriel Goldney), Mr. Ash by 45 to 5, Mr. Herapath by 28 to 23, Mr. Sanders by 28 to 20, the minority in each case consisting entirely of Conservatives. Mr. John Addington (Liberal) was also proposed, but rejected by 29 to 23. Messrs. Herapath and Sanders each received 18 Liberal and 10 Conservative votes.

Two of the original Justices (Messrs. Bright and Kington) did not qualify.

CHARITY TRUSTEES (p. 106).

Of the 61 gentlemen who have been Charity Trustees, 45 have been members of the Corporation, of whom 10 were Aldermen, and 36 **Justices of the Peace** for the city.

SECRETARIES TO THE CHARITY TRUSTEES
(p. 106).

At the election of 1853 Mr. Miller was elected by 20 votes to 4 for Mr. John Moxham.

SCHOOL BOARD (p. 115).

Of the 42 laymen who have served on the School Board, 13 have been members of the Corporation, viz., Aldermen S. V. Hare, Ford, Baker, Sir G. Edwards, Butterworth, Inskip, and Smith, Councillors L. Fry, Whitwill, Alsop, Gore, Elkins, and Lowe; 9 have been Justices of the Peace for the city, viz., Sir G. Edwards, Aldermen Hare and Baker, Colonels Savile and Woodward, and Messrs. Whitwill, Budgett, H. Thomas and Sparke Evans.

SOCIETY OF MERCHANT VENTURERS (p. 122).

This society has been for many years exclusively Conservative in politics. Mr. Robert Bruce, who died in 1874, is said by Mr. Latimer, in his "Annals of Bristol in the 19th Century," to have been the last Liberal member of it. Messrs. J. E. Lunell, M. D. Protheroe, and S. Lunell were other late Liberal survivals. The last-named died in 1876, after Mr. Bruce, but the poll books show him to have been a not very consistent politician, and he may have been a Conservative at the end of his life. In the middle of the 18th century the prevailing tone of the society was Whig.

THE COLSTON SOCIETIES (pp. 138-152).

The two oldest societies—the Colston (Parent) and the Dolphin—have always been, the former mainly, the latter exclusively, of Tory politics. The former contains a few Whig names on its roll, viz., H. O. Wills, who was President in 1822, and Messrs. T., G. E., and J. N. Sanders, each of whom declined the chair in his turn. Mr. G. E. Sanders had been a Tory in early life, and his father had filled the chair of the Dolphin. Mr. Gore-Langton, the Whig M.P. for Somersetshire (father of W. H. Gore-Langton, M.P. for Bristol) was President of the Dolphin in 1817, but his relative, the Rev. C. Gore, whose politics were more in accordance with those of the other members of the society, took the chair for him.

The Grateful Society, which is entirely non-political, was founded by, and in the earlier years of its history was almost entirely composed of, old pupils of Colston's School. The original meeting to form the society was held at the Ship Inn, November 8, 1758, and issued an appeal for support to "those who owe their well-being to that great, good man" (Edward Colston).

PARLIAMENTARY ELECTIONS (pp. 167-170).

At the election of 1654 there were two unsuccessful candidates—John Haggett, Steward of the Sheriff's Court, who was also Chief Justice of South Wales, and George Bishop, a captain in the Parliamentary army.

At the election of 1790 the Marquis of Worcester was proposed by Alderman Daniel and Lord Sheffield by Councillor Richard Bright.

At the election of 1835 Sir John Hobhouse was proposed unexpectedly on the nomination day (as stated in the text), in the hope of carrying the second seat for the Liberals, who thought to catch their opponents unprepared. The address to the electors recommending Sir John was signed by 57 prominent Liberals, headed by Mr. (afterwards Sir) C. A. Elton, of whom Mr. C. J. Thomas was the last survivor. The others were J. Cunningham, G. Thomas, J. Coates, S. Brown, G. E. Sanders, C. B. Fripp, R. Ash, T. R. Guppy, H. Visger, Michael Castle, W. Tothill, T. Powell, W. Harwood, H. Prichard, W. L. P. Taunton, R. Ricketts, R. Bruce, jun., R. Castle, E. B. Fripp, W. H. Castle, A. H. Palmer, J. Drake, F. Terrell, and W. Herapath (afterwards members of the Corporation), J. Reynolds, R. Bligh, S. Waring, John Jacques, John Hare, jun. (better known in later years as Sir John), and J. N. Sanders (afterwards Liberal candidates for the Town Council), W. Brown, T. Drake (afterwards magistrates), T. Davies (afterwards a Charity Trustee), J. W. Ricketts, T. Mills, F. Palmer (Presidents of the Anchor Society), E. Harley, jun., T. J. Manchee, the Rev. Lant Carpenter, J. Righton, E. Waring, Opie Staite, R. Bruce, sen., W. Webb, E. Thomas, T. Rees, T. Sanders, C. Castle, James Hall, R. M. Ring, C. Rittson, W. H. Terrell, T. Bromhead, T. Chamberlain, W. Roughsedge.

ALDERMEN FOR THE ANCIENT WARDS
(pp. 190-192).

The records in the Council minute books are somewhat deficient in the assignment of wards for the period between 1664 and 1689, and again between 1700 and 1736. The minutes of the Incorporation of the Poor enable me to supply some omissions and correct some errors in the text as printed on pp. 190-194:

ALDERMEN FOR THE ANCIENT WARDS.
Continued.

Trinity Ward — The succession between W. Swymmer and H. Combe should be:

    February, 1714-5, F. Whitchurch.
    October 5, 1716, R. Yate.
    1737, A. Taylor.
    February 12, 1738-9, J. Blackwell.

St. Michael.—G. Harrington was Alderman of St. Michael before October, 1623, having exchanged wards with T. Packer (St. Ewen) between March, 1620-1, and that date. C. Shuter should be inserted before A. Swymmer, with the date February, 1714-5; A. Swymmer's date should be December, 1715; and J. Becher's should be July, 1723.

All Saints—The succession between Bacheler (1702) and Elton (1739) should be:

    November, 1711, W. Whitehead.
    March, 1711-2, G. Stephens.
    February 25, 1718-9, H. Walter.
    September, 1725, J. Jefferis.
    October, 1732, J. Price.
    February, 1734-5, A. Taylor.
    November, 1837, J. Blackwell.

Redcliff.—The date of E. Mountjoy should be December, 1719, and of H. Nash, September, 1735.

St. Nicholas.—J. Elton (November, 1737) should be inserted between H. Walter and A. Taylor.

St. James.—R. Bound (March, 1711-2) should be inserted between G. Stephens and A. Elton, R. Earle (November, 1727) between N. Hickes (1719) and P. Day (1728), and the date of J. Price should be February, 1734-5.

St. Ewen.—S. Wallis (March, 1699-1700) should be inserted between J. Hickes and Sir W. Hayman; the date of J. Rich should be February, 1736-7.

St. Stephen.—The date of J. Jefferis should be October, 1732; and before him should be inserted H. Swymmer (September, 1724).

St. Maryleport. — H. Swymmer (October, 1723) should be inserted between H. Whitehead (1719) and J. Donning (1724).

St. Thomas.—The line 1667 should precede the line 1672; the date of C. Shuter should be December, 1715; "Wash" should be "Nash"; the date of J. Elton should be September, 1735, and of L. Lyde November, 1737.

THE RECORDER AND THE COMMON COUNCIL
(p. 195).

As stated in the text, the Recorder, although an Alderman by virtue of his office, was not necessarily a member of the Common Council until 1710, except during the intermission of the old Charter from 1684 to 1688. On March 6, 1689-90, the Council refused to admit the then Recorder (Serjeant Powlett), who claimed membership as a matter of right, and the minutes record that the House "broke up after a large commotion." Serjeant Powlett was subsequently (September, 1696) elected a member of the Common Council.

THE KNIGHTS (pp. 204-205).

Since the note on these pages was printed, I have ascertained that Alderman John Knight (No. 2) was a son of Edward Knight, who was second son of Alderman Francis Knight. He was consequently first cousin to the first Sir John (No. 1), who was son of Alderman George Knight, the eldest son of Francis. This appears from a conveyance of land in Bristol and Congresbury, to which Sir John, Alderman John, and his father Edward were parties, and which was enrolled in Chancery May 5, 1659, being dated December 30 in the preceding year. For this information I am indebted to Mr. Thomas Perry, of Walthamstow, who has transcribed and communicated to me an abstract of the conveyance as enrolled. "Notes and Queries" (9th series, pp. 321-322) of April 29, 1899, contains a note by me on "The Knights of Bristol," which, I think, exhausts all the facts that serve to discriminate between the various members of the family who were associated with the municipal and Parliamentary history of Bristol.

VICE CHAMBERLAINS (p. 236).

William Challoner held this office from March 2, 1668-9, to 1686, his predecessor being Arthur Hollister. Mr. Vaughan was elected "during pleasure" in 1724 (as, apparently, his predecessors were), but in January, 1735-6, it was determined to make the office subject to annual re-election, and Mr. Vaughan, on applying for re-appointment, was defeated by a majority of 5 votes, Mr. Goodwin being elected.

CORONERS (p. 236).

The following served the office before 1650:—

Hercules Phipps (date of appointment not preserved).
1602-3, February 8, John Edye (vice John Clark, removed).
1613, December 7, Peter Bysse (vice Edye, removed).
1619, April 22, William Bourne (vice Bysse, resigned).
1625-6, March 13, Walter Chester (vice Phipps, deceased).
1641, September 15, Thomas Hickes (vice Chester).
1647, July 13, Richard Ashe (vice Hickes, removed).

STEWARDS OF THE SHERIFFS' COURT (p. 237).

Between 1618 and 1643 should be inserted:—
1637-8, February 12, Thomas Greene.
1641, May 10, William Greene.

HEAD MASTERS OF THE GRAMMAR SCHOOL (p. 240).

After 1622 (Cheyney) should be inserted:
1635, November 11, Henry James.
The date of his successor (B. Man) should be September 24, 1636.

MAYOR'S CHAPLAINS (p. 244)

(1751-1758), A Mr. Gully appears to have served instead of Mr. Price during part of the year 1752.
1839-1840, Mr. Forsayth was Chaplain to Mr. Haberfield from January to November, 1839, as well as to his successor, Mr. Franklyn, from the latter date till his death.

WATER BAILIFFS AND QUAY WARDENS (p. 246).

On the amalgamation of these offices in 1861, John Douglas Wilson was appointed Deputy Quay Warden March 20, 1861; he died September 24, 1873, and was succeeded (September 29) by Frederick Lewin, who died December 13, 1884.

POSTMASTERS (p. 251).

Mrs. Fenn acted as Postmistress from her husband's death in 1788 to 1797. In the latter year she retired from the active management of the office, the business of which was conducted by Mr. Frye. She retained the official position till after the latter's death.

CLIFTON UNION (p. 253).

This Union was constituted April 9, 1836, in accordance with an Order of the Poor Law Commissioners dated March 26 in that year.

In the text the dates 1869, 1872 are obviously interchanged. Between 1869 and 1871 should be inserted 1870, September 2, William Tanner (vice Richards, resigned).

Mr. Lewis, the Second Vice-Chairman in 1883-84, died in office April 9, 1884, his successor not being appointed till the ordinary annual election in the same month.

BRISTOL COLLEGE (p. 254).

The Vice-Principal originally nominated in 1830 was Charles Smith, but he retired before the date at which the College was opened, January 24, 1831.

THE BISHOP'S COLLEGE (p. 254).

The Rev. J. R. Woodford, afterwards Bishop of Ely, was Second Master for some years under Mr. Dale.

BRISTOL INFIRMARY (pp. 256-263).

The election of officers was transferred from the general body of subscribers to a committee by new rules confirmed on January 25, 1870, and that of the honorary staff in 1891.

ERRATA AND ADDENDA.

Page 1—1836, add " J.P." to J. Savage

Page 2—1846, for " Thomas Carlisle" read " Robert Castle"

Page 5—1896, for " Leonard " read " Hare "

Pages 7, 8, 9, 61, 66—For " Burroughes " read " Burroughs "

Page 8—1853, add " Richard Bobbett Giles (C), 2 "

Page 8—1854, add " John Jones (C), 2 "

Page 10, 1892; page 35, 1887; page 110, 1892—The second name of H. W. Carter should be " Williams "

Page 12—1835, for " Llewellyn " read " Llewellin "

Page 12, 1836; page 13, 1839—Add " J.P." to G. E. Sanders, and omit those letters after W. Tothill.

Page 13—1846, omit " J.P." after R. P. King

Page 14—1876, M. K. King's votes should be 544

Page 14—1878, the votes for R. Moore and S. Cashmore should be 503 and 425 respectively

Page 14—1882, add " J.P." to W. A. F. Powell

Page 15—1897, add " J.P." to J. C. Godwin

Page 16—Note on Redcliff Ward: The number of Councillors who died in office should be 5; Mr. Price's name should be added

Page 16—1836, add " J.P." to G. Bengough

Page 17—1846, add " J.P." to R. Bright

Page 25—(Note), for " from 1889 to 1890 " read " from 1887 to 1890 "

Page 28—1840, 1841, omit " J.P." from J. George and J. Howell

Page 31—1852, the votes for J. Wetherman should be 55

Page 32—1881, 1883, add " J.P." to J. W. Hall

Page 33—For " Hale " read " Hall "

Page 35—After the election of March 20, 1891, insert 1891, Herbert Ashman (L)

Page 36—1836, add " J.P." to R. Ash

Page 40—Stapleton Ward, for " Cotterell " read " Cottrell "; Easton Ward, Mr. Verrier's first name is " Albert "; Easton Ward, for " Turner " read " Tanner "

ERRATA AND ADDENDA—*Continued.*

Page 42—1846, the votes for Mr. Bright should be 3

Page 43—1851, Mr. Whittall's name should be "Piercy"

Page 46—1889, Mr. Wall's first name should be "James"

Page 48—Second line from foot of page, for "7" read "37"

Page 49—November, 1836, add "J.P." to T. Stock

Page 54—In November, 1892, the number of Liberals and Liberal Unionists should be 22 and 2 respectively

Pages 54, 55—For votes of Councillors at the elections of 1841, 1847, 1852, see corrections on page 177

Page 56—Division of October 7, 1858, fourth line from end of paragraph, for "Webb" read "Ricketts"

Page 58—The date of Alderman Fripp's death should be "1871" (not 1891)

Page 60—The number of Masters of St. Stephen's Ringers should be 26 (not 24); and of members of the School Board 13 (not 12)

Page 61—Sir F. Wills again contested the Launceston Division in 1898; add Mr. McBayne to the West India merchants

Page 62—Add to the wine merchants, Alderman C. Edwards and Mr. Warne; to the tobacconists, Mr. F. Ricketts; to the representatives of the iron trade, Mr. Ash; of corn, Mr Holman; of the oil trade, Messrs. Jacques and T. W. Hill; of the glass industry, Alderman R. Ricketts; omit Messrs C. and C. J. Vining from those of sugar

Page 63—To representatives of wholesale grocery, add Mr McIlroy; of wholesale confectionery, Messrs. S. and J. Lucas; of brass and copper manufacture, Mr. Blisset; and to the auctioneers, Mr. Tucker

Pages 64-89—See additions on pages 267-279

Page 65—Ashman, H., add "Lord Mayor, 1899"

Page 66—Bright, R., add "President Free Port Association, 1846-50; nominated for Alderman, 1846"

Page 66—Burroughs, B. G., add "died February 12, 1898, aged 90"

Page 66—Bush, H., add Master St. Stephen's Ringers (declined), 1840

Page 67—Carter, J., date of death should be "October 26, 1892, aged 80"

Page 67—Castle, M. Hinton, add "nominated for Sheriff, 1836, 1837"

Page 69—Davies, W. W., add "President-Elect Dolphin (resigned) for 1843"

ERRATA AND ADDENDA.

Page 1—1836, add " J.P." to J. Savage

Page 2—1846, for " Thomas Carlisle" read " Robert Castle"

Page 5—1896, for " Leonard " read " Hare "

Pages 7, 8, 9, 61, 66—For " Burroughes " read " Burroughs "

Page 8—1853, add " Richard Bobbett Giles (C), 2 "

Page 8—1854, add " John Jones (C), 2 "

Page 10, 1892; page 35, 1887; page 110, 1892—The second name of H. W. Carter should be " Williams "

Page 12—1835, for " Llewellyn " read " Llewellin "

Page 12, 1836; page 13, 1839—Add " J.P." to G. E. Sanders, and omit those letters after W. Tothill.

Page 13—1846, omit " J.P." after R. P. King

Page 14—1876, M. K. King's votes should be 544

Page 14—1878, the votes for R. Moore and S. Cashmore should be 503 and 425 respectively

Page 14—1882, add " J.P." to W. A. F. Powell

Page 15—1897, add " J.P." to J. C. Godwin

Page 16—Note on Redcliff Ward: The number of Councillors who died in office should be 5; Mr. Price's name should be added

Page 16—1836, add " J.P." to G. Bengough

Page 17—1846, add " J.P." to R. Bright

Page 25—(Note), for " from 1889 to 1890 " read " from 1887 to 1890 "

Page 28—1840, 1841, omit " J.P." from J. George and J. Howell

Page 31—1852, the votes for J. Wetherman should be 55

Page 32—1881, 1883, add " J.P." to J. W. Hall

Page 33—For " Hale " read " Hall "

Page 35—After the election of March 20, 1891, insert 1891, Herbert Ashman (L)

Page 36—1836, add " J.P." to R. Ash

Page 40—Stapleton Ward, for " Cotterell " read " Cottrell "; Easton Ward, Mr. Verrier's first name is " Albert "; Easton Ward, for " Turner " read " Tanner "

ERRATA AND ADDENDA—*Continued.*

Page 42—1846, the votes for Mr. Bright should be 3

Page 43—1851, Mr. Whittall's name should be "Piercy"

Page 46—1889, Mr. Wall's first name should be "James"

Page 48—Second line from foot of page, for "7" read "37"

Page 49—November, 1836, add "J.P." to T. Stock

Page 54—In November, 1892, the number of Liberals and Liberal Unionists should be 22 and 2 respectively

Pages 54, 55—For votes of Councillors at the elections of 1841, 1847, 1852, see corrections on page 177

Page 56—Division of October 7, 1858, fourth line from end of paragraph, for "Webb" read "Ricketts"

Page 58—The date of Alderman Fripp's death should be "1871" (not 1891)

Page 60—The number of Masters of St. Stephen's Ringers should be 26 (not 24); and of members of the School Board 13 (not 12)

Page 61—Sir F. Wills again contested the Launceston Division in 1898; add Mr. McBayne to the West India merchants

Page 62—Add to the wine merchants, Alderman C. Edwards and Mr. Warne; to the tobacconists, Mr. F. Ricketts; to the representatives of the iron trade, Mr. Ash; of corn, Mr Holman; of the oil trade, Messrs. Jacques and T. W. Hill; of the glass industry, Alderman R. Ricketts; omit Messrs C. and C. J. Vining from those of sugar

Page 63—To representatives of wholesale grocery, add Mr McIlroy; of wholesale confectionery, Messrs. S. and J. Lucas; of brass and copper manufacture, Mr. Bisset; and to the auctioneers, Mr. Tucker

Pages 64-89—See additions on pages 267-279

Page 65—Ashman, H., add "Lord Mayor, 1899"

Page 66—Bright, R., add "President Free Port Association, 1846-50; nominated for Alderman, 1846"

Page 66—Burroughs, B. G., add "died February 12, 1898, aged 90"

Page 66—Bush, H., add Master St. Stephen's Ringers (declined), 1840

Page 67—Carter, J., date of death should be "October 26, 1892, aged 80"

Page 67—Castle, M. Hinton, add "nominated for Sheriff, 1836, 1837"

Page 69—Davies, W. W., add "President-Elect Dolphin (resigned) for 1843"

ERRATA AND ADDENDA—*Continued.*

Page 69—Dole, J., add " died April 20, 1899 "

Page 69—Edwards, Sir G. W., add " President Stock Exchange, 1870-1871 "

Page 69—Fisher, C., add " Warden St. Stephen's Ringers (declined) for 1855 '

Page 70—Ford, J. (Alderman), add " Warden St. Stephen's Ringers (declined) for 1840 "

Page 71—Gore, H. H., to " member of School Board, 1899," add " -1899 "

Page 71—Goss, R., add " President Stock Exchange 1859-1866 "

Page 78—Prichard, C. J. C., after " Alderman, November, 1893," add " -1898 "

Page 79—Ring, R. C., add " Clerk Haymarket, 1887-1894 "

Page 81—Visger, H., add " Treasurer County Court, 1847-1867 "

Page 93—White, G., add " President Stock Exchange, 1898 "

Page 84—Bennett, H., for " February " read " January "

Page 86—After " Gough " insert " Grant, John, Alderman, 1898 "

Page 88—Robinson, F. R., the second name should be " Ring "

Page 89—Omit C. H. Tucker (see p. 275)

Page 90—Newton, for " Bunn " read " Barrow "; and for " Hilbrough " read " Hilhouse "

Page 94—For " Borough Treasurer " read " City Treasurer "

Page 94—Clerks of the Peace, Mr. Cartwright's first name is " Frederick "

Page 95—Haven Masters, 1825, for " November 11 " read " March 9 "

Page 96—Surveyors, for " 1844 " read " 1854 "

Page 96—Sword Bearers, J. F. Edgar, for " 1797 " read " 1818 "

Page 97—Auditors, 1841, after " July 20, 1841," add " and was succeeded (August 5) by Henry Cassin "

Page 98—Assessors, for " 1843-1844, H. W. King, G. P. Hinton," read " 1843, H. W. King, George Pullin Hinton; 1844, H. W. King, James Pullin Hinton '

Page 98—After " July 10, 1850," read " and was succeeded (July 19) by Francis Short "

Page 98—1878, for " C. A. Peters " read " Charles Wintle "

Page 101—1858, for " Bigge " read " Bigg "

ERRATA AND ADDENDA—*Continued.*

Page 102—After W. M. Baker and Alfred Robinson, for "(L)" read "(L U)"

Page 104—Note (bis), for "Weare" read "Wood"

Page 104—Note, for "L. Ricketts" read "F. Ricketts"

Page 105—Add "J.P." to G. Wills, A. Baker, F. J. Fry, O. Hosegood, Sir C. Wathen, and P. J. Worsley

Page 105—T. Baker, for "Liberal" read "Liberal Unionist"

Page 105—For "21 Liberals, 2 Liberal Unionists," read "20 Liberals, 3 Liberal Unionists"

Page 106—Secretaries (Note), for "Ward" read "Wood"

Page 106—1853, after Miller add "resigned September, 1870"; 1870, after London omit "resigned September, 1870"

Page 107—For "Pole" read "Pople"

Pages 108, 109—Colonel Savile's second name is "Bourchier"

Page 110—1886, June 26, and 1884, August 17, the year should be "1885" in each place

Page 112—Mr. Trapnell's second name is "Caleb"

Pages 116 (1750, 1751) and 120 (1748)—For "Browne" read "Brown"

Page 117—1770, Mr. Williams' christian name was "Rowland"

Page 117—1778, Mr. Watson's christian name was "George"

Page 119—For "1690" read "1699"

Page 120—1732, Mr. Champion's name was "Nehemiah"

Page 120—1772, for "Hasell" read "Hazle," and for "deceased" read "not duly elected"

Page 120—1857, the date of Mr. Coles' election was November 20, 1857

Page 120—Clerks, 1857, for "January 10" read "April 9"

Page 121—First paragraph, add "Mr. Boutflower, who was the last Deputy Governor of the Incorporation, became, in 1899, Chairman of the Bristol Board of Guardians"

Page 123—Between 1629 and 1630 insert, "1630, April 6, Andrew Charlton, Common Councillor, Master, vice Browne, deceased"

Page 124—1669, omit "Common Councillor" after R. Vickris

Page 124—1671, omit all the words after John Knight, jun.

ERRATA AND ADDENDA—*Continued.*

Page 125—1689, omit "Common Councillor" after Yeamans

Page 126—1706, omit "Alderman" after Swymmer

Page 127—1745, add "Alderman" after Jefferies

Page 128—After 1794 insert, "1795, March 30, Stephen Cave, Warden, vice Jones, deceased"

Page 133—1781, for "June 4" read "June 20." (Note) The number of those elected more than once should be 29, and the name of A. Charlton should be added to those who served twice

Page 135—1830, for "W. E. Acraman" read "Henry Bush"

Page 136—1869, omit "Alderman" after H. Thomas

Page 136—1877, 1878. Mr. Chambertain's second name was "Taylor"

Page 136, 1880; Page 137, 1882—For "E. S. Robinson, J.P.," read "Edward Robinson"

Page 139—1779, for "Davies" read "David"

Page 140—1829, for "Baynburn" read "Bayntun"

Page 140—1837, for "Currick" read "Carrick"

Page 142—1816, Dr. Stock's second name was "Edmonds"

Page 148—1739, Mr. Warren's christian name was "John"

Page 150—1859, for "Gardner" read "Gardiner"

Page 151—(Bis) Alderman Thatcher's second name is "James"

Page 151—1806, add "John Blagden Hale"

Page 151—1878, for "T. W. Wickham" read "Fitzwilliam Wickham"

Page 151—1896, for "C. S. F. Abbot" read "Lucas Charles Fuidge Abbot"

Page 152—(Note) The number of those who have occupied the chair of two of the societies is 15. T. Daniel's name should be added to those who have been Presidents of the Parent and of the Dolphin. In the paragraph relating to J. Powell, for "not identical with" read "the father of"

Page 155—John Span, Warden-Elect for 1799, died February 12, 1799, and N. D. Southall, Warden-Elect for 1808, died May 20, 1808. There is no record of their successors

Page 157—W. H. Brown, Warden-Elect for 1852, died June 10, 1852

Page 158—1859-1860, for "Guy" read "Gay"

Page 158—1861-1862, for "Charles Joseph Vining" read "Joseph Collins Vining"

ERRATA AND ADDENDA—*Continued.*

Page 159—1884-1887, Mr. Goodenough Taylor's second name is "Howell"

Page 161—After S. Wharton add "Common Councillor"

Page 162—1763, 1764, the names of Messrs. Weston and Sandell should be transposed

Page 164—1860, the second name of the Rev. C. R. Davy was "Raikes"

Page 164—1874, for "Dutton" (before "Colt") read "Vaughan"

Page 165—1529-1536, add "Recorder" to T. Jubbes

Page 166—The date of W. Carr's shrievalty should be 1545-1546; W. Chester's, 1559-1560; W. Salterne's, 1574-1575; P. Langley's mayoralty 1581-1582; T. Aldworth's, 1582-1583

Page 166—1597-1598, for "T. James" read "William Ellys"

Page 169—1727, add "Alderman" to A. Elton, jun.

Page 177—At foot of page add "J. Doddridge, Barnstaple, 1646-1653; Devon, 1656-1658"

Page 179—J. O'C. Power, for "Kensington" read "Kennington"

Page 180—In "all the above held the Recordership," after "above" insert "except Sir J. Williams"; and in the same line, before "R. Kelway," insert "Thomas Jubbes"

Page 184—For "In the same week in September," read "between August 29 and September 4"

Page 184—For "1601-2" read "1600-1"

Page 187—Between April 11, 1688, and September 15, 1688, insert "August 9, 1638, Thomas Day (Whig), vice Lawford"

Page 187—August 13, 1639, for "presidency" read "precedence"

Page 189—1778, for "December 19" read "November 19"

Page 189—1822, for "Registrarship of the Court of Conscience" read "Deputy Chamberlainship"

Page 190—Trinity, 1636, for "Shore" read "Moore"; 1762, for "J. Bailey" read "G. Bailey"

Page 191—St. Michael, 1719, for "P. Clements" read "T. Clements"; 1748, for "J. Cooper" read "E. Cooper"

Page 191—All Saints, 1667, for "Wickes" read "Hickes"

Page 191—Redcliff, for "1846" read "1847"

Page 192—Castle Precincts, for "1837" read "1838," and for "1838" read "1839"

ERRATA AND ADDENDA—*Continued.*

Page 194—St. Thomas, for "January 1, 1851," read "May 14, 1850"

Page 194—In the list of senior Aldermen insert "October, 1742, J. Becher"; and alter the date of J. Denning to July, 1743

Page 195, R. Jones, for "1601-2" read "1600-1"

Page 196—1606, for "1601-2" read "1600-1," and for "1639-1640" read "1629-1630"

Page 197—1614, the date of Cecil's removal should be 1622-3, and of his death 1631

Page 198—1633, T. Hooke, for "died" read "resigned"

Page 200—1654, for "precedure" read "precedence"

Page 200—1658, for "March, 1658-9," read "February 23, 1658-9"

Page 200—1659, September, after "T. Prigg" add "re-elected August, 1663"

Page 200—1661, August, W. Colston, for "November" read "June"

Page 201—Line 8, for "October 13" read "October 30"

Page 201—1661, October 30, R. Vickris, omit "died or"

Page 202—1663, John Aldworth, add "died June 12, 1668"

Page 202—1668, June 8, for "1668" read "1669"

Page 203—1674, Sept. 1, for "Cole" read "Cale"
Page 203—1679, for "Nathaniel Webb" read "Nehemiah Webb"

Page 205—For "June 2, 1666," read "June 2, 1634"

Page 211—Line 4, for "about June, 1742," read "July 9, 1743"

Page 212—Last line, for "Bayly" read "Bailey"

Page 213—1743, for "Baker" read "Becher"

Page 216—1792, September 15, omit "on being made Receiver of Town Dues"

Page 216—1794, vice Coleman, after the year insert "September 11"

Page 217—1805, for "Registrar of Court of Conscience" read "Deputy Chamberlain"

Page 218—1811, John Hurle, omit "again elected 1811"

Page 218—1811, George Thorne; 1818, Samuel Hall; for "Tory" read "Whig"

Page 220—Note, for "Hall, sen.," read "Maze, sen."

ERRATA AND ADDENDA—*Continued.*

Page 222—1605, for "Grey" read "Guy," and for "Rowbers" read "Rowbero"

Page 222—1613, the year of Mr. Knight's previous Mayoralty was 1594-5

Page 223—Between 1654 and 1656, for "1636" read "1665"

Page 230—In the list of those who have served the office of Sheriff, insert "W. Inman" between J. F. Edgar and Sir H. Protheroe

Page 231—The date of the Earl of Leicester's election was March 22, 1569-70; of that of the Earl of Essex, January 13, 1598-9; and of Sir H. Vane, March 4, 1630-1. That of Lord Buckhurst's elevation to an Earldom was 1603-4

Page 232—Line 1, for "1574" read "Aug. 12, 1570"

Page 232—The date of T. Hannam's election was September 27, 1577

Page 233—1763. Hon. D. Barrington, for "March, 1795," read "March, 1763"

Page 233—1766, J Dunning, after "Solicitor-General" insert "1768-"

Page 233—Second line from foot of page, for "one" read "two"; and insert "R. Eyre and" before "J. Gunning." Omit the words after "Solicitor-Generalship" to the end of the sentence

Page 234—The date of Sir R. Crowder's election for Liskeard was 1849

Page 234—The date of H. Ham's appointment was August 18, 1581 (in the room of William Saxey, resigned)

Page 235—1603, for "May 3" read "September 15"

Page 235—Last line, for "prectice" read "practice"

Page 237—Stewards of Sheriff's Court, the christian name of E. Browne was "Edmund"

Page 238—Sword Bearers, the date of Mr. Whitton's election was July 22, 1623

Page 240—1622, before "Payne" insert "James"

Page 240—1697, Mr. Welsted's name was "Robert"

Page 241—The date of Mr. Franklyn's official appointment by the Corporation was Dec. 8, 1824, but he had been acting since the preceding year

Page 241—Mr. Hope was appointed pro tem. January 18, 1826, and confirmed in the following September

Page 242—City Librarian, for "1745" read "1743"

Page 242—Chaplains of St. Mark's Church, the date of Mr. Prelleur's appointment was February, 23, 1744-5

ERRATA AND ADDENDA—*Continued.*

Page 243—1787-1789, for "Wilson" read "Watson"

Page 245—Mayor's Clerks, H. Day, for "resigned 1823" read "removed October 19, 1822"

Page 246—Quay Wardens, for "1775" (bis) read "1765." The note after 1773 should precede that date

Page 247—Haven Masters, 1752, for "September 29" read "December 13"

Page 247—Corn Measurers, for "1748" read "1741"

Page 248—Secretaries to Dock Estate, 1675, for "April" read "March"

Page 249—The date of W. Harris' resignation was 1847 (not 1849)

Page 250—1660 (Note), in the sentence "was succeeded by the Marquis of Worcester," insert after "succeeded" the words "as Lord Lieutenant of Bristol"

Page 252—Official Assignees, after "till 1845" add "when he was transferred to Leeds"

Page 253—For "Davies" read "Davis"

Page 253—1863, Mr. Bowsher's name was "James"

Page 253—For "1872" read "1869"

Page 253—For "1869" read "1872"

Page 253—The date of Mr. J. B. Tanner's election as Vice-Chairman is April, 1898

Page 254—Provincial Grand Masters, for "1821, February," read "1820, June"

Page 254—Principals of Bishop's College, for "1855" read "1859"

Page 256—Physicians, 1772, after "J. Paul" add "resigned July, 1775"

Page 258—Surgeons, 1754, for "John Norman" read "Jerome Norman"

Page 259—1774, for "Linden" read "Ludlow"

Page 264—Chaplains, Mr. Marriott's name was "Walter," and Mr. Boyce's second name was "White"

Page 265—Surgeons, 1832, Mr. J. G. Lansdown's second name was "Goodale"

Page 267—1685-1686, for "Hulbert" read "Halbert"

Page 269—Acraman, for "President" read "Vice-President"

Page 269—Baker, for "1874" read "1872-1874"

Page 270—Franklyn, for "1868" read "1865"

Page 270—Fry, F. J., omit "Treasurer General Hospital"

Page 271—Haberfield, for "1847" read "1849"

Page 271—Hill, for "1893" read "1891"

ERRATA AND ADDENDA—*Continued.*

Page 272—Perry, after "1896" add "-1899"

Page 272—Sanders, for "1846-1851" read "1829-1832," and add "Chairman Water Works Company, 1846-1851"

Page 273—Wills, Sir W. H., the date of the Baronetcy should be 1893

Page 274—Baker, for "1893-1895" read "1891-1896"

Page 274—White, add "and 1851-1854"

Page 277—Barnes, for "July-October" read "January-October"

Page 280—Brooke, before "1819-1820" insert "1817-1818"

Page 282—Cecil, T., for "1630" (bis) read "1631"

Page 282—"Charleton" read "Charlton," and before "1639-1640" insert "April-November, 1630"

Page 285—Doddridge, after "Alderman," for "1658" read "1655"

Page 288—Edlys, add "M.P., 1597-1598"

Page 288—Elton, Sir A., Bart. (ii), add "M.P., Taunton, 1724-1727"

Page 290—Franklyn, R., for "Master" read "Warden"

Page 290—Franklyn, J. N., for "Norrway" read "Norroway"

Page 291—Gibbons, W., add "Master St. Stephen's Ringers, 1778"

Page 294—Hart, Sir R., line 2, after "1680-1686" insert "(Trinity)"

Page 295—"Henville" read "Henvile"; Hilhouse, J., for "1761" read "1762"; Hill, C., for "1829" read "1830"

Page 295—"Hinde" read "Hine"

Page 298—James, T., after "M.P." omit "1597-1598"

Page 305—Murcott, for "1602" read "1601"

Page 306—Rich, J., "1718-1756" read "1718-1755"

Page 307—Savage, F., omit "Master Merchant Venturers, 1841-1842"

Page 308—Speed, add "Warden Merchant Venturers, 1651-1652"

Page 309—"Swymmer, A., 1684-1688," should be a separate entry, the remaining entries under this head referring to a second A. Swymmer, who entered the Council in 1760

Page 310—Swymmer, W., the words "Treasurer Incorporation of Poor, 1711-1712," should be transferred from the first to the second of this name

Page 311—Wallis, E., for "Ezekial" read "**Ezekiel**"

ERRATA AND ADDENDA—*Continued.*

Page 312—Webb, Nathaniel (i.), for "Nathaniel" read "Nehemiah"

Page 316—Acraman, J., for "1813" read "1810"

Page 317—Ames, G. H., add "Vice-President Free Port Association, 1846-1850"

Page 318—Ash, E., the year of death should be 1818

Page 319—Ball, J. T., for "Taylor" read "Tayler"

Page 320—Beard, J. J., for "May 26" read "May 16"

Page 321—Beaufort, 6th Duke of, before "High Steward" insert "Lord-Lieutenant, 1810-1835"

Page 321—Beaufort, 8th Duke of, after "High Steward, 1854," add "-1899"

Page 321—Belce, W. C., add "Warden St. Stephen's Ringers, 1867"

Page 322—Berkeley, 3rd Earl of, for "1710-1711" read "1710-1712"

Page 323—Blackwell, J., for "1801-1802" read "1811-1812"

Page 324—Blake, Rev. W., add "Vicar Stockland-Bristol till his death"

Page 324—Bompas, C. S., for "1840-1841" read "1841-1843"

Pge 324—Boutflower, for "1898" read "1897-1898"

Page 325—Bowman, Rev. T., for "1860" read "1850"

Page 325—Bowyer, J., for "1748" read "1749"

Page 325—Bradford, G., for "June" read "January"

Page 326—Brice, W. D., for "1810" read "1820"; add "Master Merchant Venturers, 1819-1820; Clerk County Court, 1847-1849"

Page 326—Bright, H., for "1820-1826" read "1820-1830"

Page 327—for "Brown, S. W.," read "Browne"

Page 328—Bryan, G., for "1794" read "1694"

Page 328—Buckler, for "1743" read "1741"

Page 329—Burgum, add "Deputy Governor Incorporation of Poor, 1767-1768"

Page 329—Butterton, Rev. G. A., for "1639-1646" read "1839-1846"

Page 330—Castelman, for "1799" read "1779"

Page 331—Cave, Sir C. D., for "1895" read "1875"

Page 331—Challoner, W., for "1661" read "1669," and add "died 1687"

ERRATA AND ADDENDA—*Continued*.

Page 332—Omit Clarke, E. G. (on Index II., pp. 55, 274)

Page 332—Clarke, J. M., for " 1881 " read " 1886 "

Page 336—Cornish, J., for " 1855 " read " 1835 "

Page 337—Crofton, for " 1898 " read " 1895 "; and add " Rector West Bere, 1895 "

Page 337—Cross, F. R., after " 1879-1885 " insert " (Assistant Surgeon, 1878-1879) "

Page 339—Davis, G. (i.), for " May " read " August "

Page 340—Dewing, add " Rector Camerton, 1893 "

Page 341—Drew, E., add " Vice President Chamber of Commerce, 1854-1855

Page 342—Dunning, for " 1705 " read " 1706 "

Page 342—Dyer, for " 1631 " read " 1633 "

Page 343—" Edens " read " Eden "

Page 343—Edwards, Rev. W., for "1799" read "1798"

Page 345—Evans, Rev. E., add " (Vicar All Saints, Gloucester, 1875-1884; Rector Preston, Gloucestershire, 1884-1888; Vicar Bishopston, 1888) "

Page 345—Evans, J., for " 1877 " read " 1876 "

Page 345—Evans, T. M., for " Warden " read " Master "

Page 346—Fidoe, E., for " Merchant Venturers " read " St. Stephen's Ringers "

Page 346—Fisher, H., for " 1868 " (bis) read " 1858 "

Page 346—Fitzhardinge, Earl, for " 1656-1657 " read " 1856-1857 "

Page 346—Fletcher, R., for " 1870 " read " 1878 "

Page 346—For " Foster " read " Foote "

Page 346—Ford, Rev. G. E., add " Rector All Saints, Birmingham, 1893 "

Page 348—Freeling, Sir F., for " 1829 " read " 1826 "

Page 348—Fripp, E. B., for " 75 " read " 45 "

Page 350—Omit Gibbes, H. (see Index III., p. 291)

Page 350—Omit Gibbons, W. (i.)

Page 351—Glazebrook, for " 1886 " read " 1888 "

Page 252—Greethead, J., omit date of death

Page 353—Grenville, for " 1831 " read " 1832 "

Page 353—Griffiths, E., for " 1811 " read " 1821 "

Page 355—For " Hannan " read " Hannam," and for " 1585 " read " 1577 "

Page 355—Hare, H. G., add " Warden St. Stephen's Ringers (declined), 1873 "

ERRATA AND ADDENDA--*Continued.*

Page 355—Hare, W. O., Deputy Judge of Tolzey Court, 1836-1864, for " 1836 " read " 1842 "

Page 356—Harris, J. (iii.), add " Warden St. Stephen's Ringers, 1852 "

Page 356—Harris, W., for " 1849 " read " 1847 "

Page 358—Hawkswell, for " 1758 " read " 1768 "

Page 358—Heaven, J. G., for " May 3 " read " May 31 "

Page 359—Omit Hellicar, T. (See Index III., p. 294)

Page 360—Hillhouse, M., add " Dock Master, 1821-1843 "

Page 361—Hobhouse, H. (i.), for " 1756-1757 " read " 1749-1750," add " President Colston (Parent) 1768," and for " May 21, 1787," read " May 18, 1773 "

Page 363—Jackson, T., for " 1706 " read " 1716 "

Page 364—For " Jefferis " (C. T.) read " Jefferies "

Page 364—Jelf, for " 1735 " read " 1755 "

Page 365—Johnstone, Rev. R. A., add " Rector West Harndon and Ingrave, 1844-1867 "

Page 366—Jubbes, for " 1519 " read " 1529 "

Page 366—Kelway, omit "Master in Chancery, 1562"

Page 366—King, E. A., add " President Colston (Parent), 1890 "

Page 368—Langley, P., for " 1572 " read " 1571 "

Page 368—Lanseden, for " 1534 " read " 1554 "

Page 368—Lawrance, T., for " 1820 " read " 1810 "

Page 368—Lee, A., add " Vice President Chamber of Commerce, 1899 "

Page 369—Lindrea, T. T., for " Vice President " read " President," and for " 1897 " read " 1899 "

Page 369—Lippincott, Sir H. C., for " 1806 " read " 1805 "

Page 371—Ludlow, E. (i.), for " 1814 " read " 1616 "

Page 371—Lysaght, G., for " 1833, 1889," read " 1898, 1899 "

Page 372—Madan, Rev. G., add " Rector Dursley, 1865-1892 "

Page 372—Mallard, J., for " 1817 " read " 1822 "

Page 373—Mathews, E. R. N., for "1895" read "1893"

Page 374—Mereweather, J., for " 1778 " read " 1788 "

Page 376—Morley, S., add " M.P., Nottingham, 1865-1866 "

Page 376—Naish, E. H., for " Incorporation of Poor " read "Bristol Guardians "

Page 377—Newnham, W. H. C., for " Physician " read " Physician-Accoucheur "

ERRATA AND ADDENDA—*Continued.*

Page 377—Nicholls, J. F., the second name should be " Fawckner "

Page 380—Pate, Rev. H W., for " Williams " read " William "

Page 381—Pembroke and Montgomery, Earl of High Steward, for ' 1630 " read " 1635 "

Page 386—Punter, S., for " 1775 " read " 1765 "

Page 387—Reeve, A., for " July 2 " read " July 21 "

Page 389—Romilly, Sir S., for " 1818-1819 " read " July-November, 1818 "

Page 391—Savage, F., for " Warden " read " Master," and for " 1837-1838 " read " 1841-1842 "

Page 394—Smyth, Sir J. H., for " 1782 " read " 1802 "

Page 394—Somerset, E. A., for " 1781 " read " 1871 "

Page 395—Stampe, Rev. T., for " 1688 " read " 1681 "

Page 399—Thomas, Rev. V. R., for " 1790 " read " 1830 "

Page 401—Tombs, R., the date of death should be September 15, 1790

Page 402—Vaughan, James, after " 1776-1780 " add " and 1782-1784 "

Page 407—Wills, H. O., for " 1325 " read " 1826 "

[THE END.]

T. D. Taylor, Sons, and Hawkins, "Times and Mirror" Office, Bristol.

THE "BRISTOL JOURNALS" OF THE EIGHTEENTH CENTURY.

The following account of the "Bristol Journals" of the eighteenth century is reprinted with some slight alterations, from the "Bristol Times and Mirror" of August 12th, 1899. It embodies the substance of a valuable note by Mr. William George, which was first published in the "Athenæum" of August 2nd, 1881, and was reproduced in the "Times and Mirror" on the 4th of that month. The additional information is derived from Bazeley and Hyett's "Gloucestershire Bibliography," Mr. John Latimer's "Annals of Bristol," and from my own personal researches in the papers themselves.—A. B. B.

The first of the Farley papers was the "Bristol Postman," which was published by Samuel Farley in 1713, number 24 being dated July 25th in that year; it was printed at the house in St. Nicholas Street near the church. In 1725 it was discontinued, and immediately succeeded by "Farley's Bristol Newspaper," which was printed in Wine Street; number 20 is dated September 18th. On or before July 9th, 1737, the title was changed, by the insertion of the publisher's Christian name, to "Sam. Farley's Bristol Newspaper." This was superseded in 1743 by two newspapers published by the same family, and having a sort of Castor-and-Pollux existence, being issued in alternate weeks. They were named respectively "Felix Farley's Bristol Journal" and "Farley's Bristol Advertiser," the latter, as will be seen, not having a Christian name in the title. The issue of the "Journal" for March 24th, 1743-4, is numbered 17, that of the

"Advertiser" for the following week (March 31st) being 18. The last number of the "Advertiser" appeared on August 23rd, 1746, the "Journal" continuing to be issued as a weekly paper.
The number for January 9th, 1747-8, was (probably by an inadvertence) named "Felix Farley's Bristol Advertiser," but that for the following week (January 16th, 1747-8) reverted to the old designation of "Journal," dropping, however, the Christian name, and being styled "Farley's Bristol Journal"; shortly afterwards the name of the publisher was also dropped, and the title became simply "The Bristol Journal," which designation it retained unchanged till 1777. At this time the proprietors were Samuel and Felix Farley, sons of the original Samuel, and the publishing office was in Castle Green.

In March, 1752, the brothers separated, and Felix then started a rival paper under the name (which had been in use, as already stated, from 1743 to 1748) of "Felix Farley's Bristol Journal," the first number being published on March 28th. There were thus two papers appearing simultaneously under nearly the same name, "The Bristol Journal" (published by S. Farley) and "Felix Farley's Bristol Journal." The latter maintained an unbroken separate existence until incorporated with the "Bristol Times" in 1853.

In tracing the subsequent histories of the two Farley journals, I will take the older first, that, viz., carried on by Samuel, after the secession of his brother, under the name of "The Bristol Journal." Samuel did not long survive the dissolution of partnership, dying in the autumn of 1753, his brother having pre-deceased him earlier in the same year. The paper was then carried on by his niece, Sarah Farley, under the same designation, viz., "The Bristol Journal," which did not incorporate the lady's Christian name with its title until after her death. Sarah died July 12th, 1774, and was succeeded in the proprietorship and management of the paper by Hester Farley, daughter of Felix, who retired from business September 30th, 1775. She disposed of "The Bristol Journal" to Messrs. George and William Routh and Charles Nelson, from whose office, at 18, Bridge Street, it was henceforth published, the old office in Castle Green being taken from the same date by the proprietors of "Bonner and Middleton's Bristol Journal," which was then just one year old, and which subsequently became the "Bristol Mirror."

On July 12th, 1777, Mr. Nelson withdrew from the partnership, and Messrs. Routh, in order to emphasise the distinction between their paper and that bearing the name of "Felix Farley," added the name of its former proprietor, Sarah, to its title, so that it appeared thereafter as "Sarah Farley's Bristol Journal." In the course of a few years (I have not ascertained the exact date) Mr. George Routh retired, and Mr. William Routh's name appears as the sole printer and publisher in the various issues of the Bristol Directory from 1794 to 1800 inclusive. He died June 3rd, 1800, and his widow, Catherine Routh, succeeded him. In 1806 Mrs. Routh sold the paper. The "Bristol Mirror" of June 25th, 1806, contains an advertisement offering for sale a paper, of which the name is not given, but which undoubtedly was "Sarah Farley's Bristol Journal." In this advertisement it is described as having been "carried on for 90 years" in the "second great commercial and populous city in the Kingdom." I have not discovered the names of the purchasers, but the title was changed to the "Mercantile Gazette and General Intelligencer (late Sarah Farley's Bristol Journal)." The new proprietors apparently soon grew dissatisfied with their property, and the paper was again sold in July, 1807, to Messrs. Agg and Sander, proprietors of the "Western Star," and for the brief remainder of its existence it was called the "Western Star and Mercantile Gazette, late Sarah Farley's Journal."

In the Directory for 1807, John Agg's name is given as publisher of "Sarah Farley's Journal," at the old address, 18, Bridge Street. In the following year the name of Sarah Farley disappears from the Directory, and Agg's name is recorded as publisher of the "Western Star," at 43, Broadmead. On February 21st, 1809, the partnership of John Agg and James Farnham Williams, under the style of John Agg and Co., was dissolved, and on April 15th, 1809, John Agg was gazetted bankrupt. In the Directory for 1809 there is no mention of either Agg or his paper, and it may be safely assumed that the latter ceased to exist either at the end of 1808 or early in 1809, though the exact date of its final disappearance cannot now be positively fixed.

Mr. George, in the note I have already referred to, states that Sarah Farley's paper "appears to have merged in the 'Bristol Mirror,'" but I think he is in error on that point, as I can find no trace of any record either in the "Mirror" of that time, or in any other paper, confirmatory of that assumption. "Felix Farley's Journal" of September 16th, 1809, in recording the death of Mrs. Catherine Routh during the preceding week, describes her as having been the publisher of "Sarah Farley's Journal," which, it adds, "became extinct a few years since," evidently dating the decease of the paper from 1806, when it was merged in the "Mercantile Gazette."

It is somewhat remarkable that no copy of "Sarah Farley's Journal" during the last twelve years, at least, of its existence is now extant. Mr. George, in a letter to me, dated December 15, 1898, states that the latest copy with which he is acquainted is in the British Museum, dated August 3, 1793, and numbered 4,023. I have not had an opportunity of verifying this by personal inspection, but Mr. Fortescue, of the British Museum, writing to me on the day after the date of Mr. George's letter, tells me that the only copies of "Sarah Farley's Journal" in that library are those for April 27, August 3 and 10, 1782, March 3. 1784, and for the period from September to December, 1785. Mr. George is generally so accurate that I imagine Mr. Fortescue must have accidentally overlooked the copy which he names. The latest issue in Alderman Fox's library is that of December 27, 1788; the catalogue of Mr. Braikenridge's collection is entirely wanting in any entry relating to this paper, but includes six numbers of the old "Postman," those, viz., for December 19 and 31, 1715, and January 7, 14, 21, and 28, 1716. I believe I am right in saying that there are no copies of "The Bristol Journal" (afterwards "Sarah Farley's") in either the Central Free Library in King Street or the Reference Library, Queen's Road. The latest number in Mr. T. D. Taylor's collection is that for September 24, 1774. There are complete issues for several years (sometimes in the same volume with "Felix Farley") at the Commercial Rooms. The latest number in that collection is vol. 74, number 3,817, dated August 15, 1789; for the remainder of that year its place is taken by "Bonner and Middleton's Bristol Journal."

"Felix Farley's Journal," as I have already stated, was begun in March, 1752, the publishing offices being in Small Street. Felix died April 26, 1753, and the paper was carried on for some years after his death by his widow, Elizabeth Farley. (His daughter Hester, as mentioned above, took up the management of her uncle Samuel's paper, the original "Farley's Bristol Journal," on the death of his other niece, Sarah.) After Elizabeth Farley, the proprietorship of "Felix Farley's Journal" passed to Messrs. Thomas Cocking and John Rudhall, of whom the former died in July 1787, and the latter on March 10, 1803. Mr. Rudhall was succeeded by his son John Broughton Rudhall, who in October, 1805, took into partnership Mr. John Mathew Gutch, a schoolfellow of Coleridge and Lamb at Christ's Hospital.

and a man of high literary attainments, a memoir of whom is given in the "Dictionary of National Biography." This partnership was dissolved January 1, 1807, and Mr. Gutch then conducted the paper alone for several years, being afterwards joined by James Martin, who, on Mr. Gutch's retirement, in 1844, became solely responsible for the publication. The circulation had been for some years steadi'y declining, and the paper was quite unable to keep pace with its young and more vigorous Conservative rivals, the "Mirror" and the "Times," then under the able management of Messrs. John Taylor and Joseph Leech respectively. Mr. Martin found himself involved in financial difficulties, and emigrated to Australia about 1851, where he passed the remainder of his life, and died July 13, 1862. For a few months "Felix Farley's Journal" continued to struggle on, the chief proprietor during the closing months of its independent existence being the Rev. Henry Richards, rector of Horfield, until, in April, 1853, it was purchased by Mr. Leech, and incorporated with the "Bristol Times," which that gentleman, then a very young man, had started in 1839, and had continued to conduct with great energy and success.

The British Museum Library possesses a set of "Felix Farley" from 1779 to 1853, and Mr. T. D. Taylor's collection supplies the issues of previous years, with some missing numbers, from 1755 to 1765, and after 1772. Those between 1765 and 1772 are, I think, at the Commercial Rooms, with the exception of the years 1769 and 1770. It is worth remarking that I can find no trace of any extant copy of any Bristol newspaper for the year 1769 or for 1770, earlier than November 3 of the latter year, from which date Mr. T. D. Taylor possesses copies of "Sarah Farley's Journal." I am nearly sure, and Messrs. George and Latimer confirm my recollection, that a volume of either "Felix" or "Sarah Farley" (or both in one), containing the years 1769 and 1770, was at the Commercial Rooms some 15 or 20 years ago, but it has been mislaid and cannot be found.

It remains for me to add a few notes on the paper which ultimately became known as the "Bristol Mirror." In its original form this paper was called "Bonner and Middleton's Bristol Journal," the first number of which was issued by Samuel Bonner and Richard Middleton (the former of whom had been foreman to Sarah Farley, who had died in the preceding month) from their office in Castle Street, in August, 1774. On September 30, 1775, they removed their head-quarters to Castle Green, taking possession of the old office of "Farley's," afterwards

"Sarah Farley's Bristol Journal," which was vacated on the transference of the proprietorship of the latter paper to Messrs. Routh and Nelson, whose office was in Bridge Street. The partnership of Messrs. Bonner and Middleton was dissolved September 29, 1783, when the junior member of the firm (who died at the age of 82 on February 15, 1807) retired. Mr. Bonner continued to publish the journal until April 17, 1802, when he transferred it to Messrs. John Fenley and George Baylis. Mr. Bonner died at the age of 80, on September 11, 1813. The partnership of Messrs. Fenley and Baylis ceased June 25, 1803, when Mr. Baylis withdrew, his place in the firm being taken by William Sheppard. The original name of "Bonner and Middleton's Journal" was retained until the end of 1803, but on January 7, 1804, it appeared as "Fenley and Sheppard's Journal," which title it retained for three months, at the end of which period Mr. Fenley withdrew, owing to bad health. He did not long survive, dying on his passage to the West Indies, February 5, 1805. On April 14, 1804, the paper bore for the first time "The Mirror, late Bonner and Middleton's Journal," and was stated to be published "for the proprietors" by William Sheppard. The chief of these proprietors was Mr. Richard Smith, the celebrated surgeon. I do not know how many co-partners were associated with him, but the largest and possibly the only other shareholder was Mr. Thomas David, who afterwards gave his name to the present senior proprietor of the "Times and Mirror," Mr. T. D. Taylor. From this date (1804) to 1826, the "Mirror" continued to be "printed and published for the proprietors." Mr. Sheppard's name as printer and publisher made way for that of J. Desmond July 27, 1805, who in turn was succeeded by C. A. Holl, September 5, 1807, for whom, on December 31, 1809, was substituted A. Brown. Mr. Brown's name appeared as publisher "for the proprietors" till August 19, 1826; in the next issue (August 26, 1826) these words were dropped, and the name of Mr. John Taylor, the principal, and ultimately sole, proprietor, was substituted as printer and publisher. Mr. Taylor continued his control of the "Mirror" until his death, April 11, 1859, when he was succeeded by his son, the present Mr. T. D. Taylor, under whose reign was effected the amalgamation with the "Bristol Times," which resulted in the issue, on January 1, 1865, of the "Bristol Times and Mirror" as a daily Conservative newspaper, Messrs. Leech and Taylor being joint proprietors.

From the foregoing sketch it will be seen that the "Bristol Times and Mirror" traces its existence as an independent paper to the year 1752, being the direct representative of "Felix Farley's Bristol

Journal," which was then established, and has since 1853 been incorporated with the "Bristol Times," and in 1865 was merged in the present daily publication. "Felix Farley's Journal" itself being an offshoot from the original "Bristol Journal," which in turn was the successor of Samuel Farley's "Postman" of 1713, the "Bristol Times and Mirror" may be said to carry back its ancestry over a period of 186 years to a date in the very infancy of British journalism.

www.ingramcontent.com/pod-product-compliance
Lightning Source LLC
Chambersburg PA
CBHW022102300426
44117CB00007B/556